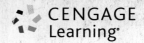

M&B, 3e
Dean Croushore

Vice President, General Manager, Social
Science & Qualitative Business: Erin Joyner

Product Director: Michael Worls

Sr. Product Manager: Steve Scoble

Content Developer: Elizabeth Beiting-Lipps

Product Assistant: Anne Merrill

Sr. Content Project Manager: Colleen A. Farmer

Media Developer: Anita Verma

Manufacturing Planner: Kevin Kluck

Senior Marketing Manager: John Carey

Production Service: MPS Limited

Rights Acquisitions Specialist: Deanna Ettinger

Text Permissions Researcher:
Sowmya Sankaran/PMG

Image Permissions Researcher:
Saranya Sarada/PMG

Sr. Art Director: Michelle Kunkler

Internal Designer: Beckmeyer Design/Pier
Design Co.

Cover Designer: Pier Design Co.

Cover Image: © Patrick Koslo/Stockbyte/
Getty Images

Inside Front Cover Images: woman with
magazine © iStockphoto.com/sdominick;
money © iStockphoto.com/alexsl; college
hangout © iStockphoto.com/A-Digit

Back Cover Image:
© iStockphoto.com/René Mansi

Title Page Images: laptop © iStockphoto
.com/CostinT; A+ © iStockphoto.com
/photovideostock; crowd © iStockphoto
.com/Leontura

For product information and technology assistance, contact us at
Cengage Learning Customer & Sales Support, 1-800-354-9706

For permission to use material from this text or product,
submit all requests online at **www.cengage.com/permissions**
Further permissions questions can be emailed to
permissionrequest@cengage.com

Library of Congress Control Number: 2013952150

Student Edition ISBN-13: 978-1-285-16796-1

Student Edition ISBN-10: 1-285-16796-1

Cengage Learning
200 First Stamford Place, 4th Floor
Stamford, CT 06902
USA

Cengage Learning is a leading provider of customized learning solutions with
office locations around the globe, including Singapore, the United Kingdom,
Australia, Mexico, Brazil, and Japan. Locate your local office at:
www.cengage.com/global

Cengage Learning products are represented in Canada by
Nelson Education, Ltd.

To learn more about Cengage Learning Solutions, visit
www.cengage.com

Purchase any of our products at your local college store or at our
preferred online store **www.cengagebrain.com**

Printed in the United States of America
3 4 5 6 7 17 16

BRIEF CONTENTS

Eyeidea/iStockphoto.com

CONTENTS

PART TWO

Fundamentals of Banking

CH13 Modern Macroeconomic Models 269

CH14 Economic Interdependence 291

PART FOUR

Monetary Policy

CH15 The Federal Reserve System 312

Thanks to my family for their support. This book was written in large part during breaks at gymnastics events, horse shows, and band competitions in which my children participated. I dedicate this book to them and especially to my wife, Claudette, whose encouragement, support, and patience with my long hours of researching and writing made it possible for me to complete this textbook.

Dean Croushore
December 2013

INTRODUCTION TO MONEY and BANKING

People say, "Money makes the world go round." Whether this is true or not, money itself does go
around the world with astonishing speed. Money has always been at the center of economic transactions—from the days when gold and silver were used for purchases to today's payments with a plastic card. No longer constrained by physical proximity, money flows around the globe through banking institutions and financial markets. This seemingly free flow of money is constrained, however, by rules under which banks and financial markets must operate, as dictated by government policy. In this chapter we will see how these policy decisions affect consumers, households, and businesses— the primary exchangers of money.

Caught up in the joy of spending, some people might think that their only contact with a bank is the occasional trip to an automatic teller machine (ATM) to withdraw cash. But banks intersect with people's lives in many ways. Banks issue the credit cards that consumers use to buy goods and services. Banks lend people money to buy cars and houses. Banks process the checks that almost everyone uses to pay their bills. Banks play a large role—sometimes obvious and sometimes invisible—in our lives every day.

Economic policy determines the rules and regulations by which banks work. If those rules are poorly designed, the banking system will not work well. For example, with efficient rules for banks, the interest rate on a car loan might be 7 percent, but if inefficient rules raise banks' costs of making loans, the interest rate might be 10 percent.

People's lives are affected by the efficiency of money and banks, and policy affects that efficiency. We readily notice the impact of policy when things go wrong—for example, during the great inflation of the 1970s or the financial crisis of 2008. Policymakers in those periods deserve blame for the results of their policymaking. But policymakers also deserve credit when things go right, such as in the late 1990s, when inflation and unemployment rates reached their lowest levels in 30 years. It is not easy to isolate the specific policy measures that cause growth or decline in the economy because there are so many interrelated factors.

This book explores the connections between the banking system and the policies governing that system; you will see how those interactions affect your lives and the economy overall. By comprehending these interactions, you will learn why financial markets and institutions are structured the way they are. You will learn how money affects the economy and begin to grasp the economic theory that demonstrates how the force of policy steers financial markets. This book emphasizes the role of the Federal Reserve System in the payments system (the way economic transactions are conducted), in regulating banks, and in setting monetary policy. By the time you have finished this book, you should understand why the financial system takes its present shape and how economic forces can change it. You also will have a framework for understanding the worldwide financial system and the world economy. This framework will enable you to comprehend economic policy and analyze the effects of different policies on financial markets and on your well-being.

Though the subject matter of money and banking is personal, it has national and international implications. People make decisions about how much money to keep in their wallets, how often to go to the bank, and whether to pay for the goods they buy by using cash, writing a check, or using a credit card, all of which are subjects in this course on money and banking. But when we consider the decisions made by millions of people and look at the overall impact of those decisions, we enter the realm of macroeconomics, where we see the impact of the sum of those individual decisions on macroeconomic variables such as the inflation rate, interest rates, the unemployment rate, and the economy's growth rate.

1-1 What Is in This Text?

This book uses economic theory and data from the U.S. and foreign economies to cover a wide variety of topics. Two aspects of this coverage are particularly noteworthy: (1) applications to everyday life and (2) the purposes and implications of government policy.

1-1a The Value of Money and Banking for Everyday Life

In early 2013, the interest rate on new car loans fell to the lowest level in history (at least since 1972 when such interest rates were recorded), at 4.8 percent. Why? Because in 2007 the economy went into recession, in fall 2008 there was a major financial crisis, and from 2009 to 2013 the economy remained very weak. The Federal Reserve (called the Fed for short) reduced the interest rate in the market in which banks borrow money from each other (the federal funds market), and the reduced interest expense faced by banks led to a decline in the interest rate on U.S. government bonds, which, in turn, determined the interest rate on new car loans. What will happen to the interest rate on new car loans in future years? No one knows yet. That depends on the Fed's future actions, the strength of the economy, and the inflation rate. Thus, if you plan to borrow to buy a car, the amount you will repay depends on what the Federal Reserve does (which we will study in Chapters 15 through 18), as well as the growth of the economy and the rate of inflation (considered in Chapters 10 to 14).

A house is the biggest purchase of most people's lives. Homebuyers usually take out a mortgage loan to buy their house and pay the loan off in 30 years, which is most of their working lives. The interest rate on a mortgage loan is influenced by a number of factors, including the Federal Reserve's monetary policy (as was the case for the interest rate on new car loans), the worldwide demand for loans, the health of the banking system, the inflation rate, and the size of the federal government's budget deficit. We will examine all these factors in this textbook so that you will know what factors influence the mortgage interest rate.

Should you invest in the stock market? Every investor wants to make the biggest profit possible, but you must understand the risks inherent in buying stocks. You do not want to make the same mistakes as those who invested heavily in technology stocks in the late 1990s and then lost a substantial portion of their wealth in 2000. This book discusses the stock market in Chapter 7. The discussion will explore what is possible and what is not possible for investors. But you also will learn that your ability to profit from the stock market depends mainly on the profits that corporations earn, which depend, in turn, on economic growth in the United States and the rest of the world; this, in turn, is discussed in Chapters 10 and 14.

Understanding what determines the interest rates on loans or what causes the stock market to fluctuate will help you make good decisions about borrowing and investing. Thus, the knowledge you gain from this book could be valuable to you in the future.

1-1b Why Is Government Policy So Crucial for Money and Banking?

Economic policy affects the entire financial system, including the amount of money in the economy, how financial securities are traded, how banks operate, how fast the economy grows, how rapidly the prices of goods and services grow over time, and what the value of the U.S. dollar is in terms of foreign currencies.

Throughout this book we will examine government policies that concern financial markets and institutions, money, banking, and the economy. In our modern financial system, government regulations and actions influence how markets perform. In some industries, such as small-appliance manufacturing, the government has very little role. However, because of externalities (situations in which one firm's decisions affect others whose interests were not taken into account by the first firm), the government plays a vital role in the financial system. For example, bank runs, which occur when many people withdraw their funds from banks at the same time, were commonplace in the 1800s and early 1900s in the United States and often led to economic downturns. The government took several steps to prevent such runs, creating several new institutions, including the system of deposit insurance in 1933.

Who are the policymakers, and why are they so important? Policy is a part of every aspect of the financial system, and thus there are many different types of policymakers. Their decisions affect the nation in many ways—some obvious and some subtle. One such institution is the Securities and Exchange Commission (SEC), which sets the rules for trading bonds and stocks. Those rules are designed to ensure that insiders (those who work in companies) do not profit by taking advantage of less knowledgeable people who purchase the bonds or stocks of those companies. In 2002, the accounting scandals that rocked several major corporations gave proof that, even with strict rules, some insiders cannot resist the temptation to defraud the system for their own gain. Now investors will shy away from investing in firms that engage in questionable accounting practices. Another important institution is the Federal Deposit Insurance Corporation (FDIC), which came into being to insure deposits at banks, helping to prevent bank runs. As a result, people poured money into banks in the financial crisis of 2008 because they knew their deposits were guaranteed by the government, even though some banks found themselves in trouble because of bad loans.

What is the Federal Reserve? The policymaking institution that we will study most carefully in this book is the Federal Reserve System, which determines the money supply, sets the rules for how checks are cleared and how banks obtain new currency, and determines what activities banks may or may not engage in and whether banks are operating in a prudent fashion. Eight times a year the Federal Reserve decides whether to take actions that increase or decrease the interest rate in a small, obscure market for overnight loans between banks (the federal funds market). That market may be small and obscure, perhaps, but the decision is vitally important to nearly everyone in the U.S. economy because it ultimately determines the interest rate you pay on your car loan, the amount of interest you receive on funds in your bank account, and the rate of inflation over the next few years. Showing the connections between that Federal Reserve decision and your life is one goal of this book.

Throughout this book we will connect the theory of money and banking to the practical decisions of policymakers and to their influence on your everyday life.

RECAP

1 The money and banking system affects your daily life by making credit cards available, by providing loans that allow you to buy a car or a house, and by enabling you to pay your bills conveniently.

2 Policy decisions affect the efficiency of the money and banking system when they cause problems, such as in the financial crisis of 2008, or when they help the economy grow rapidly, as in the 1990s.

3 The Federal Reserve is a key policymaking institution that is responsible for making sure that our system of payments works well for monitoring banks and for determining the nation's money supply.

© iStock.com/TriggerPhoto

1-2 Ten (Surprising) Facts Concerning Money and Banking

Before getting into the details of the money and banking system, here are 10 important facts about money, banking, and financial markets that may surprise you. Each of these facts will be explored more fully in later chapters. Many of them demonstrate the interdependence of policy, the money and banking system, and an individual's financial decisions.

1-2a Most Financial Formulas— No Matter How Complicated They Look—Are Based on the Compounding of Interest

Using this book, you will learn formulas that are useful in understanding financial transactions. Some look very complicated and involve fractions and terms raised to various powers. But they are all based on one idea—that the gains to investing (or the costs of borrowing) grow at a compound rate over time.

If you have ever had a bank account or taken out a loan to buy a car, you may be familiar with the concept of interest. For instance, if you put $1,000 into a savings account at a bank, and it grew to $1,600 in 10 years, the extra $600 would represent the interest you earned over those 10 years. Or if you borrowed $5,000 to buy a car and then repaid $6,000 over five years, the amount you repaid would represent the borrowed amount ($5,000) plus $1,000 in interest.

The key feature of interest is that it compounds over time, which means that interest accrues on interest from previous years. Consider what happens when you invest money. In one year, you earn some interest. The following year, you earn interest on your original investment and on your first year's interest. The next year, you earn interest on the original amount invested as well as on the interest from previous years. As the years roll on, this compounding of interest adds up.

For example, if you invest $1,000 in an investment that pays interest of 10 percent each year, you will have $1,100 after 1 year, $2,594 after 10 years, $10,835 after 25 years, and $117,391 after 50 years. Without compounding, the amount after 50 years would be just

$6,000. Thus, compounding makes a huge difference over long periods.

Once you understand compounding of interest, financial formulas of all types become easily comprehensible. For example, when you borrow the funds to buy a car, the car dealer punches a set of numbers into a computer or calculator. The calculation the dealer is performing is nothing more than the compounding of interest in reverse—your dealer is calculating the monthly payment needed to pay off the car loan, accounting for the compounding of interest. Similar calculations can be used to figure out the return you made over the past five years on your investments in the stock market, the gain you expect to make from an investment, how much you would need today to pay off your car loan, or which of two different loans you should take out.

In Chapter 2 we will examine how money flows from lenders to borrowers through financial intermediaries and markets. In Chapter 4 we will learn about compounding and the related notion of present value. We will apply these notions to interest rates (in Chapters 5 and 6) and to the stock market (in Chapter 7).

1-2b More U.S. Currency Is Held in Foreign Countries than in the United States

Naturally, U.S. citizens buy goods and services with dollars, the national currency of the United States. But more U.S. dollars circulate outside the United States than within.

Some foreigners prefer U.S. dollars because of inflation. Prices of goods in terms of their local currency keep rising rapidly over time. Instead of using their own currencies in their own countries, these people import U.S. dollars to spend. Using U.S. dollars helps them to avoid the problems caused by high rates of inflation. That inflation, in turn, is caused by their central banks (the government agencies that determine their money supplies), which allow the money supply to grow too rapidly.

Should Americans worry about all the dollars being held abroad? Not really, because our taxes are lower as a result. It costs the U.S. government about 4 cents to produce a piece of currency; so the government profits by about $19.96 for every $20 bill held overseas and $99.96 for a $100 bill. Higher government profits (which we call *seignorage*) mean lower taxes for U.S. citizens—to the tune of about $80 billion per year from 2010 to 2012.

We will discuss the uses of money and how payments are made in the United States and around the world in Chapters 3 and 11. We will look at interactions between the economies of different countries in Chapter 14.

1-2c Interest Rates on Long-Term Loans Generally Are Higher than Interest Rates on Short-Term Loans

Newspapers and business magazines often refer to "the" interest rate. In fact, there are many different interest rates, each of which is relevant for a different loan.

In general, the longer the time before a loan is paid off, the higher the interest rate. For example, a mortgage loan (a loan for buying a house) might have an annual interest rate of 3.5 percent if it is repaid in 15 years and 4.0 percent if it is repaid in 30 years. The difference in interest rates on loans that are repaid over different periods may be substantial.

To understand why long-term loans pay more interest than short-term loans, we need to consider several aspects of investing, including lender's preferences (they like to make short-term loans in case they need their money), the riskiness of the loans (long-term loans carry more risk), and the expected future changes in short-term interest rates. These elements combine to make the interest rates on long-term loans higher, almost always, than the interest rates on short-term loans.

The difference between short- and long-term interest rates is an indicator of the state of the economy and is also useful in forecasting how fast the economy will grow. We will learn all about the factors that influence interest rates on long-term compared with short-term loans in Chapter 5.

1-2d To Understand How Interest Rates Affect Economic Decisions, You Must Account for Expected Inflation

The interest rate on a bank deposit tells you how many dollars you will earn. It does not tell you how much you will be able to buy with those dollars. To figure out how much you will be able to buy when you earn interest, you must consider that the prices of the goods you buy change over time. For example, suppose that you have your eyes on a new stereo system that costs $1,100, but you have only $1,000. If you invest $1,000 and earn interest of $100 after one year, you will have the $1,100 you need. However, you can buy the stereo system only if its price has not gone up over the course of the year. If there is inflation, that is, if the average prices of goods have risen, you still may not have enough funds to make your purchase.

A person's decision about how much to save or invest depends not just on the interest rate but also on how much that person expects prices to change. The expected rate of change of prices is called the *expected inflation rate*. Thus, to understand consumer decisions about saving and investing, we need to examine both the interest rate and the expected inflation rate.

How do people form expectations about the future inflation rate? As we will see, the formation of expectations depends on circumstances. If inflation has been fairly stable over time, as it was in the United States in the 1950s and early 1960s and again in the 1990s and 2000s, expectations are likely to be based on the historical average rate of inflation. However, if inflation should begin to rise dramatically, as it did in the late 1960s and through the 1970s, or if inflation should begin to fall sharply, as it did in the early 1980s, then consumer expectations of inflation are likely to become more complicated. For example, the surprising increase in inflation that began in the late 1960s led people to examine the Federal Reserve's role in creating money, which was the source of inflation. As a result, people began monitoring the Federal Reserve's actions and adjusting their expectations about inflation according to the growth rate of the money supply.

How consumers form expectations about the future inflation rate influences their investment decisions. The most important variable determining those decisions is the *real interest rate*, which equals the nominal (or dollar) interest rate minus the expected inflation rate. The real interest rate is particularly relevant to the formation of economic policy. In periods when the expected inflation rate was based on the historical average of inflation, policymakers knew that their policies would not immediately affect expected inflation. Thus, if they wanted to affect the real interest rate, all they had to do was to change the nominal interest rate, knowing that there would be a one-for-one change in the real interest rate. However, when policymakers' actions began to influence people's expectations, policymaking became more complicated. If policymakers tried to reduce the real interest rate, expected inflation might increase, and interest rates (both nominal and real) might rise rather than fall. Thus, the effect of policy on public expectations about inflation actually made policymaking more difficult.

As we will see in Chapter 6, people's expectations of future inflation are a key variable that affects interest rates. We will explore the implications for policymaking from changes in people's expectations in Chapters 12, 13, 17, and 18.

1-2e Buying Stocks Is the Best Way to Increase Your Wealth— and the Worst

If you had wealth to invest, how would you decide what to do? Would you buy safe securities, such as U.S. government securities? Or would you take on more risk, such as buying a small business in your community? Or would you put your funds into the stock market, buying shares in U.S. corporations? Deciding what to do with your wealth depends on your willingness to take risk.

If you look at the returns that investors have made in the past few decades, you might want to invest in the stock market. Investors in the stock market made especially large gains in the 1980s and 1990s. But investing in the stock market is also very risky. Therefore, although investing in the stock market produces high returns on average, you also can lose a lot of your wealth. For example, the average stock lost 40 percent of its value from 2007 to 2009.

The stock market may seem mysterious, but it is much simpler than it first appears. Buying stocks gives you a share of ownership in America's largest corporations. As a stockholder, you get to vote on corporations' major decisions. To profit in the stock market, you need to realize both the big picture—how the stock market fits into the grand scheme of the financial system—and the little details—how likely a particular stock is to increase your wealth.

To invest efficiently, you need to understand the risks that you face in the stock market and on other investments, as we will detail in Chapter 7.

1-2f Banks and Other Financial Institutions Made Major Errors That Led to the Financial Crisis of 2008

The banking system was remarkably healthy in the 1990s and the early 2000s. Banks had substantial cushions against losses, most were very well capitalized (having a large amount of equity capital relative to potential losses on loans), and not a single bank failed in 2005 or 2006, an unprecedented event.

But in 2007, trouble began to brew. The rapid growth in housing prices led banks and mortgage brokers to become complacent about making mortgage loans, and they made many loans to people who did not have sufficient income to pay them back. The banks were counting on the houses' appreciating, so the owners could pay back the loans based on the increased value of the houses. But when housing prices stopped rising, banks began to realize that many of these subprime loans would never be repaid. As they foreclosed on such houses, housing prices fell further, making the problem even worse.

Many banks thought they had avoided any risk from subprime mortgage loans because they had sold the loans off to other firms. But they owned mortgage-backed securities, which indirectly owned subprime loans, and those securities plummeted in value as everyone in the market realized that most of the subprime loans would never be repaid. In addition, the two major government-sponsored agencies that helped finance mortgages, Fannie Mae and Freddie Mac (formally, the Federal National Mortgage Association and the Federal Home Loan Mortgage Corporation), owned so many subprime mortgages that they both went bankrupt and were taken over by the federal government.

The problems from U.S. subprime mortgages cascaded all over the world. Many investment banks were highly leveraged, having borrowed much of the funds that they invested. When losses on mortgage-backed securities became surprisingly high, the investment banks veered toward bankruptcy. As their situation became precarious, other financial firms stopped trading with them, fearing that they would default on their loan agreements. The entire financial system came to a screeching halt, as investment firms all over the world attempted to sell financial assets at the same time, causing the prices of stocks and bonds to plummet. Investors worldwide sold any risky asset and poured their funds into banks (which benefited from deposit insurance) and into U.S. government bonds. A deep recession ensued, with real GDP (gross domestic product) declining more than 8 percent (at an annual rate) in the United States, and nearly 20 percent in some Asian countries, in the fourth quarter of 2008.

The main lesson that banks and their regulators learned from the financial crisis of 2008 is to be wary when things are going well. A wise adage in banking is, "The worst loans are made in good times," which bankers seemed to have forgotten when they began to make subprime loans. Banking regulations have been strengthened since the crisis to attempt to keep banks out of trouble.

Banks like this one offer a wide variety of services for their customers, including ATM and online access 24 hours a day.

You will learn how banks operate in Chapter 8, and how deposit insurance and other regulations affect banks in Chapter 9.

1-2g Recessions Are Difficult to Predict

A recession occurs when the overall level of business activity in the economy declines persistently. In December 2007, for example, the economy entered a recession. In that month, a variety of economic indicators began to show that the economy was faltering. The number of people employed in the economy began to decline as more and more people lost their jobs and fewer new jobs were created. Not all economic variables turned down at the same time, however. The housing market had begun to decline early in 2007 and was the main cause of the recession, leading consumers to have less wealth; so they reduced their spending. The recession was fairly mild until September 2008, when the financial crisis caused most of the major sectors of the economy to decline sharply.

Because recessions cause major problems, including unemployment and declining profits, economists spend much effort attempting to forecast when they will occur. At different times, various indicators have seemed to predict recessions. Over time, however, no indicator has maintained an ability to forecast recessions. For example, if you look at declines in the stock market as a predictor of recessions, you would have predicted recessions far more often than they occurred. Another popular predictor was the difference between interest rates on two different government securities, which worked well in the 1970s and 1980s. But that indicator gave misleading forecasts in the 1990s.

Recessions simply cannot be predicted with any degree of accuracy. The best way to think about recessions is that the economy is strong at times and weak at other times. When it is weak, the economy may be more subject to falling into recession if some shock hits the economy. Such a shock might be a sudden rise in oil prices or a major change in government policy. Thus, although economists cannot predict recessions with much accuracy, they can tell you the probability that a recession is likely to occur.

We will look at how the economy grows and what might cause recessions in Chapter 10. Then we will develop several different models of how the economy works in Chapters 12 and 13.

1-2h The Federal Reserve Creates Money by Changing a Number in Its Computer System

To create additional money in the economy, the Federal Reserve, often called the Fed, for short, buys government securities from certain Wall Street firms. In exchange for the securities, the Fed increases the number in its computer system that shows how much the banks at which those Wall Street firms keep their accounts have on deposit at the Fed. Thus, money is created simply by changing a number in a computer.

Have you ever thought about where dollar bills come from? They are issued by the government, of course, but how does the government put them into circulation? The answer is that the Fed gives them to banks in exchange for reducing the number in the Fed's computer system that represents the amount of funds that banks have on deposit.

This process of money creation clearly has the potential for being abused. If the Fed creates too much money, the prices of goods and services throughout the economy will rise; that's *inflation*. Inflation is bad for the economy, so the Fed tries to reduce the amount of it.

To study how money is created, we must understand the inner workings of the Fed, which we will do in Chapter 15. We will see how the Fed controls the amount of money in the country in Chapter 16.

1-2i In the Long Run, the Only Economic Variable the Federal Reserve Can Affect Is the Rate of Inflation—the Fed Has No Effect on Economic Activity

The Federal Reserve can change the amount of money circulating in the economy—the money supply. Economists long ago discovered that when the Fed increases the money supply, the economy speeds up a bit; people buy more goods and services. Thus, when the economy is sluggish, the Fed can help the economy by increasing the money supply. The increase in the money supply causes interest rates to decline, so people buy more goods and services. On the other hand, when the economy is overheating, the Fed can reduce the money supply to slow the economy down. Doing so causes interest rates to rise, so people become more reluctant to spend.

However, there are limits on how much the Fed can do to affect economic activity. And in the long run, the economy adjusts and achieves the same level of economic activity no matter how much money is in the economy. The Fed's actions cannot affect either the long-run real interest rate or the underlying long-run growth rate of the economy. Ultimately, therefore, the only major economic variable the Fed can affect by changing interest rates and the money supply is the amount of inflation in the economy. When the Fed increases the growth rate of the money supply, the inflation rate rises; when the Fed decreases money growth, the inflation rate falls. Fear of the long-run impact of policy changes on inflation prevents the Fed from stimulating the economy very much in the short run.

We will see how the Fed's actions affect the economy in the short run and the long run in Chapter 17.

1-2j You Can Predict How the Federal Reserve Will Change Interest Rates Using a Simple Equation

We know that the Federal Reserve changes interest rates to affect economic growth in the short run and to affect inflation in the long run. But can we use that knowledge to predict what the Fed will do when it meets eight times each year to set interest rates?

Some economists think that predicting what the Fed will do is not very difficult. They note that the Fed bases its policy decisions mostly on two major variables: the output gap and the inflation rate. The *output gap* is the percentage by which real gross domestic product (GDP) is above or below its potential level. If Fed policymakers think that the economy is producing more output than is sustainable, they will raise interest rates; if they think the economy is running below par, they will lower interest rates. The inflation rate also influences policymakers' decisions. If inflation is above its target level of 2 percent, policymakers are inclined to raise interest rates; if inflation is below target, policymakers will feel comfortable reducing interest rates.

An equation that relates the interest rate to the output gap and the inflation rate is known as the *Taylor rule*, named after the economist John Taylor of Stanford University, who suggested it. Taylor showed that his equation did a good job of modeling how the Fed acted in changing interest rates in the 1980s and 1990s. The Taylor rule is used widely in the United States and in many foreign countries. Economists use the rule to show how the Fed in the United States and the central banks in other countries respond to changes in the economy through the impact of those changes on the output gap and the inflation rate. Central banks around the world use the Taylor rule as a benchmark in setting policy, often noting when and why they are deviating from the rule.

The Taylor rule is not an infallible predictor, of course. It is based on only two economic variables, whereas central banks collect data on hundreds of economic variables. The rule does not predict interest rates very well in times of crisis, such as around September 11, 2001, and during the financial crisis of 2008. But it does quite well in normal times. Thus, anyone can now predict changes in interest rates.

We will examine the Taylor rule and other recent approaches to policymaking in Chapter 18.

RECAP

Ten surprising facts about money and banking are:

1 Most financial formulas—no matter how complicated they look—are based on the compounding of interest.

2 More U.S. currency is held in foreign countries than in the United States.

3 Interest rates on long-term loans generally are higher than interest rates on short-term loans.

4 To understand how interest rates affect economic decisions, you must account for expected inflation.

5 Buying stocks is the best way to increase your wealth—and the worst.

6 Banks and other financial institutions made major errors that led to the financial crisis of 2008.

7 Recessions are difficult to predict.

8 The Federal Reserve creates money by changing a number in its computer system.

9 In the long run, the only economic variable the Federal Reserve can affect is the rate of inflation—the Fed has no effect on economic activity.

10 You can predict how the Federal Reserve will change interest rates using a simple equation.

Keep these 10 surprising facts in mind as you read through this book. They underscore the importance of understanding the interplay among money, banks, financial markets, and policymakers to explain events within the money and banking system.

Chapter Summary

1 The main goals of this book are to explain why the money and banking system takes its present shape, to explore the economic forces that may be changing that system, to examine the role of economic policy in the economy, and to explore how the money and banking system and policy decisions affect everyday life.

2 The money and banking system and policy decisions matter to you because they affect the interest rates you pay and how you save and invest. Policy decisions play a major role in determining how financial markets and institutions work, how the payments system operates, and how the activities of banks are restricted. Policy also influences how fast the economy grows in the short run and what the inflation rate is in the long run.

3 Many surprising facts arise in money and banking, such as the simple notion behind financial formulas, the location of U.S. dollars, the structure of interest rates, the importance of expected inflation, the role of the stock market, the wellbeing of banks, the causes of recessions, the mechanism for creating money, the long-run impact of monetary policy, and how easy it is to predict the Federal Reserve's actions that change interest rates.

© iStockphoto.com/Bryan Weinstein/

PART 1

MONEY and the FINANCIAL SYSTEM

The **FINANCIAL SYSTEM**
and the **ECONOMY**

At some time in your life, you may need to spend more money than you happen to have on hand—perhaps for your education, for a car, or for a house. Assuming that you don't have a fairy godmother who will drop the needed cash in your lap, where will you get the money you need? By borrowing from people who have funds available to lend. Later in life, you may be the lender, when you are setting aside savings for your retirement. At that point, you will be looking for worthy borrowers who will use your money productively in exchange for paying you a return on your savings.

As you can see, the process of saving and borrowing serves two functions. It provides funds for the person who needs an infusion of cash for a particular purchase, and it provides a way for people who have funds available to lend to earn a return on their savings. Savings are made available to borrowers in several ways. In some cases, savers transfer money directly to a borrower. In other cases, savers deposit their money in financial intermediaries, such as banks, that, in turn, lend the money to borrowers.

FIGURE 2.1 The Financial System

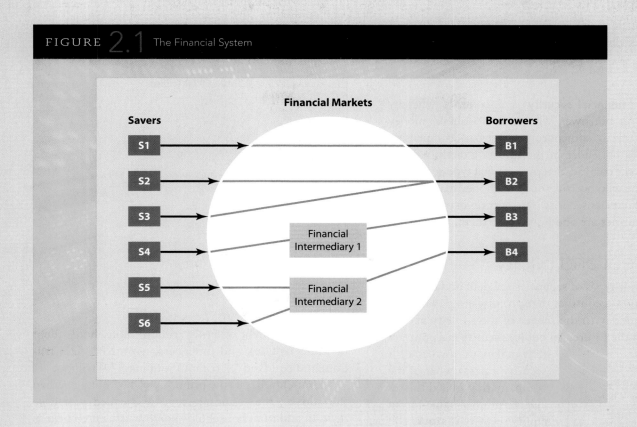

Matching those who have savings with those who want to borrow is the essential purpose of the financial system. The **financial system** consists of all the securities, intermediaries, and markets that exist to match savers and borrowers.

Figure 2.1 illustrates the components of the financial system. Many different savers transact with many different borrowers. You can see in the diagram how money flows from savers to borrowers either directly or through financial intermediaries. The diagram shows the initial flow of funds from savers to borrowers. In return, the borrowers give the savers financial securities, which are contracts that promise to repay the funds that were borrowed. All these transactions, whether involving intermediaries or not, take place in financial markets.

This chapter introduces the financial system and explains why it is an essential part of a well-functioning economy. Financial securities are a vehicle for transferring money, and we examine them first. Then we look at the role of financial intermediaries, which provide an alternative means for transferring money. Next, we discuss how supply and demand in financial markets determine the prices of securities and investigate the problems that arise when financial markets do not function efficiently. We conclude with an application to everyday life—what to consider when you invest your savings.

financial system the securities, intermediaries, and markets that exist to match savers and borrowers

2-1 Financial Securities

A financial security is a contract whereby a borrower, who seeks to obtain money from someone, promises to compensate the lender in the future. Exactly what is promised by the contract determines what type of security it is. Everyone who borrows or lends money may issue or purchase a financial security. This section explains what financial securities are and how to use them.

2-1a Debt and Equity

The two major types of securities are debt and equity. A **debt security** is a contract that promises to pay a given amount of money to the owner of the security at specific dates in the future. An **equity security** is a contract that makes the owner of a security a part owner of the company that issued the security. Another name for an equity security is **stock.**

How much debt and equity exist? At the end of 2012, a total of $82.2 trillion in debt and equity was outstanding in the United States. That amount is more than five times as much as the value of our nation's output in 2012, which was just under $16 trillion. Of the total amount of financial securities, $56.3 trillion was debt and $25.9 trillion was equity, as Figure 2.2 shows.

Who borrows using debt and equity? Households, business firms, foreigners, governments, and financial intermediaries may issue debt. Domestic and foreign business firms and financial intermediaries may also issue equity. The pie charts in Figure 2.3 show the breakdown of debt and equity by issuer. Note that business firms are the biggest issuers of securities, with debt ($12.7 trillion) and equity ($16.2 trillion) issues totaling $28.9 trillion. Next in magnitude are financial intermediaries, with debt ($13.9 trillion) and equity ($5.0 trillion) of $18.9 trillion, followed by

financial security a contract in which a borrower, who seeks to obtain money from someone, promises to compensate the lender in the future

debt security a contract that promises to pay a given amount of money to the owner of the security at specific dates in the future

equity security a contract that makes the owner of a security a part owner of the company that issued the security

stock another name for an equity security

investor the owner of a financial security

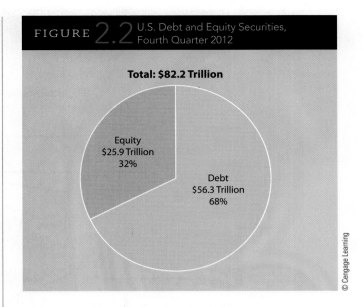

© Cengage Learning

FIGURE 2.2 U.S. Debt and Equity Securities, Fourth Quarter 2012

Total: $82.2 Trillion

Equity $25.9 Trillion 32%

Debt $56.3 Trillion 68%

governments (debt of $14.6 trillion), households (debt of $12.8 trillion), and foreigners, with debt ($2.3 trillion) and equity ($4.7 trillion) totaling $7.0 trillion.

Households borrow primarily to buy homes. When they do so, the resulting security is called *mortgage debt*. In addition, households borrow using credit cards and by taking out loans for large purchases (such as automobiles), both of which are called *consumer credit*. Over three-quarters of household debt is for mortgage loans; the remainder is consumer credit for auto loans, student loans, credit cards, and other items.

Business firms (domestic and foreign) and financial intermediaries borrow using both debt and equity. Governments, especially the federal government, borrow substantial amounts by issuing debt securities.

Who owns these securities? Again, the answer is households, business firms, foreigners, governments, and financial intermediaries. We use the term **investor** to refer to the owner of a financial security. As you can see in Figure 2.4, financial intermediaries are the dominant investors in the U.S. economy, owning 63 percent of all debt securities and 41 percent of all equity securities. The remaining securities are owned by households (18 percent), foreigners (16 percent), and governments (9 percent).

2-1b Differences Between Debt and Equity

The two major types of securities, debt and equity, differ in terms of two details that are specified in the contract: their maturity and the type of periodic payment being made. A key characteristic of debt securities

FIGURE 2.3 Debt and Equity, by Issuer, Fourth Quarter 2012

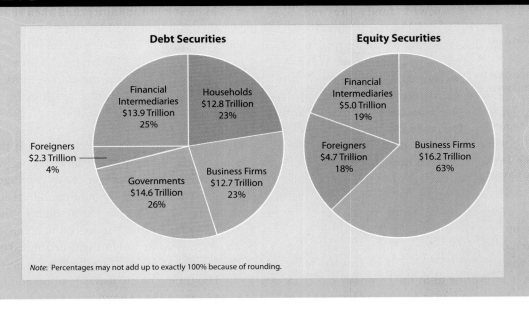

Note: Percentages may not add up to exactly 100% because of rounding.

FIGURE 2.4 Debt and Equity, by Investor, Fourth Quarter 2012

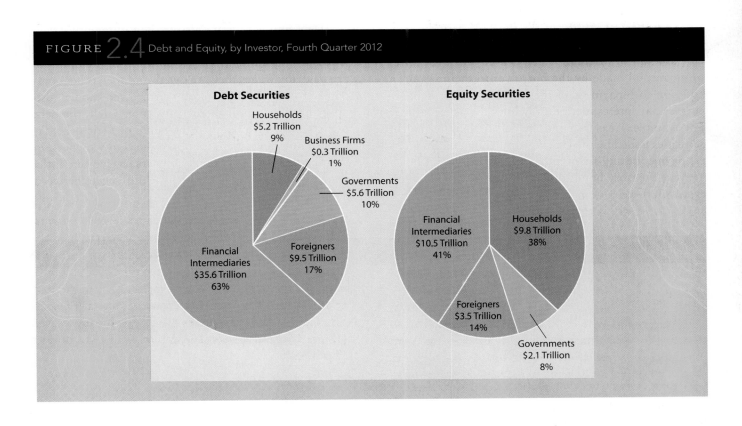

is **maturity,** which is the length of time until the borrowed funds are repaid. A debt security specifies a particular maturity date, at which time the original amount invested, which is known as the **principal,** is returned to the investor. For example, large banks sometimes lend money to each other overnight, so the maturity of the loans is one day. Debt securities issued by corporations and by governments often have much longer maturities—30 years, 40 years, or even 100 years. However, equity has no maturity; when an investor buys stock in a company, she may own it forever or until the company closes its doors. If the investor no longer wants to own equity in the company, she must find someone who wants to buy the stock; the company is under no obligation to return any money to her.

Securities also differ in the types of periodic payments they make. Debt securities promise to pay a specific amount of **interest,** which is a payment (or series of payments) made by the borrower to the investor in addition to repayment of the principal. Most debt securities pay interest periodically until the debt matures. For example, Treasury bonds, which are long-term debt securities issued by the U.S. government, make an interest payment every six months. An investor might buy a 10-year Treasury bond for $10,000 that will pay interest of $300 every six months for 10 years and then repay

the principal of $10,000 at the end of the 10 years. If the maturity of a security is short, however, it may not pay interest until maturity, and then it will pay both principal and interest in one payment. Treasury bills, which are short-term debt securities issued by the U.S. government, follow this pattern. For example, an investor might pay $9,927 for such a security in April and receive a $10,000 repayment in July. In this case, the interest received equals $10,000 − $9,927 = $73.

The periodic payment on equity is known as the **dividend.** Unlike interest, the amount of the dividend a company pays is *not* specified by the equity security. The dividend is paid from a company's earnings, but there is no set formula for the amount paid. Instead, a company can increase or decrease the amount of the dividend it pays. When earnings are high, the company often will increase the amount of its dividend. In bad times, though, it may reduce the size of its dividend or even eliminate it.

The timing of dividends paid on equity also differs across companies. The most common practice is for a company to issue a quarterly dividend. But some companies pay dividends more frequently, others pay dividends less frequently, and some pay no dividends at all.

Debt and equity are also treated differently when a company that issued both goes bankrupt. If the firm is closed and all its assets are sold off, first employees are paid any wages they are owed, and then other companies to which the bankrupt firm owed money also are paid off. Then, if there is any money left, the debt owners are paid off up to the value of their debt. Finally, if anything is left, it goes to the equity owners. In most bankruptcies, the equity owners receive very little, if anything. Table 2.1 illustrates the differences between debt and equity securities.

TABLE 2.1 Characteristics of Financial Securities

Characteristic	Security Type	
	Debt	**Equity**
Terms of contract	A promise to pay interest and to repay principal	Confers ownership to stockholder and rights to receive dividends
Maturity	A specified date in contract	No maturity date
Type of payments to security owner	Periodic interest payment and repayment of principal at maturity date	Periodic dividend payment
How are payment amounts determined?	Interest and principal amounts specified in contract	Dividend amounts determined by company and may change over time
Payments if the firm is bankrupt	Debt owners get repaid before equity owners	Equity owners get repaid after all other claimants

Why do securities differ from each other in so many ways? Because borrowers have different needs, as do investors. One company might want to borrow money for a short-term project, so it issues debt that it will repay in three years. A different company might need to finance projects that will last for a long time, so it might issue debt that it will not repay for 40 years. A new company might need a large amount of cash to get up and running, so it will sell equity to investors. A growing company might need a substantial amount of cash to build new production facilities or invest in research and development. Instead of paying out its earnings as dividends, it will reinvest them in these promising projects and choose not to pay a dividend on its equity.

A more established company may not need new facilities, so it may return most of its earnings to its investors in the form of dividends.

Similarly, investors differ in their desires, so borrowers provide different securities for different investors. Some investors may prefer to receive interest payments every six months, perhaps because they are using those payments for living expenses. Other investors may want to invest as much as possible for 30 years, so they would rather own a security that does not make periodic interest payments but just repays their principal plus a large interest payment at the end of 30 years. Borrowers design the securities they issue to make them attractive to investors.

RECAP

1 Many borrowers obtain funds from lenders by issuing debt and equity securities.

2 Borrowers include households, business firms, foreigners, governments, and financial intermediaries; lenders come from the same groups.

3 Debt and equity differ in maturity: Debt securities have a specific maturity, but equity securities do not mature. They also differ in the type of periodic payment they make: Debt securities pay interest, but equity securities pay dividends.

2-2 Matching Borrowers with Lenders

The financial system exists to match borrowers—those who issue debt and equity securities—with savers who are willing to lend. Within the financial system, matches are facilitated through two channels: direct finance and indirect finance. When savers buy securities directly from borrowers, they are using **direct finance.** But when savers invest through financial intermediaries, they are said to engage in **indirect finance.** A **financial intermediary** is a company that transfers funds from savers to borrowers by receiving funds from savers and investing in securities issued by borrowers. Figure 2.5 compares direct finance with indirect finance. In the diagram, direct finance occurs when some savers and borrowers transact directly with each other. Indirect finance occurs when savers deposit their money in financial intermediaries; those intermediaries then make loans to borrowers.

2-2a Direct Versus Indirect Finance

The distinction between direct and indirect finance is useful because each method is more efficient under some circumstances. Both direct finance and indirect finance use financial securities, and both types of transactions are conducted in financial markets. When a country's financial system is young, it usually relies more on intermediaries, so indirect finance is used more often than direct finance. Over time, however, as the economy gets larger, direct finance usually grows relative to indirect finance.

Borrowers generally have a choice of using indirect finance through financial intermediaries or using direct finance. To help you distinguish direct finance from indirect finance, consider this example. Sigfried's, Inc., is

direct finance when savers buy securities directly from borrowers

indirect finance when savers invest through financial intermediaries, which buy securities from borrowers

financial intermediary a company that transfers funds from savers to borrowers by receiving funds from savers and investing in securities issued by borrowers

FIGURE 2.5 Direct and Indirect Finance

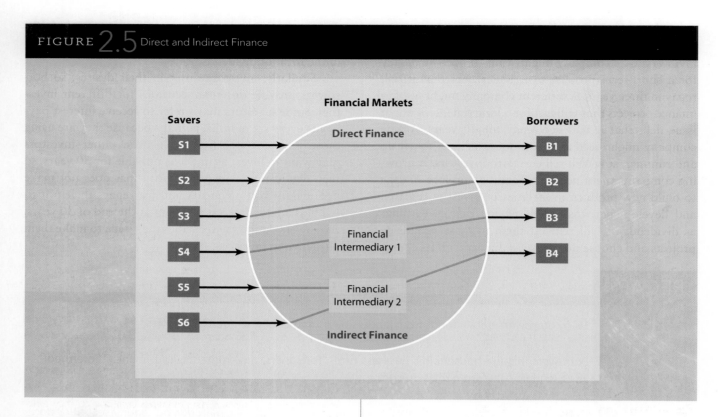

a company that produces protective covers for smartphones. The company would like to borrow to expand its production facilities in order to reduce its average cost of producing covers. It can borrow using direct finance by selling bonds directly to investors in the bond market. Alternatively, Sigfried's can try to get a financial intermediary to lend the funds. Which avenue Sigfried's chooses depends mainly on which interest rate will be lower: that on the bonds it issues via direct finance or that on the loan from the intermediary via indirect finance.

2-2b Financial Intermediaries

Financial intermediaries issue and own a large percentage of all the securities in the United States, as we saw in Figures 2.3 and 2.4. Consequently, financial intermediaries are major participants in the financial system. They also play a vital role in the economy. There are many different types of financial intermediaries, including commercial banks, savings institutions, credit unions, life insurance companies, mutual funds, pension funds, and finance companies, which we will discuss in greater detail in Chapter 9. Many intermediaries specialize in accepting deposits from households of all sizes, and they make loans to individuals, families, and small businesses.

Throughout their lives, people come into contact with financial intermediaries. When people are young, they might deposit the money from a relative's gift into a savings account at a bank. As young adults, they may borrow money for the first time to buy a car, obtaining the funds from a finance company associated with the car's manufacturer. Later in life, they might borrow money to buy a house, getting the loan from a credit union. To save for the future, they might invest in debt securities and equity securities through a mutual fund. In retirement, they might purchase an annuity from a life insurance company, which will pay them some amount every month for the rest of their lives.

2-2c Functions of Financial Intermediaries

So what, exactly, does a financial intermediary do? Intermediaries make financial transactions easier for both borrowers and savers by providing many useful services, including helping savers diversify, pooling the funds of many people, taking short-term deposits and making long-term loans, gathering information, and reducing the costs of financial transactions.

Intermediaries help savers diversify their financial investments. Diversification is the ownership of a variety of securities, and it enables investors to avoid "putting all their eggs in one basket." Consider the risks an investor would face if she could not diversify. Suppose that Sue has $1,000 to lend and that Bill asks her for a loan of $1,000. Sue might be nervous that all her money would be tied up with one borrower. If something happened to Bill's business and he could not repay the loan, Sue might lose all her money. Instead, if she took her money to a financial intermediary, it could use Sue's money, along with money from other depositors, to finance Bill and other borrowers. By pooling her savings with others and using a financial intermediary, Sue would have diversified her financial investments, spreading her money out among many different borrowers, so she would be less likely to suffer financial losses.

One type of intermediary that offers diversification is a mutual fund. A mutual fund sells equity shares in itself to many investors and pools their money to buy many different securities. Some popular mutual funds buy equity in most of the 500 largest companies in the country, so an investor who invests a few thousand dollars in the mutual fund is quite well diversified, with a financial investment spread over about 500 different companies.

Financial intermediaries pool the funds of many people. Suppose that a borrower wants a loan of $1 million, but no individual is willing or able to lend that much. The intermediary could collect the resources of 1,000 people who are willing to lend an average of $1,000 each to make the loan and thus match the borrower with savers who otherwise would not be able to get together.

Intermediaries take short-term deposits and make long-term loans. Intermediaries are able to match borrowers and savers who have different time horizons. Here is an example of how an intermediary makes home ownership possible. For most people, borrowing to purchase a house is the largest amount they will borrow in their lifetimes. A house is such a major expense that most people who take out a mortgage loan pay the loan off over most of their working lives, usually 30 years. However, very few savers want to commit their money for 30 years. Therefore, an intermediary brings together short-term savers, offering them a way to deposit money for a short time, and makes mortgage loans to home buyers for a long time. This is a potentially risky business because it requires the intermediary to constantly find new short-term depositors in order to support the long-term loans that it made.

diversification ownership of a variety of securities by an investor

Intermediaries play an important role in the economy by gathering information. Intermediaries specialize in making loans and therefore are willing to spend substantial resources investigating the creditworthiness of borrowers. If an individual saver had some small amount to lend, he would have much less incentive to find out information about borrowers. But because an intermediary is making loans continually, it remains informed about borrowers, what their businesses are, and how they will use the loan proceeds. Thus intermediaries specialize in information about borrowers.

As an example, suppose that you wanted to buy a car and needed to borrow $5,000 to do so. You would have a difficult time getting a loan that large from people on the street or even from your friends and neighbors. But a financial intermediary specializes in knowing about people such as you who borrow to buy cars. The intermediary will obtain information on your credit history and the probability that you will repay the loan. It also has lawyers who know how to deal with you in an efficient way if you do not repay the loan. Without an intermediary, you might not be able to borrow; with an intermediary, doing so is easier.

Intermediaries reduce the costs of transacting. Consider what would happen if Bill asked Sue for a loan instead of using an intermediary. Sue is unlikely to know how to analyze Bill's credit history; she might need to hire someone to help her. She also would need to hire a lawyer to write a contract to ensure that the loan would be repaid. Because an intermediary engages in thousands of similar loans each year, however, it hires workers to specialize in particular areas, such as analyzing a household's credit history or calculating a restaurant's potential for profitability.

RECAP

1 Direct finance occurs when savers and borrowers transact with each other; indirect finance occurs when savers and borrowers transact with financial intermediaries.

2 Financial intermediaries provide a number of services: helping investors diversify, pooling funds (collecting many small deposits to make a big loan), taking short-term deposits and making long-term loans, gathering information, and reducing transactions costs.

2-3 Financial Markets

So far we have seen that financial securities and intermediaries enable funds to flow from savers to borrowers. The securities are bought and sold in financial markets, and the intermediaries compete in financial markets as well. As in all markets, supply and demand determine the prices of financial securities.

2-3a The Structure of Financial Markets

A **financial market** is a place or a mechanism by which borrowers, savers, and financial intermediaries trade securities. For example, the New York Stock Exchange is a financial market in which the equity securities of many of the largest U.S. companies are traded. Similarly, in the market for U.S. government bonds, anyone can buy or sell debt securities that were issued originally by the U.S. government. If you glance at the financial pages of any major newspaper, you will see listed thousands of financial securities that are sold in many different financial markets.

Some financial markets have a central physical location at which all transactions take place, as in the case of the New York Stock Exchange. But you do not have to go there yourself; instead, you can arrange for a local broker to send instructions to buy or sell stock through a representative at the stock exchange. You also can buy and sell stock online. Many brokerages offer an online service in addition to their regular brokerage accounts, whereas other brokerages exist only as online firms.

Other financial markets are local. For example, in your hometown, there is a financial market for certificates of deposit (CDs), which are accounts offered by banks, savings institutions, and credit unions. These CD accounts usually pay more interest than regular bank accounts, but depositors must leave their money on deposit at the intermediary for a minimum amount of time, such as one or two years. Those intermediaries often advertise their rates in newspapers, trying to entice savers to deposit money in their CD accounts. Because most people find it inconvenient to have CD accounts in far-flung places, the market for CDs is usually local, with advertising in local papers being the main marketing tool.

Some markets do not have a physical location, however. Electronic communication and the Internet simplify the matching of buyers and sellers. Many markets are becoming all electronic, which greatly reduces the costs of trading. An example is the NASDAQ stock market, on which many high-tech and small-company stocks are traded. Physical markets such as the New York Stock Exchange eventually may disappear, replaced by a computer system that matches the demand and supply for every financial security.

Markets differ in another way, depending on whether the market is for a new security or for securities being resold. When a security is first issued, it is sold on the **primary market.** An investor buys the security from a borrower. Subsequently, the security may be sold by one investor to another investor, and this type of transaction can happen again and again. These sales of a security occur in the **secondary market.** This distinction is important because only sales on the primary market generate funds for the issuer of the security, as Figure 2.6 illustrates. For example, the U.S. government borrows by auctioning its bonds in the primary market. After that, investors can trade those bonds with each other in the secondary market, on which many more sales occur than on the primary market. Both investors and financial intermediaries are active participants in the secondary market.

2-3b How Financial Markets Determine Prices of Securities

Whether a financial market is centralized or localized, or whether it is a primary or secondary market, every market is similar in one regard: The prices of the goods traded in it are governed by supply and demand. The only difference between financial securities and most other goods and services is that financial securities are not consumed, so they may be bought and sold many times.

To understand how the price of a financial security is determined, consider the following example. Suppose that some borrowers wish to borrow funds today and repay the funds in a year. Let's see how a financial market could operate to get funds from lenders to these borrowers.

To keep things simple, suppose that the borrowers will repay $1,500 in one year and want to borrow as much as they can today. We will assume that there

financial market a place or a mechanism by which borrowers, savers, and financial intermediaries trade securities

primary market the market in which a security is initially sold to an investor by a borrower

secondary market the market in which a security is sold from one investor to another

FIGURE 2.6 Primary and Secondary Markets

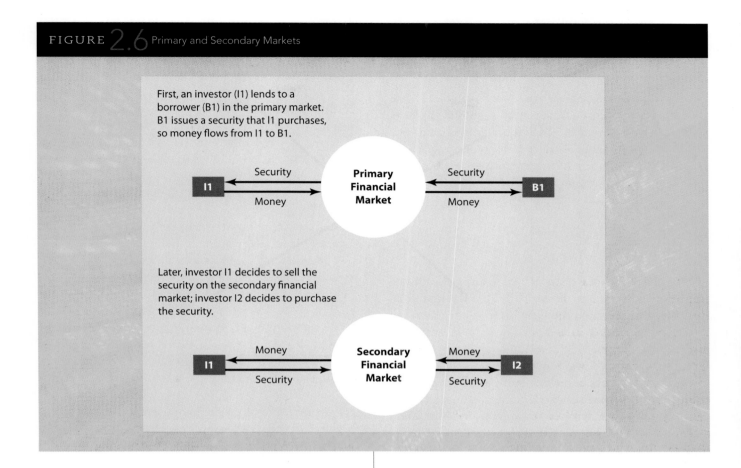

First, an investor (I1) lends to a borrower (B1) in the primary market. B1 issues a security that I1 purchases, so money flows from I1 to B1.

Later, investor I1 decides to sell the security on the secondary financial market; investor I2 decides to purchase the security.

are no periodic interest payments, just one repayment when the security matures. The amount of interest is the amount repaid ($1,500) minus the price of the security. For example, if the price of the security were $1,400, then the amount of interest would be

$$Interest = amount\ repaid - price$$
$$= \$1,500 - \$1,400 = \$100$$

Similarly, if the price of the security were $1,300, the amount of interest would be

$$Interest = amount\ repaid - price$$
$$= \$1,500 - \$1,300 = \$200$$

On the demand side of the security market, investors will want to buy more securities, the more interest they receive. Because the interest paid will be greater when the price of the security is lower, the greater will be the quantity demanded of the security. The higher the price (hence the lower the interest payment), the lower will be the quantity demanded.

On the supply side of the security market, borrowers will want to borrow more, the less interest they must pay.

Thus a lower price (higher interest payment) will cause the quantity supplied to be lower; a higher price (lower interest payment) will cause the quantity supplied to be higher.

Figure 2.7 represents this market. The quantity of the security is shown on the horizontal axis, and the price is shown on the vertical axis. The demand curve and the supply curve for the security intersect at the equilibrium price. In the graph, the equilibrium price of the security is $1,400; the equilibrium quantity is 53. At a price of $1,400, the interest on the security is

$$Interest = amount\ repaid - price$$
$$= \$1,500 - \$1,400 = \$100$$

However, the equilibrium price and quantity may vary as conditions in the market change. Consider an event that might shift the demand curve or the supply curve and thus affect the price. For example, suppose that businesses believe that the economy will soon grow more rapidly, increasing the demand for their products. They may want to obtain more equipment so that they can increase production to meet the increased demand, which may lead them to borrow more

FIGURE 2.7 Supply and Demand for a Security

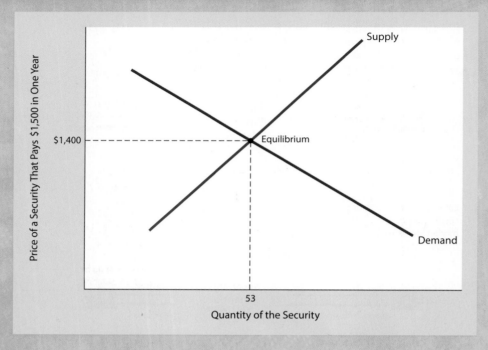

than before, which they do by increasing their supply of securities. Thus, the supply curve of securities shifts to the right.

As Figure 2.8 shows, with the supply curve shifting to the right (from S^1 to S^2), the result is a decline in the equilibrium price of the security. In the graph, the equilibrium price falls from $1,400 today to $1,350. As a result, the interest paid on the security rises from $100 to $150. (The new amount of interest is $1,500 − $1,350 = $150.) The equilibrium quantity rises to 65. Thus, an increased supply of securities leads to a higher quantity of securities sold

and a lower price. See the box "Calculating the Price of a Security" for a numerical example, using equations for demand and supply.

In the real world, financial markets are similar to the market for these $1,500 securities. Factors that change the demand or supply of the security will shift the demand curve or supply curve and thus affect the security's price. Financial markets are not much different from the markets for all other goods and services: If you can figure out what causes the demand or supply to shift, you will discover how the price of the security is likely to change.

Calculating the Price of a Security

The price of a security can be calculated if the equations describing supply and demand are known. For example, suppose that the quantity demanded for a security is

$$B_D = 380 - 0.15b$$

and the quantity supplied of the security is

$$B_S = 100 + 0.05b$$

where b is the price of the security. Then quantity demanded equals quantity supplied when b is such that $B_S = B_D$, so

$$100 + 0.05b = 380 - 0.15b$$

Adding $0.15b - 100$ to both sides of this equation and then multiplying both sides by 5 gives

$$b = 1,400$$

Thus, the equilibrium price of the security is $1,400.

FIGURE 2.8 Shift of Supply for a Security

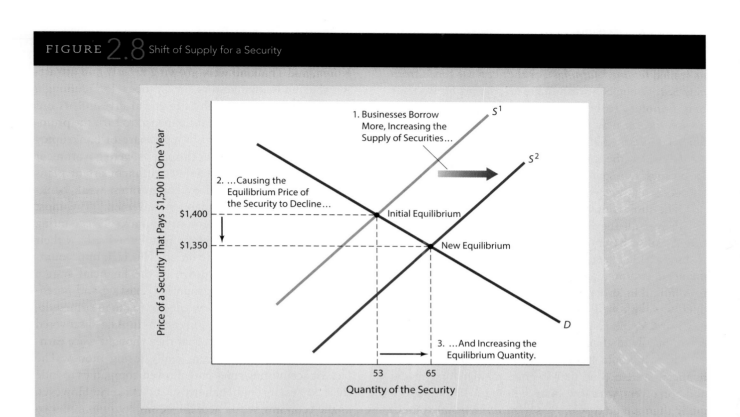

Figure 2.8 Shift of Supply for a Security

1. Businesses Borrow More, Increasing the Supply of Securities...

2. ...Causing the Equilibrium Price of the Security to Decline...

3. ...And Increasing the Equilibrium Quantity.

Price of a Security That Pays $1,500 in One Year

$1,400 — Initial Equilibrium
$1,350 — New Equilibrium

Quantity of the Security

53   65

RECAP

1 Financial markets are where financial securities are bought and sold.

2 Some financial markets are national, whereas others are local. Some exist in a physical location, whereas others exist electronically.

3 The primary market is where new securities are sold by a borrower to an investor; the secondary market is where securities are sold from one investor to another.

4 Prices of securities are determined by supply and demand.

2-4 The Financial System

While matching savers and borrowers, the financial system contributes to the health of the economy as a whole. A well-functioning financial system fosters economic growth. When the economy grows, people enjoy higher living standards, improved education, and expanded opportunities. In this section we describe the link between a financial system and economic growth, and we discuss problems that may occur when the financial system does not work efficiently.

2-4a The Financial System and Economic Growth

For an economy to grow, business firms must be able to buy capital goods such as computers, buildings, and equipment for producing output. Firms have two sources of funds. They can use funds retained from past profits (called *retained earnings*), or they can use funds from new borrowing. New firms have no past profits, so their only option is to borrow. The ability to borrow thus is essential for new firms to grow, which is one reason financial intermediation is vital for economic growth.

Consider the case of the Paradise Flower Shop. Its business is expanding, and it does not have enough trucks to deliver all the flowers that are ordered in a day. The shop is turning away business because it cannot deliver all the flowers that customers wish to order. Paradise has not yet accumulated enough profits to buy another truck. If Paradise can borrow from a financial intermediary to buy a truck, it will be able to fulfill all its orders. However, if the financial system does not work well, making it so that Paradise cannot buy a truck, the result is less business for Paradise, an economically inefficient outcome.

Thus, it would seem that a country with an efficient financial system (one that is good at matching savers and borrowers, with low costs of doing so) should grow faster than a country that has a weak financial system. Indeed, research has shown that countries with efficient financial systems tend to grow faster than countries whose financial systems do not work as well.[1]

2-4b What Happens When the Financial System Works Poorly?

When the financial system works well, business firms, households, and governments can borrow and invest at low cost. If business firms cannot borrow to build new plants or buy equipment (investment in physical capital), however, economic growth will be slow. If individuals cannot borrow to buy houses or cars, their standard of living will be lower. If people and businesses get lower returns on their financial investments and investments in physical capital, they will invest less, economic growth will decrease, and the standard of living will decline.

From time to time throughout history, financial systems have been inefficient. Some financial inefficiencies result in economic crises. Other financial inefficiencies are not as severe, but they cause the economy to grow more slowly than it would if the financial system worked better. Here are some examples.

The Asian crisis. In the mid-1990s, the economies of Hong Kong, Indonesia, Malaysia, Singapore, South Korea, and Thailand were growing rapidly and attracting the funds of investors. In October 1997, though, investors began to pull their financial investments out of Asia with urgency. What happened to turn the promise of a golden future into a nightmare of bankruptcy in these countries? Among the causes were government involvement in the financial sector, inconsistent plans for monetary policy and exchange rates, weak banking systems, and poor debt management. The most significant investor concern was a lack of accounting rules that prevented investors from knowing how their financial investments were doing. This lack of accounting rules led to a breakdown of the financial system because, without good accounting, existing and potential investors lack the knowledge to make informed decisions. In the late 1990s, investors in Asia discovered that financial investments that they thought were earning reasonable profits were really losing money. The lack of accounting rules had allowed companies to hide their losses through balance-sheet trickery. However, as the economy weakened, the losses became harder to disguise, and investors realized that their profits were much lower than they previously thought.

The Asian crisis shows that honest accounting standards are crucial. Without good accounting standards, investors will not have the information needed to assess the value of financial securities.

The savings and loan crisis. In the 1980s, the United States suffered through an episode similar to the Asian crisis when savings and loan institutions (S&Ls) began failing in large numbers. The S&Ls began to lose money when inflation rose to double-digit levels in the late 1970s and early 1980s. The S&Ls were making long-term mortgage loans, which they financed with short-term deposit accounts. A rise in inflation caused the interest rates they had to pay out on their deposit accounts to rise sharply, but their long-term mortgage loans were fixed at low interest rates. As a result, the S&Ls lost huge amounts of money. Government regulators failed to close the S&Ls promptly, so their losses multiplied substantially.

Thus, the financial system can fail if financial intermediaries do not transfer funds efficiently. In the S&L crisis, the government's delay in closing down the bankrupt S&Ls multiplied losses tremendously, distorted real estate markets throughout the country for many years, and caused the 1990–1991 recession to be much worse than it otherwise might have been.

---

[1]See Aubhik Khan, "The Finance and Growth Nexus," Federal Reserve Bank of Philadelphia. *Business Review,* January–February 2000, pp. 3–14.

Mortgages and housing. In the United States, home ownership is a common goal for most families. Prior to the financial crisis in 2008, home ownership was at an all-time high, as the U.S. financial system made mortgage loans widely available. But the financial crisis proved that U.S. lenders had extended too many mortgage loans in an unsound manner. Since 2008, it has become much more difficult for prospective home buyers to obtain a mortgage loan to buy a house. As a result, home ownership in the future is likely to occur only when the homeowners are old enough to have obtained a substantial down payment on their homes, and they are likely to begin with smaller houses and less mortgage debt.

Thus, the financial system makes an important contribution to people's standards of living. The ease of owning a home is directly related to the functioning of the financial system.

The financial crisis of 2008. In the mid-2000s, housing prices in the United States rose sharply, propelled in part by subprime lending, in which lenders provided mortgage loans to people whose ability to repay was unclear. They did so because housing prices were rising rapidly, and they expected the value of the home that was purchased to rise so much that even if the borrower did not repay the loan, the lender could take possession of the home and resell it at a tidy profit. But when home prices began to decline in 2007, the whole subprime scheme began to unravel. Many of the subprime mortgage loans had been packaged together into mortgage-backed securities, which were owned by investors all over the world. As those investors panicked and began selling their securities, the market for mortgage-backed securities crashed, and numerous investment firms suffered billions of dollars in losses. Many of those firms were highly leveraged (in some cases having assets as much as 33 times the value of their capital), so even a small decline in the value of their assets drove them to insolvency. Because mortgage-backed securities were so widespread, the panic spread all over the world and governments and central banks were forced to bail out banks and other financial institutions to prevent a complete collapse of the financial system. Nearly every industrialized country in the world went into a deep recession, and fears of another Great Depression were widespread.

The main lessons we learned from the crisis are that financial firms and borrowers need to protect themselves from becoming insolvent if house prices decline. Unregulated financial firms need to be prevented from growing so large that their failure would severely damage the economy. Government regulators need to respond more quickly when foolish financial practices, such as subprime lending, occur. The Dodd–Frank Act, passed in 2010, gave regulators more power to prevent financial firms from taking risks that could cause financial markets to crash. Included in the bill was a requirement that the Federal Reserve perform stress tests on banks, requiring banks to show that a large decline in house prices will not cause them to fail. Home buyers should also be able to withstand the effects of a large decline in home prices and should not base their home purchase decision on the assumption that home prices will always rise.

RECAP

1   An efficient financial system enables people to borrow or lend easily at low cost.

2   More efficient financial systems exist in countries with faster economic growth.

3   When the financial system is inefficient, the economy does not work as well.

What do investors care about? With so many different types of financial securities available, how do investors decide which securities they should own? In this section we look at the key factors that investors examine in determining their demand for securities.

2-4c Five Determinants of Investors' Decisions

Investors need to consider five major attributes of financial securities: expected return, risk, liquidity, taxability, and maturity.

Expected return. The most important attribute of a financial security that an investor cares about is **expected return,** which is the gain that the investor anticipates making, on average, from owning that security. We will explain the "return" part first and then show why the adjective "expected" is needed.

The **return** to a security is the income from a security plus the change in the value of the security as a percentage of the security's initial value. The return consists of two parts: current yield, which reflects the income from interest or dividends that the investor earns, and capital-gains yield, which reflects a change in the value of the security.

Current yield is the income the investor receives in some period divided by the value of the security at the beginning of that period. The income might be the interest paid on a debt security or the dividend paid on an equity security. The current yield is calculated as

$$Current\ yield = \frac{income}{initial\ value}$$

For example, suppose that an investor purchased 100 shares of PepsiCo, Inc., stock at $50 per share,

expected return the gain that an investor anticipates making, on average, from a financial security

return the income from a security plus the change in the value of the security as a percentage of the security's initial value

current yield the income the investor receives in some period divided by the value of the security at the beginning of that period

capital gain the increase in the dollar value of a financial investment in some period

capital-gains yield the capital gain divided by the value of the security at the beginning of the period

a total financial investment of 100 shares × $50 per share = $5,000. And suppose that over the course of the year, PepsiCo stock pays a dividend of $0.50 per share, so the income the investor receives is 100 shares × $0.50 per share = $50. The investor's current yield is

$$Current\ yield = \frac{income}{initial\ value} = \frac{\$50}{\$5,000} = 0.01$$

We often express return, current yield, and capital-gains yield in percentage terms by multiplying the decimal amount by 100 percent:

$$Current\ yield\ (in\ percent) = current\ yield\ (in\ decimal\ form)\\ \times 100\ percent$$

In this example, the current yield in decimal form of 0.01 also can be called a current yield of 1 percent:

$$Current\ yield\ (in\ percent)\\ = current\ yield\ (in\ decimal\ form) \times 100\ percent\\ = 0.01 \times 100\ percent\\ = 1\ percent$$

Thus, PepsiCo stock that costs $5,000 and pays a dividend of $50 over the year has a current yield of 1 percent.

The second component of the return to a security is the capital-gains yield. A **capital gain** is the increase in the dollar value of a financial investment in some period. The **capital-gains yield** is the capital gain divided by the value of the security at the beginning of the period. That is,

$$Capital\ gain = final\ value - initial\ value$$
$$Capital\text{-}gains\ yield = \frac{capital\ gain}{initial\ value}$$

In the PepsiCo stock example, suppose that one year after being purchased by the investor for $50 per share, PepsiCo stock is worth $56 per share, so the value of 100 shares is now 100 shares × $56 per share = $5,600. The capital gain is

$$Capital\ gain = final\ value - initial\ value$$
$$= \$5{,}600 - \$5{,}000 = \$600$$

The capital-gains yield is

$$Capital\text{-}gains\ yield = \frac{capital\ gain}{initial\ value}$$
$$= \frac{\$600}{\$5{,}000} = 0.12$$

or, in percentage terms,

$$Capital\text{-}gains\ yield = 0.12 = 0.12 \times 100\ percent$$
$$= 12\ percent$$

The capital-gains yield can be negative if the security declines in value. If the price of PepsiCo stock fell from $50 per share to $41 per share, the capital gain would be

$$Capital\ gain = final\ value - initial\ value$$
$$= (100\ shares \times \$41\ per\ share)$$
$$- (100\ shares \times \$50\ per\ share)$$
$$= \$4{,}100 - \$5{,}000 = -\$900$$

A negative capital gain is a capital loss. In this case, the capital-gains yield is

$$Capital\text{-}gains\ yield = \frac{capital\ gain}{initial\ value} = \frac{-\$900}{\$5{,}000} = -0.18$$

or, in percentage terms,

$$Capital\text{-}gains\ yield = -0.18 \times 100\ percent$$
$$= -18\ percent$$

The return to a financial security is the sum of the current yield and the capital-gains yield:

$$Return = current\ yield + capital\text{-}gains\ yield$$

In the example of the PepsiCo stock in the situation in which the stock price rose to $56 at the end of the year, the return is

$$Return = current\ yield + capital\text{-}gains\ yield$$
$$= 0.01 + 0.12 = 0.13 = 13\ percent$$

In the situation in which the stock price fell to $41 at the end of the year, the return is

$$Return = current\ yield + capital\text{-}gains\ yield$$
$$= 0.01 + (-0.18) = -0.17 = -17\ percent$$

Investors must make decisions about what securities to purchase before they know what the returns on the securities will be. The returns to equity securities are not known in advance because the firm's dividend payout may change over the course of a year, and so may its stock price. In the case of a debt security, an investor may not know what the return will be because the issuer of the debt may default and not make the required interest payment or principal repayment. Because of this uncertainty, an investor's decision about whether to invest in a security is based on the *expected* return, which is the return the investor expects to receive, on average.

To illustrate how to calculate the expected return, we return to our PepsiCo example. The stock price of PepsiCo is $50 at the start of the year. Suppose that the probability is 75 percent that PepsiCo's stock price will rise to $56 at the end of the year so that the return on PepsiCo stock would be 13 percent. And suppose that the probability is 25 percent that PepsiCo's stock price will decline to $41 at the end of the year so that the return on PepsiCo stock would be −17 percent. Then the expected return to PepsiCo stock is

$$Expected\ return$$
$$= (probability\ of\ high\ return \times high\ return)$$
$$+ (probability\ of\ low\ return \times low\ return)$$
$$= (0.75 \times 0.13) + (0.25 \times -0.17)$$
$$= 0.0975 - 0.0425 = 0.055 = 5.5\ percent$$

The expected return on PepsiCo stock is 5.5 percent. If all other factors were the same, an investor would rather buy a security with a high expected return than one with a low expected return. However, an investor must consider other factors, the most important of which is the risk to the investment.

Risk. The second determinant of financial investment decision making is risk. The **risk** to a security is the amount of uncertainty about the return to that security. What causes the return to be uncertain? The main causes of uncertainty are default by the issuer of a debt security,

risk the amount of uncertainty about the return on a security

How to Calculate a Security's Expected Return

The expected return to a security that has many different possible returns can be found by following these steps:

1. Multiply each return by its probability.
2. Add up the results from step 1.

The sum found in step 2 is the expected return. A general formula for the expected return to a security is

$$E = p_1 X_1 + p_2 X_2 + \cdots + p_N X_N \qquad \text{(1)}$$

where there are N possible outcomes, and a given outcome X_i ($i = 1, 2, \ldots, N$) occurs with probability p_i. The sum $p_1 + p_2 + \cdots p_N$ must equal 1 because probabilities must add up to 100 percent.

For example, suppose a security has four possible returns: a return of 1 percent with probability 0.4, 2 percent with probability 0.3, 3 percent with probability 0.2, and 5 percent with probability 0.1. Note that the probabilities add up to one ($0.4 + 0.3 + 0.2 + 0.1 = 1.0$), as required. The expected return, using Equation (1), is

$$
\begin{aligned}
E &= p_1 X_1 + p_2 X_2 + \cdots + p_N X_N \\
&= (0.4 \times 1\%) + (0.3 \times 2\%) + (0.2 \times 3\%) + (0.1 \times 5\%) \\
&= 0.4\% + 0.6\% + 0.6\% + 0.5\% = 2.1\%.
\end{aligned}
$$

---

an unexpected change in the dividend paid on an equity security, a change in the price of a security, and an unexpected change in the inflation rate.

First, an investor in debt securities should realize that the issuer of a security may be unable to pay the interest or repay the principal when due. When the issuer fails to make such a payment, it is in **default.** (See the Data Bank box "Default Risk on Debt.") If a company borrows using equity, no explicit payment is promised, so default is not an issue.

Second, investors in equity securities face the risk that the dividend payout may change unexpectedly. For example, General Motors Corporation (GM) paid dividends of $2 per share each year from 2000 to 2005, then cut its dividend to $1 per share in 2006. After paying a dividend of $0.25 per share early in 2007, GM stopped paying a dividend altogether because of substantial losses that it was incurring. The company declared bankruptcy in 2009 and was restructured in 2010, and existing shares of GM stock became worthless. Investors can never know for certain how much income they will receive from dividends.

Third, investors face the risk of a change in the price of a security. The risk of a change in the market price of a security cuts both ways—there is *upside risk* (the chance that the price will rise) and *downside risk* (the chance that the price will decline). The amount of risk from a change in the market price of a security varies across types of securities. Some securities, such as debt securities that mature within three

default the situation when the issuer fails to make a payment promised by a debt security

standard deviation a measure of the risk to a security

months, have almost no such risk because they will soon pay a given amount to their owners. Other securities, such as equity securities in industries whose profits are volatile, are very risky. Some of the risk to a security is correlated with the risk to other securities. For example, the prices of many stocks rise and fall together. But every security also has its own independent risk. For example, the stock price of GM fell from $72.68 per share at the start of 2000 to $19.42 per share at the start of 2006, then plummeted to $3.20 at the start of 2009, and the stock had no value in mid-2010. In the chapters that follow, we will examine in greater detail the risk to a change in the market price of a security.

A fourth source of risk is a change in the inflation rate. Almost all securities sold in the United States pay interest or dividends in dollars. But because the amount of goods and services that those dollars can buy depends on the inflation rate in the economy (the change in the average price of goods and services), those financial securities pay a risky return. Sue knows that her security will pay her $1,500 in one year, but she does not know how much she will be able to buy with that amount of money. If inflation is low, she will be able to buy more; if inflation is high, she will not be able to buy as much. (For more on this topic, see the Data Bank box "How Much Risk Do Investors Face from Inflation?")

Given all the sources of risk, investors must decide what securities they want to buy. They must ask themselves: Is the expected return worth the risk? How much additional expected return is needed to justify taking on additional risk?

Quantifying risk is not easy. The most widely used measure of risk is the **standard deviation**. The idea

Risk is a part of life. Every person can choose how much risk to take. Some workers, such as the worker shown here removing asbestos from a house, choose to take a substantial amount of risk. They are compensated for doing so by earning higher wages. Similarly, in financial markets, an investor may decide to take on additional risk to obtain a higher expected return.

behind the standard deviation is to determine how far the different possible returns are from the expected return. To measure the standard deviation, we follow these steps:

1. Calculate the difference (or "deviation") of each return from the expected return.
2. Square each of those differences (that is, multiply it times itself).
3. Multiply those squared differences by the probability that the return occurs.
4. Add all the numbers from step 3 for all the possible returns.
5. Take the square root of the sum in step 4.

The reason for squaring the deviations is to give a greater weight to deviations that are bigger. As a result, if we compare the standard deviation on two different securities, the measure will be higher for a security whose deviations are bigger—that is, whose returns differ from the expected value by more. And this is precisely what we mean by risk.

How to Calculate the Standard Deviation of the Return to a Security

The calculation of standard deviation may be easier to understand with the following formula, using the same terms that were used in Equation (1):

$$\text{Standard deviation} = \{[\text{probability of outcome 1} \times (\text{deviation of outcome 1})^2]$$

$$+ [\text{probability of outcome 2} \times (\text{deviation of outcome 2})^2]$$

$$+ \cdots + [\text{probability of outcome N} \times (\text{deviation of outcome N})^2]\}^{1/2}$$

$$= [p_1(X_1 - E)^2 + p_2(X_2 - E)^2 + \cdots + p_N(X_N - E)^2]^{1/2} \tag{2}$$

where there are N possible outcomes and E comes from Equation (1). Note that raising a term to the ½ power means taking the square root.

We can observe how the market for debt treats default risk by comparing interest rates on the debt of companies that are strong financially (and thus unlikely to default) with interest rates on the debt issued by companies that are not as strong financially. Because investors care about the likelihood of a company defaulting on its debt, they pay research firms to rate the financial strength of different companies. Those ratings, which are carried out by firms such as Moody's Corporation and Standard & Poor's Corporation, give each company a rating, with an A rating being better than a B rating, and so on. Within each rating class are finer gradations. Within the A class, the strongest companies are given a rating of Aaa, then those that are not quite as strong are rated Aa, and then those that are slightly worse are rated A. For companies with a B rating, the companies are rated Baa, then Ba, and then B. Companies with a relatively high chance of default are rated Caa, then Ca, and then C, which is the lowest grade. (This is the rating scale for Moody's; other rating firms have slightly different scales.)

The ratings are not perfect, but they are useful to investors. The companies that supply the ratings spend resources and time gathering information, so they provide more comprehensive data than an investor could find on his own. And if you look in the financial pages, you will note that the interest rate paid on bonds is higher, the lower the bond rating. For example, suppose that we examine the interest rates on Aaa debt compared with Baa debt (Figure 2.A) across time. On average, the difference in interest rates between Aaa and Baa debt is 1.00 percentage point (from January 1956 to March 2013). However, if we look at a plot of the difference between the interest rates (Figure 2.B), which we call a *risk spread* because it shows the difference in interest rates because of risk, we can see that it has changed substantially over time. The risk spread (the Baa interest rate minus the Aaa interest rate) was the smallest in January 1966, at just 0.32 percentage point, and it was the largest in December 2008, at 3.38 percentage points. Most of the changes in the risk spread depend on the overall state of the economy, which can be seen by looking at the vertical blue bars, which denote time periods in which the economy was in a recession. Note that the risk spread rises sharply in most recessions and then declines when the recession is over. This is what we should expect because more companies go bankrupt in recessions than any other time, so the differences in default risk between companies rated Aaa and Baa are magnified.

FIGURE 2.A Interest Rates on Aaa versus Baa Bonds

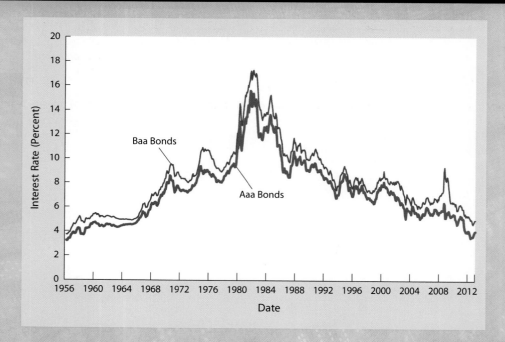

FIGURE 2.B Risk Spread (Aaa versus Baa)

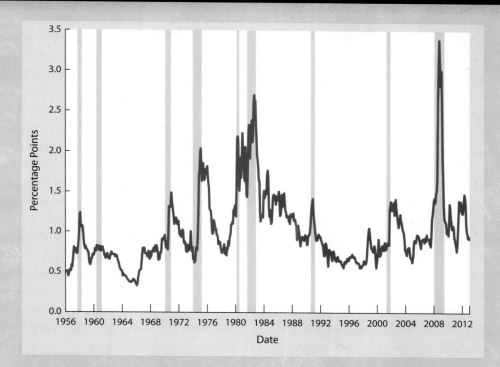

Even when times are good, some companies go bankrupt and default on their debt. For example, in 2006, 29 companies defaulted on debt securities. Investors in debt securities lost $7 billion as a result. Of course, when the economy is not do-ing well, default risk is even greater. In 2009, 265 companies defaulted on $628 billion in debt.

All investors must be mindful of default risk when choosing how to invest.

Source: Data on corporate defaults from Standard and Poor's, "Default, Transition, and Recovery: 2011 Annual Global Corporate Default Study and Rating Transitions" on the Internet at **www.standardandpoors.com** on March 21, 2012.

Figure 2.C shows data from 1954 to 2012 on economists' expectations (gathered from a survey) about the inflation rate over the coming year compared with the inflation rate that actually occurred.

The figure shows several periods in which the actual inflation rate rose sharply relative to the expected inflation rate. Some of those episodes are associated with dramatic rises in oil prices, as was the case in the mid-1950s, 1973–1975, 1979–1980, 1990, 2003–2005, and 2007–2008. Occasionally, the inflation rate rises unexpectedly for some reason other than a hike in oil prices, as in the late 1960s, when both monetary and fiscal policies were expansionary and led to increased inflation. Sometimes, the inflation rate turns out to be lower than expected. For example, in the early 1980s, inflation fell dramatically, but the forecasters did not think it would fall as much as it did, nor did they expect it to stay that low.

But you also will note that from 1990 to the mid-2000s, inflation did not move in a very surprising way. In that period, the forecasters expected slightly higher inflation than actually occurred, but the forecasts were not off by much. There have been no significant periods in which inflation differed by more than a few tenths of a percentage point from what was expected. Worse forecasts were made around 2006–2007, when oil prices first rose sharply and then fell dramatically, causing the inflation rate to spike up to over 5 percent and then decline significantly to less than 1 percent. Overall, though, the risk that the inflation rate would be different from what was expected was a factor in the past two decades, but not nearly to the extent it had been in the preceding 30 years.

The risk that the inflation rate will differ from the expected inflation rate is not trivial, as this graph shows. Expected inflation is the forecast for the inflation rate in consumer prices from the Livingston Survey of economists. Actual inflation in consumer prices spikes up during oil-price shocks; such shocks are clearly not forecastable. In addition to the oil-price shock periods, inflation forecasts miss the mark on some other occasions.

FIGURE 2.C Actual and Expected Inflation

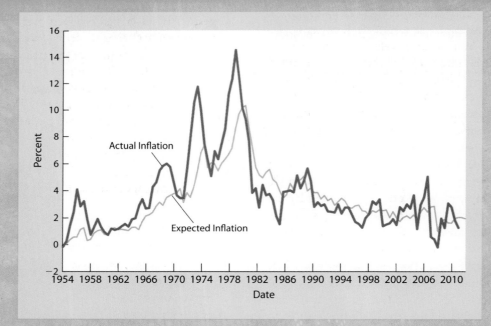

Let's return to our example of PepsiCo stock to calculate the standard deviation of its return. There was a 75 percent chance (0.75) that PepsiCo stock would return 13 percent (0.13) and a 25 percent chance (0.25) that it would return −17 percent (−0.17), and we calculated that the expected return was 5.5 percent (0.055). The standard deviation of the return to PepsiCo stock is

$$
\begin{aligned}
\text{Standard deviation} &= \{[\textit{probability of outcome } 1 \times (\textit{deviation of outcome } 1)^2] \\
&\quad + [\textit{probability of outcome } 2 \times (\textit{deviation of outcome } 2)^2]\}^{1/2} \\
&= \{[0.75 \times (0.13 - 0.055)^2] + [0.25 \times (-0.17 - 0.055)^2]\}^{1/2} \\
&= (0.0042 + 0.0127)^{1/2} = 0.0169^{1/2} = 0.13 = 13 \textit{ percent}
\end{aligned}
$$

The standard deviation of the return to a security is a useful measure of risk. When the standard deviation of one security's return is higher than the standard deviation of another, the first security is riskier. For example, if the standard deviation of Coca-Cola's stock return were 15 percent, then Coca-Cola stock would be riskier than PepsiCo stock.

Liquidity. The third determinant of investors' decisions is liquidity. Some investors buy securities and hold them until they mature. But many other investors buy and sell securities periodically. If Sue owns a security that pays $1,500 on July 1 but wants to sell it before then, she will need to find someone else to sell the security to.

The **liquidity** of a security refers to how easy it is to buy or sell the security in the secondary market when you want to without incurring significant costs. Securities that are easy to buy and sell at low transactions costs are considered very liquid; an example is stock in Ford Motor Company or a short-term government debt security such as a three-month Treasury bill. Securities that have high transactions costs or take a significant amount of time to buy and sell are considered illiquid; an example is a debt security sold by the government of a small town. Some securities cannot be sold to another investor at all. Such a security is known as a **nonmarketable security** because it cannot be resold in a secondary market. An example is a U.S. Savings Bond, which you can redeem at a bank but cannot sell to someone else. But most securities can be sold to another investor; such a security is called a **marketable security.**

In the equity market, liquidity differs among stocks, affecting the demand for them. Equity of the most well-known companies trades in a very large market.

Any time you want to trade, you can find someone to buy stock from or sell stock to. But there are many smaller companies whose stock is not traded frequently. If you own stock in these companies, it may be very difficult to sell it when you want to. Thus, an investor is better off (other factors equal) owning a stock that is liquid.

Taxes. The fourth determinant of investors' decisions is taxes. The interest and dividends paid on securities are subject to taxation. Thus, although we said earlier that investors care about their expected return, it would be more accurate to say that they care about their **after-tax expected return,** which is the expected return that remains after taxes are paid. Thus, an investor's decision about what securities to own depends on his tax bracket.

For example, an investor who has a tax rate of 40 percent and expects to earn a return of 6 percent before taxes has an after-tax expected return of

$$
\begin{aligned}
\text{After-tax expected return} &= \textit{pretax expected return} - (\textit{tax rate} \\
&\quad \times \textit{pretax expected return}) \\
&= (1 - \textit{tax rate}) \times \textit{pretax expected return} \\
&= (1 - 0.4) \times 0.06 = 0.6 \times 0.06 = 0.036 = 3.6 \textit{ percent}
\end{aligned}
$$

Investors in high tax brackets have discovered some ways to reduce their tax burden. For example, the federal government does not tax the returns on certain financial investments, such as interest paid on debt securities issued by state and city governments, so some investors find it desirable to buy such debt. There are a number of other securities that investors desire to own because they do not have to pay as much in taxes. Because of this, investors often consult with tax advisors in making their decisions.

Maturity. The fifth determinant of investors' decisions is maturity. Some investors who are young but already saving for retirement may want to own securities that will not mature for a long time. Other investors may not want to lock their money up for a long period

liquidity how easy it is to buy or sell a security in the secondary market when you want to without incurring significant costs

nonmarketable security a security that cannot be sold to another investor

marketable security a security that can be sold to another investor

after-tax expected return the expected return after taxes are paid

of time in case they need the cash. As a result, many investors favor securities with short times to maturity. To attract investors to lend for long periods, borrowers offer higher interest rates than on securities with short times to maturity.

2-4d Choosing a Financial Investment Portfolio

Given that investors care about expected return, risk, liquidity, taxes, and maturity, how should an investor choose what securities to invest in? An investor's **portfolio** is the collection of securities the investor owns. An investor must choose a portfolio based on her own circumstances (such as age and wealth) and preferences (how much risk to take).

An investor with a portfolio of securities should look at the risk to the entire portfolio, not the risk to any single security in the portfolio. In fact, one reason for holding a portfolio of securities rather than just a single security is to decrease risk. Holding just one security is very risky because the value of the investor's wealth will increase or decrease with the profits in that single firm or industry. An investor owning a diversified portfolio with securities from a number of different firms and industries has a less risky portfolio because when one industry fares poorly, another is probably doing well, so they offset each other. Thus, investors should think about how to diversify their portfolios so that they are not subject to the risk in a single industry.

By buying different combinations of securities, investors can reduce their risk substantially, although they can never eliminate all risk. Risk that can be eliminated by diversification is known as **idiosyncratic risk** (or **unsystematic risk**). Investors usually attempt to eliminate idiosyncratic risk if they can do so at low cost. The remaining risk is known as **market risk** (or **systematic risk**), which is risk that cannot be reduced by diversification. An investor in equity securities who owns 20 or more stocks in a variety of industries probably has removed most of the idiosyncratic risk; the remaining risk is the risk to the overall stock market.

Other than choosing to diversify, the major decision investors must make in creating a portfolio is the tradeoff between expected return and risk. In equilibrium in the financial market, riskier securities offer higher expected returns than safer securities because most investors do not like risk. Thus, an investor could have a relatively safe portfolio with a low expected return, or the investor could own a relatively risky portfolio with a high expected return. Is there an optimal portfolio? According to financial theory, the answer is no. People who do not like risk should hold less risky portfolios; people who do not mind risk should hold riskier portfolios. *No* portfolio is right for everyone. Every person has a different attitude toward risk and therefore a different optimal portfolio.

You probably know someone who is very risk averse—a person who is very cautious, who always likes to know what is going to happen, and who rarely takes a chance in life. Such a person is better off owning financial securities that have very little risk. You also may know someone who enjoys risk—the type of person who might go skydiving, ride a motorcycle, or go bungee-jumping. Such a person is better off buying risky financial securities. There is no one right or wrong investment strategy. What is right for each person depends on the degree to which he or she tolerates risk.

portfolio the collection of securities an investor owns

idiosyncratic (unsystematic) risk risk that can be eliminated by diversification

market (systematic) risk risk that cannot be removed by diversification

RECAP

1 Expected return is the gain an investor anticipates making, on average, on a security both from interest or dividends and from a change in the value of the security.

2 Risk arises from the possibility of default by the issuer of a debt security, an unexpected change in the dividend paid on an equity security, an unexpected change in the price of a security, and a change in the inflation rate. Risk is measured by the standard deviation of the return to a security.

3 Investors choose their portfolios based on the expected return, risk, liquidity, taxes, and maturity of the securities in the market; their personal circumstances and preferences; and how the different securities fit together.

Review Questions and Problems

Review Questions

1 What are the main features that distinguish debt from equity? Is there more debt or equity outstanding in the United States?

2 What are the main roles that financial intermediaries play in the financial system?

3 Compare and contrast direct finance and indirect finance. Which is more likely to have a larger share of the total financial market in a mature economy? In a young economy? Why?

4 What is the difference between a primary market and a secondary market? Which market is bigger for equity securities?

5 What is the relationship between the efficiency of a financial system and the rate of economic growth?

6 How do investors calculate the expected return on a security?

7 Describe the major types of risks to financial securities, and give a specific example of each. How do investors measure risk?

8 Describe and explain three factors other than expected return and risk that affect the demand for financial securities.

9 What is liquidity, and why do investors care about it?

10 Why is it usually better for an investor to own 100 different stocks rather than 1?

Numerical Exercises

11 Julia is considering buying stock in *only one* of the following companies: (i) Uninvest.com, which runs a Web site geared toward older people's retirement income and has a 10 percent probability of returning 20 percent this year and a 90 percent probability of returning 7 percent, or (ii) Speculate, Inc., which invests in derivative securities and has a 50 percent chance of returning 0 percent this year and a 50 percent chance of returning 50 percent.

  a What are the expected returns to investing in Uninvest and Speculate?

  b What are the standard deviations of the returns to Uninvest and Speculate?

  c If Julia is very risk-averse, which company's stock should she buy?

  d If Julia is risk-neutral (that is, she does not worry about risk at all), which company's stock should she buy?

12 In the market for debt securities that promise to pay $1,500 in one year, the quantity demanded is

$$B_D = 250 - 0.15b - 20W_t - 10W_{t+1}$$

where b is the price of a security, W_t is a variable equal to 1 if the economy is in an expansion today and 0 if the economy is in a recession today, and W_{t+1} is a variable equal to 1 if the economy is expected to be in an expansion next year and 0 if the economy is expected to be in a recession next year. The quantity supplied of the security is

$$B_S = 50 + 0.05b + 40W_t + 20W_{t+1}$$

Calculate the equilibrium price and quantity of the security for each of the following situations:

  a The economy is in *recession* today and is expected to remain in *recession* next year.

  b The economy is in an *expansion* today and is expected to be in *recession* next year.

  c The economy is in *recession* today and is expected to be in an *expansion* next year.

  d The economy is in *expansion* today and is expected to be in an *expansion* next year.

13 Suppose that a security costs $1,500 today.

  a Calculate the percentage return on the security if the payoff to the security in one year is $1,000, $1,500, $2,000, or $2,500. (*Note:* This is the total amount returned to the investor, so you may just calculate the total return and not worry about how this is split up between current yield and capital-gains yield.)

  b If each of the outcomes in part *a* is equally likely, calculate the expected return on the security.

  c Calculate the standard deviation of the return on the security. (Again, assume that each of the outcomes in part *a* is equally likely.)

(*continued*)

14 Suppose that a security costs $3,000 today and pays off some amount b in one year. Suppose that b is uncertain according to the following table of probabilities:

b:	$3,000	$3,300	$3,600	$3,900	$4,200
Probability:	0.1	0.2	0.3	0.2	0.2

  a Calculate the return (in percent) for each value of b. (*Note:* You may just calculate the total return and not worry about how this is split between current yield and capital-gains yield.)

  b Calculate the expected return (in percent).

  c Calculate the standard deviation of the return.

  d Suppose that an investor has a choice between buying this security or purchasing a different security that also costs $3,000 today but pays off $3,300 with certainty in one year. How is an investor's choice of which security to purchase related to his degree of risk aversion?

15 In each of the following scenarios, which security should an investor buy? Assume that the securities are identical in all ways except as described below. Explain your answer.

  a Security A has an expected return of 12 percent, whereas security B has an expected return of 10 percent.

  b Interest on security C is 10 percent and is taxable, whereas interest on security D is 7 percent and is not taxable, and the investor's tax rate is 40 percent.

  c Security E has a 20 percent chance of default, whereas security F has a 15 percent chance of default.

  d Security G and security H are both debt securities that cost $1,000 and mature in one year. An investor incurs a transactions cost of $50 to purchase security G, which has an expected return of 8 percent. An investor incurs no transactions cost to purchase security H, which has an expected return of 5 percent.

Analytical Problems

16 If you look in the financial pages of the newspaper, you will see that interest rates differ dramatically for different bonds. For each of the following situations, which bond would you expect to have a higher interest rate? Explain your reasoning.

  a A U.S. government bond or a bond issued by Ford Motor Company, given that the market for U.S. government bonds is more liquid

  b A U.S. government bond or a bond issued by IBM Corp., given that state and local governments cannot tax the interest earned on U.S. government bonds

  c A bond issued by Microsoft Corporation or by Microsmart.com, given that Microsmart.com is near bankruptcy

  d A 3-month government bond or a 30-year government bond, given that investors prefer short-term investments

17 Suppose that you are an investor who owns a portfolio of investments in stocks and bonds. You are currently satisfied with your portfolio; it is perfect for you, given your degree of aversion to risk. Suddenly, an event occurs that increases the riskiness of all the securities in your portfolio. Are you likely to modify your portfolio? If so, how?

18 If you observe news reports about financial markets for some time, you will notice that investors pay a tremendous amount of attention to economic data releases from the government. Why do you think that this is the case? What are investors concerned about? What would happen in financial markets if investors thought that there was a much higher probability than before that a recession would occur soon?

CHAPTER 3

Ariel Skelley/Alamy

MONEY
and PAYMENTS

Money plays a unique role in the financial system as the item used to buy goods and services.

Policymakers must manage the amount of money in the economy to keep inflation in check. In this chapter we will examine money in detail. After describing the role that money plays in the economy, we will look at the way we use money to make transactions and examine how the payments system evolved. Because the money supply—the total amount of money in circulation—is directly related to the level of prices and so the growth rate of the money supply is directly related to the rate of inflation, policymakers must measure the money supply and its growth rate. Many different financial securities can be called "money," so when we want to count the money supply, we first must determine what types of money to include. We end this chapter with an application to everyday life that examines what people do with their change and how this affects the government's production of money.

3-1 How We Use Money

The use of money is nearly as old as humanity itself. Some type of money has existed since ancient times, even in the most unsophisticated economies. Clearly, there must be something about money that makes it hard to do without. Yet, if you think of the dollar bill in your wallet, it is nothing but a piece of paper with words and pictures printed on it. So why is it valuable?

To answer this question, we need to look closely at the various roles money plays in society. We give these roles different names: (1) medium of exchange, (2) unit of account, (3) store of value, and (4) standard of deferred payment.

3-1a Medium of Exchange

Money's most prominent role is as a **medium of exchange,** which means that people use money by giving it in exchange for goods and services. This function of money is universal. In its role as a medium of exchange, money makes exchanges easier by reducing **transactions costs,** which are the costs of trading, such as time spent shopping and negotiating.

Without money of some kind, the economy would be much less efficient. To demonstrate, imagine a world in which you had to trade the goods that you produced with others to get goods that they produced. This kind of trade is called *barter.* If you were a baker, you would have to haul around loaves of bread with you while you were looking to buy some meat. Not only that, you would need to find a butcher who wanted to trade his meat for your bread. This situation is called a *double coincidence of wants* because two producers must each want what the other produces. Most likely, because your barter trade would be so time-consuming, you would purchase a much smaller variety of goods and make many of your own goods instead. Rather than specializing in a particular occupation, you would grow your own food and make your own clothing because trade would be so difficult.

Money's use as a medium of exchange allows people to specialize in producing goods and services. They can then sell their goods or services for money and then use that money to buy other goods and services that they want. This results in more efficient production and reduced transactions costs.

A vivid example of how a medium of exchange improves transactions efficiency occurred during World War II in the German prisoner-of-war (POW) camps that held Allied soldiers. The prisoners received packages from the International Red Cross containing canned food, candy bars, and cigarettes. The prisoners often received items that they did not want, and they traded them to others. Relatively quickly, though, the need for something to serve as a medium of exchange became clear, and since the prisoners did not have any currency in prison camp, cigarettes fit the bill nicely.

Cigarettes have good properties for use as a medium of exchange: They are homogeneous (all the same), relatively durable, portable, and worth a small enough amount that most transactions could be undertaken in units of whole cigarettes. How do these attributes make cigarettes a useful medium of exchange? First, cigarettes are homogeneous, which is desirable because the amount traded is easily verified. If something being used for money does not come in standard units, people must spend time and effort verifying how much each unit is worth, as might be the case if gemstones were used, for example. Second, cigarettes are relatively durable, so they can survive many exchanges without being damaged. Other items might be damaged more easily or deteriorate over time; for example, bread would serve poorly as money because it gets moldy in a short time. Third, cigarettes are light and easy to carry around, so they are convenient to use. By contrast, using heavy objects as money would require more effort. For example, if wood logs were money, you would not carry them with you, but every time you wanted to buy something, you would go home and drag back the right number of logs; the payment process would be more cumbersome. Fourth, each cigarette is a small unit of value, so change is made easily. A pack of cigarettes is more suitable as money than larger objects, such as the food items, because it is so easy to split up. These four attributes make trades easier and reduce the overall costs of transacting. Thus, people in the POW camps began to buy and sell food items in exchange for cigarettes. Even nonsmokers carried cigarettes with them so that they could buy things when they wanted to.

The movements of prices in this POW economy are interesting to observe as well. Because food and cigarettes normally were distributed on the same day every week, both became scarcer as the days after a

medium of exchange
the function that money serves when people exchange money for goods and services

transactions costs
costs of trading, such as time spent shopping and negotiating

distribution day elapsed. As the supply of both goods and cigarettes declined over the week, it was not obvious whether the prices of food items in terms of cigarettes would rise or fall. In fact, the prices of food items usually rose sharply on delivery day and then fell throughout the week. Patient prisoners could profit by waiting to buy food until later in the week. (For more on lessons about money learned from the POW camps, see the box titled "Gresham's Law and Money in POW Camps.")

This example illustrates the idea that every economy, no matter what its situation, needs something as a medium of exchange. Prior to the twentieth century, most economies settled on the use of some rare item, such as gold or silver, but as in the POW camps, almost anything will do for money in a pinch as long as it is *accepted* as money. Gold and silver have been popular historically as money because they can be minted into coins of standard size and weight, and the coins are homogeneous, durable, portable, and available in various denominations to make change.

No matter what the benefits or shortcomings of a medium of exchange, public acceptance is the key to its success. The object used as money may be intrinsically worthless. Our currency today has no value in and of itself (it is nothing more than cheap paper with colored ink on it), but because we all accept it as the medium of exchange, it is valuable.

3-1b Unit of Account

The second role that money plays is as a **unit of account,** which means that it serves as the item in which prices are denoted. When you go into a store in the United States, all the prices are listed in terms of dollars. Because money is a medium of exchange, it only makes sense to list prices in terms of money. If, instead of dollars, another item such as bread were the unit of account, we might find that a pair of shoes would cost 50 loaves of bread, a phone call might cost 2 loaves of bread, and so on. But if bread costs $2 per loaf, it would be confusing and awkward to keep prices in units of bread and not dollars.

unit of account the function that money serves when prices are denoted in terms of money

In certain circumstances, money is not the unit of account. One case is when barter trade is being arranged. For example, some people want to trade tickets to a sports event in exchange for tickets to another sports event. Classified ads in newspapers or on online sites such as Craigslist at times contain offers for these types of trades. And some people try to evade taxes by bartering instead of paying for something with money.

A second case in which money is not the unit of account occurs in countries where prices are changing rapidly. In a number of Latin American countries in the 1970s and 1980s, inflation was very high. Shopkeepers decided that instead of changing the prices on their goods every day, they would list their prices in terms of U.S. dollars, whose value was more stable. With prices listed in dollars (which is the unit of account) but payments made in the local currency (the medium of exchange) such as Argentine pesos, all the shopkeeper had to do was to find out the exchange rate between dollars and pesos several times a day and then multiply each price in terms of dollars by the number of pesos per dollar (the exchange rate) to find out how many pesos to charge. Other than these fairly rare circumstances, however, the unit of account is the same as the medium of exchange.

3-1c Store of Value

Money also serves as a store of value, at least for short periods. Money functions as a **store of value** when people keep money for some period instead of spending it or investing it.

Why do people use money as a store of value rather than keeping all their money in the bank, where it could earn interest? The main reason is that holding money reduces transactions costs. It would be costly to visit the bank every time you wanted to buy something, especially when shopping opportunities arise that you do not know about in advance. If you keep enough money in your wallet, you will be prepared and can purchase things whenever you want.

store of value the function that money serves when people keep money for some period instead of spending it or investing it

hyperinflation a very high rate of inflation, often taken to be 50 percent per month (13,000 percent per year) or higher

Of course, you probably will not want to keep very much cash with you. You probably will want to invest funds that you are unlikely to spend within a reasonable period of time so that you can earn interest. Thus, you must decide how often to go to the bank to get money and how much money to get each time. If there were a free automatic teller machine (ATM) on every corner, you probably would carry less cash around with you; because going to the ATM is costly, you keep more money with you. Thus, there is a tradeoff between the opportunity cost of holding money (which is the interest you forego by having cash in your pocket instead of investing it) and the transactions costs of going to the bank to get money when you need it. Problems of deciding how much cash to carry around with you are often solved, in recent years, by the widespread use of credit and debit cards, which eliminates the need for cash.

The tradeoff between holding money and investing is affected by inflation. The higher the rate of inflation, that is, the faster your money is losing value, the more you will want to either spend your money or keep it invested and earning interest, and the less money you will want to hold.

Occasionally a country suffers from **hyperinflation,** which is a very high rate of inflation, often taken to be an inflation rate exceeding 50 percent per month, or 13,000 percent per year. For example, in Germany after World War I, the annual inflation rate reached 32,400 percent; one German mark in August 1922 bought the same amount of goods as 10,200,000,000 marks in November 1923. In Hungary from August 1945 to July 1946, the purchasing power of the Hungarian currency, the pengo, fell by a factor of 3.81 octillion—that is, 3,810,000,000, 000,000,000,000,000,000,000! More recently, Bolivia in early 1985 had an annual inflation rate that reached 116,000 percent. Needless to say, when the value of money is declining this rapidly, no one wants to use money as a store of value. People spend their money as soon as possible or deposit it in a bank account that protects them from inflation.

The following anecdote illustrates how ineffective money is as a store of value during hyperinflation. As the story goes, in an economy that was in a hyperinflation, a man took a wheelbarrow full of money to the bank one day. The wheelbarrow would not fit through the door of the bank, so the person went inside the bank to get some help. When he came back out, the wheelbarrow was gone, but the money was sitting on the curb!

So money works well as a store of value, at least for the short run, for small amounts, and under normal circumstances. People face a tradeoff between holding more money, which is convenient but which earns no interest, and holding less money but incurring the transactions costs of going to the bank to get cash more often. This tradeoff favors holding less money as the inflation rate rises because money loses value more quickly.

3-1d Standard of Deferred Payment

There is one final, less-well-known function of money, which is money's role as a standard of deferred payment. Money is used as a **standard of deferred payment** whenever you buy something one day and pay for it later, and the repayment you make is denoted in terms of money. For example, if you buy a car, you usually do not pay cash but rather take out a loan and pay for the car over time. Money acts as a standard of deferred payment because you agree to pay off the loan with money.

In many countries, such as the United States, the law states that money is **legal tender,** which means that a lender must accept it in the repayment of debts. U.S. currency is explicit about this, since the phrase, "This note is legal tender for all debts, public and private," is printed on the front. The legal tender law requires people to use money as a standard of deferred payment unless a loan agreement specifically indicates some other repayment.

Thus, money is a very useful invention. It serves as a medium of exchange, unit of account, store of value, and standard of deferred payment. However, the physical existence of money is not the only thing that matters. Money is part of a broader structure in society that we call the *payments system,* which is the focus of the following section.

standard of deferred payment the function that money serves when people buy something one day and pay for it later, and the repayment is denoted in terms of money

legal tender the condition that a lender must accept money in the repayment of debts, by law

RECAP

1 For something to serve as a medium of exchange, it must be widely accepted in that role. Ideally, the medium of exchange is homogeneous, durable, easy to transport, and exists in small denominations.

2 Money serves as a unit of account when prices of goods are quoted in terms of money. Except for barter and times of hyperinflation, money is the unit of account.

3 Money serves as a short-term store of value because people do not want to run to the bank whenever they want to buy something, so they keep some money in their wallets. Doing so thus reduces their costs of transacting because money allows them to buy things when spending opportunities arise.

4 Money serves as a standard of deferred payment because loans are repaid in terms of money.

3-2 The Payments System

The **payments system** is the set of mechanisms used for making transactions. Money allows people to make exchanges within the payments system.

The economy works well if the payments system functions efficiently, and it is unlikely to perform well if it is hard to make payments. The payments system has changed over time, and improvements have occurred to facilitate transactions. In particular, improvements in computer technology and communications have increased the efficiency of the payments system.

In this section we use a different scheme to categorize money. We identify inside and outside money, and in doing so, we trace the evolution of the payments system.

3-2a Outside Money

We start our discussion of the payments system by analyzing **outside money.**

payments system the set of mechanisms used for making transactions

outside money money created by the government or by nature, not by groups or institutions in the private sector

This is money created by the government (such as dollar bills) or by nature (such as gold or silver), not by groups or institutions in the private sector (such as checking accounts).

Commodity money. Consider first an economy in which some metal, typically gold or silver, is used as money. Money of this type is called **commodity money** (or **full-bodied money**) because its value as money equals its value as a material, such as the value of gold used in jewelry. A 1-ounce gold coin is worth whatever the market price is for an ounce of gold.

Gold, silver, and other metals have been used as money throughout history. Coins made of metal circulated as early as the seventh century B.C. The Romans greatly improved the efficiency of the minting process, and coins have circulated in nearly every economy since then. Metallic money has a number of drawbacks, however, the main one being that large quantities are not portable. It is difficult to use metallic money to settle large transactions because large sums are heavy and hard to transport. Not only that, but countries that have used metals as money have suffered tremendous bouts of inflation when new discoveries of the metal were made. For example, the California gold rush in 1849 led to an increase in the amount of gold circulating, which caused a huge increase in the prices of goods in terms of gold. Therefore, although many early economies used metal as money, its disadvantages led people to search for a better money.

One way to correct the problem that metal is too heavy to use for large transactions is to substitute paper money that is fully backed by metal and redeemable for metal. Rather than hauling the metal around to pay your bills, a bank or government could issue pieces of paper that represented a particular amount of metal and could be exchanged for that amount of metal. This is the type of system the United States had for many years under the "gold standard" (as it was from 1879 to 1934), when each paper dollar could be redeemed for a certain amount of gold. People could make large transactions more easily, but these paper notes still left the economy subject to wild fluctuations in the price of the metal and thus with serious

economic problems. While the U.S. currency was on the gold standard, prices rose at times and fell sharply at other times.

Fiat money. The next logical step was to break the link between the paper currency and metal. The United States began doing so in 1934 when it went off the gold standard, under which anyone could exchange paper money for gold. From 1934 to 1971, we were instead on the gold *exchange* standard, under which individuals in the United States could not redeem paper currency for gold, but foreign governments could (and did at times, causing the U.S. gold stock to shrink). All links between gold and dollars were broken in 1971, when President Nixon took the country off the gold exchange standard. Once the link between paper currency and metal was broken, the system became one of **fiat money,** because the money has value in large part by the government's fiat—that is, because the government decrees that it has value for the payment of taxes. Public acceptance of fiat money also matters because people will not use a currency as money if the inflation rate is very high, even if the government wants them to.

Fiat money was a brilliant innovation, reducing the costs of producing money. Producing money out of metal in a commodity money system was costly because people spent much time and resources digging the metal out of the ground, and the government had to ensure the quality of the metal and mint it into coins. When the government substituted fiat money for commodity money, though, production costs fell substantially. The cost of printing a dollar bill, or even producing a dollar coin whose metal content is worth just a few cents yet whose value is one dollar, is much lower than the cost of producing a dollar coin whose metal content is worth a dollar. So think of fiat money as being an efficient process for creating cash, which consists of coins and paper currency, that then provides useful functions (medium of exchange, unit of account, and so on) in the economy.

Despite its benefits, fiat money is not without problems. Most people do not keep large sums of cash in their houses because they fear loss or theft. The use of cash also requires that the government produce the right amount of it so that prices in the economy are fairly stable, a job entrusted to the Federal Reserve (also called the Fed) in the United States. In addition, the government must keep other people from being able to produce similar money *(counterfeits),* or the real money will decline in value.

Different countries use varying amounts of cash in transacting. In the United States, we use about half as much cash per person as people do in Europe, and Europeans, in turn, use about one-quarter as much cash as the Japanese. Countries with less efficient banking and financial systems use even more cash.

3-2b Inside Money

There are other types of money besides outside money. We call these other kinds of money **inside money** because they are created in the private sector. An example of inside money is a checking account held at a bank. Because you can write a check to buy things, your checking account represents money; it serves as a medium of exchange. Therefore, money in checking accounts is called *inside money* because it is created in the banking system. We will trace the steps in the process of creating inside money in Chapter 16. For now, consider checking account balances to be money created by the private sector. Other types of inside money also exist, including money-market mutual funds and other types of accounts at financial intermediaries that allow a depositor to spend her funds quickly.

Checking accounts have advantages that cash does not. Unlike cash, if checks are lost or stolen, it does not matter as long as they are not signed by the account holder. And people depositing checks often can be traced in the case of fraud. Checks can be made out for any possible amount, so you do not have to worry about the size of the transaction, be it 50 cents or $50,000. After checks (or their electronic images) have been returned to their owners, they provide receipts for payments.

Although inside money has many powerful advantages, it is a more complicated method of payment than cash. Checking accounts only work well if the banking system can clear checks efficiently—in other words, there must be an efficient payments system.

Consider the check-clearing process of a typical transaction. If Judy Jasko from Juniper, New Jersey, writes a check payable to Carol Conrad from Cascade, California, Carol will deposit the check in her bank in California, which will make an image of the check and send the image to Judy's bank, which will transfer funds to Carol's bank through its account at the Federal Reserve.

In addition to paper checks, a number of other types of inside money exist, some of which work with new technology. The oldest method is traveler's checks, which are a hybrid between currency and paper checks. Like checks, they require a signature, which helps to prevent their misuse if they are lost or stolen, but because they are prepaid, they do not require an elaborate clearing mechanism. Credit cards were invented after traveler's checks, but they have grown dramatically in terms of the amount used in payments over the last 20 years. A credit card, as the name suggests, is really a mechanism by which a short-term loan is made, allowing a shopper to purchase goods or services today and to pay at a later date.

Electronic technology is used in many other types of inside money, including debit cards, stored-value cards, e-cash, and electronic checks. Debit cards take money directly from your checking account and deposit it in a merchant's account when you buy goods and services. Stored-value cards allow you to prepay some amount and then spend it whenever you want, eliminating the need to carry cash with you. E-cash makes it convenient to buy goods from Internet retailers. Electronic checks are just checks made payable electronically.

For very large payments, the Federal Reserve and banks have systems other than the check-clearing system in place that can handle such payments efficiently. An example is Fedwire, which connects banks to the Fed and allows real-time payment of large dollar amounts of cash or securities. The average Fedwire transaction is about $5 million in cash or securities. Fedwire is fast and cheap, so banks like to use it. It is called a *real-time* payment system because transactions clear immediately, whereas most other transactions in the banking system (including all paper checks) clear at the end of the business day.

All these forms of electronic money, however, are open to fraud and security lapses. What if someone breaks the code in the bank's computer and steals all the money from your account? What if something goes wrong with the stored-value card, and it does not work? How can you prove you paid for something if you do not get a receipt or have a canceled check as proof? Despite these concerns, most people have had a good experience with electronic forms of money and payments, and they continue to grow in popularity. Check writing has been declining sharply in recent years.

inside money money that is created in the private sector

1 Outside money is money created by the government or nature, such as paper currency, coins, gold, and silver. Gold and silver are outside money that is commodity money because their value as money equals their value in other uses. Fiat money is outside money that is worth more in exchange for goods and services than the value of the materials of which it is made.

2 Inside money is money created by the private sector, mainly by banks. Funds in checking accounts are inside money, as are funds in other accounts at financial intermediaries.

3 Inside money requires a national payments system for clearing transactions. Checks go through an electronic clearing process that occurs very rapidly.

4 Other than paper checks, a number of types of inside money exist, including traveler's checks, credit cards, debit cards, stored-value cards, e-cash, and electronic checks.

3-3 Counting Money

The amount of money in the economy influences the inflation rate and the level of economic activity. Because the Federal Reserve must determine how much money circulates, it must count the amount of money people have and decide how fast to allow the amount of money in circulation to grow over time as the economy grows.

Because there are so many different types of money, there is not a simple way to count the amount of money. As a result, we must consider a number of options for how to count money properly.

3-3a Measuring the Money Supply

Earlier we said that money played four roles: medium of exchange, unit of account, store of value, and standard of deferred payment. Which financial assets in the economy fulfill these roles? Clearly, money in the form of coins or paper currency and amounts in checking accounts serve all four roles. But there are many different stores of value besides coins, paper currency, and funds in checking accounts, so we may want to count them as well. In most retail stores, you can choose among many different mediums of exchange. You can choose to pay in currency, write a check, or use a credit card. Let's think about each of these methods in turn to decide whether they should be included in a measure of the amount of money or not.

Clearly, coins and paper currency are money. They fulfill all the roles of money. We even gave them a special name: outside money. So coins and paper currency will be included in all our measures of money.

What about funds deposited in a checking account? Those funds represent inside money because they were created by banks, not by the government. Should they count in our measures of money? They probably should because they fulfill all the functions of money. The problem is that not all the money in a person's checking account is used for purchases. For example, to save on transactions costs, many people keep some minimum amount in their accounts, say, $1,000, so they do not incur bank charges. Should we count the $1,000 as money or not? The role of funds used to meet a minimum-balance requirement makes them much more of a long-term store of value than a medium of exchange. Indeed, some people who formerly had separate checking and savings accounts have combined them into one large account, so should all that money be counted?

Finally, what about credit cards? They appear to be a medium of exchange because they are used to pay for goods and services, so perhaps they should be counted as well. But what should we count? Should we count the amount transacted in a given month? Should we count the total credit line on the card? The answers to these questions are not clear, but one way to think about credit cards is that they represent borrowing rather than making a payment. When you charge dinner to your credit card, you receive goods in exchange for signing a piece of paper showing that you are borrowing the amount of the dinner's cost from the credit-card company. You do not really pay for the dinner until you pay your credit-card bill. Therefore, an easy solution is to simply ignore credit cards in our calculations of money because people must later use money to pay off their credit-card bills.

There are many different types of accounts at banks other than checking accounts. They differ in their properties in terms of how much interest they pay, service charges, and minimum balances. Some accounts, such as certificates of deposit (CDs), even have a time to maturity, so you cannot always withdraw your money when you want it. But most fill at least some of the functions of money. The question is this: How do we decide which of those accounts to include in our measure of money and which to exclude?

One way that we might decide what bank accounts to include in a measure of money is to consider their **liquidity,** which means how quickly and easily they can be used to purchase goods and services. (Note that this is a different, though related, type of liquidity than we used in our discussion of financial securities in Chapter 2, where liquidity referred to the ease with which an investor could buy or sell a security in the market.) Coins and paper currency are the most liquid forms of money because they can be used anywhere to buy goods. Traveler's checks are nearly as liquid; they are a bit more cumbersome to use than currency because they must be signed and the signature verified, and as a result, some merchants will not accept them. Funds in checking accounts are only slightly less liquid because a person generally can buy most things by writing a check, or else he can go to the ATM to withdraw cash from his checking account and spend it. Money in savings accounts at banks is a bit less liquid still because you must go to the bank to withdraw the funds before you can spend them. Money in an account such as a money-market mutual fund is fairly liquid because you can write checks against your balance, but usually the amount spent must exceed some minimum amount (such as $250) before such checks can be used. Money deposited in CD accounts is even more difficult to spend because if the money is withdrawn before the CD's maturity date, you bear a substantial interest penalty. Still, if you needed the funds quickly, you could get them.

In addition to liquidity, what also may matter for determining how we count money is the size of the account. Small amounts in bank accounts most likely are owned by individuals and probably are used in transactions. Large amounts, though, are less likely to be spent and probably represent savings instead.

Thus, examining both the liquidity and size of various bank accounts is a logical way to think about how to count the amount of money in the economy. As we now show, these are the attributes that the Federal Reserve uses in its official measures of money.

3-3b The Federal Reserve's Monetary Aggregates

The Federal Reserve measures the money supply in the United States so that it knows how much money is circulating and can determine whether the amount of money is sufficient for people to make payments but not so large as to cause inflation. The Fed measures the money supply following a system based mainly on the liquidity and size of the different types of money. Rather than choosing just one measure of money, the Fed calculates several different measures of money, which may be useful to different analysts for different purposes. Each different measure is called a **monetary aggregate**—a measure of the total supply of money in the economy—although each adds together different types of money.

The Fed's narrowest monetary aggregate is **M1,** which consists of coins, paper currency, traveler's checks, and amounts in checking accounts. These are all the most liquid types of money, so M1 represents money that can be spent quickly and easily. This is obviously the case for coins and paper currency, so their inclusion in M1 is natural. Traveler's checks are included in M1 because they are just about equal to currency in terms of their acceptance in transactions. M1 includes all the amounts in checking accounts because the Fed cannot separate the amount that people plan to save from the amount they plan to use for transactions.

For a long time, nearly all transactions included one asset that was in M1. In the past two decades, however, as the payments system has evolved, this has

liquidity how quickly and easily a type of money can be used to purchase goods and services

monetary aggregate a measure of the total supply of money in the economy

M1 the Federal Reserve's measure of money consisting of coins, paper currency, amounts in checking accounts, and traveler's checks

changed. Now people who are planning to make large transactions in the near future do not keep the money in their checking accounts. Instead, they keep the funds in accounts that earn more interest and then transfer the funds when they are ready to make the transaction.

M2 the Federal Reserve's measure of money consisting of M1 plus amounts in savings accounts, money-market mutual funds (held by individuals), and small time deposits (under $100,000)

Some high-interest accounts even permit check writing, even though they are used mostly for savings. For this reason, the Fed has a broader measure of money that includes some of these accounts.

M2 is a measure of money that incorporates funds in other accounts that can be accessed quickly for spending but are not quite as liquid as the items in M1. **M2** thus includes M1 plus amounts in savings accounts, money-market mutual funds (held by individuals), and small time deposits (under $100,000). There are a number of different types of savings accounts, including passbook savings accounts, which people with small amounts of money can use but which pay very little interest, and money-market deposit accounts, which require larger balances, pay more interest, and allow checks to be written against them. Money-market mutual funds (MMMFs) are investment funds that buy high-quality short-term debt securities (with low default risk), such as Treasury securities and commercial paper sold by large corporations. Small time deposits are accounts such as CDs, in which the depositor agrees to keep her money invested for a certain period of time (such as a year) in exchange for a higher rate of interest than on an account from which the funds could be withdrawn at will.

All the different measures of money and the components are illustrated in Figure 3.1. The graph shows that M2 is over four times the size of M1. The largest component of M1 is checkable deposits, which are sometimes called transactions deposits. The next largest component of M1 is currency and coins. Traveler's checks are just a fraction of M1 and have been declining so much in recent years that they are too small to show up in Figure 3.1. Savings deposits are the largest component of M2, followed in size by M1, then retail MMMFs, and then small time deposits; the latter two are similar in size.

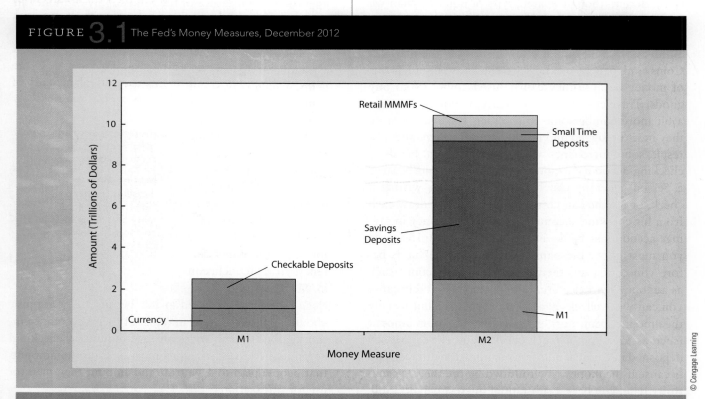

FIGURE 3.1 The Fed's Money Measures, December 2012

The graph shows the Fed's two measures of money and the components of each in December 2012. The components of each money measure are based on liquidity and size. M1's largest component is checkable deposits, followed by currency (including coins), and then traveler's checks, which are too small to show up in the graph. M2's largest component is savings deposits, followed by M1, then retail MMMFs, and then small time deposits.

© Cengage Learning

A comparison of amounts in each measure in December 2002 and December 2012 is shown in Table 3.1. M1 has increased in the past decade by an average of 7 percent per year. M2 has grown slightly slower at about 6 percent per year. Looking at individual components, traveler's checks, small time deposits, and retail money-market mutual funds have declined over the past decade, whereas all the other components have increased, with savings deposits and checkable deposits having grown the most rapidly at about 9 percent per year, on average.

We would expect the differing measures of the money supply to move together if interest rates on different accounts do not change much. However, long-term interest rates have declined in recent years, relative to short-term interest rates, so people are putting more funds in checking and savings accounts and less funds in time deposits and money-market mutual funds.

To see how the growth rates of the monetary aggregates have changed over time, Figure 3.2 shows a plot of them since 1960. You can see that from 1960 to 1985 they grew at different rates, but when the growth rate of one measure increased, the other often did as well. However, since 1985, M1 has shown a different pattern from M2, often growing more rapidly when M2 was growing less rapidly, and vice versa. We normally expect the amount of money to increase as the economy grows, but in 1996 and 1997, as the economy grew rapidly, the growth rate of M1 was negative, which means that the amount of M1 declined. On the other hand, M1 increased sharply early in the 1990s when the economy was growing slowly. In large part this is explained by the foreign demand for currency, which is a very large proportion of M1. In the early 1990s, Eastern Europe was in crisis and imported much U.S. currency to use as a store of value until their governments and economies stabilized. M1 and M2 grew rapidly during the financial crisis of 2008 and its aftermath, as people sought safety for their funds in bank accounts that were insured by the FDIC.

3-3c The Case of the Missing Currency

Table 3.1 shows that in 2012 there was over $1 trillion of currency (and coins) in circulation. This figure averages out to over $3,000 for every man, woman, and child in the United States. Do you keep that much cash around? Probably not. So where is all the currency?

Economists at the Federal Reserve have sought to figure out where the money is. Their research suggests that in recent years, about two-thirds of cash is held in foreign countries.

People in foreign countries like to use U.S. dollars, especially in times of crisis when their local currencies may become worthless. Also, wherever there are high rates of inflation, people often switch to using a more stable currency, such as the U.S. dollar, as a store of value. When the Soviet Union was breaking up in the early 1990s, major U.S. banks shipped planeloads of

TABLE 3.1	The Money Supply in 2002 and 2012 (trillions of dollars)			
		December 2002	December 2012	Average Annual Growth Rate
M1	Currency and coins	0.63	1.09	6
	Traveler's checks	0.01	0.00	–7
	Checkable deposits	0.61	1.40	9
	Total M1	1.25	2.50	7
M2	M1	1.25	2.50	7
	Savings deposits	2.78	6.71	9
	Small time deposits	0.89	0.63	–3
	Retail MMMFs	0.85	0.64	–3
	Total M2	5.77	10.48	6

Note: The components may not add up exactly to M1 or M2 because of rounding.

© Cengage Learning

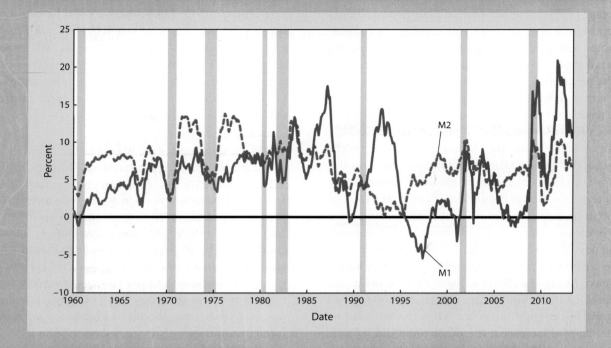

The graph shows the growth rates of the different monetary aggregates over time from January 1960 to March 2013. All grow at different rates, but when the growth rate of one measure increases, usually the other one does as well. However, since 1985, M1 has shown a different pattern from M2, often growing more rapidly when M2 is growing less rapidly, and vice versa. Blue shaded areas indicate recessions.

U.S. currency to Eastern Europe because the demand for it was so high. The Federal Reserve is able to count some of these exports of currency and thus can get a rough count of how much currency is abroad. Finally, in recent years, some countries have made their currencies completely exchangeable with U.S. dollars, so the currencies circulate together, and so such countries import many dollars.

In fact, the average American does not hold $3,000 in currency. Instead, people in many foreign lands hold U.S. dollars as a store of value. This practice, however, complicates the relationship between the monetary aggregates and U.S. economic activity. As a result, because about 40 percent of M1 is currency, of which much is in foreign countries, many economists do not use the M1 measure in economic analyses.

RECAP

1 The Federal Reserve's monetary aggregates are based on the liquidity and size of various bank accounts.

2 M1 is the measure of money whose components are the most liquid and smallest in size, consisting of coins, currency, traveler's checks, and checking accounts. M2 includes items of slightly less liquidity or larger size than those in M1 and consists of M1, small time deposits, retail MMMFs, and savings deposits.

3 More than half of all U.S. currency is located in foreign countries.

What do you do with your change? When you receive change, especially pennies, do you spend them? Or do you take them home, throw them in a box or a jar, and forget about them? Many Americans let coins pile up at home, so the government must produce more of them all the time.

Davis Barber/Photo Edit

People tend to stockpile their coins and not spend them. Machines such as this Coinstar device, found in grocery stores and other retail outlets, provide consumers with a convenient way to return their coins to circulation, and they help reduce the overall demand for new coins.

Under our fiat money system, the government makes a profit, known as *seignorage revenue*, on every coin that is issued. Even on the most expensive coin it produces, the Sacagawea golden dollar, the U.S. government earns seignorage revenue of about 90 cents.

But there are costs to the government of large fluctuations in the demand for coins. A shortage of coins can wreak havoc on our payments system, which is based on a steady supply of coins for making change. In 1999 and 2000, the United States found itself running short of coins, especially quarters and pennies.

The source of the problem was a new program to produce quarter dollars that depicted scenes or historical events from one of the 50 states on the back. The plan, passed by Congress, was to produce quarters for one state at a time, about every 10 weeks, for 10 years. When the state quarters were first produced, they were moderately popular, about what the U.S. Mint (which produces coins) and the Federal Reserve (which distributes coins) had expected. Then their popularity grew dramatically in the latter half of 1999, and the U.S.

Mint found itself running out of capacity to produce enough coins to meet demand.

As the demand for the state quarters grew in 1999, people began hoarding the quarters and spending other coins, including nickels, dimes, and old quarters. Because there simply were not enough quarters to meet demand, however, the demand for other coins began to rise. The demand for nickels and dimes rose sharply, and even some shortages of pennies occurred. During the shortages, banks were unable to obtain enough coins for their customers, either from other banks or from the Federal Reserve. In some cases, the Federal Reserve rationed the amount of coins it was willing to sell to banks because it could not get enough coins from the U.S. Mint.

In 2000, the shortages occurred again, in part because some U.S. Mint production capacity was devoted to producing the new Sacagawea golden dollar. Finally, in 2001, coin demand subsided, and the shortages disappeared.

A practical difficulty that many people face in getting rid of their piles of coins is that banks in recent years have stopped providing coin-wrapping services. Many banks require you to wrap your coins yourself in heavy paper containers designed for that purpose; most people do not want to bother. In response, companies such as Coinstar have placed thousands of coin-counting machines in supermarkets and other retail stores around the country. With these machines, you can dump all your change into the machine, and the machine will give you currency in exchange, less a service charge (a percentage of the value of your coins) that allows the company to pay for the machines and to make a profit from doing so. As the number of such machines has increased, the demand for new coins has declined.

Thus, when you look at the piles of coins you keep around your room, consider who is making a profit—the U.S. government. When you let those coins pile up, you are effectively making an interest-free loan to the government. You may find it worth your while to get rid of your coins periodically at your bank or your local supermarket coin machine, especially if there is a general shortage of coins.

1 People build up piles of change, especially pennies, because they do not want to bother carrying them around for spending.

2 With so many coins being hoarded and not spent, the government must produce billions of new coins every year. The government profits on producing those coins.

3 Shortages arise when there is a sudden change in people's demand for coins. In 1999 and 2000, shortages occurred when new coins—the new state quarters and the Sacagawea dollar—were produced.

4 Coin shortages are a function of people's unwillingness to spend their change and the lack of avenues for recirculating coins. The shortages may become history if enough people return their change through their banks or by using coin machines.

Review Questions and Problems

Review Questions

1 What are the four main functions of money? Describe each role, and give an example of how money works and how it might not work.

2 Why should we consider transactions costs in examining the role that money plays in society?

3 How does a high rate of inflation affect money in all its different roles?

4 Define hyperinflation, and explain the economic problems associated with it.

5 How does commodity money differ from fiat money? Give an example of each.

6 What is the difference between inside money and outside money? Give an example of each.

7 How might the payments system evolve over time to reduce transactions costs for society?

8 Are credit-card balances considered money? Why or why not?

9 Define the Federal Reserve's two measures of money, and explain how they differ.

10 Why did coin shortages occur in 1999 and 2000?

Numerical Exercises

11 Carlotta Crone withdraws $500 from her checking account and deposits it in a two-year CD. How does this transaction affect M1 and M2?

12 Get a copy of the latest *Federal Reserve Bulletin* at your library (or go to the Internet at **www .federalreserve.gov**), and find the most recent data on M1 and M2. How have these aggregates been growing in the past year compared with the values in Figure 3.2? If you can, download the data from the Internet, or enter them by hand into a spreadsheet, and see if you can plot the data to compare with Figure 3.2. Can you explain why the growth rates have changed recently?

13 Some economists argue that the Federal Reserve has caused recessions by reducing money growth too much. Do you see any evidence in Figure 3.2 in support of the proposition that slow money growth is associated with recessions? Explain.

Analytical Problems

14 Money has existed in even the most ancient economies. What are the main reasons that societies use money?

15 In the POW economy, what do you think happened to the prices of goods as the end of the war drew near? Two factors to consider are that the German supply lines were disrupted, so Red Cross packages could not reach the POW camps regularly, and Allied bombing attacks began to get closer to the camps.

16 Imagine that a new government in the United States declared all existing currency valueless and made the use of money illegal. What would happen to transactions? What would happen to economic activity?

17 If you wanted to construct a model predicting the growth in the demand for U.S. currency, what would be the main factors you would include? List at least five variables, and explain whether an increase or decrease in each variable would cause an increase in the demand for currency.

18 Should the government encourage or discourage people from hoarding coins and not spending them? In your answer, consider the government's profits from producing coins as well as society's overall welfare. Is it beneficial to society to produce coins that pile up unproductively in people's homes?

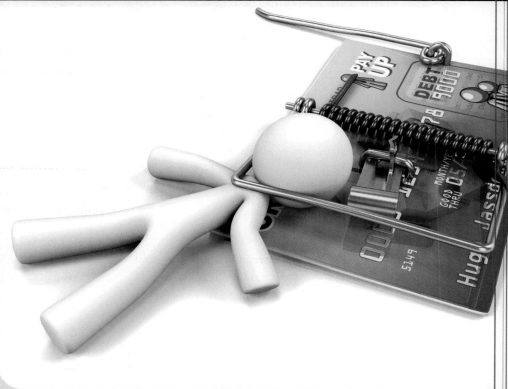

PRESENT
VALUE

Suppose that you are walking through the mall one day and find yourself listening to some credit-card

salesperson's pitch about how "our card features a low, low interest rate, offered only to you because your credit is so good." Half his words are jargon, discussing "APRs" and "finance charges" that are nearly incomprehensible to the average human. If you think that you are being fleeced, you are probably right. However, there are laws on the books designed to protect consumers. Unfortunately, financial transactions are so complicated that you may not know what kind of deal you are really getting.

Financial transactions, from the simplest to the most complex, are based on a single idea—that cash is going from one person to another at different times. The cash received or paid at different dates is worth different amounts. Thus, the main concept to understand is the value of a dollar today compared with a dollar at some date in the future.

Suppose that you win the state lottery, and you have the choice of receiving a lump sum of $75,000 or payments of $10,000 for eight years. Which should you select? If winning the lottery seems like a flight of fancy, you will still face similar financial decisions. More likely, you will have to make decisions such as these: Should I buy or lease a car? Am I better off with a 15-year mortgage or a 30-year mortgage? Should I invest in bonds or stocks? Is it preferable to put money in certificates of deposits (CDs) or a money-market mutual fund?

You might wonder what the answers to these questions have to do with financial markets, valuing financial securities, and determining the returns to financial investments. They all have to do with the concept of present value. This concept allows us to measure the value of cash paid or received over time, and we can use the results of our analysis to make prudent personal decisions, as well as to analyze the values of financial securities.

In the first part of the chapter we develop the present-value formula and use it to evaluate cash flows that occur at different times. In this way we can compare different types of securities that have different amounts of cash flow at different dates. Then we look at how people can use the present-value formula to make decisions. This analysis continues our investigation of financial markets and their role in channeling funds from savers to borrowers. We then see how we can use the concept of present value to look backward at past returns or forward at future returns. Finally, we apply our knowledge of present value with practical advice on how to negotiate a car lease.

4-1 The Present Value of One Future Payment

Would you rather have $100 today or $105 one year from now? Should you subscribe to a magazine for six months or three years? The answers to these questions are all made easier by a simple analytical device known as present value. The **present value** of an amount to be received in the future is simply the amount of money you need to invest today to yield the given future amount. The method of present value lets you compare flows of money received or paid at different times.

4-1a Investing, Borrowing, and Compounding

The concept of present value is based on two main ideas: (1) you can determine how much money you have available at different times by borrowing or saving, and (2) interest is earned on past interest. The first idea says that if you want more money today, you can borrow, and if you want more money in the future, you can save. Thus, you can determine how much money you have today or at any date in the future by deciding how much to borrow

and save over time. The second idea is that interest grows over time because of compounding. For example, if you invest your money in a debt security, you earn interest. In the future, you earn interest on the interest from earlier years. The following examples will help illustrate both these ideas.

First, compare money today with money in one year. Suppose that you have $100 today that you want to save for the future. If you deposit the money in a bank account, you earn a 4 percent annual interest rate. The amount of your deposit ($100 in this case) is the principal amount of your financial investment. In general, the **principal** of any financial investment is the amount you invest in a financial security or deposit in a financial intermediary. In one year, the amount of interest you will earn equals the principal amount of your financial investment ($P = \$100$) times the interest rate ($i = 0.04$), where the interest rate is expressed in decimal terms.

present value the amount of money you need to invest today to yield a given future amount

principal the amount of money invested in a financial security or deposited in a financial intermediary

$$Interest = principal \times interest\ rate$$
$$= P \times i$$
$$= \$100 \times 0.04 = \$4$$

LONDON—JULY 2007: Anthony Kiedis of the American rock band Red Hot Chili Peppers performs on stage during the Live Earth concert held at Wembley Stadium on July 7, 2007, in London. Live Earth was a 24-hour, seven-continent concert series taking place on 7/7/07, bringing together more than 100 music artists and 2 billion people to trigger a global movement to solve the climate crisis.

Adding the $4 of interest to the amount of principal, $100, gives a total of $104, which is the value of the financial investment at the end of one year.

It is often useful to add the interest to the principal in one step. That is,

$$\text{Amount of investment at end of year} = (principal \times interest\ rate) + principal$$
$$= (P \times i) + P$$
$$= (i \times P) + (1 \times P) = (1 + i) \times P$$

In our example we could find the value of the financial investment in just one step:

$$\text{Amount of financial investment at end of year}$$
$$= (1 + i) \times P$$
$$= (1 + 0.04) \times \$100 = 1.04 \times \$100 = \$104$$

Suppose that you sold your collection of Red Hot Chili Peppers CDs to someone who offered you either $100 today or $105 in one year. Which would you take? Suppose that if you received $100 today, you would put the money in the bank at a 4 percent annual interest rate, as described above. Then you would have $104 at the end of the year. In that case, you would rather receive $105 in one year because $105 is bigger than $104.

So far, our examples have involved investing, but the calculations are the same

compounding earning interest on interest that was earned in prior years

for borrowing. If you borrow $100 for one year at an annual interest rate of 4 percent, you will owe $104 at the end of the year. Therefore, all the same formulas apply for borrowing as they do for investing—but you will pay the money instead of receiving it.

Second, consider compounding over several years. When you invest for more than one year, **compounding** occurs because you earn interest in later years on the interest you earned in earlier years. Interest in one year adds to the principal value in subsequent years. As an example, suppose that you deposit $100 in a bank account for two years at a 4 percent annual interest rate. Call the original amount of principal $P = \$100$. In the first year, as we just saw, you earn $4 in interest and have $104 at the end of the year. Call the amount of principal you have at the end of one year $P_1 = \$104$. In the second year, you now earn interest of

$$Interest = principal \times interest\ rate = P_1 \times i$$
$$= \$104 \times 0.04 = \$4.16$$

At the end of the second year, you have

$$\text{Amount of financial investment at end of year}$$
$$= (1 + i) \times P_1$$
$$= (1 + 0.04) \times \$104 = 1.04 \times \$104 = \$108.16$$

If not for compounding, you would have earned $4 in interest in the second year, just as you did in the first year. But because you earn interest on the first year's interest, the amount you earn in the second year is higher (by 16 cents) than your earnings in the first year.

In this example, to find the amount you would have after one year, we calculated the amount

$$\text{Amount after one year} = (1 + i) \times P$$
$$= 1.04 \times \$100 = \$104$$

Then we used that as the new amount of principal and calculated

$$\text{Amount after two years} = (1 + i) \times P_1$$
$$= 1.04 \times \$104 = \$108.16$$

We could combine these two separate calculations into one, as shown here:

$$\text{Amount after two years} = (1 + i) \times P_1$$
$$= (1 + i) \times amount\ after\ one\ year$$
$$= (1 + i) \times (1 + i) \times P = (1 + i)^2 \times P$$
$$= 1.04^2 \times \$100 = \$108.16$$

The squared term shows that you have received interest on your principal in the first year and then interest on that whole amount in the second year, including interest on the first period's interest. That is compounding!

We can generalize this specific example. The value of a financial investment after N years (where N can be any positive number) is

$$\text{Value after } N \text{ years} = (1 + i)^N \times P \qquad \text{(1)}$$

where i is the annual interest rate, and P is the principal amount of the financial investment.

People often are amazed when they first realize how much difference compounding can make when carried out over a long period of time. For example, suppose that you invest $1,000 in a security that pays interest of 8 percent each year (and in which the interest is reinvested at 8 percent). You may not be too impressed after five years because the value of your $1,000 investment is $1.08^5 \times \$1,000 = \$1,469$. And after 10 years your investment has grown to only $1.08^{10} \times \$1,000 = \$2,159$; so you are hardly rich. However, if you keep your investment going for a longer time, compounding begins to matter. After 25 years, your investment is worth $1.08^{25} \times \$1,000 = \$6,848$; after 50 years, it is worth $1.08^{50} \times \$1,000 = \$46,902$; and after 100 years, your investment is worth a whopping $1.08^{100} \times \$1,000 = \$2,199,761$. Thus, it pays to be a long-term investor! If you borrow, the amount you owe also compounds, which is one reason that many people get themselves into debt trouble with credit cards. For example, if you put $1,000 on your credit card and let it grow without paying it off, it may grow to several thousand dollars in just a few years, thanks to compounding and the high interest rates that most credit cards charge.

4-1b Discounting

Now that we have seen how compounding works and how investing or borrowing can determine how much money you have at different dates, here is a closely related question: How much money today is worth a given amount of money at a future date?

First, consider as an example one payment in one year. How much would you be willing to give up today in exchange for receiving $104 in one year? Your answer to this question should depend on what you would do with the money if you had it today. Suppose that if you had the money today, you would deposit it in the bank at an annual interest rate of 4 percent. How much would you need to have today to get $104 in one year? The answer, of course, is $100,

which we determined in the example in the preceding section; $100 of principal invested for one year at a 4 percent annual interest rate yields $104 at the end of the year. Thus, you would be willing to give up $100 today to get $104 in one year. Therefore, the present value to you of $104 in one year equals $100.

Now let us make the idea of present value more general rather than focusing on this specific example. How do we calculate the present value of some amount F that you will receive one year from now? The present value is just the principal amount P that you need to invest today to have F at the end of the year. That is, we need to determine P such that

$$(1 + i) \times P = F$$

where i is the interest rate on a bank account where you would invest the money if you had it today. If we divide both sides of this equation by $1 + i$, we find that

$$P = \frac{F}{1+i} \qquad \text{(2)}$$

Thus, we calculate the present value by dividing the future value by a **discount factor** (in this case, $1 + i$). This process is **discounting.**

In our example, $F = \$104$ and $i = 0.04$. Using these values in Equation (2) yields

$$P = \frac{F}{1 + i} = \frac{\$104}{1.04} = \$100$$

This is the same result we found earlier.

To find the present value, you must answer two questions: (1) What would you do with money today so that it is available for you to spend in the future? (2) How much would you earn on such an investment? Often, when we want to calculate present value, we answer question 1 by saying that we would put the money in the bank and earn interest on it. The discount factor is then 1 plus the interest rate on our bank account. In many cases, investors are comparing two financial investments that are very similar, for example, two different debt securities with just slight differences in payments or maturity dates. In these cases, the appropriate discount factor of one debt

discount factor the amount by which a future value is divided to obtain its present value, which equals $(1 + i)^N$ for an amount to be received or paid in N years, where i is the rate of discount

discounting the process of dividing a future value by the discount factor to obtain the present value

security is one plus the interest rate paid on the other debt security. However, some people may invest money in other ways; for example, they may put their money in the stock market. In such a case, the discount factor would be 1 plus the return people expect to earn on stocks. For this reason, the term i in Equation (2) will be called the **rate of discount** rather than the interest rate in our discussion from now on.

Equation (2) is worth studying carefully because it yields two insights. First, for a given discount factor $(1 + i)$, the higher the future value F is, the higher the present value P will be because more money in the future is worth more today. Second, for a given future value F, the higher the discount factor $(1 + i)$ is, the lower the present value P is because the discount factor is the denominator of the fraction in Equation (2). When the discount factor is larger, you are dividing the future value by a larger number, so the present value is smaller.

To demonstrate, suppose that we consider again the present value of $104 to be received in one year. We saw earlier that when the rate of discount is 4 percent (i = 0.04), the present value is $100. If the rate of discount were smaller—say, 0 percent—then the discount factor also would be smaller (1.00). In this case, the present value is

$$P = \frac{F}{1 + i} = \frac{\$104}{1.00} = \$104$$

The present value is larger because the discount factor is smaller.

On the other hand, if the rate of discount were larger—say, 10 percent—then the discount factor would be larger (1.10), so the present value decreases:

$$P = \frac{F}{1 + i} = \frac{\$104}{1.10} = \$94.55$$

These results show that if the rate of discount were to decline from 4 to 0 percent, the present value would rise from $100 to $104. If the rate of discount were to rise from 4 to 10 percent, the present value would fall from $100 to $94.55. Thus, the *present value is inversely related to the rate of discount*. Because the discount factor is 1 plus the rate of discount, the present value is also inversely related to the discount factor. When the rate of discount or discount factor rises, present value falls; when the rate of discount or discount factor falls, present value rises. This is a key insight of the present-value formula.

rate of discount the term i in the discount factor

discount bond a debt security with just one payment

Second, consider one payment more than one year in the future. Suppose that an amount is to be received more than one year in the future. As with a payment being received one year in the future, we ask this: What principal amount is needed today to yield the future amount?

We learned in our discussion of compounding that the amount you have after N years of an investment paying annual interest rate i that started with principal amount P is $(1 + i)^N \times P$. Thus, if we want to have some amount F after N years, then we need to find the amount P such that $(1 + i)^N \times P = F$. Dividing both sides of this equation by $(1 + i)^N$ gives us the present value of an amount F being received N years in the future:

$$P = \frac{F}{(1 + i)^N} \qquad \text{(3)}$$

In this case, the discount factor is $(1 + i)^N$, where i is the rate of discount.

For example, if you are to receive $108.16 in two years, and the interest rate on your bank account is 4 percent, what is the present value? Using Equation (3), it is

$$P = \frac{F}{(1 + i)^N} = \frac{\$108.16}{1.04^2} = \$100$$

This is the same example we worked with in the earlier section "Investing, Borrowing, and Compounding."

You can even find the present value of amounts that will be received far in the future. For example, $1,000 to be received in 20 years (with a rate of discount of 4 percent) has a present value of

$$P = \frac{F}{(1 + i)^N} = \frac{\$1,000}{1.04^{20}} = \$456.39$$

You can see that because of compounding, the present value of an amount to be received far in the future is much less than the future amount, even with a fairly low rate of discount. If the rate of discount were higher, the present value would be even lower. In this example, if the rate of discount were 10 percent, the present value of $1,000 to be received in 20 years would be

$$P = \frac{F}{(1 + i)^N} = \frac{\$1,000}{1.10^{20}} = \$148.64$$

A number of financial securities make just one payment at a future date rather than a number of payments over time. A debt security with just one payment is a **discount bond.** The U.S. government sells Treasury bills, which mature in one year or less, by this method. In the next section, we will look at how to calculate the present value for multiple payments over time.

1 You can determine how much money you have available to spend at different dates by borrowing or investing.

2 When you invest, your earnings grow at a compound rate; when you borrow, your debt grows at a compound rate.

3 Present value is calculated by discounting, that is, dividing an amount to be received in the future by a discount factor.

4 To find the present value of a future amount, you must know (1) what you would do with the money today so that it is available for you in the future and (2) how much you would earn on such an investment (for example, what interest rate you would earn), which determines the rate of discount.

5 For a given discount factor, the higher the future value, the higher the present value is.

6 For a given future value, the higher the rate of discount, and hence the higher the discount factor, the lower the present value is. Present value is inversely related to the rate of discount or the discount factor.

7 For a payment to be received N years in the future, the discount factor is $(1 + i)^N$, where i is the rate of discount.

4-2 The General Form of the Present-Value Formula

Thus far we have found the present value of just one payment that is to be received either in one year or in several years. We can use those results to find the present value of many payments that will be received over time. The main principle is that the present value of many payments over time is the sum of the present values of each individual payment.

For example, suppose that you are to receive $100 in one year, $150 in two years, and $200 in three years. As before, assume that if you had the money today, you would deposit it in a bank at an interest rate of 4 percent. The present value of your payments is the present value of $100 in one year, plus the present value of $150 in two years, plus the present value of $200 in three years:

$$P = \frac{\$100}{1.04^1} + \frac{\$150}{1.04^2} + \frac{\$200}{1.04^3} = \$96.15 + \$138.68$$
$$+ \$177.80 = \$412.63$$

In general, when you are evaluating many payments being received over time, you can use Equation (3) for each payment and add them up. Thus, if you are evaluating a set of payments of F_1 in one year, F_2 in two years, and so on out to F_N in N years, where the rate of discount is i, the present value is

$$P = \frac{F_1}{(1 + i)^1} + \frac{F_2}{(1 + i)^2} + \cdots + \frac{F_N}{(1 + i)^N} \qquad \textbf{(4)}$$

Equation (4) is the **present-value formula,** an equation that can be used to calculate the present value of almost any financial security. As in the case of a single payment, a higher future amount (that is, an increase in one of the F amounts) will yield a higher present value. Also, a higher rate of discount or discount factor will yield a lower present value.

We will now see how this general form of the present-value formula can be used to evaluate the value of different types of financial securities. To aid in this

present-value formula
an equation that can be used to calculate the present value of almost any financial security

evaluation, we describe the flow of payments from a financial security using a timeline.

4-2a Timelines to Describe Payment Amounts

A convenient way to describe the payments promised by a financial security is to use a timeline, which is a graphic device that shows payment amounts over time. For example, if you were promised a payment of $104 in one year, the timeline would look like this:

Time (Years)	0	1	2	3	4	
Payment		$104				

The timeline for a payment of $108.16 in two years is

Time (Years)	0	1	2	3	4	
Payment			$108.16			

Many financial securities have more complicated timelines. In the following sections we will examine some fairly common types of securities: perpetuities, fixed-payment securities, and coupon bonds. In each case, we show the timeline and then calculate the present value.

4-2b The Present Value of a Perpetuity

Some financial securities never mature, so the timeline goes on forever, as do the payments that are entered into the present-value formula. One example of such a security is a share of stock in a corporation. We will analyze the present value of shares of stock in Chapter 7. In addition, some debt securities pay interest forever and never repay principal; such a bond is commonly called a **perpetuity**. Suppose that a perpetuity pays interest of $100 per year forever. The timeline is

perpetuity a debt security that pays interest forever and never repays principal

Time (Years)	0	1	2	3	4	5	6	7	...
Payment		$100	$100	$100	$100	$100	$100	$100	...

The dots in the timeline indicate that the payments go on forever.

To find the present value of the perpetuity, we use Equation (4) but let the payments go on forever. Suppose that the interest rate on a different perpetuity that an investor also could buy is 5 percent, so we use 5 percent as the rate of discount. The present value is

$$P = \frac{F_1}{(1+i)^1} + \frac{F_2}{(1+i)^2} + \frac{F_3}{(1+i)^3} + \cdots$$
$$= \frac{\$100}{1.05^1} + \frac{\$100}{1.05^2} + \frac{\$100}{1.05^3} + \cdots$$
$$= \$95.24 + \$90.70 + \$86.38 + \cdots$$

You might think that because the payments continue indefinitely, the present value must be infinite. However, this is not the case. The present value of each payment is less than the one before (note that each succeeding term is equal to the term before it multiplied by 1/1.05). So the sum of the present values of the payments is finite. You could use a spreadsheet program to add up the first several hundred terms in this expression, and you would find that the sum of the terms is getting higher and higher as additional terms are added, but the sum is converging to $2,000. Appendix 4.A shows why the sum converges to $2,000.

More generally, the present value of a perpetuity that pays amount F each year forever is

$$P = \frac{F}{i} \tag{5}$$

where i is the rate of discount. In this example, since $F = \$100$ and $i = 0.05$,

$$P = \frac{F}{i} = \frac{\$100}{0.05} = \$2,000$$

4-2c The Present Value of a Fixed-Payment Security

Many securities, especially loans made to consumers such as automobile and mortgage loans, are set up so that the principal amount is repaid gradually over time, a process called **amortization.** In many cases the amortization of the principal is done so that the dollar payment on the security is the same every year; such a security is called a **fixed-payment security.**

For example, a small automobile repair business might borrow money for some new diagnostic equipment, with a loan agreement that requires it to pay $700 at the end of each of the next four years, at which time the loan is completely paid off. The timeline is

Time (Years)	0	1	2	3	4	5	6
Payment		$700	$700	$700	$700		

To calculate the present value of a fixed-payment security, we again apply the present-value formula in Equation (4), but now all the payments are the same. Suppose that the interest rate on similar loans in the market is 7 percent; we use 7 percent as the rate of discount. Then the present value is

$$P = \frac{F_1}{(1+i)^1} + \frac{F_2}{(1+i)^2} + \cdots + \frac{F_N}{(1+i)^N}$$
$$= \frac{F}{(1+i)^1} + \frac{F}{(1+i)^2} + \cdots + \frac{F}{(1+i)^N}$$
$$= \frac{\$700}{1.07^1} + \frac{\$700}{1.07^2} + \frac{\$700}{1.07^3} + \frac{\$700}{1.07^4}$$
$$= \$654.20 + \$611.41 + \$571.41 + \$534.03$$
$$= \$2,371.05$$

We can develop a more compact formula for the present value of a fixed-payment security, as described in Appendix 4.B. A security that pays the amount F at the end of each of the next N years, when the rate of discount is i, has a present value of

$$P = \frac{F}{(1+i)^1} + \frac{F}{(1+i)^2} + \cdots + \frac{F}{(1+i)^N}$$
$$= F \times \frac{1 - [1/(1+i)]^N}{i} \qquad (6)$$

For the case of the fixed-payment security of $700 each year for four years (so $N = 4$) when the rate of discount is 7 percent, the present value is

$$P = \frac{\$700}{1.07^1} + \frac{\$700}{1.07^2} + \frac{\$700}{1.07^3} + \frac{\$700}{1.07^4} = \$700 \times \frac{1 - (1/1.07)^4}{0.07}$$
$$= \$700 \times \frac{0.237105}{0.07} = \$2,371.05$$

Note that this is the same answer that we derived earlier when we took the present value of each payment and added them together. Although the calculations we did here may not seem much easier than the calculations we performed earlier when we found the present value of each payment separately, using Equation (6) is much easier if the number of payments is very large.

For example, imagine that you take out a 30-year mortgage loan to buy a house. In this case the loan requires payments of $7,000 each year for 30 years. If the interest rate on mortgages in the market is 7 percent, then the present value of the loan is

$$P = \frac{F}{(1.07)^1} + \frac{F}{(1.07)^2} + \cdots + \frac{F}{(1.07)^{30}} = \$7,000 \times \frac{1 - (1/1.07)^{30}}{0.07}$$
$$= \$7,000 \times \frac{0.868633}{0.07} = \$86,863.30$$

This calculation is much simpler than calculating the present value of 30 different terms and adding them together.

4-2d The Present Value of a Coupon Bond

Many debt securities sold by corporations and the U.S. government take the form of a coupon bond. A **coupon bond** pays a regular interest payment until the maturity date, at which time the face value is repaid. Such bonds are called coupon bonds because many years ago the interest payment was made only after the investor delivered a coupon that was attached to the printed bond certificate. These days, such payments are made automatically, with most transactions accomplished electronically. The **face value** is the amount repaid by the bond at maturity; it is usually called face value and not principal for a fairly subtle reason: Often such bonds are sold in the primary market

amortization a process in which the principal amount of a security is repaid gradually over time

fixed-payment security a security in which the dollar payment on the security is the same every year so that the principal is amortized

coupon bond a security that pays a regular interest payment until the maturity date, at which time the face value is repaid

face value the amount repaid by a coupon bond at maturity

for slightly different amounts than their face value. For example, the U.S. government will sell a Treasury note with a $10,000 face value and a stated interest rate of 5 percent of the face value per year. Then the government will sell the note in an auction and allow market demand to determine the price; for example, it might sell for $9,956. Because the price is less than the face value, investors who buy the security will earn slightly more than the stated interest rate of 5 percent. The investor's principal amount is $9,956, but the face value of the bond is $10,000. (Note: this is called an *original issue discount* in the financial markets.)

Let's look at an example of a coupon bond. Suppose that a coupon bond pays $100 of interest each year for five years and then returns the face value of $1,000 at the end of the fifth year. The timeline looks like this:

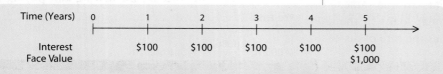

In this case we use the timeline to show the amount of interest and face value separately, which may be helpful in finding the present value. If an investor's best alternative to investing in this particular bond is to invest in a similar bond that pays an interest rate of 10 percent, then we can use the present-value formula with rate of discount $i = 0.10$ to find the value of the bond:

$$P = \frac{F_1}{(1+i)^1} + \frac{F_2}{(1+i)^2} + \cdots + \frac{F_N}{(1+i)^N}$$

$$= \frac{\$100}{1.10^1} + \frac{\$100}{1.10^2} + \frac{\$100}{1.10^3} + \frac{\$100}{1.10^4} + \frac{\$100}{1.10^5} + \frac{\$1,000}{1.10^5}$$

$$= \$90.91 + \$82.65 + \$75.13 + \$68.30 + \$62.09 + \$620.92$$

$$= \$1,000.00$$

Note that the coupon bond looks like a combination of a fixed-payment security and a single payment of the face value at maturity. Thus, for a coupon bond making an interest payment of F each year for N years and then repaying the face value V at the end of N years, the timeline is

The present value of the coupon bond is

$$P = \frac{F}{(1+i)^1} + \frac{F}{(1+i)^2} + \cdots + \frac{F}{(1+i)^N} + \frac{V}{(1+i)^N}$$

The present value of the interest payments can be found using Equation (6), so the present value of the coupon bond is

$$P = \left\{ F \times \frac{1 - [1/(1+i)]^N}{i} \right\} + \frac{V}{(1+i)^N} \qquad (7)$$

In the preceding example with $F = \$100$, $i = 0.10$, $V = \$1,000$, and $N = 5$, the present value is

$$P = \left\{ F \times \frac{1 - [1/(1+i)]^N}{i} \right\} + \frac{V}{(1+i)^N}$$

$$= \left\{ \$100 \times \frac{1 - (1/1.10)^5}{0.10} \right\} + \frac{\$1,000}{1.10^5} = \$379.08 + \$620.92 = \$1,000.00$$

Note that this is the same value we calculated earlier, but Equation (7) is often an easier equation to use than Equation (4). For example, if $N = 30$, then Equation (4) has 30 terms to be calculated, whereas Equation (7) still has only two terms.

4-2e The Present Value When Payments Occur More Often than Once Each Year

When we introduced the present-value formula, the examples we used had periodic payments that were made once each year. However, in reality, many financial securities require payments at more frequent intervals. Stocks usually pay dividends quarterly, government bonds pay interest semiannually, homeowners make mortgage payments monthly, and automobile owners make payments on their car loans monthly. Because interest compounds (that is, interest is paid on past interest), we need to account for the frequency of the payments in our present-value calculations.

To adjust the present-value formula to allow for payments being made more often than once a year, we redefine the length of the time period for the analysis. In Equation (4), which shows the general form of the present-value formula, each amount to be received in the future is divided by a discount factor that equals $(1 + i)^N$, where i is the rate of discount, and N is the number of years in the future at which the payment is to be received. In setting up that equation, we dealt only in whole years, so the time period for the analysis was one year. Now we modify the time period for the analysis to be monthly, quarterly, semiannually, or however long the time is between payments. We also modify the rate of discount from an annual basis to one that represents the rate of discount for the relevant time period.

For example, consider a 30-year mortgage loan with monthly payments of $735 and an annual interest rate of 9 percent. The time period for the analysis will be monthly because a payment is made each month. The loan matures in 30 years $\times$ 12 months/year = 360 months. The annual interest rate is 9 percent = 0.09. To turn this into a monthly rate of discount to use in the present-value formula, divide the annual interest rate by the number of months each year, which in this case is 0.09/12 = 0.0075. Because a mortgage loan is a fixed-payment security (one that is amortized with a fixed payment each period), we can use Equation (6), so the present value of the mortgage loan is

$$P = F \times \frac{1 - [1/(1 + i)]^N}{i} = \$735 \times \frac{1 - (1/1.0075)^{360}}{0.0075} = \$735 \times \frac{0.932114}{0.0075} = \$91,347.17$$

The present value of the loan is $91,347.17, which represents the amount you are borrowing and paying off over time.

RECAP

1 The general form of the present-value formula, given by Equation (4), can be used to evaluate a wide variety of financial securities and other payments over time.

2 A timeline is a graphic device showing the values of payments received at different dates.

3 A perpetuity makes periodic payments forever, but the principal is never repaid.

4 A fixed-payment security is one in which the principal is amortized (paid off) over the life of the security so that the payments are identical each year until maturity.

5 A coupon bond makes regular interest payments until the maturity date, at which time the face value is repaid.

6 The present-value formula can be used to find the present value of payments that occur more often than once each year by following these steps:

   a. Determine the number of periods each year in which a payment is made (2 for semiannual payments, 4 for quarterly payments, 12 for monthly payments).

   b. Divide the annual interest rate by the number of periods per year to determine the rate of discount.

   c. Multiply the number of years until maturity by the number of payments per year to determine the number of periods until maturity.

   d. Employ the appropriate version of the present-value formula, using the result in step b for the rate of discount and the result in step c for the time until maturity:

   Equation (3) for a discount bond or other security with just one payment
   Equation (5) for a perpetuity
   Equation (6) for a fixed-payment security
   Equation (7) for a coupon bond
   Equation (4) for a security that does not fit into any other specific case

4-3 Using Present Value to Make Decisions

We now have examined a variety of different types of securities, what their timelines look like, and how their present values are calculated. But you might be wondering, "Why do we calculate present value?" When we introduced present value at the beginning of this chapter, we said, "The present value of an amount to be received in the future is simply the amount of money you would need to invest today to yield the given future amount. The method of present value lets you compare flows of money received or paid at different times." In discussing present value, we also noted that to make a calculation of present value, you need to decide on two things: (1) What would you do with the money today so that it is available for you to spend in the future? (2) How much would you earn on such an investment? You can use the answers to these questions to calculate the present value of a financial security or of some money that is to be paid to you in the future. You will be able to use the present-value formula to make decisions. You also will be able to use the ideas behind present value to answer questions that cannot be tackled by plugging numbers into a standard equation.

4-3a Comparing Alternative Offers

Suppose that you are buying a car. You go to one dealer, who works up a deal in which you pay $3,740 each year for three years for the car. Another dealer gives you a deal in which you will pay $2,870 each year for four years. Which is the better deal for you? How to approach this problem may not be obvious. Think about what you would do if you took the second offer, in which you pay less each of the first three years but must pay for a fourth year. Suppose that you would take the money that you would save in each of the first three years (the amount is $3,740 − $2,870 = $870) and put it into a savings account paying 6 percent interest so that you could make the payment in the fourth year. Then we can calculate the present value of both options using a discount rate of 6 percent to see which is the cheapest. The payment amounts of each option are shown in this timeline:

The first option, paying $3,740 each year for three years, has a present value of

$$P = \frac{\$3,740}{1.06^1} + \frac{\$3,740}{1.06^2} + \frac{\$3,740}{1.06^3} = \$3,528.30$$
$$+ \$3,328.59 + \$3,140.18 = \$9,997.07$$

The second option, paying $2,870 each year for four years, has a present value of

$$P = \frac{\$2,870}{1.06^1} + \frac{\$2,870}{1.06^2} + \frac{\$2,870}{1.06^3} + \frac{\$2,870}{1.06^4}$$
$$= \$2,707.55 + \$2,554.29 + \$2,409.71$$
$$+ \$2,273.31$$
$$= \$9,944.86$$

Since the present value of the second option is lower than the present value of the first, the second option is a better deal for you. Therefore, you should take the second deal, save the difference between the two annual payments in each of the first three years, and you will have enough to make the payment in the fourth year with some extra funds left over.

Another common use of the present-value formula arises when an investor wants to buy a coupon bond. Different bonds have different payment amounts over time, making comparisons among them difficult. By using the present-value formula, however, you can determine if a particular bond is better to buy than another one. Suppose that you could buy a new bond in the primary market with five years to maturity that pays $800 per year and that has a principal value equal to its face value of $10,000 (that is repaid at the maturity date) and thus an annual interest rate of 8 percent. Alternatively, you could buy a bond in the secondary market from another investor that pays $600 each year for five years and repays principal of $10,000 at the end of the fifth year. What is the most you would be willing to pay the other investor for the bond in the secondary market? To answer this question, think about your alternative opportunity: If you do not buy the bond in the secondary market, you will buy the new bond in the primary market. You should use the interest rate on the new bond as the rate of discount in determining the present value of the bond in the secondary market.

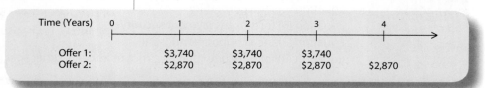

Time (Years)	0	1	2	3	4
Offer 1:		$3,740	$3,740	$3,740	
Offer 2:		$2,870	$2,870	$2,870	$2,870

Then the present value of the bond in the secondary market, using Equation (7), is

$$P = \left\{ F \times \frac{1 - [1/(1 + i)]^N}{i} \right\} + \frac{V}{(1 + i)^N}$$

$$= \left[\$600 \times \frac{1 - (1/1.08)^5}{0.08} \right] + \frac{\$10,000}{1.08^5}$$

$$= \$2,395.63 + \$6,805.83 = \$9,201.46$$

Because the present value of the payments on the bond in the secondary market is $9,201.46, that amount is the most you should be willing to pay for the bond. If the bond's owner asks for more than that, do not buy it; if the bond's owner asks for less than that, buy it immediately!

4-3b Buying or Leasing a Car

One of the situations in which consumers can apply the present-value formula is when they decide whether to purchase or lease a car. Personal finance advisors in the media often address this decision, and because they do not understand the present-value formula, they often give bad advice. For example, here is what one columnist had to say: "Dealers make more on leases because such payments, plus what the dealer gets selling the car after you turn it in, are more than he'd get in an old-fashioned sale."

Here is the example used by the columnist to explain his reasoning. Suppose that you could either buy a car for $17,990 or lease it for $149 per month plus a down payment of $2,800. Which is the better deal financially? If you lease, you pay $149 for 24 months plus the $2,800 down payment, which totals $6,376 over the two years. When you lease, you have the option to buy the car at the end of the two-year lease period for a specified amount, in this case $14,154. Thus, if you lease for two years and then buy the car, you will spend a total of $6,376 + $14,154 = $20,530. According to the columnist, because you could have purchased the car initially for $17,990, the dealer has made an extra profit of $20,530 − $17,990 = $2,540 from the lease.

This analysis is incorrect, however. It ignores the present value of the payments that are being made. Money paid today is worth more than money paid in the future. Thus, we must use the present-value formula, discounting future payments, to analyze the cost of the lease.

First, let us look at the present value of the monthly payments. Suppose the interest rate on auto loans is 8 percent. Because your choice is between borrowing and leasing, using a rate of discount of 8 percent in

In negotiating to buy or lease a car, buyers must understand the concept of present value. If they understand the present-value formula, they will be better able to compare alternative offers and to decide whether to buy the car or lease it.

the present-value formula makes sense for evaluating a lease. Because the lease payment is $149 per month for 24 months, we need to express the rate of discount in monthly terms as

Monthly rate of discount = annual interest rate ÷ 12

$$= 0.08 \div 12 = 0.006667$$

Using these numbers in the present-value formula for a fixed-payment security, Equation (6), the present value of the monthly payments is

$$P = F \times \frac{1 - [1/(1 + i)]^N}{i} = \$149 \times \frac{1 - (1/1.006667)^{24}}{0.006667} = \$149 \times \frac{0.1474}{0.006667} = \$3,294$$

Second, the $14,154 paid when you buy the car at the end of the lease must be discounted because it is paid 24 months in the future. It is just a single payment, so its present value, using Equation (3), is

$$P = \frac{F}{(1 + i)^N} = \frac{\$14,154}{1.006667^{24}} = \frac{\$14,154}{1.1729} = \$12,068$$

Thus, the present value of the $14,154 purchase price of the car in 24 months is $12,068. Notice that the difference between $14,154 and its present value of $12,068 is over $2,000. This amount alone accounts for most of the supposed "extra profit" earned by the dealer on a lease.

Now that we have everything in terms of present value, we can compare the cost of the lease with the alternative of buying the car. The total present value of the lease is the sum of the present values of the purchase price (after two years), the lease payments, and the down payment:

Present value of lease = $3,294 + $12,068 + $2,800 = $18,162

This is not too much different from the price of $17,990 to purchase the car initially. The difference between these amounts, $172, is less than one-tenth the amount that the columnist suggested ($2,540) when he failed to calculate the present value of all the terms.

Thus, when we calculate the present value of a lease, we see that the cost of a lease followed by a purchase when the lease expires is not much different from the price for purchasing the car initially. The lease represents nothing more than an alternative method of getting the services of a car—renting it rather than buying it. Using the present-value formula shows that, on the financial side of things, the differences between buying and leasing are fairly small, in contradiction to what the newspaper columnist argued.

There are, however, a number of other differences between leasing and buying a car. One major advantage to a consumer who leases is that the consumer gets an option to purchase the car at a set price. She then can drive the car for several years (the time to maturity of the lease) and decide for herself if the car is worth owning. In addition, she can look at the market at the time the lease expires. If the car is worth more than the buyout price, she will buy the car and perhaps sell it in the market. If the car is worth less than the buyout price, she can either turn the car in or negotiate with the lease owner, usually a bank, for a lower price. Thus, the buyout option for the car can be very beneficial for the consumer, so it is worth money to her. (For more information on this topic, see the last section in this chapter, "Application to Everyday Life: How to Negotiate a Car Lease.") For people who like to own a new car for a few years and then replace it, a lease makes sense because it reduces their transactions costs in buying and selling cars frequently. However, if you want to keep a car for a long time, leasing is less useful because when the lease expires, you need to engage in another round of

interest-rate risk the risk of a change in the price of a security in the secondary market because of a change in the market interest rate

transactions to buy the car. In addition, depending on your personal circumstances, leasing has a number of other disadvantages. With a lease, you have no ownership in the car, so you may feel that you are paying every month without building up any ownership rights. Also, leases come with a limit on the number of miles you can drive the car, often 15,000 to 18,000 miles per year. If you exceed the limit, you must pay some amount (these days, often 10 to 20 cents per mile over the limit) to the car dealer to reflect the increased depreciation on the car. If you drive a lot, you are probably better off buying the car. Also, if your car is damaged, you will have to pay the car dealer to repair the damage if you turn the car in at the expiration of the lease. And car dealers like leases because they encourage people to lease new cars when the leases on their old cars expire.

All these considerations are important in your decision about whether to buy or lease a car. One thing that you do not need to worry about, though, is that somehow leases are inherently more expensive than buying a car. The financial differences are fairly small. Thus, you should consider leasing a car if you want new cars frequently and do not drive too much; otherwise, buying a car may be a better choice for you.

4-3c Interest-Rate Risk

Another way to use the present-value formula is to examine **interest-rate risk,** the risk of a change in the price of a security in the secondary market because of a change in the market interest rate. You will recall from Chapter 2 that such risk occurs because a change in the price of a security causes the investor to receive capital gains or to suffer capital losses.

Consider this example: Suppose that you decide to purchase a coupon bond that has five years to maturity, pays $100 in interest each year, and repays its face value of $1,000 at the end of five years. The timeline of the bond is

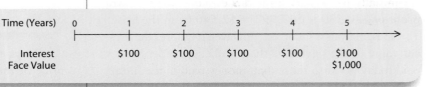

Time (Years)	0	1	2	3	4	5
Interest		$100	$100	$100	$100	$100
Face Value						$1,000

What is the present value of your bond? Suppose that the current market interest rate on other coupon bonds that mature in five years is 10 percent. Using Equation (7), the present value is

$$P = \left\{ F \times \frac{1 - [1/(1 + i)^N]}{i} \right\} + \frac{V}{(1 + i)^N} = \left[\$100 \times \frac{1 - (1/1.10)^5}{0.10} \right] + \frac{\$1,000}{1.10^5}$$

$$= \$379.08 + \$620.92 = \$1,000.00$$

Now suppose that, suddenly and unexpectedly (just after you have purchased your bond), the interest rate in the market for five-year bonds such as yours rises to 20 percent. What is the present value of your bond now? Using the present-value formula with the higher rate of discount, the present value of your bond is now

$$P = \left\{ F \times \frac{1 - [1/(1 + i)]^N}{i} \right\} + \frac{V}{(1 + i)^N} = \left[\$100 \times \frac{1 - (1/1.20)^5}{0.20} \right] + \frac{\$1,000}{1.20^5}$$

$$= \$299.06 + \$401.88 = \$700.94$$

Thus, the rise in interest rates in the market reduced the present value of your bond from $1,000 to about $700, a significant decline. If you were to now try to sell the bond in the market, you would find a buyer only at a price of $700.94. Why did the value of your bond fall? Essentially, you own a bond that promises to pay a return of 10 percent per year for five years, but market opportunities have changed so that someone buying a new bond could earn interest of 20 percent. Because your bond now pays an interest rate that is much lower than the market interest rate, your bond is worth less. If you want to sell the bond, you will have to reduce the

price well below the bond's face value of $1,000 to induce someone to buy it.

Similarly, a drop in the market interest rate results in an increase in the present value of your bond. For example, if the market interest rate falls to 5 percent, your bond's present value changes to

$$P = \left\{ F \times \frac{1 - [1/(1 + i)]^N}{i} \right\} + \frac{V}{(1 + i)^N} = \left[\$100 \times \frac{1 - (1/1.05)^5}{0.05} \right] + \frac{\$1,000}{1.05^5}$$

$$= \$432.95 + \$783.52 = \$1,216.47$$

In this case, the decline in the market interest rate causes a rise in the present value of the bond. Now someone comparing your bond with other, similar bonds in the market would be willing to pay you as much as $1,216.47 for your bond. For additional examples of how other changes in the market interest rate affect the price of this bond, see the box "The Relationship Between the Market Interest Rate and the Price."

These examples show that the present value of a coupon bond is affected by changes in interest rates paid on similar coupon bonds. Would an investor ever pay more than the present value of a bond to purchase the bond? This is not very likely because the investor could spend less on another bond and thus get a better deal. Would an investor ever sell a bond for less than its present value? Not if the market contains many buyers because it should be possible to find someone willing to pay an amount equal to the present value for

The Relationship Between the Market Interest Rate and the Price

In the case of the bond with a $1,000 face value that matures in five years and pays a coupon of $100 each year, analyzed in this section, we can look at many different market interest rates and see how much the price of the bond (which equals the present value) is affected.

Market Interest Rate	Bond Price
1%	$1,436.81
2%	$1,377.08
3%	$1,320.58
4%	$1,267.11
5%	$1,216.47
6%	$1,168.50
7%	$1,123.01

Market Interest Rate	Bond Price
8%	$1,079.85
9%	$1,038.90
10%	$1,000.00
11%	$963.04
12%	$927.90
13%	$894.48
14%	$862.68
15%	$832.39
16%	$803.54
17%	$776.05
18%	$749.83
19%	$724.81
20%	$700.94

the bond. Thus, if a bond never sells for more or less than its present value, any transactions must occur at a price equal to the present value. Because the price of a bond equals its present value, and because present value is inversely related to the market interest rate, we conclude that the price of a bond is inversely related to the market interest rate. Interest-rate risk is one of the major sources of risk to a security that we examined in Chapter 2. Now you know how to use the present-value formula to determine the magnitude of such risk.

4-4 Using the Present-Value Formula to Calculate Payments

In many financial transactions, the borrower and lender do not need to calculate the present value because they already know it. Instead, they need to calculate, for a given interest rate, the amount of money to be paid back. For example, if you want to buy a car for $20,000, and you would like to borrow the money from a bank and pay it back with monthly payments for the next five years, how large will your monthly payment be? To answer questions such as these, we use the present-value formula, but we solve for the future payments, given the interest rate and the present value.

To illustrate how this can be done, consider the example of a car loan in which you borrow $20,000 for five years. Suppose that the annual interest rate is 9 percent. What monthly payment would be required to pay off the loan? The type of security is a fixed-payment security. With an interest rate of 9 percent on an annual basis, the monthly interest rate is $0.09 \div 12 = 0.0075$. Because the loan is to be paid off over five years and

there are 12 months per year, the maturity of the loan is 5 years × 12 months per year = 60 months.

The present-value formula for a fixed-payment security is Equation (6):

$$P = \frac{F}{(1 + i)^1} + \frac{F}{(1 + i)^2} + \cdots + \frac{F}{(1 + i)^N} = F \times \frac{1 - [1/(1 + i)]^N}{i}$$

Because we wish to find F, given values for i, P, and N, we can use algebra to modify the equation in this way. Multiply both sides of the preceding equation by $i/\{1 - [1/(1 + i)]^N\}$ and rearrange terms to get

$$F = P \times \frac{i}{1 - [1/(1 + i)]^N} \tag{8}$$

Now, with $P = \$20,000$, $i = 0.0075$, $N = 60$, the monthly payment is

$$F = \$20,000 \times \frac{0.0075}{1 - (1/1.0075)^{60}} = \$20,000 \times \frac{0.0075}{0.3613} = \$20,000 \times 0.020758 = \$415.17$$

In a similar way, you can calculate payment amounts for other types of securities using Equation (3) for a security with just one payment, Equation (5) for a perpetuity, and Equation (7) for a coupon bond.

To use the present-value formula to calculate future payments, follow these steps:

1 Determine the type of security.

2 Determine the amount being borrowed.

3 Determine the time period between payments.

4 Determine the appropriate interest rate.

5 Determine the number of periods until maturity.

6 Use the appropriate form of the present-value formula, depending on the type of security in step 1 and the period between payments in step 3, based on the result in step 4 for the interest rate, the result in step 5 for the time to maturity, and the result in step 2 for the present value P. Then solve for the future payment amount F.

4-5 Looking Forward or Looking Backward at Returns

In many situations we want to know the future return to owning a security. In other situations we want to know our return in the past. In this section we will see how the present-value formula can be used either to look forward at the future return to a security or to look backward at a security's past return.

Here are some examples in which someone would like to look forward at future returns or backward at past returns: (1) An investor has received a forecast of a firm's future profits and would like to calculate the expected return to owning stock in the company. (2) A student has been offered several different student loans with different upfront fees and would like to evaluate which is the best deal. (3) As a person heads into retirement, she would like to know the interest rate she will earn on a retirement annuity (a type of debt security that makes monthly payments for the rest of the owner's life). (4) An investor purchased stock in a company 27 years ago, received dividend payments over time, and then sold the stock and would like to know if the return was better or worse than the average stock return in the market.

We can use the present-value formula to answer all these questions, all of which require us to calculate the term i in the present-value formula (Equation 4), which is repeated here:

$$P = \frac{F_1}{(1 + i)^1} + \frac{F_2}{(1 + i)^2} + \cdots + \frac{F_N}{(1 + i)^N}$$

If we know P and we know all the payments (F_1, F_2, . . . , F_N), we will be able to calculate i. In what follows, we look at some examples to see how i is calculated in a number of different situations. When we used the present-value formula for discounting, we called i the *rate of discount*. But when we solve the present-value formula to calculate i, the calculated value of i may be called different things, including *past return* in a backward-looking situation and *expected return* or *yield to maturity* in forward-looking situations.

The backward-looking concept is **past return,** which is the average annual return that a security or a portfolio of securities has produced in the past. As we learned in Chapter 2, returns consist of two components: current yield and capital-gains yield. We will now learn how to use the present-value formula to calculate the past return on an investment for any period.

The first of the forward-looking concepts, expected return, was defined in Chapter 2 as the expected gain from both income (interest or dividends) and capital gains as a percentage of the amount invested. As we saw

past return the average annual return that a security or a portfolio has produced in the past

in Chapter 2, expected return accounts for the possibility that an expected payment may not be made.

The second forward-looking concept is **yield to maturity,** which is the average annual return that an investor will receive on an investment if it is held until it matures. Yield to maturity and expected return differ in two ways: (1) Expected return can be calculated on equity securities or debt securities, but yield to maturity can be calculated only on debt securities because equity

yield to maturity the average annual return to a security if you purchase the security in the market today and hold it until it matures

securities have no maturity date. (2) Yield to maturity is calculated assuming that the issuer of the debt security does not default, whereas expected return accounts for the probability of default.

Past return, expected return, and yield to maturity are all calculated using the present-value formula, Equation (4), or some variant of it, such as Equations (2), (3), (5), and (7), in which you plug in the payments made by the security on the right-hand side of the equation and the price on the left-hand side and solve for the term i. If the payments (the F terms) in the formula already have been made, then the calculated value of i is the past return. If the payments are expected future payments, then the calculated value of i is the expected return. If the payments are the promised payments from a debt security, then the calculated value of i is the yield to maturity (note that the calculation ignores the chance of default). Let's see how we can calculate past return, expected return, and yield to maturity with payments similar to those we analyzed when we looked at present value.

4-5a One Payment in One Year

When one payment is being made in one year, the value of i can be calculated by rewriting Equation (2). Equation (2) is

$$P = \frac{F}{1 + i}$$

Rearranging terms, we get

$$i = \frac{F}{P} - 1 \qquad \textbf{(9)}$$

For example, consider a one-year security that sells for $1,000 and repays $1,050 at the end of the year. The value of i is

$$i = \frac{F}{P} - 1 = \frac{\$1,050}{\$1,000} - 1 = 1.05 - 1 = 0.05 = 5 \text{ percent}$$

In this example, if this is a debt security that you buy for $1,000 and that promises to pay you $1,050 in one year, then the calculation shows that your yield to maturity is 5 percent. Alternatively, suppose that this is a debt security that you bought one year ago for $1,000 and that matures, paying you $1,050 today, or an equity security that you bought one year ago for $1,000 and sell today for $1,050 and that paid no dividends. In either case, your past return is 5 percent. Another possibility is that this is a debt security that you buy for $1,000 today and that has an expected payoff of $1,050 at maturity in one year. This could arise if the security offers an interest rate of 9 percent, but there is a 3.7 percent probability that the company will default and not make the interest payment or repay your principal. Thus, there is a 96.3 percent chance that the security will pay you $1,090 and a 3.7 percent chance that the security will pay you nothing. So the expected payment in one year is

$$(0.963 \times \$1,090) + (0.037 \times \$0) = \$1,050$$

With an expected payment in one year of $1,050, the expected return on the security is 5 percent. Thus, in all three of these situations, the past return, expected return, and yield to maturity would be 5 percent.

4-5b One Payment More Than One Year in the Future

If a security makes one payment more than one year in the future, the appropriate present-value formula is Equation (3):

$$P = \frac{F}{(1 + i)^N}$$

As in the case of one payment being made in one year, we can solve this equation for i in terms of P and F:

$$i = \left(\frac{F}{P}\right)^{1/N} - 1 \qquad \textbf{(10)}$$

For example, suppose that you are a top executive at a corporation that offers you, as part of your compensation package, either $500,000 in cash today or shares of the company's stock that you expect will be worth $2 million in three years, which is the first date at which you are allowed to sell them. If you took the cash, what expected return from investing the cash would you need to equal the expected value of the stock in three years? The expected value of the stock in three years is $F = \$2$ million. The alternative is to take cash of $P = \$500,000$. The maturity date is $N = 3$ years. Thus, the expected return you would need to earn by investing the cash is

$$i = \left(\frac{F}{P}\right)^{1/N} - 1 = \left(\frac{\$2,000,000}{\$500,000}\right)^{1/3} - 1 = 4^{1/3} - 1 = 1.59 - 1 = 0.59 = 59 \text{ percent}$$

You would need to invest the cash and earn a 59 percent annual return over the next three years for the cash to be worth as much as the stock in three years. Why would a company offer you such a good deal on its stock? Because the company knows that your skills are immensely valuable and that you will increase the firm's profits over the next three years as a result of your abilities. The company wants to make it worth your while to stay in its employ for the next three years and does not want you to work for anyone else.

4-5c Perpetuity

In the case of a perpetuity, finding the past return, expected return, or yield to maturity requires that we operate on Equation (5):

$$P = \frac{F}{i}$$

Multiplying both sides by i and dividing by P gives

$$i = \frac{F}{P} \qquad (11)$$

For example, if you spend $1,400 on a perpetuity that pays $70 each year, your yield to maturity is

$$i = \frac{F}{P} = \frac{\$70}{\$1,400} = 0.05 = 5 \text{ percent}$$

We can call this the yield to maturity, even though the perpetuity never matures, because 5 percent is your yield each year forever. Of course, if there were some probability that the firm that sold the perpetuity would go bankrupt, then your expected return would be less than the yield to maturity.

4-5d Fixed-Payment Security

With a fixed-payment security, calculation of the implied interest rate when you know the annual payment amount and the price of the security requires a modification of Equation (6). That equation was

$$P = \frac{F}{(1 + i)^1} + \frac{F}{(1 + i)^2} + \cdots + \frac{F}{(1 + i)^N}$$
$$= F \times \frac{1 - [1/(1 + i)]^N}{i}$$

If we divide both sides of the equation by F, we get

$$\frac{P}{F} = \frac{1 - [1/(1 + i)]^N}{i} \qquad (12)$$

There is no way to write this out in terms of i as a function of just P and F, so we can use the "guess, test, and revise method" to find i given any P and F. For example, suppose that we have a fixed-payment business loan in which we borrowed $P = \$10,000$ and will repay $2,500 each year for five years. What is the yield to maturity that the lender earns? Because $P/F = \$10,000/\$2,500 = 4$, we need to search for the value of i that makes the right-hand side of the equation equal 4. A guess of $i = 0.10$ makes the right-hand side equal 3.79; a guess of $i = 0.07$ makes the right-hand side equal 4.10; a guess of $i = 0.08$ makes the right-hand side equal 3.99; and a guess of $i = 0.079$ makes the right-hand side equal 4.00. Therefore, this fixed-payment security has a yield to maturity of 7.9 percent. In practice, we use computers to calculate the yield to maturity, not the "guess, test, and revise" method.

4-5e Coupon Bond

Suppose that you are considering the purchase of a coupon bond that pays $100 per year for five years, repays its face value of $1,000 at the end of the fifth year, and has a current price of $950. You would like to calculate the bond's yield to maturity. If we plug the payments and price into the present-value formula for a coupon bond (Equation 7), we get

$$P = \left\{ F \times \frac{1 - [1/(1 + i)]^N}{i} \right\} + \frac{V}{(1 + i)^N}$$

$$\$950 = \left\{ \$100 \times \frac{1 - [1/(1 + i)]^5}{i} \right\} + \frac{\$1,000}{(1 + i)^5}$$

Because the terms that include i are raised to a power, solving this equation is best accomplished using a computer. Alternatively, you could use the guess, test, and revise" method. Using either method, you will find that $i = 0.114$ solves the equation almost exactly. Putting this into percentage terms, the yield to maturity is 11.4 percent. You could make a similar calculation for a coupon bond's expected return or past return as well.

4-5f Payments Made More Frequently Than Once Each Year

The method used in the preceding sections can be used to calculate the past return, expected return, or yield to maturity for a security that makes a payment more often than once each year. The calculated value of i will be expressed on the basis of a period that is shorter than one year. However, normally, we express returns and yields in terms of annual rates, which can be done in this case by multiplying the result for i by the number of periods each year.

For example, suppose that you buy a debt security that pays you $1,000 in six months, for which you pay $975 today, and you would like to know the yield to maturity. According to the formula for one payment that we derived earlier, the yield to maturity is

$$i = \frac{F}{P} - 1 = \frac{\$1,000}{\$975} - 1 = 1.0256 - 1 = 0.0256 = 2.56 \text{ percent}$$

To express this as an annual yield, multiply the yield for six months by 2 (because there are two six-month periods in a year):

$$\text{Yield to maturity at annual rate} = 0.0256 \times 2 = 0.0512 = 5.12 \text{ percent}$$

(For an analysis of the legal requirements for how banks must report interest rates on bank accounts when interest is paid more than once each year, see the Policy Insider box "Annual Percentage Yield.")

Policy →IN← sider   Annual Percentage Yield

To clarify how much interest you earn when you deposit your savings in a bank, the Truth-in-Savings Act requires the bank to tell you the annual percentage yield on your deposit, which is an interest rate that accounts for compounding. *Annual percentage yield* (APY) is the annual interest rate that would give you the same amount from investing for one year with annual compounding as you would earn with more frequent compounding at the stated annual interest rate. For example, if you invest $1,000 in a security that pays you an annual interest rate of 8 percent with monthly compounding, at the end of the year you will have

$$\$1,000 \times \left(1 + \frac{0.08}{12}\right)^{12} = \$1,083.00$$

because the monthly interest rate is 0.08/12, and there are 12 months for which your investment is compounded. What annual interest rate would give you the same amount at the end of the year? From Equation (9),

$$i = \frac{F}{P} - 1 = \frac{\$1,083.00}{\$1,000} - 1 = 0.083 = 8.3 \text{ percent}$$

Thus, the APY is 8.3 percent, which is slightly higher (because of the monthly compounding) than the stated annual interest rate of 8 percent.

As we saw in this example, the APY differs from the annual interest rate when compounding occurs more than once a year. It reflects compounding according to the formula

$$APY = \left(1 + \frac{i}{X}\right)^{X} - 1 \qquad (13)$$

where i is the stated annual interest rate, and compounding occurs x times per year. Raising the term $1 + (i/x)$ to the power x calculates the discount factor for one year.

Here is an example that will show how the APY might be useful to a saver. Imagine that you have $1,000 to deposit in a bank. Suppose that Bank A offers you a CD that promises you an interest rate of 5.7 percent with annual compounding if you keep your money deposited there for three years. (CDs are bank accounts in which the bank pays you a higher interest rate than you would get on a regular savings account. However, you must agree to leave your money invested for a certain length of time, and you pay a penalty if you withdraw your money before that time.) Bank B not only offers a lower interest rate (5.6 percent) on a similar CD but also offers monthly compounding. Suppose that you think that there is no chance that either bank will fail to make the payments on either CD, so the expected return equals the yield to maturity. Which bank offers a higher expected return?

When compounding is annual, the stated annual interest rate equals the APY, so Bank A is offering you a CD with an APY of 5.7 percent. For Bank B, the stated annual interest rate is 5.6 percent ($i = 0.056$), and interest is compounded monthly, so $x = 12$. Then the annual percentage yield is

$$APY = \left(1 + \frac{i}{X}\right)^X - 1 = \left(1 + \frac{0.056}{12}\right)^{12} - 1$$
$$= 1.0575 - 1 = 0.0575 = 5.75 \text{ Percent}$$

Because banks are required by law to use this method to calculate the APY, you can compare the APYs for the two banks to see that Bank B offers a slightly higher expected return because its APY is higher. In general, you will be able to compare the APY offered by one bank with that offered by another, and you can choose the investment with the highest APY.

Borrowers, however, are not as fortunate. Government regulations set forth in the truth-in-lending laws require banks to report the *annual percentage rate* (APR) so that borrowers can attempt to compare interest rates on different loans. The APR may be misleading for loans with upfront fees, however, because banks may choose to include or not include certain fees and because paying off a loan early leads to a higher APR than the stated one. And for open-end loans, such as credit-card loans and home equity lines of credit, the APR does not incorporate compounding. So reporting is very misleading.

RECAP

1 We can use the present-value formula to look at a security's past return, expected return, or yield to maturity.

2 Calculation of past return, expected return, and yield to maturity requires solving the present-value formula for the term i.

How to negotiate a car lease When car dealers calculate lease payments on a new car, they usually use an approximation of the present-value formula. With a few clicks of calculator buttons, they can tell you what your lease payment will be. You, as a well-informed student of money and banking, understand the present-value formula much better than your car dealer does. But could you, on the spot (sitting in a dealer's showroom), calculate the monthly payment on a deal to lease a car? If you can, you have the power to negotiate a great deal for yourself. If you do not know how to do it, you may be throwing money away. Here we show you how car dealers calculate the payments and how close that calculation is to the present-value formula.

The information the car dealer uses to calculate the monthly lease amount includes the cost of the car; the "residual value," which is the estimated value of the car when the lease expires (and is equal to the buyout option if you buy the car when the lease expires); the number of months in the lease; and the interest rate. Then the dealer follows these steps:

1. Calculate the monthly depreciation = (cost of car − residual value) ÷ number of months in lease.
2. Calculate the monthly finance charge = (cost of car + residual value) × (interest rate ÷ 24).
3. Add the monthly depreciation to the monthly finance charge, and then multiply that sum by (1 + tax rate on leases) because most state governments tax automobile leases.

Let's see how this works in practice. Imagine that a car dealer is going to lease you a Ford Mustang for three years, and you have negotiated a price of $23,000 for the car (it is always best, in negotiations, to bargain on the price of the car first and then to decide on leasing once you have done that). Suppose that the residual value after three years is $13,400, the annual interest rate is 8 percent, and the sales tax rate is 9 percent on leases. Then the steps are

1. Monthly depreciation = ($23,000 − $13,400) ÷ 36 = $266.
2. Monthly finance charge = ($23,000 + $13,400) × (0.08/24) = $121.
3. Total payment (with 9 percent sales tax) = ($266 + $121) × 1.09 = $423.

How does this dealer's approximation work, and how does it relate to the present-value formula? Think about it this way. You are borrowing the cost of the car for three years and then giving back the car at the end of the third year for its residual value. Thus, you are taking out a fixed-payment loan that amortizes over 36 months an amount equal to the difference between the cost of the car and the present value of the residual. In the example, that amount is

$$\$23{,}000 - \frac{\$13{,}400}{(1 + 0.08/12)^{36}} = \$12{,}451$$

Using Equation (8), this gives a monthly payment of

$$F = P \times \frac{i}{1 - [1/(1 + i)]^N} = \$12{,}451 \times \frac{0.08/12}{1 - \{1/[1 + (0.08/12)]^{36}\}} = \$390.17$$

After multiplying this amount by 1.09 to account for the sales tax, we have a monthly payment of $425. Therefore, in this example, the car dealer's approximation ($423) is very close to the result given by the present-value formula ($425).

Why is the dealer's approximation so close to the result from the present-value formula? The first part of the formula, the monthly depreciation charge, seems sensible—you must pay for the amount that the car depreciates over the lease period. The second part, though, the monthly

finance charge, might seem odd. Why is the cost of the car added to the residual value and then multiplied by the annual interest rate divided by 24? Let's answer this question intuitively. First, what is the monthly interest rate for a given annual interest rate? It is the annual interest rate divided by 12. (Note that the equation says 24, so we still need to explain why we are off by a factor of 2.) Second, think about how much you are borrowing over the course of the lease period. At the start of the lease period, you are borrowing an amount equal to the cost of the car, so you should pay interest on that full amount. However, over the lease period, you pay for the car's depreciation, so by the end of the lease period, you should be paying interest just on the residual value. Thus, the principal amount you are borrowing is declining from an amount equal to the cost of the car to an amount equal to the residual value. The average amount you are borrowing over the lease period thus is equal to the average of the cost of the car and the residual value, which can be calculated as

(Cost of car + residual value) ÷ 2

To get the monthly finance charge, multiply the average principal amount times the monthly interest rate:

[(Cost of car + residual value) ÷ 2] × (annual interest rate ÷ 12)
= (cost of car + residual value) × (annual interest rate ÷ 24)

This is the formula in step 2 above.

What lessons have we learned from this exercise? First, you can see that, in the real world, people make approximations to formulas such as the present-value formula to simplify calculations. Yet the idea of present value is still the economic notion that underlies the calculation. Thus, you need not get too hung up on precise formulas; it is far better to have an intuitive understanding of how things work. Second, you have gained some practical knowledge that you can use in the future. Now that you understand what the car dealer is doing, you can feel comfortable in negotiations. You are in the driver's seat!

RECAP

1 Car dealers use an approximation to the present-value formula in determining lease payments.

2 To negotiate an automobile lease properly, you need to have the following information for a proposed deal: the cost of the car, the residual value of the car at the end of the lease, the length of the lease, and the interest rate.

Review Questions and Problems

Review Questions

1 Explain the basis for the present-value formula (Equation (4)). Tell why each term looks the way it does. If the rate of discount is zero, how does the formula simplify?

2 What is the relationship between present value and the rate of discount for a given future value?

3 Would you believe a banker who told you that if you invested $1,000 in her bank, you would be a millionaire someday? How can this happen?

4 What is the relationship between present value, future value, and the interest rate in the case of a perpetuity?

5 What does it mean to amortize a loan?

6 Is it better (financially) to buy or lease a car?

7 Why are security prices and interest rates inversely related?

8 How should you determine the appropriate rate of discount to use in the present-value formula?

9 Suppose that I buy a 10-year bond today for $1,000 and that the interest rate when the bond is issued is 5 percent. The day after I buy the bond, the market interest rate on 10-year bonds rises to 7 percent. If I keep the bond for the full 10 years until it matures, what is the bond's average annual return?

10 What information do you need to be able to negotiate an automobile lease? Do you need any other equipment, such as a calculator, financial tables, or anything else?

Numerical Exercises

11 If the rate of discount is 20 percent,
  a Would you rather receive $100 today or $120 in one year?
  b Would you rather receive $205 today or $240 in one year?
  c Would you rather receive $500 in one year or $610 in two years?

12 Suppose that you are considering the purchase of a security that has the following timeline of payments:

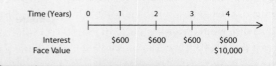

Time (Years)	0	1	2	3	4
Interest		$600	$600	$600	$600
Face Value					$10,000

  a How much would you be willing to pay for this security if the market interest rate is 6 percent?
  b Suppose that you have just purchased the security, and suddenly the market interest rate falls to 5 percent. What is the security worth?
  c Suppose that one year has elapsed, you have received the first payment of $600, and the market interest rate is still 5 percent. How much would another investor be willing to pay for your security?
  d Suppose that two years have elapsed since you purchased the security, and you have received the first two payments of $600 each. Now suppose that the market interest rate suddenly jumps to 10 percent. How much would another investor be willing to pay for your security?

13 You have just won a $25 million lottery prize, which pays you $1 million (tax-free) every year for the next 25 years. Have you really won $25 million? What have you won if the rate of discount is 5 percent? (*Note:* You will get your first $1 million payment today and your last $1 million payment 24 years from now.)

14 Find the yield to maturity of the following securities:
  a A security paying $1,000 in one year, for which you pay $926 today.
  b A security paying $80 one year from now and $1,080 two years from now, for which you pay $1,050 today.
  c A security paying $50 every six months for the next five years (beginning six months from now), plus the return of the face value of $1,000 at the end of the five years, for which you pay $1,000 today.

(continued)

15 Your newest book, "50 Shades of Gray Recession Bars," is being considered by a publishing house, which offers you an advance of $100,000 today, plus $50,000 at the end of each of the next two years. Call this Plan A.

   a What is the present value of the payments from the publisher, given your rate of discount is 2 percent? Show your work. You may round to the nearest dollar.

     Your literary agent thinks you should make a counteroffer, in which you receive nothing today but receive $3 at the end of each of the next two years for each book you sell during the year. Call this Plan B.

   b If you think you will sell 35,000 books a year during each of the next two years, what is the present value of your earnings under Plan B? Show your work. You may round to the nearest dollar.

   c If your publisher thinks you will sell 30,000 books a year during each of the next two years, what is the present value of your earnings under Plan B? Show your work. You may round to the nearest dollar.

   d Which plan is best for you, based on your expected sales? Which plan is best for your publisher, based on its expected sales? Which plan will you and your publisher agree to, or will you have to negotiate further? Explain.

16 Consider a coupon bond that pays $200 every year and repays its principal amount of $10,000 at the end of 10 years. If the rate of discount is 2 percent, what is the present value of the bond?

Analytical Problems

17 Which would you rather be holding if there is a decline in interest rates: a debt security that matures in 10 years or one that matures in three months? Why? (*Note:* Assume that the interest rates on both securities change by the same amount; for example, suppose that both fall by 2 percentage points.)

18 Why is the monthly payment on a car lease lower than the monthly payment on a car loan for the same car and the same time to maturity?

Appendix 4.A

Deriving the Present-Value Formula for a Perpetuity

To derive the present-value formula for a perpetuity, we begin by considering the fact that it consists of an infinite sum of related terms. First, consider the finite sum of N terms:

$$a + a^2 + a^3 + \cdots + a^N$$

If we multiply that sum by $(1 - a)$, we get

$$(1 - a) \times (a + a^2 + a^3 + \cdots + a^N) = a + a^2 + a^3 + \cdots$$
$$+ a^N - a^2 - a^3 - a^4 - \cdots$$
$$- a^N - a^{N+1} = a - a^{N+1}$$

Now, as we make N get larger and larger, the term a^{N+1} will get smaller and smaller and closer to zero if a is positive and less than one because a number less than one raised to higher powers gets closer and closer to zero. Thus, if we think about the infinite sum

$$a + a^2 + a^3 + \cdots$$

then we have shown that

$$(1 - a) \times (a + a^2 + a^3 + \cdots) = a$$

as long as $0 < a < 1$. Now divide both sides of this expression by $1 - a$ to get

$$a + a^2 + a^3 + \cdots = \frac{a}{1 - a}$$

In the case of the present value of $100 per year received indefinitely with a rate of discount of 5 percent, the present value is

$$P = \frac{\$100}{1.05^1} + \frac{\$100}{1.05^2} + \frac{\$100}{1.05^3} + \cdots$$
$$= \$100 \times \left(\frac{1}{1.05^1} + \frac{1}{1.05^2} + \frac{1}{1.05^3} + \cdots \right)$$

The term in parentheses looks like the expression derived earlier, where $a = 1/1.05 = 1/(1 + i)$. Thus, we know that the term in parentheses equals

$$\frac{a}{1 - a} = \frac{1/(1 + i)}{1 - [1/(1 + i)]}$$

$$= \frac{1}{(1 + i) \times \{1 - [1/(1 + i)]\}}$$

$$= \frac{1}{1 + i - 1} = \frac{1}{i}$$

This is part of the general formula for the present value of a perpetuity, which we use in Equation (5). In our example, the present value is

$$P = \frac{\$100}{1.05^1} + \frac{\$100}{1.05^2} + \frac{\$100}{1.05^3} + \cdots$$

$$= \$100 \times \left(\frac{1}{1.05^1} + \frac{1}{1.05^2} + \frac{1}{1.05^3} + \cdots \right)$$

$$= \$100 \times \frac{1}{0.05} = \$100 \times 20 = \$2,000$$

Appendix 4.B

Deriving the Present-Value Formula for a Fixed-Payment Security

In developing the formula for a perpetuity, we used a formula that will allow us to calculate the present value of a fixed-payment security in one step. In Appendix 4.A we established the equation

$$(1 - a) \times (a + a^2 + a^3 + \cdots + a^N) = a - a^{N+1}$$

If we divide both sides of the equation by $1 - a$, we get

$$a + a^2 + a^3 + \cdots + a^N = \frac{a - a^{N+1}}{1 - a} = \frac{a}{1 - a} - \frac{a^{N+1}}{1 - a}$$

Because $a = 1/(1 + i)$,

$$1 - a = 1 - \frac{1}{1 + i} = \frac{1 + i}{1 + i} - \frac{1}{1 + i} = \frac{i}{1 + i}$$

In Appendix 4.A we showed that

$$\frac{a}{1 - a} = \frac{1}{i}$$

Thus,

$$a + a^2 + a^3 + \cdots + a^N = \frac{a}{1 - a} - \frac{a^{N+1}}{1 - a}$$

$$= \frac{1}{i} - \frac{[1/(1 + i)]^{N+1}}{i/(1 + i)}$$

$$= \frac{1 - [1/(1 + i)]^N}{i}$$

This is the main term in Equation (6).

i love images/Jupiter images

The **STRUCTURE** of **INTEREST RATES**

Economists are constantly trying to predict recessions. In a recession, the economy stops growing, people lose jobs, and stock prices fall. Among the most noticeable indicators that a recession may occur is the yield curve. The yield curve is a diagram of the interest rates on debt securities with different times to maturity. When the yield curve is inverted, indicating that interest rates on long-term bonds are lower than interest rates on short-term bonds, conditions are ripe for recession.

In this chapter we will learn about the structure of interest rates—why the interest rates on various debt securities differ from each other and what those differences mean. We will compare interest rates on short-term bonds with those on long-term bonds to see how the relationship between such interest rates reflects economic events. We will study why investors care about the time to maturity of bonds and evaluate the implications of differing times to maturity on interest rates. Finally, we will focus on the policy question of whether or not we can forecast recessions by examining interest rates, especially the yield curve.

5-1 What Explains Differences in Interest Rates?

On a given day, a borrower might find that the interest rate on a loan for a new car is 7 percent, whereas the interest rate on a business loan is 11 percent, and the interest rate on a credit card is 14 percent. Why are the interest rates so different? Supply and demand affect the prices of debt securities and thus interest rates, as discussed in Chapter 2. Digging deeper, we know that investors evaluate securities based on certain characteristics, such as expected return, risk, maturity, liquidity, and taxation, so all those factors affect the demand for securities. Borrowers also consider the same characteristics in the debt securities they sell, which thus affect how many securities they supply. As a result, when expected return, risk, maturity, liquidity, or taxation change, so do supply and demand; in addition, changes in the tastes or preferences of investors and borrowers affect supply and demand and hence security prices. Let's look at these shifts in supply and demand, beginning with a survey of the types of debt securities.

5-1a The Many Different Types of Debt Securities

If you flip through the financial pages of a newspaper, you will see listings for hundreds of different debt securities, some of which are shown in Table 5.1. The debt securities listed differ in many ways, and the yield to maturity, or interest rate, on each is different, as the table shows. These differences in interest rates stem from the characteristics of those securities and how those characteristics influence demand and supply.

In the table, you can see a variety of debt securities divided into three main categories: personal saving via indirect finance, personal borrowing via indirect finance, and saving (by people, business firms, governments, and foreigners) via direct finance. The yield to maturity shown for each security reflects the national average.

Personal saving via indirect finance. The category of personal saving via indirect finance includes certificates of deposit (CDs) of differing maturities and money-market deposit accounts. CDs are securities in which the saver buys the security for a given time to maturity, earning interest at the specified rate. The saver is allowed to withdraw the invested funds before the security matures, but a substantial financial penalty comes with doing so. An alternative investment is a money-market deposit account at a bank, which has no specified maturity, so funds can be withdrawn at any time. These accounts allow the investor to write checks against the account balance, but investors must deposit some minimum amount when the account is opened (often $1,000 to $2,000) and are limited to three withdrawals each month. Banks and other financial intermediaries offer both CDs and money-market deposit accounts to their customers.

Personal borrowing. People borrow in a variety of different ways. Among the debt securities available to them are various types of home loans, automobile loans, and credit-card loans. Three different types of home loans are listed in Table 5.1. The most common type is a fixed-rate mortgage with 30 years to maturity. The term *fixed-rate* means that the interest rate remains the same over the 30-year duration of the mortgage. An alternative type of mortgage is an adjustable-rate mortgage. The mortgage with a one-year adjustable rate is a home loan that is paid off over 30 years but for which the interest rate and the payment amount are adjusted each year. Usually the interest rate is tied to some average measure of market interest rates, such as the average yield to maturity on one-year Treasury securities (compiled by the Federal Reserve), although other interest rates also can be used as the basis for the adjustment. As an example, an adjustable mortgage rate might be set on March 1 each year by a formula such as

New interest rate for the year = average interest rate on one-year Treasury securities over the preceding month plus 2.75 percent

When the interest rate is set for the year, a new monthly payment is determined using the present-value formula; thus, a homeowner's monthly mortgage payment changes once each year. Usually, adjustable-rate mortgages have a maximum interest rate to protect homeowners from paying a very high interest rate. Generally, adjustable-rate mortgages are popular when market interest rates are temporarily high and are expected to decline soon, so homeowners can get a lower rate in subsequent years. Another type of home loan is a home equity loan. In this type of arrangement, a family that owns its home can borrow money using the home as collateral.

TABLE 5.1 Examples of Different Debt Securities and Their Yields to Maturity

Category	Type of Security	Yield to Maturity (percent)
Personal saving (indirect finance)	Certificate of deposit (CD) with 5 years to maturity	0.52
	CD with 6 months to maturity	0.35
	CD with 3 months to maturity	0.21
	Money-market deposit account at bank	0.47
Personal borrowing (indirect finance)	Mortgage, 30 years to maturity, fixed rate	3.43
	Mortgage, 1-year adjustable rate	2.51
	Home equity loan	5.12
	Auto loan	2.29
	Credit card	15.27
Saving (direct finance)	U.S. Treasury security with 3 months to maturity	0.05
	U.S. Treasury security with 1 year to maturity	0.11
	U.S. Treasury security with 5 years to maturity	0.68
	U.S. Treasury security with 10 years to maturity	1.67
	U.S. Treasury security with 29 years to maturity	2.89
	U.S. Treasury security with 30 years to maturity	2.88
	Government agency security with 1 year to maturity	0.20
	Government agency security with 20 years to maturity	2.75
	Corporate bond rated Aaa	1.81
	Corporate bond rated Baa	3.08
	Mortgage-backed security with 30 years to maturity	2.40
	Local government bond	1.99
	Foreign government bond with 10 years to maturity	4.88
	Commercial paper	0.23

Note: Each yield to maturity is the national average for that type of debt security. Securities are divided into those used by people for saving via indirect finance through banks, those used by people for borrowing via indirect finance through banks, and those used by many different investors for saving via direct finance. If there is no maturity date, the current stated interest rate is shown rather than the yield to maturity. These interest rates were reported in April 2013.

People also borrow to purchase cars, and they borrow using credit cards. When someone borrows to buy a car, the car is collateral for the loan. If the person fails to make the payments on time, the financial intermediary that lent the funds can repossess the car and sell it in the market to get its money back. Credit cards, on the other hand, involve no collateral. If a borrower cannot repay the credit-card lender, the lender cannot seize any of the borrower's assets. Instead, the lender must go to court to get the court to force the borrower to repay the loan, which is a more expensive process than repossessing collateral.

Saving via direct finance. Savers, including individuals, business firms, governments, and foreigners, can invest using direct finance, buying debt securities issued by many different borrowers. The U.S. government is the world's largest borrower; to finance its spending, it sells securities with many different times to maturity, some of which are shown in Table 5.1. Some other government-related companies also sell debt securities, which are called *government agency securities*. Corporations sell debt securities of different types, and those with better financial ratings (such as Aaa, which indicates a low risk of default) have different yields to maturity than those with lower financial ratings (such as Baa). Some corporate securities are backed with particular types of assets that serve as collateral, such as securities backed by mortgages (called *mortgage-backed securities*). In those securities, the financial intermediaries that own the assets (in this case, mortgage loans) sell them off to another company (such as the Federal National Mortgage Association, a company that makes home ownership more affordable) that sells securities to investors. The interest paid on those securities comes from the mortgage payments. The process of turning assets such as mortgages into securities sold to investors is called **securitization.**

Many local governments also borrow substantial amounts in financial markets, usually for capital-improvement projects. Foreign governments sometimes borrow in the United States, although only large, developed countries such as Japan and Germany are able to sell debt securities using direct finance; smaller countries such as Argentina often borrow via indirect finance from U.S. financial intermediaries. Finally, to raise short-term funds, large corporations sell debt securities called *commercial paper,* which usually matures in one to two months. Commercial paper is often traded in the secondary market and used by investors as a liquid security for temporary cash flows of several hundred thousand to several million dollars.

> **securitization** the process by which financial intermediaries that own assets (such as mortgage loans) sell them off to another company, which in turn sells bonds to investors; the interest payments on those bonds are paid from the interest payments on the original assets (such as mortgage payments)

5-1b Demand and Supply in the Secondary Market Affect Interest Rates

The debt securities listed in Table 5.1 differ in terms of yield to maturity. What explains those differences? The answer is differences in risk, liquidity, taxation, and time to maturity, which are the major characteristics of securities that investors care about.

Risk. One source of difference in yields to maturity on debt securities is risk. Some debt securities are more risky than others. For an investor to choose a riskier security instead

of one that is less risky, there must be the promise of some benefit. Most often that benefit is a higher expected return on the riskier security, which means that it must have a higher yield to maturity. For example, note that the interest rate on credit cards (15.27 percent) is much higher than the interest rate on automobile loans (2.29 percent) or on fixed-rate mortgages (3.43 percent). Both automobile loans and mortgage loans have relatively little risk to the financial intermediary that offers the loan because the house or the car serves as collateral for the loan, whereas a credit card has no collateral. This difference is reflected in the interest rates. In a similar way, risk affects the yields to maturity on bonds. Note that a U.S. Treasury security with one year to maturity has a yield to maturity of 0.11 percent, whereas a government agency security with one year to maturity has a yield to maturity that is slightly higher at 0.20 percent. The difference reflects a slightly higher default risk for the government agency. In addition, note the large differences between corporate bonds with different levels of risk. A corporate bond with an Aaa rating is fairly safe from default risk and has a yield to maturity of 1.81 percent. A corporate bond with a Baa rating has a somewhat higher risk of default and thus has a higher yield to maturity of 3.08 percent.

Liquidity. Another source of difference in yields is liquidity. Investors would rather own securities that are more liquid because the costs of trading them are lower than for less liquid securities. As a result, the yield to maturity of less liquid securities must be higher to induce investors to hold them instead of more liquid securities.

In the market for Treasury securities of a given time to maturity, the security that was issued most recently in the primary market—called the **on-the-run security**—is used by many investors for buying and selling either to speculate or to combine with other securities to reduce the risk in their portfolios. As a result, its market is very liquid. The yield to maturity of an on-the-run security is usually a bit lower than the yield to maturity of an **off-the-run security,** which is a security that is not the most recently issued. For example, an on-the-run Treasury security with 30 years to maturity has a yield to maturity of 2.88 percent, whereas an off-the-run

on-the-run security the U.S. Treasury security (for a given time to maturity) that was issued most recently in the primary market

off-the-run security a U.S. Treasury security that is not the most recently issued

basis point one-hundredth of a percentage point

Treasury security with 29 years to maturity has a yield to maturity of 2.89 percent, a difference of 0.01 percentage point. The difference equals 1 basis point (a **basis point** is one-hundredth of a percentage point).

Taxation. How taxes affect yields also can be seen in Table 5.1. Note that the yield to maturity on a local government bond (issued by a city or state government) is low—only 1.99 percent—primarily because interest earned on local government bonds is exempt from federal income taxes. However, the bonds pose some risk of default because a city or a state may go bankrupt. Most city and state governments that issue bonds have credit ratings somewhere between corporate credit ratings Aaa and Baa. To see the impact of taxability, we can compare the yield to maturity of corporate bonds rated Aaa and Baa (1.81 and 3.08 percent) with that on local government bonds (1.99 percent). Because investors must pay taxes on interest earned on corporate bonds but not on local government bonds, they are willing to accept the lower interest rate on the local government bonds because of the tax savings, and the difference in yields to maturity reflects the tax rate faced by investors.

Time to maturity. The other difference among the debt securities in Table 5.1 is time to maturity. Note that the time to maturity affects the interest rate substantially because a CD with five years to maturity pays 0.52 percent, whereas one with six months to maturity pays 0.35 percent and one with only three months to maturity pays just 0.21 percent. Similarly, the yields to maturity on Treasury securities vary from 0.05 percent for one with just three months to maturity up to 2.89 percent for one with 29 years to maturity. Moreover, a government agency security with 20 years to maturity has a much higher yield (2.75 percent) than one with one year to maturity (0.20 percent). We will examine the relationship between yield to maturity and time to maturity in greater detail in the section entitled "The Term Structure of Interest Rates."

What changes the yields on different debt securities? The differences between yields to maturity on different debt securities can change over time. For example, a company might do very well when economic times are good, but the risk that the company will default on its debt securities increases substantially when the economy goes into a recession. As you might imagine, if the economy is doing well when such a company issues debt securities that mature in a few years, investors do not worry too much about the risk of default. However, if the odds of a recession occurring are high, then the risk of default will cause investors to reduce their demand, resulting in a fall in the price and thus a higher interest rate on such securities. The same types of effects can arise when investors' perceptions of risk change, even if there is no actual change in a borrower's financial condition.

Consider, for example, what happened to interest rates in the United States in 2010. The European Central Bank decided to bail out the government of Greece, to keep it from defaulting on its debt. Investors began to worry whether that default would lead the governments of other countries to default on their debt as well. Existing investors sold off their securities in secondary markets, and investors who had been considering such investments chose not to invest. The sudden increase in supply and decrease in demand caused the prices of these securities to decline, as shown in Figure 5.1. The decline in the prices of the securities caused an increase in their yields to maturity because yields to maturity and bond prices are inversely related. Thus,

a change in investors' perceptions (in this case, an increase in perceived risk to a security) can cause the price of a security to decline and its yield to maturity to rise.

In a similar way, differences in maturity and taxability or changes in investors' preferences or tastes for different securities can affect the demand for securities and thus their price.

5-1c Supply in the Primary Market Affects Interest Rates

When borrowers issue debt securities, their decisions are shaped by the same characteristics of securities as those that affect investors who buy the securities. Borrowers would like to borrow as cheaply as possible, so they would like the expected return (and thus the interest rate) to be low, whereas investors would like it to be high. Borrowers are concerned with default risk, just as investors are. They worry that they will not be able

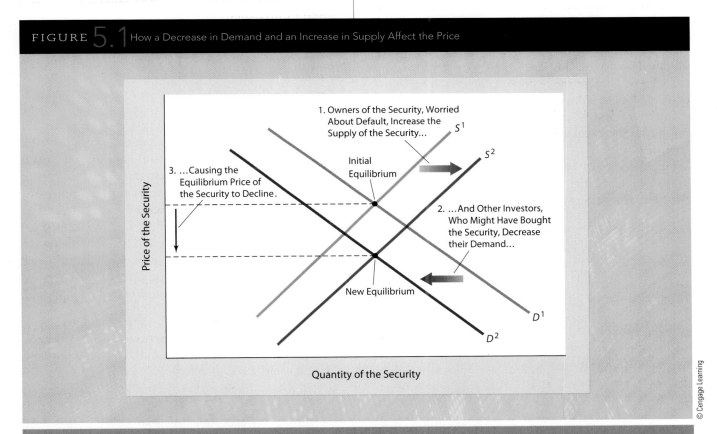

FIGURE 5.1 How a Decrease in Demand and an Increase in Supply Affect the Price

1. Owners of the Security, Worried About Default, Increase the Supply of the Security... S^1

S^2

Initial Equilibrium

3. ...Causing the Equilibrium Price of the Security to Decline.

Price of the Security

2. ...And Other Investors, Who Might Have Bought the Security, Decrease their Demand...

New Equilibrium

D^1

D^2

Quantity of the Security

© Cengage Learning

When investors worry about an increased risk that borrowers will default, as happened when the European Central Bank bailed out the Greek government in 2010, the supply of securities in the secondary market increases [the supply curve shifts right ($S^1 \rightarrow S^2$)] and the demand decreases [the demand curve shifts left ($D^1 \rightarrow D^2$)]. As a result, the equilibrium price of the security declines.

to repay interest when due and that they will default on the securities, which would then cause problems for them if they tried to borrow in the future. They are also concerned about maturity because they need to manage their incoming and outgoing flows of cash. Thus, they would like to match the timing of their borrowing with their need for cash to pay employees and to buy capital equipment for new projects, for example.

To see how supply matters, consider what happened in October 2001, when the U.S. Treasury Department, which manages the U.S. federal government's finances, announced that it would stop selling U.S. Treasury securities with 30 years to maturity (a decision that was reversed in 2006). The Treasury Department argued that investors mostly bought and sold Treasury securities with 10 years to maturity, so investors no longer needed the 30-year security. In addition, the prospect of future government budget surpluses meant less need for long-term borrowing by the government. The abrupt elimination of the supply of new 30-year Treasury securities in the primary market led to a big jump in the price of the securities in the secondary market on the day of the announcement, as shown in Figure 5.2. In the figure, the announcement of a cutoff of future supply in the primary market causes current owners of the security to reduce their supply in the secondary market and other investors to increase their demand. The result is a sharp rise in the price of the securities and thus a decline in the yield to maturity.

Data confirm the theory, as you can see in Figure 5.3. The price of 30-year Treasury bonds in the secondary market rose by over $5 for every $100 in face value on the day of the Treasury announcement. The yield to maturity fell from 5.22 to 4.88 percent on that day. (Changes in the yields on 2-year and 10-year securities are shown in the graph as well, so you can see that the yield on the 30-year security changed much more than the yield on other securities.) Thus, changes in supply in the primary market for a security can have significant effects on the prices of securities and yields to maturity in the secondary market.

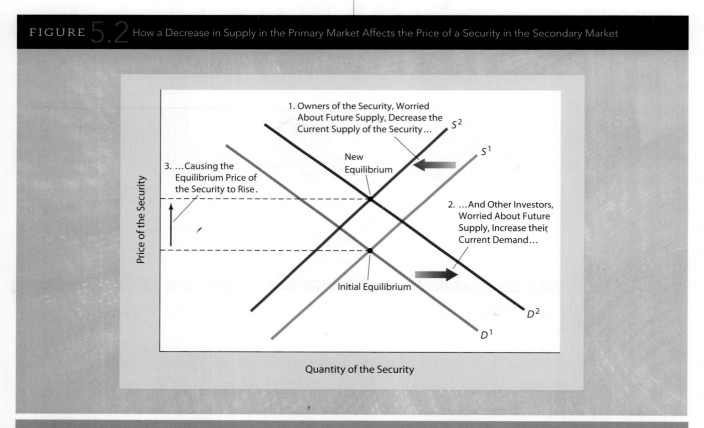

FIGURE 5.2 How a Decrease in Supply in the Primary Market Affects the Price of a Security in the Secondary Market

When the supplier of a security reduces the supply in the primary market, as in October 2001 when the U.S. government announced that it would no longer sell 30-year Treasury bonds, investors worry that they will not be able to obtain long-term bonds in the future. So they reduce their current supply [the supply curve shifts left ($S^1 \rightarrow S^2$)] and increase their current demand [the demand curve shifts right ($D^1 \rightarrow D^2$)] in the secondary market. The result is a rise in the equilibrium price of the security.

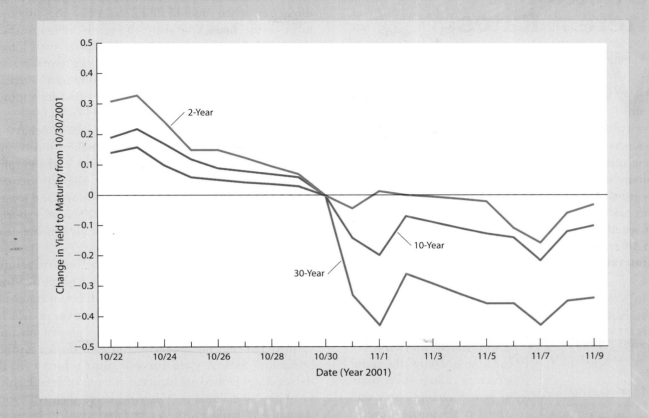

On October 31, 2001, the U.S. Treasury surprised investors by announcing that it would no longer sell securities with 30 years to maturity. The graph plots the yields to maturity on 2-year, 10-year, and 30-year Treasury securities from October 22 to November 9, 2001, minus the yield of each security on October 30, just before the announcement. Thus, the graph indicates changes in the yield of each security around the time of the announcement. The yields were all falling gradually in the days prior to the announcement. On the day of the announcement, the yields all declined sharply, but the biggest impact was on the 30-year securities, whose yield fell about 0.3 percentage point.

RECAP

1 Hundreds of debt securities are in existence, serving the needs of many different borrowers and lenders.

2 Demand explains many of the differences in yields on debt securities. Investors care about expected return, risk, liquidity, time to maturity, and taxability; differences in securities along these lines lead to differences in yields to maturity.

3 Supply explains some of the differences in the yields to maturity on different securities. Changes in the supply of Treasury securities illustrate how much the supply of securities in the primary market can matter in the secondary market.

5-2 The Term Structure of Interest Rates

We have now established that interest rates differ for securities with differing characteristics, including expected return, risk, time to maturity, liquidity, and taxability. Economists find the differences in interest rates because of differing times to maturity particularly insightful in analyzing the economy and in predicting how rapidly the economy will grow. Therefore, the remainder of this chapter will focus on issues related to the time to maturity of debt securities. The relationship between interest rates with differing times to maturity is the **term structure of interest rates.**

How can we analyze the term structure of interest rates? First, we can examine data on interest rates with different times to maturity to see how the term structure changes over time or how it changes over the course of the business cycle. Second, we can use our theory of what investors want from Chapter 2 and our theory of present value from Chapter 4 to see if we can explain the data on the term structure.

term structure of interest rates the relationship between interest rates with differing times to maturity

yield curve a plot of interest rates for a given date for debt securities with different times to maturity in which the yield to maturity is shown on the vertical axis and the time to maturity is shown on the horizontal axis

5-2a Data on the Term Structure of Interest Rates

The most direct way to learn about the term structure of interest rates is to look at data on interest rates for securities with different times to maturity. Doing so reveals some interesting patterns, as we can see in Figure 5.4. In the figure, you can see the fluctuations in market interest rates that have occurred over time for both short-term interest rates (represented here with the interest rate on three-month Treasury securities) and long-term interest rates (represented by the interest rate on 10-year Treasury securities). (Both the interest rates plotted are really the yield to maturity on securities in the secondary market; whenever we refer to the *interest rate* in discussing the *term structure*, we mean the *yield to maturity*.) Short- and long-term interest rates generally move in the same direction; when one declines, so does the other—most of the time. You also can see in the figure that short-term interest rates are usually lower than long-term interest rates. The volatility of short-term interest rates, though, is greater than that of long-term interest rates; the short-term interest rate rises and falls more sharply over time.

Prominent in Figure 5.4 is the abnormal behavior of the two interest rates around periods of recession, which are indicated by vertical blue bars in the graph. During recessions, and sometimes slightly before recessions begin, the interest rates on short- and long-term debt securities become closer. Then the short-term interest rate declines dramatically during the recession.

A different way to learn about the term structure of interest rates is to plot the data for a given day for interest rates on debt securities with different times to maturity. Doing so results in a **yield curve,** in which the interest rate (yield to maturity) is shown on the vertical axis and the time to maturity is shown on the horizontal axis. A yield curve is most informative if the securities plotted are identical in terms of default risk, taxability, and liquidity. The yield curve then tells you what the difference in interest rates is solely because of time to maturity. Most plots of the yield curve are based on Treasury securities because they are the only debt securities that are nearly identical in default risk, taxability, and liquidity.

Figure 5.5 illustrates the yield curve (on U.S. Treasury securities) for February 15, 1997. Notice that it slopes upward, meaning that debt securities with longer times to maturity have higher yields to maturity. An upward-sloping yield curve is the most common, for reasons that we will soon discuss.

Figure 5.6 shows the shapes of the same yield curve on different dates. Note that the yield curve sometimes slopes upward and other times downward; sometimes it is steep, and other times it is flat. The overall level of interest rates also changes over time (compare 1981, with interest rates of 13 to 15 percent, to 2013, with interest rates of 0.10 to 3.18 percent), but we will explain those differences in Chapter 6; in this chapter we will focus on the slope of the yield curve.

Our quick look at the data gives us a number of facts to explain. Can we develop a theory of the behavior of short- and long-term interest rates, especially their usual upward slope and their behavior around

FIGURE 5.4 Short- and Long-Term Interest Rates

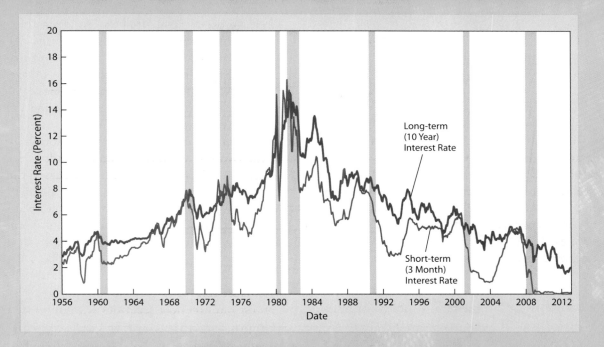

The graph plots the interest rates over time on a short-term (three-month) Treasury security and a long-term (10-year) Treasury security. Recessions are indicated by blue vertical bars.

FIGURE 5.5 Yield Curve for February 15, 1997

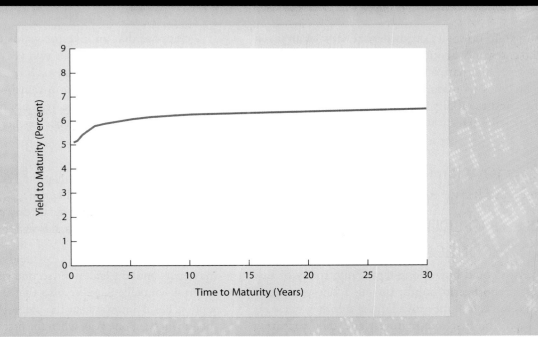

This yield curve (on U.S. Treasury securities) slopes upward because debt securities with longer times to maturity have higher yields to maturity. This is the most common shape of the yield curve.

FIGURE 5.6 Yield Curves, Mid-February, Every Four Years, 1977 to 2013

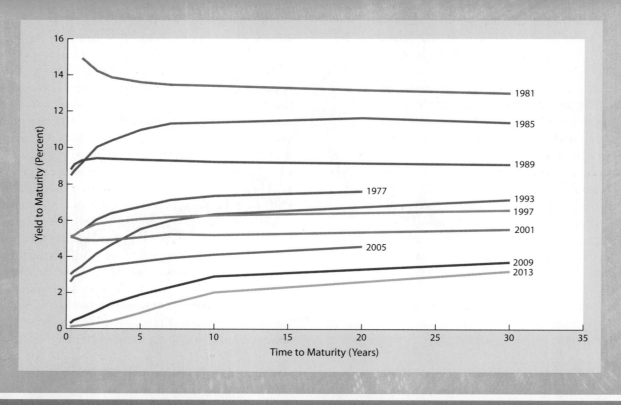

The graph shows the yield curve (for U.S. Treasury securities) in mid-February every four years, illustrating a wide variety of shapes. Note that the yield curve sometimes slopes upward and other times slopes downward; sometimes it is steep, and other times it is flat.

recessions? To do so, let's consider the view of an investor who cares only about expected return and is considering several alternative financial investments that have different times to maturity but the same default risk, liquidity, and taxability (so that we can exclude other differences in interest rates).

5-2b How Investors Choose Between Short- and Long-Term Securities

An investor could buy a long-term bond today or buy a series of short-term bonds, buying a one-year bond today, taking the money and buying another one-year bond when the first one matures, and then repeating this process. Which option is better? Let's try to answer this question by taking the simplest possible case, comparing a two-year bond to two one-year bonds.

Suppose that an investor wants to buy a bond and keep her funds invested for two years. She could either buy a two-year bond today or buy a one-year bond today, take the proceeds from that bond after one year, and then buy another one-year bond a year from now. The following timeline illustrates her options:

Time	Today	End of One Year	End of Two Years
Option			
A:	Buy Two-year Bond		Get Funds Back
B:	Buy One-year Bond	Buy One-year Bond	Get Funds Back

Suppose that the two-year bond does not make any payments until the end of the second year and compounds interest annually. Suppose also that if the investor takes option B, she knows what the interest rate on a one-year bond will be in one year, when the first one-year bond matures. The interest rates on the various bonds are as follows: The interest rate today on the two-year bond is i_2^0, the interest rate on a one-year bond today is i_1^0, and the interest rate on a one-year bond purchased in one year is i_1^1. In the notation for interest rates, the subscript means the time to maturity on the bond (one or two years), and the superscript refers to the time at which the investment is made—a 0 means "today" and a 1 means "one year from now." See the box "The Notation Used in Describing Interest Rates" for a quick reference guide to the notation.

In this example, an investor with principal amount P who compares the two options might reason in the following way: "With option A, I can buy the two-year bond today, and at the end of two years, I would have $P \times (1 + i_2^0)^2$. Alternatively, with option B, I can invest in two successive one-year bonds, and at the end of two years, I would have $P \times (1 + i_1^0) \times (1 + i_1^1)$. Because the principal amount P multiplies both interest rate terms, it can be taken out of the analysis, and I will buy the two-year bond if $(1 + i_2^0)^2$ is larger than $(1 + i_1^0) \times (1 + i_1^1)$. Otherwise, I will buy the one-year bond today and buy another one-year bond in a year."

Thus, the choice of which bond to buy today depends on the interest rates. It should be obvious that if i_2^0 is greater than both i_1^0 and i_1^1, the investor will buy the two-year bond. Or if i_1^0 and i_1^1 are both greater than i_2^0, the investor will buy the one-year bonds. However, if one of the one-year interest rates is greater than the two-year rate and the other is less, the investor must perform the calculation described in the preceding paragraph to determine which bond to buy today.

Table 5.2 lists some examples of two- and one-year bonds with different interest rates. The table also includes the calculations to determine which bond to buy today. In the first row, the interest rates on the two-year bond and the two one-year bonds are the same, so the investor can buy either bond today and will get the same return. In the second and third rows, you can see that it is better for the investor to earn 5 percent

interest in two years than to earn 4 percent one year and 5 percent another year. In the last two rows, the one-year bonds give the investor a higher return.

Investors often find it convenient to use an approximation of the return from their financial investments, calculating the average interest rate of each investment, rather than the calculations shown in Table 5.2. The approximation entails taking the average interest rate for the one-year bonds and comparing it with the interest rate on the two-year bond. The approximation works because compounding is small in most cases, but an investor would not want to use this approach in complicated situations with many periods, in which compounding is likely to be more important. Rather than comparing $(1 + i_2^0)^2$ with $(1 + i_1^0) \times (1 + i_1^1)$, it is easier to compare i_2^0 with $[(i_1^0 + i_1^1)/2]$. The results in Table 5.2 are identical in terms of whether an investor would choose the two-year bond or the one-year bonds no matter which method (exact or approximation) is used, as Table 5.3 shows.

In this analysis we made two assumptions that simplified matters: no transactions costs and no uncertainty about future interest rates. Let's examine the consequences of relaxing those assumptions.

First, we assumed that the investor did not bear any transactions costs. However, buying securities usually entails some fees paid to an investment firm to cover the costs of the transaction (which may be as high as 1 or 2 percent of the transaction's value). Transactions costs are likely to be higher if an investor buys two one-year bonds than if the investor buys one two-year bond. Thus, transactions costs might push people toward buying long-term bonds as opposed to short-term bonds. However, in recent years, improved efficiency in the financial sector (especially computerized trading) has made this factor much less important than ever before because transactions costs in financial markets have been declining significantly.

The Notation Used in Describing Interest Rates

When we write notation for interest rates in this chapter, we use the italic letter i to stand for interest rate, a subscript to denote the time to maturity on the security, and a superscript to denote the purchase date, which is the number of years in the future when the security will be purchased. The notation is

i_N^s — purchase date (number of years in the future)

— time to maturity (number of years)

For example, the notation i_3^1 refers to the interest rate on a security that is purchased one year from now and has a time to maturity of three years (which means that it matures four years from now).

TABLE 5.2 Comparing Interest Rates on One- and Two-Year Bonds

i_2^0	i_1^0	i_1^1	$(1 + i_2^0)^2$	$(1 + i_1^0) \times (1 + i_1^1)$	Buy Two-Year Bond or One-Year Bond Today?
0.05	0.05	0.05	1.1025	1.1025	Either
0.05	0.05	0.04	1.1025	1.0920	2-year bond
0.05	0.04	0.05	1.1025	1.0920	2-year bond
0.05	0.05	0.06	1.1025	1.1130	1-year bond
0.05	0.04	0.07	1.1025	1.1128	1-year bond

Note: The table shows the interest rates on a two-year bond purchased today (i_2^0), a one-year bond purchased today (i_1^0), a one-year bond purchased in one year (i_1^1), the amount the investor has after two years from buying the two-year bond ($(1 + i_2^0)^2$), the amount the investor has after two years from buying two successive one-year bonds [$(1 + i_1^0) \times (1 + i_1^1)$], and the decision the investor makes about whether to buy the two-year bond today or a one-year bond today.

TABLE 5.3 Comparing Interest Rates on One- and Two-Year Bonds: An Approximation

i_2^0	i_1^0	i_1^1	$\dfrac{i_1^0 + i_1^1}{2}$	Buy Two-Year Bond or One-Year Bond Today?	Does Approximation Give the Same Result as Exact Formula?
0.05	0.05	0.05	0.05	Either	Yes
0.05	0.05	0.04	0.045	2-year bond	Yes
0.05	0.04	0.05	0.045	2-year bond	Yes
0.05	0.05	0.06	0.055	1-year bond	Yes
0.05	0.04	0.07	0.055	1-year bond	Yes

Note: The table shows the interest rates on a two-year bond purchased today (i_2^0); a one-year bond purchased today (i_1^0); a one-year bond purchased in one year (i_1^1); the average interest rate on the two successive one-year bonds [$(i_1^0 + i_1^1)/2$]; the decision the investor makes about whether to buy the two-year bond today or a one-year bond today by comparing i_2^0 to $(i_1^0 + i_1^1)/2$; and whether the approximation yields the same result as the exact calculation used in Table 5.2.

The second assumption we made is that the investor knows what the interest rate on a one-year bond will be in the future (see the Data Bank box "How Accurate Are Expectations of Short-Term Interest Rates?" to investigate the validity of this assumption). However, it is impossible to be certain of future interest rates. Indeed, Wall Street investment firms devote substantial resources to predicting future interest rates. An investor who feels uncertain about the level of future interest rates will find making a choice between short- and long-term bonds difficult. Often such uncertainty will encourage an investor to buy the longer-term bond that matches the period she wants to keep the money invested.

Our discussion of the term structure here also assumes that investors in bonds do not have a "preferred habitat," that is, investors are willing to purchase bonds of different times to maturity. Some investors, however, may prefer or be required to purchase bonds of a particular time to maturity. If so, then our theory will still work as long as enough other investors do not have a preferred habitat and will try to profit when interest rates are not aligned according to our complete theory of the term structure.

5-2c What Determines the Term Structure of Interest Rates in Equilibrium?

Our objective in this analysis is to determine a relationship between short- and long-term interest rates. To simplify matters initially, we will assume that there are no transactions costs and that investors can predict short-term interest rates accurately. In such circumstances, the long-term interest rate is equal to the average of current and expected future short-term interest rates on securities that cover the same period as the long-term security. Because expectations of future short-term interest rates affect long-term interest rates, this theory is known as the **expectations theory of the term structure of interest rates.**

DataBank → How Accurate Are Expectations of Short-Term Interest Rates?

In discussing the yield curve, we assumed that people could forecast short-term interest rates fairly well. Is this a reasonable assumption? We can investigate that issue by comparing people's forecasts of interest rates with the actual rates.

To show how well forecasts track actual interest rates, we use the *Survey of Professional Forecasters*, which is a widely known and well respected quarterly survey of economists' expectations. The survey asks forecasters to predict interest rates on three-month Treasury securities for the current quarter, one quarter ahead, two quarters ahead, three quarters ahead, and four quarters ahead.

To see how accurate the forecasts are, we plot the one-quarter-ahead and four-quarter-ahead forecasts and compare them with the actual values in Figure 5.A. In this graph, you can see that the forecasts move fairly well with the actual movements in the interest rate. However, the forecasters made persistent errors in a few periods: the early 1980s, the mid-1980s, the early 1990s, the early 2000s, and the late 2000s. Thus it appears that large declines in interest rates are difficult to forecast.

FIGURE 5.A Forecasts of Short-Term Interest Rates

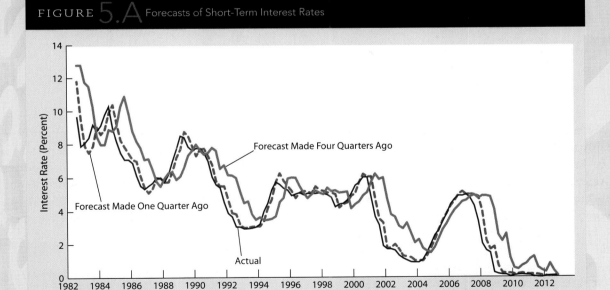

This graph plots forecasts of a short-term interest rate (on three-month Treasury securities) made one quarter earlier and made four quarters earlier compared with the actual values. The forecasts track the actual movements in the interest rate, but the forecasts made four quarters earlier are clearly worse than those made one quarter earlier. In a few periods, the forecasters made persistent errors: the early 1980s, the mid-1980s, the early 1990s, the early 2000s, and the late 2000s.

(continued)

A second way to examine forecast accuracy is by means of a scatter plot of the forecast compared with the actual value of the interest rate. Such a comparison appears in Figure 5.B for the forecast made one quarter earlier. The plot shows a 45-degree line, which makes the graph easy to interpret. If the forecasts are close to the actual values, the points will lie directly on the 45-degree line. Forecasts that are higher than actual will be above the line, whereas forecasts that are less than actual will be below the line. As you can see, these forecasts seem quite accurate, since almost all the points are close to the 45-degree line.

What about forecasts that are formed one year ahead of time? As you might imagine, these forecasts are not as accurate as those formed just one quarter ahead of time. Still, as Figure 5.C suggests, they are not too bad, which you can tell because the points are fairly symmetric around the 45-degree line. Occasionally, the forecasts are not very good, as you can see when the forecast differs from the actual by 3 percentage points or more. But there does not appear to be any systematic error in forecasting. Overall, the forecasts of interest rates appear to be reasonably accurate and useful for showing how investors think about future interest rates.

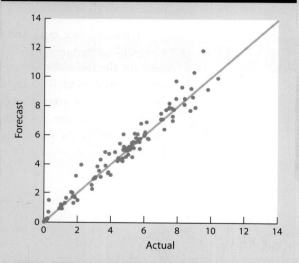

FIGURE 5.B — Scatter Plot of Actual Interest Rate versus Forecast Made One Quarter Ago

This graph shows a scatter plot of the forecast made one quarter ago compared with the actual value of the interest rate. If the forecasts are close to the actual values, the points will lie directly on the 45-degree line. Forecasts that are higher than actual will be above the line, whereas forecasts that are less than actual will be below the line. These forecasts seem quite accurate, since almost all the points are close to the 45-degree line.

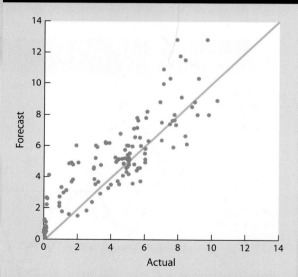

FIGURE 5.C — Scatter Plot of Actual Interest Rate versus Forecast Made One Year Earlier

This graph shows forecasts that are formed one year ahead of time, which are not quite as accurate as those formed just one quarter ahead of time. The points are fairly symmetric around the 45-degree line, so they are fairly accurate, but occasionally the forecasts differ from the actual by 3 percentage points or more.

Let's see how the expectations theory might work in practice using a simple example. Suppose that investors face no transactions costs and have perfect forecasts of future short-term interest rates. Consider bond A, which matures in two years, with the following timeline:

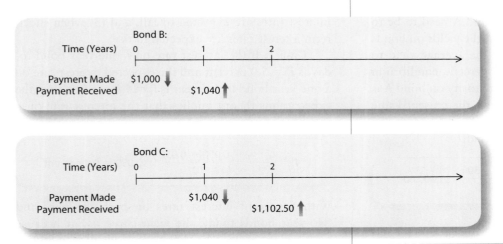

Bond A:

| Time (Years) | 0 | 1 | 2 |

Payment Made $980 ↓

Payment Received $1,102.50 ↑

(Note: In the timeline, the upward-pointing arrow denotes a payment received or a cash inflow; a downward-pointing arrow denotes a payment made or a cash outflow. The arrows help you keep track of which way the money is flowing.)

Suppose that the alternative for investors who want to spend their funds in two years is to buy bond B with one year to maturity today, then take the funds they receive from bond B after one year and invest in bond C, which is a one-year bond. The timelines for bond B and bond C are

Bond B:

| Time (Years) | 0 | 1 | 2 |

Payment Made $1,000 ↓

Payment Received $1,040 ↑

Bond C:

| Time (Years) | 0 | 1 | 2 |

Payment Made $1,040 ↓

Payment Received $1,102.50 ↑

Given these timelines for the bonds, we can use the present-value formula to find the yield to maturity on each bond using Equation (10) from Chapter 4. With just one payment of amount F being made in N years with principal amount P, the yield to maturity is

$$i = \left(\frac{F}{P}\right)^{1/N} - 1$$

Bond A has $F = \$1,102.50$, $P = \$980.00$, and $N = 2$, so the yield to maturity on bond A is

$$i_2^0 = \left(\frac{F}{P}\right)^{1/N} - 1 = \left(\frac{\$1,102.50}{\$980.00}\right)^{1/2} - 1 = 0.061 = 6.1 \text{ percent}$$

Bond B has $F = \$1,040$, $P = \$1,000$, and $N = 1$, so the yield to maturity on bond B is

$$i_1^0 = \left(\frac{\$1,040}{\$1,000}\right)^{1/1} - 1 = 0.040 = 4.0 \text{ percent}$$

Bond C has $F = \$1,102.50$, $P = \$1,040.00$, and $N = 1$, so the yield to maturity on bond C is

$$i_1^1 = \left(\frac{\$1,102.50}{\$1,040.00}\right)^{1/1} - 1 = 0.060 = 6.0 \text{ percent}$$

If the investor buys bond A, the yield to maturity is 6.1 percent for the two years. If the investor buys bond B today and bond C in one year, the yield to maturity is the average of the two yields on the one-year bonds, which is

$$\frac{4.0 + 6.0}{2} = 5.0 \text{ percent}$$

Because the yield to maturity is higher for bond A than bonds B and C, the investor will buy bond A. However, as more investors buy bond A, the quantity demanded of bond A rises at the existing price in the market. This causes the demand curve to shift to the right, raising the price of bond A, as Figure 5.7 illustrates. The shift in demand continues until the yield to maturity on bond A equals the average yield to maturity on bonds B

FIGURE 5.7 How Demand for a Bond Shifts to Restore Equilibrium

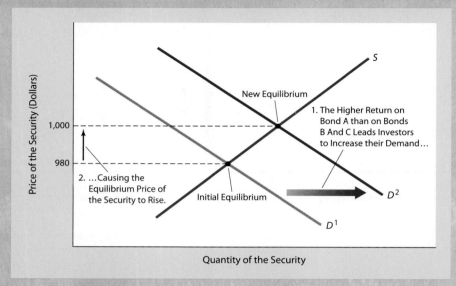

Investors compare the interest rate on a long-term bond with the average interest rate on successive short-term bonds, increasing their demand for whichever offers the highest return. In the graph, at the initial price of $980, the interest rate on bond A is higher than the average rate on bonds B and C, so investors increase their demand for bond A. As they do so, the price of bond A rises to $1,000. At that price, the interest rate on bond A is equal to the average rate on bonds B and C, so $1,000 is the equilibrium price.

and C. What would the price of bond A need to be to reach equilibrium if we assume that the yields on bonds B and C do not change? Because the average yield to maturity of bonds B and C is 5.0 percent, equilibrium will be reached when the yield to maturity on bond A is 5.0 percent. Because the price equals the present value of the bond, we can use Equation (3) from Chapter 4 to calculate the present value of the bond:

$$P = \frac{F}{(1 + i)^N} = \frac{\$1,102.50}{1.05^2} = \frac{\$1,102.50}{1.1025} = \$1,000.00$$

The result of this exercise is that with a given set of interest rates (yields to maturity) on current and future one-year bonds, the equilibrium yields to maturity and prices of longer-term bonds can be calculated. Shifts in the demand for and supply of bonds cause the prices of the bonds to adjust until equilibrium is reached.

We have seen how demand and supply in the bond market can relate the interest rates on bonds with differing times to maturity to each other. We can now see what this means for the shape of the yield curve based on the expectations theory of the term structure. We consider three basic cases: (1) when short-term interest rates are not expected to change, (2) when short-term

interest rates are expected to fall, and (3) when short-term interest rates are expected to rise.

Case 1: If the interest rate on a one-year bond today is $i_1^0 = 5.0$ percent and the expected interest rate on a one-year bond in one year is $i_1^1 = 5.0$ percent, then the expectations theory implies that the interest rate on a two-year bond today is

$$i_2^0 = \frac{i_1^0 + i_1^1}{2} = \frac{0.050 + 0.050}{2} = 0.050 = 5.0 \text{ percent}$$

With 5 percent interest rates on both the one- and two-year bonds today, the yield curve is flat because both points plotted have the same yield to maturity (Figure 5.8a). *Note that the yield curve is a plot of current interest rates (i_1^0 and i_2^0) and does not show expected future interest rates such as i_1^1.*

Case 2: If the interest rate on a one-year bond today is $i_1^0 = 6.0$ percent, but the interest rate on a one-year bond one year from now is expected to be $i_1^1 = 4.0$ percent, then the expectations theory implies that the interest rate on the two-year bond will be

$$i_2^0 = \frac{i_1^0 + i_1^1}{2} = \frac{0.060 + 0.040}{2} = 0.050 = 5.0 \text{ percent}$$

FIGURE 5.8 Yield Curves of Different Shapes

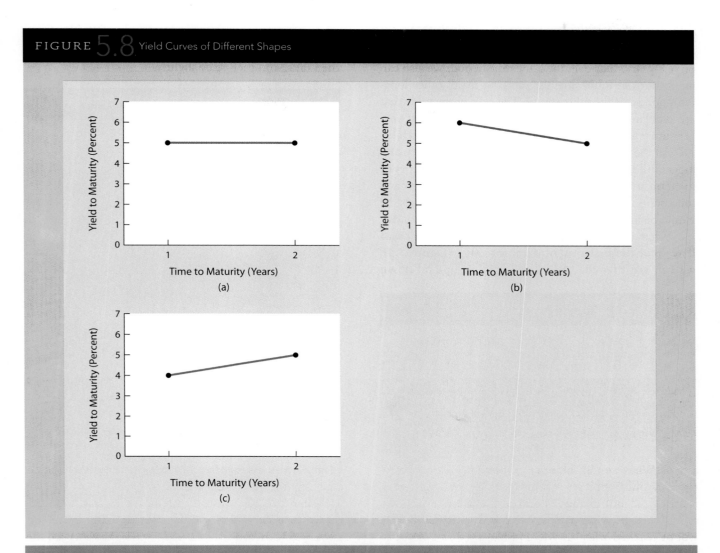

(a) Flat Yield Curve. When the yields to maturity on one-year and two-year securities are both 5 percent, the yield curve is flat. **(b) Downward-Sloping Yield Curve.** When the yield to maturity on a one-year security is 6 percent and the yield to maturity on a two-year security is 5 percent, the yield curve is downward sloping. **(c) Upward-Sloping Yield Curve.** When the yield to maturity on a one-year security is 4 percent and the yield to maturity on a two-year security is 5 percent, the yield curve is upward sloping.

The yield curve is downward sloping because it shows a 6.0 percent interest rate on a one-year bond (i_1^0) and a 5.0 percent interest rate on the two-year bond (i_2^0), as Figure 5.8b shows.

Case 3: If the situation were reversed and the interest rate on the one-year bond is $i_1^0 = 4.0$ percent today, but the interest rate on a one-year bond in one year is expected to be $i_1^1 = 6.0$ percent, then the interest rate on the two-year bond would be

$$i_2^0 = \frac{i_1^0 + i_1^1}{2} = \frac{0.040 + 0.060}{2} = 0.050 = 5.0 \text{ percent}$$

The yield curve then would slope upward, as shown in Figure 5.8c. Table 5.4 summarizes the interest rates and the resulting slope of the yield curve for each of the cases.

If we extend this analysis to consider longer times to maturity, the same types of relationships between interest rates must hold. Given those relationships, if we know the expected interest rates on future one-year bonds, we can figure out the interest rates for all long-term bonds.

For example, consider the following path over time for the one-year interest rate. Imagine that the interest rate on a one-year bond is 5.0 percent in 2013, 6.0 percent in 2014, 7.0 percent in 2015, 6.0 percent in 2016, and so on, as shown in the first column of interest rates in

Table 5.5. Then we can calculate the interest rates on all longer-term bonds by figuring out the average interest rate on one-year bonds over the same time period. We also can figure out the future interest rates on many other long-term bonds, as the table shows. The cells in the table that are left blank cannot be filled in unless we know what one-year interest rates will be for bonds sold in 2023 and later.

All the interest rates with two years to maturity and longer in Table 5.5 are based on the expectations theory of the term structure of interest rates. Given a choice of any time period over which an investor might buy bonds, he would be indifferent to any combination of these bonds.

What does the yield curve look like in this case? If we plot the first row of data, for 2013 (Figure 5.9), we can see that the yield curve has an up-and-down pattern. Fluctuations in future one-year interest rates over time lead to a yield curve that rises for a while, then falls, and then rises slightly.

| TABLE 5.5 | Equilibrium Interest Rates on Bonds with Differing Times to Maturity |

Date	Time to Maturity (years, interest rates in percent)									
	1	2	3	4	5	6	7	8	9	10
2013	5.0	5.5	6.0	6.0	5.8	5.5	5.1	5.0	5.0	5.1
2014	6.0	6.5	6.3	6.0	5.6	5.2	5.0	5.0	5.1	
2015	7.0	6.5	6.0	5.5	5.0	4.8	4.9	5.0		
2016	6.0	5.5	5.0	4.5	4.4	4.5	4.7			
2017	5.0	4.5	4.0	4.0	4.2	4.5				
2018	4.0	3.5	3.7	4.0	4.4					
2019	3.0	3.5	4.0	4.5						
2020	4.0	4.5	5.0							
2021	5.0	5.5								
2022	6.0									

Note: In this table, the interest rates on one-year bonds sold in the years 2013 to 2022 are given, as shown in the column in which the time to maturity is one year. The equilibrium interest rates on longer-term bonds are calculated from the one-year interest rates using the expectations theory of the term structure.

| TABLE 5.4 | Interest Rates and the Slope of the Yield Curve in Equilibrium |

Case	i_1^0	i_1^1	i_2^0	Slope of Yield Curve
1	5.0%	5.0%	5.0%	Flat
2	6.0%	4.0%	5.0%	Downward sloping
3	4.0%	6.0%	5.0%	Upward sloping

Note: The table's entries show the equilibrium interest rate on a security with two years to maturity purchased today (i_2^0), given interest rates on a one-year bond purchased today (i_1^0) and a one-year bond purchased in one year (i_1^1), in each of three cases. The resulting slope of the yield curve is shown in the last column.

| FIGURE 5.9 | Yield Curve with Fluctuating Short-Term Interest Rates |

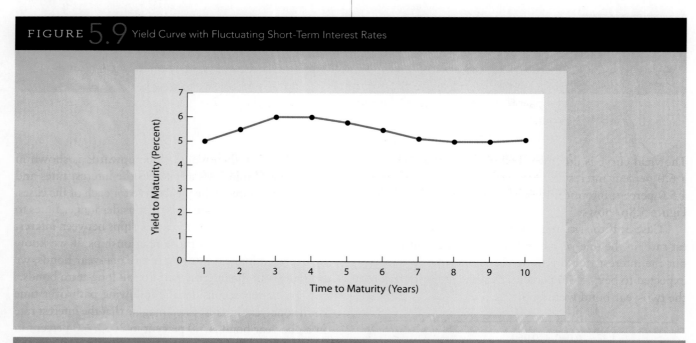

This graph plots the yield curve based on the interest rates in the first row of Table 5.5, which are generated using the expectations theory of the term structure of interest rates. The yield curve has an up-and-down pattern because of fluctuations in future one-year interest rates.

Equilibrium Interest Rates Under the Expectations Theory of the Term Structure

The expectations theory of the term structure says that, in equilibrium, the long-term interest rate on a debt security today equals the average of current and future short-term interest rates. This equality will hold for any time to maturity. We can calculate the relationship between any long-term interest rate and the interest rates on any combination of short-term securities that give the same overall time to maturity. Here are some examples:

$$i_2^0 = \frac{i_1^0 + i_1^1}{2}$$

Investing in two successive one-year bonds must give the same average interest rate as buying a two-year bond today.

$$i_3^0 = \frac{i_1^0 + i_1^1 + i_1^2}{3}$$

Investing in three successive one-year bonds must give the same average interest rate as buying a three-year bond today.

$$i_3^0 = \frac{(2 \times i_2^0) + i_1^2}{3}$$

Investing in a two-year bond today and a one-year bond in two years must give the same average interest rate as buying a three-year bond today.

$$i_3^0 = \frac{i_1^0 + (2 \times i_2^1)}{3}$$

Investing in a one-year bond today and a two-year bond in one year must give the same average interest rate as buying a three-year bond today.

$$i_4^0 = \frac{i_1^0 + i_1^1 + i_1^2 + i_1^3}{4}$$

Investing in four successive one-year bonds must give the same average interest rate as buying a four-year bond today.

RECAP

1 An investor has many different ways of investing in debt securities—buying a long-term bond or buying a series of successive short-term bonds. In comparing these options, the investor looks at the payoff to each option, which can be approximated by looking at the average interest rate on each.

2 The expectations theory of the term structure says that, ignoring transactions costs and uncertainty about future short-term interest rates, the interest rate on long-term bonds equals the average of current and future short-term interest rates.

5-3 The Term Premium

When we look at data on actual yield curves over long periods, we observe that they slope upward most of the time. However, we also notice that there are often periods in which short-term interest rates are not expected to change, but the yield curve still slopes upward. This contradicts the expectations theory, which suggests that yield curves should slope upward and downward about the same amount of time. The expectations theory says that if short-term interest rates are not expected to change, the yield curve should remain flat. Thus, the theory is missing something because it does not match what we observe in the data.

Our analysis of the expectations theory of the term structure was based on the assumption that investors care only about the yield to maturity in selecting among bonds with different times to maturity, and we ignored transactions costs and the uncertainty about future short-term interest rates. But both transactions costs and uncertainty about future interest rates should lead investors to prefer longer-term bonds over shorter-term bonds, which would make the yield curve slope downward, on average. Therefore, something still must be missing in our theory that will help to explain the usual upward slope of the yield curve.

The missing link in the expectations theory is an assumption about how investors treat risk. The expectations theory assumes that investors worry about their returns alone, but investors also care about other characteristics of bonds, notably the risk that a change in market interest rates will cause the price of a bond to change substantially. And this risk is greater on long-term bonds than on short-term bonds, as we will see. If that risk is strong enough, it will cause investors to prefer owning short-term bonds over long-term bonds, thus explaining why the yield curve usually slopes upward.

We can modify the expectations theory by factoring in risk to account for the usual upward slope of the yield curve. Risk can be accounted for by considering a term premium that is added onto the interest rates on longer-term bonds. The **term premium** refers to the difference between the interest rate on a longer-term bond and the average interest rate on shorter-term bonds; this difference arises from interest-rate risk. In other words, the interest rate on a long-term bond equals the average interest rate on shorter-term bonds (based on the expectations theory) *plus* a term premium that reflects the additional interest-rate risk associated with the long-term bond.

term premium the difference between the interest rate on a longer-term bond and the average interest rate on shorter-term bonds, which arises from interest-rate risk

5-3a The Increased Interest-Rate Risk of Long-Term Debt Securities

One of the main sources of risk to a security is interest-rate risk: the risk that the market value (or price) of the security will change as the rate of discount in the present-value formula changes. What affects that rate of discount? Our discussion of present value showed that the rate of discount is determined by the returns that can be earned on alternative financial investments. Because a given change in the rate of discount affects the present value of long-term securities more than the present value of short-term securities, longer-term bonds have more interest-rate risk than shorter-term bonds.

To understand the intuition for this result, think about a bond that will mature tomorrow. If the market interest rate rises today, the price of the bond will not change much because all the principal will be returned in one day, and the principal then can be reinvested at the higher interest rate. Thus, a bond with almost no time to maturity has very little interest-rate risk. On the other hand, if you buy a bond with a yield to maturity of 5 percent that does not mature for 30 years, and suddenly the market interest rate rises to 10 percent, the price of your bond will fall substantially because it is paying much less interest than a new bond would pay. Thus, interest-rate risk is low for bonds with little time to maturity and high for bonds with a long time to maturity.

To illustrate why longer-term bonds are riskier than shorter-term bonds, let's examine some numerical examples. Suppose that we consider a number of bonds that are alike except in their times to maturity. Let's see how much their prices change when the market interest rate suddenly falls from 8 to 7 percent. To illustrate this, we look at bonds with maturities from 1 to 10 years, 15 years, 20 years, 25 years, and 50 years. Each bond has a principal and face value of $1,000 and was issued at a coupon interest rate of 8 percent, so the annual interest payment on each bond is $1,000 \times 0.08 = 80.

For a particular market interest rate i, the present value of a bond with time to maturity of N years is given by

$$P = \frac{\$80}{(1+i)^1} + \frac{\$80}{(1+i)^2} + \cdots + \frac{\$80}{(1+i)^N} + \frac{\$1,000}{(1+i)^N}$$

The present value of the bond can be calculated from Equation (7) in Chapter 4:

$$P = \left[F \times \frac{1 - \left(\frac{1}{1+i}\right)^N}{i} \right] + \frac{V}{(1+i)^N} = \left[\$80 \times \frac{1 - \left(\frac{1}{1+i}\right)^N}{i} \right] + \frac{\$1,000}{(1+i)^N}$$

Note that when the market interest rate is $i = 0.08$, the present value is $1,000, no matter what the time to maturity. To see this, note that we can rearrange the terms of the present-value equation to get

$$P = \frac{\$80 \times \left[1 - \left(\frac{1}{1.08}\right)^N\right]}{0.08} + \frac{\$1,000}{1.08^N} = \frac{\$80 - \left[\$80 \times \left(\frac{1}{1.08}\right)^N\right]}{0.08} + \frac{\$1,000}{1.08^N}$$

$$= \frac{\$80}{0.08} - \frac{\$80 \times \frac{1}{1.08^N}}{0.08} + \frac{\$1,000}{1.08^N} = \$1,000 - \frac{\$1,000}{1.08^N} + \frac{\$1,000}{1.08^N} = \$1,000$$

Note that the terms containing N all drop out of the equation.

When the rate of discount falls to 0.07 because the yield to maturity on alternative bonds in the market declines, the terms containing N do not drop out of the equation. The present value of the bond's payments is now

$$P = \frac{\$80 \times \left[1 - \left(\frac{1}{1.07}\right)^N\right]}{0.07} + \frac{1,000}{1.07^N} = \frac{\$80 - \left[\$80 \times \left(\frac{1}{1.07}\right)^N\right]}{0.07} + \frac{\$1,000}{1.07^N}$$

$$= \frac{\$80}{0.07} - \frac{\$80 \times \frac{1}{1.07^N}}{0.07} + \frac{\$1,000}{1.07^N} = \$1,142.86 - \frac{\$1,142.86}{1.07^N} + \frac{\$1,000}{1.07^N}$$

$$= \$1,142.86 - \frac{\$142.86}{1.07^N}$$

In this equation, the higher N is, the larger the denominator of the last term will be. This makes the last term smaller, so the present value will be larger. Thus, bonds with more time to maturity will have a higher present value than bonds with less time to maturity. Consequently, when the market interest rate falls from 8 to 7 percent, the present value of a long-term bond rises more than the present value of a short-term bond.

Table 5.6 shows the present value of the bond, as well as the percentage increase in the present value of the bond because of the decline in the market interest rate, for selected times to maturity from one to 50 years.

Note that the present values shown in Table 5.6 become smaller as the time to maturity shortens and become larger as the time to maturity increases. In a competitive market, the price of the bond will equal its present value. Thus, a decline in the market interest rate from 8 to 7 percent has a much bigger effect (in terms of the percentage change in the price) on long-term bonds than on short-term bonds. *In general, for a given change in interest rates on all bonds, the prices of long-term bonds are affected more than the prices of short-term bonds.*

TABLE 5.6 Present Value of a $1,000 Bond When the Market Interest Rate Declines from 8 to 7 Percent		
Time to Maturity (years)	**Present Value**	**Percentage Change in Present Value**
1	$1,009.35	0.9
2	$1,018.08	1.8
3	$1,026.24	2.6
4	$1,033.87	3.4
5	$1,041.00	4.1
6	$1,047.67	4.8
7	$1,053.89	5.4
8	$1,059.71	6.0
9	$1,065.15	6.5
10	$1,070.24	7.0
15	$1,091.08	9.1
20	$1,105.94	10.6
25	$1,116.54	11.7
50	$1,138.01	13.8

Note: The entries in the column labeled "Present Value" show the present value of a coupon bond paying $80 each year with a face value of $1,000 and time to maturity shown in the first column.

Figure 5.10 further illustrates this idea. The graph shows four bonds with different times to maturity: 1 year, 3 years, 5 years, and 10 years. All four bonds have a principal and face value of $1,000 and a coupon interest rate of 8 percent, so each pays an annual coupon payment of $80. The horizontal axis shows the current market interest rate, with the price of each bond shown on the vertical axis. When the market interest rate is 8 percent, the bond price is $1,000 for bonds of every maturity. If the market interest rate falls below 8 percent, the prices of all four bonds rise, but the prices of bonds with longer times to maturity rise more than the prices of bonds with shorter times to maturity. Conversely, if the market interest rate rises above 8 percent, the prices of all four bonds fall, but

the prices of bonds with longer times to maturity fall more. Thus, for a given change in market interest rates on bonds of all maturities, the prices of long-term bonds are affected more than the prices of short-term bonds. Therefore, long-term bonds are riskier than short-term bonds.

5-3b How Do We Incorporate a Term Premium in Our Analysis?

To demonstrate how we include the term premium in our analysis, reconsider the case of an investor who is comparing a two-year bond with two one-year bonds. If the investor did not care about risk but only about the expected return, then in equilibrium the interest

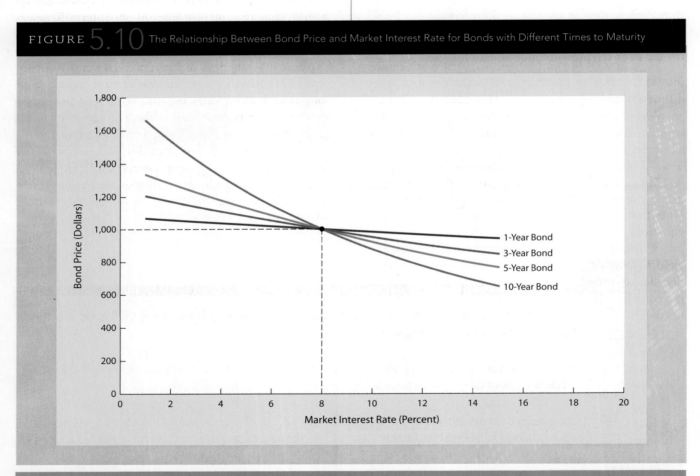

FIGURE 5.10 The Relationship Between Bond Price and Market Interest Rate for Bonds with Different Times to Maturity

This graph shows the prices of four coupon bonds with different times to maturity: 1 year, 3 years, 5 years, and 10 years. All four bonds have a face value of $1,000 and a stated interest rate of 8 percent, so each pays an annual coupon payment of $80. The horizontal axis shows the current market interest rate, with the price of each bond shown on the vertical axis. When the market interest rate is 8 percent, the bond price is $1,000 for bonds of all four maturities. If the market interest rate falls below 8 percent, the prices of all four bonds rise, but the prices of bonds with longer times to maturity rise more than the prices of bonds with shorter times to maturity. Conversely, if the market interest rate rises above 8 percent, the prices of all four bonds fall, but the prices of bonds with longer times to maturity fall more.

rates on the bonds would be related according to the equation

$$i_2^0 = \frac{i_1^0 + i_1^1}{2}$$

However, if there is a term premium on the two-year bond, then this equation must be modified to include an extra term:

$$i_2^0 = \frac{i_1^0 + i_1^1}{2} + i_2^{tp}$$

where the superscript *tp* means "term premium." The term premium will be positive if the increased riskiness of long-term bonds is more important to investors than the impact of lower transactions costs and reduced uncertainty on long-term bonds relative to short-term bonds.

How large is the term premium? Theoretically, the longer the time to maturity, the larger the term premium is likely to be because interest-rate risk is greater. In addition, the term premium changes over time, depending on how much interest-rate risk there is. For example, if you look at a period such as the 1990s, in which interest rates remained constant for long periods, then you can imagine that market risk was small, as were term premiums. (See the Data Bank box "The

Term Premium When Short-Term Interest Rates Are Not Expected to Change" for an attempt to calculate the size of the term premium.) In the late 1970s and early 1980s, though, interest rates were moving quite dramatically over time, so risk was great, and so were term premiums.

Economists believe that this theory, in which the interest rate on a long-term bond consists of a term premium added onto the average interest rate on short-term bonds, provides a good explanation of the yield curve. According to the theory, unless short-term interest rates are expected to decline significantly, the yield curve will slope upward—that is, we should expect long-term interest rates to be higher than short-term interest rates. Indeed, this is what we see in the data. For example, if you look at Figure 5.4, you will see that the interest rate on long-term Treasury securities is almost always higher than the interest rate on short-term Treasury securities. If there were no term premium, the interest rates would be the same, on average. The theory also explains why changes in interest rates occur together; that is, when short-term interest rates increase, so do long-term interest rates because the major portion of the long-term interest rate is the average of expected short-term interest rates. Thus, a rise in current and expected short-term interest rates should be accompanied by a similar rise in long-term interest rates. These types of changes occur with regularity over the business cycle, as we will see next.

RECAP

1 The expectations theory of the term structure implies that yield curves should be flat, on average, but in fact they usually slope upward.

2 The usual upward slope of the yield curve can be explained by a term premium that results from the increased risk of long-term debt securities.

3 Long-term debt securities have more interest-rate risk than short-term debt securities because an equal change in the market interest rate on all debt securities has a bigger effect on the prices of long-term bonds than it does on the prices of short-term bonds.

4 To incorporate a term premium into our analysis of long-term interest rates, follow two steps:

a. Calculate what the long-term interest rate would be according to the expectations theory.
b. Add a term premium to the result from part a. The longer the time to maturity, the larger the term premium is.

One way to examine the size of the term premium is to look at periods when forecasts show no change in short-term interest rates. If we look at a consistent set of forecasts, such as those from the *Survey of Professional Forecasters* (see the Data Bank box "How Accurate Are Expectations of Short-Term Interest Rates?"), we can look for periods in which short-term interest rates are not expected to change very much. There are not very many periods in which the interest rate on three-month Treasury securities is expected to change by one-tenth of a percentage point or less over the coming year, but such small expected changes occurred in forecasts made on five occasions in the 1980s and 1990s: in the fourth quarter of 1985, the third quarter of 1995, the second quarter of 1996, the third quarter of 1998, and the first quarter of 1999. To get an idea of the size of the term premium, we can look at the expected short-term interest rates compared with longer-term interest rates. The following table shows the range of the expected interest rates on the three-month Treasury security in the current quarter up to four quarters in the future compared with the current interest rate on two-year Treasury securities and 10-year Treasury securities at the time the forecasts were made. The term premiums shown in the table are equal to the interest rate on the long-term security (two-year or 10-year) minus the highest interest rate on three-month Treasury securities being forecast over the next four quarters.

Calculating the Term Premium When Short-Term Interest Rates Are Not Expected to Change Very Much

Date	3-Month Bonds Range of Expected Rates	2-Year Bonds Interest Rate	2-Year Bonds Term Premium	10-Year Bonds Interest Rate	10-Year Bonds Term Premium
1985:Q4	7.15% to 7.23%	8.66%	1.43%	9.92%	2.69%
1995:Q3	5.48% to 5.54%	5.53%	−0.01%	6.57%	1.03%
1996:Q2	5.03% to 5.09%	6.01%	0.92%	6.65%	1.56%
1998:Q3	4.99% to 5.09%	5.34%	0.25%	5.40%	0.31%
1999:Q1	4.38% to 4.45%	4.93%	0.48%	5.03%	0.58%
Average			0.6%		1.2%

You can see in this table that even when short-term interest rates are expected to change little over the coming year, longer-term bonds almost always have a positive term premium. The term premium is smaller on two-year bonds than on 10-year bonds, but it also varies substantially over time.

The term premium in the table averages 0.6 percentage points on two-year bonds and 1.2 percentage points on 10-year bonds, so the term premium is higher on longer-term bonds, as we might expect. These results confirm that the expectations theory of the term structure is not correct. To explain the data, long-term interest rates must contain a term premium. But the term premium appears to change over time.

5-4 The Yield Curve and the Business Cycle

The business cycle, which is the fluctuation of the economy about its long-term trend, influences how much consumers and businesses save and borrow. Their savings affect the demand for debt securities, and their borrowing affects the supply of debt securities. As a result, the yield curve is affected by the business cycle.

In a recession, both saving and borrowing decline, but borrowing usually declines more than saving. As a result, the supply curve of debt securities shifts to the left more than the demand curve does, as shown in Figure 5.11. The result is an increase in the price of debt securities and thus a decline in the yields to maturity of existing securities and a decline in the interest rates on new securities. But which falls more, interest rates on short-term securities or long-term securities?

To answer this question, consider what happens when the recession ends and the economy recovers. Both saving and borrowing rise, but borrowing rises more than saving, so prices of debt securities fall, and interest rates rise. Because short-term interest rates fall in recessions and rise in expansions, and because long-term interest rates are the average of current and future short-term interest rates plus a term premium, long-term interest rates will not fall as much in recessions as short-term interest rates do. To see this, refer to Table 5.5 and note that the interest rates on short-term securities change much more than the interest rates on long-term securities.

Now that we have established that short-term interest rates change more over the business cycle than long-term interest rates do, we can ask this: What should the yield curve look like over the business cycle? Suppose that the economy is near the start of a recession. At the beginning of recessions, short-term interest rates are usually high and are going to decline as the recession occurs. Because short-term interest rates are going to decline, if it were not for the term premium, long-term interest rates would be lower than short-term interest rates, and the yield curve

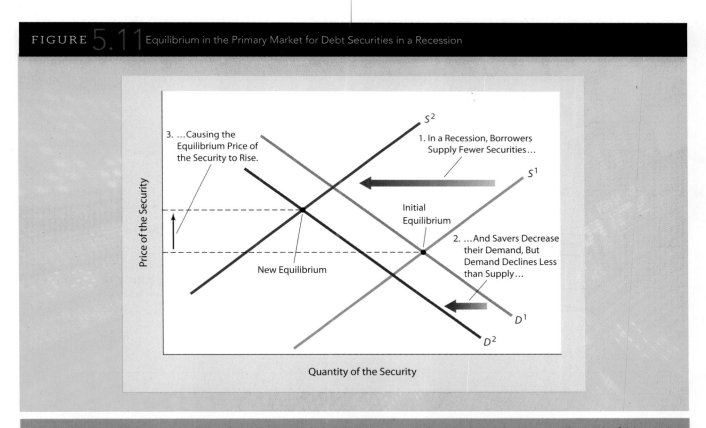

FIGURE 5.11 Equilibrium in the Primary Market for Debt Securities in a Recession

3. ...Causing the Equilibrium Price of the Security to Rise.

1. In a Recession, Borrowers Supply Fewer Securities...

S^2

S^1

Initial Equilibrium

2. ...And Savers Decrease their Demand, But Demand Declines Less than Supply...

New Equilibrium

D^1

D^2

Price of the Security

Quantity of the Security

This graph shows that in a recession, both saving and borrowing decline, but borrowing usually declines more than saving, so the supply of debt securities shifts to the left more than the demand. The result is an increase in the price of debt securities and thus a decline in the yields to maturity of existing securities and the interest rates on new securities.

would slope downward. When we include the term premium in the analysis, we have to determine whether the term premium will be bigger or smaller than the likely decline in the short-term interest rate over the course of the recession. If the term premium is small, the yield curve may be downward sloping, in which case we say that we have an **inverted yield curve.** If the term premium is large, then the expected decline in short-term interest rates leads to a fairly flat yield curve or perhaps one with a slight upward slope, but not nearly as steep as it is early in economic expansions.

Does this description match our observations? Let's look at the yield curves in the month before the start of the last seven recessions (Figure 5.12). As you can see, the yield curves are fairly flat or inverted, which suggests that people anticipated the recession or at least believed that the economy was slowing and that short-term interest rates would be declining.

What should the yield curve look like after a recession has ended and the economy has begun to improve?

At such a time, people expect short-term interest rates to begin rising. Thus, long-term interest rates should exceed short-term interest rates both because short-term interest rates are expected to rise and because of the term premium. If we look at the yield curve one year after the start of the economic expansion, as shown in Figure 5.13, we can see that the yield curves are much steeper. The steep upward-sloping yield curves suggest that people are expecting short-term interest rates to rise, which is what typically happens early in an expansion.

Finally, what does the yield curve look like in the middle of an economic expansion? At that time, there may be little reason to expect interest rates to rise, so the only reason for an upward slope to the yield curve would come from the term premium. If we look at the yield curves in the third year of economic expansions, we see that the curves are not as steep as at the start of the expansions but are steeper than before recessions (Figure 5.14). The exception is November 2004, at which time the yield curve was fairly steep after the expansion had been going on for three years. Most likely, the yield curve was steep in November 2004 because short-term interest rates had just begun to rise, much later than usual for an economic expansion.

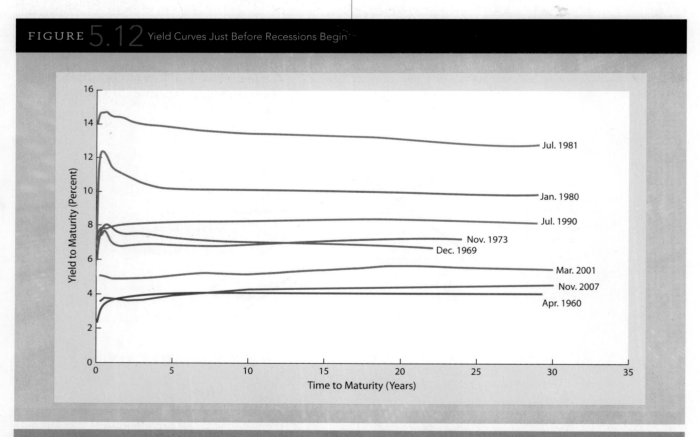

FIGURE 5.12 Yield Curves Just Before Recessions Begin

This graph shows the yield curves in the month before the start of the last eight recessions. In most cases, the yield curves are fairly flat or inverted, which suggests that people anticipated the recession or at least believed that the economy was slowing and that short-term interest rates would be declining.

FIGURE 5.13 Yield Curves One Year After Economic Expansions Begin

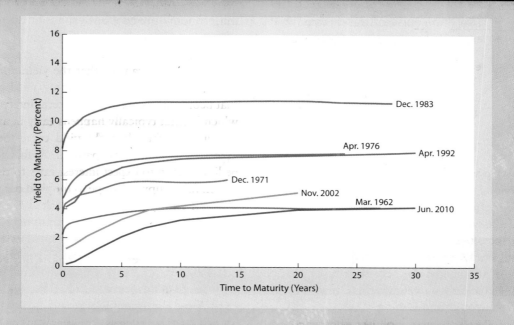

The graph shows the yield curves one year after the start of the economic expansions. Yield curves are much steeper after an economic expansion has begun than they are just before a recession begins. The steep upward-sloping yield curves suggest that people are expecting short-term interest rates to rise, which is what typically happens early in an expansion.

FIGURE 5.14 Yield Curves Three Years After Economic Expansions Begin

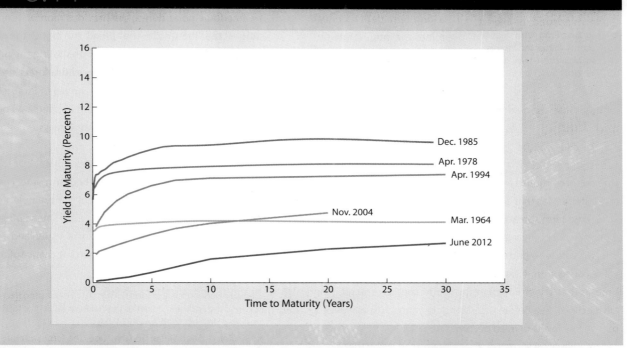

This graph shows yield curves in the third year of economic expansions. The curves are not as steep as at the start of the expansions but are usually steeper than before recessions.

Policy → Perspective   Can the Term Spread Help Predict Recessions?

Because recessions affect consumers and businesses in many ways, people would like to be able to forecast when they will occur. Can we use our theory about the yield curve to predict recessions?

Plotting yield curves over long periods of time is difficult because there are too many data points to make out a clear pattern. To simplify matters, we can look at a **term spread,** which is the interest rate on a long-term debt security minus the interest rate on a short-term debt security. If the spread is positive, the yield curve slopes upward, whereas if the spread is negative, the yield curve slopes downward.

term spread the interest rate on a long-term debt security minus the interest rate on a short-term debt security

Let's look at the term spread for the data that we used earlier in Figure 5.4. In that figure, the short-term interest rate was that on three-month Treasury securities, whereas the long-term interest rate was that on 10-year Treasury securities. Figure 5.15 shows the term spread, along with blue recession bars to show when the economy was in recession.

Do you see a pattern in this figure? Notice that in the early stages of economic expansions, the spread is fairly high. Over time, as the economic expansion progresses, the spread generally declines. Just before recessions, the spread usually declines to very low levels or even becomes negative.

Is a negative spread or a very low spread a sign that a recession is coming? Not necessarily. You might notice that the graph shows several false signals. For example, in late 1966, the spread became negative, but there was no recession. In late 1998 as well, the spread was very low, yet a recession did not occur.

But how likely is a recession when the spread is low or negative? Obviously, the probability of a recession is much larger when the spread is low than when it is high because no recession has occurred when the spread has been above 1 percentage point during the previous month. Researchers suggest that the smaller the spread, the higher the chance is of a recession in the coming year.[1] Forecasting the probability of recession using the yield curve provides forecasts that may even be superior to those from the Survey of Professional Forecasters. A spread of −0.5 percent implied a 40 percent chance of recession in late 2000; and a recession began in March 2001.

Researchers looking at national economies in foreign countries have reported similar results, although in other countries the recession probabilities are different. For example, in Japan, the spread matters significantly less, with a spread of −4 percent associated with a 33 percent chance of recession and a spread of +4 percent associated with a 19 percent chance of recession.[2]

[1] Glenn D. Rudebusch and John C. Williams, "Forecasting Recessions: The Puzzle of the Enduring Power of the Yield Curve," *Journal of Business and Economic Statistics,* 2009, pp. 492–503.

[2] Henri Bernard and Stefan Gerlach, "Does the Term Structure Predict Recessions? The International Evidence." *International Journal of Finance and Economics,* 1998, pp. 195–215.

Of the European countries, the United Kingdom and France are somewhat less sensitive to the spread, whereas Germany and Belgium are very sensitive to it.

In recent years, some economists have placed less faith in use of the term spread as a predictor of recessions because models that used the spread and other variables completely missed the recession of 1990–1991. The spread was quite low before the recession, as you can see in Figure 5.15, but not nearly so low as it was in previous recessions. In addition, the spread began rising about a year before the recession started. Also, on several other occasions the spread reached low levels without a recession occurring.

Probably the best way to view the yield curve's or term spread's value in predicting recessions is that it affects the probability of a recession. Many indicators, including the yield curve, provide useful information about economic weakness. However, no single indicator is definitive; they simply suggest the likelihood of a recession.

So does the term spread matter? A low or negative spread may indicate one of two possible scenarios, both of which increase the odds of a recession.

First, as we saw in the preceding section, when people expect a recession, they expect lower short-term interest rates in the future, so long-term interest rates may be below short-term interest rates. If we look at the level of interest rates before the yield curve became inverted (see Figure 5.4), we see that short-term rates were rising, whereas long-term rates were not rising as much. Rising short-term rates often occur when monetary policy is becoming tighter; that is, when the Federal Reserve is slowing the growth of the money supply to reduce the economy's growth rate. Thus, people may expect a recession or slow growth because monetary policymakers are attempting to slow down the economy.

Second, a low or negative spread may reduce lending by banks. For example, a temporary rise in short-term interest rates (possibly caused by tighter monetary policy) will not cause long-term interest rates to rise very much. Because banks borrow money for short periods and lend money for longer periods, they get squeezed. They now pay more interest on their deposits but do not receive more interest on their existing loans. As a result, they may need to sell some securities or reduce the amount of loans they make. Thus, the amount of

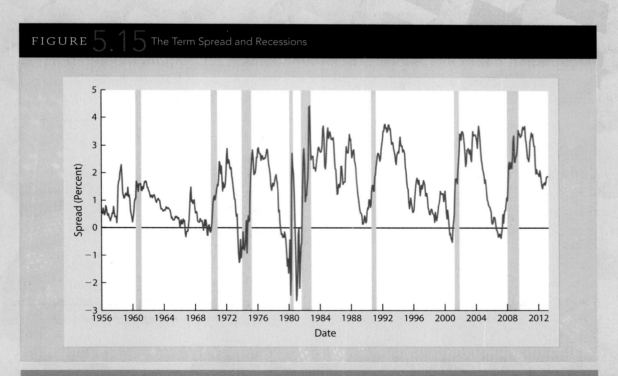

FIGURE 5.15 The Term Spread and Recessions

This graph shows the term spread between a short-term interest rate (that on three-month Treasury securities) and a long-term interest rate (that on 10-year Treasury securities), along with blue recession bars to show when the economy was in recession. The term spread gets smaller before recessions and rises during recessions.

(continued)

lending available to businesses is likely to decline, causing the economy's growth to slow.

To summarize, there are theoretical reasons why low or negative spreads explain slow growth or even recessions. As our charts showed, though, such spreads are closely—but not perfectly—associated with recessions. Nonetheless, a low or negative term spread in the market indicates that the odds of recession have risen.

RECAP

1 The slope of the yield curve, measured by the term spread, is helpful in analyzing the probability that a recession will occur.

2 The term spread helps to predict recessions either because of tighter monetary policy or because of a decline in bank lending.

Review Questions and Problems

Review Questions

1 Why is the interest rate on a credit card usually higher than the interest rate on an automobile loan?

2 Why is the interest rate on a security sold by a city government usually less than the interest rate on a security sold by a corporation if both have comparable default risk?

3 Why is the interest rate on an on-the-run security usually less than the interest rate on an off-the-run security?

4 Explain what a yield curve shows. What must be held constant among the bonds whose interest rates are shown on a yield curve?

5 Explain why investors might compare the interest rate on a long-term bond with the expected future interest rates on short-term bonds.

6 Describe the shape of the yield curve if investors think that short-term interest rates are likely to increase in the future. Why does the yield curve have this shape?

7 What is a term premium, and why does it exist?

8 What characteristics of a debt security determine the size of its term premium?

9 Is the term premium constant over time? If not, why not?

10 What is the shape of the yield curve at the start of a recession? At the start of an economic expansion? In the middle of an economic expansion?

Numerical Exercises

11 Suppose that a corporate bond with a Baa credit rating and five years to maturity has a yield to maturity of 8 percent. Suppose that the government of the city of Udwellum, which has a Baa credit rating, issues a bond with the same time to maturity in a market that is just as liquid as the market for corporate bonds. Suppose that investors have a federal tax rate of 30 percent. Calculate the interest rate that Udwellum should pay on its bonds if they will yield the same after-tax rate of return to investors as comparable corporate bonds. Show your work.

12 Compare a two-year bond with two successive one-year bonds in a situation in which an investor buys a one-year bond today and then another one-year bond when the first matures. Suppose that the two-year bond has an interest rate of 8 percent each year.

a Now consider the pattern of interest rates on the one-year bonds listed below and explain whether an investor should buy the two-year bond or the one-year bond today, assuming that the only thing that matters to the investor is the amount of money he has at the end of the two years. In each case, how much would an investor have at the end of two years if he invested $1,000 today?

(i) The one-year interest rate today is 7 percent; the one-year interest rate will be 9 percent one year from now.

(ii) The one-year interest rate today is 5 percent; the one-year interest rate will be 11 percent one year from now.

(iii) The one-year interest rate today is 3 percent; the one-year interest rate will be 13 percent one year from now.

(iv) The one-year interest rate today is 0 percent; the one-year interest rate will be 16 percent one year from now.

b From these results, is it reasonable to compare the average interest rates on alternative financial investments? (In other words, how reasonable is the assumption that we can compare average interest rates on short-term bonds with the interest rate on long-term bonds instead of using the exact method?)

13 You are given the following information on the bond market:

Money available on January 1, 2013: $1,000

Interest rates on January 1, 2013, on bonds of different maturities: one year, 4 percent; two years, 5 percent; three years, 5.5 percent; four years, 6 percent

Note: Consider these to be bonds that compound the interest at the rate given, that is, the three-year bond pays $1,000 \times 1.055^3$ at maturity.

(*continued*)

Expected future interest rates on one-year bonds:

January 1, 2014: 6.5 percent

January 1, 2015: 7 percent

January 1, 2016: 9 percent

Investment horizon: four years, ending
     January 1, 2017

What should an investor buy to yield the largest stream of expected income over the period from January 1, 2013, to January 1, 2017?

14 How would your answer to question 13 change if there is a $10 transactions cost for every bond purchased? In other words, if an investor has $1,000 now, she can spend only $990 on a bond because $10 goes for transactions costs. Each time she buys a new bond, she incurs the $10 fee.

15 Suppose that the interest rate on a one-year bond is 7 percent today and the interest rates expected on one-year bonds in the future are 6 percent in one year, 5 percent in two years, and 4 percent in three years.

  a According to the expectations theory of the term structure, what are the interest rates today on a two-year bond, a three-year bond, and a four-year bond?

  b If the term premium is equal to 0.5 percent times the number of years to maturity of a bond for times to maturity of two, three, and four years, what are the interest rates today on a two-year bond, a three-year bond, and a four-year bond? (Assume no term premium on one-year bonds.)

16 Using Table 5.5, show the derivation of each of the following entries:

  a The interest rate of 5.1 percent on a bond sold in 2013 that matures in seven years.

  b The interest rate of 4.4 percent on a bond sold in 2016 that matures in five years.

  c The interest rate of 4.5 percent on a bond sold in 2020 that matures in two years.

Analytical Problems

17 Which would you rather hold if there is a decline in interest rates: long-term bonds or short-term bonds? Why?

18 What would happen to the yield curve if investors were concerned about stability in foreign countries and rushed their money into the United States to buy long-term Treasury securities? How would you expect the term premium to change?

19 If the newspaper reported that the interest rate on 10-year Treasury securities was 5 percent and the interest rate on three-month Treasury securities was 6 percent, would it be a good time to invest in the stock market? Explain your reasoning.

20 If capital gains are taxed at a lower rate than interest income, would the determination of yields to maturity be affected? Consider the case in which a change in the market interest rate has occurred in an early year in the life of a bond, after which the market interest rate remains constant. You are considering two bonds: a used one with a capital gain or loss versus a new one paying interest at the market rate. Would it matter for your decision about which bond to buy whether the market interest rate today was lower or higher than the original interest rate on your bond?

21 Nora the novice investor wants to invest her money for the next year. She is thinking of buying a bond with 20 years to maturity instead of a bond with one year to maturity because the interest rate on 20-year bonds is 6 percent and the interest rate on one-year bonds is only 5.5 percent. As her investment advisor, what would you suggest that Nora think about in making her decision?

22 Consider the following four debt securities, which are identical in every characteristic except as noted:

W: A corporate bond rated Aaa

X: A corporate bond rate Baa

Y: A corporate bond rated Aaa with a shorter time to maturity than bonds W and X

Z: A corporate bond rated Aaa with the same time to maturity as bond Y that trades in a more liquid market than bonds W, X, or Y

List the bonds in the most likely order of the interest rates (yields to maturity) of the bonds from highest to lowest. Explain your work.

CHAPTER 6

Chris Bott/Alamy

REAL INTEREST RATES

Investors do not care about how many dollars they earn on their financial investments.

What they really care about is what they can buy with their investment earnings. Analyzing how many goods and services an investor can buy requires accounting for inflation.

In this chapter we examine the real interest rate, which is the interest rate adjusted for inflation (expected or actual). Economic research suggests that real interest rates are a key determinant of decisions by businesses to invest in physical capital and decisions by individuals about consuming and saving, and they may be the best variable to look at in interpreting changes in monetary policy. As former Federal Reserve Chairman Alan Greenspan put it in testimony before Congress in 1993, "One important guidepost is real interest rates, which have a key bearing on longer-run spending decisions and inflation prospects." We will see what real interest rates are, how inflation affects them, and why inflation is public enemy number one to investors. We will then develop a version of the present-value formula in real terms. Next, we will examine the historical data on real interest rates and see how they respond to changes in the inflation rate and how they change during recessions. Finally, we will look at an application to everyday life, investigating how the combination of taxes and inflation reduces returns on financial investments.

6-1 What Are Real Interest Rates?

If you invest $1,000 in a debt security at a 6 percent interest rate and earn $60 in interest in a year, are you better off financially at the end of the year than you were at the beginning? Even though you have $60 more at the end of the year than you did at the start, you actually might be worse off if the inflation rate is more than 6 percent. For example, if the inflation rate is 10 percent over the year, then your interest gives you 6 percent more dollars, but each dollar is worth 10 percent less in terms of what it can buy, so the value of your wealth declines by 4 percent.

To fully understand events in financial markets, we must adjust all our calculations of interest rates and returns to account for the change in the prices of goods and services; that is, we must adjust for inflation.

Suppose that an investor earns a 13 percent return one year and a 7 percent return the next year. Which year was better? You might think the answer is obviously the first year because the return that year was higher. If inflation was 20 percent the first year and only 5 percent the second year, however, the investor actually did better, in inflation-adjusted terms, in the second year. An accurate measure of well-being is based on the amount of goods and services an investor can buy, not on the number of dollars that she earns. To account for inflation in financial matters, we use the concepts of real interest rates and real returns.

Until now, when we have discussed interest rates, we have looked only at the **nominal interest rate,** which is the amount of interest paid on a debt security in nominal (dollar) terms as a percentage of the principal (in dollar terms). The **real interest rate** is the nominal interest rate adjusted for expected or actual inflation (over the period until the debt security matures). Most often expected inflation is the measure used to adjust the nominal interest rate, not actual inflation, because what matters for

nominal interest rate the amount of interest paid on a debt security in nominal (dollar) terms as a percentage of the principal (in dollar terms)

real interest rate the nominal interest rate adjusted for expected or actual inflation

expected real interest rate the nominal interest rate adjusted for expected inflation; also called the **ex-ante real interest rate**

When a consumer buys goods or services with a credit card, as this woman is doing, the real interest rate she pays depends on both the nominal interest rate and the expected inflation rate. Consumers need to understand the concept of the real interest rate to be fully aware of the economic costs of borrowing.

people's decisions to borrow or lend is what they think they will be paying or earning in inflation-adjusted terms when they take out a loan or invest their funds. Because this measure of the real interest rate is based on expected inflation—and not actual inflation—it is called the **expected real interest rate.** The expected real interest rate is sometimes called the **ex-ante real interest rate** because the term *ex ante* means "before the fact."

How do we adjust the nominal interest rate to account for expected inflation to calculate the expected real interest rate? Formally, we represent the expected real interest rate on a loan or a bond as

$$r = \frac{1 + i}{1 + \pi^e} - 1 \qquad (1)$$

where i is the nominal interest rate, r is the expected real interest rate, and π^e is the expected rate of inflation. Intuitively, you can see that this equation divides the amount of dollars an investor would have after earning nominal interest rate i for one year $(1 + i)$ by an amount that represents the expected increase in the price level in that year $(1 + \pi^e)$. Therefore, the expected real interest rate represents the expected increase in purchasing power of a financial investment in terms of the real goods and services that it can buy. See Appendix 6.A for an example and derivation of Equation (1).

Equation (1) is a bit cumbersome to use, but if the i and π^e terms are all fairly small, then the following approximation works well:

> Expected real interest rate = nominal interest rate − expected inflation rate

or

$$r = i - \pi^e \qquad (2)$$

For example, if the nominal interest rate is 6 percent and the expected inflation rate is 4 percent, the expected real interest rate is approximately $r = 0.06 - 0.04 = 0.02 = 2$ percent.

To see why this approximation works, add 1 to both sides of Equation (1) to get

$$1 + r = \frac{1 + i}{1 + \pi^e} \qquad (3)$$

expected inflation

If we multiply both sides of this equation by $1 + \pi^e$, we get

$$(1 + r) \times (1 + \pi^e) = 1 + i \qquad (4)$$

Multiplying out the terms on the left-hand side of the equation gives

$$1 + r + \pi^e + (r \times \pi^e) = 1 + i$$

Now subtract $1 + \pi^e + (r \times \pi^e)$ from both sides of the equation to get

$$r = i - \pi^e - (r \times \pi^e)$$

The last term is very small as long as the expected real interest rate and expected inflation rate are fairly small (for example, if they are less than 5 percent, then the approximation is off by less than one quarter of one percentage point). Thus, we often use Equation (2) in our calculations, but keep in mind that when expected inflation and the expected real interest rate are high, we will need to use Equation (1) to get a reasonable value for the expected real nominal interest rate.

The other measure of the real interest rate that economists sometimes use is based on the actual inflation rate rather than the expected inflation rate in Equation (1) or Equation (2). When the real interest rate is based on actual inflation, it is called the **realized real interest rate** or the **ex-post real interest rate**. (The term *ex post* means

"after the fact.") The expected real interest rate is more relevant to investors and business firms than the realized real interest rate because investment decisions must be made before anyone knows the actual inflation rate. Therefore, when a business firm borrows and uses the proceeds to invest in equipment, it must guess what the inflation rate will be in the future, which explains why inflation expectations are so important in economics.

The realized real interest rate may not influence people's decisions, but an investor may find it useful to calculate after the fact to see how well he did financially when he borrowed or lent. In fact, in the absence of nominal capital gains and losses, the realized real interest rate is the same as the real past return on an investment. It is a measure of an investor's gain in real wealth as a percentage of the principal amount invested.

The equations for the realized real interest rate are just like the equations for the expected real interest rate, but they contain a term for the actual inflation rate instead of the expected inflation rate:

Realized Real Int-Rate

$$rr = \frac{1 + i}{1 + \pi} - 1 \qquad (5)$$

inflation

or the approximation

$$rr = i - \pi \qquad (6)$$

where rr is the realized real interest rate, and π is the actual inflation rate.

For example, if Ivy invests \$1,000 in a debt security that matures in one year and pays a 5 percent nominal interest rate, then she will receive an interest payment of

$$\$1,000 \times 0.05 = \$50$$

at the end of the year. She also receives her principal back, so she has \$1,050 at the end of the year. If actual inflation turns out to be 7 percent, then the value of Ivy's wealth of \$1,050 is lower than it was at the beginning of the year because her \$1,050 now buys fewer goods and services than her \$1,000 did at the beginning of the year. Thus, the realized real interest rate tells us how many more goods and services Ivy can buy with her \$1,050.

realized real interest rate the nominal interest rate adjusted for actual inflation; also called the **ex-post real interest rate**

If actual inflation is 7 percent, then Ivy's realized real interest rate is

$$rr = i - \pi = 0.05 - 0.07 = -0.02 = -2\ percent$$

Thus, even though investors make decisions based on the expected inflation rate, the performance of their financial investments depends on the actual inflation rate.

6-1a The Impact of Unexpected Inflation on Real Interest Rates

How much of a problem is caused by unexpected inflation? Let's consider an example that compares the expected real interest rate and the realized real interest rate to see how unexpected inflation affects the difference between them. Suppose that a business firm is making a physical capital investment in new equipment that costs $100,000. Further, suppose that the firm can borrow the $100,000 for one year at a nominal interest rate of 9 percent and that it expects the inflation rate in the coming year to be 3 percent. What is the expected real interest rate on the loan? From Equation (2), the expected real interest rate equals the nominal interest rate of 9 percent minus the expected inflation rate of 3 percent, which equals 6 percent:

$$r = i - \pi^e = 0.09 - 0.03 = 0.06 = 6\ percent$$

So the firm knows that in real (inflation-adjusted) terms, the project must return a profit of at least 6 percent to be worthwhile. The real returns to many projects are unaffected by inflation because when inflation is higher than expected, the revenues from the project rise, but so do the costs. Thus, a firm usually calculates expected real returns on projects and compares them with the expected real interest rate on the loan needed to finance the project.

What happens if the inflation rate does not match expectations? In this case, the realized real interest rate can tell us who gained and who lost from unexpected inflation. Suppose, for example, that the inflation rate turned out to be zero over the year. Now, the firm would be paying an interest rate of 9 percent on the loan, with no inflation, so the realized real interest rate would be 9 percent, which equals the interest rate (9 percent) minus the actual inflation rate (0 percent). Thus, the firm would have to pay back more than it expected to because it had expected to pay only 6 percent in real terms. Therefore, inflation that is lower than expected

hurts the borrower (the firm) and helps the lender (the bank). On the other hand, if the inflation rate turned out to be 6 percent over the year, the realized real interest rate would be 3 percent, which equals the 9 percent nominal interest rate minus the 6 percent actual inflation rate. In this case, with the inflation rate higher than expected, the borrower (the firm) is better off, and the lender (the bank) is worse off. The firm repays the loan to the bank with money that is worth less because of unexpected inflation.

With a numerical example such as this, we can see that when actual inflation differs from expected inflation, the expected real interest rate differs from the realized real interest rate. From Equations (2) and (6) we can see the exact amount by which they differ. Because we know from Equation (2) that

$$r = i - \pi^e$$

then adding the term π^e to both sides of the equation and rearranging terms gives

$$i = r + \pi^e \qquad (7)$$

Also, because from Equation (6)

$$rr = i - \pi$$

then adding π to both sides of the equation and rearranging terms gives

$$i = rr + \pi \qquad (8)$$

Because we have expressions for i in both Equation (7) and Equation (8), we can set the right-hand sides of those equations equal to each other:

$$r + \pi^e = rr + \pi$$

Rearranging the terms, we see that

$$r - rr = \pi - \pi^e \qquad (9)$$

Thus, whenever $\pi < \pi^e$, then $r < rr$; when $\pi = \pi^e$, then $r = rr$; and when $\pi > \pi^e$, then $r > rr$. For example, if the actual inflation rate is 1 percent less than expected, then the realized real interest rate will be 1 percent more than the expected real interest rate. If the actual inflation rate is 2 percent more than expected, then the realized real interest rate will be 2 percent less than the expected real interest rate.

In general, unexpectedly low inflation helps lenders and hurts borrowers; unexpectedly high inflation helps borrowers and hurts lenders.

6-1b Why Inflation Risk Is a Problem for Investors

Investors who buy financial securities do not like unexpectedly high inflation, because their financial investments usually give them payments in dollar terms, the value of which is reduced by inflation. Investors also hate the unpredictability of inflation because it increases the risk to the real return on their financial investments.

To see why investors dislike inflation so much, consider the example of Bobby Bonds, who has purchased $10,000 in debt securities that mature in one year and have a yield to maturity of 4 percent, paying $400 in interest at the end of the year.

Suppose that the inflation rate had been 3 percent for several years, so Bobby and other investors expect the inflation rate to continue to be 3 percent. Bobby's expected real interest rate is

$$r = i - \pi^e = 0.04 - 0.03 = 0.01 = 1 \, percent$$

However, if the inflation rate were to rise to 6 percent instead of staying steady at 3 percent, Bobby's realized real interest rate would be

$$rr = i - \pi = 0.04 - 0.06 = -0.02 = -2 \, percent$$

A realized real interest rate of −2 percent means that Bobby's $10,400 at the end of the year buys 2 percent fewer goods and services than Bobby could have purchased with his $10,000 at the beginning of the year.

Of course, Bobby would like the outcome if the inflation rate turned out to be less than 3 percent. For example, if the inflation rate were zero, the realized real interest rate would be

$$rr = i - \pi = 0.04 - 0.00 = 0.04 = 4 \, percent$$

With such a high realized real interest rate, Bobby can buy 4 percent more goods and services at the end of the year than he could have purchased at the beginning of the year. Thus, Bobby is happy whenever the inflation rate is less than expected. In general, investors do not like unexpectedly high inflation, but they do like unexpectedly low inflation, as the example suggests.

Because investors do not like risk, it is not just the inflation rate that matters to them but also the riskiness of inflation. Consider two situations, the first with a lower risk to the inflation rate than the second.

Case 1: There is a 25 percent chance that the inflation rate will be 0 percent, a 50 percent chance that the inflation rate will be 3 percent, and a 25 percent chance that the inflation rate will be 6 percent. Given these probabilities, we can calculate the expected inflation rate. Recall the formula for expected value from Equation (1) in Chapter 2:

$$E = p_1 X_1 + p_2 X_2 + \cdots + p_N X_N$$

where the p terms are the probabilities of the outcomes given by the X terms. The expected inflation rate equals the sum of the probabilities of each possible inflation rate multiplied by that inflation rate. The expected inflation rate is thus

$$\pi^e = p_1 \pi_1 + p_2 \pi_2 + \cdots + p_N \pi_N = (0.25 \times 0.00) + (0.50 \times 0.03)$$
$$+ (0.25 \times 0.06)$$
$$= 0.0 + 0.015 + 0.015 = 0.03 = 3 \, percent$$

Because Bobby earns a nominal interest rate of $i = 4$ percent, his expected real interest rate is

$$r = i - \pi^e = 0.04 - 0.03 = 0.01 = 1 \, percent$$

A second way to calculate Bobby's expected real interest rate is to find the expected value of the realized real interest rate. Bobby's realized real interest rate depends on the actual inflation rate, as we found earlier: $rr = 4$ percent when actual inflation is $\pi = 0$ percent, $rr = 1$ percent when $\pi = 3$ percent, and $rr = -2$ percent when $\pi = 6$ percent. Given these numbers and given the probabilities of the different actual inflation rates, Bobby's expected real interest rate is

$$r = (0.25 \times 0.04) + (0.50 \times 0.01) + (0.25 \times -0.02)$$
$$= 0.01 + 0.005 - 0.005 = 0.01 = 1 \, percent$$

Note that this is identical to the expected real interest rate that we found by subtracting the expected inflation rate from the nominal interest rate. Either method can be used, and both give the same result.

The risk to Bobby's real return is given by the standard deviation, derived as Equation (2) in Chapter 2. Recall the formula for standard deviation:

$$\text{Standard deviation} = \{[\textit{probability of outcome } 1 \times (\textit{deviation of outcome } 1)^2]$$
$$+ [\textit{probability of outcome } 2 \times (\textit{deviation of outcome } 2)^2] + \cdots$$
$$+ [\textit{probability of outcome } N \times (\textit{deviation of outcome } N)^2]\}^{1/2}$$
$$= \{[p_1 \times (X_1 - E)^2] + [p_2 \times (X_2 - E)^2] + \cdots + [p_N \times (X_N - E)^2]\}^{1/2}$$

Using this with the probabilities and outcomes that Bobby faces, noting that Bobby's expected return is 1 percent (which equals 0.01), we can calculate the risk to Bobby's real return in case 1 as

$$S_1 = \{[p_1 \times (r_1 - r)^2] + [p_2 \times (r_2 - r)^2] + \cdots + [p_N \times (r_N - r)^2]\}^{1/2}$$
$$= \{[0.25 \times (0.04 - 0.01)^2] + [0.50 \times (0.01 - 0.01)^2] + [0.25 \times (-0.02 - 0.01)^2]\}^{1/2}$$
$$= 0.0212 = 2.12 \textit{ percent}$$

Case 2: Suppose that there is a 35 percent chance that the inflation rate will be 0 percent, a 30 percent chance that the inflation rate will be 3 percent, and a 35 percent chance that the inflation rate will be 6 percent. In this case, there is a larger probability of either a higher or lower inflation rate, so the risk of inflation is bigger. Let's see how this affects the risk to Bobby's real return.

The expected inflation rate is unchanged:

$$\pi^e = (0.35 \times 0.00) + (0.30 \times 0.03) + (0.35 \times 0.06) = 0.0 + 0.009 + 0.021 = 0.03 = 3 \textit{ percent}$$

For each possible inflation rate, Bobby's realized real interest rate remains the same as it was before because the outcomes are the same; only the probabilities have changed. Thus, Bobby's expected real interest rate is

$$r = (0.35 \times 0.04) + (0.30 \times 0.01) + (0.35 \times -0.02)$$
$$= 0.014 + 0.003 - 0.007 = 0.01 = 1 \textit{ percent}$$

which is also the same as in case 1. However, the risk to Bobby's expected real interest rate in case 2 is different from what it was in case 1; now it is

$$S_2 = \{[p_1 \times (r_1 - r)^2] + [p_2 \times (r_2 - r)^2] + \cdots + [p_N \times (r_N - r)^2]\}^{1/2}$$
$$= \{[0.35 \times (0.04 - 0.01)^2] + [0.30 \times (0.01 - 0.01)^2] + [0.35 \times (-0.02 - 0.01)^2]\}^{1/2}$$
$$= 0.0251 = 2.51 \textit{ percent}$$

In this example, the higher risk of inflation translates into a higher risk to Bobby's real return, with a standard deviation of 2.51 percent in case 2 compared with a standard deviation of 2.12 percent in case 1. Because investors generally prefer to avoid risk to their real returns, they dislike uncertainty about inflation as well as inflation itself.

Investors and borrowers have several ways in which they try to avoid the problems of unexpected inflation and inflation uncertainty. First, they can share the risk of changes in the inflation rate. For example, adjustable-rate mortgages allow the interest rate on a loan to adjust periodically. As the inflation rate changes, market interest rates change, and the interest rate on an adjustable-rate mortgage changes, as we will see in the box titled "How Adjustable-Rate Mortgages Work." Second, they can agree to borrow or lend in real terms rather than in nominal terms (which we discuss next).

6-1c How Inflation-Indexed Securities Work

Investors do not like the risk posed to them by inflation. You might wonder why borrowers and lenders do not agree to make interest payments in real terms instead of in dollar terms. That is, rather than making an interest payment of $500, the borrower and lender could agree that the payment will be $500 plus an amount that adjusts when actual inflation is higher or lower than expected. This type of real interest payment would alleviate the problems with unexpected inflation and would appear to benefit both borrowers and lenders.

In 1997, following this logic, the U.S. government introduced a new set of securities, called _Treasury Inflation-Protected Securities_ (TIPS), with payments to be made in real terms rather than in nominal terms. The adjustment for inflation is not perfect, but the real interest payments on the securities are fairly constant over time.

Inflation-indexed securities work like this: When you buy them, you are guaranteed a fixed real payment until the security matures. You get a basic real interest rate (for example, 3 percent). In addition, the nominal value of your principal increases as inflation occurs so as to maintain the real value of your principal. Interest is paid every six months. In addition, the value of your principal is also adjusted every six months, even though you will not receive that amount until the security matures.

For example, suppose that on January 15, 2014, you buy a 10-year inflation-indexed Treasury security for $10,000. The security has a stated (real) annual interest rate of 3 percent and makes interest payments twice a year. The inflation adjustment is based on a measure of inflation over the period in question. Suppose that the inflation index value is 102.0 on January 15, 2014, and is 103.0 on July 15, 2014, when you are to receive your first interest payment. First, we calculate the inflation-adjusted principal value on July 15, 2014, which equals the original principal value times the ratio of the inflation index values:

How Adjustable-Rate Mortgages Work

Most people who buy homes do so by taking out mortgage loans, which they pay off over a long time, often 30 years. Adjustable-rate mortgages are an alternative to traditional fixed-rate mortgages in which payments are fixed in dollar terms. With an adjustable-rate mortgage, the interest rate changes every year, depending on the movement of an index of interest rates in the market. Are adjustable-rate mortgages beneficial to homeowners or to the banks (or other financial intermediaries) that offer them?

The idea behind adjustable-rate mortgages is that no one can accurately predict inflation or interest rates over 30 years. Yet that is what both a homeowner and a bank must do if they agree to a 30-year fixed-rate mortgage loan. With a fixed-rate loan, the bank agrees to lend the homeowner money for 30 years, but the bank's source of funds is deposits in checking accounts, savings accounts, certificates of deposit, and other accounts that mature in a short time. Thus, if nominal interest rates in the market rise (perhaps because the expected inflation rate rises), the bank will find itself lending money to the homeowner at an interest rate that is below the rate on its deposits, and thus the bank will lose money. Because of this risk, the fixed-rate mortgage interest rate that a bank offers to homeowners is higher than it would otherwise be if there were no such risk.

What causes fluctuations in banks' cost of funds? One factor in the short run is the business cycle because the interest rates that banks pay to depositors vary with the state of the economy (that is, whether the economy is in an expansion or a recession). The most important factor, however, is the expected inflation rate. Because the expected inflation rate is fairly slow to rise or fall and is quite persistent, banks bear a large risk from changes in the expected inflation rate.

Is there a way to reduce the risk so that banks could offer lower mortgage interest rates? One way is for the homeowner and the bank to share the risk, which is what an adjustable-rate mortgage does. If market interest rates that determine the bank's cost of funds rise, so does the mortgage interest rate. If those market interest rates fall, so does the mortgage interest rate. The rises and falls in the mortgage interest rate represent increased risk to the homeowner and lower risk to the bank, but in return, the bank can offer a lower mortgage interest rate on average over time. Thus, homeowners who have the ability to handle fluctuations in their mortgage payments can benefit from adjustable-rate loans.

In theory, then, the adjustable-rate loan is a useful device for reducing the risk to banks in the mortgage market. In practice, however, there are difficulties. Although the lower average interest rate on adjustable-rate mortgages should make them attractive to homeowners, many homeowners do not want to be subject to so much risk in their mortgage payments, so they never take out such loans. Other people are willing to obtain adjustable-rate mortgages when interest rates are high because they think interest rates will decline in the future and then their mortgage payments will decline. However, when interest rates are low, most people obtain fixed-rate mortgages because they think interest rates will not decline any further, so they want to lock in a low mortgage rate for the long term. Thus, although in principle adjustable-rate mortgages could benefit both homeowners and banks, in practice, such mortgages are not used very much during periods with low interest rates.

$$\text{Inflation-adjusted principal} = \text{original principal} \times \text{ratio of inflation indexes}$$
$$= \$10,000 \times \frac{103.0}{102.0}$$
$$= \$10,000 \times 1.009804$$
$$= \$10,098.04$$

Second, we calculate your interest payment by multiplying the inflation-adjusted principal amount by the semiannual interest rate:

$$\text{Interest payment} = \text{inflation-adjusted principal} \times \text{semi-annual interest rate}$$
$$= \$10,098.04 \times \frac{0.03}{2}$$
$$= \$10,098.04 \times 0.015$$
$$= \$151.47$$

For future payments, a similar procedure is followed. For example, the second interest payment will be made on January 15, 2015. If the inflation index value is 104.0 at that time, then we can calculate the inflation-adjusted principal as

$$\text{inflation-adjusted principal} = \text{original principal} \times \text{ratio of inflation indexes}$$
$$= \$10,000 \times \frac{104.0}{102.0}$$
$$= \$10,000 \times 1.019608$$
$$= \$10,196.08$$

Your second interest payment is

$$\text{Interest payment} = \text{inflation-adjusted principal} \times \text{semiannual interest rate}$$
$$= \$10,196.08 \times \frac{0.03}{2}$$
$$= \$10,196.08 \times 0.015$$
$$= \$152.94$$

To compare these interest payments with those of a bond making a nominal interest payment, consider a calculation of the bond's past return. If we assume for simplicity that the interest rate on similar inflation-indexed securities remains 3 percent, your bond's market value should equal its inflation-adjusted principal of $10,196.08. We can then use Equation (4) in Chapter 4, with $N = 2$, $P = \$10,000$, $F_1 = \$151.47$, and $F_2 = \$152.94 + \$10,196.08 = \$10,349.02$, where the interest rate i is the semiannual interest rate (because each period is six months). Thus, we must solve this equation in terms of the nominal interest rate i to find out what interest rate on a nominal bond would give the same present value as the inflation-indexed bond. That is,

$$\$10,000 = \frac{\$151.47}{(1 + i)^1} + \frac{\$10,349.02}{(1 + i)^2}$$

We can plug this equation into a computer to find a value of i of 0.0249. Multiplying this semiannual rate by 2 to find the annual interest rate gives

$$\text{Annual nominal interest rate} = 0.0249 \times 2 = 0.0498$$
$$= 4.98 \text{ percent}$$

Thus, owning the inflation-indexed security paying a 3 percent real interest rate would yield the same return as owning a nominal security paying a 4.98 percent nominal interest rate. The advantage to the investor, however, is a reduction in risk to the real return on the financial investment.

Two practical issues make inflation-indexed securities less than ideal. First, the data on the inflation rate for the year are not known immediately, but investors do not want to wait to receive their payments. Thus, there is a slight difference in timing between what the bond pays and what the inflation rate is; the inflation adjustment is based on the consumer price index from three months earlier. Having this lag in the data allows everyone to know what their payments will be and gives the government time to calculate the payments well in advance of when they will be made. And the difference in timing is not so important because most of the inflation-indexed securities have a long time to maturity—5, 10, and 20 years.

The second issue is the way taxation is handled. To make the inflation-indexed securities comparable with securities with nominal payments in terms of how they are taxed, an investor is taxed not just on the real interest income but also on the amount that the principal value of the inflation-indexed security adjusts as compensation for inflation. The payment to compensate an investor for inflation by increasing the principal value of the security is taxable in the year in which the inflation occurs, but the security does not actually make the payment until the bond matures. Thus, if the principal value of an investor's security increases by $2,000 because of inflation, the investor is required to pay taxes on that amount before the $2,000 is even received. If this tax provision were eliminated, inflation-indexed securities would be much more attractive to investors.

Should an investor buy these inflation-indexed securities rather than similar ones that pay a fixed nominal interest rate? In principle, investors should find the inflation-indexed securities more attractive (except for the tax disadvantage discussed in the preceding paragraph) because their real return is less risky. As 16 years have now passed since such bonds were introduced, investors are now more comfortable with them, and the bonds are now held by many investors all over the world.

RECAP

1	The expected real interest rate is the nominal interest rate adjusted for expected inflation.
2	The realized real interest rate is the nominal interest rate adjusted for actual inflation.
3	When inflation is lower than expected, the realized real interest rate is higher than the expected real interest rate, so borrowers are worse off and lenders are better off.
4	When inflation is higher than expected, the realized real interest rate is lower than the expected real interest rate, so borrowers are better off and lenders are worse off.
5	Investors dislike increases in inflation because the realized real interest rate is lower than the expected real interest rate. Investors dislike uncertainty about inflation because such uncertainty increases the risk to their real return.

6-2 Real Present Value

Time (Years)	0	1	2	3	4
Payment			$108.16		

We have been using the term *real interest rate* loosely to focus on the idea that we need to adjust nominal interest rates for inflation. Now that we have established that concept, we can apply the idea to many related measures, including past return, expected return, and yield to maturity. The basis for all these measures is the present-value formula from Chapter 4. We can use the same formulas as in Chapter 4 but use real (inflation-adjusted) terms instead of dollar terms.

To express the present-value formula in real terms, all we need to do is use a real interest rate in the formula and write down all dollar amounts in inflation-adjusted terms. Here is an example from Chapter 4 to illustrate how this can be done. We calculated the present value of a payment of $108.16 in two years, which has this timeline:

To calculate the present value of this amount, we used the present-value formula for one payment received N years in the future, which is Equation (3) in Chapter 4:

$$P = \frac{F}{(1 + i)^N}$$

We plugged in the dollar amount of the future payment ($F = \$108.16$) and the rate of discount ($i = 0.04$), and calculated the present value:

$$P = \frac{\$108.16}{1.04^2} = \$100$$

Now let's run through the present-value calculation in real terms. First, we adjust the future payment

past inflation discount factor for every dollar's worth of goods and services bought at an earlier date, how much money it would take now to buy the same amount of goods and services after N years of inflation at rate π

future inflation discount factor for every dollar's worth of goods and services bought today, how much money it will take in N years to buy the same amount of goods and services when the average future inflation rate is π^e

amount for inflation. Then we use the real interest rate in place of the nominal interest rate.

To adjust the future payment amount for inflation, we need to develop an inflation discount factor that accounts for changes in the prices of goods and services over time. Suppose that the expected inflation rate is 3 percent per year for the next two years. To adjust the dollar amount of the future payment, we must figure out how much the value of one dollar changes over the two years; that is, how much would you need in two years to purchase the same amount of goods and services, on average, as $1 could buy today? To calculate this, we use the same idea of compounding that we used in Chapter 4 because prices grow at a compound rate, just as the value of financial investments do. Each year, the cost of $1 of the average good rises by the inflation rate times $1; that is, an inflation rate of 3 percent means that it takes $1 \times 0.03 = \$0.03$ more to buy the same amount of goods as before, or a total of $1.03. If the inflation rate is also 3 percent in the second year, then after two years it would take

$$\$1.03 \times \$1.03 = \$1.0609$$

to buy the same amount of goods and services as $1 could buy two years earlier. In this example, then, the real payment amount in two years equals

$$\frac{\$108.16}{\$1.0609} = \$101.95$$

Here, the expected real interest rate, according to Equation (1), is

$$r = \frac{1+i}{1+\pi^e} - 1 = \frac{1.04}{1.03} - 1 = 1.0097 - 1 = 0.0097$$

The real present value is thus

$$P = \frac{\$101.95}{(1+0.0097)^2} = \frac{\$101.95}{1.0195} = \$100$$

Note that the real present value is equal to the nominal present value. Thus, we get the same present value whether we use the formula in nominal terms or in real terms.

Moving away from the example to a more general situation, we would like to know, for every dollar's worth of goods and services bought at an earlier date, how much money it would take now to buy the same amount of goods and services after N years of inflation at rate π; that amount is the **past inflation discount factor.** Just as interest compounds, so do the prices of goods and services, so the past inflation discount factor equals

$$\text{Past inflation discount factor} = (1+\pi)^N$$

This inflation discount factor can be used in looking at past returns to see what the real return on an investment was. If an investor is considering the purchase of a security, however, the relevant inflation discount factor depends on the expected inflation rate. The **future inflation discount factor** is

$$\text{Future inflation discount factor} = (1+\pi^e)^N$$

We can divide any dollar amount received in the future by the future inflation discount factor to determine the real amount to be received.

The second adjustment that we must make to the present-value formula is to use the real interest rate in place of the nominal interest rate. Once we replace dollar amounts with real amounts, we need to discount those amounts based on a real rate of discount.

To see how the present-value formula in nominal terms is related to the present-value formula in real terms, let's look at the equation for the general form of the present-value formula in dollar terms, which is Equation (4) from Chapter 4:

$$P = \frac{F_1}{(1+i)^1} + \frac{F_2}{(1+i)^2} + \cdots + \frac{F_N}{(1+i)^N}$$

where F_1 is the dollar amount to be received in one year, F_2 is the dollar amount to be received in two years, and so on, and i is the nominal interest rate.

Now, let's divide each term on the right-hand side of this equation by the same amount on the top and the bottom, namely, by the future inflation discount factor for the appropriate number of years (although, if you wanted to calculate the past return, you would want to use the past inflation discount factor instead). We then have

$$P = \frac{F_1/(1 + \pi^e)^1}{(1 + i)^1/(1 + \pi^e)^1} + \frac{F_2/(1 + \pi^e)^2}{(1 + i)^2/(1 + \pi^e)^2} + \cdots + \frac{F_N/(1 + \pi^e)^N}{(1 + i)^N/(1 + \pi^e)^N}$$

We define some new terms that represent the future payment amounts in real terms:

$$f_1 = F_1/(1 + \pi^e)^1, f_2 = F_2/(1 + \pi^e)^2, \ldots, f_N = F_N/(1 + \pi^e)^N$$

where f_1 is the expected real payment in one year, f_2 is the expected real payment in two years, and so on. Now if we substitute $1 + r = (1 + i)/(1 + \pi^e)$ from Equation (3), we obtain the real present-value formula:

$$P = \frac{f_1}{(1 + r)^1} + \frac{f_2}{(1 + r)^2} + \cdots + \frac{f_N}{(1 + r)^N} \quad \textbf{(10)}$$

This formula can be used in the same ways as described in Chapter 4 for the nominal present-value formula. We can use the real present-value formula to find all of the following:

- The present value P of given future real amounts (the f terms) for a given expected real interest rate r
- Future real amounts (the f terms) given an expected real interest rate r and a current principal value P
- The average past return r given real income received (the f terms) and the original amount invested P
- The expected future return r given expected future income (the f terms) and the original amount invested P
- The real yield to maturity of a security r given future promised payments (the f terms) and the current price of the security P

For example, in Chapter 4 we examined a one-year security that an investor purchased for $P = \$1,000$ and which paid $F = \$1,050$ at the end of the year. The past nominal return was calculated using Equation (9) from Chapter 4:

$$\begin{aligned} i &= \frac{F}{P} - 1 \\ &= \frac{\$1,050}{\$1,000} - 1 = 0.05 = 5 \ percent \end{aligned}$$

The past nominal return of 5 percent does not really tell you everything you would like to know, however, because it does not account for inflation. To calculate the past real return, we must adjust for inflation by using Equation (10) and then solve for the value of r.

From Equation (10), with only one payment

$$P = \frac{f}{1 + r}$$

where $f = F/(1 + \pi)$. Multiplying both sides of the equation by $1 + r$, dividing both sides by P, and subtracting 1 from each side of the equation gives

$$r = \frac{f}{P} - 1 \quad \textbf{(11)}$$

Suppose that the inflation rate over the year was 4 percent. Then $f = F/(1 + \pi) = \$1,050/1.04 = \$1,009.62$. Using this in Equation (11) gives

$$\begin{aligned} r &= \frac{f}{P} - 1 \\ &= \frac{\$1,009.62}{\$1,000} - 1 = 0.00962 = 0.962 \ percent \end{aligned}$$

Thus, the nominal past return is 5 percent, but the real past return is slightly less than 1 percent. In a similar way, we can calculate expected real return or real yield to maturity on a debt security. In all cases, we just need to replace the nominal payment amounts by the real payment amounts.

RECAP

1 The present-value formula can be put into real terms by dividing nominal payments by an inflation discount factor and by using a real rate of discount.

2 The real present-value formula can be used to calculate the real past return, the real expected return, and the real yield to maturity.

6-3 What Affects Real Interest Rates?

If we could figure out what causes real interest rates to change, we could make better investment decisions. For example, if the expected real interest rate is low today, an investor would like to know if he should hold off purchasing long-term bonds until the expected real interest rate rises. We will consider two factors that may cause changes in expected real interest rates: changes in the expected inflation rate and changes in the strength of the economy over the business cycle. We will consider other factors that cause changes in real interest rates in Chapters 12 and 13, when we discuss complete macroeconomic models. Before getting to those factors, let's see how we measure real interest rates.

6-3a Measuring Real Interest Rates

To measure expected and realized real interest rates, we need data on the nominal interest rate, the actual inflation rate, and the expected inflation rate. For the first two, national averages are readily available from the Federal Reserve and government statistical agencies. Measuring the expected inflation rate is more difficult, but we can use forecasts of the future inflation rate from surveys of economists. Research has shown that these survey forecasts are useful for this purpose. With these data in hand, we can calculate both the expected real interest rate from Equation (2) and the realized real interest rate from Equation (6).

We begin by looking at real interest rates on one-year Treasury securities, for which we have data from the fourth quarter of 1968 on. We use the one-year-ahead forecast of inflation [using the gross domestic product (GDP) price index] from the *Survey of Professional Forecasters*. Subtracting the expected inflation rate from the nominal interest rate on one-year bonds gives the expected real interest rate shown in Figure 6.1. Doing the same calculation but using the actual inflation rate rather than the expected inflation rate gives us a measure of the realized real interest rate.

For much of the period shown in the graph, the expected and realized real interest rates moved together fairly closely. Those are periods in which inflation

---

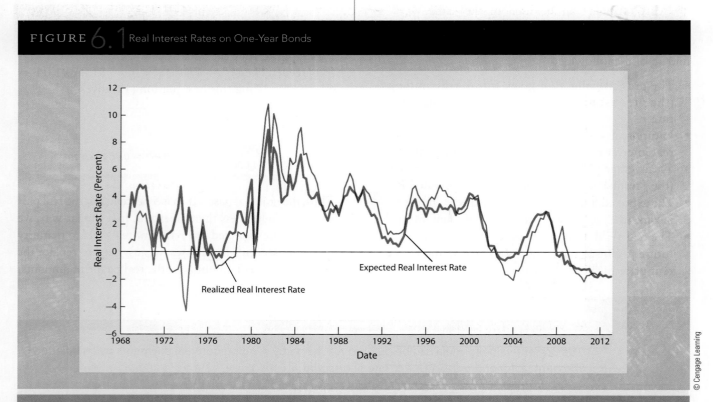

FIGURE 6.1 Real Interest Rates on One-Year Bonds

© Cengage Learning

This graph shows the expected real interest rate and realized real interest rate on Treasury securities with one year to maturity. Divergences between the two measures are sometimes quite large, as in the late 1960s and early 1970s. For much of the period, however, the expected and realized real interest rates moved together fairly closely.

forecasts were reasonably accurate because actual infla-tion matched up with expected inflation. There are a few times, however, such as the late 1960s and early 1970s, when the expected real interest rate differed substan-tially from the realized real interest rate. Note that in the period from 1972 to 1974, realized real interest rates generally were negative, but expected real interest rates were positive. This was one of the most difficult periods in U.S. economic history largely because of the rise in oil prices engineered by OPEC. Forecasters were far from the mark with their projections of inflation, and the economy was in a deep recession.

In a similar way, we can analyze real interest rates on 10-year Treasury securities (Figure 6.2). In this graph, we do not have good data on 10-year inflation forecasts until 1979, so the series on the expected real interest rate does not begin until then. The series on the realized real interest rate starts in 1968 but ends in early 2003 because we have to wait 10 years to know what actual inflation is over a 10-year horizon. For example, for a 10-year bond sold in 2006, we must wait until 2016 to find out what actual inflation was over the life of the bond. Thus, with

data only through early 2013 when this graph was cre-ated, we can compare the expected real interest rate only with the realized real interest rate from 1979 to early 2003. In that period, the realized real interest rate exceeded the expected real interest rate most of the time because the forecasters in the 1980s did not realize that inflation would be lower than it was in the 1970s, and they were slow to reduce their long-term inflation fore-casts. The result was that the actual inflation rate was much lower than the expected inflation rate, causing the realized real interest rate to be higher than the expected real interest rate. However, for 10-year bonds sold from the mid-1990s to early 2003, the expected and realized real interest rates are very similar.

Can we reach any general conclusions about real interest rates from these data? First, note that in the 1970s, real interest rates generally were very low. This may not be surprising because the economy was weak for much of the decade, especially after 1973, and we will see shortly that weak economic growth is often ac-companied by low real interest rates. In the early 1980s, real interest rates generally were quite high. Real interest

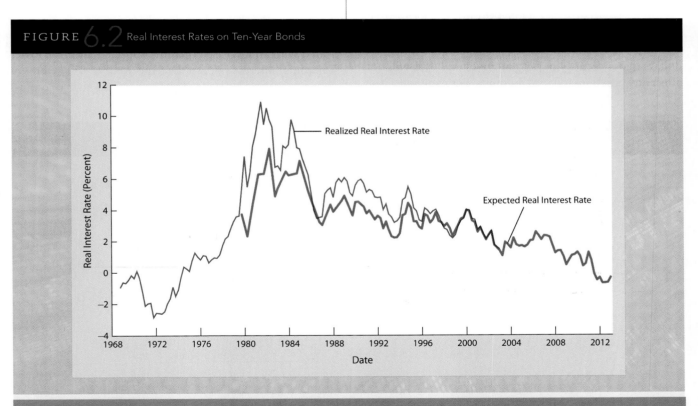

FIGURE 6.2 Real Interest Rates on Ten-Year Bonds

This graph shows the expected real interest rate and the realized real interest rate on Treasury securities with 10 years to maturity. Over the period for which the data exist for both real interest rates, the realized real interest rate is almost always higher than the expected real interest rate because actual inflation turned out to be lower than the expected inflation rate. However, since the mid-1990s, the expected real interest rate has been very similar to the realized real interest rate.

rates were stable from the mid-1980s to the late-1990s, but fluctuated dramatically in the 2000s and have been negative for much of the period since 2000.

6-3b How Do Expected Real Interest Rates React to Changes in the Expected Inflation Rate?

When the expected inflation rate changes, what happens to the expected real interest rate? Because investors and lenders base their decisions on the expected real interest rate, it seems logical that a rise in the expected inflation rate would lead to a rise in the nominal interest rate, with the expected real interest rate unchanged. This idea was stated most clearly by Irving Fisher, a Yale University economist who rose to prominence in the early 1900s. The **Fisher hypothesis** states that an increase in the expected inflation rate will cause an increase in the nominal interest rate but will not change the expected real interest rate. The idea is that if an increase in the inflation rate is fully anticipated, it will affect the dollar prices of goods and the number of dollars that a security pays to an investor, but it will not affect any inflation-adjusted amounts. For example, if the

Fisher hypothesis the argument that an increase in the inflation rate, in equilibrium, will cause an increase in the nominal interest rate but will not change the expected real interest rate

inflation rate is 3 percent instead of 2 percent, all dollar payments will be 1 percent higher. With dollar payments adjusting by the exact amount of the change in the inflation rate, real payments do not change, and neither does the expected real interest rate. In the real present-value formula [Equation (10)], the real payments do not change, so the expected real interest rate does not change.

For example, suppose that the expected real interest rate is 4 percent. If the expected inflation rate were zero, the nominal interest rate would be 4 percent. However, if the expected inflation rate were 3 percent, the nominal interest rate would be 7 percent. And if the expected inflation rate were 6 percent, the nominal interest rate would be 10 percent. In other words, for different expected inflation rates, the expected real interest rate does not change, and the nominal interest rate adjusts one-for-one with the expected inflation rate.

In earlier chapters (both Chapters 2 and 5) we plotted the supply and demand for a bond, with the price of the bond on the vertical axis, as shown in Figure 6.3a. However, since we learned in Chapter 4 that the price of a bond and the nominal interest rate are inversely related, we also could plot the supply and demand curves with the nominal interest rate on the vertical axis. The inverse relationship between the price and the interest rate, however, means that a higher price, which is associated with an increased quantity supplied, means a lower nominal interest rate, so the supply curve will be downward sloping. Similarly, a lower price (and higher nominal

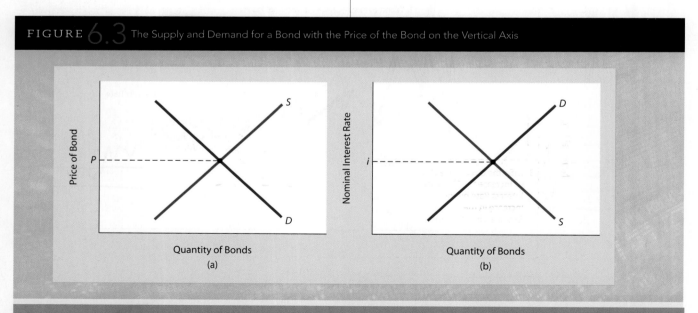

FIGURE 6.3 The Supply and Demand for a Bond with the Price of the Bond on the Vertical Axis

(a) This graph shows the supply and demand for a bond when we have plotted the price of the bond on the vertical axis. The supply curve slopes upward, and the demand curve slopes downward. **(b)** This graph shows the supply and demand for a bond when we have plotted the nominal interest rate on the vertical axis. The supply curve slopes downward, and the demand curve slopes upward.

interest rate) is associated with an increased quantity demanded, so the demand curve slopes upward. Figure 6.3b shows the relationship with an upward-sloping demand curve and a downward-sloping supply curve.

What happens if the expected inflation rate increases? A rise in the expected inflation rate would shift both the demand and supply curves up by an amount equal to the change in the expected inflation rate, so the nominal interest rate would change by the amount of the change in the expected inflation rate. In Figure 6.4, the demand for bonds is initially D^1, and the supply of bonds is initially S^1. When the expected inflation rate rises, people who demand bonds would demand the same quantity of bonds if the expected real interest rate were the same, which would occur if the demand curve shifted up by the amount of the change in the expected inflation rate. Thus, the vertical distance between the old demand curve D^1 and the new demand curve D^2 is equal to the amount by which the expected inflation rate changes. The same is true for the shift of the supply curve from S^1 to S^2. Because both demand and supply curves have shifted up by the same amount, the nominal interest rate is higher by that amount, which is the

change in the expected inflation rate. Under these conditions, the Fisher hypothesis is true.

The Fisher hypothesis suggests that changes in the expected inflation rate do not affect expected real interest rates. We saw in Figures 6.1 and 6.2, however, that the expected real interest rate changes significantly over time. The change in expected real interest rates over time does not disprove the Fisher hypothesis because other economic variables change over time, not just the expected inflation rate. For example, in periods when the inflation rate rose quickly and sharply, the expected real interest rate often rose. Look at the periods from 1973 to 1975 and from the late 1970s to early 1980s shown in Figure 6.2. As noted earlier, the rise in the inflation rate in those periods was caused by large increases in oil prices because OPEC restricted the supply of oil. These increases in oil prices caused the inflation rate to rise, but they also had many other effects on the economy, which shifted the demand and supply of bonds. As a result, expected real interest rates changed not because of the rise in the expected inflation rate but because of the impact of the oil-price shocks on the demand and supply of bonds beyond those caused by the higher inflation rate.

FIGURE 6.4 Shifts in Supply and Demand for a Bond When Expected Inflation Increases

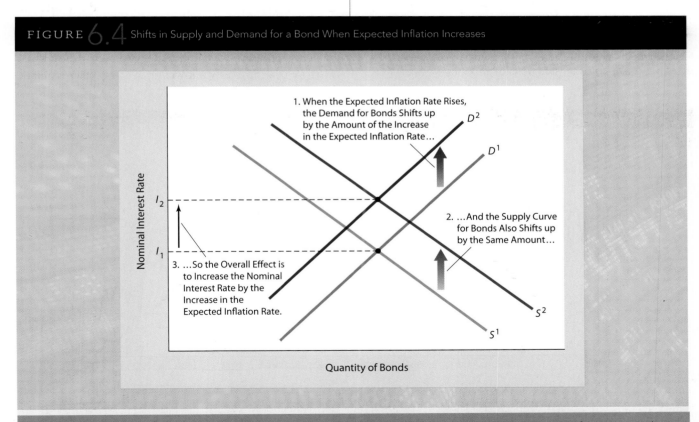

1. When the Expected Inflation Rate Rises, the Demand for Bonds Shifts up by the Amount of the Increase in the Expected Inflation Rate...

2. ...And the Supply Curve for Bonds Also Shifts up by the Same Amount...

3. ...So the Overall Effect is to Increase the Nominal Interest Rate by the Increase in the Expected Inflation Rate.

This graph shows that when the expected inflation rate rises, both demand and supply curves for bonds shift up by the amount of the increase in the expected inflation rate. The result is that the nominal interest rate also increases by that same amount, consistent with the Fisher hypothesis.

What the Fisher hypothesis really says is that nominal interest rates will adjust one for one with the expected inflation rate if the only economic variable that changes is the expected inflation rate. When there are changes in economic variables other than the expected inflation rate that affect the supply and demand for debt securities, the expected real interest rate does change.

6-3c What Happens to Expected Real Interest Rates in a Recession?

In a recession, nominal interest rates usually decline, as we saw in Chapters 2 and 5. Is the same true of expected real interest rates? Economic theory does not provide a clear answer. In a recession, we expect less borrowing because business firms are not investing in new plants and equipment. The resulting decline in the supply of debt securities should lower the expected real interest rate. However, people also may save less because their incomes decline in the recession. The resulting decline in the demand for debt securities should raise the expected real interest rate. Because demand and supply curves both shift to the left, the impact on the expected real interest rate is ambiguous.

To settle the issue of whether expected real interest rates are affected in a recession, we must look at the data because economic theory does not provide a definitive answer. Let's begin by reproducing the data on short- and long-term expected real interest rates from Figures 6.1 and 6.2 with recession bars so that we can see how the state of the business cycle affects expected real interest rates (Figure 6.5). In each of the seven recessions shown, the short-term expected real interest rate (on one-year bonds) fell sharply. In all but one recession it declined by about 4 percentage points. (The exception was the recession of 1990–1991, when the short-term expected real interest rate fell by only about 2 percentage points.) The long-term expected real interest rate (on 10-year bonds) also declined in each recession but not by as much as the short-term rate did. Thus, it appears that in recessions both demand and supply for bonds decrease, but the supply declines more than the demand, so expected real interest rates fall.

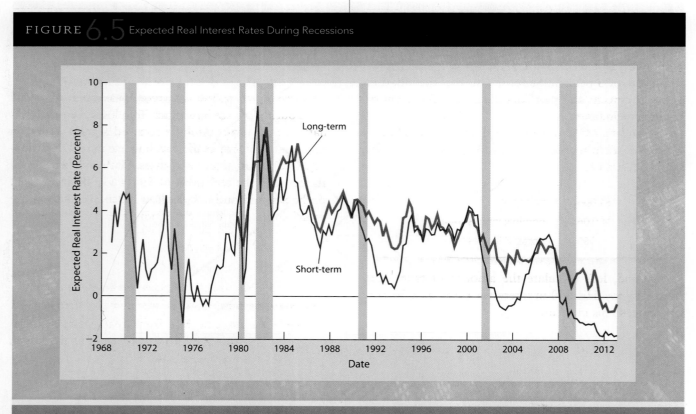

FIGURE 6.5 Expected Real Interest Rates During Recessions

This graph plots the expected real interest rates on one- and 10-year Treasury securities, with blue bars denoting periods of recession. Note that the short-term expected real interest rate declines sharply during most recessions, but the long-term expected real interest rate does not decline as much.

1 We measure real interest rates using national average data on interest rates and actual inflation plus survey data on expectations of inflation.

2 Measures of real interest rates show that they were low in the 1970s, high in the early 1980s, and stable at a moderate level since the mid-1980s.

3 According to the Fisher hypothesis, a rise in the expected inflation rate, with no other changes in the economy, will lead to a rise in the nominal interest rate, with no change in the expected real interest rate. Observing the Fisher hypothesis in the data is difficult because changes in the expected inflation rate usually are caused by changes in other economic variables that affect expected real interest rates.

4 In a recession, the expected real interest rate on short-term bonds usually declines sharply, whereas the expected real interest rate on long-term bonds does not fall as much.

How inflation and taxes reduce investors' returns

How inflation and taxes reduce investors' returns Taxes are a major concern of investors because they take a big bite out of investment returns. Inflation has particularly large effects on investors as well because of how it interacts with the tax system.

Application TO EVERYDAY LIFE

To look at the effect of taxes on interest rates, we will start with a simple example. Suppose that Tom buys a one-year debt security for $1,000 with a nominal interest rate of 6 percent. Suppose also that the inflation rate is 3 percent and that Tom must pay 30 percent of his income in taxes.

First, let's see how well Tom does in nominal (dollar) terms. At a nominal interest rate of 6 percent, he earns interest of

$1,000	principal
× 0.06	nominal interest rate
$60	nominal interest income

Second, let's calculate the amount of taxes that Tom will pay. His $60 in interest is taxed at a 30 percent rate, so his taxes are

$60	nominal interest income
× 0.30	tax rate
$18	taxes

Third, let's find out how much Tom earns in dollar terms after taxes:

$60	nominal interest income
−$18	taxes
$42	after-tax nominal interest income

Fourth, let's see how much Tom loses because of inflation. Tom might think he received a good return on his investment, but he did much worse in real (inflation-adjusted) terms than he realizes. With a 3 percent inflation rate, the real value of Tom's $1,000 investment declines significantly. To see how much, we multiply the principal amount by the inflation rate:

$1,000	principal
× 0.03	inflation rate
$30	loss of principal value because of inflation

Fifth, we can calculate Tom's real interest income, which is his nominal interest income minus the loss of principal value because of inflation:

$60	nominal interest income
−$30	loss of principal value because of inflation
$30	real interest income

Sixth, we can calculate Tom's after-tax real interest income in either of two ways. We can take his real interest income and subtract the amount of taxes he pays. Alternatively, we can take his after-tax nominal interest income and subtract the loss of principal value because of inflation. As you can see in the calculations below, both give the same figure for Tom's after-tax real interest income:

$30   real interest income
−$18   taxes
$12   after-tax real interest income

or

$42   after-tax nominal interest income
−$30   loss of principal value because of inflation
$12   after-tax real interest income

Thus, the $42 that Tom receives after taxes is really only a net gain of $12; this is his realized increase in wealth after taxes and after adjusting for inflation.

To see the end result of this exercise and what it means, let's examine where the $60 nominal interest income goes. Note that Tom receives just $12 in after-tax real interest income, the government gets $18 of tax revenue, and inflation effectively eats up $30 of Tom's income. The percentages of Tom's income that go to each are

Tom:

$$\frac{\text{After-tax real interest income}}{\text{Nominal interest income}} = \frac{\$12}{\$60} = 0.20 = 20 \ percent$$

Government:

$$\frac{\text{Taxes}}{\text{Nominal interest income}} = \frac{\$18}{\$60} = 0.30 = 30 \ percent$$

Inflation:

$$\frac{\text{Loss of principal value}}{\text{Nominal interest income}} = \frac{\$30}{\$60} = 0.50 = 50 \ percent$$

Even more alarming are the shares of Tom's real interest income:

Tom:

$$\frac{\text{After-tax real interest income}}{\text{Real interest income}} = \frac{\$12}{\$30} = 0.40 = 40 \ percent$$

Government:

$$\frac{\text{Taxes}}{\text{Real interest income}} = \frac{\$18}{\$30} = 0.60 = 60 \ percent$$

Out of Tom's $30 in real interest income, he gets 40 percent, whereas the government gets 60 percent, which means that the effective tax rate is 60 percent, not 30 percent. (adjusted for inflation)

How can the government earn more than the investor when the tax rate is only 30 percent? The government earns so much because it taxes Tom on his nominal (dollar) income rather than his real income. As a result, when we account for inflation, the effective real tax rate is much higher than the stated tax rate because the government is taxing nominal income, including income received to compensate for inflation.

This increase in the effective tax rate when inflation occurs led economist Martin Feldstein of Harvard University and the National Bureau of Economic Research (NBER), a leading authority on the effects of taxes, to argue that ". . . the interaction of existing tax rules and inflation causes a significant . . . loss even at a low rate of inflation."[1]

Feldstein argues that the effective tax rate increases with the rate of inflation, as demonstrated by the numerical example. Thus, the effective tax rate is identical to the stated tax rate only if the inflation rate is zero. For example, suppose that the inflation rate were zero and the nominal interest rate were 3 percent, with the tax rate at 30 percent. Then Tom's $1,000 would earn nominal interest income of $30, which also would be his real income. The tax rate of 30 percent would yield $9 in taxes, and Tom's after-tax income would be $21, which also would equal his after-tax real income. The government's effective real tax rate is just 30 percent (because $9/$30 = 0.30), which is the same as the stated tax rate.

Feldstein argues that the tax rules combined with inflation impose a significant cost on society. The cost arises because the higher the inflation rate, the higher the effective tax rate is, and economists have shown that higher tax rates reduce economic efficiency. Note that in our earlier example the effective tax rate was twice the stated tax rate—and that was for an inflation rate of just 3 percent! Because inflation increases the effective

[1] Martin Feldstein, "The Costs and Benefits of Going from Low Inflation to Price Stability," in *Reducing Inflation: Motivation and Strategy*, edited by Christina Romer and David Romer (Chicago: University of Chicago Press, 1997), p. 153.

tax rate, Feldstein argues, people save and invest less when inflation is high than they do when inflation is low. As a result, he suggests, even reducing inflation from a fairly low rate (2 percent) to an even lower rate (zero) would lead to a large social benefit, worth as much as 1 percent of the economy's GDP per year.

If the government's effective tax rate is double the stated tax rate when the inflation rate is just 3 percent, imagine what happens when the inflation rate is even higher. Consider some realistic numbers from the 1970s in the United States. Suppose that Tom invested $1,000 at an interest rate of 12 percent, but inflation was 10 percent, and Tom is again in the 30 percent tax bracket.

First, let's calculate Tom's income in nominal (dollar) terms. At an interest rate of 12 percent, he will earn interest of

$1,000	principal
× 0.12	nominal interest rate
$120	nominal interest income

Second, calculate the amount of taxes:

$120	nominal interest income
× 0.30	tax rate
$36	taxes

Third, calculate after-tax nominal interest income:

$120	nominal interest income
−$36	taxes
$84	after-tax nominal interest income

Fourth, calculate the loss to principal because of inflation:

$1,000	principal
× 0.10	inflation rate
$100	loss of principal value because of inflation

Fifth, Tom's real interest income is

$120	nominal interest income
−$100	loss of principal value because of inflation
$20	real interest income

Sixth, calculate Tom's after-tax real income:

$20	real interest income
−$36	taxes
−$16	after-tax real interest income

or

$84	after-tax nominal interest income
−$100	loss of principal value because of inflation
−$16	after-tax real interest income

Therefore, the $84 that Tom receives after taxes is really a net loss of $16—his wealth actually declines after taxes and after adjusting for inflation. Tom's real interest income is just $20, but he must pay taxes of $36. This means that the government is taxing his real income at a rate exceeding 100 percent!

Because increased inflation caused the effective tax rate to rise, after-tax realized real interest rates were negative in the United States and throughout the world during the 1970s. These negative realized real interest rates created a tremendous distortion in the economy, discouraging saving and investment and causing the world economy to grow more slowly than it otherwise would have grown.

To study the size of the impact of inflation on expected real interest rates, we use our analysis in the example and write it in general terms using expected inflation instead of actual inflation. Suppose that P is the principal amount invested, i is the nominal interest rate, t is the tax rate, and π^e is the expected inflation rate. Nominal interest income equals the interest rate times the principal value:

$$\textit{Nominal interest income} = i \times P$$

Taxes equal the tax rate times nominal interest income:

$$\textit{Taxes} = t \times i \times P$$

After-tax nominal interest income is nominal interest income minus taxes:

$$\textit{After-tax nominal interest income} = (i \times P) - (t \times i \times P)$$
$$= (1 - t) \times (i \times P)$$

The expected loss of principal value because of inflation is the expected inflation rate times the principal amount:

$$\text{Expected loss of principal value} = \pi^e \times P$$

After-tax expected real interest income is after-tax nominal interest income minus the expected loss of principal value because of inflation:

$$\text{After-tax expected real interest income} = [(1 - t) \times (i \times P)] - (\pi^e \times P)$$
$$= \{[(1 - t) \times i] - \pi^e\} \times P$$

The after-tax expected real interest rate is after-tax expected real interest income divided by the principal amount:

$$r_a = [(1 - t) \times i] - \pi^e \qquad \textbf{(12)}$$

Similarly, the after-tax realized real interest rate on a financial investment is

$$rr_a = [(1 - t) \times i] - \pi \qquad \textbf{(13)}$$

Notice that in Equation (12) if the nominal interest rate i and the expected inflation rate π^e rise by the same amount, as in the Fisher hypothesis, the after-tax expected real interest rate would decline as the expected inflation rate rises. Some examples are shown in Table 6.1, which also shows the expected real interest rate ($r = i - \pi^e = 3$) for comparison, using a tax rate of $t = 0.30$. Notice that each row of the table has the same

expected real interest rate, but the after-tax expected real interest rate declines as inflation rises.

You might ask: Why doesn't the interest rate adjust when expected inflation is higher to account for taxation? That is, suppose that the demand and supply curves for bonds both shift to keep the after-tax expected real interest rate unchanged. In that case, both the demand curve and the supply curve in Figure 6.3 would shift up when the expected inflation rate increased, and equilibrium would occur with an unchanged after-tax expected real interest rate. However, because the government taxes nominal interest income, this would mean a higher before-tax expected real interest rate and hence an increase in the nominal interest rate larger than the amount by which the expected inflation rate rose.

To see this, suppose that we vary the expected inflation rate as we did in Table 6.1 but now ask the question: What nominal interest rate would be needed to give the same after-tax expected real interest rate? The answers are shown in Table 6.2.

Note that in this table we see some dramatic changes. As the expected inflation rate rises, the nominal interest rate must rise much more than the increase in the expected inflation rate to maintain an unchanged after-tax expected real interest rate. In the table, each increase of the expected inflation rate by 3 percentage points leads to an increase in the expected real interest rate by about 1.3 percentage points. For example, when the expected inflation rate rises from 3.0 to 6.0 percent, the expected real interest rate rises from 4.1 to 5.4 percent, an increase of 1.3 percentage points.

To sum up, it seems likely that the demand and supply for debt securities depend more on the after-tax expected

TABLE 6.1	How the After-Tax Expected Real Interest Rate Varies with the Expected Inflation Rate When the Expected Real Interest Rate Is Constant		
Expected Real Interest Rate r	Expected Inflation Rate π^e	Nominal Interest Rate i	After-Tax Expected Real Interest Rate r_a
3.0	0.0	3.0	2.1
3.0	3.0	6.0	1.2
3.0	6.0	9.0	0.3
3.0	9.0	12.0	−0.6

Note: All interest and inflation rates are in percent. The table takes as given the data in the first two columns on the expected real interest rate r and expected inflation rate π^e and then generates values for the nominal interest rate i using Equation (2) ($i = r + \pi^e$) and the after-tax expected real interest rate r_a using Equation (12) $r_a = [(1 - t) \times i] - \pi^e$. The tax rate is $t = 0.3$.

After-Tax Expected Real Interest Rate r_a	Expected Inflation Rate π^e	Nominal Interest Rate i	Expected Real Interest Rate r
2.0	0.0	2.9	2.9
2.0	3.0	7.1	4.1
2.0	6.0	11.4	5.4
2.0	9.0	15.7	6.7

Note: All interest and inflation rates are in percent. The table takes as given the data in the first two columns on the after-tax expected real interest rate r_a and the expected inflation rate π^e. Values for the nominal interest rate i are generated using Equation (12) $[r_a = [(1 - t) \times i] - \pi^e$, so $i = \frac{r_a + \pi^e}{1 - t}]$, and the expected real interest rate r is generated using Equation (2) ($r = i - \pi^e$). The tax rate is $t = 0.3$.

real interest rate than on the before-tax expected real interest rate. The next question is: Can policymakers do something to avoid the problems caused by the interaction of inflation and taxation?

Clearly, if there were no taxes on financial investment income, there would be no distortion. Eliminating taxes on financial investment incomes, though, is not feasible without a major change in the structure of the tax system. However, two smaller changes might help:

- Modify the tax system so that taxes are imposed on real, rather than nominal, interest income.
- Reduce inflation to zero.

The tax system could be modified to tax only real financial investment income in the following way: (1) find how much a financial investment earns in dollar terms in a year, (2) multiply the inflation rate over the course of the year by the amount invested to calculate the loss of principal value because of inflation, (3) subtract the amount in part 2 from the amount in part 1 to calculate the real amount of income, and (4) multiply the amount in part 3 by the tax rate to find the amount of taxes.

This procedure to tax real interest income rather than nominal interest income eliminates the distortion from the interaction of inflation and the tax system. But there could be some practical difficulties in implementing such a tax system. First, people would have to agree on the appropriate inflation rate to use. Of the many different measures of inflation, each has some desirable properties and some undesirable properties. Second, the calculation of taxes in this new system is more complicated than the calculations in today's tax system. What if, for example, you invested money midyear or sold your financial investment midyear? This would seem to require a daily calculation of inflation, which is impossible to generate with any degree of precision. Thus, there might be some practical difficulties.

There is a second way to avoid the problem of taxes interacting with inflation: Reduce inflation to zero, and keep it there. If there were no inflation, there could be no distortion. Further, even if inflation varied a bit over time, if it averaged zero, there likely would be little distortion from the tax system.

What are the chances that our economy can achieve a zero inflation rate? Progress has been made toward that goal, in that inflation has been declining for the last two decades. If such progress continues, we may very well see an inflation rate near zero before too much longer. If inflation could be reduced to zero, we would eliminate the problem of the distortion to the economy caused by the interaction of taxation and inflation.

You might think that a third solution to the problem would be the introduction of inflation-indexed bonds. In fact, in the 1990s, the U.S. government did begin selling bonds whose dollar interest payments and principal were indexed to inflation. (See the section entitled "How Inflation-Indexed Securities Work" for more details.) As inflation occurs, the government increases the dollar value of the principal to compensate for inflation. But do these bonds prevent the interaction of taxes and inflation? Not really. They just guarantee a particular *realized* real interest rate that is identical to an *expected* real interest rate. Inflation-indexed bonds thus eliminate inflation risk from the real return on bonds, but they do not prevent the interaction of inflation and the tax system because the government still taxes the implied nominal return on the bonds, not the real return! In other words, the government compensates investors when inflation occurs but then taxes the payments that compensate investors for inflation. Thus inflation-indexed bonds are beneficial to investors because they eliminate inflation risk, but the tax system still taxes their nominal return rather than their real return. Consequently, inflation-indexed bonds fail to solve the main problem.

RECAP

1 Inflation interacts with the tax system, affecting savings and investment and thus distorting the market for debt securities.

2 One way to eliminate the distortion is for the government to modify the tax system to tax only real returns.

3 A second solution is for the Federal Reserve to reduce the inflation rate to zero.

Review Questions and Problems

Review Questions

1 Explain the difference between the expected real interest rate and the realized real interest rate. Which is more relevant for decision making? Why? Which is more relevant for determining whether a borrower or lender is better or worse off because of unexpectedly high or low inflation? Why?

2 Describe the overall movements of short- and long-term real interest rates over the past 30 years. Are real interest rates roughly constant over time?

3 What is the Fisher hypothesis? Is there convincing evidence for or against it?

4 Why do investors dislike inflation?

5 During recessions, do expected real interest rates increase or decrease? Explain why. What are the major forces acting on expected real interest rates in recessions?

6 How does inflation interact with the tax system to affect the after-tax expected real interest rate?

7 Under what circumstances does the effective tax rate on real interest income differ from the government's stated tax rate? Why does it differ?

8 Explain how the expected real interest rate must adjust when the expected inflation rate changes if market conditions are such that the after-tax expected real interest rate is unchanged.

9 Describe two ways the government could eliminate the interaction of inflation with the tax system.

10 Why don't inflation-indexed bonds eliminate the interaction of inflation with the tax system?

Numerical Exercises

11 In each of the following situations, explain whether borrowers or lenders are worse off, better off, or equally well off because of unexpected inflation.

  a Expected inflation one year ago was 4 percent; actual inflation over the year turned out to be 7 percent.

  b Expected inflation one year ago was 5 percent; actual inflation over the year turned out to be 3 percent.

  c The nominal interest rate on a loan was 8 percent; the expected real interest rate on the loan was 4 percent; actual inflation over the year turned out to be 3 percent.

  d The nominal interest rate on a loan was 8 percent; the expected real interest rate on the loan was 5 percent; actual inflation over the year turned out to be 3 percent.

12 Suppose that the demand for and supply of bonds both change with the state of the business cycle. In economic expansions, the demand for bonds is given by the equation

$$D = 200 + 2{,}000r$$

and the supply of bonds is

$$S = 500 - 1{,}000r$$

where r is the expected real interest rate. In recessions, however, both the demand for and supply of bonds is lower:

$$D = 150 + 2{,}000r$$
$$S = 300 - 1{,}000r$$

  a Given these equations, what is the equilibrium expected real interest rate in economic expansions?

  b Given these equations, what is the equilibrium expected real interest rate in recessions?

  c If the expected inflation rate is 4 percent in economic expansions, what is the equilibrium nominal interest rate in economic expansions?

  d If the expected inflation rate is 2 percent in recessions, what is the equilibrium nominal interest rate in recessions?

13 Suppose that the Fisher hypothesis holds for an economy that has an expected real interest rate of 2 percent. For each of the expected inflation rates of 0, 2, 4, 6, and 8 percent, calculate the nominal interest rate and the after-tax expected real interest rate if the tax rate is 30 percent.

14 Suppose that conditions in the economy are such that the after-tax expected real interest rate is described by the equation

$$r_a = a \times g$$

where a is a number that depends on how people value their consumption in one period compared with another period, and g is the growth rate of

(continued)

the economy. The number *a* equals 1 when people prefer consumption to be balanced, with the same amount of consumption each period; *a* may be bigger than 1 when people prefer consumption today over consumption in the future, with *a* being larger and larger the more impatient people are.

a Suppose that $a = 2$, $g = 0.02$, the inflation rate is expected to be steady at $\pi = 0.03$, and the tax rate is 0.40. What are the values of the equilibrium nominal interest rate and the before-tax expected real interest rate?

b Beginning with the situation in part a, if the growth rate of the economy increases to 0.04, what are the new values of the equilibrium nominal interest rate and the before-tax expected real interest rate?

c Beginning with the situation in part a, if the tax rate in the economy is reduced to 0.25, what are the new values of the equilibrium nominal interest rate and the before-tax expected real interest rate?

d Beginning with the situation in part a, if the expected inflation rate declines to 0.01, what are the new values of the equilibrium nominal interest rate and the before-tax expected real interest rate?

e From these results, what general conclusions can you draw about the relationship between the nominal interest rate and the rate of economic growth, the tax rate, and the inflation rate? What about the relationship between the before-tax expected real interest rate and the rate of economic growth, the tax rate, and the inflation rate?

15 Hans lives in a country that taxes only real interest income. When Hans calculates his taxes at the end of the year, he writes down on a form how much he invested and multiplies that amount times the inflation rate for the year to arrive at his "inflation compensation amount." Hans subtracts the inflation compensation amount from his interest income to find his taxable interest income.

a In 2013, Hans invested C40,000 and earned C2,000 in interest income, where C stands for "credits," which is the monetary unit of the country in which Hans lives. If the inflation rate in 2013 was 4 percent and Hans pays taxes equal to 25 percent of his income, how much will Hans pay in income tax on his interest income? What is Hans's before-tax realized real interest rate? His after-tax realized real interest rate?

b In 2014, Hans invested C50,000 and earned C5,000 in interest income. If the inflation rate in 2014 was 6 percent (and Hans still has a tax rate of 25 percent), how much will Hans pay in income tax on his interest income? What is Hans's before-tax realized real interest rate? His after-tax realized real interest rate?

c Suppose that Hans had to pay taxes on his nominal interest income instead of his real interest income. Repeat the analysis in parts a and b under this assumption. Does it make much difference if taxes are based on nominal income instead of real income?

Analytical Problems

16 An alternative type of mortgage loan is called a price-level-adjusted mortgage (PLAM), which sets all mortgage payments and the principal amount of the mortgage in real rather than nominal terms. Thus, if the inflation rate was 10 percent in a certain year, the monthly payment would be increased by 10 percent in dollar terms, and the principal value of the mortgage loan also would be increased by 10 percent in dollar terms. Who gains from this type of mortgage: the homeowner or the bank or both? Explain. Who bears the inflation risk?

17 Suppose that both the supply and demand for bonds depended only on the after-tax expected real interest rate, which is independent of the expected inflation rate. What is the effect of higher expected inflation on the bond market? (*Hint:* Because taxes are imposed on nominal interest income, bond demanders pay the tax, and bond suppliers have their taxes reduced by an equal amount because they can deduct the interest expense.) How does the amount of tax paid change when actual inflation is higher than expected inflation? Who gains and who loses from inflation?

18 When inflation is unexpectedly high, the stock prices of banks usually decline sharply. Can you explain why?

19 Why would anyone lend money if there were a negative after-tax expected real interest rate?

Appendix 6.A

Deriving Equation (1) for the Expected Real Interest Rate

Consider someone with principal of $P = \$1,000$ who buys a one-year bond paying a nominal interest rate of $i = 6$ percent. In one year, the person earns interest of $P \times i = \$1,000 \times 0.06 \times \$60$. The total amount that the person has after one year is $(1 + i) \times P = 1.06 \times \$1,000 = \$1,060$.

Now, let's think about how many goods and services those dollars can buy. Suppose that there is only one good in the economy, which costs $100 when the person purchases the bond and is expected to cost $103 after one year. In general, think of the price evel as $CPI_1 = 100$ at the beginning of the year and expected $CPI_2 = 103$ at the end of the year. At the beginning of the year, the person could use the $1,000 to buy 10 goods because $P/CPI_1 = \$1,000/100 = 10$ goods. At the end of the year, after earning interest,the person expects to buy 10.29 goods because $(1 + i) \times P/CPI_2 = \$1,060/103 = 10.29$ goods.

We will now translate this increase in the number of goods that the investor expects to purchase after one year into an expected real interest rate. Notice that in this situation the expected inflation rate equals 3 percent because the price of the good is expected to rise from $100 to $103. Thus the expected inflation rate is $\pi^e = (103 - 100)/100 = 0.03 = 3$ percent. In general terms, using the consumer price index (CPI), we would define the expected inflation rate as $\pi^e = (CPI_2 - CPI_1)/CPI_1 = CPI_2/CPI_1 - 1$. Note that $1 + \pi^e = CPI_2/CPI_1$, a fact that we will use in a moment.

At the end of the year, the investor expects to buy 10.29 goods, compared with 10 goods at the beginning of the year. Thus, the expected real interest rate is the percentage increase in the number of goods that can be purchased, which is $(10.29 - 10)/10 = 0.029 = 2.9$ percent. In equation terms, this amount equals

$$r = \frac{\{[(1 + i)P]/CPI_2\} - (P/CPI_1)}{P/CPI_1} = \frac{1 + i}{CPI_2/CPI_1} - 1 = \frac{1 + i}{1 + \pi^e} - 1$$

The following breakdown might be easier to follow:

	The Example in Dollars	Matching Equation
Principal:	$1,000	P
Nominal interest rate:	0.06 = 6 percent	i
Interest:	$1,000 × 0.06 = $60	$P \times i$
Total dollar amount after one year:	$1,000 + $60 = $1,060 = $1,000 × 1.06	$(1 + i) \times P$
Number of goods that can be purchased each year:	Price in year 1 = $100/good	CPI_1
	Expected price in year 2 = $103/good	CPI_2
	In year 1, $1,000 buys $1,000/100 = 10 goods	P/CPI_1
	In year 2, $1,060 buys $1,060/103 = 10.29 goods	$(1 + i) \times P/CPI_2$
Expected inflation rate:	$\pi^e = (103 - 100)/100$ $= 0.03 = 3$ percent	$\pi^e = (CPI_2 - CPI_1)/CPI_1$ $= CPI_2/CPI_1 - 1$ Note that $1 + \pi^e = CPI_2/CPI_1$
Percentage increase in the number of goods you can buy:	$\dfrac{10.29 - 10}{10} = 0.029$ $= 2.9$ percent	$r = \dfrac{\{[(1 + i)P]/CPI_2\} - (P/CPI_1)}{P/CPI_1}$ $= \dfrac{1 + i}{CPI_2/CPI_1} - 1 = \dfrac{1 + i}{1 + \pi^e} - 1$

Scott Eells/Bloomberg/Getty Images

STOCKS and OTHER ASSETS

Stock prices are the focus of most business news and a yardstick for measuring the success of corporations.

Nearly half of all Americans now own stock, but few people understand what determines the return on financial investment in the stock market.

In early 2013, as the market rose to record levels, some economists argued that stocks were overvalued—that stock prices were too high and were likely to fall. But what determines the level of stock prices? How do analysts determine when the market is overvalued? And how can investors decide where to invest? Answering these questions requires an understanding of the efficiency of stock markets, how stock prices reflect corporate earnings, how interest rates affect stock prices, and how people's attitudes toward risk change over time. The answers are important to policymakers as well because movements in the stock market are likely to affect the economy.

In this chapter we examine how the stock market works, the major influences on stock prices and returns, and data on stock prices and returns over time since 1875. Next, we look at whether investors can follow profitable financial investment strategies. We close the chapter with an application to everyday life to show how an investor should compare stocks with other financial investments, such as bonds or real estate.

7-1 The Stock Market

It is almost impossible to listen to the TV business news or to read the financial section of a daily paper without hearing how the stock market performed that day or finding out how events affected the stock price of a particular company. Why are people so interested in the stock market?

The stock market is the clearest barometer of the economy's health. Stock prices reflect the optimism or pessimism of investors. When stock prices are high, most people enjoy economic prosperity.

7-1a Issuing and Investing in Stock

Corporations issue stock because they want to raise funds to invest in capital improvements such as new equipment or production facilities (investment in physical capital). People invest in stock because they want to own a piece of the corporation, thus making a claim on the profits of the firm (financial investment). The investors benefit when the firm pays dividends or when the firm's stock rises price. (Of course, they lose when the stock declines price.)

Investors who own stock in a corporation are called **shareholders** or **stockholders,** which means that they are part owners of the firm. Shareholders are entitled to receive any dividends paid by the firm, and they have the right to vote on key decisions affecting the corporation, especially choosing its board of directors. The board of directors, in turn, chooses the management team of the corporation, headed by the president or chief executive officer (CEO) and the chief financial officer (CFO). If shareholders do not like what the management team of the firm is doing, they can ask the board of directors to request a change in the firm's strategy or to change the management team. If shareholders remain unsatisfied, they may elect a new board of directors. Alternatively, shareholders may decide to sell their shares to other investors.

A shareholder who no longer wants to own stock in a particular company must find another investor to sell the stock to. To facilitate the sales and purchases of stock between investors, stock exchanges exist. Simply put, a **stock exchange,** or **stock market,** is a place where people buy or sell stocks. There are a large number of stock exchanges, although we focus on the largest and most well-known. Some stock exchanges exist as physical places, as is true of the New York Stock Exchange, which is located in a building in lower Manhattan. Other stock exchanges do not have a fixed physical location, such as the National Association of Securities Dealers Automated Quotation (NASDAQ) stock exchange, which exists through a network of computers.

Because there are thousands of corporations, each with its own stock price, analyzing whether stock prices are rising or falling in general requires some way of averaging. Averaging stock prices is accomplished through the use of stock indexes. A **stock index** is a number that represents the average price of a collection of stocks. Some of the best known indexes are the Dow Jones Industrial Average (the Dow), the Standard & Poor's 500 (the S&P 500), the Russell 2000, and the Wilshire 5000, each of which represents the average price of its group. The Dow represents the average price of 30 major industrial companies. The S&P 500 covers 500 major companies in the country, including those in the Dow plus 470 others. The Russell 2000 index measures the average stock price of 2,000 small firms. The Wilshire 5000 (a misleading name because it really consists of over 6,500 stocks of companies of all different sizes) shows the average price of the broadest collection of stocks in any index because it includes every company with U.S. headquarters whose stock price is available and whose stock trades in the United States. There are many indexes for various segments of the market (for example, stock in financial companies), so an

shareholders investors who own stock in a corporation; also called **stockholders**

stock exchange a place where people buy or sell stocks; also called a **stock market**

stock index the average price of a collection of stocks

The existence of a strong secondary market for stocks is vital to the health of corporations. In this photo, top Facebook managers, including founder and CEO Mark Zuckerberg, celebrate Facebook's initial public offering of stock on the NASDAQ exchange in 2012. Corporate executives maintain strong relationships with stock exchanges and market traders.

mutual fund an investment company that pools the funds of many investors and buys a large number of different stocks (or other securities)

index fund a mutual fund that tries to mimic a stock index, such as the S&P 500

investor can readily find out how stocks in any particular sector are doing or how a particular stock is doing compared with other stocks in the same sector.

Indexes of stock prices may be misleading because they do not provide information on dividends, which are needed for calculating the total return. For example, if the Dow rose 3 percent in a year, you might not think that you received a very good return. But if those stocks paid dividends of 2 percent, your total return would be 5 percent, much better than you thought just looking at the rise in the index. Table 7.1 gives you some recent data on

the total returns to the four different indexes that we have been discussing.

In general, stock indexes move in the same direction at the same time. But the different indexes show quite different total returns. For example, there are clearly periods when the stocks in the S&P 500 significantly outperformed those in the Dow (2012) or when the Russell 2000 stocks outperformed those in the S&P 500 (2010).

Many investors would like to own a number of different stocks so that their financial investments will be diversified, but they may have neither the resources nor the interest in picking individual stocks. Such investors benefit by investing through a **mutual fund,** which is an investment company that pools the funds of many investors and buys a large number of different stocks (or other securities). Mutual funds exist to help investors diversify at low cost.

Many large investment companies offer a wide variety of mutual funds. Each is run by a different set of investment managers, and each may have slightly different objectives, catering to the needs of different investors. Some mutual funds, known as **index funds,** try to mimic a stock index, such as the S&P 500. Because of transactions costs, their returns may differ from those of the index, but not by more than 1 percentage point and often by much less than that. For example, over the decade from March 2003 to March 2013, the Vanguard 500 Index Fund Investor Shares fund had an average annual return just 0.11 percent below that of the S&P 500 index.

7-1b An Investor's View of Stock Returns and Prices

Investors care about making profits on their stock investments. They want to buy stocks that are going to provide them with higher returns than other stocks. Thus, they would like to own stocks that pay high

TABLE 7.1	Total Returns on Stock Indexes (in percent)				
	Year				
Index	**2008**	**2009**	**2010**	**2011**	**2012**
Dow Jones Industrial Average	−31.9	+22.7	+14.1	+8.4	+10.2
S&P 500	−37.0	+26.5	+15.1	+2.1	+16.0
Russell 2000	−33.8	+27.2	+26.9	+2.1	+16.4
Wilshire 5000	−37.2	+28.6	+17.5	+1.1	+16.4

© Cengage Learning

dividends or whose prices are likely to rise more than other stocks. To do so, investors need to understand how dividends are set and what determines a stock's price. Both dividend payments and a firm's stock price depend on the profits the firm earns today and is likely to earn in the future.

A share of stock gives an investor partial ownership of the corporation that issued the stock. The stockholder has the right to vote on key issues at an annual meeting, including approval of the firm's board of directors. Through the board of directors, the stockholders tell the company's management team what to do.

Most investors, of course, do not own stock in order to control the company but rather because they think that the firm will be profitable in the future. Their ownership stake entitles them to a share of those profits. When a firm earns profits, stockholders benefit in two ways. First, the firm may pay out part of its profits to shareholders in the form of dividends. Second, the firm may retain some of the profits to use for investing in new capital improvements and equipment, generating more profits in the future. Higher future profits will cause investors to bid up the stock's price.

Thus, there are two parts of an investor's total return from owning stock in a company: the dividend yield (equivalent to current yield, as we discussed in Chapter 2) and the capital-gains yield.

The dividend yield on stock is the amount of dividends received over the period D_t divided by the price of the stock at the end of the previous period P_{t-1}:

$$\text{Dividend yield} = \frac{D_t}{P_t}$$

The period here could be a day, a week, a month, a quarter, or a year. Because most firms pay dividends once each quarter, we usually analyze the returns to a stock on a quarterly or sometimes an annual basis. For example, General Electric (GE) stock might pay a dividend of $0.20 per share on March 31, June 30, September 30, and December 31. Adding the four dividend payments together, we see that a GE shareholder would have received $0.80 in dividends for the year. Thus, if GE's price was $40 per share on December 31 of the prior year, then for the first quarter (from January through March), GE's dividend yield was

$$\text{First-quarter dividend yield} = \frac{D_t}{P_{t-1}} = \frac{\$0.20}{\$40} = 0.005 = 0.5 \text{ percent}$$

For the year as a whole, GE's dividend yield was

$$\text{Annual dividend yield} = \frac{D_t}{P_{t-1}} = \frac{\$0.80}{\$40} = 0.02 = 2.0 \text{ percent}$$

The capital-gains yield on the stock is the percentage increase in the price of the stock:

$$\text{Capital-gains yield} = \frac{P_t - P_0}{P_0}$$

Suppose that GE's price rose from $40 per share on December 31, 2012, to $45 per share on March 31, 2013, and then ended the year at $50 per share on December 31, 2013. For the first quarter, GE's capital-gains yield was

$$\text{First-quarter capital-gains yield} = \frac{P_t - P_{t-1}}{P_{t-1}} = \frac{\$45 - \$40}{\$40} = 0.125 = 12.5 \text{ percent}$$

For the year as a whole (from January to December), GE's capital-gains yield was

$$\text{Annual capital-gains yield} = \frac{P_t - P_{t-1}}{P_{t-1}} = \frac{\$50 - \$40}{\$40} = 0.25 = 25.0 \text{ percent}$$

The total return to the stock equals the dividend yield plus the capital-gains yield, so the total return to the stock is

$$\text{Total return} = \frac{D_t}{P_{t-1}} + \frac{P_t - P_{t-1}}{P_{t-1}} \qquad \textbf{(1)}$$

In our GE example, the total return for the first quarter is

$$\text{First-quarter total return} = \frac{D_t}{P_{t-1}} + \frac{P_t - P_{t-1}}{P_{t-1}} = 0.005 + 0.125 = 0.13 = 13.0 \text{ percent}$$

For the year as a whole, the total return is

$$\text{Annual total return} = \frac{D_t}{P_{t-1}} + \frac{P_t - P_{t-1}}{P_{t-1}} = 0.02 + 0.25 = 0.27 = 27.0 \text{ percent}$$

Just as we did in the case of debt securities, we can compare the total return that an investor expects to earn (the expected total return) with the total return the investor actually earns (the realized total return). However, as we will see later in this chapter and in the next one, the returns to stocks are very uncertain because capital gains change so much from year to year (or sometimes from day to day). As a result, when we examine the returns to stock, we generally look at realized total returns. Only when we examine a very long run investment period do we focus on expected total returns.

How investors view dividends. An investor wants to get the highest total return on a financial investment, so when a firm earns profits, it seems natural that an investor should want to receive some of those profits in the form of dividends. Should an investor care about how much of a firm's profits she receives in the form of dividends as opposed to how much the firm retains for investment in physical capital? There are advantages and disadvantages for investors when firms distribute their profits as dividends. One advantage of receiving dividends is that the investor receives some of the cash flow generated by the firm directly, which may be important to investors who need money for living expenses. If the firm retains the profits instead of paying out dividends, the price of the stock should rise, so the investor could sell some of her shares to get cash. Selling shares, however, especially in small quantities, may be inconvenient and costly. (On the other hand, some investors find dividends annoying because they must then decide how to reinvest the dividends; to help out, some companies offer dividend reinvestment plans that automatically invest the dividends in new shares of stock.) A second advantage of receiving dividends is that because the firm must pay out some dividends, the firm must generate sufficient cash flow to make the dividend payment. Such dividend payments reassure investors that the firm is profitable and that it remains relatively healthy. A firm that pays no dividends might squander resources and hide losses from investors.

Despite these advantages of receiving dividends, one major disadvantage looms much larger: taxes. When an investor receives dividends, he must pay taxes on them (unless the investor owns the stock in a tax-advantaged account (an IRA or 401(k) plan) on which taxes need not be paid until retirement when payouts from the retirement fund are received). However, if the price of the stock rises because the firm earns profits and does not pay dividends, the investor gets an equal increase in (pretax) wealth but may pay fewer taxes (or no taxes at all) and thus is better off. Recent increases in tax rates on wealthier taxpayers may encourage firms to minimize their dividend payments, to reduce the tax burden on their shareholders.

How capital-gains taxes lead to the lock-in effect. In addition to paying taxes on dividends, investors also must pay taxes on their realized capital gains. Realized capital gains are taxed, but implicit capital gains are not. **Realized capital gains** are profits that an investor receives by actually selling stock. **Implicit capital gains** are those that have been accrued but not yet realized—they are paper profits. If I buy GE stock at a price of $20 per share, and the price subsequently rises to $30, I have earned $10 per share in implicit capital gains. Only when I sell the stock are those capital gains realized and subsequently taxed.

The favorable tax treatment of implicit capital gains encourages stockholders to keep their stocks for a long time. This tax policy thus reduces the efficiency of the stock market, for it forces investors, in deciding which stocks to own, to consider not just which stocks will provide the greatest returns but also whether they can avoid capital-gains taxes by holding stock longer. This problem is known as the **lock-in effect** because investors who own stock that has appreciated significantly feel locked into holding that stock forever.

Consider the following example. Suppose that Andrea bought stock in IBM a few years ago at $20 per share, after which it rose over time to $50. Now Andrea thinks that IBM's price will rise only 10 percent in the coming year, whereas GE's price, currently at $50, will rise by 15 percent because GE's profits will increase in coming years. If Andrea did not have to worry about capital-gains taxes, she would sell her IBM stock immediately and buy GE stock. She would expect to profit by earning an extra 5 percent (or $2.50 per share) by owning GE instead of IBM.

realized capital gains profits that an investor receives by actually selling stock

implicit capital gains capital gains that have been accrued but not yet realized

lock-in effect the idea that investors who own stock that has appreciated significantly feel locked into holding that stock forever to avoid paying capital-gains taxes

Suppose, however, that Andrea faces a 15 percent tax rate on her capital gains. If she sells her IBM stock today, she must pay taxes of 15 percent on her capital gains of $30, which comes to $4.50 per share. The $4.50 per share to be paid in taxes outweighs the $2.50 gain from buying stock in the company with the higher return. Thus, Andrea is locked into keeping her IBM stock.

The lock-in effect is worrisome to economists because it prevents stocks from being priced efficiently. If there were no lock-in effect, investors would change their portfolios, increasing the supply of IBM stock and the demand for GE stock, so the price of IBM stock would fall and the price of GE stock would rise. But the lock-in effect may reduce trading in both stocks, and so stock prices may not be based solely on investors' perceptions of the profitability of different corporations. The market then may reflect distorted information about companies' prospects. The lock-in effect was reduced in 2003 when federal tax law was changed to make the maximum tax rate on capital gains on stock (held for at least one year) equal to 15 percent, which is less than one-half the tax rate imposed on other income of taxpayers in the top tax bracket. However, for very high income earners (taxable income exceeding $400,000 for a single taxpayer or $450,000 for married couples filing jointly), the capital-gains tax rate was increased to 20 percent in 2013.

How inflation affects stock returns. A macroeconomic variable that has a major effect on investors' stock returns is inflation. Investors do not care about how much they earn in dollars—they care about how much they can buy with those dollars. Thus, to see what an investor earns from investing in stock, we need to subtract the inflation rate from the investor's after-tax total return.

We examined the after-tax real interest rate in Chapter 6. A parallel treatment for stocks can be developed but is slightly more complicated because taxes need to be paid only on realized capital gains, not implicit capital gains. However, the same principles apply to stocks as they did to debt securities.

To illustrate how much taxes and inflation matter, consider again the example in which an investor purchased GE stock at a price of $40, received dividends of $0.80 per share, and sold the stock at the end of the year for $50 per share. Ignoring taxes and inflation, we calculated a return of 27.0 percent. Now suppose that the inflation rate is 5 percent and that the tax rate on both dividends and capital gains is 15 percent (or 0.15).

For each share of GE stock that the investor purchased, her dividend income is $0.80 per share and her capital gains are

$$\text{Capital gains} = \text{sale price} - \text{purchase price}$$
$$= \$50 - \$40 = \$10$$

Thus her total income (dividends plus capital gains) is $0.80 + $10.00 = $10.80. Her taxes on those dividends and capital gains are

$$\text{Taxes} = \text{tax rate} \times \text{income from dividends and capital gains}$$
$$= 0.15 \times \$10.80 = \$1.62$$

After-tax income per share equals

$$\text{After-tax income} = \text{dividends} + \text{capital gains} - \text{total taxes}$$
$$= \$0.80 + \$10.00 - \$1.62 = \$9.18$$

The loss of principal value to inflation equals

$$\text{Loss of principal value to inflation} = \text{inflation rate} \times \text{principal value}$$
$$= 0.05 \times \$40.00 = \$2.00$$

The investor's after-tax real income equals

$$\text{After-tax real income} = \text{after-tax income} - \text{loss of principal value to inflation}$$
$$= \$9.18 - \$2.00 = \$7.18$$

The investor's after-tax real return is her after-tax real income as a percentage of her principal:

$$\text{After-tax real return} = \frac{\text{after-tax real income}}{\text{principal}}$$
$$= \frac{\$7.18}{\$40.00} = 0.1795 = 17.95 \text{ percent}$$

Thus, the return of 27.00 percent is cut substantially to 17.95 percent once we account for taxes and inflation. Therefore, an investor needs to examine the effect that taxes and inflation have on the return because the difference between pretax nominal returns and after-tax real returns may be substantial.

TABLE 7.2	Alternative Stock Investment Strategies			
Return		**Average Annual Return**	**Return Minus Costs**	**Return Minus Costs and Taxes**
Strategy A Index fund: lower return lower capital gains, less trading		6.2%	5.9%	5.5%
Strategy B Mutual fund: higher return, higher capital gains, more trading		8.3%	6.6%	5.3%

How investors can boost stock returns by reducing taxes and transactions costs. Investors can improve their after-tax real returns if they carefully determine their financial investment strategy based on their tax rates and costs of trading, determining how much and how often to buy and sell stocks.

To see how much the trading strategy matters, suppose that we compare the returns available to several different financial investment strategies. Strategy A is to invest in an S&P 500 index fund that receives dividends from the stocks it owns but does not realize many capital gains. An investor receives dividends from the index fund each year, from which he pays taxes and reinvests the rest. Strategy B is to invest in a mutual fund that not only has higher returns than an index fund, but also has higher costs, and realizes more capital gains each year. Suppose that the investor's tax rate on dividends and capital gains is 15 percent. Suppose that transactions costs are 0.25 percent for the index fund and 1.5 percent for the mutual fund. Suppose also that the mutual fund gives the investor capital gains that are 2 percent higher each year than the index fund. We will use the actual returns to the S&P 500 from 1972 to 2012 to evaluate the results, which are shown in Table 7.2.

Comparing just the average annual return is quite misleading. Accounting for costs reduces the returns substantially, more so for strategy B than for strategy A. But the impact of taxes is even larger than that of costs. The average return is substantially lower after we include both transactions costs and taxes. Thus, an investor can boost his return by minimizing transactions costs and avoiding taxes. Avoiding taxes can be done by investing in a tax-favored account, such as a retirement plan, or simply by not buying or selling stocks very much (a great benefit of index funds or mutual funds that mainly buy stocks and hold them), thus avoiding capital-gains taxes and transactions costs. This strategy suggests that investors avoid strategies that require a lot of buying and selling.

7-1c Historical Returns and Stock Prices

For investors to make informed choices, they need to know how stocks have fared as an investment in the past. Therefore, now that we have considered some of the issues relevant to investors in the stock market (for example, dividend payments, capital gains, inflation, and taxes), we look at the data on stock returns and the movements of stock prices over time. Because the role of dividends has been changing in recent years, it makes sense for us to focus not on dividends but on a firm's earnings (or profits). After all, a firm's earnings are the fundamental source of value to a stockholder. In addition, we are going to focus on the stock market as a whole rather than on an individual stock or a small portfolio of stocks because research in the field of finance has shown that most investors would do best if they owned shares of a mutual fund with many stocks in it.

For similar reasons, the risk of any particular stock to an investor cannot be viewed in isolation but must be related to the investor's other stocks. If an investor owns stock in three different companies, including one in the computer industry, adding stock in Apple is going to increase her risk because she is already sensitive to the risks in the computer industry. However, if she owns stock in 50 different companies, none of which are in the computer industry, adding stock in Apple could reduce her risk because doing so increases the diversification of her portfolio.

When an investor is well diversified, the risk she faces is basically the risk that the entire stock market will rise or fall. For the remainder of this section, therefore, we will keep our analysis simple by assuming that investors diversify completely by buying a piece of the entire stock market through an index fund that tracks the S&P 500 index.

How would an investment in such a mutual fund have fared historically? The answer can be seen in Figure 7.1, which shows the level of stock prices in January each year from 1875 to 2013, as measured by the S&P 500

FIGURE 7.1 Real Stock Prices, January 1875 to January 2013

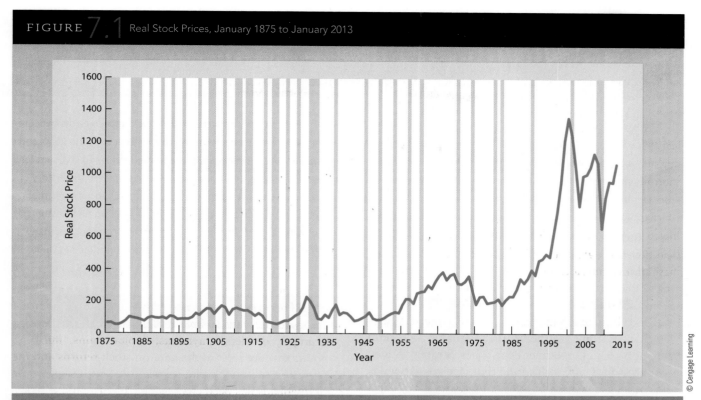

This graph shows the level of stock prices in January each year from 1875 to 2013, as measured by the S&P 500 index (prior to 1957, the S&P composite index), adjusted for inflation. Vertical blue bars denote recessions. The graph shows that inflation-adjusted stock prices are volatile, going through long periods in which they rise and other long periods in which they are stagnant or decline.

index (prior to 1957, it was the S&P composite index and had only 90 stocks, not 500), adjusted for inflation. The graph shows that inflation-adjusted stock prices are volatile. After peaking in 1906, the market declined, falling to about one-third its 1906 value by 1921. In the 1920s, stock prices rose sharply, peaking in 1929 at about four times their level in 1920. The stock market crash in October 1929 and the Great Depression, however, kept the level of stock prices below their 1929 level until 1959. Thus, an investor who had purchased stock in 1929 would have had a negative or zero real capital gain on her stock for 30 years! In 1948, just after World War II, the stock market's inflation-adjusted value was about 40 percent of its value in 1929. As the postwar period progressed, stock prices rose, especially as corporate profits grew in the 1950s and early 1960s.

However, by the mid-1960s, the stock market began to stagnate and then dropped sharply in the deep recession of 1973 to 1975, falling nearly 50 percent in two years. In fact, after peaking in 1966, it took the market 24 years to return to the level it reached that year. Inflation-adjusted stock prices began to appreciate in 1983, and they continued to do so for the following two decades. They increased sharply in the late 1990s (from

1995 to 2000), with an average increase of 23 percent each year, but fell substantially in 2001 and 2002, before rebounding from 2003 to 2007. (For more on the run-up of stock prices in the late 1990s and the decline in the early 2000s, see the Data Bank box "The Explosion of Tech Stocks in the Late 1990s and Their Implosion in the Early 2000s.") But the financial crisis of 2008 caused real stock prices to decline 39 percent from January 2008 to January 2009. Stock prices rose substantially in 2009, 2010, and 2012, but in January 2013 they were still 6 percent below their peak in January 2007.

The overall message of Figure 7.1 is that inflation-adjusted stock prices change dramatically over time, going through long periods in which they rise and other long periods in which they decline or stagnate. The blue recession bars in the graph show that declines in stock prices are closely associated with downturns in the economy.

Of course, investors do not care about the level of stock prices themselves; they care about the total return. By using data on the dividend yield and adjusting for inflation, we can calculate the real return to the S&P 500, as shown in Figure 7.2. (Unfortunately, we cannot easily calculate the after-tax return because investors have different tax rates.) The graph shows that real stock returns

DataBank → The Explosion of Tech Stocks in the Late 1990s and Their Implosion in the Early 2000s

The U.S. stock market went through a boom-bust cycle in the late 1990s and early 2000s, especially in the market for technology stocks. What caused the boom and bust? Explaining such short-run movements in the stock market is quite difficult. From October 1998 to March 2000, the NASDAQ stock index, which is heavily weighted with technology stocks, more than tripled in value. Some Internet-related stocks rose in price more than 10-fold in that period. It seemed like every investment in these stocks turned to gold.

But the story ended unhappily for many investors because the prices of tech stocks began to plummet in spring 2000, and the NASDAQ index fell sharply and then remained stagnant for months (Figure 7.A). As has happened so often in the history of speculative investing, momentum carried financial investment in the tech sector beyond its justifiable level. Some investors got out when prices became too high for their comfort, but many other investors were hurt when the market declined in value.

FIGURE 7.A Stock Prices, January 1998 to July 2002

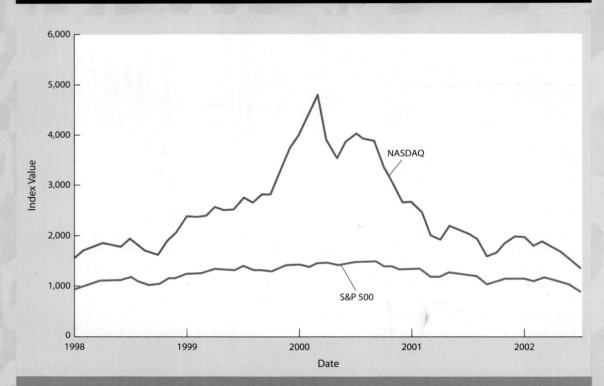

This graph shows the monthly average value of the S&P 500 index and the NASDAQ index from January 1998 to July 2002. The NASDAQ index appreciated sharply from late 1998 to early 2000 and then declined for over two years; its level in July 2002 was only 28 percent of its peak value in March 2000. The S&P 500 index did not have nearly so dramatic a swing, peaking in August 2000; its value in July 2002 was 61 percent of its peak value.

No doubt some of the run-up in the sector was justified, because tech stocks showed great promise for future profitability. But the rise in the stock prices was too large to be justified by reasonable expectations of future corporate profits. Investors began to realize that a company that sells discounted airline tickets is unlikely to be worth more than the airlines it served. As investors lost their faith, stock prices began to fall. In addition, a number of speculators were hoping to hop on the bandwagon for a while and get out of the market just before it fell. Some did, but others did not.

Fads and fashions in investing come and go. However, as Burton Malkiel put it in his op-ed piece in 2000, "Eventually, every stock can only be worth the value of the cash flow it is able to earn for the benefit of investors. In the final analysis, true value will win out."[1]

[1] Burton G. Malkiel, "Nasdaq: What Goes Up . . ." *Wall Street Journal*, April 14, 2000.

FIGURE 7.2 Real Stock Returns, Annual, 1875 to 2012

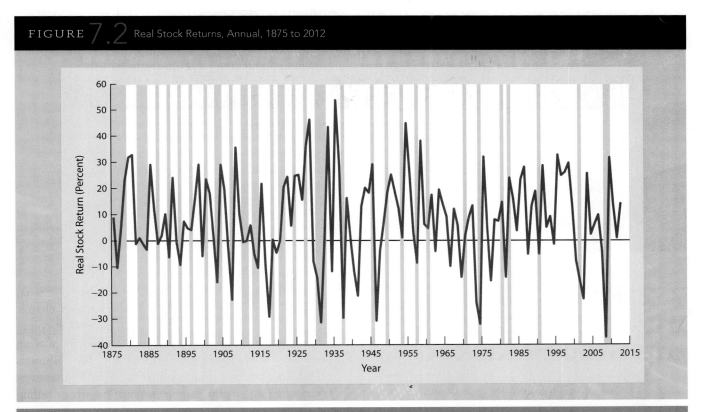

This graph shows stock returns (on the S&P 500 index), adjusted for inflation, each year from 1875 to 2012. The graph shows that real (inflation-adjusted) stock returns are very erratic from year to year.

are very erratic from year to year. The average annual real return from 1875 to 2012 is 6.4 percent. Returns in a particular year range from a high of 54 percent in 1935 to a low of −37 percent in 2008. Notice that in the last half of the 1990s, returns to the stock market were very high, averaging 25 percent each year—representing the largest total return for five consecutive years since 1929. As the blue recession bars in the figure indicate, negative returns to stocks often occur during recessions.

An investor might wonder whether, after a string of years in which returns to the stock market were high,

she should sell her stock because stock prices are too high and are likely to fall. An investor who thought this might have sold her stocks when the market peaked in 1999, which would have been, in retrospect, a smart move. Getting the timing right, however, is crucial. What if the investor sold her stocks in 1994 when real stock prices were two and a half times their level in 1980? She would have missed the run-up in stock prices and the high returns in the late 1990s. With returns as erratic as those shown in Figure 7.2, no one can time the market.

1	Stock exchanges are valuable because they efficiently match buyers and sellers of corporate stock.
2	Stock indexes show the average price for groups of stocks.
3	Mutual funds help investors to diversify their financial investments at low cost.
4	The total return to a stock equals its dividend yield plus its capital-gains yield.
5	The tax disadvantage of receiving dividends explains their unpopularity among some investors. Other investors, however, like the cash flow provided by dividends.
6	The structure of capital-gains taxes causes investors to lock into their financial investments, so much so that the stock market may fail to reflect information about companies' future prospects.
7	Inflation and taxes reduce the total returns to stocks substantially.
8	Investors can boost their total returns by reducing taxes and transactions costs.
9	Stock prices (adjusted for inflation) are volatile and go through long periods in which they rise and other long periods in which they decline or stagnate.
10	Annual stock returns are volatile and decline in recessions.

7-2 How Can an Investor Profit in the Stock Market?

Among all markets for goods and services, stock markets are studied the most by economists because they are closer to the vision of an ideal market than nearly any other. An ideal market would have many buyers and sellers, each of whom knows all the relevant information about the items being traded; there would be no transactions costs for buying or selling; and there would be no other reasons why people buy or sell other than their own wants and needs. If the stock market met these ideal conditions, stock prices would have particular characteristics. Specifically, the stock market would conform to the **efficient markets hypothesis,** which states that prices fully reflect all available information. We will examine what this hypothesis implies about how stock prices change over time, determine how close the stock market comes to confirming the hypothesis, and then look at how an investor should choose what to invest in. We will focus on whether an investor has a profitable trading strategy by considering whether any method of buying or selling stocks would give the investor a higher return (adjusted for risk) than buying a stock index fund would provide.

efficient markets hypothesis the idea that stock prices fully reflect all available information

7-2a The Efficient Markets Hypothesis and Stock-Price Movements

The efficient markets hypothesis assumes that the stock market is deep (with many buyers and sellers) and liquid (easy to buy or sell at any time). In such circumstances, new information that becomes available, such as Intel announcing an increase in computer chip sales, immediately affects the demand and supply of the stock and thus its price. In this example, if Intel's increased

chip sales exceeded investors' expectations, we would expect the demand for Intel stock to increase, causing the stock price to rise. On the other hand, if Intel's chip sales increased, but the increase was less than investors expected, then the demand for Intel's stock would decline, as would its stock price. Thus only unexpected news causes stock prices to change. If Intel's chip sales were exactly what the market expected, the stock price would not change.

The efficient markets hypothesis sometimes is combined with the assumption that investors do not care about risk. Under such an assumption, stock prices move randomly; they are said to follow a **random walk.** This means that the movements of stock prices from day to day, year to year, or decade to decade are not predictable.

7-2b Are Stock Prices Unpredictable?

We need to look at data to see if stock prices are predictable or not. If they are unpredictable, we may conclude that the efficient markets hypothesis holds, that investors on average do not care about risk, and that stock prices follow a random walk. If stock prices are predictable, then they do not follow a random walk, and we may conclude either that stock markets are not efficient or that investors on average do care about risk.

Research shows that stock prices are somewhat predictable. The most important evidence that stock prices are predictable comes in several forms: (1) There is a significant relationship between the return on stocks in one week and their return the following week, (2) the movement of stock prices of companies over time is much greater than the changes in the earnings of those companies, and (3) high returns to a particular stock in one period generally are associated with low returns in a later period.

All three of these phenomena would not occur if stock prices followed a random walk. Because stock prices are predictable, we may conclude that either investors care about risk or that stock markets are not efficient.

There is some evidence that the predictability of stock prices occurs because some markets are not efficient because they lack enough participants. When researchers look at stock data, they find that the return to stocks in one week is correlated with the return in following weeks. However, the correlation has been declining over time as the stock market has become larger and more liquid. Predictability is mostly apparent in stock in small companies, whose markets do not have as many participants as the markets for stock in large companies. In addition, some of the findings of predictability in stock prices depend on the use of data from before World War II, when the stock market was smaller and presumably less liquid. These findings suggest that the stock market was not efficient in the past but has become more efficient as it has grown in size.

Another way to see whether the predictability of stock prices is due to risk aversion or to inefficiency is to account for risk and see if stock prices remain predictable. Doing so leads to the study of anomalies.

7-2c Are Stock Returns Predictable Only Because of Risk?

Is there any clear-cut evidence that the stock market is not efficient, especially if we consider that investors are likely to be averse to risk? Some economists do not think that there is such evidence, but others cite the existence of anomalies as evidence that stock markets are not efficient. **Anomalies** are observations that do not fit a model. In looking at stock prices, anomalies are cases in which there are predictable patterns to stock prices that investors could exploit, even accounting for risk aversion.

> **random walk** the idea that movements of stock prices from day to day, year to year, or decade to decade are not predictable
>
> **anomalies** incidents of predictable patterns to stock prices that investors could exploit, even accounting for risk aversion

In studying stock prices and total returns, and accounting for risk very carefully, economists have discovered many anomalies, the most prominent of which are these:

- Stock in small firms has a higher risk-adjusted return than stock in large firms.
- Stocks have higher than average returns in early January.
- Stock prices do not change as much as they should when firms announce changes in their earnings.
- The day of the week has an effect on a stock's return; in particular, returns are lower over a weekend, and the best time to sell a stock is late on Wednesday or Friday, whereas the best time to buy a stock is late Tuesday or Thursday.
- There is a relationship between the price-earnings ratio (the stock's price per share divided by its profits per share over the last year) of a firm and its expected return.
- Firms that pay no dividends or pay high dividends yield higher returns than firms that pay low dividends.

Many other anomalies have been discovered as well. The question is: What do they mean for an investor? Their existence implies that markets may not be perfectly efficient. But do they mean that an investor can make a profit from them? Anomalies may exist but not provide profit opportunities for several reasons: (1) An anomaly may be based on an inaccurate model of risk, (2) the search for anomalies is so pervasive that some anomaly always would be discovered even in a world with perfectly random stock prices, and (3) the anomalies may be too small to profit from, especially if they arise because markets lack depth and liquidity.

A claim that there is an anomaly in stock prices depends on a model of risk. Take the first anomaly on the preceding list, for example, that stocks in small firms have higher risk-adjusted returns than stocks in large firms. To measure the risk-adjusted returns of stocks, a researcher must specify how investors adjust for differences in risk because we know that the total returns to stock in small firms are, on average, riskier than for larger firms. If a researcher underestimates how much return is needed to compensate an investor for the added risk of owning stock in a small firm, the research findings will be questionable. What models do economists use to account for risk?

One popular model of risk is the **capital asset pricing model (CAPM),** which models the return to a stock as depending on how risky the stock is compared with the market average. The CAPM says that the return to a particular stock equals the return on a risk-free bond, plus a coefficient times the average excess return on stocks over bonds, plus a term representing unsystematic risk. The model is represented in a formula as

$$R_t^i = r_t + \beta^i(R_t - r_t) + \varepsilon_t^i \qquad (2)$$

In this equation, the term on the left-hand side (R_t^i) is the realized return to holding stock i at date t. There may be thousands of stocks, so imagine numbering them all and letting the term i tell you what stock it is that you are holding; for example, $i = 1{,}573$ might represent Hewlett-Packard Corporation. We can look at this equation for any period we want it to represent; that is, it could be daily, monthly, quarterly, yearly, or any other period. Suppose, for example, that we wanted to look at monthly data; then $R_{January1978}^{1.573}$ would represent the total return to Hewlett-Packard stock in January 1978.

The other terms in Equation (2) are

r_t = the interest rate on a risk-free bond, usually a Treasury security

β^i = a coefficient that must be estimated statistically using data on R_t^i, r_t, and R_t

R_t = the average return to all stocks in the market, and

ε_t^i = the part of the return that is unexplained by the model, called unsystematic risk

The CAPM suggests that the return to a stock above the risk-free interest rate has two sources of risk: (1) **systematic risk,** which is the risk to a stock's return that is attributable to the fluctuations in the overall stock market, and (2) **unsystematic risk,** which is the risk to the stock's return that is not explained by movements in the market as a whole. Systematic risk is represented in Equation (2) by the coefficient β^i multiplied by the market's excess return, $R_t - r_t$, which is the amount by which the average return on the stock market exceeds that on Treasury securities. The term ε_t^i represents unsystematic risk (also called *idiosyncratic risk*), which is risk to a stock that can be reduced in an investor's portfolio if the investor holds a diversified portfolio with many different stocks. Systematic risk (also called *market risk*) cannot be diversified away in that manner; this is the risk that arises from holding any stocks at all.

When $\beta^i = 1$, the stock's return tends to move in tandem with the stock market as a whole. Some stocks are much more volatile than the market, though, and they have $\beta^i > 1$. Stocks that are less volatile than the market as a whole have $0 < \beta^i < 1$. Investors often discuss a company's "beta," which is β^i in our equation. A stock with a smaller beta (in magnitude) has less systematic risk than one with a larger beta; that is, as returns on the stock market rise or fall, returns on stock with a lower beta do not fluctuate as much as returns on stock with a higher beta. β^i can even be negative for a stock whose price moves in the opposite direction of the market as a whole.

In the CAPM, the only source of systematic risk comes from the overall movement of the stock market. This may not be good enough, however, because there are many sources of risk in the economy. The prices of different stocks are likely to respond in differing ways depending on the exact nature of the event that influences the economy. For example, the economy may experience a downturn if oil prices rise or if there is a slowdown in the economies of our foreign trading partners. In either case, the average stock price is likely to fall. The stock prices of electric companies likely will fall if oil prices rise because oil is a key input in the production of electricity. But prices of electric-company stock are less likely to be affected if foreign demand declines because most of the electricity sales in this country are to domestic customers. The CAPM cannot distinguish between these different sources of an economic slowdown.

For this reason, the **arbitrage-pricing theory (APT)** was developed as an alternative to the CAPM. The idea is similar, but the APT allows for more sources of systematic risk than just the stock market's excess return. The return to a particular stock using the APT equals the return on a risk-free Treasury bond, plus a beta coefficient times each factor, plus unsystematic risk:

$$R_t^i = r_t + \beta^{1i}f_t^1 + \beta^{2i}f_t^2 + \cdots + \beta^{ki}f_t^k + \varepsilon_t^i \qquad (3)$$

In this equation, k different factors affect the return to the stock, and they all can change over time. One factor could be the market's excess return, $R_t - r_t$, which is the only factor in the CAPM (so the APT and the CAPM are the same if that is the only factor). However, other factors may matter. Thus, the APT could include many sources of risk in determining the return for a given stock.

The CAPM and APT are used widely in studies of stock-price anomalies. When a researcher finds an anomaly, however, how do we know that the anomaly is not just a symptom of the CAPM or APT being inadequate models of risk? The answer is that we do not know, but improving these models is difficult.

So what does all this mean for how efficient the stock market is? Economists have sought to develop the best models of risk possible, yet the anomalies still exist, which suggests that the stock market may not be efficient.

7-2d A Random Walk with a Crutch

Given all the research testing the efficient markets hypothesis and anomalies, what can we conclude about whether an investor has profit opportunities in the stock market? The most realistic view is that the market works extremely efficiently when conditions are right and that it works less efficiently in some situations. For a large corporation with millions of shares of stock outstanding that are traded heavily every day, the market is very efficient. For a small company that gets little attention from investors, the market is not likely to work as well because the transactions and information costs exceed the value to investors of learning about the stock and buying it. Burton Malkiel of Princeton University has coined a phrase for the little inefficiencies that arise in the stock market, arguing that prices are not totally random but rather follow a "random walk with a crutch." Malkiel's notion is that although the market is close to being efficient, it is not wholly efficient.

We might even go a step further and argue that perfectly efficient markets cannot exist. If they did—that is, if there were never any profit opportunities in the market—no one would expend any effort to gather information about corporations and their profit opportunities. But then how

arbitrage-pricing theory (APT) a model of stock prices that allows for more sources of risk than just the stock market's excess return

would new information be revealed and translated into changes in prices? And why would investors do anything except buy and hold a portfolio of typical stocks? Under this type of interpretation, it is the lack of efficiency that keeps investors in the market. Of course, if markets were too inefficient, more people would seek to invest, and that would reduce the inefficiency. Thus, there must be some equilibrium amount of inefficiency in the market—enough to make it interesting and slightly profitable but not so much that huge profits could be made. In such an equilibrium, we also should expect specialization—those who are good at gathering information and figuring out what it means for firms' future profits (such as investment firms on Wall Street) will make slightly larger-than-average returns as a payoff to their specialization, whereas those who trade on rumors and fads will earn lower-than-average returns.

What is the average investor to do? If an investor has a lot of time to do research on different companies and their prospects, there could be a payoff. However, as John Bogle notes, "You rarely, if ever, know something the market does not."[2] Therefore, most investors would be better off letting investment professionals do the research for them, for example, by putting their money into mutual funds, which also provide diversification.

Will any mutual fund do? Probably not, because some are better than others at collecting information on companies and figuring out which stocks to buy or sell. In fact, the average mutual fund does worse than the market average once fees are accounted for. Bogle found that over a 23-year period in which the stock market rose an average of 12.0 percent per year, the average mutual fund's return (after deducting fees) was just 10.8 percent per year. The average mutual fund actually earned average returns of 13.0 percent before fees and costs, which is slightly better than the market average, but the cost of fees paid to the managers and the costs of trading averaged 2.2 percent per year. Thus the net return was over a percentage point less than the market's return per year. And Malkiel's research shows that index funds do better than 80 percent of all mutual funds each year.[3]

fundamental value the present value of expected earnings of a company or of all companies in the stock market as a whole

[2] John C. Bogle, *Bogle on Mutual Funds* (New York: Dell Publishing, 1994), p. 305.

[3] Burton G. Malkiel, "The Efficient Market Hypothesis and Its Critics." *Journal of Economic Perspectives* 17 (Winter 2003), pp. 59–82.

Thus, an investor needs to either figure out what mutual fund will do better than average or else buy an index fund that yields the market return. Bogle was founder and chairman of the Vanguard Group, which sells many different kinds of mutual funds, including index funds. But he thinks that for most investors, index funds are the way to go. It is difficult to know in advance which mutual fund will be better than average. Because the costs of index funds are low, they will give an investor a return close to the market return. And an average historical return of 6.4 percent, after adjusting for inflation, is not bad for a passive activity. An investor can just sit back and let the money flow in (although accepting the risk that the money also could flow out).

7-2e What Determines Average Stock Prices and Returns?

If the stock market follows a random walk with a crutch, then individual stock prices are predictable. However, an investor also might want to know what determines the overall level of stock prices at some date and what return he should expect to earn from investing in stocks. He also might want to know if there are good times to buy or to sell stocks as a whole. For example, in the late 1990s, stock prices rose sharply, making many investors and researchers wonder if the market was overvalued and would crash. Could a savvy investor accurately predict swings in the market as a whole? If so, he could move his financial investments into some other asset, such as cash, just before the crash and invest in stocks again after the crash when stock prices were set to rise.

To investigate whether an investor can predict swings in the market, we begin by examining the present value of the stock market. Then we can look at whether the historical data on the prices of stocks are consistent with that present-value calculation.

An investor buys stocks because she expects to receive dividend payments or because she expects capital gains or both. But the firm's ability to pay dividends and investors' willingness to pay a high price for a stock depend on the company's earnings (profits). Consequently, we look at earnings as the main determinant of stock prices.

We can use the present-value formulas from Chapter 4 to evaluate the present value of expected earnings of the stock market as a whole. When we calculate this present value, the result is the **fundamental value** of the market. We can compare the fundamental value with actual stock prices to see how close they are. If stock prices (measured by an index such as the S&P 500) exceed their fundamental value, the market is **overvalued.** If the value of the stock market is below its fundamental value, it is **undervalued.**

One theory about the stock market is that investors have **rational expectations,** which means that investors use all the information available to them about companies' future prospects in determining their buying and selling decisions. If people have rational expectations, stock prices always equal their fundamental value. An alternative theory, which we will call **irrational expectations,** argues that the stock market goes through periods in which stock prices rise higher than their fundamental value and other periods in which stock prices fall below their fundamental value. These differences between stock prices and their fundamental value provide profit opportunities for savvy investors. As we will see, proving which of these theories is correct is very difficult.

The fundamental value of stocks equals the present value of expected future corporate earnings. Based on the present-value formula [see Equation (4) in Chapter 4], the value of the stock market is

$$V = \frac{e_1}{(1 + R)^1} + \frac{e_2}{(1 + R)^2} + \frac{e_3}{(1 + R)^3} + \cdots$$

where e_i is the expected earnings of the firms in the stock market at the end of the ith year (that is, e_1 is expected earnings one year from now, e_2 is expected earnings two years from now, and so on), and R is the rate of discount. Think of the stock market as being represented by an index, such as the S&P 500. Then the measure of expected earnings is the sum of expected earnings of the 500 firms in the index.

To simplify the model, suppose that we assume that earnings are expected to grow at a constant rate over time and that e_0 is last year's actual earnings. Then letting g represent the growth rate of earnings over time, we can use the results in Appendix 4.A to find that

$$V = \frac{1 + g}{R - g} \times e_0 \qquad (4)$$

This formula is convenient because it is based on earnings from the previous year (e_0), which are

known, the investor's rate of discount (R), and the expected growth rate of earnings (g), which an investor can forecast, perhaps by looking at data from previous years.

How well does the model explain the movement of stock prices? To find out, we need to compare the model's predictions with the data on actual stock market values.

If we look at earnings data from 1875 to 2012 and insert those data into Equation (4), the values for V are the fundamental values of the stock market over time. We can plot the values for V (Figure 7.3) obtained by this process (labeled *Model* in the figure) and compare these values with the actual value of the stock market (labeled *Actual* in the figure). The year is shown on the horizontal axis, and the stock value for that date is shown on the vertical axis using a logarithmic scale. Stock prices have risen so much from 1875 to 2013 that if we do not use a logarithmic scale, the movements of the lines in the early years are difficult to see. Using a logarithmic scale helps the graph to show the movements in stock prices in all years. It also has the advantage of showing how trends have changed because a constant growth rate of stock prices shows up as a straight line on a logarithmic scale.

The model apparently tracks the stock market fairly well over time. There are a few periods in which, if the model is correct, you might conclude that stock prices were undervalued (that is, actual stock prices were less than the model predicted)—in the 1910s, much of the 1950s, and from 1973 to 1985. The market was overvalued in the 1890s, the 1960s, and most of the 1990s and 2000s.

The model implies that the stock market has gone through long periods of overvaluation or undervaluation. If the model is true, then investors do not have rational expectations, and it is possible to make profits using the model (buying stocks when they are

overvalued a situation in which stock prices exceed their fundamental value

undervalued a situation in which stock prices are below their fundamental value

rational expectations a theory that investors use all the information available to them about companies' future prospects in determining their buying and selling decisions, in which case stock prices always equal their fundamental value

irrational expectations a theory that investors do not have rational expectations, so the stock market goes through periods in which stock prices rise higher than their fundamental value and other periods in which stock prices fall below their fundamental value

FIGURE 7.3 Real Stock Prices: Actual Compared with Model

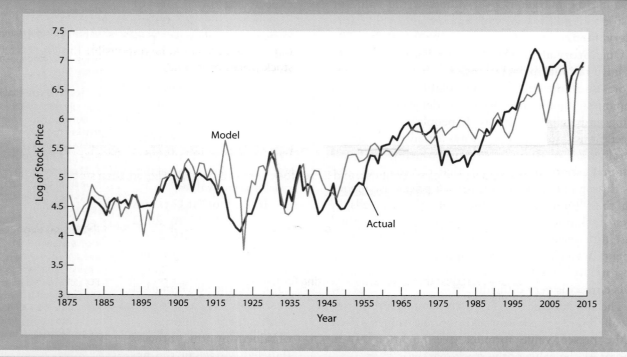

This graph shows the log level of the S&P 500 index compared with the log level implied by the model based on constant earnings growth and a constant rate of discount from 1875 to 2013. The model fits reasonably well, but there are periods of overvaluation and undervaluation.

undervalued and selling them when they are overvalued). However, the model makes several assumptions that may not be true.

The first shortcoming of the model is that it assumes constant earnings growth over time, but the data show that the growth rate of earnings varies from year to year. A second shortcoming of the model is that it assumes a constant rate of discount, but there are some reasons why the rate of discount might have changed over time, especially because investors have changed their views about taking risk.

In fact, one event probably had more impact on people's attitudes toward the stock market than any other: the stock market crash of October 29, 1929. It is widely blamed as the cause of the Great Depression by those who lost their jobs or their fortunes. These same people taught their children and grandchildren about the evils of the stock market. And it took 30 years for the S&P 500 index to return to its 1929 level (adjusted for inflation). Only recently have people begun to realize that many other factors contributed to the Great Depression, not just the

stock market crash. Investors in recent years seem more willing to accept the risk in the stock market. However, that willingness may have changed after the dramatic declines in stock prices in the financial crisis of 2008.

Economists have helped people learn more about the risks and returns to the stock market. Books about the stock market and investing by economists such as Jeremy Siegel and industry leaders like John Bogle are prominent examples. As people have learned more, the influence of the Great Depression has declined, and the rate of discount also may have declined.

The rate of discount probably rose sharply after the stock market crash of 1929. Then, at some point around 1980, it probably declined and may have declined again in the 1990s. John Cochrane of the University of Chicago put it well in 1997 when he said, "We could interpret the recent run-up in the market as the result of people finally figuring out how good of an investment stocks have been for the last century, and building institutions that allow wide participation in the stock market. If so, future returns are likely to be much lower."[4]

However, we have no way of knowing whether the rate of discount really fell or not because we cannot observe it directly. If you believe in irrational expectations, you believe that the stock market goes through periods of overvaluation (as in 1929, 1987, and 1999) and undervaluation (as in 1919, 1953, and 1982). This is a hypothesis that cannot really be tested, but you *can* bet on it (or against it) by choosing how you invest. If you believe in rational expectations, then the stock market always equals its fundamental value, and changes in the rate of discount could be responsible for large swings in stock prices over time.

RECAP

1 If investors do not care about risk, and if the stock market is deep and liquid, then stock prices follow a random walk and are not predictable.

2 Research shows that stock prices are predictable, so either the market is not efficient or investors care about risk.

3 Anomalies suggest that even after adjusting for risk, stock prices are predictable, so the stock market is not efficient.

4 The inefficiencies in the stock market may be so difficult to exploit that most investors are likely to do better by buying an index fund.

5 We can estimate the stock market's fundamental value using the present-value formula.

6 If people have rational expectations, the stock market's value always equals its fundamental value.

7 A simple model that assumes that both the growth rate of expected earnings and the rate of discount have been constant over time matches the overall movements of stock prices. In some periods, though, such as the late 1990s, the model shows that the stock market's value exceeded its fundamental value.

8 The simple model may not show the correct fundamental value either because expected earnings growth is not constant or because the rate of discount is not constant or both.

Comparing stocks with bonds and other financial investments
An investor will consider more than just stocks in deciding what to invest in. The investor might compare returns on stocks to those on bonds and then might consider other assets, such as real estate, precious metals, or buying a small business.

Application TO
EVERYDAY LIFE

[4]John H. Cochrane, "Where Is the Market Going? Uncertain Facts and Novel Theories," Federal Reserve Bank of Chicago *Economic Perspectives*, November/December 1997, p. 32.

	Average Return	Standard Deviation
Stocks	7.1%	16.5%
Short-Term Treasury Securities	1.5%	2.3%

7-2f Comparing Stocks with Debt Securities: The Equity Premium

The main alternative financial investments to stocks are debt securities. If we compare their returns, we see that, on average, stocks have had much higher returns over time than debt securities.

Table 7.3 shows the average annual real (adjusted for inflation) return on stocks compared with short-term Treasury securities from 1960 to 2012. The average annual return to the stock market exceeds the return to short-term Treasury securities by 5.6 percentage points. Thus, stocks provide a return that is significantly larger than the returns on short-term bonds. Researchers have shown that stock returns are significantly higher than the returns on long-term bonds, as well.

This difference between the returns on stocks and on other financial investments is called the **equity premium** because the market pays a premium (extra return) to investors who hold equity securities (stocks) compared with those who hold debt securities.

The right-most column of Table 7.3 helps to explain why the equity premium exists. It shows the standard deviation, the measure of risk defined in Chapter 2, of the return to the different financial investments. You can see that the return on stocks is significantly more risky than the return on Treasury securities. Because of the higher risk to stocks, people will hold stocks only if, on average, they are compensated for taking that risk by receiving a higher average return.

When the equity premium was discovered, economists were surprised about its size. A positive

equity premium the average amount (in terms of percentage return) by which the return on stocks exceeds the return on debt securities

equity-premium puzzle the surprising result that people will not pay much to avoid risk in everyday situations, but when it comes to the stock market, people are willing to give up large potential returns to stocks in order to buy safer Treasury securities

equity premium is appropriate because stocks are riskier than bonds. The question is this: Why is the equity premium so large? As an investor, how much extra return do you need to compensate you for the additional risk you bear when you buy stocks?

The size of the equity premium depends on the tradeoff investors make between risk and return. Economists have devoted substantial research efforts to examining that tradeoff. One way economists look at the issue is by observing how much insurance people buy. Also, economists have tried experiments in which they put people in risky situations and asked them how much they would be willing to pay to avoid the risk or how much they would be willing to bet on some gamble. The results of all this research show that people do not like risk, but they are not willing to pay very much to avoid such risk.

What has surprised economists is that this research on people's attitudes toward risk is inconsistent with the size of the equity premium. In fact, the equity premium is about two or three times larger than the research on risk suggests that it should be. That is, if economists' standard model of risk were correct, stocks should have a return that is about 2 or 3 percent higher than the return on bonds; in fact, however, the difference in returns has been about 5.6 percent over the last 50 years. Thus, it seems very odd that people will not pay much to avoid risk in everyday situations, but when it comes to the stock market, people are willing to give up the tremendous potential returns to stocks in order to buy safer Treasury securities. Economists use the term **equity-premium puzzle** for this mystery. To explain the high return on stocks, economists have had to change their models of how people behave toward risk and how they make spending decisions. (See the box titled "Is the Equity Premium So High Because the United States Is Lucky?" for one possible explanation of the high U.S. equity premium.)

The equity premium may have declined somewhat in the 1990s and 2000s for such reasons as (1) people thought the risks of a severe recession were lower than before (until the financial crisis of 2008), (2) the average tax rate on investment income has fallen, and (3) transactions costs have become lower. In addition, there is some evidence that the equity premium has declined in the past three decades because technology has made it easier for investors to diversify through mutual funds, thus reducing the risk to stock portfolios.

In summary, the equity premium tells us that the return to stocks exceeds the return to bonds. Despite this, many investors hold portfolios that are fairly balanced between stocks and bonds, which suggests that they are frightened by the risk to the stock market. Other

Is the Equity Premium So High Because the United States Is Lucky?

If you had invested $1 in the U.S. stock market 75 years ago (and reinvested the dividends you earned), your stock would be worth $118 today (adjusted for inflation). In some countries, however, a dollar invested in the stock market 75 years ago would give you less than a dollar today. Why does the United States have such a high equity premium compared with most other countries?

Phillippe Jorion and William Goetzmann found that the stock markets of many countries have been damaged by financial crises, political uprisings, and wars.[5] In some cases, investors lost everything, and in others, their returns were low for decades. The United States simply may be lucky in not having experienced any such events since the Great Depression.

One possible explanation for the high U.S. returns is that stock returns in all countries suffer from what economists call a "peso problem." The name comes from the first example of the phenomenon, which was related to the value of the Mexican peso. The idea is that investors account for events that may occur some day but have not yet occurred. In the case of the Mexican peso, interest rates in Mexico were persistently higher than interest rates in the United States. So why didn't investors borrow money in the United States and lend it in Mexico? The answer is that investors were worried about a sudden change in the exchange rate between the peso and the dollar. The exchange rate was fixed by the government, but investors thought that the government might allow it to change. (As we will see in Chapter 14, it can be very expensive for a government to maintain a fixed exchange rate.) For the period in which the peso remained fixed against the dollar, investors were persistently wrong; they gave up profit opportunities from borrowing in the United States and lending in Mexico. Eventually, though, the peso was devalued against the dollar, and the investors were proven correct.

Thus, one argument about why stock returns in the United States have been so high is that there is a peso problem. People have continued to expect some very bad outcomes that have not yet taken place. People worry that events such as the stock market crashes in October 1929, October 1987, and fall 2008 will happen while they are holding much of their wealth in stocks. As a result, they are reluctant to hold stocks, even though the expected return is high. In the rest of the world, in fact, stock market crashes and financial problems have occurred much more frequently than in the United States. The question to ask yourself as an investor is this: Is the United States *lucky*, or is it *better* in some ways than other countries? If all countries face the same risks, then the United States has had a higher average return only by luck. As John Cochrane put it, "Was it obvious in 1945 that the United States would not slip back into depression, but would instead experience a half century of growth never before seen in human history?"[6] However, it may be that there is something about the U.S. economy and financial system that makes it less susceptible to major financial problems than other countries. If so, then investors should invest more of their wealth in the stock market than has been the case historically.

[5] Phillippe Jorion and William Goetzmann, "Global Stock Markets in the Twentieth Century," *Journal of Finance* 54 (June 1999), pp. 953–80.

[6] John H. Cochrane, "Where Is the Market Going? Uncertain Facts and Novel Theories," Federal Reserve Bank of Chicago *Economic Perspectives*, November/December 1997, p. 7.

investors, however, have sought financial investments other than stocks and bonds.

7-2g Other Assets as Investments

In addition to stocks and bonds, investors may invest in many other assets. Alternatives include real estate, precious metals such as gold and silver, and small business firms.

Real estate (housing) is often the most important investment that people make. But houses (at least those occupied by their owners) differ from stocks and bonds. For one thing, while stocks and bonds can give a return only in the form of money, houses also can give a return in terms of shelter. Like stocks and bonds, real estate also can appreciate in price, so capital gains are possible.

Investors also can compare the returns on real estate to the returns on stocks. In the high-inflation environment of the 1970s and early 1980s, real estate was a good investment because its value kept pace with inflation and because there was a tax advantage to owning real estate. Over time, as inflation has declined, the advantages to owning real estate have declined. Real estate also requires constant upkeep and maintenance, something that need not be done with stocks and bonds. On the other hand, there is a tax advantage to owning real estate because part of the returns (in terms of the shelter benefits of the house) are not taxed, whereas the returns to stocks and bonds are taxed. The data show that the returns to owning stocks are significantly higher than the average annual appreciation of housing prices over the last 25 years. Thus, while a house is a great asset, it should be purchased more for its value in providing shelter than for its investment role.

If we look at data on the amounts that people invest in stocks, bonds, and real estate, we see that people's stock portfolios now represent a larger share of their wealth than 10 years ago, and housing represents a smaller share. Nevertheless, real estate remains the top asset owned by the average household and represents 25 percent of total wealth, compared with 19 percent for stocks.

What about other assets, such as gold and silver? Precious metals are great investments during times of rising inflation, as in the 1970s. For example, from 1971 to 1980, gold yielded a real return of 26 percent per year, and silver yielded 23 percent per year, which compare favorably with stocks, whose total return averaged −1.1 percent per year. Other than that nine-year period, however, the returns to both gold and silver have been mediocre. Over the period from 1975 to 2012, the real return to gold was 3.5 percent per year, whereas the real return to silver was 2.1 percent per year. Stocks, on the other hand, had a real return averaging 7.3 percent per year.

One last alternative investment worth considering is direct investment in a business, usually a small firm. There are no good data on the returns to such investments. Owning all or part of a small business can be very lucrative but entails much more risk than stocks. Thus, if you are not risk averse, and if you love to work hard to get a small business operating, an active business venture may be the route for you. Most investors prefer a more passive role, so they are better off investing in stocks and bonds.

7-2h How Investors Can Diversify Their Portfolios

Given what we know about the returns to different portfolios, what is the average investor to do? Most investors with families will have most of their wealth tied up in their houses. Diversification is difficult because houses represent such a large fraction of most people's lifetime earnings. However, in retirement savings accounts and pension plans, people have the opportunity to invest in financial securities. The average investor is well served in having a diversified portfolio containing a mix of stocks (probably including some in foreign countries) and debt securities (perhaps including some inflation-indexed securities to help protect against increases in inflation). The more risk averse the investor, the smaller should be the share of the portfolio in stock.

Looking beyond strictly financial securities, the best investment a person can make is in his or her own human capital (that is, skills, knowledge, and education) and the human capital of his or her children. The returns to human capital in recent years have far exceeded the returns to financial securities of any type. If investors who study the stock market and then buy individual stocks would devote the same amount of time to learning new skills or obtaining additional training or education, the payoff in terms of higher future wages likely would be tremendous.

RECAP

1 Calculations of the equity premium show that the return to stocks has been much higher than the return to debt securities since 1960.

2 The equity premium exists because the returns to stocks are significantly riskier than the returns to debt securities.

3 The equity premium seems to be too large for the difference in risk between equity and debt.

4 People invest in assets other than stocks and bonds, including real estate, precious metals, and small business firms. None of the other assets provides returns as high as those on stocks or bonds in the long run. However, they may provide high returns during particular short-term periods (the 1970s for gold, silver, and real estate) and may have other desirable properties.

Review Questions and Problems

Review Questions

1 What is the role of a stock exchange? Give two examples of stock exchanges and explain how they differ.

2 How does the lock-in effect cause the stock market to be inefficient?

3 Why is it important for an investor to diversify? How does a mutual fund help an investor achieve this goal?

4 Describe three major stock indexes. In what ways are they similar? In what ways are they different?

5 What is the longest period the stock market took to return to its previous peak after declining? What is the shortest period in which the stock market doubled in value?

6 Why does frequently buying and selling stocks lead to lower returns?

7 What is the efficient markets hypothesis? What are the most important characteristics of markets that are necessary for them to be efficient?

8 How do stock prices behave if stock markets are efficient and if investors do not care about risk?

9 Describe three anomalies in the stock market. In what way are they anomalous?

10 What are the basic ideas that motivate the CAPM and the APT? Which theory is more general? Explain.

Numerical Exercises

11 A stock was priced at $150 per share at the end of 2009. The following table shows dividends per share paid during each year and the price of the stock at the end of the year for the following four years:

Year	Dividends Paid During Year	Stock Price at End of Year
2010	$3.00	$125
2011	$3.00	$150
2012	$3.50	$155
2013	$4.00	$200

For each year from 2010 to 2013, calculate the dividend yield, the capital-gains yield, and the total return to the stock. Express your calculations in percentage terms.

12 Suppose that an investor purchased 100 shares of IBM stock at a price of $100 on December 31, 2012. During the year 2013, IBM paid dividends of $2.00 per share, and at the end of the year, the investor sold the stock at a price of $115.

  a If there were no taxes or inflation, what was the total return?

  b If there were no taxes but inflation was 5 percent, what was the real return?

  c If the tax rate was 15 percent on dividends and capital gains, what was the after-tax real return?

13 Some people have the opportunity to invest in stocks in a tax-advantaged retirement plan, such as a 401(k) plan. Consider the difference between Andy, who is able to save in a tax-advantaged plan, and Ben, who must pay taxes on his return each year. Both invest $100,000 in the same mutual fund at the same time and always reinvest their earnings in the fund. Suppose that the return on the mutual fund is 7 percent each year and that the tax rate is 15 percent. (Note that Ben must pay taxes each year on his earnings, so he can reinvest only his after-tax earnings; Andy, however, pays the 15 percent tax rate when he retires and withdraws his funds.)

  a How much do Andy and Ben each accumulate over 10 years?

  b How much do Andy and Ben each accumulate over 30 years?

14 Suppose that the CAPM is a good model of risk in the stock market. Suppose also that the average excess return on stocks is 10 percent and that the risk-free interest rate is 1 percent. What would you expect to be the return to stocks with each of the following beta coefficients?

  a -0.5

  b 0.3

  c 1.0

  d 2.0

15 Suppose that the following version of the APT is a good model of risk in the stock market. Consider

(*continued*)

Review Questions and Problems (continued)

three factors: the stock market's excess return in percentage points, the change over the last year in the price of oil in dollars, and the spread between 10-year Treasury bonds and three-month Treasury bills in percentage points. Suppose that the stock market's average excess return is 9 percent and that the average risk-free interest rate is 1 percent, the average change in the price of oil is $0.25, and the average spread between 10-year Treasury bonds and three-month Treasury bills is 1.25. Each of the following stocks has the beta coefficients shown in the table below:

	β^{1i}	β^{2i}	β^{3i}
Armstrong	1.5	−0.5	0.8
McDonald's	1.0	−0.2	0.6
Shell Oil	0.3	1.5	0.4

a What is the expected return to each of the three stocks?

b If the market's excess return were to be above average by 1 percent (that is, it rose 10 percent in a particular year instead of the usual 9 percent), what would you expect the effect to be on the return to each of the three stocks?

c If the price of oil were to fall by $3.00 in a particular year (that is, $3.25 less than the average change of +$0.25), what would you expect the effect to be on the return to each of the three stocks?

d If the interest-rate spread rose to 2.00 percent in a particular year (that is, 0.75 percentage point higher than average), what would you expect the effect to be on the return to each of the three stocks?

16 Which of these three stocks would you rather own if your rate of discount is 5 percent?

a A stock that currently earns $2 per share whose earnings are growing 3 percent each year.

b A stock that currently earns $1 per share whose earnings are growing 4 percent each year.

c A stock that currently earns $5 per share whose earnings are growing 2 percent each year.

Analytical Problems

17 If you want to trade stocks on the floor of the New York Stock Exchange, you must purchase a "seat," which is really a license to buy or sell stocks. Can you explain why the price of such seats rose sharply in the 1980s and early 1990s but has been declining rapidly in recent years?

18 If the government invested a portion of the Social Security trust fund in the stock market, would you expect people to change the way they invest their other savings? That is, suppose that someone currently has a portfolio with a $50,000 investment in the stock market and $25,000 in debt securities. Now suppose that their share of the Social Security trust fund is $30,000, and the government invests it all in the stock market. How might someone adjust his or her own portfolio in response?

19 If the efficient markets hypothesis is true, is it worthwhile for an investor to spend a lot of time investigating different companies to decide what to invest in?

20 Suppose that investors were stubborn and pessimistic about corporate earnings growth, so they consistently forecast lower earnings than actually materialized. How might this affect the return to the stock market? Do you think that the equity premium would be higher or lower than if investors' expectations were accurate?

21 Rodney the researcher theorizes that people become pessimistic on Friday the thirteenth. Consequently, he studies the data on the stock market to see what happens to the average return on Friday the thirteenth for the last 40 years. He finds that the return is slightly lower than average on those days, even accounting for risk through the CAPM or the APT. Is this an anomaly? Now consider Danny the data digger. He looks at the average return on each day of the month, comparing the average return on the first of the month with that on the second, then the third, and so on, through the thirty-first. He finds that the returns are lower than average on the thirteenth (just like Rodney) and higher than average on the twenty-seventh. Whose evidence is more convincingly an anomaly, Rodney's or Danny's?

Henryk Sadura/Alamy

▶ FUNDAMENTALS
of BANKING

© iStockphoto.com/Dcdebs

How
BANKS
WORK

As financial intermediaries, banks perform the key function of transferring funds from savers to borrowers.

Banking has had the reputation of being a conservative and staid business, but economic conditions over the last decade, changes in financial regulations, and improvements in computing and telecommunications have presented the banking industry with challenging opportunities for innovation.

The goal of this chapter is to describe how banks operate. We start by describing the role banks play in the financial system, especially how they handle information. We show that differences in the information known by banks and their borrowers lead to problems that banks solve using a variety of techniques. We also look at the balance sheets of banks and examine how banks profit from the services they provide. The chapter closes by describing what banks did when the Fed began paying interest on reserves during the financial crisis of 2008.

8-1 The Role of Banks

What is a bank? A **bank** is a financial intermediary that accepts deposits from savers and makes loans to borrowers. Many types of intermediaries perform both these services: commercial banks, thrift institutions (savings banks and savings-and-loan associations), and credit unions. In this chapter we lump them together and call them all *banks* because they have become increasingly alike over the years; we will discuss the differences among them in Chapter 9.

Because banks are efficient in combining small deposits from savers to make larger loans to borrowers, they have a special role in the financial system. Specifically, they provide liquidity for people and for businesses, both borrowers and lenders. Banks are efficient at matching savers and borrowers because banks are particularly adept at (1) pooling funds and (2) gathering information about borrowers.

Banks attract funds from individuals with small amounts to invest and pool those savings to buy financial securities that are available only in large denominations. For example, an individual saver would not have enough savings to make a loan to a corporation, but a bank can combine that saver's deposit with the deposits of others to make a loan for $1 million.

Banks specialize in gathering information. If you wanted to earn interest on your savings, you could loan your money directly to a small business such as Joe's Garage, but then you would have to worry about your savings, wondering if you would ever get your money back. What a bank offers in this situation is a knowledge of Joe's Garage and all the other small business firms in town. The bank studies how these firms operate and what their financial condition is. When you want to invest your savings, you can deposit them confidently in the bank; the bank guarantees you a certain amount of interest on your savings, and the bank makes the loan to Joe's Garage. This is an efficient process; the bank specializes in knowing about small business firms so that you do not have to.

Imagine if banks did not exist and you were too worried about risk to lend money to Joe's Garage. Then your money would remain under your mattress, and Joe's Garage would go out of business because it lacked the funds to buy needed equipment. If there were many businesses like Joe's Garage and many people unwilling to lend, businesses would have trouble expanding, and the economy would not grow very fast. Banks allow the economy to be stronger and to grow faster, allowing more jobs to be created and letting businesses expand more easily.

8-1a Asymmetric-Information Problems

Banks gather information about potential borrowers to determine their ability to repay loans. Bankers realize, however, that individuals and businesses seeking loans are going to "put their best foot forward." That is, they are likely to provide selective information that would induce the bank to approve the loan. For example, a business firm might ask its best customer to order extra product just before the firm asks for a loan so that the bank will think that the firm's orders are growing rapidly. Borrowers know more about their prospects than the bank does, and so the bank must devote time and resources to learn about the borrower. This situation, in which one party in a transaction knows more than another, is called **asymmetric information.**

Asymmetric information causes two problems: (1) adverse selection and (2) moral hazard. Adverse selection comes from asymmetric information that arises before a contract is agreed on; moral hazard comes from asymmetric information that arises after a contract is agreed on. These problems also apply to transactions other than bank loans, and we will present examples that do not apply to banks before explaining how they affect banks.

Adverse selection. Adverse selection occurs when people or firms that are worse than average risks are more likely to enter a contract that is offered to everyone; in banking it means that bad borrowers are more likely to seek a loan than good borrowers.

A good example of adverse selection is the used-car market. People whose new cars turn out to be lemons are more likely to sell them in the used-car market than

> **bank** a financial intermediary that accepts deposits from savers and makes loans to borrowers; includes commercial banks, savings banks, savings-and-loan associations, and credit unions
>
> **asymmetric information** a situation in which one party in a transaction knows more than another
>
> **adverse selection** the problem that people or firms that are worse than average risks are more likely to seek out loans than borrowers that are better than average risks

people whose new cars work well. Therefore, the selection of used cars is adverse; the market for used cars contains cars of lower than average quality. Thus, when you are shopping for a used car, you must be concerned about the risk of buying a car that does not run well.

In banking, the problem is similar. Suppose that a bank offers loans at high interest rates. The problem is that people or firms that are good credit risks will not want to pay a high interest rate; only people or firms that cannot obtain loans elsewhere will apply for such loans. Thus, if the bank makes a loan to anyone who asks, it should expect that many of the loans will not be repaid. In short, the least desirable borrowers from the bank's point of view are the ones most likely to want to borrow money at a high interest rate.

Potential borrowers can be either good or bad. Good borrowers are likely to use the proceeds of a loan productively and pay the loan back. Bad borrowers are less likely to do so. The asymmetric-information problem is that the borrowers know which camp they fall into, but the banks do not. Banks have to sort out the good borrowers from the bad; doing so is one of their main functions. Adverse selection arises because bad borrowers are more likely to ask for a loan than good borrowers.

Moral hazard. The term **moral hazard** may seem unusual, but the two words describe the problem. The word *moral* means that the correctness of people's behavior is in question. *Hazard* means that this behavior can cause harm. In a situation of moral hazard, the existence of a contract changes the behavior of a party to the contract, doing harm to the other party.

We can observe moral hazard in the behavior of people when they insure property. Imagine, for example, that you were completely insured against all automobile accidents. In such a case, you might drive more recklessly than if you had to pay for car repairs that resulted from an accident. Or if you insured the contents of your home against theft, you might become careless about locking up your house. You drive recklessly or leave your home unlocked because you know that you are fully insured; your knowledge about the effort you put into securing

your house is a source of asymmetric information. You cause harm to other drivers by your recklessness. You cause harm to other insurance policyholders because your bills for car repairs or loss from theft are paid by the insurance company, which gets the funds from insurance premiums on policyholders. Thus, moral hazard causes increased costs to other drivers and higher premiums to insurance policyholders.

Moral hazard arises in banking if the firm receiving a bank loan behaves differently because it has the loan than if it didn't have the loan, in a way that harms the bank. For instance, suppose that Joe, the owner of Joe's Garage, comes to Barry, the owner of Barry's Bank, with a loan request. Joe tells Barry that business is so good that he could increase his profits if he could double the size of his building, but he needs a loan of $500,000 to do so. Joe might show Barry all his financial statements from the past few years and assure Barry that if he got the loan and built the bigger building, he would earn an extra $500,000 in profit the first year and could repay the loan quickly.

Here we have a situation in which there is asymmetric information. All the information about Joe's prospects comes from Joe himself, and Barry has not verified it. If Barry makes the loan, based only on Joe's claims about his business, he might be in for a shock. With $500,000 available to him, Joe might spend the money building an addition to his garage that makes his life more pleasant (such as putting in a room for a pool table and a large-screen TV) but will not be of use in generating additional profits. If Joe did not have access to the funds provided by the loan, he would not have built the pool room.

Solutions to asymmetric-information problems. How do banks avoid the asymmetric-information problems of moral hazard and adverse selection? They begin by gathering as much information as possible about potential borrowers. The more information they have, the more they reduce asymmetric-information problems because they come to know nearly as much about the borrower's prospects as the borrower does.

In addition to gathering information, banks impose restrictions on borrowers to constrain their behavior. These restrictions are (1) requiring collateral, (2) requiring certain amounts of net worth, and (3) writing covenants into the loan contract.

One common restriction is the pledge of something of value as collateral for the loan. **Collateral** is an asset that a borrower promises to give to the bank if that borrower is unable to repay the bank's loan. The court

moral hazard the situation in which the existence of a contract changes the behavior of a party to the contract; for example, if a firm receiving a bank loan behaves differently because it has the loan than if it didn't have the loan, in a way that harms the bank

collateral an asset that a borrower promises to give to the bank if that borrower is unable to repay the bank's loan

system enforces the promise, so it is legally binding. For example, if a small-business owner wants to take out a loan for $100,000, the bank might ask him to put up his house as collateral for the loan. In the case of most loans that consumers take out to buy houses or cars, the house or car itself is the collateral. Often the collateral is worth more than the loan amount, so the bank is well protected against loss.

Collateral reduces the problem of moral hazard and the bank's risk in making a loan. The borrower has no incentive to abscond with the funds because if he does, he will lose his collateral, which is of greater value than the funds that were borrowed. The only exception occurs when the value of the collateral falls sharply after the loan is made. For example, from 2007 to 2009, the first-ever nationwide decline in housing prices occurred, causing many home borrowers to owe more than their homes were worth. In such a case, if the borrower defaults on the loan, the bank takes possession of the home, but the fall in the home's value means that the bank will suffer a loss.

A second restriction that banks impose on borrowers to reduce asymmetric-information problems is to have the borrower maintain a certain net worth. This restriction prevents existing borrowers from engaging in moral hazard because they must repay the loan if their net worth falls below a certain level. Net-worth requirements for new borrowers also can help to reduce adverse selection. (However, net-worth requirements lead to the quip that banks lend only to people who don't really need the money.)

Loan covenants also reduce asymmetric-information problems. A **covenant** is a legally enforced part of a loan contract that requires the borrower to act in a certain way or to use the borrowed funds for a particular purpose. Because the borrower has a legal obligation to honor the covenant, the bank has some assurance that the funds will be used as the borrower stated they would be when she made the loan request. For example, one common covenant requires a firm that borrows from a bank to keep its checking account at the bank; such a covenant helps the bank make sure that the firm is not engaging in dubious transactions (and also may help the bank profit from the fees it charges and the interest it can earn on the firm's deposits).

Reducing adverse selection is perhaps the most difficult task a banker faces. The task is especially daunting over the course of the business cycle. Many firms look profitable when the economy is growing rapidly. During a recession, however, some firms go bankrupt. A banker must be skilled at interpreting financial statements that show how the firm has performed over many years to determine how likely it is that the firm will experience financial difficulties during economic downturns. A well-known banking adage is that most bad loans are made in good times. In many cases, loans that went bad did so only because of a downturn in the overall economy. Thus, a banker must think about not only what a firm's financial condition is today but also what it will look like if economic conditions deteriorate.

8-1b Failures of the Banking System

Banks are key players in the financial system and the economy. But their performance is not always flawless, and when banks encounter problems, they cause inefficiencies in the transfer of funds from savers to borrowers and disruptions in the economy. We will describe three recent breakdowns in the banking system that had detrimental effects: the savings-and-loan crisis, the credit crunch of the early 1990s, and the financial crisis of 2008.

The savings-and-loan crisis. Savings-and-loan associations (S&Ls) once made half the nation's home mortgage loans, but their share of the mortgage market has fallen to less than one-fifth today. S&Ls existed to take deposits (mostly in the form of savings accounts) and make loans to people for purchasing houses. The government helped them in this noble cause by giving them certain advantages over other banks, such as the right to pay a slightly higher interest rate on some types of deposits than commercial banks were allowed to pay.

However, the activities of S&Ls were risky. First of all, they were lending money to borrowers in their local areas only and for home mortgages only. Thus, their portfolios were undiversified both geographically and in the types of assets they owned. Thus, their portfolios were very risky. A downturn in the local economy or in housing values would reduce the value of an S&L.

Second, S&Ls attracted short-term deposits but made long-term loans. For the most part, the money that the S&Ls were using to lend for mortgages came from savings accounts, in which people were paid a fixed rate of interest but generally could withdraw their funds at any time, and certificates of deposits

covenant a part of a loan contract that requires the borrower to act in a certain way or to use the borrowed funds for a particular purpose

(CDs), which paid a higher interest rate than savings deposits but had to be left in the S&L for a fixed amount of time, usually one to three years. However, the mortgage loans made by S&Ls generally were for 30 years. Thus, the S&Ls were providing a service to people by obtaining short-term funds (because depositors did not want their money tied up for too long) and making long-term loans for houses. These activities also put the S&Ls at great risk because if interest rates rose substantially and remained high, they would have to pay more on their deposits than they were earning on their home loans. In the 1970s, managers of S&Ls could look at the past history of interest rates and not be too concerned because high interest rates usually did not last too long.

Unfortunately for the S&Ls, past history was a poor guide to predicting interest rates. In the second half of the 1970s, the Federal Reserve allowed inflation to creep higher and higher. As inflation rose, and as people began to expect higher inflation, nominal interest rates throughout the economy started to rise. S&Ls were in a bind because the interest rates they had to pay their depositors were rising, whereas the interest they received on long-term home loans that they had made in the past was fixed at lower rates. Consequently, many of the S&Ls suffered losses.

The crisis intensified in late 1979. At that time, the Federal Reserve finally decided to reduce inflation, and it sharply reduced the growth rate of the money supply, driving interest rates up sharply. The huge rise in interest rates was catastrophic for S&Ls. They had to issue new CDs at even higher rates because competitive pressures made those rates rise with interest rates in general. The S&Ls began suffering huge losses. Altogether, S&Ls lost several billion dollars in a very short time because of the change in interest rates.

So far this is not a very pleasant story. It is a classic case in banking in which a set of institutions based their decisions on historical behavior, in this case the behavior of interest rates. Never before had interest rates risen to such high levels and remained so high for so long. The S&Ls had taken on risks that led to losses when interest rates rose in this way. Had the S&Ls that were most severely affected by high interest rates been declared bankrupt and closed their doors, the entire episode would have been just a footnote in history. Unfortunately, what happened next turned the footnote into an entire chapter.

When the S&Ls suffered losses in the late 1970s and early 1980s, the normal course of events would have been that the banking regulators would close those whose condition had deteriorated sufficiently. In this case, the regulators were the Federal Home Loan Bank Board (FHLBB) and the Federal Savings-and-Loan Insurance Corporation (FSLIC), both of which no longer exist. The FHLBB established the rules under which S&Ls operated, and the FSLIC insured S&L depositors against loss. When an S&L went bankrupt, the FSLIC would pay the depositors and sell off the S&L's assets to recoup the money or sell the entire S&L to a bank that wanted to expand. Only after it had done so would the S&L's bondholders and stockholders get any of their invested funds back. For this reason, the regulators require S&Ls to have substantial equity capital (the value of the equity initially paid by shareholders when the S&L was started plus retained earnings accrued over time). In this way, if the S&L fails, the stockholders, not the government, will lose their money. Society benefits when stockholders bear the risk of a bank failure because it gives stockholders the incentive to monitor the bank and make sure that it is not acting irresponsibly, behavior that we have identified as moral hazard.

In the early 1980s, looking at the carnage of S&Ls throughout the country whose balance sheets had been destroyed by high interest rates, economists and accountants knew that many of the S&Ls were in financial difficulty. At one point, the FHLBB and FSLIC could have declared over half the S&Ls bankrupt. For various reasons, though, the S&Ls were not shut down. The regulators allowed them to remain open by adding fictional "regulatory capital" to their balance sheets, which they could add to their equity capital. In a sense, it was not the S&Ls' fault that they failed but rather the dramatic and unprecedented change in interest rates. Politicians were not happy that many S&Ls were bankrupt, because the government had supported home ownership through laws that effectively subsidized the S&L industry. And of course, politicians received many campaign contributions from S&Ls. The result was political pressure on the regulators to not close down the S&Ls.

The S&Ls blamed their woes on economic conditions and the banking regulations that forced them to take so much risk. They were required to make local home loans, which caused their portfolios to lack diversification. Therefore, in 1980, the government enacted new laws at their request allowing the S&Ls to expand both geographically and in the types of loans they made. The size of accounts covered by deposit insurance was raised from $40,000 to $100,000, thus keeping wealthy depositors from pulling out of the

S&Ls. And the S&Ls were allowed to sell brokered CDs offering high interest rates to attract large deposits. In addition, because fixed-rate mortgage loans contributed to the S&Ls' woes, the government allowed S&Ls to begin offering variable-rate mortgages, which allow the interest rate and monthly payment on a mortgage to change as interest rates in the bond market change, thus reducing the risk to S&Ls from rising interest rates.

At this point regulators and legislators created a moral-hazard problem. We now had a situation in which S&Ls were bankrupt but knew that the regulators were not about to close them down. A banker at one of these S&Ls had two choices: (1) keep investing conservatively, hoping for a decline in interest rates so that some day profits would make up for past losses, or (2) make risky loans, hoping for a big, quick profit. In the second case, an investment in risky loans meant making loans at high interest rates to borrowers who had a substantial probability of defaulting on the loans. If default occurred, the FSLIC, not the S&L's owners, would pick up the tab because the S&L was already bankrupt. On the other hand, if the speculative investments were successful, the banker would be a hero for saving the institution and probably would get a huge raise and bonus. The incentive was clear: Bet the entire S&L on a big payoff.

Because these S&Ls were technically bankrupt but still engaging in banking activity, they came to be known as "zombies" or "zombie thrifts." They were the walking dead of the banking industry, and they destroyed everything in their wake. Because they began competing with banks for business loans, banks were sucked into speculative lending as well. S&Ls began making loans for office buildings far from home. A speculative frenzy in real estate ensued in many cities, which in turn helped cause the credit crunch of the 1990s (discussed next). And the S&Ls marched on, desperate to survive, yet continuing to act irresponsibly.

In situations such as these, there is always a day of reckoning. The S&Ls managed to remain afloat for several years, losing more and more money. Finally, the government responded by closing some of them. A few had taken big gambles and won, and those institutions survived. Most, however, were shut down when the recession of 1990 took hold and legislation to restructure the banking industry was enacted in the early 1990s. The number of S&Ls declined from over 4,000 in the 1970s to about 3,000 by the mid-1980s and to under 500 by 1999. The drop was especially sharp in the early 1990s as the S&L crisis was resolved.

Altogether, the S&Ls left the FSLIC responsible for losses estimated at $153 billion, most of which resulted from moral hazard.[1] Of course, the FSLIC was just an

---

[1]Timothy Curry and Lynn Shibut, "The Cost of the Savings and Loan Crisis: Truth and Consequences," *FDIC Banking Review*, December 2000, pp. 26–35.

insurance fund, which obtained its money through a fee imposed on S&Ls, but the fund had nowhere near enough money to cover the S&Ls' losses. So where did the money come from to pay off the depositors? Eventually, the government sold bonds to borrow the money from the public. Ultimately, the bonds were paid off in part with taxpayers' money and in part by imposing fees on the rest of the banking industry. Thus, U.S. citizens bore the cost in the form of higher prices for banking services and higher taxes than otherwise would have been the case.

The lessons learned by the banking industry and by banking regulators were clear. First, banks should be careful about the risks they are taking; unprecedented events sometimes occur. Second, regulators must close weak financial institutions quickly, or their actions will cause moral-hazard problems. Third, the structure of regulations must allow for the risk that banks take and not force them into positions where they cannot adjust.

The credit crunch of the early 1990s. A **credit crunch** occurs when banks do not lend money as they ordinarily would but rather have much higher requirements for borrowers to qualify for loans than normal. It is harder for borrowers to qualify for credit, so banks do not lend as much. A credit crunch occurred from 1990 to 1992. It arose in part because of lax lending standards in the preceding few years. In the late 1980s, a combination of favorable tax laws, a booming economy, and competition from failing S&Ls that needed to make money quickly encouraged banks to make loans that turned out to be problematic. Despite growing vacancies, banks made loans for the construction of new office and apartment buildings in major cities. When the economy moved into a recession in 1990, many banks realized that they would never be repaid for these real estate projects. At the same time, new legislation was passed that increased the amount of equity capital that banks had to hold and thus could not use to make loans.

The result was a significant decrease in the number of loans that banks made to businesses. Because of the overbuilding of office space and apartment buildings in large cities, banks were unwilling to lend for those types of projects. Because the higher capital requirements

credit crunch a situation in which banks do not lend money as they ordinarily would but rather have much higher requirements for borrowers to qualify for loans than normal

were tied to the riskiness of a bank's assets, banks were scrambling to modify their portfolios to hold more safe assets (such as Treasury securities) and fewer risky assets (such as business loans). Thus, the banking system failed, at least for a time, to deliver funds from depositors to borrowers.

Research studies showed that small businesses felt the brunt of the credit crunch. Unlike large firms, which can raise capital by issuing stocks or bonds in capital markets, small businesses rely on bank loans to finance their operations. Because bank loans were difficult to secure, many small businesses failed to grow, and others went out of business completely.

The financial crisis of 2008. In 2007, house prices began to decline in the United States, leading millions of people to find themselves owing more on their mortgages than their houses were worth. As many of those people found themselves unable or unwilling to repay their mortgage loans, many banks faced much larger losses on mortgage loans than they had anticipated. As investors in the market began to fear massive failures of banks, they began to withdraw their investments in the financial sector of the economy. The stock prices of banks began to plummet, and the entire stock market fell with them. The mild recession that the country was in suddenly became much worse in fall 2008. Numerous banks and other financial companies failed or were forced to merge with others, and investors all over the world began to pull out of any risky investments and seek the safety of U.S. government bonds.

Such a flight to safety had grave consequences for the U.S. and world economies. With investors seeking only very safe investments, thousands of firms that were perceived as risky were forced to close their doors because they could not obtain financing. In the fourth quarter of 2008, the shutting down of all risky markets caused a sharp decline in international trade, so that GDP declined 9 percent (at an annual rate) in the United States, but over twice that much throughout most of Asia because of the decline in U.S. purchases of goods exported from those countries. The Federal Reserve tried to help by buying a variety of financial assets in the market and extending loans to many banks and other financial firms that were not in danger of bankruptcy, as well as a few that were deemed so large that their failure would endanger the financial system, such as the insurance firm AIG. The federal government also made numerous loans to financial firms, such as mortgage lenders Fannie Mae and Freddie Mac, and many banks that were in trouble.

The financial crisis of 2008 occurred in large part because mortgage lenders had become complacent. From the mid-1990s to the mid-2000s, house prices had increased dramatically and there appeared to be no end in sight. Lenders were willing to extend mortgage loans to just about anyone who wanted one, making subprime loans (to borrowers who were high risks), and even making so-called NINJA loans (to people with No Income, No Job, or Assets). Such loans were predicated on house prices continuing to rise, which led banks to believe that they had plenty of collateral in case of a loan default. But when house prices began to decline in 2007, those loans quickly went bad.

The financial crisis was made much worse by the fact that numerous financial firms were highly leveraged. The investment bank Bear Stearns, for example, was forced to merge with another firm after suffering losses on numerous mortgage-related assets. Bear Stearns had assets of 34 times its capital, which meant that a 3 percent decline in the value of its assets wiped out its entire capital base. Other investment banks faced similar situations; many merged with commercial banks

Jin Lee/Bloomberg/Getty Images

and were then forced to de-leverage to meet regulatory requirements, thus selling off many assets at once and causing asset prices to decline still further. The government kept a number of firms, including Bear Stearns, from declaring bankruptcy, fearing that the failure of such firms would lead to a deepening of the crisis. But by preventing them from going under, the government risked increasing moral hazard by such firms in the future, as they now know that they are too big for the government to let them fail. They may make riskier investment decisions as a result.

In the stock market, as investors all tried to change from investing in risky assets to safer assets, the attempt by so many investors to sell assets all at once caused prices to plummet. Stock returns in 2008 were the lowest ever (since 1875 when accurate records of overall stock prices were first kept). In part, many investors had placed their investments with mutual funds or hedge funds. As they asked for their shares to be redeemed, the mutual funds and hedge funds had no choice but to sell their assets in the market, even at very low prices. On numerous days in fall 2008, the stock market declined by several percentage points in the last half-hour of trading, as mutual funds and hedge funds tried to sell their assets before the end of the trading day.

The main lingering concern at banks in the aftermath of the financial crisis was what to do with all the bad assets on their books. The government developed a fund, called the TARP (Troubled Asset Relief Program), with which it hoped to buy the bad assets from banks, then recapitalize them, so banks could get back to the business of making good loans to sound borrowers. But the TARP didn't work out as planned because the number of troubled assets was so large. If the government bought only some of them at low prices, all the other similar assets would have to be revalued on banks' books at the low prices, and many more banks would have to declare bankruptcy. An attempt to rework that plan began in mid-2009, but in 2008, the government had used the funds to simply invest in banks and give them capital in exchange for sharing in their future profits.

The Dodd–Frank Act, passed in 2010, attempted to remedy the problems that caused the financial crisis by reining in the mortgage industry, adding regulations on firms that pose a risk to the financial system, protecting consumers from predatory practices, and imposing new rules to keep banks safer. (We will discuss the Dodd–Frank Act in more detail in Chapter 9.)

1	Banks provide liquidity to borrowers and lenders by pooling funds and gathering information about borrowers.
2	Banks face two asymmetric-information problems: adverse selection and moral hazard. Adverse selection occurs because undesirable borrowers are more likely to apply for bank loans than desirable borrowers. Moral hazard occurs because borrowers use borrowed funds in ways other than the bank intended.
3	Banks counter asymmetric-information problems using collateral, net-worth requirements, and covenants.
4	The savings-and-loan crisis arose when inflation rose to high levels in the late 1970s. Bankrupt S&Ls were not closed by regulators, and the resulting moral-hazard problem led them to invest speculatively, causing their losses to multiply.
5	The credit crunch of the early 1990s occurred when the economy entered a recession and new regulations forced banks to reduce the risk of their assets. The credit crunch mostly affected small businesses, which were unable to obtain bank loans.
6	The financial crisis of 2008 was a direct result of failures in the banking system. Banks made low-quality mortgage loans, which turned bad when house prices began declining. Banks and other large financial firms were bailed out by the government, which may encourage future moral hazard.

8-2 How Do Banks Earn Profits?

We have stated that banks attract deposits from savers and use those funds to make loans, but we have not explained how banks make decisions that lead to profits. In this section we go behind the scenes to describe how banks decide how much to lend and how they influence the amount of funds flowing into the bank and the amount flowing out. Banks earn profits by borrowing funds from depositors at one interest rate and lending those funds to borrowers at a higher interest rate.

8-2a A Bank's Balance Sheet

Let's consider the fictional example of Barry's Bank. Barry's Bank owns some assets on which it earns interest and has some liabilities on which it pays interest. The bank also has some equity capital, which equals the initial payments to the firm when it first sold stock plus earnings that the firm has retained and not paid out as dividends.

We list equity capital on the right-hand side of the balance sheet because accounting rules are set up so that

$$Assets = liabilities + equity\ capital \qquad (1)$$

Suppose that Barry's Bank has a balance sheet that looks like this:

Balance Sheet for Barry's Bank
(amounts in millions of dollars)

Assets		Liabilities + Capital	
Reserves	129	Transactions deposits	123
Securities	348	Nontransactions deposits	1107
Loans	933	Borrowings	187
Other assets	330	Other liabilities	125
		Equity capital	198
Total assets	1740	Total liabilities + capital	1740

The balance sheet for Barry's Bank is fairly typical of U.S. banks in terms of the split of its assets between the different asset categories and the split of its liabilities between the different types of liabilities (in fact, it is based on the U.S. average for commercial banks and savings institutions in 2010). Let's look at each of these categories of assets and liabilities in turn.

The smallest asset category, but one that is quite important, is **reserves,** which equal the bank's vault cash and its deposits at the Federal Reserve. As the name makes clear, vault cash is simply the amount of cash (currency and coins) that the bank has in its own vault. Banks also keep money on deposit at their local Federal Reserve Bank. (The 12 Federal Reserve Banks span the country, and banks may keep deposits at one of the Fed branches.) Keeping deposits at the Fed is convenient because when all banks have money on deposit at the Fed, they can all clear their transactions through the Fed, and a simple computer program can take care of all the accounting. If Barry's Bank owes Charlie's Credit Union $57,000, the institutions tell the Fed to take the funds from Barry's Bank's account at the Fed and put it into Charlie's Credit Union's account. All that happens is a change of two numbers in the Fed's computer system. Thus, no bank needs to transfer cash to another bank; they simply adjust their account balances at the Fed.

The second category of assets is securities other than loans, which are mainly debt securities because banks generally are restricted from holding equity securities (as we will discuss in Chapter 9). Banks hold a large number of debt securities, which provide a good source of liquidity. When banks need cash, they can sell securities in the market quickly and at low cost.

Banks earn most of their profits from the third asset category—loans. A bank that makes good loans will earn a significant profit; banks that make loans that are not repaid realize losses. For Barry's Bank, loans are over 50 percent of assets. Banks prosper or fail by their ability to make good loans to individuals and businesses. The average bank makes about 20 percent of its loans to business firms, 60 percent of its loans for the purchase of real estate (mainly home mortgages and mortgages on business buildings), and 20 percent for consumer loans (such as automobile loans and credit card loans).

On the liability side, the first item for Barry's Bank is transactions deposits. Transactions deposits are funds in checking accounts of various types. You might think that money in checking accounts is the main source of a bank's funds, but it represents less than 10 percent of the total.

The second liability item is nontransactions deposits, which total over 70 percent of Barry's Bank's liabilities. These are deposit accounts that do not offer check writing, the largest of which are savings deposits (passbook savings accounts) and time deposits (CDs), as well as deposit accounts with limited check writing, such as money-market deposit accounts (MMDAs) that have a limit of three check transactions per month.

The third type of liability is borrowings. Banks may borrow from each other, they may borrow from the private sector, or they may borrow from public-sector institutions such as the Federal Home Loan Banks (FHLBs) or the Federal Reserve. Borrowings are about 12 percent of Barry's Bank's liabilities.

Equity capital consists of the value of shareholders' investment in the bank. The bank's original equity capital came into existence when the bank initially sold its stock in its initial public offering. Over time, as the bank earned profits, it returned some of the profits to the shareholders in the form of dividends and kept the rest, called *retained earnings*, which were added to the bank's equity capital.

Every entry onto the balance sheet must be made to ensure that the equality in Equation (1) holds. For example, suppose that someone walks into the bank and deposits $3,000 in cash into a checking account. On the asset side of the balance sheet, reserves rise by $3,000. On the liability side, transactions deposits rise by $3,000. The balance sheet changes as shown here:

reserves a bank's vault cash plus its deposits at its Federal Reserve bank

Change in Balance Sheet for Barry's Bank (dollars)	
Assets	**Liabilities + Capital**
Reserves +3,000	Transactions +3,000 deposits

Another example is that if the bank makes a loan to a business customer for $150,000, loans rise by $150,000 on the asset side of the balance sheet, and transactions deposits rise by $150,000 on the liability side of the balance sheet because the bank makes the funds it lends available in the business's checking account:

Change in Balance Sheet for Barry's Bank (dollars)

Assets		Liabilities + Capital	
Loans	+150,000	Transactions deposits	+150,000

Suppose that a bank customer wrote a check for $90,000 to someone with an account at another bank. Barry's Bank would reduce the customer's balance by $90,000 and would transfer $90,000 in funds to the other bank, thus reducing its reserves. Then the balance sheet for Barry's Bank would change in this way:

Change in Balance Sheet for Barry's Bank (dollars)

Assets		Liabilities + Capital	
Reserves	−90,000	Transactions deposits	−90,000

If someone moved funds from his checking account into his money-market deposit account, the balance sheet would change like this:

Change in Balance Sheet for Barry's Bank (dollars)

Assets	Liabilities + Capital	
	Transactions Deposits	−60,000
	Nontransactions Deposits	+60,000

If the bank went to the government securities market and sold $250,000 in government bonds (in exchange for cash, which is counted as reserves), the balance sheet would change like this:

Change in Balance Sheet for Barry's Bank (dollars)

Assets		Liabilities + Capital
Reserves	+250,000	
Securities	−250,000	

As our last example, suppose that the bank borrows $500,000 from the FHLB (at a low interest rate), obtaining cash (transaction 1). It then lends those funds to a customer at a higher interest rate (transaction 2). The customer then spends the funds (transaction 3). Each of these transactions is recorded on this balance sheet:

Change in Balance Sheet for Barry's Bank (dollars)

Transaction		Assets	Liabilities + Capital	
1	Reserves	+500,000	Borrowings	+500,000
2	Loans	+500,000	Transactions deposits	+500,000
3	Reserves	−500,000	Transactions deposits	−500,000

If we net out the offsetting amounts in this example, the total change in the bank's balance sheet is this:

Change in Balance Sheet for Barry's Bank (dollars)

Assets		Liabilities + Capital	
Loans	+500,000	Borrowings	+500,000

In effect, the bank borrowed at a low interest rate and lent at a higher rate.

8-2b Reserve Accounting

Banks manage their funds by adjusting the size of their reserves. Reserves are also a key variable for monetary policy because the Fed's actions affect banks' reserves. Keep in mind that

> Reserves = vault cash + deposits at the Federal Reserve $\quad$ **(2)**

By law, banks are required to maintain a certain amount of reserves. The required amount of reserves equals a percentage of the deposits in a bank's transactions accounts. Required reserves in 2013 were determined according to Table 8.1.

In the case of Barry's Bank, with $123 million in transactions deposits, required reserves would be calculated as follows: Because the bank has more than $79.5 million in transactions deposits, it will be required to hold no reserves on some of its deposits, 3 percent reserves on some, and 10 percent reserves on some, as the following breakdown shows:

> *Required reserves*
> $0.00 \times \$12.4 \text{ million} = \$0$
> $+ 0.03 \times (\$79.5 - \$12.4) \text{ million} = \$2,013,000$
> $+ 0.10 \times (\$123.0 - \$79.5) \text{ million} = \$4,350,000$
> $= \$6,363,000$

The first line shows that the bank is not required to hold any reserves against the first $12.4 million of its transactions deposits. The reserve requirement is 3 percent on deposits between $12.4 million and $79.5 million, so the bank must hold $0.03 \times (\$79.5 - \$12.4)$ million $= 0.03 \times \$67.1$ million $= \$2,013,000$ in reserves against those deposits, as the second line shows. Subtracting $79.5 million from $123.0 million shows that the bank has $43.5 million on which it must hold reserves of 10 percent. Those required reserves are $0.10 \times (\$123.0 - \$79.5)$ million $= 0.10 \times \$43.5$ million $= \$4.35$ million. So, the bank's total reserve requirement is $\$2,013,000 + \$4,350,000 = \$6,363,000$.

TABLE 8.1 Reserve Requirements for 2013

Amount of Bank's Transactions Deposits	Reserve Requirement
The first $12.4 million	0 percent
Amounts from $12.4 to $79.5 million	3 percent
Amounts over $79.5 million	10 percent

Note: The cutoff amounts ($12.4 and $79.5 million in 2013) are adjusted by formula each year to reflect the nationwide growth of transactions accounts in the banking system.

© Cengage Learning

Thus, Barry's Bank would be required to hold reserves of $6,363,000, given that it has $123 million in transactions deposits. The requirements do not force banks to hold exactly that amount of required reserves continuously on a daily basis; rather, they may average their reserve holdings (and their transactions deposit amounts) over a two-week period. Therefore, they must meet their reserve requirements on average every two weeks.

Because Barry's Bank's balance sheet shows that it has $129 million in reserves, it has sufficient reserves to meet its requirements. In fact, it has $122,637,000 more reserves than are required, because $129,000,000 − $6,363,000 = $122,637,000.

What does a bank do when it has more reserves than required? In such a situation, the bank is said to have excess reserves. The amount of **excess reserves** equals a bank's total reserves minus its required reserves. The bank can use its excess reserves in five ways: (1) hold them, (2) lend them in the federal funds market, (3) deposit them at the Fed's Term Deposit Facility, (4) buy securities with them, and (5) make new loans with them. The first option, holding excess reserves, is a safe practice, and since October 2008 the Fed has paid interest on excess reserves held at the Fed. The second option, lending the reserves in the federal funds market, is attractive because the costs of doing so are low, and the bank earns interest. The **federal funds market** is the market in which banks with excess reserves lend them to banks that desire additional reserves. The market is called the federal funds market because transactions take place entirely on the Federal Reserve's computer system; the Fed simply records the transaction and credits the borrowing bank with additional reserves in its account at the Fed, removing the reserves from the account of the lending bank. The interest rate in the federal funds market is called the **federal funds rate.** The choice between holding reserves and lending them in the federal funds market has become more complicated since late 2008, as described in the later section "Interest on Reserves."

A new option that became available to banks in 2010 is to deposit their excess reserves at the Federal Reserve's Term Deposit Facility. The Fed designed this facility to help it manage the total volume of reserves in the economy. Banks offer reserves in a competitive auction process that determines the interest rate on the deposits that are kept at the Fed for a predetermined amount of time, such as four weeks. Because banks agree to keep the deposits at the Fed for several weeks, the interest rate is likely to be higher than the interest rate on reserves or the federal funds rate.

The other two options for using excess reserves are buying securities or making new loans. Because these options will tie up the excess reserves for a long period, a bank will buy securities or make new loans only if it thinks that it will have excess reserves for some time; if the excess reserves are not expected to be available for long, the bank will lend in the federal funds market.

Banks that are short of reserves have five sensible options: (1) borrow in the federal funds market, (2) borrow from the Fed at the discount window, (3) sell some securities, (4) reduce loans outstanding, or (5) issue some CDs. One last option is not sensible: A bank could remain short of reserves, but it would be fined substantially by the Fed. No bank ever chooses this option.

If the shortfall of reserves appears to be just a short-term problem, the bank likely will borrow in the federal funds market. It also might borrow funds from the Federal Reserve. The Federal Reserve offers loans to banks at its **discount window;** the interest rate on such loans is called the **discount rate.** Banks in good financial condition can borrow at a lower discount rate than banks in poor condition.

If the shortfall of reserves appears to be long-lived, the bank will choose to modify its assets or liabilities to bring its reserves into balance. The easiest way to increase reserves is to sell off some securities, thus gaining the cash to meet the reserve requirements. Alternatively, the bank might reduce the number of loans it has outstanding by not renewing some loans when they come due or perhaps even selling some of its loans to another bank. Finally, the

excess reserves a bank's total reserves minus its required reserves

federal funds market the market in which banks with excess reserves lend them to banks that desire additional reserves

federal funds rate the interest rate in the federal funds market

discount window the place where banks can request loans from the Federal Reserve

discount rate the interest rate a bank pays on a loan from the Fed's discount window

Those Pesky ATM Fees

For many years, banks provided ATM access for free. Banks realized that it was much less expensive for them to maintain ATMs than it was to provide tellers, and bank customers liked the convenience of getting money whenever they wanted to. In the 1990s, however, banks began charging people to use their ATMs. Mostly, a bank charges a customer who uses the bank's ATMs but does not have an account at that bank.

Why was ATM use free for many years? Banks wanted to encourage people to use the ATMs and to become accustomed to how they worked. Cynics might even argue that banks wanted people to get hooked on ATMs so that they could raise the fees for using them once people were addicted. However, there was a good rationale for free ATM use initially. An ATM is part of a network that is not valuable if every ATM is isolated from every other one. The value in the network comes when customers have access to their funds no matter where they are in the world. Thus, as banks built larger and larger networks, keeping fees low helped to encourage the networks to grow.

Banks began charging fees for ATM use once the ATM network was big enough. The fees keep small banks from becoming free riders on the network. Without fees, a small bank that contributed nothing to the ATM network could take advantage of the network's existence without adding to it. The fee charged by the ATM's owner to the customer of the small bank pays for the convenience of having the ATM. If there were no fees, banks would have little incentive to provide their own ATMs but instead would ask customers to use the ATMs of other banks.

Some people complain that ATM fees are unfair because they preferred the situation when they could use ATMs for free. With the fees in place, most customers can go to their own banks' ATMs to avoid a fee or pay the fee to another bank to use its ATMs if that is more convenient. The choice is theirs. In any event, if there were no fees, there would be far fewer ATMs available.

Getty Images/Jupiterimages

ATMs provide convenience for many bank services, especially withdrawing cash. In recent years, banks have increased fees for using ATMs from other banks. Although they are unpopular with bank customers, such fees help banks to maintain a large network of ATMs.

---

bank might offer a higher interest rate on its time deposits (CDs) to attract additional funds into the bank.

8-2c Bank Profits

How does a bank earn profits? The bank's income mostly comes from interest it receives from borrowers who take out loans and from the securities the bank owns. Only cash assets do not pay interest. In addition, banks earn income from fees charged for various other services, such as for use of automatic teller machines (ATMs), for safe deposit boxes, for managing investments for wealthy people or for retirement accounts, or for providing banking services by phone or via the Internet. (For an example of how banks earn fees for services, see the box titled "Those Pesky ATM Fees.")

From all the income it earns, the bank must cover its costs of operations (including overhead and wages for its workers) and pay interest to its depositors. The difference between the income and expenses is the bank's profits. Because most of the bank's assets earn interest, and because the bank must pay interest on most of its liabilities, the size of its profit depends mainly on the **spread,** which is the difference between the average interest rate on the assets and the average interest rate on the liabilities.

spread the difference between the average interest rate on a bank's assets and the average interest rate on its liabilities

Why Are Interest Rates on Credit Cards So High?

In the 1990s and 2000s, interest rates on most securities declined substantially from the levels they reached in the 1980s. One exception was the interest rates on credit cards, which remained stubbornly high. Why did the interest rates on credit cards not decline when other interest rates were falling? Economists have identified three main reasons: adverse selection, inelastic demand, and changes in the characteristics of credit-card holders.

Perhaps the most interesting reason that credit-card interest rates have remained so high is adverse selection. Banks that have sent out mass mailings offering credit cards at a below-average interest rate have found that many of the people who apply for such offers are very bad risks; that is, they are very likely to default on their cards. Default is so high that the bank cannot make a profit on the new cards. On the other hand, when banks offer credit cards at high rates, people who are bad risks are less attracted to the card offer, and those who get the cards pay an interest rate high enough that the bank can profit even though some customers default. People who are good risks may not worry about the high rates because they usually pay off their balances each month and thus do not pay interest anyway.

Another reason that credit-card interest rates are high is that the demand for cards is fairly inelastic; that is, the quantity demanded does not change very much

as the interest rate changes. Thus, people's use of credit cards does not respond very much to a change in the interest rate. Therefore, why should a bank lower its interest rate if it knows that it will not gain many additional customers from doing so? People tend to be slow to shop around for a new card even if a bank raises the interest rate on their current card. As a result, banks find that they do not lose many customers when they increase the interest rate on their cards. Banks often find it profitable to offer people new cards with low "teaser" interest rates for several months, hoping the people will build up a large credit balance; the banks then raise the interest rate substantially.

The third reason that credit-card interest rates remain high is that the mix of people who use credit cards has been changing over time. Forty years ago, when credit cards began to become popular, a person had to have a fairly high income just to qualify for a card, and defaults were rare. Over time, banks have extended credit cards to people with lower and lower incomes, including students. Naturally, default rates have risen because people with lower incomes are more likely to be adversely affected by some event in their lives, such as losing their jobs, and not be able to pay off their credit cards. As a result, banks charge higher interest rates to counteract the higher default risk and still be able to make a profit.

Competition from other banks limits the profits a bank can earn by changing the spread. If a bank tries to increase its spread by setting the interest rate it pays on its CDs much lower than its competitors, it would find depositors switching to other banks. If it charged an interest rate on loans that was much higher than its competitors, borrowers would go elsewhere. Competition keeps interest rates (on both loans and deposits) similar across banks. In fact, the more vigorous the competition among banks, the smaller will be the spread between the interest rates on loans and the interest rate on deposits. In big cities where large banks compete with each other, the spread is much narrower than in rural areas where there is not much competition. (For an analysis of how competition may not lower interest rates, see the box titled "Why Are Interest Rates on Credit Cards So High?")

The forces of competition, however, are changing the banking industry. Especially because of the advent of new technology, a bank that operates with large volumes will be able to reduce its costs by taking advantage of economies of scale and scope. Economies of scale occur when a firm's average costs decline as its volume of sales increases, whereas economies of scope occur when a firm branches out into different products and is able to reduce its costs in doing so. Because banks with many customers can run efficient computer systems and use the Internet to provide additional services, they have lower costs than small banks that may use older technology and lack a presence on the Web. As a result, medium-sized and large banks are merging and becoming larger, whereas small banks are remaining small. The spreads of the large banks are shrinking as they compete with each other, whereas small banks serve customers less efficiently (fewer ATMs, fewer electronic services) and at greater cost.

The FDIC compiles statistics on the spread between the average interest rate banks receive on their assets and the average interest rate they pay on their deposits. The spread was just under 4 percent until 1991, when new banking regulations raised banks' costs, causing the spread to rise to about 4.3 percent. It has gradually declined since 1991 and is about 3.7 percent today. But competition causes the spread to vary across banks depending on their size. There are almost 7,000 small banks in the United States, each with less than $1 billion in assets in 2010. These small banks face less competition than larger banks, and have spreads that average about 3.8 percent. Medium-sized banks, with assets between $1 billion and $10 billion, and large banks with assets above $10 billion, had a spread of 3.7 percent. The difference in spreads between small, medium-sized, and large banks was more pronounced when interest rates were higher than they were in 2010, with spreads generally being smallest for large banks and with small banks having the largest spreads. So banking is an industry in which location matters, and small banks do not face the same competitive pressures that large banks do.

default risk the possibility that a bank's loan customers might not repay their loans as specified in the loan agreement or that the issuer of securities (other than loans) the bank owns will not pay interest or principal when due; also called **credit risk**

interest-rate risk the risk that a change in market interest rates will affect the value of financial assets

Does the competitive pressure faced by large banks cause them to earn lower profits than small banks? The answer is not obvious without looking at the data because even though the spreads are smaller for large banks, they are more efficient, so their costs are lower. To see which banks are more profitable, we look at the return on equity; that is, we take each bank's profits and divide by the amount of their equity capital. In 2010, the 100 largest banks were the most profitable, averaging about 7 percent return on equity. Medium-sized and small banks did not do very well, averaging about a 1 percent return. So even though the spread is large for small and medium-sized banks, they operate with higher costs than large banks, and thus did not have higher returns.

8-2d The Risks Banks Take

Banks' profits are not guaranteed. Indeed, banks face a number of risks in their day-to-day operations, the most important of which are default risk and interest-rate risk.

Default risk, also called **credit risk,** is the possibility that a bank's loan customers might not repay their loans as specified in the loan agreement or that the issuer of securities (other than loans) the bank owns will not pay interest or principal when due. Every bank expects that a few of its loans will go into default because a borrower's financial condition may change. For example, the firm may make a bad investment decision; or the firm's customers may find a better product available, and the demand for the firm's product may decline substantially; or a person with a mortgage loan may become unemployed and be unable to make the required monthly payment. Default risk generally increases during a recession because many firms may suffer losses at once and thus have trouble making loan or interest payments. Default risk rose dramatically during the financial crisis of 2008 because of the deep recession and the sharp decline in house prices, which led many homeowners to default on their mortgages.

Interest-rate risk arises when market interest rates change, thus affecting the value of a bank's assets—both loans and securities. It was interest-rate risk that caused so much trouble in the savings-and-loan industry in the late 1970s and early 1980s because the S&Ls made long-term mortgage loans at low interest rates and then suffered losses on those loans as interest rates rose sharply.

Banks face several other risks, such as the risk that a large depositor suddenly will withdraw its funds; the risk that an official of the bank will steal money from the bank or its customers; the risk that a major system within the bank, such as its computer system, will break down; and the risk that the foreign-exchange rate will change when the bank has a number of loans to foreign countries.

How does a bank handle all these risks? Banks set up a variety of controls to ensure the safety and soundness of the bank's funds. Redundant accounting systems and frequent audits reduce the risk of fraud. Comprehensive analysis of potential risks can help the bank to understand its risks clearly. However, the two main types of risks, default risk and interest-rate risk, require special care.

To reduce the impact of default risk, the bank ensures that it has a diversified portfolio so that the failure of one firm or several firms in a single industry will not hurt the bank too badly. In addition, banks can decide how much default risk they are willing to take; they can make only very safe loans at low average interest rates, or they may make riskier loans at higher interest rates. In most banks, a loan committee composed of top officers of the bank examines every potential loan and decides if the loan represents an appropriate risk for the bank, denying loans that do not meet their standards.

To reduce interest-rate risk, a bank tries to manage its assets and liabilities to reduce the sensitivity of its profits to changes in interest rates. If the bank had assets with the same time to maturity as its liabilities, then changes in interest rates would not affect the bank's overall portfolio very much. Interest rates on both assets and liabilities would change at the same time, so the bank's spread would remain fairly constant. For example, if the S&Ls in the late 1970s and early 1980s had deposits that did not mature as soon, the increase in interest rates in general would not have led to such quick and dramatic losses for the S&Ls. As it was, most of the interest rates on their deposits rose immediately, causing the S&Ls' spread to become negative, and thus it became impossible for the S&Ls to make a profit.

How do banks manage their assets and liabilities to try to equalize their time to maturity? One way is to sell off some of their assets. These days, many banks originate loans (that is, they agree to a loan with a customer and provide the loan), especially mortgages or automobile loans, and then sell the loans off to investors in a process known as **securitization.** In this way, the investors, rather than the bank, bear the risk of a change in interest rates. The bank might take the funds it receives from investors and buy securities or some other assets that do not have such a long time to maturity so that the time to maturity of its assets will match that of its liabilities. Another way to equalize the time to maturity of assets and liabilities is to purchase derivative securities that allow the bank to hedge against a movement of interest rates that would cause it to suffer losses. For example, if a rise in interest rates of 5 percentage points would cause the bank to lose $100 million, it could buy a derivative contract that would pay the bank $100 million in the event that the interest rate rose 5 percentage points.

securitization the process by which a bank sells a loan (which it made previously) to investors

RECAP

1 A bank's balance sheet shows the bank's assets, liabilities, and equity capital. Assets equal liabilities plus equity capital.

2 Bank reserves equal vault cash plus deposits at the Fed. A bank must hold enough reserves to meet its reserve requirements, which are based on the amount of deposits in transactions accounts held at the bank.

3 A bank with excess reserves may hold them, lend them in the federal funds market, deposit them in the Fed's Term Deposit Facility, buy securities with them, or make new loans with them.

4 A bank that has reserves less than its required reserves must eliminate its reserve shortfall by borrowing in the federal funds market, borrowing from the Fed at the discount window, selling some securities, reducing its loans outstanding, or issuing some CDs.

5 A bank earns profits largely on the spread between the interest rate it charges borrowers and the interest rate it pays to depositors.

Before October 2008, banks did not earn interest on reserve balances that they held at the Federal Reserve. As a result, banks had the incentive to keep their reserve balances as low as possible. In fact, banks developed special types of accounts to keep their reserve balances artificially low. The reduction in banks' reserve balances created some operational problems for them because they needed a lot of reserves to clear transactions but tried to limit the amount of reserves that they held at the end of the day. Banks essentially borrowed from the Fed during the day (balances known as daylight overdrafts), then reduced their reserves to the bare minimum at the end of the day.

The situation changed dramatically in the financial crisis of 2008. In the midst of the crisis, the Fed wanted to encourage banks to hold more reserves for safety, so it persuaded Congress to allow the Fed to begin paying interest on reserves immediately. The payment of interest on reserves began in October 2008 and changed banks' behavior dramatically, as Figure 8.1 shows. In the graph, you can see that as soon as the Fed began to pay interest on reserves, banks' demand for reserves increased sharply. During the crisis, the Fed was also making more loans available to banks, lending to them against a variety of collateral, such as commercial paper and mortgage-backed securities, so the supply of reserves also increased sharply, beginning in September 2008.

Figure 8.1 shows that bank reserves, which had been fairly steady at $40 to $45 billion each month from January 2000 to August 2008, suddenly jumped to $100 billion in September 2008, then to $300 billion in October (when the Fed began paying interest on reserves), then to $600 billion in November, and to over $800 billion in December. Required reserves rose only slightly, to about $60 billion in this period, so most of the added reserves were in the form of excess reserves, on which the Fed agreed to pay interest (although interest rates were very close to zero, so the Fed did not pay very much interest to the banks). Quantitative easing by the Fed in 2009 to 2013 raised bank reserves from $800 billion at the end of 2008 to over $1,800 billion in early 2013.

In the future, the fact that the Fed is willing to pay interest on reserves gives the Fed another mechanism for

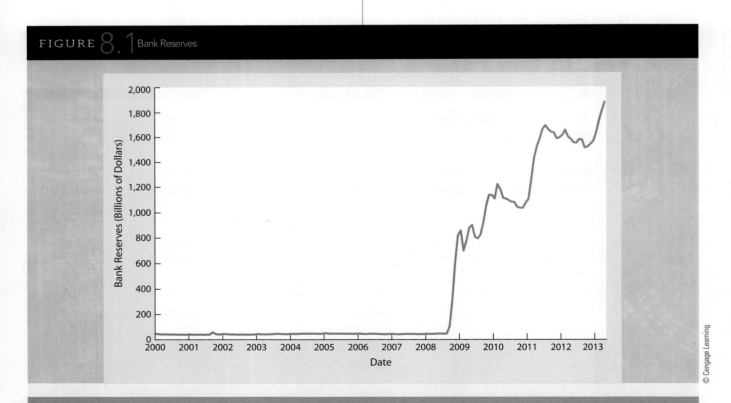

FIGURE 8.1 Bank Reserves

Bank reserves were fairly steady, between $40 billion and $45 billion in nearly every month between January 2000 and August 2008. But bank reserves rose dramatically in the financial crisis of 2008, as the Fed made loans to banks to make up for the lost liquidity in financial markets and the Fed also began paying interest on reserves in October 2008.

© Cengage Learning

affecting the money supply and the amount of reserves that banks hold. The Fed could vary the interest rate it pays on reserves to be lower than the federal funds rate, so that banks would have a choice between lending to other banks at the federal funds rate or keeping excess reserves and earning a somewhat lower interest rate. In the financial crisis of 2008 and in early 2009, banks all wanted to maintain many reserves for safety, so they kept large quantities of excess reserves and few loans were made to other banks. But as the economy improves, banks will have more choice about whether to hold or to lend their excess reserves.

RECAP

1 Before October 2008, banks took out daylight overdrafts every day.

2 When the Fed began paying interest on reserves, banks immediately increased their demand for reserves and the Fed increased its supply of reserves, mainly because of the poor condition of banks in the financial crisis.

3 The Fed can now use the interest rate on reserves as a policy instrument to affect the amount of reserves in the banking system.

Review Questions and Problems

Review Questions

1. Describe two services that banks provide at which they are particularly efficient.

2. What are the two main types of asymmetric-information problems? Give an example of each.

3. List the major ways that banks attempt to solve asymmetric-information problems. Why are such measures necessary?

4. Explain how high inflation in the late 1970s and early 1980s led to the S&L crisis. What other events contributed to the crisis?

5. What caused the credit crunch in the early 1990s?

6. Describe the major assets and liabilities on a bank's balance sheet. Give an example of each.

7. Explain the major options available to a bank that is short of reserves. What determines which option a bank is likely to choose?

8. What is the spread, and why is it such an important concept for banks?

9. Why did banks desire to hold many excess reserves in late 2008 during the financial crisis?

10. How can the Fed affect the amount of reserves that banks hold? What interest rates can it change to manipulate the quantity of reserves?

Numerical Exercises

11. Look in the latest *Federal Reserve Bulletin* (or on the Internet at the Federal Reserve Board's Web site: **www.federalreserve.gov**), and find the current set of reserve requirements that banks must meet. Then calculate the reserve requirements for banks with the following amounts of transactions deposits. Calculate both the marginal reserve requirement (the additional amount of required reserves per dollar of additional transactions deposits) and the average reserve requirement (required reserves divided by transactions deposits). Consider four banks with the following amounts of transactions deposits:

    a. $3.8 million
    b. $28.9 million
    c. $193.0 million
    d. $5.7 billion

12. The balance sheet of a bank follows. Suppose that the reserve requirement is 3 percent on the first $30 million of checkable deposits and 10 percent on checkable deposits in excess of $30 million. (Amounts on the balance sheet are in millions of dollars.)

Assets		Liabilities + Capital	
Reserves	$15.9	Transactions deposits	$180.0
Loans	$150.0	Equity capital	$ 20.0
Securities	$34.1		
Total	$200.0	Total	$200.0

   a. Calculate the bank's excess reserves.

   b. Suppose that the bank sells $5 million in securities to get new cash. Show the bank's balance sheet after this transaction. What are the bank's excess reserves?

   c. Suppose that the bank makes a loan to a customer equal to the amount of its excess reserves from part b. Show the bank's balance sheet before the customer spends the proceeds of the loan. What are the bank's excess reserves?

   d. Now suppose that the customer spends the proceeds of the loan. Show the bank's balance sheet, and calculate its excess reserves.

13. Consider the example of Barry's Bank described on pages 166 to 169. Show the changes in Barry's Bank's balance sheet for each of the options for using the excess reserves discussed on page 169. Show the amount of excess reserves remaining in the bank after each option.

14. In a recent year, a bank earned $37 million in interest on its assets of $462 million, it paid out $23 million in interest on its liabilities (excluding capital) of $416 million, and it paid its workers $8 million in total compensation. Calculate the bank's spread and its return on equity.

Analytical Questions

15 During a credit crunch, small firms appear to be harmed more than large firms are. Explain why this is true. Can you relate this result to asymmetric-information problems?

16 In the financial crisis of 2008, the government raised the amount of deposits that is insured by the Federal Deposit Insurance Corporation (FDIC) to $250,000 per person from its previous level of $100,000. What are the pros and cons of such a change?

17 If the Fed pays interest on reserves equal to the federal funds interest rate, would banks ever lend to each other in the federal funds market, given that loans in the federal funds market are made with no collateral requirements? How could the Fed encourage loans in the federal funds market while still paying interest on reserves?

18 Bankers have numerous methods for reducing their risk, such as requiring collateral for loans and imposing covenants. Yet when recessions occur, banks usually suffer losses on loans that are not repaid. Explain how competition between banks might prevent them from protecting themselves completely against risk. Do you think that it would be a good idea for the government to regulate banks and keep them from competing very vigorously so that they would take less risk?

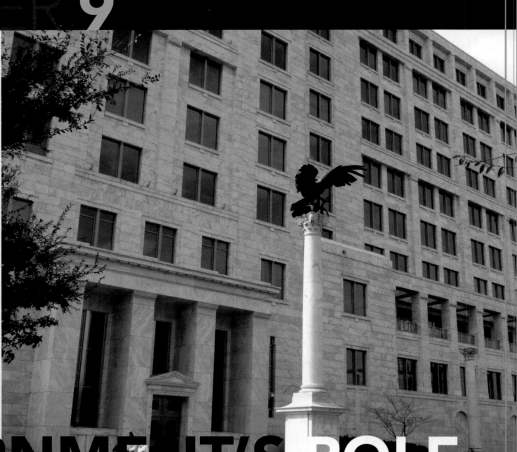

GOVERNMENT'S ROLE
in BANKING

Banks are special. They are essential to the operation of the payments system and the circulation of money.

Their willingness to make loans affects the ability of firms to buy new machinery and equipment and of households to buy houses and cars. Because of their unique nature, banks are more closely regulated than any other industry. To prevent problems in banks from disrupting the economy, government authorities supervise and regulate bank activities. This chapter takes up the question of who these authorities are and why they play such a prominent role in the banking system. We will look at how the government regulates banks by establishing the rules under which banks operate and how the government supervises banks by asking them for information about their activities and telling them when they are not acting properly. The Policy Perspective at the end of the chapter discusses how the government decides whether banks can merge. It covers a case study of a merger of large banks and considers the question of whether the government should try to keep banks from merging and getting bigger.

9-1 Regulation of Banks

The government regulates very few industries as heavily as banking. In this section we will investigate why the government regulates them so heavily, how it achieves its regulatory goals, the costs to banks of such regulation, and the restrictions that banks face.

9-1a Why Does the Government Regulate Banks?

The government regulates the banking industry more heavily than other industries for five reasons:

- To reduce the externalities caused by bank problems
- To keep banks small
- To prevent bank runs
- To ensure that payments flow through the banking system efficiently
- To stabilize the money supply

Reducing externalities. A bank is more than just a business. A bank is a participant in the financial system, and when a bank functions successfully, it transfers funds from lenders to borrowers efficiently, helps payments flow through the economy, and helps the economy grow. When an ordinary business (such as Enron or Circuit City) goes bankrupt, the firm's workers may lose their jobs and the firm's stockholders suffer a loss of wealth, but the damage is limited. When a bank fails, not only are the people who work for the bank and who own the bank harmed but so also are many of the people and businesses who were customers of the bank. In addition, the failure of one bank may hurt other banks. Thus, banks are different from other firms because their success or failure has broader consequences. These externalities justify more government attention and regulation than for an ordinary business firm.

Keeping banks small. Americans' fear of concentrated financial power dates back to the country's origins. That fear reached a peak in the early 1900s when the government dismantled huge industrial companies with monopoly power, such as John D. Rockefeller's Standard Oil Corporation and J. P. Morgan's railroad trust. Over the years, the government has passed numerous regulations to keep banks fairly small, with limits on their size and their power. For example, the fear that large banks might take deposits out of a small town and lend the funds in the city, retarding economic growth in the town and favoring the city, is a major cause of restrictions on bank branching (see the Policy Insider box "How Today's Banking System Reflects Yesterday's Regulations"). Even in 1994, when legislation effectively allowed all banks to operate in any state, it limited the amounts of deposits that can be controlled by any one bank within a state.

Preventing bank runs. Bank runs occurred periodically in the United States in the nineteenth and early twentieth centuries. In a **bank run,** many depositors go to a bank at the same time to withdraw their money. Because the bank has used depositors' funds to make long-term loans, it cannot give all depositors their money back at once. As a result, the bank may be forced to borrow funds from somewhere else, but if there is no one to lend to the bank, it may not be able to pay depositors their funds.

> **bank run** a situation in which many depositors go to a bank at the same time to withdraw their money
>
> **contagion** the spread of a bank run from one bank to another

Why do people participate in bank runs? If Andy thinks his bank might go bankrupt and he will lose his money, he might withdraw his funds. If Bonnie believes Andy, she might withdraw her money too. If Carl has no reason to think the bank will go bankrupt but notices that Andy and Bonnie withdrew their funds, he might worry that other people will soon withdraw their funds. If he is the last one to act, the others will get their money out, and he will lose all his money. Thus, even though he thinks the bank is in good shape, he does not want to take the risk that he will be left holding the bag, so he withdraws his funds as well. Once a few people pull their money out of a bank, many others will follow.

The worst feature of bank runs is that they tend to spread from one bank to another, a condition known as **contagion.** If depositors engage in a run on one bank, depositors at other banks may worry that their bank will be next. If their worry translates into action and each depositor tries to get his funds out before everyone else, the result will be another run on another bank. Before long, every bank may suffer a run, and many will close their doors.

Not only are bank runs bad, but also the possibility of a bank run reduces the flow of funds to banks. When a bank run is possible, a depositor might feel that her money is not safe in a bank. If banks get few deposits, they can make few loans. As a result, business firms will not be able to obtain the loans they need to invest and grow, so the economy will not produce as much

Although many banking regulations have come and gone over the years, their mark on the American banking system remains and can be seen in the number and location of banks. The history of the regulation of commercial-bank branching is a prime example. From 1864, when the national banking system was established, until 1927, when the McFadden Act was passed, commercial banks with a national charter from the Comptroller of the Currency were forbidden to have any branches. So the term *national* referred to the fact that they had a national charter from the federal government instead of a charter from a state government. The term did not indicate that they had a national geographic presence. The McFadden Act allowed national banks to have branch locations if the bank was located in a state in which banks with state charters were allowed to have branches (some states allowed their banks to have branches, whereas others did not) and allowed them to have additional offices in the same city as their main office. The result was that national banks in a few states had branches, but most did not. You might find it odd that a "national" bank would have offices in only one city, but that was the situation for decades. Essentially, state law determined the degree of branching allowed to banks.

However, banks must serve the needs of their customers, and as business corporations expanded geographically, banks wanted to establish offices to serve the needs of those companies. Banks tried to avoid the regulations against branching by creating a new corporate structure—the bank holding company—that would own several banks within a state or across state lines. The banks argued that the other banks within the holding company were not branches at all, just wholly owned subsidiaries of the bank holding company. In 1956, though, the Bank Holding Company Act forbade bank holding companies to branch across state lines through the bank holding company structure unless the state permitted it. However, at that time, no states permitted banks to do so.

Banks finally were allowed to branch across state lines in 1982 (when the Garn–St. Germain Act was passed), thanks to the savings and loan (S&L) crisis. The change in law was needed to deal with the many failing S&Ls. To prop up the banking industry, the government allowed banks to buy failing thrifts or commercial banks in other states, figuring that healthy banks would leap at the chance to expand their territory and would inject new capital into the failing banks. In 1989, the ability of banks to acquire S&Ls was expanded (by the Financial Institutions Reform, Recovery, and Enforcement Act), so banks could acquire even healthy S&Ls. Finally, in 1994, new legislation (the Interstate Banking and Branching Efficiency Act) threw out all the old restrictions, allowing nationwide branching without restriction, except in a state that forbids all interstate branching.

The impact of all this regulation of branching is that U.S. banks generally are smaller than their counterparts throughout the rest of the world. Most U.S. banks started with offices in just one city. As recently as 1975, only 14 states allowed statewide branching, a few states allowed a bank to have one branch office, and some other states allowed branching in counties adjacent to the bank's main office. As the restrictions gradually weakened over time, banks began to expand. Even in the 1990s, though, only a few banks had locations in more than a handful of states. Even today, only a few banks have a significant presence nationwide. By comparison, countries such as Canada, Germany, France, and Japan have several huge banks that operate nationwide and often have branches in many other countries.

The economic impact of the restrictions on bank branching was to keep most banks inefficiently small. The restrictions also prevented well-run banks from expanding to compete with poorly managed banks. (Not surprisingly, those poorly managed banks worked hard to convince politicians to pass laws preventing branching.) As the geographic restrictions faded, increased competition helped weed out weak banks and allowed strong banks to grow.

payments system the mechanisms by which cash, checks, and electronic payments flow from buyers to sellers

output as it would if firms could borrow more easily.

Making the payments system work efficiently. Another goal of the government is to make the payments system work efficiently. The term **payments system** refers to the mechanisms by which cash, checks, and electronic payments flow from buyers to sellers. Most transactions are paid in a way that goes through the banking system. You pay the street vendor in cash, but he deposits the funds in

In the United States, the existence of many small banks, such as this one in Taos, New Mexico, helps to reduce the concentration of financial power in the country. Historically, U.S. banking regulations have helped ensure the continued existence of small banks, but in recent years, banks have been allowed to merge across state lines to reduce costs and increase efficiency, at the cost of increased financial concentration.

his bank account at the end of the day. You pay your rent with a check, which is deposited in your landlord's bank at the end of the day, which sends it to your bank the next day, which withdraws the funds from your account. You pay the bookstore with your credit card, which sends a transaction report electronically to its bank, which sends it to the bank that has your credit-card account. Also, banks supply people with the currency and coins they need. People want the checks they deposit into the bank to be cleared quickly. All these transactions are part of the payments system.

Because banks are an integral part of the payments system, government oversight of banks ensures that the system operates well and that payments are carried out expeditiously. The government supervises banks to be sure that they operate soundly so that the failure of a bank does not cause a hardship on people making payments to one another.

Controlling the money supply. A final reason for government regulation of banks is that the government wants to control the amount of money in circulation. If too much money is available, the economy will suffer from inflation; if too little money is available, interest rates will be high, and business firms may not be able to borrow for needed equipment and machinery, so the economy will slow. To control the amount of money in circulation, the government must monitor the money that banks create and find ways to affect

the total money supply. We will discuss control of the money supply in Chapter 16.

9-1b How Does Government Regulation Achieve Its Goals?

A number of government regulations have been introduced over the years to enable the government to achieve its goals for the banking system (for a timeline of important laws regulating banking, see the Policy Insider box "A History of Major Banking Regulations"). The government:

- Supervises banks to reduce externalities
- Restricts mergers and bank activities to keep banks small
- Provides a federal safety net to prevent bank runs
- Offers services to ensure efficient payments
- Requires banks to hold reserves to control the money supply

Supervising banks to reduce externalities. To prevent the failure of a bank, especially a large one, the government supervises banks carefully to be sure they are sound. For some large banks, as many as three different government agencies may request documents from them and review their policies and procedures. Any activity that banks engage in may be reviewed by these government agencies, so banks cannot freely conduct business as they please. Furthermore, responding to this supervision costs the bank valuable time and resources. For example, the Call Report that a commercial bank must file quarterly is 40 pages long and requires the bank to provide the government with detailed statistics on its assets, liabilities, and profits. A recent estimate suggests that the cost of filling out paperwork to comply with government regulations is about 13 percent of a bank's total costs (other than paying interest on liabilities), which makes a significant impact on a bank's bottom line.

Restricting mergers and bank activities to keep banks small. To keep banks small, the government enforces a variety of laws that prevent banks from merging and that limit the activities a bank engages in. Thus, banks are not allowed to operate like other business firms. They cannot enter many markets where they could earn profits unless the law specifically allows them to do so.

Many of the restrictions on banks that have existed in the past 70 years were enacted as a result of the Great Depression in the 1930s. In that period, many people lost their jobs, and businesses were unable to borrow to

1864   National Bank Act

Creates the system of national banks to be chartered by the Comptroller of the Currency and establishes a uniform currency

1913   Federal Reserve Act

Creates the Federal Reserve System and gives it the responsibility as a lender of last resort

1927   McFadden Act

Requires national banks to abide by state branching laws; allows national banks to have additional offices in the same city as their main office

1933   Glass–Steagall Act

Establishes the Federal Deposit Insurance Corporation (FDIC); prohibits commercial banks from investment banking activities; prohibits banks from owning commercial firms and vice versa; prohibits interest payments on demand deposits

1956   Bank Holding Company Act

Gives the Federal Reserve authority to regulate bank holding companies and prevents bank holding companies from branching across state lines

1977   Community Reinvestment Act

Encourages banks to meet the credit needs of their communities; examinations of Community Reinvestment Act compliance can be used when banks wish to expand or merge

1980   Depository Institutions Deregulation and Monetary Control Act

Allows payment of interest on transactions accounts of individuals (not businesses); phases out interest-rate ceilings on deposits; makes all depository institutions subject to reserve requirements; gives thrifts the ability to own a wider range of assets; raises deposit insurance ceiling to $100,000

1982   Garn–St. Germain Act

Allows strong banks to buy failing banks in other states; allows banks to offer money-market deposit accounts; allows thrifts to invest up to 10 percent of portfolios in riskier assets such as stocks and real estate

1989   Financial Institutions Reform, Recovery, and Enforcement Act

Abolishes the Federal Savings and Loan Insurance Corporation (FSLIC) and gives responsibility for thrift deposit insurance to the FDIC; creates the Office of Thrift Supervision; sets up institutions to deal with failed S&Ls

1991   Federal Deposit Insurance Corporation Improvement Act

Creates scheme of risk-based deposit insurance premiums; requires FDIC to use least-cost method for dealing with bank failures; created new structure of capital requirements for banks, causing many to increase capital

1994   Interstate Banking and Branching Efficiency Act

Phases in interstate branching and allows interstate bank mergers, unless a state prohibits them

1999   Gramm–Leach–Bliley Act

Repeals Glass–Steagall Act, allowing banks to sell insurance and engage in some investment banking activities; allows banks to form financial holding companies that may sell insurance, invest in real estate, and engage in other activities that had been prohibited

2010   Dodd–Frank Act

Establishes Financial Stability Oversight Council to reduce risks to the financial system and Bureau of Consumer Financial Protection to keep financial institutions from taking advantage of consumers; strengthens regulations to prevent bad mortgage originations; subjects financial institutions other than banks to regulatory oversight if their failure might cause financial instability

---

buy new equipment or buildings. Much of the blame was placed on a poorly functioning banking system. Banks had made two serious errors that caused their depositors to lose their funds. First, banks in the 1920s also could serve as investment banking firms (selling marketable securities, both stocks and bonds, in the primary market), and they were reported to have pushed bad securities on their customers, who suffered losses as a result (just as some brokerage firms pushed bad technology stocks on their customers in the late 1990s). Second, banks sometimes owned companies that were engaged in businesses other than banking. When those businesses went bankrupt, the bank suffered losses. To prevent these problems from recurring, the government passed legislation to both separate banking from the securities industry and to keep banks separate from firms that did not do banking.

In response to the banking problems that arose in the Great Depression, the Glass–Steagall Act was passed into law in 1933 and remained in force until 1999, when it was repealed. The **Glass–Steagall Act** prohibited banks from underwriting securities or buying and selling securities for their customers (except through special trust companies) or selling mutual funds. Such restrictions were enacted because, during the boom period of the 1920s, some banks stuffed their customers' accounts with poor-quality stocks that they were underwriting and had their customers take much bigger risks than the customers desired. While these deceptive bank practices did not matter too much as long as stock values were rising, they caused great harm to bank customers when the stock market crashed in October 1929 and throughout the 1930s, when the stock market remained depressed.

Opponents of the Glass–Steagall Act pushed for its repeal almost immediately, and opposition to the law continued for 66 years. Banks tried various innovations to get around the law, but they were unable to do so successfully. Banks argued that they could take advantage of economies of scope (reductions in average cost from producing a wider variety of services) if they were able to underwrite securities and sell them directly to their customers. However, those supporting the Glass–Steagall Act argued that letting banks engage in investment banking would extend deposit insurance coverage to firms that were not banks, and they claimed that banks would again have a conflict of interest between their needs to underwrite stocks and to serve their banking customers.

The Glass–Steagall Act (along with the Bank Holding Company Act, passed later) also prevented banks from owning commercial firms and prohibited commercial firms from owning banks. (*Commercial firms* are business firms that sell products other than banking services.) Thus, basically, the laws prevented banks from engaging in any business but banking. Banks could not own subsidiary firms that sold products other than banking services, nor could firms that were not banks own a bank.

Over the years, opponents of Glass–Steagall made numerous arguments to repeal the separation of banking and commerce. Proponents of repeal argued that repeal would lead to higher capital levels, lower operational and information costs, economies of scope, greater international competitiveness, and better opportunities for diversification. Opponents of such a change, however, argued that if banks could own commercial firms, they would have greater monopoly power, there would be increased risk to banks from problems at their affiliates, deposit insurance effectively would apply to commercial firms, unprofitable commercial firms might cause the banks that owned them to suffer losses, and problems at commercial firms that were part of banks could affect the electronic payments system.

> **Glass–Steagall Act**
> the law, passed in 1933, that kept banks out of the securities industry

Despite the apparent clarity of the law restricting banking and commerce, bankers managed to find ways to avoid the restriction. Because the law defines a bank as an institution that takes deposits and makes loans, some commercial firms created *nonbanks*. These were enterprises that either took deposits or made loans but did not do both and thus were not subject to the same restrictions as banks. Officially, therefore, the commercial firm did not own a bank, but the nonbank it owned could make loans just as a bank would.

Practical considerations also led to cracks in the separation of banking and commerce. Because small towns were not served well by insurance companies, the government allowed banks to sell insurance in a town with fewer than 5,000 residents. Banks began selling insurance in small towns but then sold it to customers all over the country from the small-town office. Banks also were allowed to sell securities and insurance in limited amounts if they organized their business so that the securities and insurance parts of the firm were separate operating subsidiaries of the banks. Finally, the banking authorities allowed commercial firms to buy S&Ls in the aftermath of the S&L crisis in the 1980s.

In part, the banks were able to play off one banking authority against the other. In particular, they were able to get the U.S. Treasury Department and the Federal Reserve (Fed) to battle with each other over which activities would be allowed and how they would be supervised. The Treasury wanted to allow banks to be able to engage in more nonbanking activities through operating subsidiaries, but the Fed wanted greater firewalls (accounting structures to keep firms separate so that the finances of one firm would not affect the other) between companies and subsidiaries. Of course, politics was involved as well. One piece of proposed legislation would have given all the power for regulating banks to the Treasury; of course, the Federal Reserve argued against this. However, the result of these turf fights was that changes in banking law were slow to develop.

Passage of the **Gramm–Leach–Bliley Act** in 1999 greatly reduced the restrictions facing banks. It replaced the Glass–Steagall Act almost entirely, allowing banks to engage in investment activities, as well as to sell insurance, and allowing banks to own commercial firms for the purpose of reselling them. However, it kept in place restrictions on banking and commerce; banks still can affiliate only with companies in businesses related to banking, securities, and insurance.

To engage in the newly permissible activities, banks have to choose how to reorganize their corporate structures. They can choose to organize as a **financial holding company (FHC)** in which a parent company, the FHC, owns a bank and owns separate nonbanking companies, such as a securities underwriting firm, an insurance agency, a securities agency (such as a stock brokerage), an insurance underwriting firm, or a merchant banking firm (a firm allowed to buy commercial firms temporarily and then sell them within 10 years). A banking firm may own an insurance underwriter or a merchant banking firm only by forming an FHC. The other activities are permissible through a bank holding company, which owns subsidiary companies that engage in securities underwriting or sell insurance or securities. The law limits the amount of nonbanking activities the bank or FHC can engage in.

Banks were delighted to have these new opportunities available to them, but most did not rush to take on newly permissible nonbanking activities when the law went into effect in early 2000. Many were uncertain about exactly how the banking regulators would interpret the new law. They also were reluctant to take on new risks without understanding them fully. As a result, the conversion to the FHC organization for banks has been evolving slowly. However, the Gramm–Leach–Bliley Act is an expansion of the banking industry's competitive abilities in the long run.

After many decades of laws that increased the ability of banks to expand in size, banks' ability to expand was limited by the Dodd–Frank Act in 2010. That law set a limit to prevent a bank from merging with others if the merger would increase its liabilities to more than

Gramm–Leach–Bliley Act the law, passed in 1999, that allowed banks back into the securities (and insurance) industries

financial holding company (FHC) a new financial structure, created by the Gramm–Leach–Bliley Act, in which a company can own a bank, a securities firm, and an insurance company

lender of last resort the service provided by the government that lends funds to a bank when needed

10 percent of national bank liabilities. The effect of the law will certainly be to prevent the spread of national megabanks that would pose great risks to financial stability if they were to fail. Since the financial crisis, lawmakers have been debating whether to restrict the activities of banks further, to reduce their risk of failure.

Providing a federal safety net to prevent bank runs. How can bank runs be prevented? The government has set up several methods for doing so: providing deposit insurance, acting as a lender of last resort, and not allowing large banks to fail.

Deposit insurance is a powerful method for preventing bank runs. Under deposit insurance, people and firms that have funds in a bank account will not lose their funds if the bank fails. The government provides deposit insurance through the Federal Deposit Insurance Corporation (FDIC) so that depositors know that their funds are completely safe (up to a $250,000 limit for each person per bank). Thus, there is no need for people to run to the bank to withdraw their money even if they think the bank might fail because they know that they will get their money back. Under normal circumstances, the funds to support the FDIC come from the banks themselves, which must pay into the insurance fund. But there is also an implicit government subsidy because the government declares that in an emergency it will back up the FDIC and pay off depositors even if the FDIC runs out of funds. During the financial crisis of 2008, the FDIC limit was increased from $100,000 to $250,000 for each person per bank because bank runs were starting among people who had over $100,000 in certain banks; the increase in the limit stopped those runs.

Another way to prevent bank runs is for the government to stand ready to provide money to banks whenever a bank run occurs. Then people would have no reason to fear that they would not be able to withdraw their funds at any time, so they would not participate in a bank run. When the government provides such funds, it serves as the **lender of last resort.** The responsibility for serving as the lender of last resort belongs to the Federal Reserve, which lends to solvent but illiquid banks through the discount window (a *solvent* bank is one with positive equity capital; an *illiquid* bank is one that does not have enough cash on hand to meet the demands of its customers). A bank with a temporary problem that prevents it from borrowing from other banks can borrow instead from the Fed at the discount window. The Fed's loans to the bank are fully backed by collateral (usually government securities owned by the bank), so there is little risk to the Federal Reserve. Instead, the discount window allows banks to borrow when other sources of liquidity have dried up. During the financial crisis of 2008, the Fed used its lender-of-last-resort authority to make many loans to banks that were solvent but faced liquidity problems.

Providing deposit insurance and serving as a lender of last resort are complicated by asymmetric-information problems. Moral hazard arises from both deposit insurance and the lender-of-last-resort function. When a bank knows that its depositors do not care what the bank does because their deposits are insured by the government, the bank might make riskier investments. If these risky investments fail, the government will pick up the tab. Similarly, a bank that can borrow from the government if it gets into trouble may take more risks than it would if it could not borrow at the discount window. In addition, adverse selection may arise, because badly run banks borrow from the government, whereas well-run banks do not.

To prevent these asymmetric-information problems, the government must supervise and regulate banks. The main idea of the government's supervision and regulation of banks is that it is willing to insure deposits for or provide loans to banks that are solvent and well run but will close banks that are insolvent or badly run. Thus, a bank that needs funds because of a temporary cash-flow problem or because of some short-run crisis is a good candidate for a government loan. A badly run bank that is losing money and headed for bankruptcy is one that the government does not want to lend to and whose deposits the government does not want to insure.

The existence of the discount window benefits the banks and the Fed. Banks benefit because they know that they always have a backup source of liquidity that they can call on in an emergency; a common example is the failure of a computer system that prevents a bank from transferring funds when needed. The Fed benefits because the existence of the discount window helps the payments system work well even in a crisis. The discount window helps to accomplish this goal by giving the Fed the ability to act as a lender of last resort for many banks in the event of a financial crisis.

Indeed, the Fed has used this power aggressively to offset potential problems in the financial system in the past few decades. For example, when the stock market crashed in October 1987, the Fed provided discount-window loans to financial institutions with temporary liquidity problems; by doing so, it prevented the stock market crash from causing banks to fail. When the Russian government defaulted on its debt and the hedge fund Long-Term Capital Management went bankrupt in 1998, fear by investors caused them to stop their normal buying and selling of debt securities. Banks had trouble obtaining funds through normal channels, so the Fed made discount loans available to offset the decline in liquidity in financial markets. Another example arose in 1999 as participants in financial markets became concerned that the Y2K rollover would create huge problems for financial institutions. The Fed was on the scene, offering a number of possible solutions, including discount-window loans for banks that needed them. Perhaps the most dramatic example of the value of the discount window came on September 11, 2001, when the payments system suffered disruptions after several large banks in Manhattan were damaged and could not clear payments and the banks' transportation network could not operate normally because planes were grounded. The Fed responded by making loans to many banks that could not obtain their expected flow of funds—an amount exceeding $45 billion on the day after the attacks.

One other piece of the safety net for banks is that the government will not allow large banks to go bankrupt; this is known as the **too-big-to-fail policy.** The government knows that if one of the largest banks in the country were to fail, the payments system would be disrupted, many business firms that use the bank to obtain funds would face a cash-flow crisis, and fear of other banks failing could cause a bank run. As a result, the government will not allow such a large institution to fail but instead will make loans to keep it afloat.

too-big-to-fail policy a policy under which bank regulators will not close a bank that is deemed to be so large that its closure would affect the financial system and cause other banks to fail; instead, the government will make loans to the bank to keep it afloat

When is a bank considered to be too big to fail? Many banks and other financial institutions are considered too big to fail if banking authorities determined that failure of one of them would seriously hurt the banking industry or the economy. For example, in 1984, Continental Illinois, the seventh largest bank in the country, with $41 billion in assets, had made a series of bad loans. It had billions of dollars in deposits that were not covered by deposit insurance (because they exceeded the limit of $100,000 per account), including deposits from 2,300 small banks. As Continental's bad loan losses became apparent, uninsured depositors began withdrawing their funds, putting even more pressure on Continental. Continental appeared to be heading for a bank run, which might have spread to other large banks with loan losses. To prevent a bank run from developing, the FDIC added capital to the bank and took over its bad loans. In the end, Continental was saved, and neither depositors nor creditors lost any money. However, Continental's shareholders felt the brunt of the loss, losing most of their equity.

In the financial crisis of 2008, many major U.S. banks found themselves with a shortage of liquidity. They suffered large losses on their portfolios of mortgages and mortgage-backed securities, leading many investors to sell their stock and causing their stock prices to decline sharply. The largest bank failure was that of Washington Mutual, which was a fairly large subprime lender and held mortgage loans as its main asset. But a number of other major banks were weakened substantially. In 2009, the Fed helped one of the country's largest banks, Wachovia, which had foolishly purchased a large subprime mortgage lender the year before, merge with the much stronger bank, Wells Fargo. Clearly, the Fed was using its too-big-to-fail policy to merge a weak bank with a stronger bank, to prevent the financial crisis from worsening.

When a bank is closed by government authorities (which happens when it becomes insolvent, that is, when the bank's equity capital falls below zero), the FDIC must decide what to do with the bank's assets and how to pay off creditors and depositors who are owed money. There are essentially three choices: (1) payoff, (2) purchase and assumption, and (3) assistance. In the payoff transaction, the FDIC closes the bank, sells off the assets, pays off insured depositors first, and then pays off creditors of the bank if funds remain. In a purchase-and-assumption transaction, the FDIC finds a buyer for the bank, giving the buyer the good assets of the bank, and assumes the bad loans of the bank. In an assistance transaction, the FDIC keeps the bank open and lends funds to it so that it survives. An assistance transaction usually means that

shareholders lose their stake in the bank, depositors and creditors lose nothing, and the FDIC has some losses. In the past, under the too-big-to-fail policy, the FDIC often used assistance transactions, on the grounds that they prevented uninsured depositors from causing a bank run. The number of bank failures rose sharply in the 1980s, however, as you can see in Figure 9.1, depleting the deposit insurance funds. As a result, the government passed a new law in 1991 requiring the FDIC to use the least costly transaction method when banks fail. In effect, the law makes creditors and uninsured depositors in a bank share the loss suffered by the bank before FDIC funds are used unless the FDIC, the Fed, and the Secretary of the Treasury agree to protect them. This raises the risk of a bank run, even though it saves the FDIC money. From 1993 to 2007, the FDIC made no assistance transactions, but in the financial crisis in 2008–2009, the agency used the assistance method to rescue 13 banks with a total of $3.2 trillion in assets. The least costly transaction is usually purchase and assumption, which was used in over 90 percent of commercial bank and thrift failures since 1993.

Offering services to ensure efficient payments. The second government program that benefits banks is the payments services the Fed provides to banks, as we discussed in Chapter 3. A well-functioning payments system provides benefits to banks because it lowers their costs. The Fed ensures that payments will clear in a timely and efficient manner. Thus, banks do not need to maintain their own systems for clearing checks and obtaining cash for their customers.

Requiring banks to hold reserves to control the money supply. To control the money supply, the government must be able to affect the flows of money through the banking system (as we will discuss in greater detail in Chapter 16). One way the government achieves this control is by requiring banks to hold a certain level of reserves, based on the amounts of transactions accounts they have. As discussed in Chapter 8, the Fed can now manipulate banks' reserves by changing the federal funds rate and the interest rate that it pays on reserves.

9-1c Do Banks Receive a Net Subsidy from the Government?

Given the costs and benefits of banking regulation, what is the balance between them? Do banks receive a net subsidy from the government? Or do the costs exceed the benefits? In testimony before Congress concerning modernizing the financial system in the late 1990s, then Fed Chairman Alan Greenspan argued that there was a net subsidy

FIGURE 9.1 Failures of Commercial Banks and Thrifts

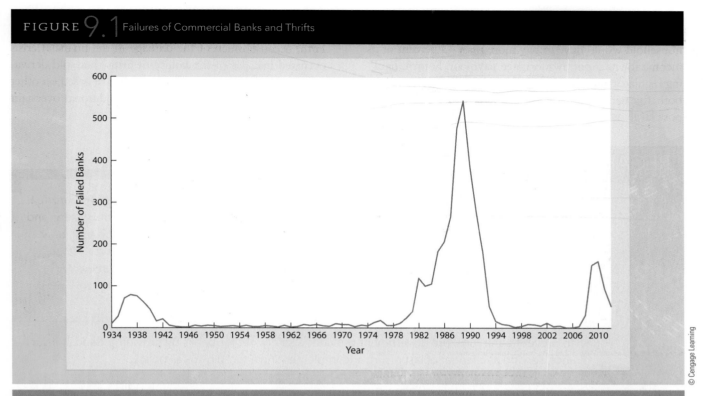

This graph shows the number of commercial banks and thrifts that have failed since 1934. Although there were many bank failures in the Great Depression in the 1930s, there were far more in the 1980s, especially failures of thrifts (in particular, S&Ls). The financial crisis of 2008 led to many bank failures.

© Cengage Learning

to banks—that the benefits to banks exceeded the costs. However, the U.S. Treasury Department argued that the costs were higher than the Fed indicated, so there was no net subsidy. Whatever the answer to this question, it is clear that both the benefits and the costs to banks of government regulation of the banking system are substantial. At the same time, it is also clear that consumers and businesses benefit substantially from government's role because the payments system has operated with greater efficiency since these programs were put in place. Bank runs, which occurred frequently in the late 1800s and early 1900s, have been eliminated almost completely. Financial crises that led to severe recessions were commonplace before World War I; such crises are now much less common and have far less impact on the economy. That's why most economists and policymakers were stunned by the financial crisis of 2008 and the impact it had on the economy. In 2010, the U.S. government passed the Dodd–Frank Wall Street Reform and Consumer Protection Act to attempt to prevent financial institutions from engaging in practices that led to the financial crisis. First, greater regulatory oversight of the mortgage industry was put in place. Many of the bad mortgage loans that were made were not made by established banks but by mortgage brokers who made the deal

for a mortgage loan to a bad borrower, collected a fee, sold the mortgage off to someone else, and had no responsibility or concern for the quality of the loan after that. The government has changed the rules to attempt to ensure that whoever originates a mortgage loan has responsibility for the quality of the loan, even if it is securitized. Second, because much of the crisis occurred because firms like Bear Stearns were so highly leveraged and because their failure would have wreaked havoc with the entire financial system, the government has created a Financial Stability Oversight Council to keep such large firms from behaving recklessly and endangering the rest of the economy. Those large firms have been designated as Systemically Important Financial Institutions (SIFIs), and they are subject to additional regulation and supervision. Such firms are required to develop living wills that describe how they could be dissolved if they were to go bankrupt. Third, to protect consumers, the government created a new agency, the Consumer Financial Protection Bureau (CFPB). The CFPB enforces consumer financial protection laws, educates consumers about abusive financial practices, and engages in research about consumer finances. For example, the CFPB operates a Web site that allows consumers to report complaints about financial institutions, it provides education about student loans, and it requires that banks use a sensible rule for mortgage loans by forbidding such loans if a household would have to pay more than 43 percent of its income for its monthly mortgage payment. Fourth, banking regulators increased capital and liquidity requirements both for banks and for other financial institutions that pose large risks to the economy if they fail. Regulators also added a rule to keep banks from engaging in risky investment activities, such as through unregulated hedge funds. Fifth, because much of the damage in the financial crisis occurred because of the failure of firms that sold derivative securities (securities whose returns are based on other securities), Dodd–Frank put in place additional oversight and regulation of derivatives.

RECAP

1	Banks are regulated because the government wants to reduce the externalities caused by bank failures, to keep banks small, to prevent bank runs, to ensure the efficiency of the payments system, and to control the money supply.
2	To reduce the externalities caused by bank failures, the government supervises banks closely.
3	To keep banks small, the government restricts mergers and bank activities.
4	To prevent bank runs, the government provides a safety net for banks by providing deposit insurance, serving as a lender of last resort, and implementing a too-big-to-fail policy.
5	To ensure the efficiency of the payments system, the government offers services to banks.
6	To control the money supply, the government requires banks to hold a certain level of reserves.

9-2 Supervision of Banks

Perhaps the greatest cost facing banks is the close supervision of their activities by banking authorities. Banking authorities examine banks periodically, require them to file reports about their condition, and sometimes surprise them with new requests for information.

9-2a Bank Supervisors

Who are the bank's supervisors? This depends on the structure of the bank and how it is chartered. A *charter* is a bank's application for going into business. A new bank can choose whether to be chartered as a commercial bank, a thrift institution (savings bank or S&L), or a credit union. The bank also may choose whether to be chartered by

dual banking system a system in which a bank may choose whether to be chartered by federal government authorities or by a state government

the federal government or a state government. The United States is said to have a **dual banking system** because banks have this choice of being chartered either by the federal or the state government.

A bank that wishes to become a commercial bank may do so through either the federal government or a state government but not both. A commercial bank that gets a charter from the federal government obtains its charter through the Office of the Comptroller of the Currency (an agency of the U.S. Treasury Department)—the bank then is called a *national bank*. If the commercial bank gets its charter from a state government (the state in which its headquarters are located), it is called a *state bank*. A national bank must become a member of the Federal Reserve System and must have FDIC insurance, so the Comptroller, the Fed, and the FDIC all supervise the bank. A state bank usually is required to obtain FDIC insurance, and it may choose to become a member of the Federal Reserve System. Most choose not to join the Fed system because they do not lose much by not joining, and, by doing so, they avoid having an additional supervisor (the Fed). Thus, state banks are supervised by the state's banking department

FIGURE 9.2 Banking Supervisors

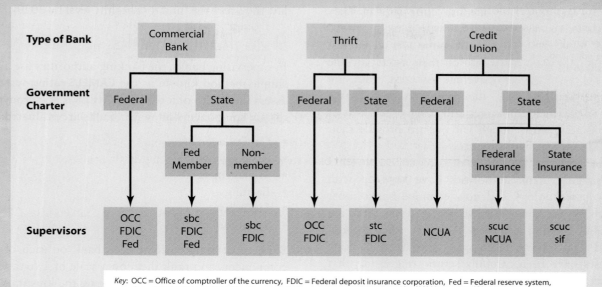

This figure shows the different types of banks, the choices they have (about who charters them, who insures them, and whether they join the Federal Reserve System), and who their supervisors are.

and the FDIC, plus the Fed if the state bank joins the Federal Reserve System. Figure 9.2 provides a listing of all the bank regulators and which banks they supervise.

With so many bank authorities, the result could be duplication of effort, but the authorities agree that just one of them will be the main supervisor of each bank. The Federal Reserve supervises all financial holding companies (FHCs), bank holding companies (corporations that own one or more banks), and state member banks (state-chartered banks that have joined the Federal Reserve System); the Comptroller of the Currency supervises national banks that are not in FHCs or bank holding companies; and the FDIC is the main supervisor for state banks that choose not to join the Federal Reserve System. However, the Fed supervises most of the largest banks, whereas the FDIC has mostly very small banks under its supervision.

A bank may not want to be chartered as a commercial bank—it may prefer to be organized as a thrift institution or a credit union. Thrifts are chartered at the federal level or by a state government. Just like commercial banks, thrifts must have FDIC insurance. In general, thrifts have a more liberal charter than banks and can engage in activities that commercial banks cannot, including owning or being owned by a commercial

firm. However, they can have a maximum of 20 percent of their assets in the form of commercial loans and must have 65 percent of their assets in the form of mortgage or consumer loans to qualify for special funding from a Federal Home Loan Bank.

Credit unions get their charters from the National Credit Union Association (NCUA) at the federal level or a state government credit-union agency at the state level. They are insured by the National Credit Union Share Insurance Fund (NCUSIF), which is similar to the FDIC, or in a few states by a state or private insurance fund. The lender of last resort for credit unions is not the Federal Reserve, as it is for banks and thrifts, but NCUA's Central Liquidity Facility.

Other than who supervises and regulates them, what are the differences among commercial banks, thrifts, and credit unions? The answer is—not much. Commercial banks and thrifts are quite similar in many ways, although by historical development, thrifts generally have a greater proportion of their assets as home mortgages and have less in the form of commercial loans. Credit unions are most often run as nonprofit organizations, so they are often exempt from taxes, giving them a slight competitive advantage over commercial banks and thrifts.

In general, however, the methods by which all three types of institutions operate are quite similar. They profit by having a spread between the average interest rate on their assets and the average interest rate on their liabilities that is large enough to pay their employees and cover other costs of doing business, with enough left over to provide their shareholders a reasonable return.

In recent years, the nature of bank supervision has been changing. Bank authorities have kept up with changes in technology and now examine banks more thoroughly concerning their overall risk levels. They are increasingly looking into how banks are using technology and what risks technology poses for them. Banking authorities have been carefully scrutinizing banks that have accepted large sums of cash from their customers in a nationwide crackdown on money laundering and a hunt for sources of funding for terrorist activities.

9-2b Deposit Insurance

There also have been changes in the past decade in the deposit insurance system. Following the S&L debacle of the 1980s, the government changed the structure of the FDIC to ensure that it would not face the same fate as the FSLIC. In response to the moral-hazard problem caused by deposit insurance, the government established a set of risk-based deposit insurance premiums in 1993. In this system, riskier banks must pay larger amounts into the deposit insurance fund than safer banks. Banks with safer portfolios are acknowledged and rewarded.

Although banking authorities worried that banks were weak as the decade of the 1990s began, the changes in regulation and the requirements that banks strengthen their balance sheets paid off later in the decade. By the end of 1997, the FDIC had nearly $40 billion in its fund, totaling 1.4 percent of all insured deposits. By law, reaching this level meant that banks with low risk levels no longer needed to pay any deposit insurance premiums at all. In fact, until the financial crisis of 2008, in recent years less than 1 in 10 banks was considered to be risky enough to require payments into the fund. Thus, the entire banking system by the end of the 1990s had returned to health, diminishing the worries of banking authorities. The banks even went through the recession of 2001 without major losses. Of course, the financial crisis of 2008 changed the health of the deposit insurance system dramatically. In 2009, bank failures exhausted the FDIC Deposit Insurance Fund, and funds were supplied by the government to keep the FDIC from failing. The FDIC then increased the assessments on banks and is required by the Dodd–Frank law to restore the fund to a healthy level by 2020.

9-2c Rating Banks

In supervising banks, the banking authorities use a fairly simple method known as the **CAMELS rating system** to assess the health of a bank. CAMELS is an acronym for the six components on which banks are evaluated:

- Capital adequacy
- Asset quality
- Management
- Earnings
- Liquidity
- Sensitivity to risk

Bank supervisors evaluate each bank on each of these components and rank them on a scale of 1 to 5, with 1 being the highest rating and 5 being the lowest. A rank of 1 means that the supervisor has no concerns about the bank's performance on that component, whereas a rank of 5 means that the supervisor is extremely concerned.

Capital adequacy is evaluated by comparing various measures of a bank's capital to its assets. A bank is required to hold more capital if its assets are relatively risky and less capital if its assets are relatively safe. Asset quality is rated by looking at the collateral a bank has for its loans and the completeness of the documentation for each loan. Management is rated by the examiners' view of the managers' awareness of the bank's activities and strategic direction, the controls they have in place to ensure good performance, and their oversight of the bank's operations. Earnings are judged by the bank's returns over time. Liquidity is evaluated in terms of the bank's ability to get cash when it needs it; for example, a bank that borrows from the discount window too often may be downgraded in this category. Sensitivity to risk is evaluated by examining how the bank's profitability is affected by changes in market interest rates.

A bank is rated on all these components and then given an overall rating as well. The ratings are used by the banking supervisors to determine whether a bank is allowed to engage in some activities (those with CAMELS ratings near 1 are allowed more freedom than those with CAMELS ratings near 5). In addition, the supervisors discuss the evaluation and the CAMELS ratings with the bank and make suggestions for improvement. However, the CAMELS ratings are not revealed publicly.

Perhaps the most complex of the CAMELS components is the measure of capital adequacy. Bank supervisors like banks to have a lot of equity capital because then the stockholders of the bank have a strong stake in making sure the bank performs well and because the stockholders would lose all their funds before the deposit insurance fund (such as the FDIC) would suffer any losses if the bank failed. Thus a bank with a lot of capital is not likely to ever need government funds. Bank supervisors around the world use a common measurement standard for capital adequacy, based on an agreement known as the *Basel Accord*. The supervisors use the amounts reported on a bank's balance sheet to determine if the bank's capital is adequate for the amount of risk it undertakes.

The problem with the capital requirements is that they do not really reflect the risk of the assets very well because there are no gradations within categories. Bankers know that some loans are much riskier than others, yet for meeting capital requirements, all loans get the same weight. To implement a better system, however, would require that banking authorities know much more about the quality of different loans—far more than they are likely to know. The U.S. banking regulators and others from around the world reached agreement on a second Basel Accord, known as Basel II, which was being implemented just before the financial crisis began in 2008. Under the proposal, large U.S. banks would be allowed to develop their own models of risk and could in principle reduce their capital requirements substantially if they could show that their assets were not very risky. This system was about to be put into place when the financial crisis of 2008 made it clear that banks' models of risk were inadequate. In early 2009, the banking regulators forced many large banks to raise additional capital, based on uniform stress tests (evaluating how the banks would do if the recession worsened), even though the banks'

internal models said such capital was not necessary. International banking regulators decided to scrap Basel II almost completely and instead, in 2010's Basel III agreement, imposed higher capital requirements on banks all over the world. So, instead of giving banks more freedom, the regulators are now being tougher on banks and keeping them under tighter regulatory control.

In addition to the CAMELS ratings and compliance with the capital requirements, banks also are subject to supervision as to their compliance with the **Community Reinvestment Act (CRA)**. The CRA requires banks to serve their local communities. The act was a response to banks' bad behavior in the past in which some engaged in *redlining*. Redlining is the practice of refusing to make loans in certain locations, usually inner cities. Redlining effectively discriminates against people based on where they live and is related to the racial characteristics of the neighborhoods. Now, by law, a bank must show that it does not discriminate on the basis of location. Banks are given ratings of outstanding, satisfactory, needs work, or substandard. In recent years, about one-quarter of banks were rated outstanding, almost three-quarters were ranked satisfactory, and only a few were rated as needing work or substandard. However, this is one area about which banks complain that they must donate money to community groups to ensure a good rating but that those donations serve no real business purpose. On the other hand, people in neighborhoods that were redlined will tell you that the CRA changed banks' behavior for the better.

> **Community Reinvestment Act (CRA)** a law requiring banks to serve their local communities; the purpose of the law is to prevent discrimination, especially on the basis of race, in granting credit

RECAP

1 Banks are subject to scrutiny from a variety of different supervisors, depending on what type they are (commercial bank, thrift, or credit union), how they are chartered (federal or state), who insures them (FDIC or NCUSIF), and whether they are members of the Federal Reserve System.

2 Banks pay deposit insurance premiums depending on the riskiness of their assets, as determined by their government supervisors.

3 Banks are rated according to the CAMELS system, which examines their capital adequacy, asset quality, management, earnings, liquidity, and sensitivity to risk.

4 Banks must comply with the Community Reinvestment Act, which requires them to make loans in areas where they take deposits.

Can policymakers play a role in shaping the banking system of the future? Or should they stay out and let the industry evolve naturally, allowing mergers such as Wachovia's merger with Wells Fargo or Bank One's merger with JPMorgan Chase?

To answer these questions, we will look at the regulations governing mergers and acquisitions of banks. We will see how banking authorities analyze mergers using the merger between Wachovia and Wells Fargo as a case study. We also will look at economists' research that seeks to explain how mergers affect bank profitability to answer the question: Do bank profits rise after mergers because their costs are lower or because they have more monopoly power?

Herfindahl–Hirschman Index (HHI) a statistic used to measure the amount of competition in a banking market

The government can stop mergers between banks, just as it can stop mergers between commercial firms. According to the Clayton Antitrust Act of 1914, the government can prevent a merger that would "substantially lessen competition" in an industry. In practice, the banking authorities must make a decision about what it means to substantially lessen competition. They follow the guidelines of the U.S. Department of Justice, with some modifications to allow for the unique nature of banking.

9-2d Evaluating Bank Mergers

In evaluating mergers of banks (or acquisitions of one bank by another), the authorities consider (1) the effect on competition, (2) the adequacy of the financial and managerial resources of the new bank, (3) the ability of the bank to meet the convenience and needs of the community, and (4) whether the banks provided complete information about the merger or acquisition to the banking authorities. We will focus most of our attention on the first factor because that is the major one that matters for antitrust purposes.

In calculating the effect of a merger or acquisition on competition, banking authorities must decide how to define the relevant market—in terms of both products and geography—and then define what it means to substantially lessen competition in that market. First, because banks compete with each other for deposits, the authorities look at the amounts of deposits of the banks participating in the merger or acquisition.

Next, the *geographic market* has come to be defined as "boundaries of mutually exclusive predefined economically integrated regions." The idea is that banks compete in relatively local economies. Generally, the banking authorities use the Rand-McNally Company's economic areas, called *RMAs,* or they perform special surveys to determine the geographic area.

In determining how much a proposed merger "substantially lessens" the amount of competition in a market, banking authorities use a statistic known as the **Herfindahl–Hirschman Index (HHI).** The HHI is defined as

$$HHI = s_1^2 + s_2^2 + \cdots + s_N^2 \qquad (1)$$

The terms on the right-hand side of the equation are the squared values of the market shares (expressed in percentage points) of each of the banks. That is, if the total amount of deposits in the market is D and the amount of deposits in bank i is d_i, then $s_i = 100 \times d_i/D$. Because there are N banks, $d_1 + d_2 \cdots d_N = D$, so $s_1 + s_2 + \cdots + s_N = 100$.

For example, suppose that there were three banks in the market, with deposits totaling $D = \$500$ million. Suppose that the largest bank had deposits of $d_1 = \$250$ million, the next largest had deposits of $d_2 = \$150$ million, and the smallest had deposits of $d_3 = \$100$ million. Then their market shares are $s_1 = 100 \times \$250$ million$/\$500$ million $= 50$ percent, $s_2 = 100 \times \$150$ million$/\$500$ million $= 30$ percent, and $s_3 = 100 \times \$100$ million$/\$500$ million $= 20$ percent. Note that $d_1 + d_2 + d_3 = \$250$ million $+ \$150$ million $+ \$100$ million $= \$500$ million $= D$, and $s_1 + s_2 + s_3 = 50 + 30 + 20 = 100$. The HHI is $50^2 + 30^2 + 20^2 = 3,800$.

Note that if there were just one bank in a market, the HHI would have a value of 10,000 because the market share of the one bank is 100 percent, so HHI $= 100^2 = 10,000$. Under conditions of perfect competition, there would be a large number of competitors, each with a market share that is infinitesimally small, so HHI $= 0$. Thus, the HHI always will be somewhere between 0 and 10,000.

To demonstrate how the HHI measures competitiveness, imagine that there were five firms, each with 20 percent of the market. Then HHI $= 20^2 + 20^2 + 20^2 + 20^2 + 20^2 = 400 + 400 + 400 + 400 + 400 = 5 \times 400 = 2,000$. Or suppose that there were 10 firms, each with 10 percent of the market. Then HHI $= 10^2 + 10^2 + 10^2 + 10^2 + 10^2 + 10^2 + 10^2 + 10^2 + 10^2 + 10^2 = 10 \times 100 = 1,000$.

According to the guidelines used by the banking authorities, mergers or acquisitions could be challenged if, after the merger or acquisition, the HHI would become greater than 1,800 and if the change in the HHI would exceed 200 or if the new bank would have more than 35 percent of the deposits in the market. There is no particular magic to these numbers; they are just values that, based on the experience of the government authorities, lead to substantial monopoly power. In addition, a bank being formed by a merger must not have more than 10 percent of the nation's deposits or 30 percent of a state's deposits; that rule may soon be binding as more and more large banks merge. In 2008, Wells Fargo's acquisition of Wachovia raised its share of national deposits from 4.2 percent to 9.9 percent. However, because banks have tried to get around this rule by reducing deposits in clever ways, the Dodd–Frank Act added another consideration: a merger can be stopped if the new bank would hold more than 10 percent of the nation's total banking *liabilities* (as opposed to 10 percent of the nation's *deposits*).

How competitive is the banking system? To find out, let's look at actual data on HHIs for banking markets. The average HHI across all the different RMAs in the United States is about 1,600. It has been increasing gradually over time, however—15 years ago it was about 1,400. In nearly 30 percent of the banking markets, the HHI exceeds 1,800, so those markets are considered to be concentrated. Most big cities have HHIs in the range of 1,000 to 1,800, but eight cities have HHIs in excess of 3,000, which means that banks there are very highly concentrated. Note, however, that the banking authorities have no power to break up a bank that has a monopoly; they can only prevent the bank from merging with or acquiring another bank.

In deciding how to calculate these statistics, however, the banking authorities have some leeway to use their judgment about the circumstances in a particular market. For example, if several commercial banks propose to merge, usually only the deposits of the commercial banks (not thrifts or credit unions) in the market are used in calculating the size of the market. In some places, however, thrifts compete with commercial banks for certain types of loans and deposits, so some fraction (often 50 percent) of their deposits may be included in the calculation of the total amount of deposits in the market.

The banking authorities also may consider other mitigating factors in allowing a merger. For example, they may consider if there is active competition from other banking organizations, such as thrifts and credit unions, in evaluating the merger of commercial banks. In addition, they may consider the ease and attractiveness of entry into the banking market, the existence of competition from outside the geographic region, the possibility that the new institution will be able to reduce costs significantly through economies of scale (reductions in average cost from selling more services), the number and strength of the new banks' competitors, whether or not a bank being acquired might be in financial trouble, and any plans by the new bank to reduce its market share by selling off some branch offices. Thus, the banking authorities may allow a merger even if it does not meet the HHI or market-share guidelines if the authorities determine that mitigating factors are strong enough.

If the merger violates the guidelines (either for HHI or market share), and if mitigating factors are not strong, then the main banking supervisor (most often the Federal Reserve) will simply say that it disapproves of the merger and will not allow it to proceed. The bank could sue the Fed and allow the courts to determine if the Fed is right or wrong to disallow the merger. Or if the Fed allows a merger but the U.S. Department of Justice disagrees with the Fed, then the Justice Department may sue the bank to stop the merger. Most often the Fed, the other banking authorities, and the Justice Department together determine what assets or branch offices the new bank must dispose of in order for the merger or acquisition to be approved.

9-2e The Merger of Wachovia and Wells Fargo

To show how the merger approval process works, we examine the merger between two of the largest banks in the country—Wells Fargo and Wachovia—which occurred in 2008. At the time of the merger proposal, Wells Fargo (headquartered in San Francisco) was the fifth-largest bank in the country, with about $600 billion in assets and operations in 23 states. Wachovia (headquartered in Charlotte, North Carolina) was the third-largest bank in the country, with over $800 billion in assets and operations in 21 states. Together, and after divestiture of some assets as described below, the new bank would have over $1.3 trillion in assets, which would make it the second-largest bank in the country.

Because the new bank was to be organized as a bank holding company, the Federal Reserve was the banking supervisor mainly in charge of determining whether the merger would be allowed. It began investigating all the factors relevant to the merger as soon as the merger was

announced. As part of the process, the Fed solicited comments about the merger from interested members of the public. However, because the merger came in the middle of the financial crisis and the banking regulators feared that Wachovia might fail, the process was expedited. An objection to the merger came from Citibank, which had wanted to acquire Wachovia itself and sued in court to prevent the merger; the lawsuit did not succeed.

In analyzing the competitiveness of banks affected by the merger, the Fed analyzed the 49 banking markets in which both Wells Fargo and Wachovia had operations. In 37 of the 49 markets, the merger would not violate any of the guidelines based on the HHI or other guidelines. In 2 markets, the HHI showed that the market would be unconcentrated (HHI less than 1,000); in 27 markets, there would be moderate concentration (HHI between 1,000 and 1,800); and in 8 markets, the market would be concentrated (HHI above 1,800) but the change in the HHI would be less than 200. In 12 markets, the new HHI would exceed the guidelines. In 5 of those markets, the Fed required the new bank to sell some of its branches to bring the HHI within the guidelines. In 7 markets, all of which were small cities, even after divestiture of branches, the new banks' HHI would exceed the guidelines or else the bank would have a market share exceeding 35 percent in that

market. In each of those 7 markets, the Fed determined that mitigating factors, especially competition from credit unions, meant that the merger would not unduly affect competition.

Concerning the other requirements for approval of the merger (adequacy of the financial and managerial resources of the new bank, ability of the bank to meet the convenience and needs of the community, and whether the bank provided complete information about the merger or acquisition to the banking authorities), all were passed satisfactorily.

9-2f The Impact of Mergers on Bank Profits

Usually, bank profits rise after a merger. The banks argue that higher profits come about because the bigger (merged) bank is able to reduce its costs significantly by gaining economies of scale and scope. It is also possible, though, that the reduced competitiveness of the banking industry could lead to higher profits. What is the source of the higher profits, reduced costs or a reduction in competition?

Researchers studying this issue have found that an answer is not easy to come by. The problem is that after mergers, most banks increase both their risk and their expected return. To some extent, therefore, the higher profits they earn are because they are becoming riskier institutions. But research also shows that banks do, in fact, increase their efficiency and reduce their costs, which supports banks' claims.

Over the years, different research findings have been developed, and banking economists have debated them intensely. In fact, it seems likely that both reduced costs and reduced competition have boosted banks' profits. Neither factor alone is dominant.

RECAP

1. The government evaluates bank mergers on the basis of the effects on competition, the adequacy of the financial and managerial resources of the new bank, the ability of the bank to meet the convenience and needs of the community, and whether the bank provided complete information about the merger or acquisition to the banking authorities.

2. The effect of a merger on competition is based on the Herfindahl–Hirschman Index (HHI), which is the sum of the squared shares of deposits in a banking market.

3. A merger can be challenged if the HHI after the merger would exceed 1,800 and if the change in the HHI would exceed 200 or if the new bank would have a market share exceeding 35 percent. However, mitigating factors also may be considered.

4. When Wachovia merged with Wells Fargo, the Fed required the banks to sell a number of branches for the merger to be allowed.

5. Banks' profits increase after mergers both because costs are reduced and because competition is reduced.

Review Questions and Problems

Review Questions

1 Describe the ways in which the government provides a safety net for banks. How has that safety net evolved over time?

2 What is the government's role in the payments system, and how does that help banks?

3 Describe the major costs that banks face because of the government's role in banking.

4 Describe the methods by which bank failures are handled by the banking authorities. In which method is the government most likely to absorb losses?

5 What features of existing law were repealed by the Gramm–Leach–Bliley Act? What restrictions on banking remained after the new law was passed?

6 Describe the different types of financial institutions and which banking authorities supervise them.

7 What is the CAMELS rating system? Describe each of the elements of the system in general terms.

8 Describe the ways in which the Dodd–Frank Act changes banking regulation.

9 What is the Community Reinvestment Act? Why do banks complain so much about it?

10 What four main factors determine whether a bank merger or acquisition will be allowed?

Numerical Exercises

11 The banking market in Athens, Ohio, currently has four banks with market shares of 60 percent, 20 percent, 15 percent, and 5 percent. The two smallest banks have proposed merging. Under the standard merger guidelines of the Federal Reserve and the Justice Department, is the merger likely to be approved? Why or why not? In your answer, be as quantitative as possible.

12 The city of Puni has 10 banks of various sizes. Bank A has 18 percent of all Puni's deposits, bank B has 15 percent, bank C has 12 percent, bank D has 10 percent, the next five banks have 8 percent each, and the smallest bank has 5 percent. Suppose that banks A and D propose a merger at the same time that banks B and C propose a merger. You, as the banking structure analyst at the Federal Reserve, must analyze the competitive situation and determine whether either or both of the mergers should be allowed. Write up your analysis as a recommendation to the Federal Reserve Board, which will use your analysis to make a decision. Be sure that your answer includes the numerical considerations relevant to the case.

13 Suppose a banking market consists of banks that have the following shares of the market: 34 percent, 16 percent, 13 percent, 10 percent, 9 percent, 8 percent, 4 percent, 4 percent, and 2 percent.

a Calculate the HHI. Show your work.

b Suppose the largest bank wants to merge with the smallest bank. Calculate the new HHI (after the merger). Show your work.

c Would such a merger be acceptable, according to standard Justice Department guidelines? Explain why or why not.

Analytical Problems

14 When a small bank has financial problems, the banking authorities are likely to close it down, leading to substantial losses for uninsured depositors and the bank's stockholders. Yet a big bank in the same trouble may be saved by the banking authorities. Is this a sensible solution? Can it be defended on the grounds of economic efficiency? What about on the grounds of equity (fairness)?

15 In foreign countries it is quite common for banks to own nonfinancial companies and vice versa. Do the U.S. laws restricting banking and commerce cause U.S. banks to be at a competitive disadvantage internationally? What are the benefits of such restrictions?

16 Would bank supervision be made easier if banks' CAMELS ratings were made available publicly? What might be the downside of public announcement of such ratings?

17 Why are mergers of large banks located in different geographic regions more likely to be approved than mergers of smaller banks located in the same region?

Stasys Eidiejus/Shutterstock.com

PART 3

► MACROECONOMICS

CHAPTER 10

ClassicStock/Alamy

ECONOMIC GROWTH
and
BUSINESS CYCLES

*One of our main goals in this textbook is to explain
how monetary policy affects the overall economy.*

To set the stage for evaluating monetary policy, we need to understand the key elements of macroeconomics. Macroeconomists usually divide the economy into two main parts, both of which we consider in this chapter: (1) long-run trend growth of output and (2) fluctuations of output around its long-run trend, known as the *business cycle*. Output is usually measured by real gross domestic product (GDP), which is the total amount of goods and services produced in the economy.

Looking at the long run tells us about the trend in output. Because the growth rate of trend output exceeds the growth rate of the population, later generations will consume more goods and services than earlier generations did. For example, today we enjoy twice the standard of living (measured as output per person) as in 1965. Why does output grow over time? As we will see, output growth comes from growth in productivity, capital (equipment and machinery), and labor. Continued increases in output growth will be responsible for continued improvements in the standards of living of our children and our children's children.

But output does not increase along a steady upward path; it moves by fits and starts. In the short run, output fluctuates around its long-run trend. During a recession, output declines, firms lay off workers, and some firms even go out of business. If you are looking for a job in a recession, you may find it difficult to find a suitable position—or any position at all. If you are a small-business owner, you may find that banks are reluctant to make you a loan, and you also may find that you have fewer customers. During an expansion, output is growing, you may find it easy to find a job, and banks will be competing with each other to make a loan to you.

Figure 10.1 shows the differences between the long- and short-run views of output in the U.S. economy. The erratic line in the graph is quarterly output (measured by real GDP) for the 15-year period from the first quarter of 1969 to the fourth quarter of 1983. We use a logarithmic scale to reflect the fact that the variable being plotted is growing over time; on a logarithmic scale, a variable growing at a constant rate appears as a straight line. The straight line in the graph is a trend line that shows the long-run path of real output over those 15 years; it indicates that output was growing at an average annual rate of 2.7 percent. Thus, in the long run, output grew over that 15-year period at a rate of 2.7 percent, but it did so in an erratic fashion, with output fluctuating above and below the trend line in the short run.

FIGURE 10.1 Output in the U.S. Economy, Quarterly, 1969:Q1 to 1983:Q4

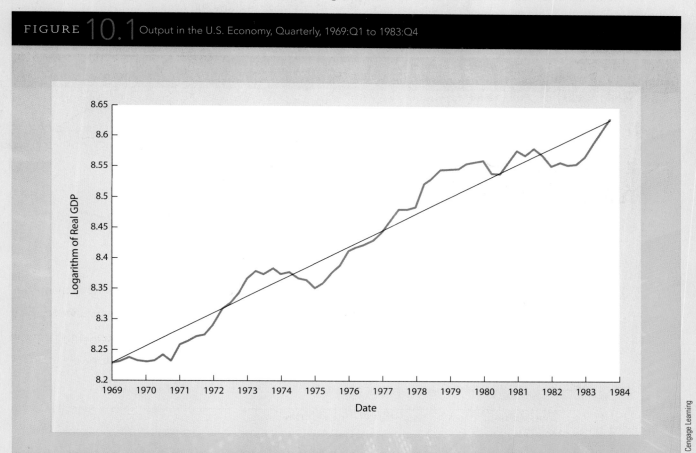

© Cengage Learning

This graph shows the differences between the long- and short-run views of output in the U.S. economy. The erratic line in the graph is quarterly output (measured by real GDP) from the first quarter of 1969 to the fourth quarter of 1983. The data are plotted on a logarithmic scale because a variable growing at a constant rate appears as a straight line. The straight line in the graph is a trend line that shows the long-run path of output over those 15 years.

In this chapter we will look at both long- and short-run movements of the economy's output. We start by discussing trend output growth, focusing on productivity and increases in capital and labor as the variables that contribute most to the economy's overall growth. We then turn our attention to the short run and study the business cycle. The stages of the business cycle show how the economy is deviating from its long-run path. The chapter closes with an application to everyday life that shows how the economy's growth rate affects your future income.

10-1 Measuring Economic Growth

Economists seek to understand economic growth because it is responsible for increases in living standards. If we can identify the variables that cause the upward trend in output, we can recommend actions that ensure a higher future standard of living.

Output has not followed the same trend over time. Figure 10.2 illustrates the long-term movements of output since 1950, again plotted on a logarithmic scale like that used in Figure 10.1. The period from 1950 to 1970 showed the fastest growth, with output growth averaging 4.1 percent per year. From 1971 to 1982, output growth averaged just 2.7 percent per year. And from 1983 to 2007, output grew 3.3 percent per year on average. The long-term effects of the Great Recession from 2007 to 2009 are not yet clear, but real GDP grew at an annual rate of only 0.5 percent from the end of 2007 to the end of 2012.

Because output growth is beneficial to society in so many ways, economists study the variables that contribute to growth. By understanding these variables and their contribution to growth, we can ensure that government policies promote growth rather than retard it. The key

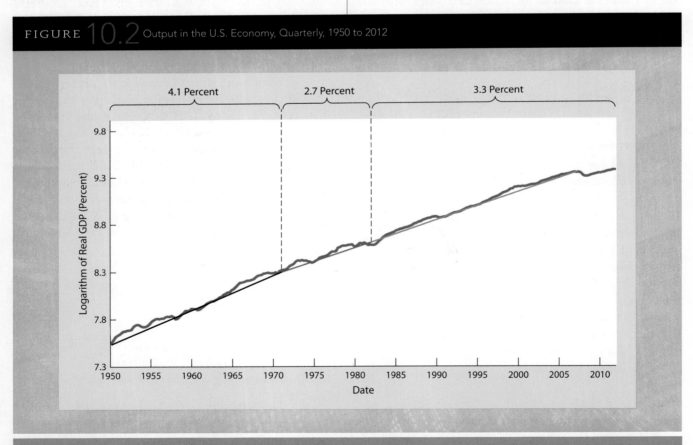

FIGURE 10.2 Output in the U.S. Economy, Quarterly, 1950 to 2012

This graph illustrates the long-term movements of output since 1950 on a logarithmic scale. Output growth averaged 4.0 percent from the third quarter of 1950 to 1970, 2.7 percent from 1971 to 1982, and 3.3 percent from 1983 to 2007.

variables that are responsible for output growth are the economy's resources—labor and capital—and productivity, which tells us how much output is produced by capital and labor.

We face major problems in studying growth, however, because the data on the amount of capital goods in the economy are not measured accurately. Those inaccurate measurements arise because it is difficult to estimate precisely how rapidly capital goods depreciate, and it is also difficult to measure their quality, as we will discuss in more detail later. Therefore, we will take two different routes in our analysis of economic growth. The first relies only on data on the amount of labor used in producing goods and services, which is measured much more accurately than capital. The second uses the flawed data on capital as well as data on labor.

10-1a A View of Economic Growth Based on Labor Data

We measure the amount of labor in the economy in a number of ways, including the number of employed workers and the amount of hours they work. In the long run, what determines the amount that labor grows in the economy? As with all economic markets, there are two sides to the labor market: supply and demand.

The supply of workers, called the **labor force**, consists of people who are either employed (they have jobs) or unemployed (they desire to have jobs):

> *Labor force = employed people + unemployed people*

The labor force is not the entire population because many people cannot work or choose not to work. If we subtract those who are too young to work (under 16 years of age), in the military, or in institutions (such as prisons) separate from the population, we get the number of people in the working-age noninstitutional civilian population (hereafter called the *working-age population*). Of those in the working-age population, some are not in the labor force because they are in school, some are working without explicit pay inside the home, and some are retired. The ratio of the labor force to the working-age population is called the **labor-force participation rate**:

> *Labor-force participation rate = $\dfrac{labor\ force}{working\text{-}age\ population}$*

The labor-force participation rate is a useful measure because it tells us the percentage of the population that wants to work. If the labor-force participation rate were constant, then the labor force would grow at the same rate as the population. In fact, however, the labor-force participation rate changes substantially over time, as you can see in Figure 10.3. The labor-force participation rate was relatively constant from the end of World War II to the mid-1960s. The rate increased substantially from the mid-1960s to 2000, especially as women entered the labor force in increasing numbers. Since 2001, the rate has been declining at a rate of about 0.4 percent per year, most notably because young people are staying in school longer.

The other side of the employment equation is demand. Workers must find jobs, so they care about the performance of business firms. When firms are not growing and making profits, they do not hire many new workers, so the number of employed people as a percentage of the labor force is low. In periods of economic growth, on the other hand, the number of employed people as a percentage of the labor force is high.

With both supply and demand in the picture, we can now illustrate how the population is split up into the labor force and the employed, as shown in Figure 10.4 using data for the fourth quarter of 2012. The 315.2 million people in the population were split between those in the working-age population, totaling 244.2 million, and those who are young, in the military, or in institutions, totaling 71.0 million. The working-age population of 244.2 million is divided into those in the labor force (155.5 million) and those not in the labor force (88.7 million). The labor-force participation rate therefore is

> *Labor-force participation rate* $= \dfrac{labor\ force}{working\text{-}age\ population}$
> $= \dfrac{155.5\ million}{244.2\ million}$
> $= 0.637$
> $= 63.7\ percent$

Of the 155.5 million in the labor force, 143.3 million were employed, and 12.2 million were unemployed.

A commonly used measure of the condition of the labor market is the **unemployment rate**, which is the number of unemployed workers as a fraction

labor force the supply of workers, which consists of people who are either employed (they have jobs) or unemployed (they desire to have jobs)

labor-force participation rate the ratio of the labor force to the working-age population

unemployment rate the number of unemployed workers as a fraction of the labor force

FIGURE 10.3 U.S. Labor-Force Participation Rate, Monthly, 1950 to 2012

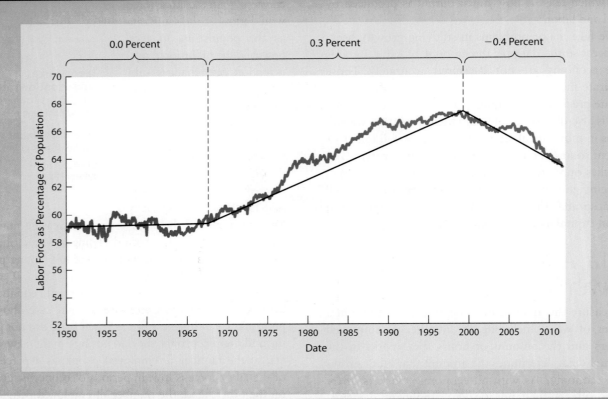

This graph shows the U.S. labor force participation rate since 1950. The rate was fairly steady from 1950 to the mid-1960s, grew about 0.3 percent per year from the mid-1960s to 2000, and has been declining at a rate of about 0.4 percent per year since then.

of the labor force. In the fourth quarter of 2012, with unemployment of 12.2 million and a labor force of 155.5 million, the unemployment rate was:

$$Unemployment\ rate = \frac{Unemployed}{Labor\ force}$$
$$= \frac{12.2}{155.5}$$
$$= 0.078$$
$$= 7.8\ percent$$

The unemployment rate of 7.8 percent means that 7.8 percent of everyone who wants to work is unemployed, nearly one of every 13 people in the labor force. Figure 10.5 shows the unemployment rate over time. The trend in the unemployment rate is fairly erratic, with a fairly flat trend before 1970, a rising trend in the 1970s, a falling trend in the 1980s and the 1990s, and an unclear trend in the 2000s. In fact, forecasting the unemployment rate in the long run is quite difficult because the long-run trend is so uncertain.

Because of the erratic nature of the unemployment rate, macroeconomists prefer to look at the level of nonfarm payroll employment as a short-run guide to the strength of the economy. Nonfarm payroll employment data come from a survey of business firms, whereas the unemployment rate and labor-force participation rate come from a survey of households. As a result of the two different surveys, the data sometimes conflict, but generally macroeconomists believe the survey of business firms is more accurate.

Figure 10.6 shows the level of nonfarm payroll employment from 1950 to 2012. Its growth rate is fairly steady over time at about 1.8 percent per year, on average. Nonfarm payroll employment is correlated in the short run with GDP growth.

The actual amount of work provided by workers depends not just on the number of people employed but also on the number of hours each person works. This is so because in boom times, workers often will be asked to work overtime hours (more than their normal amount of hours each week). In slack times, overtime work is

FIGURE 10.4 Population, Labor Force, and Employment in 2012:Q4

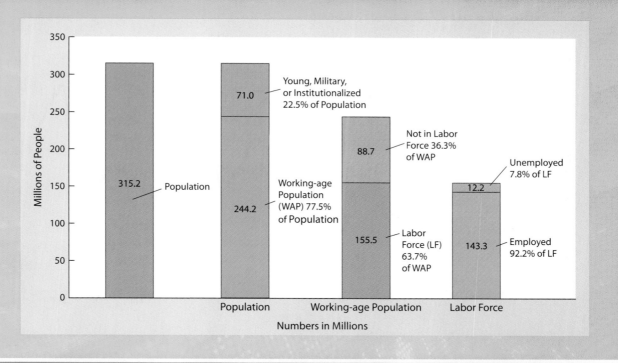

This graph shows the breakdown of the U.S. population into various labor-market segments, including the working-age population, the labor force, employed, and unemployed.

rare, and many workers are asked (or told) to reduce the amount of time they work. Hours worked are plotted in Figure 10.7. You can see that the total number of hours worked in the economy rose at a fairly steady pace since 1950. (Note that the data on hours worked are for the nonfarm business sector, not the overall economy, because those are the only data available.)

Supply and demand together determine the number of hours worked and the overall wage rate paid to workers. As with any other market, increases in labor demand cause increases in the wage rate (the price of labor) and in the number of hours worked (the quantity of labor). Of course, the demand for workers also depends on their productivity, which we turn to next.

Labor productivity is simply output divided by the number of hours worked. It tells you how much output the economy gets from one hour of labor effort. This is the measure used most often when we talk about productivity growth.

To see how output is related to labor productivity and the amount of hours worked, consider the following equation:

$$Output = \frac{output}{hours\ worked} \times hours\ worked \tag{1}$$
$$= labor\ productivity \times hours\ worked$$

The top line of the equation is valid because in the right-hand side of the equation the two *hours worked* terms cancel each other out, so the equation just says that output equals output. By writing the equation in this way, however, we can see how productivity and hours worked together determine output.

Because we are concerned mainly with the growth rates over time of output, labor productivity, and hours worked, we can transform Equation (1) in terms of growth rates. Note that the growth rate of terms multiplied by each other is the sum of the growth rates. Thus, because labor productivity and hours worked multiply each other on the right-hand side of Equation (1), we add their growth rates when

labor productivity
a measure of productivity per worker, calculated as output divided by the number of hours worked

FIGURE 10.5 The Unemployment Rate, 1950 to 2012

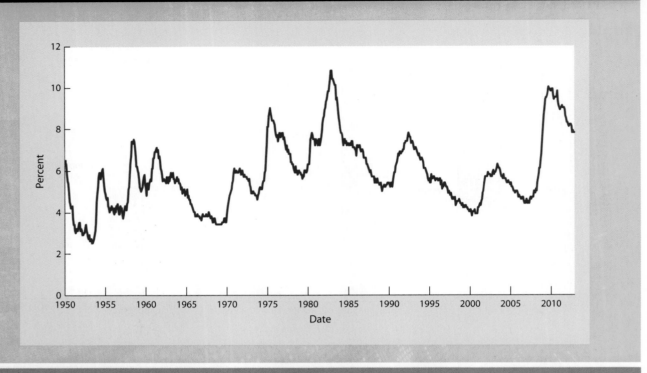

The trend in the unemployment rate is fairly erratic over time. The unemployment rate was generally flat over time before 1970, rose in the 1970s, fell in the 1980s and the 1990s, and was erratic in the 2000s. In fact, forecasting the unemployment rate in the long run is quite difficult because the long-run trend is so uncertain.

FIGURE 10.6 Nonfarm Payroll Employment, 1950–2012

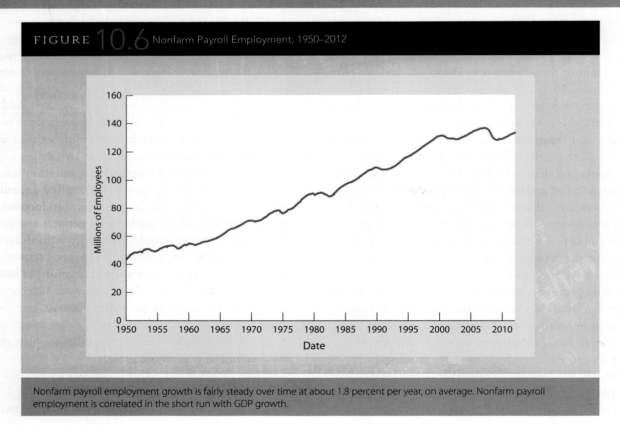

Nonfarm payroll employment growth is fairly steady over time at about 1.8 percent per year, on average. Nonfarm payroll employment is correlated in the short run with GDP growth.

FIGURE 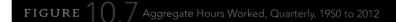 10.7 Aggregate Hours Worked, Quarterly, 1950 to 2012

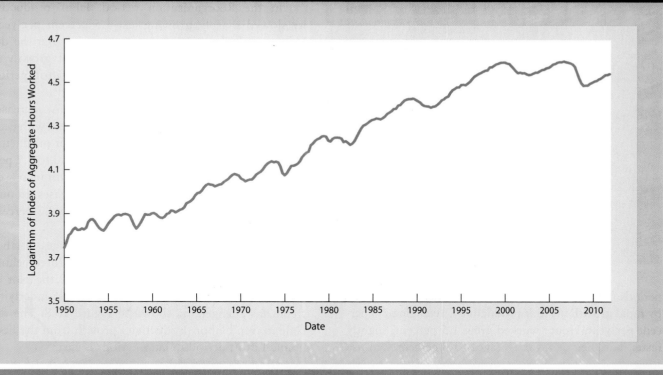

The total number of hours worked in the economy has risen at a fairly steady pace since 1950.

determining the growth rate of output. The growth-rate form of Equation (1) is

> Output growth = labor productivity growth + growth of hours worked
> %Δ Output = %Δ labor productivity + %Δ hours worked   **(2)**

We use the symbols %Δ to stand for the growth rate or percentage change in a variable.

Growth of hours worked tends to be fairly stable over time, as we saw in Figure 10.7. Thus, the changes in trend output growth that have occurred over time are attributable to changes in trend labor productivity growth.

Because the data on output shown in Figure 10.2 show breaks in trend around the end of 1970 and the end of 1982, we can identify three distinct periods since World War II: 1950 to 1970, 1971 to 1982, and 1983 to 2007; data since 2008 have behaved differently and may represent a new period, but there is not yet enough data to be sure. The first period, from 1950 to 1970, we call the *Economic Liftoff.* That period began after World War II as the United States became the strongest economy in the world. The second period, from 1971 to 1982, we call the *Reorganization.* In that period, the U.S. economy struggled to reinvent itself because of higher oil prices, high inflation, and poor macroeconomic policies, and a

transition from manufacturing to services. The third period, from 1983 to 2007, we call the *Long Boom.* That period is one in which the economy grew steadily, unemployment declined steadily, income and wealth grew sharply, and the United States again became the dominant economic force in the world (see the Data Bank box "Why Is the Economy More Stable in the Long Boom?"). Whether the long boom ended with the financial crisis of 2008 remains to be seen.

We can see how the changes between these periods in trend labor productivity growth have affected trend output growth in Table 10.1. Because we want to break output growth into labor productivity growth and growth in hours worked, and the data on the latter two series are available only for the nonfarm business sector, the measure of output we use (output of the nonfarm business sector) is slightly different from that used in Figure 10.2 (real GDP). The difference of 0.2 to 0.3 percentage points in output growth arises mainly because output growth of farms and the government sector differed from output growth in the rest of the economy.

Table 10.1 illustrates the large swings in labor productivity and the changes in hours worked that led to the changes in trend output growth across the three postwar

TABLE 10.1	Contributions to Output Growth in Three Postwar Periods (average annual growth rates, in percentage points)		
Period	Output Growth	= Labor Productivity Growth +	Growth in Hours Worked
Economic Liftoff			
1950 to 1970	4.1	2.6	1.5
Reorganization			
1971 to 1982	2.9	1.5	1.4
Long Boom			
1983 to 2007	3.7	2.2	1.5
Full Period			
1950 to 2012	3.5	2.1	1.3

Note: Output growth may not exactly equal the sum of labor productivity growth and growth in hours worked because of rounding. Data in this table are for the nonfarm business sector, not the entire economy.

© Cengage Learning

labor productivity growth was so strong, however, output grew at a rapid annual rate of 4.1 percent.

In the Reorganization period, labor productivity slowed sharply, growing just 1.5 percent per year. Hours worked grew 1.4 percent per year. But the decline in labor productivity caused output growth to tumble from 4.1 percent in the Economic Liftoff period to 2.9 percent in the Reorganization period.

The Long Boom from 1983 to 2007 saw increases in both labor productivity and hours worked, with each contributing to faster output growth. Labor productivity growth increased by 0.7 percentage point to 2.2 percent per year, whereas hours worked growth increased slightly to 1.5 percent per year. Those increases led output growth to rise 0.8 percentage point to 3.7 percent per year.

Because Table 10.1 suggests that changes in labor productivity growth are the main driving force behind changes in trend output, we can examine the plot of data on labor productivity to see how its underlying trend has changed, as shown in Figure 10.8. The decline in trend labor productivity growth from the Economic Liftoff period to later periods is clear.

periods. The Economic Liftoff period was characterized by rapid growth in labor productivity, averaging 2.6 percent per year. Hours worked grew 1.5 percent, slightly faster than their postwar average of 1.3 percent. Because

FIGURE 10.8 Labor Productivity, Quarterly, 1950 to 2012

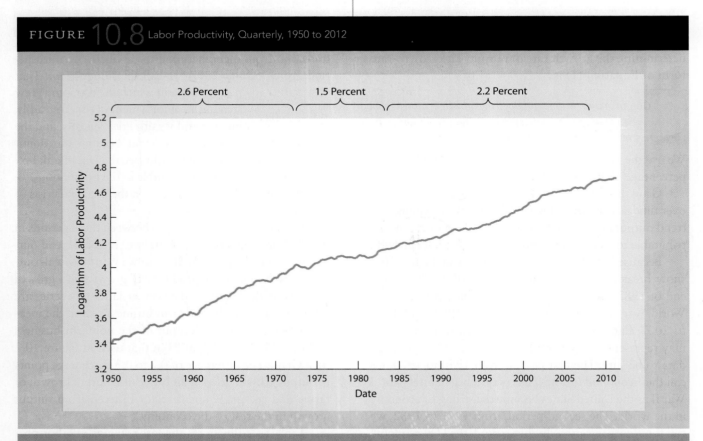

Labor productivity grew at an average annual rate of 2.6 percent from 1949 to 1970, slowed to an average annual rate of 1.5 percent from 1970 to 1982, and then grew faster from 1982 to 2008, averaging 2.2 percent per year.

An examination of many economic variables suggests that the Long Boom period is different from the other years since the end of World War II. The economy appears to be much less volatile in the sense that many economic variables are closer to their trend lines than before. For example, output growth, as shown in Figure 10.A, has been remarkably steady in the Long Boom compared with earlier periods.

What accounts for the more stable performance of the economy in the Long Boom? We would like to be able to answer this question as a guide to our future. If the stability is caused by good government policies, for example, that would be useful to know so that the government could keep those policies in place. If the stability is caused by changes to the structure of the economy, such as more efficient financial markets, the change in output from goods to services, or advances by businesses in managing inventories, that would be useful to know so that we could encourage the private sector to continue such developments. If the stability is simply luck, in the sense that we have not been hit by major shocks,

such as the sharp rise in oil prices in the 1970s or major wars such as the Korean War in the 1950s and the Vietnam War in the 1960s, that would be useful to know so that we do not attribute the stability to other factors and can employ diplomacy to prevent such catastrophic events in the future.

Unfortunately, finding out exactly what caused the stability of the Long Boom is not easy. In recent years, a number of economists have attempted to do so, with mixed results. The clearest study was done by economists Jim Stock and Mark Watson in 2003.[1] They found that the increased stability in the economy occurred not just for output but also for many subsectors of the economy, such as consumer spending and business capital investment spending. The change seems to have happened all at once some time between the fourth quarter of 1982 and the third quarter of 1985 (around the time of the start of the Long Boom), although it is difficult to pin down the exact date when the economy stabilized. Perhaps surprisingly, Stock and Watson did not find that much of the increased stability in the economy came from changes

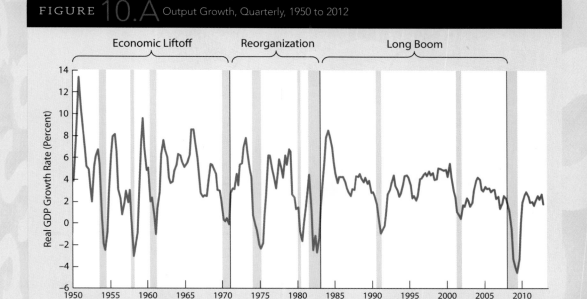

FIGURE 10.A Output Growth, Quarterly, 1950 to 2012

This graph shows that the growth rate of output was fairly steady in the Long Boom (other than the sharp drops in the two recessions). In both the Economic Liftoff period and the Reorganization period, output growth was much more volatile, and even more so after the end of the Long Boom in 2008.

(continued)

in how the economy operates, whether because of the shift from goods to services, or better inventory management, or more efficient financial markets. While all three of those changes in how the economy operates help the economy run more smoothly, they did not help much in making the economy more stable. Stock and Watson also found that improved monetary policy was responsible for reducing inflation but was responsible for only a fraction of the increased stability in the economy. Instead, for whatever reason (perhaps just good luck), the economy became less volatile. This graph shows that the growth rate of output was fairly steady in the Long Boom (other than the sharp drops in the two recessions). In both the Economic Liftoff period and the Reorganization period, output growth was much more volatile. The Long Boom probably ended in 2008 with the financial crisis and the subsequent very sharp drop in GDP growth.

Morintoons Syndicate/The Miami Herald

[1]"Has the Business Cycle Changed? Evidence and Explanations," in *Monetary Policy and the Economy: Adapting to a Changing Economy*, Federal Reserve Bank of Kansas City, pp. 9–56.

This view of economic growth based on labor data shows how changes in labor productivity growth and the quantity of hours worked have affected the trends in output growth and is useful in characterizing the broad changes in the U.S. economy over the past 50 years. However, it does not offer much insight into why the growth rate of labor productivity has changed over time. Is it because of increased capital per worker, better organization of work, or better technology? To answer this question, we must consider the factors other than labor that cause output to grow over time.

10-1b A View of Economic Growth Using Data on Both Labor and Capital

Other factors of production besides labor contribute to output, particularly capital. Capital includes the buildings and equipment that firms use to produce output. Sometimes, but not often because we lack reliable data, economists consider additional factors besides labor and capital, such as energy, entrepreneurial ability, and land.

If we think of the economy's output as being produced by capital and labor, we might posit a relationship such as this:

$$Y = F(K, L) \qquad (3)$$

where Y is output, F is a production function that relates the amount of capital and labor to the amount of output, K is the amount of capital in the economy, and L is the amount of labor. Economists who have examined the data on output, capital, and labor often find that the following more specific equation fits the data well:

$$Y = A \times K^a \times L^{1-a} \qquad (4)$$

In this equation, K is raised to the power a, and L is raised to the power $1 - a$. (The data for the United States suggest that a has been roughly constant for decades at about 0.3.) The equation shows how changes in the quantity of capital and labor contribute to output. The term A is known as **total factor productivity (TFP)** because it explains changes in output that are not attributable to changes in either the quantity of capital or the quantity of labor and thus must be due to overall productivity changes.

The growth-rate form of this equation can be used to show how TFP growth contributes to output growth. Because the growth rate of a product is the sum of the growth rates, the growth version of Equation (4) is

$$\%\Delta Y = \%\Delta A + (a \times \%\Delta K) + [(1 - a) \times \%\Delta L]$$
Output growth = TFP growth + (a × growth rate $\qquad (5)$
of capital) + [(1 − a) × growth rate of labor]

This equation shows that a 1 percentage point increase in TFP growth (with capital and labor unchanged) leads to a 1 percentage point increase in output growth. However, note that an increase in the growth rate of just capital or just labor would not lead to an equal increase in output growth. For example, if the growth rate of capital increased by 1 percentage point (with no change in TFP growth or labor growth), and if $a = 0.3$, then output growth would increase by 0.3 percentage point. Or if the growth rate of labor increased by 1 percentage point (with no change in TFP growth or capital growth), then output growth would increase by 0.7 percentage point (because $1 - a = 0.7$). However, if both capital growth and labor growth increased by 1 percentage point (with no change in TFP growth), then output growth would increase by

> **total factor productivity (TFP)** a measure of productivity that explains changes in output other than those attributable to the amount of labor and capital, which is calculated by estimating the contributions of the quantity of capital and the quantity of labor to total output and then figuring out what is left over

$$
\begin{aligned}
\textit{Percent change in output growth} &= (a \times \textit{increase in capital growth}) + [(1 - a) \\
&\quad \times \textit{increase in labor growth}] \\
&= (0.3 \times 1\%) + (0.7 \times 1\%) \\
&= 1 \textit{ percent}
\end{aligned}
$$

If both labor and capital increased by one percentage point, so would output.

To see how economists calculate TFP growth from the available data, subtract the last two terms from both sides of Equation (5) and switch sides of the equation to obtain

Economists have difficulty measuring changes in total factor productivity because of technological advances, especially in computers. When Intel develops new chips that are more powerful than older ones, government statisticians face difficulties in measuring how such a change affects productivity.

	Output	Labor Productivity	Total Factor Productivity (TFP)	Capital	Labor
Economic Liftoff (1950 to 1970)	4.1	2.6	1.6	3.9	1.5
Reorganization (1971 to 1982)	2.9	1.5	0.4	4.7	1.5
Long Boom (1983 to 2007)	3.7	2.2	1.1	4.1	1.9
Overall (1950 to 2011)	3.5	2.1	1.1	4.0	1.5

$$\%\Delta A = \%\Delta Y - (a \times \%\Delta K) - [(1 - a) \times \%\Delta L] \qquad (6)$$

Given data on output growth, the growth rate of capital, and the growth rate of labor, we can calculate the growth rate of TFP using Equation (6). However, remember that the data available on capital are not very reliable, so we must be cautious in using and interpreting these measures of TFP. The problem with data on capital is that we do not know precisely how fast the capital depreciates, and we would like to adjust the data for changes in quality, but measuring capital quality is very difficult. For example, Intel's Core i7 processor is substantially faster than a Core Duo chip from just three years ago. Someone running complicated mathematical programs would notice a huge difference, but someone doing word processing would hardly notice any difference at all. Thus, as personal computers (PCs) with Core i7 chips replace older PCs, how can we determine the amount that capital has changed? Also, although we measured hours worked in our discussion of labor productivity, a better measure of the amount of labor that is used in Equation (6) is available—one that adjusts for the quality of labor. The adjustment for labor quality is not as problematic as the adjustment for the quality of capital, but still some

guesswork is involved. Clearly, as workers over time have become more educated, a given hour of work produces more; an hour worked by a highly trained worker surely produces more output than an hour of work by a novice. Thus, the data used in calculating TFP account not just for hours worked but also for the quality of those hours.

Table 10.2 shows output growth, labor productivity growth, and TFP growth, as well as the growth rates of quality-adjusted capital and labor, over the three major economic periods since World War II. TFP has grown about 1.1 percent per year, on average, from 1950 to 2011. In the Economic Liftoff period, TFP grew at a 1.6 percent annual rate; in the Reorganization period, it grew just 0.4 percent per year; and in the Long Boom, it grew 1.1 percent. Note that these changes in TFP growth parallel the changes in labor productivity growth, suggesting that the same factors are responsible for both measures. In each period, labor productivity growth was about 1 percentage point higher than TFP growth.

Because the changes in the growth rate of TFP parallel those of labor productivity, the major change affecting output growth across the three periods is the change in productivity; there is relatively little impact from changes in the growth rates of capital and labor.

RECAP

1 Based on data from the labor market, changes in trend output growth arise mainly from changes in labor productivity growth across periods of economic liftoff, reorganization, and the long boom.

2 Based on data on both labor and capital, changes in trend output growth also arise mainly from changes in total factor productivity (TFP) growth.

10-2 Business Cycles

In this section we switch gears and look at economic performance over shorter time periods. We now examine the fluctuations in output around its long-run trend. Output can fluctuate around its long-term trend as a result of changes in prices of key resources such as oil, disruptions in the financial system, and government policies. Referring to Figure 10.2, the preceding section on economic growth explained the trend lines; this section on business cycles will explain the fluctuations of real output around the trend lines.

10-2a What Is a Business Cycle?

A **business cycle** is the short-term movement of output and other key economic variables (such as people's incomes and the number of people employed) around their long-term trends. What do business cycles look like? First, let's draw a hypothetical picture to help us identify some characteristics of business cycles. If we were to plot the movement of output (measured by real GDP) over time, it might look something like Figure 10.9. Output varies over time around its long-term trend.

An economic **expansion** occurs when output is rising, along with other key variables such as income and employment. The end of the expansion occurs when output, income, and employment hit a **peak** and begin to decline. A **recession** is a period when output, income, and employment are declining. The recession ends when those variables hit a **trough** and begin to rise. A particularly bad recession (in which output declines much more than usual for a recession) is called a **depression**. The last depression in the United States occurred in the 1930s; in the Great Depression, 1 of every 4 workers was unemployed, which is much worse than

business cycle the short-term movement of output and other key economic variables around their long-term trends

expansion the state of the economy in which output is rising, along with other key variables such as income and employment

peak the end of an expansion, when output, income, and employment begin to decline

recession a period when output, income, and employment are declining

trough the end of a recession, when output, income, and employment begin to rise

depression a particularly bad recession, in which output declines much more than usual for a recession

FIGURE 10.9 The Business Cycle

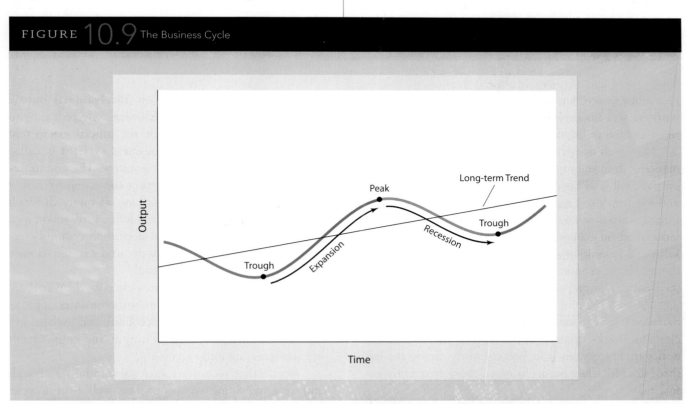

Over the course of the business cycle, output varies over time around its long-term trend. An economic expansion occurs when output is rising. A recession occurs when output hits a peak and begins to decline. The recession ends when output hits a trough and begins to rise.

FIGURE 10.10 Output in the U.S. Economy, Quarterly, 1950 to 2012

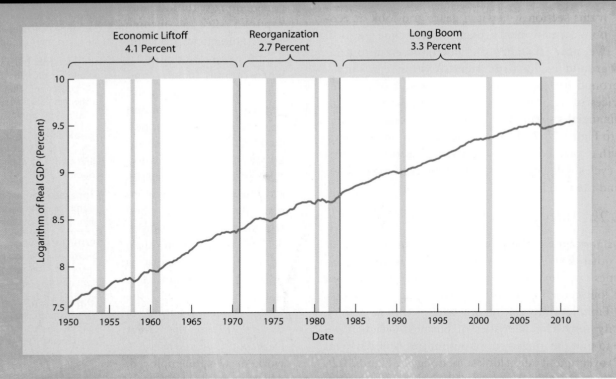

This graph plots output over time since 1950. Output growth averaged 4.1 percent in the Economic Liftoff period, 2.7 percent in the Reorganization period, and 3.3 percent in the Long Boom. There are both expansions and recessions within each of the three periods, although there are more recessions (and they last longer) in the Reorganization period than in the Long Boom period. The vertical blue bars show when recessions have occurred, which line up with declines in output.

recessions since then, during the worst of which 1 in 10 workers was unemployed. Output declined 30 percent from its high point in 1929 to its low point in 1933.

How well does Figure 10.9 match the actual performance of the economy? Look at Figure 10.10, which plots output (real GDP) over time and includes the trend lines and the periods (Economic Liftoff, Reorganization, and Long Boom) that we discussed while looking at the long-term trends in economic growth. There are both expansions and recessions within each of the three periods, although there are more recessions (and they last longer) in the Reorganization period than in the Long Boom period.

The vertical blue bars in Figure 10.10 show when recessions have occurred. You can see that output declines for several quarters in each recession. You also will notice that recessions have become fairly rare in the last three decades; they occurred much more frequently before that.

Notice that the actual data in Figure 10.10 are much more erratic than appears in Figure 10.9, making it difficult to determine when an expansion or recession is taking place. For this reason, the National Bureau of Economic Research (NBER) has selected a number of economic experts to be the official group that determines the state of the business cycle; it is called the *Business Cycle Dating Committee*. The committee makes a judgment about whether the economy is in a recession or expansion by looking at many different macroeconomic variables. They define a *recession* as a period in which "a significant decline in economic activity spreads across the economy and can last from a few months to more than a year."[2]

NBER's business-cycle dates since World War II are shown in Table 10.3. The table shows the dates of peaks and troughs, the lengths of recessions and expansions, and the percentage change in output and employment in each recession and expansion.

Notice that recessions vary substantially in length and severity. Some recessions last well over a year,

[2]This language comes from the NBER's Web site (as of June 9, 2013): **www.nber.org/cycles/recessions.html**.

TABLE 10.3 U.S. Business-Cycle Dates

RECESSIONS

Date of Peak	Date of Trough	Length of Recession (months)	Percent Change in Output (peak to trough)	Percent Change in Employment (peak to trough)
Economic Liftoff				
November 1948	October 1949	11	−1.6	−5.0
July 1953	May 1954	10	−2.5	−3.1
August 1957	April 1958	8	−3.1	−4.0
April 1960	February 1961	10	−0.5	−2.3
December 1969	November 1970	11	−0.2	−1.2
Reorganization				
November 1973	March 1975	16	−3.2	−1.6
January 1980	July 1980	6	−2.2	−1.1
July 1981	November 1982	16	−2.6	−3.1
Long Boom				
July 1990	March 1991	8	−0.3	−1.1
March 2001	November 2001	8	0.7	−1.2
December 2007	June 2009	18	−4.7	−5.4

EXPANSIONS

Date of Trough	Date of Peak	Length of Expansion (months)	Percent Change in Output (trough to peak)	Percent Change in Employment (trough to peak)
Economic Liftoff				
October 1949	July 1953	44	28.7	17.7
May 1954	August 1957	39	13.5	8.5
April 1958	April 1960	24	11.7	7.4
February 1961	December 1969	106	51.2	33.0
Reorganization				
November 1970	November 1973	36	16.4	10.7
March 1975	January 1980	58	23.2	18.5
July 1980	July 1981	12	4.4	2.0
Long Boom				
November 1982	July 1990	92	37.3	23.7
March 1991	March 2001	120	40.6	22.2
November 2001	December 2007	73	17.2	5.4

whereas others last six to eight months. The longest and most severe recession was the one from December 2007 to June 2009. However, the length of a recession is not always a good guide to its severity. One of the shortest recessions (August 1957 to April 1958) had one of the the largest declines in output and employment. The recession in 2001 was unusually mild. Output actually increased 0.7 percent during the recession (the only recession on record in which output increased rather than decreasing), whereas employment declined 1.2 percent. Similarly, expansions also vary in length and strength. Although the expansion that began in March 1991 was clearly the longest of all time, it did not lead to the greatest increase in output or employment among expansions. The expansion from May 1954 to August 1957 also was weak in terms of the increase in output and employment. The expansion from November 2001 to December 2007 was one of the weakest in terms of employment growth.

The NBER business-cycle dating committee usually waits for some time to pass before declaring that the economy is in a recession or that a recession has ended. For example, the committee announced in April 1991 that a recession had begun in July 1990; that is nine months later. And they determined in December 1992 that the recession had ended in March 1991; that is 21 months later! The reason they wait so long is that a decision about when a recession has begun must stand the test of time, but data often are revised substantially. Thus, the committee waits until the data indicate fairly clearly when a recession began or ended.

In addition to the decline in output that occurs in recessions and the rise in output that occurs in expansions, two other facts characterize the business cycle: (1) Many economic variables move together, and (2) many economic variables deviate from their long-term growth trends for substantial periods.

First, many economic variables move in the same direction at the same time. For example, spending by consumers on goods and services tends to rise and fall at the same time as spending by businesses on new capital. This comovement of macroeconomic variables is a hallmark of business cycles. Some variables move in opposite directions, but their timing is about the same; for example, the unemployment rate rises in recessions and falls in expansions, whereas the growth rate of real GDP declines sharply in recessions and rises sharply when expansions begin, as you can see in Figure 10.11. Notice that in recessions the two variables move in opposite directions. After expansions are a few years old, however, the variables do not seem closely related

to one another because the unemployment rate usually declines and output growth sometimes rises and sometimes declines.

Second, most macroeconomic variables tend to stay above trend or below trend for some time, as we saw in the hypothetical case for output in Figure 10.9. Thus, when we look at the data on output in Figure 10.10, we see that recessions are not times when output declines for just one quarter but times when it declines for several quarters in a row. Even during a recession, there might be one quarter when output rises, but then it might decline the next quarter. Thus, NBER's official method of looking at the business cycle says that a downturn in economic activity usually must last for at least six months to be called a recession.

10-2b The Causes of Business Cycles

What causes business cycles? Unfortunately, economists do not have a good answer. Instead, they have a number of partial answers. Here are a few of them:

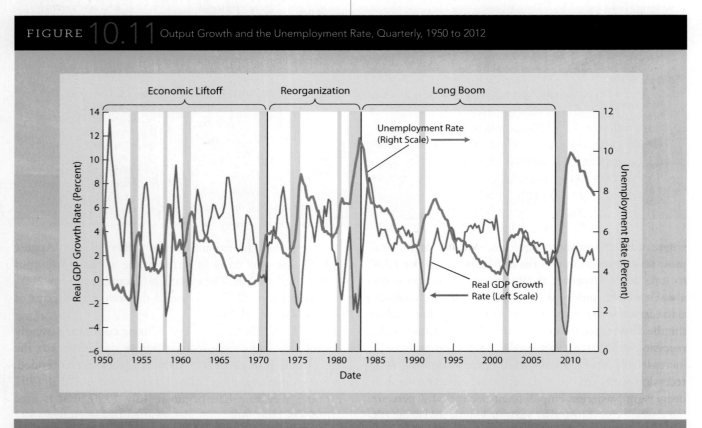

FIGURE 10.11 Output Growth and the Unemployment Rate, Quarterly, 1950 to 2012

Many economic variables move together over the business cycle. The unemployment rate and the growth rate of output generally move at the same time, especially in recessions. The unemployment rate rises in recessions and falls in expansions, as this graph shows. The growth rate of output falls sharply in recessions and rises sharply when recessions end.

1. Erratic growth of the money supply
2. Swings of optimism and pessimism that cause business investment in capital goods to fluctuate
3. Sudden changes in productivity growth
4. Changes in the prices of key factors of production such as oil

The first answer, that erratic growth of the money supply is the main cause of business cycles, is suggested by a group of economists known as **monetarists.** Monetarists attribute the business cycle to changes in the amount of money in the economy, and they have a good deal of evidence to support their case. Most compelling is the large decline in the money supply that occurred during the Great Depression. Particularly onerous was an increase in the reserve requirements on banks in 1936 and 1937, which led them to curtail lending, thus choking off the economy's recovery and lengthening the depression. In addition, in many other cases reductions in the growth rate of the money supply occurred shortly before recessions began. More recently, in the late 1980s, the Federal Reserve had been reducing money growth for a year from spring 1988 to summer 1989 and then began to ease up for about a year. But the slower money growth during that year may have made the economy vulnerable, and it went into recession when the price of oil rose in mid-1990.

Not all economists accept the monetarists' claim that changes in the money supply cause recessions. Many find it hard to believe that changes in money have so great an impact on business cycles; they expect that money should affect prices and inflation, with little effect on any real (inflation-adjusted) variables. Other economists have developed statistical models of the economy and found money's role to be of limited importance.

A second possibility is that the main cause of business cycles is waves of optimism and pessimism that cause business investment in capital goods to fluctuate. This is one possibility raised by **Keynesians,** who follow the ideas of British economist John Maynard Keynes. They argue that if you examine data on business cycles, capital investment spending rises and falls substantially. It is hard to point to particular reasons why capital investment spending changes; it simply does so. Thus, Keynesian economists suggest that businesses become optimistic or pessimistic, perhaps without any good reason, and this is the cause of business cycles.

However, Keynesian economics is not just about the optimism or pessimism of business firms and their capital investment decisions. Investment in capital goods is just one component of the economy's **aggregate demand,** which is the demand for all goods and services in the economy at a given time (more on this in Chapter 12). Thus, in a broader context, Keynesians claim that shifts in aggregate demand—whether from changes in spending by businesses on new capital, spending by consumers, government spending, or spending on our exports by foreigners—are the main cause of business cycles. Of course, this just pushes the question one step deeper: Why does aggregate demand change, and how does that lead to a business cycle? Keynesians believe that the key element in business cycles is the economy's inability to return to equilibrium immediately following a shift in aggregate demand because wages and prices are sticky and do not adjust right away (we will analyze equilibrium and Keynesian theory in more detail in Chapter 12). Skeptics of Keynesian theory argue that businesses should find it less costly to adjust wages or prices than to lay off workers, so it is hard to see why wage and price stickiness can be the cause of recessions.

A third explanation for business cycles is that sudden changes in productivity (TFP, in particular) are the main source of the business cycle. This theory is called **real business cycle (RBC) theory.** It has been developed by a number of economists over the past 30 years, most prominently by Edward Prescott. Prescott and his colleagues have shown that changes in productivity in RBC models can explain 70 percent of the business-cycle fluctuations in the United States. Real business cycle theory and monetarism are both theories whose main adherents are called **classical economists** because, unlike Keynesian economists, they believe the economy will return to equilibrium quickly without the need for government intervention.

Productivity is susceptible to numerous types of sudden changes,

monetarists economists who believe that erratic growth of the money supply is the main cause of business cycles

Keynesians economists who follow the ideas of British economist John Maynard Keynes; they believe that the key element in business cycles is the economy's inability to return to equilibrium immediately following a shift in aggregate demand because wages and prices are sticky and do not adjust right away

aggregate demand the demand for all goods and services in the economy at a given time

real business cycle (RBC) theory a theory that business cycles are caused by shocks to productivity

classical economists economists who believe the economy will return to equilibrium quickly without the need for government intervention or shocks. For example, some firms might adopt more efficient production methods. This may reduce output temporarily, causing a recession, while new, more efficient firms start up and old firms are eliminated. Eventually, however, it leads to faster economic growth. Or another possibility is that new and improved products are produced, thus increasing people's well-being and increasing trend output.

To see how a sudden change in productivity could lead to a change in economic output, consider the following example. Suppose that a pharmaceutical company develops a new drug that is much superior to older drugs. The company's productivity rises, in the sense that the same amount of capital and labor as before is used to produce a better (more valuable) product. The firm wants to sell more of this new drug, so it increases its capital and hires more workers. Thus, capital investment spending rises, as does overall economic output. Because more workers are hired and thus have higher incomes, they spend more. Because it takes some time before all the adjustments are made, the rise in consumer spending, capital investment, and output last for a while, and all three variables change in the same direction at the same time.

Critics of RBC theory say that productivity shocks are *not* the main force behind the business cycle. They argue that what the RBC theorists are calling productivity shocks are not changes in productivity at all. Consider a business firm that sees the demand for its product declining. It cannot sell all the output it is currently producing, so it slows down its production lines to produce less. Should it fire some of its workers as well because they are not needed for production? Probably not, especially if the slowdown in the demand for the product is temporary. After all, the firm had to train the workers and has invested time and effort into making them productive. If it fired workers every time demand slowed down a bit, it would need to devote additional resources to train new workers every time demand increased. However, if the firm keeps the workers on the payroll and produces less output, then the firm's output per hour worked declines. If output per hour worked declines at many firms, the aggregate data show a decline in productivity at the same time the economy enters a recession, even though the recession was caused by a decline in demand, not a decline in productivity. Because RBC theory fails to account for the intensity with which labor is used, it may incorrectly attribute the cause of a recession to a decline in productivity rather than to a decline in demand.

The fourth possible cause of business cycles is a change in the prices of resources, most prominently the price of oil. For example, a fall in the price of oil led to rapid U.S. economic growth in 1998 and 1999. Also, the rise in the price of oil that occurred during the Gulf War when Iraq invaded Kuwait was a major cause of the recession of 1990 to 1991. In fact, economist James Hamilton has argued that almost every recession in the last 50 years was preceded by a sharp increase in the price of oil. It is hard to deny Hamilton's argument because the data show an increase in the price of oil before every recession, except for the one in 1960, which saw only a very small rise in the price of oil.

However, Hamilton's theory about the impact of oil prices on output is also not completely convincing. After all, oil is not all that important to our economy. Why, indeed, should the economy suffer a recession and lose hundreds of billions of dollars in output because it has to pay several billion more dollars to buy oil at a higher price? Economists who have developed models of the various factors of production, including oil, find it hard to reconcile oil's overall value in the economy with an ability to cause a recession. In addition, recessions failed to occur after some very large increases in oil prices in the past.

Given all these theories and the problems with each, what can we conclude? Each theory has a valid point, and each should be taken seriously. But none of the theories, alone, is capable of explaining business cycles fully and completely. Perhaps we should consider all these theories as potential explanations of business cycles. Also, we might think that negative movements of these factors (that is, slower money growth, business pessimism, a decline in productivity, or higher oil prices) could make the economy more vulnerable to other shocks. For example, in 1988 and 1989, the Federal Reserve reduced money growth to constrain inflation, which may have made the economy fairly vulnerable. Then the start of the Gulf War pushed the economy over the edge and into recession. (For one view of the notion that economies become vulnerable to recessions, see the Data Bank box "The Anxious Index.")

Thus, we will not isolate a single factor as the cause of the business cycle but instead think about all these factors together. Keep in mind also that the business cycle is just the short-term path around the economy's long-term growth trend, which is determined by the growth theory that we discussed in the preceding section.

How does economic growth affect your future income?

Is economic growth good for you? To examine this question, let's look at the relationship between the income of workers and growth of the economy (in terms of real GDP).

Application TO EVERYDAY LIFE

When the economy grows, output is higher, so someone must be earning more income because payment for goods goes to workers and the owners of capital. To find out who gains when the economy grows, we will examine the data on compensation of workers per hour worked. By **compensation** we mean wages and salaries plus benefits earned by workers. We look at compensation instead of just at wages and salaries because in the last few decades an increasing amount of what a worker earns is not in the form of wage payments but rather in the form of health benefits, life insurance, and stock options. As we did throughout this chapter, we can look at the data to see how the growth in compensation over time is related to the growth of output and labor productivity in the three periods: Economic Liftoff, Reorganization, and the Long Boom. Table 10.4 shows the results of doing so, with the variables expressed in inflation-adjusted terms.

The table shows that in the period of Economic Liftoff, compensation growth nearly equaled the growth in labor productivity, with both averaging over 2.5 percent per year. In the Reorganization period, labor productivity growth slowed substantially, averaging just 1.5 percent per year, but compensation growth declined even more, averaging just 1.1 percent over that period. Surprisingly, in

compensation wages and salaries plus benefits earned by workers

TABLE 10.4	Growth of Output, Productivity, and Compensation in Three Postwar Periods (average annual inflation-adjusted growth rates)		
Period	**Output**	**Labor Productivity**	**Compensation per Hour**
Economic Liftoff 1950 to 1970	4.1	2.6	2.7
Reorganization 1971 to 1982	2.9	1.5	1.1
Long Boom 1983 to 2007	3.7	2.2	1.2
Full Period 1950 to 2012	3.5	2.1	1.6

Our discussion of the business cycle in this chapter suggests that there is no single main cause of recessions. Therefore, at any given time, we must view the economy as having some probability of falling into a recession. Events that weaken the economy increase the chance that the economy will enter a recession.

Almost no recession has ever been explicitly forecast. Economic forecasters are reluctant to go out on a limb and predict actual declines in output. But forecasts of the probability that output will decline often increase after bad economic news is revealed.

New York Times reporter David Leonhardt coined the term "anxious index" to refer to the probability of a decline in real GDP, as reported by forecasters in the Federal Reserve Bank of Philadelphia's quarterly *Survey of Professional Forecasters*. This survey asks panelists for their forecasts for output (real GDP) and many other macroeconomic variables. If you look at the forecasts for real GDP, you see that just before recessions, the forecasters generally predict slower growth of real GDP but never fully anticipate a recession. However, the survey also asks for the forecasters' views of the probability that real GDP will decline in the quarter in which the survey is taken and in each of the following four quarters. The anxious index tracks the forecasters' estimates of the probability of a decline in real GDP in the quarter after a survey is taken. For example, in the survey taken in the fourth quarter of 1987, just after the stock market crashed precipitously, the anxious index was 30 percent, which means that forecasters believed that there was a 30 percent chance that real GDP would decline in the first quarter of 1988.

Figure 10.B shows how the anxious index has changed over time since 1970. The graph shows that the index often rises significantly before the start of recessions. A recent example is what happened in the second half of 2007. In the third quarter survey of 2007 (which was taken in mid-August), forecasters began to sense that financial troubles might lead to a downturn, and the anxious index rose to 17 percent. By the fourth quarter survey of 2007 (taken mid-November) the forecasters raised the odds of a decline in real GDP to 23 percent, and to 43 percent in the first quarter survey of 2008. As it turned out, the National Bureau of Economic Research declared that a recession started in December 2007.

The graph shows that the anxious index is a fairly good indicator of when recessions are likely to begin. The index sometimes gives false signals, such as when it rose in 1984, 1986, 1987, and 1996. However, when the index rises above 20 percent, a recession often follows, so the index appears to be a useful guide to recessions. Note that the index generally continues rising as the recession goes on and then falls when the economy is nearing a trough and the next expansion is about to begin.

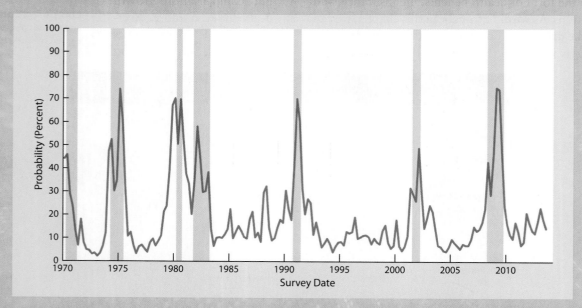

FIGURE 10.B The Anxious Index, Probability of Decline in Real GDP in Quarter After Survey Date

This graph shows the probability of a decline in real GDP in the quarter after the survey date shown on the horizontal axis, as determined by panelists in the *Survey of Professional Forecasters*. The index rises sharply just before recessions, although it also rises sharply sometimes when no recession follows.

the Long Boom, even though labor productivity growth picked up to 2.2 percent, compensation did not keep up, averaging just 1.2 percent.

The slow growth of compensation in the Long Boom is not explained easily. Economists generally would like to believe that workers are compensated as their productivity rises. This view is supported by the data in the Economic Liftoff period and is reasonably accurate for the Reorganization period. Clearly, however, this view has been mere wishful thinking during the Long Boom. Perhaps the decline in the number of workers in labor unions that has occurred over the last few decades is responsible. As unionization has declined, the owners of capital, rather than workers, now capture a bigger share of economy's total income. Alternatively, increased low-wage foreign competition might be suppressing the growth of U.S. workers' compensation as more and more American businesses relocate operations overseas rather than increase wages at home.

Even with relatively slow growth of compensation in the Long Boom, the standard of living of workers today is better than in the past. The compensation per hour of a worker in 2010 was *twice* what a worker earned in 1960. Obviously, if workers' compensation grows at an average rate of just 1.2 percent per year, as it did during the Long Boom, the standard of living will not increase nearly as rapidly as it did during the Economic Liftoff period, when compensation grew 2.7 percent per year. Still, even at the 1.2 percent growth rate, in 30 years a worker will earn over 40 percent more than before. Thus, economic growth is good for workers—but not as good as it used to be. And because workers' compensation has been growing slowly, owners of capital have received a greater share of income.

RECAP

1 Economic growth, especially growth in labor productivity, affects people's incomes.

2 In the Long Boom, compensation per hour did not rise nearly as rapidly as labor productivity.

3 Economists do not have a good explanation for the slowdown in compensation growth.

Review Questions and Problems

Review Questions

1 What are the two major determinants of the overall growth of the economy according to the view of economic growth based on labor data?

2 In the long run, what determines employment growth in the economy?

3 What are the three main postwar periods in which trend output and productivity have varied?

4 How much did the labor-force participation rate increase in the United States in the 1990s compared with the previous 15 years?

5 What is the unemployment rate? How is it measured?

6 Describe the differences between labor productivity and total factor productivity.

7 Can changes in trend TFP growth help to explain changes in trend output growth?

8 What is a business cycle? What group determines the official starting and ending dates of business cycles in the United States?

9 What are the main causes of business cycles? Is there one main cause?

10 Why should workers care about increases in labor productivity?

Numerical Exercises

11 Suppose that the country of Bigu has a population of 127 million, of which 83 million are in the working-age population. Of those, 25 million are not in the labor force and 52 million are employed.

  a Calculate the working-age population as a percentage of the population.

  b Calculate the labor-force participation rate.

  c Calculate the unemployment rate.

12 Suppose we wish to decompose output growth into that part due to growth in hours worked and that part due to growth in labor productivity. In the table below are data on output and hours worked at the end of each decade (in the fourth quarter).

Output and Hours Worked

Date	Output	Hours Worked
1959:Q4	1864	49.15
1969:Q4	2900	58.88
1979:Q4	4173	70.16
1989:Q4	5710	83.14
1999:Q4	8251	97.63
2009:Q4	9563	88.36

  a Calculate the growth of output and hours worked in each decade (that is, from the fourth quarter of the tenth year of the previous decade to the fourth quarter of the tenth year of each decade). Show your work and calculate each growth rate in percentage points with one decimal place.

  b From your calculations in part a, calculate the growth rate of labor productivity (that is, the growth rate of output per hour worked) in each decade. You may use a sensible approximation. Show your work.

  c Which decade shows the fastest growth in output? The slowest? Which decades show the fastest and slowest growth in output per hour? Can you interpret these results in a historical context?

13 Suppose that in 2013 a country has capital of 450 units, labor of 5,000 units, and output of 10,000 units. In 2014, the country has capital of 480 units, labor of 5,050 units, and output of 10,300 units. In both years, $a = 0.2$ in Equation (4). Calculate the level of TFP in both years and the growth rate of TFP from 2013 to 2014.

14 In the country of Bigcap, the coefficient in Equation (4) is $a = 0.3$, the capital stock is growing 10 percent per year, employment is growing 1 percent per year, and output is growing 5 percent per year. In the country of Smallcap, the coefficient in Equation (4) is $a = 0.1$, the capital stock is growing 3 percent per year, employment is growing 2 percent per year, and output is growing 4 percent per year. In which country is TFP growing the fastest? Explain your answer and interpret what the result means.

15 If you started a job at age 21 earning $30,000 per year and your salary increased 5 percent each year, how much would you be making by the time you retired at age 70? What if your salary increased only 3 percent per year?

Analytical Problems

16 Which economy is better off, country A, in which output is growing 6 percent per year with population growth of 4 percent per year, or country B, in which output is growing 4 percent per year with population growth of 1 percent per year? Explain your answer.

17 What happens to each of the following variables in economic expansions?

a Output per hour worked

b Hours worked per worker

c Employment as a fraction of the labor force

d Labor force as a fraction of the population

In each case, provide an economic rationale for your answer. Given all these results, what happens to output growth in expansions?

MODELING MONEY

This chapter resumes the study of money that began in Chapter 3. We now take the functions of money from that chapter (medium of exchange, store of value, unit of account, and standard of deferred payment) and incorporate them into a series of models to show how those functions affect the demand for money. Economists like to create models to help them understand the basic driving forces in the economy. Ultimately, we want the models of money we develop to help us understand the effects of monetary policy—both how the Federal Reserve (Fed) affects interest rates and the macroeconomic consequences of their doing so.

No single model can capture everything we would like to know about money, so we develop several different models that we can use for different purposes. The first model we work with shows how the demand for money depends on people's spending, the level of prices of goods and services, and the nominal interest rate. Incorporating this first model into a larger model that also analyzes the supply of money, we can investigate how changes in the supply of money affect the nominal interest rate in the short run. We then build a third model that incorporates time, the purpose of which is to show how the effects of changes in the money supply lead to different changes in the nominal interest rate in the short and the long run. In addition to learning about money's role in the economy and how it interacts with other economic variables such as income, prices, and nominal interest rates, these models will help us to build more complete macroeconomic models in Chapters 12 and 13.

After developing these models of money, our policy issue looks at the data on money, income, prices, and nominal interest rates to test the models. We find that the data are consistent with the implications of the models despite many changes over time in the way people use money and the types of money they use.

11-1 The ATM Model of the Demand for Cash

Economists use models to understand how the overall economy and its individual markets work. To help us picture how people decide on the amount of money to hold, we build a model that examines one person's money-holding decision. In this model we examine how a person chooses the amount of money to hold based on her spending habits, the transactions costs of obtaining cash from a bank's automated teller machine (ATM), and the nominal interest rate.

In this model we consider just the demand for cash, not for the other components of the money supply discussed in Chapter 3. We also simplify the model by assuming that there is just one nominal interest rate, not many interest rates, as discussed in Chapter 5. In addition, we consider here just the nominal interest rate, not the real interest rate from Chapter 6. These types of simplifications are used often by economists in developing models. Such simplifications may be relaxed when a researcher desires to expand the model and make it more realistic, but it is usually desirable to fully understand a simple model first before adding complications.

The model examines the decisions of one person, Tracy, who earns income and decides how much cash she will carry and how much to keep on deposit at the bank. Suppose that Tracy's monthly paycheck is automatically deposited into her bank account. She is a creature of habit who spends $20 in cash every day on meals and other small purchases. The rest of her income is automatically deducted from her bank account to

PictureNet/Corbis

People use cash to purchase goods and services. A key decision they must make is how often to go to the ATM to get the cash they need. That decision is the focus of the ATM model of the demand for cash, which in turn is a building block for more complicated models of the demand for money.

pay for housing, utilities, and her automobile loan. The question is this: How often should she go to the ATM to get cash?

Consider all the factors that might influence Tracy's decision. We would include the costs (in terms of both time and money) of going to the ATM, the amount Tracy spends, the possibility of losing her cash or being robbed, and the opportunity cost of holding cash instead of having the money in the bank where it earns interest.

We can illustrate the pattern of Tracy's cash holdings (Figure 11.1) if she visits the ATM every T days. For example, if $T = 1$, then Tracy goes to the ATM every day; if $T = 7$, then Tracy visits the ATM once a week. The amount that she withdraws depends on how often she goes. Because she spends $20 every day, the amount she withdraws from the ATM is $20 \times T$. Thus, if she goes to the ATM every day (that is, if $T = 1$), then she will withdraw $20. But if she goes just once a week ($T = 7$), she will take out $140 at a time. In that case, each day her cash balance falls by $20 until on the seventh day it goes to $0, so she goes to the ATM and takes out another $140. Thus, Figure 11.1 shows a sawtooth pattern to her cash holdings.

For Tracy to determine the best number of times to go to the ATM, she needs to compare the cost of going to the ATM more often with the opportunity cost of holding cash. The more often she goes to the ATM, the more time and money she spends on making trips back and forth. The opportunity cost of holding cash depends on the nominal interest rate and the possibility of having her cash lost or stolen. Let's consider each of these costs in turn.

Tracy incurs several costs when she withdraws cash from the ATM. First, her bank may charge her a fee every time she withdraws money at the machine, especially if the most convenient machine belongs to a bank other than the one where Tracy keeps her account. Second, Tracy may have to travel to the ATM if it is not located near her home or workplace. Or she may have to wait in line at the ATM, so there is a cost in terms of her time. Suppose that it costs Tracy $0.50 every time she uses the ATM; this includes both the value of her time and the explicit monetary costs. Obviously, the more often she goes to the ATM (the smaller T is), the greater Tracy's yearly cost of going there will be. For example, if Tracy goes to the ATM every day ($T = 1$), her cost would be $0.50 \times 365 = $182.50 over the course of a year. However, if she goes to the ATM once a week, her cost would be just $0.50 \times 52 = $26.00. In general, because there are 365 days in a (non-leap) year, Tracy will go to the bank $365/T$ times, so her total explicit cost of going to the ATM will be $365/T \times $0.50 = $182.50/T$.

What about the opportunity cost of holding cash, which earns no interest, compared with keeping money in her banking account? Suppose that Tracy's bank account pays annual interest of 5 percent. Although calculating how much interest Tracy will earn would not seem to be an easy task because Tracy's bank account

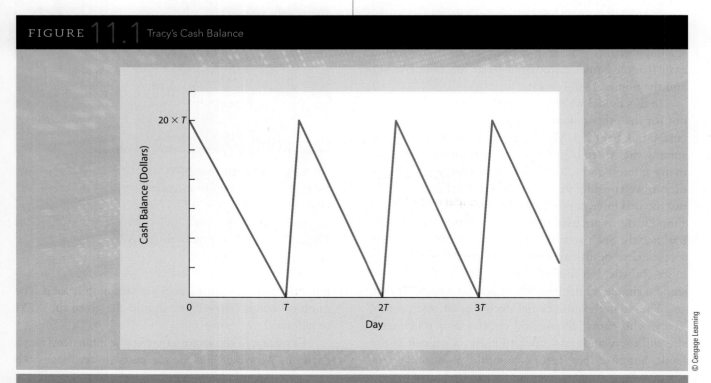

FIGURE 11.1 Tracy's Cash Balance

This graph shows the amount of cash being held over time by Tracy, who goes to the ATM every T days to get cash, withdrawing $20 \times T$. For example, if $T = 1$, then Tracy goes to the ATM every day and withdraws $20; if $T = 7$, then Tracy visits the ATM once a week and withdraws $140. As time passes, she spends money, so her cash balance declines until she visits the ATM once again.

© Cengage Learning

balance changes every day, we can calculate the opportunity cost of money using a simple approximation. Notice in Figure 11.1 that Tracy's cash holdings rise to $20.00 × T when she goes to the bank and then decline steadily to zero. Thus, Tracy's average cash holdings are midway between $0 and $20.00 × T. This average is just [$0 + ($20.00 × T)]/2 = $10.00 × T. Tracy's opportunity cost is the interest she does not earn because she holds cash, which equals her average cash balance times the nominal interest rate: $10.00 × T × i. If the nominal interest rate is 5 percent (or 0.05) per year, then Tracy's opportunity cost of holding cash is $10.00 × T × 0.05 = $0.50 × T. Therefore, if Tracy goes to the ATM every day (T = 1), she holds a small amount of cash every day, and her annual opportunity cost is just $0.50 × 1 = $0.50. If Tracy goes to the ATM weekly (T = 7), her annual opportunity cost would be $0.50 × 7 = $3.50.

Let's also assume that Tracy does not like to have large amounts of cash with her. She thinks that if she carries around a lot of cash, she might lose it, or it might be stolen. Suppose that Tracy lives in a rough neighborhood and thinks that the odds of her cash being stolen or lost are about 25 percent per year. Thus, the expected cost of losing her money or having it stolen is equal to her average cash balances times 25 percent, or $10.00 × T × 0.25 = $2.50 × T.

Now let's combine both the explicit costs and the opportunity costs. The total cost for the year when Tracy's cash balance averages $10.00 × T is

$$\text{Cost} = \text{cost of going to ATM} + \text{opportunity cost} + \text{expected cost of loss or theft}$$
$$= (\$182.50/T) + (\$0.50 \times T) + (\$2.50 \times T) \qquad \textbf{(1)}$$
$$= (\$182.50/T) + (\$3.00 \times T)$$

All Tracy needs to do now is to find the number of days between trips to the ATM that minimizes her annual cost. To do this, we plot the annual cost of holding cash for different values of T in Figure 11.2[1]. For small values of T, you can see that Tracy's costs are fairly high. She goes to the ATM so often that the $0.50 cost per visit is the dominant cost. As T rises above 1, this cost falls. Eventually, however, as T gets larger and larger, the opportunity-cost term and the expected cost from possible loss or theft begin to dominate, and the total cost increases as T increases.

The total cost of holding cash is minimized when Tracy goes to the ATM every eight days. On each visit,

[1]We will show the number of trips that minimize the cost using graphical methods; this can also be done using calculus.

she will withdraw $160 (because she needs $20 per day for eight days). You can see this graphically in Figure 11.2. We also show this result numerically in Table 11.1. The smallest annual cost of holding cash balances occurs when T = 8 days.

Because Tracy goes to the ATM every eight days, she withdraws $160 each time. Eight days later, at the end of the day, she has no money left. Thus, over the eight days, her cash balances average $80. Tracy's average cash balance over time is considered her demand for money.

We have now calculated Tracy's demand for money under the assumptions that she wanted to spend $20.00 each day, that the nominal interest rate was 5 percent, that the cost of going to the ATM was $0.50, and that the probability of loss or theft was 25 percent. We can now use the model to find out how her demand for money varies with changes in (1) the nominal interest rate, (2) the cost of going to the ATM, (3) her spending, and (4) the probability of loss or theft.

Suppose that the nominal interest rate is 10 percent instead of 5 percent, which means that the opportunity cost of holding cash is higher. Recall that Tracy's opportunity cost is $10.00 × T × i, which is now $10.00 × T × 0.10 = $1.00 × T. With this opportunity cost, Equation (1) is modified, so Tracy's total cost is

$$\text{Cost} = (\$182.50/T) + (\$1.00 \times T) + (\$2.50 \times T) \qquad \textbf{(2)}$$
$$= (\$182.50/T) + (\$3.50 \times T)$$

The increase in the opportunity cost causes the total costs of holding cash to rise, as shown by the line labeled *Higher interest rate* in Figure 11.3. As you might imagine, Tracy now has the incentive to go to the ATM more often. Indeed, now (with a higher nominal interest rate) she minimizes her costs if she visits the ATM every seven days, instead of every eight days when the nominal interest rate was lower. Because Tracy goes to the ATM only every seven days, she withdraws 7 × $20 = $140 each time, and her average cash balance is $140/2 = $70. Thus, a higher nominal interest rate reduces Tracy's demand for money from $80 to $70.

Tracy's demand for cash also can be affected by changes in the costs of going to the ATM, by changes in the amount she spends each day, or by changes in the risk of loss or theft. Suppose that the cost of going to the ATM were to increase to $1.00 per visit instead of $0.50. Then, as shown by the line labeled *Higher ATM costs* in Figure 11.3, Tracy's annual cost of holding

FIGURE  11.2 Tracy's Costs of Holding Cash Balances

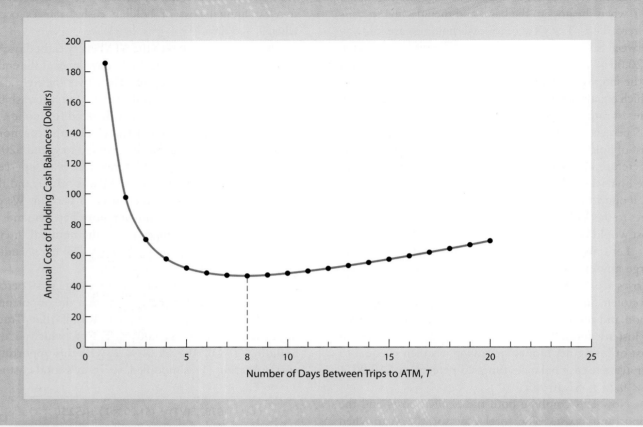

This graph shows the total annual cost that Tracy incurs from holding cash balances, which depends on how frequently she goes to the ATM. Tracy minimizes her costs by going to the ATM every eight days.

TABLE 11.1 Tracy's Annual Costs and the Frequency of Visits to the ATM

Frequency of Visits (T days)	Amount Withdrawn	Annual Costs
1	$20.00	$185.50
2	$40.00	$97.25
3	$60.00	$69.83
4	$80.00	$57.63
5	$100.00	$51.50
6	$120.00	$48.42
7	$140.00	$47.07
8	$160.00	$46.81
9	$180.00	$47.28
10	$200.00	$48.25

© Cengage Learning

cash rises for any given *T*. In this case, her costs are minimized when she goes to the ATM every 11 days, withdrawing $220 each time. This conclusion is logical: A person will use the ATM less often the more expensive it is to use. In this case, Tracy's demand for money would be $220 ÷ 2 = $110, an increase over the $80 in the baseline situation. Thus, higher ATM costs increase the demand for money.

What if Tracy's income was higher and she spent $40 each day instead of $20? In this case she will be carrying larger cash balances, so the opportunity cost and the cost of having money lost or stolen loom larger, as you can see by the line labeled *Higher spending* in Figure 11.3. The result, with the numbers given, is that Tracy will now go to the ATM every six days, withdrawing $240 each time. Again, intuitively, it makes sense that if you spend more, you will withdraw

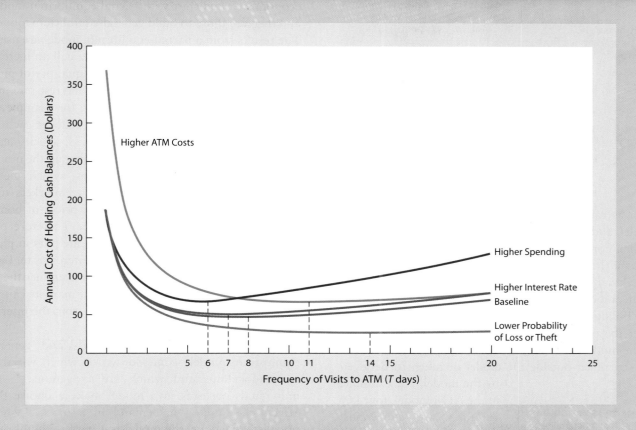

This graph shows the total annual cost that Tracy incurs from holding cash balances under a number of alternative assumptions about spending, the nominal interest rate, costs, and the probability of loss or theft. The baseline is the same as in Figure 11.2, in which Tracy goes to the ATM every eight days. If ATM costs are higher, Tracy will visit the ATM every 11 days. If the nominal interest rate is higher, Tracy's costs are higher and the opportunity cost of holding cash is higher, so Tracy gets cash more frequently, visiting the ATM every seven days. If Tracy spends more, she will need to get cash more often, every six days in this case. If the probability of loss or theft is lower, Tracy will visit the ATM less often, every 14 days in this case.

more money at a time, and the ATM fees will not be as significant as before compared with the opportunity costs, so you will go to the ATM more often. In this case, Tracy's demand for money would be $240 ÷ 2 = $120, an increase over the $80 in the baseline situation. Thus, increased spending increases the demand for money.

Finally, what if Tracy moves to a safer neighborhood, reducing the probability that her money is lost or stolen to 5 percent? The opportunity cost of holding cash declines, so Tracy will hold more cash, which means she will go to the ATM less often. In this scenario, Tracy goes to the ATM just once every 14 days, as the line labeled *Lower probability of loss or theft* shows. She withdraws $20 × 14 = $280 each time. In this case, Tracy's demand for money would be $280 ÷ 2 = $140,

an increase over the $80 in the baseline situation. Thus, the reduced probability of loss or theft increases the demand for money.

The example of Tracy teaches us that the demand for money depends on the nominal interest rate, the costs of obtaining cash, the amount of spending, and the probability of loss or theft, as Table 11.2 shows.

These results are based on the assumption that a person spends the same amount each day. Of course, this assumption is a bit extreme because people also hold money in case they need it for an unexpected expense. Thus, uncertainty about our spending also matters. Nonetheless, this model illustrates a number of the main factors influencing money demand.

The ATM model is a simple one in which we analyze just one person's decision. Beginning with a model

TABLE 11.2 Variables Affecting Quantity of Money Demanded

An Increase in	Causes Time Between ATM Visits to	Causes Quantity of Money Demanded to
Nominal interest rate	Decrease	Decline
ATM costs	Increase	Increase
Spending	Decrease	Increase
Probability of loss or theft	Decrease	Decline

Note: A *decrease* in the variable would lead each entry in the table to change in the opposite direction.

such as this, however, we can add complexity to the model and build up to a complete macroeconomic model. For example, we could model a business firm's demand for cash as well, and combine the models of individual cash demand and business cash demand to create a more complete model.

Building more complete models requires us to consider the two types of economic variables we include in the models. An **exogenous variable** is a variable that is determined outside the model or taken to be given by the model. For example, in the ATM model, four key variables are exogenous: the nominal interest rate, Tracy's daily spending, the cost of a visit to the ATM, and the probability of loss or theft. An **endogenous variable** is a variable that is determined within the model. Three variables in the ATM model are endogenous: the number of days between visits Tracy makes to the ATM, the amount she withdraws each time, and her average cash balances.

The types of variables in a model determine how general the conclusions of the model are. A **general-equilibrium model** is one in which all the key macroeconomic variables are endogenous. In a **partial-equilibrium model,** some

exogenous variable a variable that is determined outside the model or taken to be given by the model

endogenous variable a variable that is determined within the model

general-equilibrium model a model in which all the key macroeconomic variables, such as the nominal interest rate, are endogenous; a model in which all prices are endogenous in markets where individuals or firms make a choice that affects the supply or demand in those markets

partial-equilibrium model a model in which some key macroeconomic variables, such as the nominal interest rate, are exogenous; a model in which individuals or firms make a choice that affects the supply or demand in a market whose price is exogenous

key macroeconomic variables are exogenous. Thus, the ATM model is a partial-equilibrium model because the nominal interest rate is exogenous. In building models, economists often start with partial-equilibrium models and then use those to build general-equilibrium models. The results from a partial-equilibrium model are useful for answering questions such as: How will an increase in the nominal interest rate affect the quantity of money demanded? However, the nominal interest rate may be affected by the demand for money; for example, an increase in the nominal interest rate reduces each individual's quantity of money demanded, which means that the total quantity demanded (adding up the money demand of each individual) declines, which means a greater total supply of funds in other markets such as the bond market, which raises the prices of bonds, which reduces the nominal interest rate. Therefore, paradoxically, a higher nominal interest rate puts in place events that lead to a lower nominal interest rate. Only with a general-equilibrium model that examines the interaction of supply and demand in all markets can we determine the equilibrium that arises from the interaction of all markets.

The difference between partial- and general-equilibrium models comes down to which variables are endogenous and which are exogenous. If the individuals or firms in a model make a choice that affects the supply or demand in a market whose price is exogenous, the model is a partial-equilibrium model; if that price is endogenous, the model is a general-equilibrium model. In the ATM model, Tracy determines the amount of money she holds and how much she keeps on deposit in her bank account. The amount she keeps in her bank account is part of the supply of funds to the banking deposit market and thus influences the nominal interest rate paid on funds in bank accounts. The nominal interest rate is the price in that market, and because the nominal interest rate is exogenous, the ATM model is a partial-equilibrium model. To develop a general-equilibrium model, we need to extend the ATM model to make the nominal interest rate endogenous.

Broadly speaking, economists prefer to work with general-equilibrium models whenever they can because their results are more believable and can be applied to a wider variety of problems. However, partial-equilibrium models are useful as the building blocks of general-equilibrium models. One must be careful, however, not to generalize too much from a partial-equilibrium model; only a general-equilibrium model provides a complete analysis.

11-2 The Liquidity-Preference Model

The ATM model presents a picture of one person's demand for money and the main variables (spending, the nominal interest rate, transactions costs, and the probability of loss or theft) that affect money demand. But the model is a partial-equilibrium model and can give us no sense of the feedback effects of money demand on nominal interest rates. In other words, in the ATM model, the nominal interest rate affects the quantity of money demanded, but money demand does not affect the nominal interest rate. If we wish to develop a general-equilibrium model of money demand, we need to make the nominal interest rate in the model endogenous. We can do so by examining both the supply of and demand for money.

The **liquidity-preference model** is a model in which money demand and supply determine the nominal interest rate. (Again, we assume only one interest rate in the economy, abstracting from the real world because there are, in fact, many different interest rates, as we learned in Chapter 5. We also consider the demand for and supply of cash and consider just the M1 supply of money, ignoring the components of M1 other than cash.) We assume that people invest in bonds, earning nominal interest rate *i*, or hold cash, which earns no interest, so a person's demand for money depends on the nominal interest rate. Just as in the ATM model, money demand also depends on spending. However, we will neglect the transactions costs of going to the ATM and the probability of loss or theft. Instead, we use the result from the ATM model and suppose that the quantity of money demanded depends on the nominal interest rate and the amount of spending.

We also can generalize from an individual's decisions and consider instead the money demand of all people taken together. We assume that the amount people spend depends on their real incomes and the level of prices of goods and services (higher incomes or higher prices lead to higher spending). We assume that the total supply of money is determined by the Federal Reserve.

> **liquidity-preference model** a model in which money demand and supply determine the nominal interest rate

To illustrate how this model works, we use a graph of the supply of and demand for money. To find the demand curve, consider all the possible different nominal interest rates, and calculate the quantity of money demanded by everyone for each nominal interest rate; this result can be plotted as a money-demand curve, such as in Figure 11.4, labeled M^D. As we learned from the ATM model, a higher nominal interest rate *i* means a lower quantity of money demanded, so the money-demand curve slopes downward. The slope of the curve depends on how sensitive the demand for money is to the nominal interest rate. If the quantity of money demanded changes substantially for a 1 percentage point change in the nominal interest rate, the money-demand curve will be fairly flat; if the quantity of money demanded does not change very much for a 1 percentage point change in the nominal interest rate, the money-demand curve will be fairly steep.

The location of the money-demand curve depends on the other variables that affect people's demand for money—incomes and the prices of goods and services. When people have higher incomes, spending will be higher in dollar terms, so people's demand for money will be higher (as we learned in the ATM model), and the money-demand curve will be farther to the right.

FIGURE 11.4 The Liquidity-Preference Model of Money

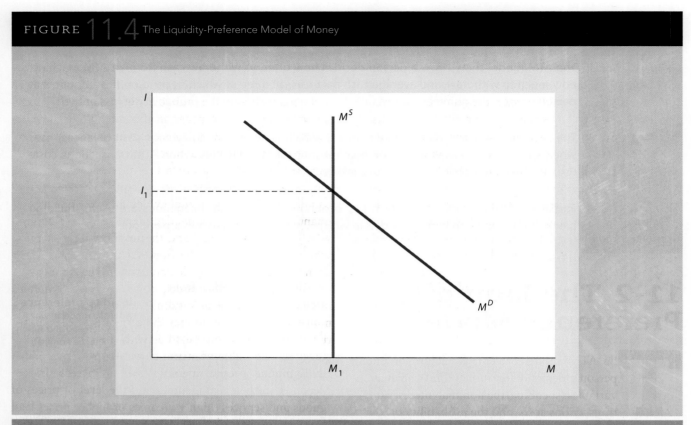

This graph plots the supply and demand curves for money against the nominal interest rate. In equilibrium, the nominal interest rate is i_1 and the quantity of money is M_1.

The same is true when prices are higher; with higher prices but the same real incomes and spending, people need more money (in nominal terms) to buy the goods and services they want. A money-demand curve that is farther to the right means that for a given nominal interest rate, money demand is higher. Similarly, when people's incomes are lower or prices are lower, the money-demand curve will be farther to the left.

On the supply side of the market, the Federal Reserve determines the money supply. In our model, we assume that the Fed decides on the quantity of money supplied and that its decision is not affected by the nominal interest rate. As a result, the money-supply curve (M^S in Figure 11.4) is vertical because a vertical line indicates that the variable on the vertical axis has no effect on the variable on the horizontal axis.

The point at which the supply and demand curves for money intersect, where the quantity supplied equals the quantity demanded, is the equilibrium point. As shown in Figure 11.4, this occurs when the nominal interest rate is i_1 and the quantity of money is M_1. (Here, the subscript 1 refers to an initial equilibrium; later, we will examine shifts in the curves, denoting variables with subscript 1 to refer to the initial equilibrium and using subscript 2 to refer to a new equilibrium. Do not confuse the equilibrium quantity of money M_1 with the measure of money M1 that we examined in Chapter 3.)

What would happen if the nominal interest rate were above i_1? If so, then the quantity of money demanded would be less than the quantity of money supplied because the quantity of money demanded is lower when the nominal interest rate is higher, whereas the quantity supplied is not affected. Because bonds are the alternative to money, people would use their excess money to purchase bonds. This would cause the quantity of bonds demanded to exceed the quantity of bonds supplied, thus raising the price of bonds. A rise in the price of bonds implies a decline in the nominal interest rate. (Recall the inverse relationship between bond prices and nominal interest rates from Chapter 4.) This process would continue until equilibrium was restored, with the nominal interest rate declining to i_1. Similarly, if the nominal interest rate were below i_1, market forces would increase it back to i_1.

By modeling the supply of money and adding up the demand for money of everyone, we have transformed the ATM model in which the nominal interest rate is exogenous into a model in which the nominal interest rate is endogenous. Thus, we have moved part of the way to changing the model from a partial-equilibrium model to a general-equilibrium model. Still, the liquidity-preference model is not a general-equilibrium model, because the prices of goods and services remain exogenous. However, economic theory indicates that the money supply affects prices. Thus, to complete the process and develop a general-equilibrium model, we must make prices endogenous, which we will do shortly in a dynamic model.

In the liquidity-preference model, the exogenous variables are people's real incomes, the prices of goods and services, and the quantity of money supplied. The endogenous variables are the quantity of money demanded (which depends on people's spending and the nominal interest rate), the nominal interest rate and the equilibrium quantity of money (both of which are determined by the intersection of the demand and supply curves for money), and people's spending (which is determined by their real incomes and the prices of goods and services). We can use the model to examine how changes in the exogenous variables affect the endogenous variables.

What happens to the endogenous variables in the model when the money supply (an exogenous variable) increases? Because spending depends on people's real incomes and the prices of goods and services, both of which are exogenous (and thus not affected by a change in the money supply), a change in the money supply cannot affect people's spending in this model. Because the quantity of money supplied is exogenous and the quantity of money demanded equals the quantity of money supplied in equilibrium, then the increased quantity of money supplied must lead to an equal increase in the equilibrium quantity of money demanded. Because the quantity of money demanded depends on spending, which does not change, and the nominal interest rate, which is endogenous, the nominal interest rate must change to equate money demand and money supply.

Therefore, in this model, how would the nominal interest rate change in response to an increase in the money supply? Suppose that the economy is in equilibrium, as shown in Figure 11.5, with the money-supply curve M_1^S and money-demand curve M^D, so the equilibrium nominal interest rate is i_1. After an increase in the

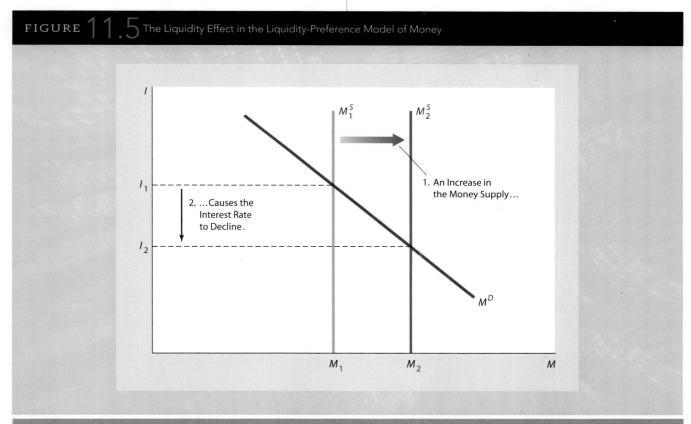

FIGURE 11.5 The Liquidity Effect in the Liquidity-Preference Model of Money

1. An Increase in the Money Supply...

2. ...Causes the Interest Rate to Decline.

This graph shows the effect of an increase in the money supply in the liquidity-preference model of money. The economy begins in equilibrium with the money-supply curve M_1^S and the money-demand curve M^D, so the equilibrium nominal interest rate is i_1. An increase in the money supply from M_1^S to M_2^S causes the nominal interest rate to decline, leading to an increase in the quantity of money demanded. The new equilibrium nominal interest rate is i_2, where $i_2 < i_1$, and the new equilibrium quantity of money is M_2, where $M_2 > M_1$.

money supply from M_1^S to M_2^S, nominal interest rate i_1 no longer equates the quantity of money supplied with the quantity of money demanded. Because the quantity of money supplied is higher than the quantity of money demanded at the existing nominal interest rate, the nominal interest rate must decline to restore equilibrium, causing an increase in the quantity of money demanded. Because the nominal interest rate declines, people will hold fewer bonds and hold more money. The new equilibrium nominal interest rate is i_2, where $i_2 < i_1$, and the new equilibrium quantity of money is M_2, where $M_2 > M_1$.

The decline in the nominal interest rate when the money supply increases is the key result in the liquidity-preference model. It is commonly thought to be the main short-run effect of expansionary monetary policy: *When the Fed increases the money supply, the nominal interest rate declines. Conversely, when the Fed decreases the money supply, the nominal interest rate rises.* The inverse relationship between the money supply and the

liquidity effect the inverse relationship between the money supply and the nominal interest rate

nominal interest rate is known as the **liquidity effect** because it explains what happens when the amount of liquidity (the money supply) increases or decreases.

The liquidity effect is a key prediction of the liquidity-preference model. When we look at data on nominal interest rates and money supply, we see that increases in the money supply are almost always accompanied by declining nominal interest rates on short-term bonds, and decreases in the money supply are almost always accompanied by rising nominal interest rates on short-term bonds, at least in the short run.

As recessions and expansions occur over the business cycle, people's incomes fall and rise. We can use the liquidity-preference model to analyze the impact on nominal interest rates of these changes in people's incomes. When people's incomes rise in the expansionary part of the business cycle, they want to spend more, so they want more money to carry out more transactions, and thus they increase their demand for money. We show this increase in the demand for money graphically in Figure 11.6; the money-demand curve shifts to the right from M_1^D to M_2^D. Because the money supply

FIGURE 11.6 The Effect of Increased Income in the Liquidity-Preference Model of Money

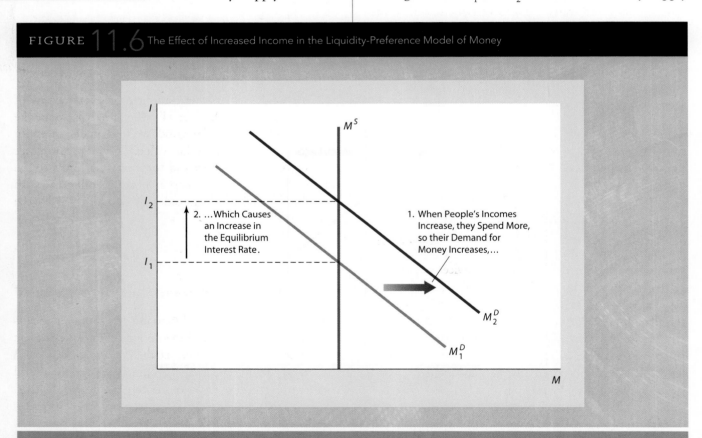

This graph shows the effect of an increase in the demand for money caused by increased income. The rise in income means people want to spend more, and thus they increase their demand for money, causing the money-demand curve to shift to the right from M_1^D to M_2^D. Because money supply does not change, the quantity of money demanded cannot change. Thus, the equilibrium nominal interest rate increases, from i_1 to i_2, so the higher nominal interest rate reduces the quantity of money demanded to just offset the increase in the demand for money caused by people having higher income.

does not change, the quantity of money demanded cannot change. Thus, the equilibrium nominal interest rate must increase, as the figure shows, so the higher nominal interest rate reduces the quantity of money demanded to just offset the increase in the demand for money caused by people having higher incomes. This positive relationship between income and nominal interest rates is consistent with our observation of increases in nominal interest rates that occur during economic expansions. Similarly, in recessions, the demand for money declines, leading to a decline in the nominal interest rate, which is also consistent with our observations.

We also can use the liquidity-preference model to analyze the effects of changes in the prices of goods and services. When prices increase, people will need more money to buy the same amount of goods. Thus, a rise in prices leads to an increase in the demand for money. But by how much does the demand for money increase? If there are no changes in the amounts of goods and services people buy, then people will want more money in proportion to the increase in prices. That is, if prices all double, people will want to hold twice as much money for transactions. We conclude that the demand for money itself is proportional to prices. We can express this relationship in an equation:

$$M^D = P \times m(Y, i) \qquad (3)$$

where M^D is the total quantity of money demanded (the sum of the quantity of money demanded by each individual), P is the price level (described in the next paragraph), and m is a function relating the nominal interest rate i and people's total real income Y to their demand for money.

The price level is a measure, usually reported by a government statistical agency, of the average price of goods and services at a particular date. Such a measure reports the average price of goods and services at that date relative to the average in a base year, which is arbitrarily assigned a price level value of 100. To create its measure, the government collects price data on thousands of goods and services each month and then follows statistical procedures to determine the average price. The choice of a base year is arbitrary; currently, the national income and product accounts use a base year of 2005 for price indexes for gross domestic product. For example, the government measure of the average price level in 2012 was 115.4, which means that prices, on average, were 15.4 percent higher in 2012 than they were in 2005. The value of P we use in Equation (3) is the government's measure of the price level in a particular year divided by 100. The

value of P we would use in Equation (3) for 2012 is $115.4/100 = 1.154$.

Here is a more specific example of a money-demand function where we specify the function m in a particular way:

> **real money-demand function** the function $m(Y, i)$, which is a useful summary of the relationship between the real demand for money, real income, and the nominal interest rate

$$M^D = P \times [(0.125 \times Y) - (75 \times i)] \qquad (4)$$

where M^D is in billions of dollars, Y is in billions of constant dollars, and i is in percentage points. This equation says that the demand for money is proportional to the price level and that, quantitatively, the demand for money depends on total income and the nominal interest rate. For example, suppose that $P = 1.12$, $Y = 7,000$, and $i = 5$. Then the demand for money in billions of dollars is

$$
\begin{aligned}
M^D &= P \times [(0.125 \times Y) - (75 \times i)] \\
&= 1.12 \times [(0.125 \times 7,000) - (75 \times 5)] \\
&= 1.12 \times (875 - 375) \\
&= 560
\end{aligned}
$$

Another way to think about prices is in terms of real money demand. After all, when we ask about the demand for a particular good, we look at the quantity of goods, not their dollar value. Similarly, shouldn't we think about the demand for money in terms of the goods it can buy rather than in terms of dollars? We can do this by dividing both sides of Equation (3) by the price level. This gives

$$\frac{M^D}{P} = m(Y, i) \qquad (5)$$

In this equation, the real demand for money depends on total real income and the nominal interest rate. The function $m(Y, i)$ is known as the **real money-demand function.** The real money-demand function is a useful summary of the relationship between the real demand for money, real income, and the nominal interest rate; it is particularly useful because it is not affected by changes in the money supply or the prices of goods and services. Thus, the real money-demand function helps economists to analyze how much money people want even when the money supply and prices change over time.

1 The liquidity-preference model makes the nominal interest rate an endogenous variable by considering both the demand for and supply of money.

2 In the liquidity-preference model, an increase in the money supply causes a decline in the nominal interest rate; a decline in the money supply causes an increase in the nominal interest rate.

3 According to the liquidity-preference model, in an economic expansion, as people's incomes rise, they spend more, so the demand for money increases and the nominal interest rate rises; in a recession, the nominal interest rate declines.

4 Nominal demand for money is proportional to the prices of goods and services; real demand for money depends positively on real income and negatively on the nominal interest rate.

11-3 The Dynamic Model of Money

The liquidity-preference model describes changes in the demand for money and the supply of money at a point in time, so it is a static model. A **static model** is one that does not allow variables to change over time. If we want to allow variables to change over time, in particular to change in one direction in the short run and in another direction in the long run, we need to use a dynamic model. A **dynamic model** is one that allows variables to change over time.

Why do we need to use a dynamic model of money? First, money functions as a store of value in addition to being a medium of exchange. Therefore, if we want to assume that people choose between holding money and bonds, where bonds serve only as a store of value, then we must include time in our model. Second, two key macroeconomic variables that affect people's well-being are the inflation rate and the nominal interest rate. The inflation rate is the percentage change in prices over time, and the nominal interest rate is the cost of borrowing funds at one date and repaying those funds at a later date. Both variables depend on time. Third, economists have found that many economic variables change one way in the short run and another way in the long run, so we need a model with time to distinguish short-run effects from long-run effects.

In the dynamic model of money, we allow more variables to be endogenous, and thus fewer variables are exogenous. In the static liquidity-preference model, the exogenous variables were people's incomes, the prices of goods and services, and the money supply. The endogenous variables were the nominal interest rate, the quantity of money demanded, the equilibrium quantity of money, and people's spending. In the dynamic model, people's incomes and the prices of goods and services are endogenous variables. Thus, the only exogenous variable is the money supply. Because every price variable in a market that would be affected by people's decisions is endogenous, this is a general-equilibrium model. Also, because there are now so many endogenous variables, we are going to simplify the model and focus only on the impact on those variables of a change in the money supply.

In any dynamic model, we start with the economy in a **steady state,** in which the key variables in the model are constant or else growing at a constant rate. The steady state is the long-run equilibrium of the model, which describes what the endogenous variables in the model will do if they are not disturbed by any other variable in the model.

static model a model that does not allow variables to change over time

dynamic model a model that allows variables to change over time

steady state the long-run equilibrium of a model, which describes what the endogenous variables in the model will do if they are not disturbed by any other variable in the model; the key variables in the model are constant or else they are growing at a constant rate

Shocks to variables in the model can affect other variables in the short run and sometimes even in the long run. A **shock** is a change to a variable in a model that causes other variables to deviate from their long-run equilibrium values in the short run (or to differ over time from the path they would take in a steady state) or in the long run. In analyzing a dynamic model, we are interested in how shocks of different types lead to changes in various economic variables. Thus, we usually begin analyzing a dynamic model by finding its steady state; then we determine how shocks affect the model in both the long run and the short run.

Suppose that many people in the economy are choosing how much money and how many bonds to hold as time goes on. To make the prices of goods and services endogenous, we make three assumptions. We assume that (1) prices adjust slowly when the money supply changes, (2) in the long run prices change proportionally with a change in the money supply, and (3) in the short run a decline in the nominal interest rate causes people to buy more goods and services than they would buy otherwise. So people's spending and incomes rise temporarily.

What is the steady state in this model? Suppose that the money supply—the model's only exogenous variable—is constant over time and that trend output is constant. With no shocks to the money supply, the price level is constant, so the inflation rate is zero. Both the nominal supply of money and the nominal demand for money are constant as well, and so is the nominal interest rate.

11-3a The Effects of an Increase in Money Supply

What happens in the short run if the money supply increases? As in the static liquidity-preference model, a one-time increase in the money supply leads to a liquidity effect, which is short-lived. The decline in the nominal interest rate stimulates spending, causing income to increase for a while. After some time, however, prices in the economy start rising until they reach a point that is higher by the same percentage as the increase in the money supply. In the long run, income and spending return to the level they were prior to the increase in the money supply. The price level, money supply, and demand for money are proportionately higher, but all other variables are the same as before the increase in the money supply.

If we were to trace out the movement of the nominal interest rate over time, we would see it decline when the money supply first increased as a result of the liquidity effect. Over time, though, as prices begin to rise, the demand for money would increase. Because the lower nominal interest rate increases spending, the demand for money increases further. The increase in the demand for money causes the nominal interest rate to increase.

These changes are illustrated in Figure 11.7. Panel (a) shows the movement of the nominal interest rate over time, whereas panel (b) shows the corresponding static view of the liquidity-preference model at three different dates. Panel (a) shows that in the first period the nominal interest rate is i_1, whereas panel (b) shows the money supply at M_1^S and the demand for money at M_1^D. Then the Fed increases the money supply to M_2^S, causing the nominal interest rate to decline over time to i_2. Because the figure in panel (b) can represent only a one-time equilibrium, you have to imagine gradual movements of the lines in panel (b) leading to the change in the nominal interest rate in panel (a). As some time passes, the lower nominal interest rate leads to increased spending and incomes and a higher price level, causing the money-demand curve to shift upward gradually to M_3^D, thus returning the nominal interest rate to i_1. In this situation, the demand for money and the money supply (in nominal terms) have increased in the same proportion as the price level, so, in real terms, all the variables in the economy are the same as they were before.

Because the variables in the model all affect one another, disentangling which variable causes what to happen is difficult. To understand all these effects, we would need to write out equations for each of the variables and see how they relate to each other. In addition, the sizes and timing of the effects depend on the underlying relationships in the model. For example, suppose that the price level adjusts very rapidly. Then in Figure 11.7 the variables will adjust very quickly to their final equilibrium, with the nominal interest rate not changing very much along the way. Alternatively, if the price level takes a very long time to adjust, then we would have a long-lived liquidity effect, with the nominal interest rate remaining low for a long time. Thus, the results shown in panel (a) of the figure may vary considerably. Indeed, economists have studied the conditions under which different speeds and magnitudes of adjustment occur and have found that these adjustments differ over time.

We have already studied the liquidity effect, which showed that an increase in the money supply causes the nominal interest rate to decline. In our discussion of Figure 11.7, we noted two changes that led to shifts

shock a change to a variable in a model that causes other variables to deviate from their long-run equilibrium values in the short run (or to differ over time from the path they would take in a steady state) or in the long run

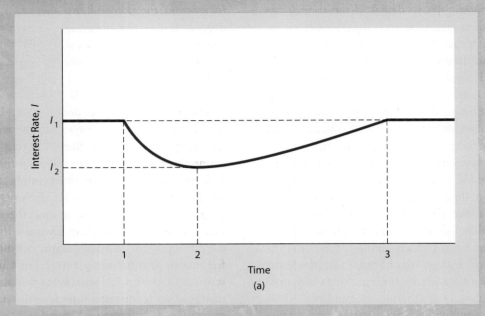

(a)

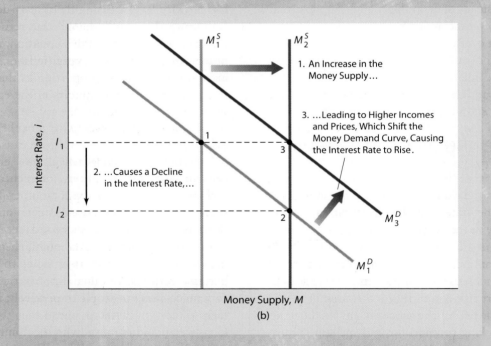

1. An Increase in the Money Supply...

3. ...Leading to Higher Incomes and Prices, Which Shift the Money Demand Curve, Causing the Interest Rate to Rise.

2. ...Causes a Decline in the Interest Rate,...

Money Supply, M

(b)

This graph shows how the nominal interest rate, shown in panel (a), and the demand and supply curves for money, shown in panel (b), change over time in response to an increase in the money supply. Panel (a) shows that the economy is initially in equilibrium until time 1 with the nominal interest rate at i_1, whereas panel (b) shows the money supply at M_1^S and the demand for money at M_1^D. At time 1, the Fed begins to increase the money supply, which reaches M_2^S at time 2. The increase in the money supply causes the nominal interest rate to decline over time to i_2. As time passes, the lower nominal interest rate leads to increased income and a higher price level, causing the money-demand curve to shift up. At time 3, the money-demand curve has shifted to M_3^D, thus returning the nominal interest rate to i_1.

in the money-demand curve: a rise in people's incomes and a rise in the price level. Equation (3), which says that $M^D = P \times m(Y, i)$, makes clear why the money-demand curve shifts. Increases in the price level increase the demand for money, leading to a higher nominal interest rate, which is the **price-level effect.** Increases in income also increase the demand for money, leading to a higher nominal interest rate, which is the **income effect.** Thus, the path over time that the nominal interest rate takes in Figure 11.7a really depends on how quickly prices adjust, thereby determining the size and timing of the price-level effect and how much and how quickly people's incomes change, in turn determining the income effect. The price-level effect and the income effect move the nominal interest rate in the opposite direction of the liquidity effect between time 1 and time 3 in Figure 11.7a. The liquidity effect dominates at first, so the nominal interest rate declines from time 1 to time 2. The price-level effect and income effect overcome the liquidity effect from time 2 to time 3, so the nominal interest rate rises.

11-3b The Effects of an Increase in the Growth Rate of the Money Supply

Often we observe a change not just in the level of the money supply but in its growth rate over time as well. Suppose that instead of just a one-time increase in the money supply, we think about an economy in which the money supply increases continuously over time. Suppose, for instance, that after a period in which the money supply was constant, it suddenly began to grow at a rate of 5 percent per year. In this situation, instead of just a one-time increase, the money supply continues to grow over time.

To analyze this situation, let's first consider what the final steady state is likely to be and then trace the short-term changes over time. In the long run, the 5 percent growth rate of the money supply is likely to lead to inflation of 5 percent, for reasons we will discuss in more detail later (in Chapters 12 and 13). We will assume that because the inflation rate was zero when the money supply was constant, an increase in the growth rate of the money supply to 5 percent would lead to an inflation rate of 5 percent. If there were no change in the real interest rate, then a 5 percentage point higher inflation rate should lead to a higher

nominal interest rate by 5 percentage points. Thus, we should expect the nominal interest rate to rise by 5 percentage points. This is the Fisher hypothesis that we discussed in detail in Chapter 6.

Is there likely to be a liquidity effect? If people do not anticipate the change in the growth rate of the money supply and it takes them a while to realize that inflation will rise, then there might be an initial liquidity effect. However, with such a dramatic change in the growth rate of the money supply, the liquidity effect is likely to be short-lived. As people begin to see prices rising and inflation continuing, the demand for money will increase, and the nominal interest rate will rise. Figure 11.8 represents the overall movement of the nominal interest rate over time. In the long run, the nominal interest rate is higher than it was when the growth rate of the money supply was lower.

Other short-term changes are possible. For example, if people anticipate the increased growth rate of the money supply and they expect inflation to rise quickly, then the nominal interest rate also will rise quickly, and there may be no liquidity effect, as shown in Figure 11.9. In this situation, the nominal interest rate rises to its new long-run level, with no short-run decline as in Figure 11.8.

This dynamic model tells us more about the effects (on output, inflation, and the nominal interest rate) of a change in the money supply than the static liquidity-preference model we discussed earlier. In both models there is an effect from increased liquidity; when the money supply increases, the nominal interest rate may decline. The size of that effect, however, depends on the dynamic response of other variables, such as the length of time it takes for people to perceive a rise in expected inflation or to adjust prices. Thus, people's expectations about inflation and the flexibility of prices play key roles in the model. The implications of differing degrees of price flexibility and different assumptions about expectations will be examined in larger models in Chapters 12 and 13. (To explore some additional implications of models of money demand, see the box titled "Microeconomic Foundations of Money and the Friedman Rule.")

price-level effect the situation when a higher nominal interest rate results from an increase in the price level that increases the demand for money

income effect the situation when a higher nominal interest rate results from an increase in income that increases the demand for money

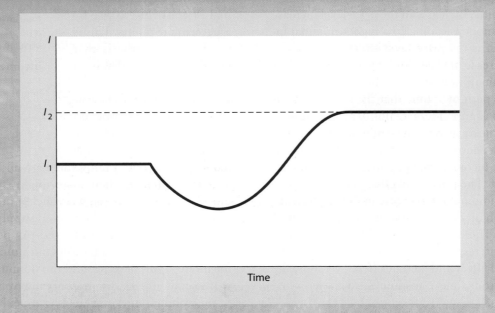

This graph shows how the nominal interest rate changes in response to an increase in the growth rate of the money supply. If people do not anticipate the change in the growth rate of the money supply and it takes them some time to realize that inflation will rise, then there will be an initial liquidity effect. But the liquidity effect is likely to be short-lived. As people begin to see prices rising and inflation continuing, the demand for money will increase, and the nominal interest rate will rise above its initial level.

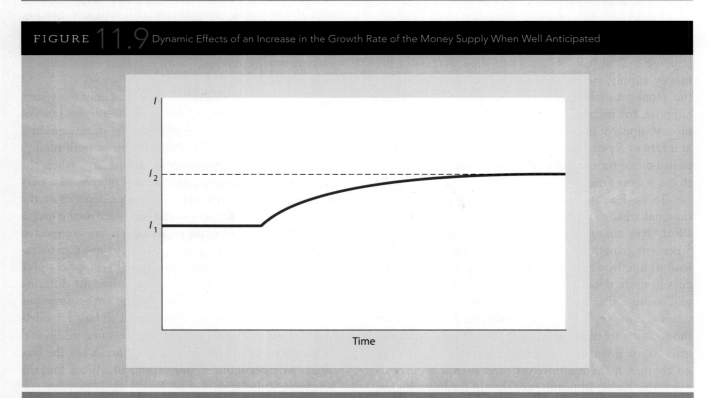

This graph shows how the nominal interest rate changes in response to an increase in the growth rate of the money supply when people anticipate the increase. If people expect inflation to rise quickly, then the nominal interest rate also will rise quickly, and there may be no liquidity effect.

1   A dynamic model allows variables to change over time.

2   The dynamic model of money can be analyzed in the long run by determining the model's steady state, in which all variables are constant or growing at a constant rate.

3   A change in the money supply causes a liquidity effect, which affects the nominal interest rate. An increase in the money supply leads to a lower nominal interest rate; a decrease in the money supply leads to a higher nominal interest rate.

4   In the long run, a one-time change in the money supply leads to a proportionate change in the price level and no change in real variables or the nominal interest rate. A permanent change in the growth rate of the money supply leads to a permanent change in the nominal interest rate and an equal change in the inflation rate.

Policy→Perspective   Using Models of Money Demand in Practice

In our present system of fiat money, the value of money depends on what it can buy, which depends on the supply of money relative to the demand. Therefore, an agency such as the Federal Reserve, which has the duty to determine the supply of money in setting monetary policy, must understand what determines the demand for money so that it can supply the appropriate amount. Thus, the Fed must know how much money people want to hold.

How helpful is the theory of the demand for money in understanding data on money and nominal interest rates? Can the models of the demand for money explain movements over time in the data on money or forecast future demand for money? To investigate these issues, we need to test the conclusions of the models using data.

Economists develop simple theoretical models so that they can understand the key forces that affect demand and supply. When they look at the data, however, they must make the models more complicated to deal with the facts. For example, nearly every theoretical model of money assumes that there is only one type of money. We learned in Chapter 3, though, that the many different bank accounts differ in their degree of liquidity and could be counted as money. So what measure of money in the data corresponds to the concept of

money in the model? There is no clear answer to this question. In practice, researchers choose one of two procedures: (1) They use a measure of money that seems most closely related to the theoretical model, or (2) they make the theoretical model more complicated so that it matches the data more closely.

We would like to use data on money to answer questions based on theory, such as these: How sensitive is the demand for money to changes in nominal interest rates? How stable is the demand for money? The latter question is often phrased as, Do the relationships between money and other variables, such as nominal interest rates, change substantially over time?

Because economic variables such as income grow over time, there is one complication to our data analysis. You may recall from Chapter 7 that because stock prices were growing over time, we had to take the logarithm of the stock price at each date to more easily show how stock prices changed over time. Taking logarithms of variables that grow over time is useful statistically as well. Thus, most analyses of the data on the demand for money begin with Equation (5) and then take the logarithm of the demand for money and income on both sides of the equation and assume that the resulting equation is a linear one. (But the analysis usually does not take the logarithm of the nominal interest rate because it does not grow over time

(continued)

like the other variables.) That is, the equation for the demand for money is

$$log(MD/P) = \alpha + \beta i + \gamma \, log(Y) + \varepsilon \qquad (6)$$

In this equation, the logarithm of real demand for money M^D/P depends on a constant term α, the nominal interest rate i in percentage points times its coefficient β, the logarithm of real income Y times its coefficient γ, and a final term called an *error term* ε. The error term represents shocks to the demand for money other than changes in the variables in the equation. The idea is that income and the nominal interest rate are the main factors affecting the demand for money, with everything else that affects it being included in the error term.

To estimate the coefficients of this equation, researchers use econometric methods. **Econometrics** is the use of statistical techniques on economic data to investigate how economic variables are related. The key statistical method used is called **regression analysis,** in which the coefficients of an equation such as Equation (6) are calculated by finding values for them that make the error term in the equation have certain desirable properties. In particular, regression analysis finds the values of the coefficients such that the sum of the squared error terms is as small as possible. This is all done on a computer, which can perform a large number of calculations rapidly, so estimating the coefficients takes just seconds.

This type of estimation method for Equation (6) or some version of it has been used by many researchers over time with mixed results. The exact variable being used to represent money (M1 or M2) matters, the estimated coefficients seem to change over time, and the error term in the equation does not behave randomly—suggesting that some key variables are absent from the model. In addition, when the model (or a variation of it) has been used to forecast the demand for money, the forecasts seem far from the mark.

econometrics the use of statistical techniques on economic data to investigate how economic variables are related

regression analysis the key method in econometrics in which the coefficients of an equation are calculated by finding values for them that make the sum of the squared error terms as small as possible

Economist Laurence Ball showed that much of the earlier research had a major statistical problem. Researchers who estimated versions of Equation (6) used data that began in 1959 (when the Fed's data on monetary aggregates begin). Because many of these studies were done in the 1970s and 1980s, the data did not cover a very long period. And, as Ball showed, over that period, interest rates and income both generally were rising together. This creates a statistical problem because then the computer program used in the regression analysis cannot easily calculate the coefficients on income and the nominal interest rate.

However, in the early 1980s, nominal interest rates began a long overall decline as inflation decreased. Thus, by the mid-1990s, there was over a decade's worth of new data on the relationship between the demand for money, income, and the nominal interest rate that help the computer's regression-analysis program produce better estimates of the coefficients in Equation (6).[2] With those additional data, Ball was able to estimate the coefficients more precisely than earlier researchers did. Ball's estimates, using the M1 measure of money, were

$$log(M^D/P) = -0.05i + 0.5 \, log(Y) \qquad (7)$$

that is, in Equation (6), $\beta = -0.05$ and $\gamma = 0.5$.

What is particularly interesting about these estimates is that they are smaller by half than most researchers found before. But they seem to be much more stable than the values earlier researchers found; that is, they are less sensitive to minor variations in the variables being used and to the exact method of regression analysis that is used.

We can use Equation (7) to examine the impact on the real demand for money (the variable on the left-hand side of the equation) when one of the variables on the right-hand side of the equation changes. With the real demand for money on the left-hand side written in logarithms, a change in the demand for money because of a change in a variable on the right-hand side can be interpreted as a percentage change. Thus, given this equation, if the nominal interest rate were to rise by 1 percentage point, the real demand for money would fall by 0.05, or 5 percent. Because the logarithm of income is on the right-hand

[2]Laurence Ball, "Another Look at Long-Run Money Demand," *Journal of Monetary Economics* 47 (2001), pp. 31–44.

side of the equation, it also can be interpreted as a percentage change. If income rose by 1 percent, the coefficient of 0.5 in the equation implies that the real demand for money would rise by 0.5 percent. The percentage change in one variable divided by the percentage change in another variable is called the *elasticity* of the first variable with respect to the second. In this case, we would say that the elasticity of the real demand for money with respect to income is 0.5. (Only the coefficient on income is an elasticity, not the coefficient on the nominal interest rate, because in Equation (6) we took the logarithm of output, but we did not take the logarithm of the nominal interest rate. Sometimes economists call the coefficient on the nominal interest rate a *semielasticity* because the idea is similar to an elasticity.)

Are Ball's estimates as reported in Equation (7) believable? They correspond to values that most economists would consider sensible theoretically. Ball himself noted, however, that his empirical work ignored one key factor: the changing technology of money.

If technology has changed, we would expect that the demand for money would fall. In the ATM model, we noted that as the cost of a trip to the ATM fell, people would withdraw cash more often, so money demand would decline. Thus it seems that we might expect the coefficients in Equation (7) to change over time to reflect this, whereas Ball assumed that the coefficients were constant over time. We need more data than we have yet to be able to test the hypothesis that the coefficients have changed in response to banking innovations.

Therefore, we are not very certain of the role played by improved technology and how it affects money demand. However, at least after Ball's empirical work, we have more precise estimates of the demand for money than before, assuming that changes in technology have not changed the demand for money too much. (To see how the Federal Reserve has estimated the demand for money in practice, see the Policy Insider box "Can the Federal Reserve Accurately Forecast the Demand for Money?")

Policy →IN← sider — Can the Federal Reserve Accurately Forecast the Demand for Money?

In our present system of fiat money, the Federal Reserve, which has the duty to determine the supply of money, must understand what determines the demand for money so that it can supply the appropriate amount. Federal Reserve economists have created a detailed procedure for estimating the demand for money.

The Fed's empirical procedure is described in a paper by Fed economists George Moore, Richard Porter, and David Small.[3] They estimate a model of the demand for M1 and M2 and each of their components. We will examine just the demand for M2, which has been the Fed's focus for most of the past two decades.

Two equations describe the demand for M2. First, one equation describes the long-run relationship between demand for M2 and other variables. That equation shows that demand for M2 is proportional to the price level and related to

aggregate income and the opportunity cost for M2. The long-run equation is not always satisfied in the short run, but the variables in the model will adjust so that the equation holds in the long run. The second equation describes the factors that influence the growth rate (rather than the logarithm of the level as in the first equation) of the demand for M2 in the short run. These include the past growth rate of the demand for money, past values of growth in consumer spending, and the past value of the nominal interest rate. The equations are related because the short-run demand for money depends in part on how close the long-run equation is to being satisfied.

The long-run equation for M2 is

$$log(M2_t) = \alpha + log(y_t) + \beta \, log(R_t - r_t) + \gamma t + e_t \quad \textbf{(A)}$$

where $M2_t$ is the nominal (dollar) amount of M2 at time t, α is a constant term, y_t is nominal income, R_t is the nominal interest rate on three-month Treasury bills, r_t is the average nominal interest rate on the components of M2, and e_t is an error term.

(continued)

[3]"Modeling the Disaggregated Demands for M2 and M1: The U.S. Experience in the 1980s," in *Financial Sectors in Open Economies: Empirical Analysis and Policy Issues* (Washington, DC: Board of Governors of the Federal Reserve System, 1990), pp. 21–105.

The term γt represents a time trend t times the coefficient γ that represents the effects of long-term changes in the demand for money over time (and could be useful in capturing the changes in technology that Ball's model did not).

Use of nominal income in the model is controversial because real income is more relevant in economic theory and is the variable used by most other researchers. Nominal income also is assumed to have a coefficient of 1, which the Fed researchers found to fit the data well. The term $R_t - r_t$ represents the opportunity cost of holding money because it is the difference in return from holding money instead of a short-term bond. Calculating a value for r_t is complicated because it is a weighted average of the returns on all the different components of M2, where the weights are determined by the relative quantities of each asset in M2.

The short-run equation differs from the long-run equation in several ways. First, it is based on the growth rate of each term rather than on the logarithm of the level. Second, it includes the past value of the demand for M2 on the right-hand side of the equation. Finally, because the system of the two equations must be related to each other, it includes the error term from the long-run equation. The resulting short-run equation looks like this:

$$m2_t = \alpha + be_{t-1} + dm2_{t-1} + f\%\,\Delta(R_t - r_t)$$
$$+ g_0 c_t + g_1 c_{t-1} + g_2 c_{t-2} + \varepsilon_t \qquad \textbf{(B)}$$

where $m2_t$ is the growth rate of M2 at time t, the symbols $\%\Delta$ stand for "percentage change in," and c_t is the growth rate of nominal consumption spending at time t. Note that e_{t-1} in this equation is the error term from one quarter ago from Equation (A).

This modeling effort seemed promising at first. The model given by Equations (A) and (B) performed well for several years after it was developed. The Fed used the model to forecast the demand for M2, and it was quite accurate for a short time. Soon, however, the equation began to falter, as forecasts using the model were far from the mark. Perhaps the cause was the switch that people made into bond and stock mutual funds, as we discussed in Chapter 3. Or it may have been improved technology, which allowed people to switch between assets more readily in response to changes in nominal interest rates. Whatever the reason was, it caused the Fed's model to miss the mark badly.

These problems with the model actually were predicted in advance by critics of the model when it first appeared. Academic economists were critical of the research by Moore, Porter, and Small, worrying that it was based on a partial-equilibrium model and thus would work in the short run but not in the long run. They also worried that people's expectations of inflation did not play a key role in the model, even though such expectations are crucial in models such as our dynamic model of the demand for money.

Because of the difficulties faced by the model in the 1990s, the Fed downplayed the importance of setting the money supply. Although the Fed explicitly set targets for M1 and M2 in the 1980s and 1990s, it has not set such targets since February 2000, in part because it has no confidence in its ability to explain or forecast the demand for money. Former Fed Chairman Alan Greenspan noted: "The value of fiat money can be inferred only from the values of the present and future goods and services it can command. And that, in turn, has largely rested on the quantity of fiat money created relative to demand."[4] Unfortunately, the Fed lacks a very reliable guide to how much fiat money to create. As a result, the Fed uses other methods to determine the money supply, which we will discuss in Chapter 18, after we investigate models of the entire economy and the causes and consequences of inflation.

[4]Alan Greenspan, "The History of Money: Remarks at the Opening of an American Numismatic Society Exhibition, Federal Reserve Bank of New York," January 16, 2002.

Microeconomic Foundations of Money and the Friedman Rule

Economic researchers have developed a number of different models of how people use money. When such models describe how individuals choose how much money to hold, the models are said to have microeconomic foundations of money. These models provide insights that can be applied to models of the economy as a whole, just as we use the results of the ATM model in the liquidity-preference model and the dynamic model.

Models of the microeconomic foundations of money include (1) transactions-cost models, in which people hold money to avoid the transactions costs of going to the bank, as we saw in the ATM model earlier; (2) search models, in which people are modeled as searching for sellers of goods, so they need to hold money so that they are ready to purchase goods when they find them; (3) cash-in-advance models, in which people must obtain cash one period in advance of purchasing goods; (4) shopping-time models, in which holding more money reduces the time it takes to shop so that there is a tradeoff between the opportunity cost of holding money and shopping time; and (5) overlapping-generations models, in which trade between people of different generations requires the use of money.

One of the most difficult tasks faced by researchers in their work on the microeconomic foundations of money is generating a liquidity effect. In the simple versions of all the models just described, an increase in the growth rate of the money supply does not lead to a decline in the nominal interest rate; instead, the nominal interest rate rises because of a higher expected inflation rate. Thus, researchers have spent much time and energy trying to show how a liquidity effect can arise in such models. Doing so generally requires the introduction of a number of complications to the model, such as some mechanism that prevents an immediate return to equilibrium following a shock to the growth rate of the money supply.

An interesting result that arises from nearly all the models of the microeconomic foundations of money is that the optimal rate of inflation—that is, the inflation rate that is best for the economic agents in the models—is slightly negative. In other words, in these models, deflation is optimal. This result is known as the *Friedman rule* because Milton Friedman first described it in his 1969 book on the optimal amount of money the Fed should issue.[5] The intuition for the result is fairly simple: The cost of producing new money is close to zero, so the government should issue it until the costs equal the benefits to people of holding money. Because people's main alternative to holding money is to hold bonds, which earn a nominal interest rate, then the ideal situation is for the return to holding money to be the same as the return to holding bonds, which will occur when the inflation rate equals the negative of the real interest rate on bonds. In such a situation, the nominal interest rate on bonds will be zero.

The Friedman rule, which arises from the nature of the models of the microeconomic foundations of money, contrasts sharply with current views of policymakers, who think deflation is a situation to be avoided at all costs. They cite the recent case of the Japanese economy, which has had deflation and very slow economic growth for over a decade. Perhaps either the theory or the policymakers are missing some key aspect that might reconcile the two views.

[5]Milton Friedman, "The Optimum Quantity of Money," in *The Optimum Quantity of Money and Other Essays* (Chicago: Aldine, 1969), pp. 1–50.

RECAP

1 Econometric methods can be used to test the ability of models of the demand for money to forecast accurately.

2 Instability in estimates of the money-demand function may have arisen because of statistical problems resulting from the fact that income and nominal interest rates had risen together over time in early data. Later data from the early 1980s through the mid-1990s enabled researchers to estimate the equation for the demand for money more precisely.

3 The demand for money is estimated to decline 5 percent in response to a 1 percentage point increase in the nominal interest rate. Also, the elasticity of the demand for money with respect to income is estimated to be 0.5. These estimates are more precise than those found by earlier research but ignore the possibility that technology has changed the demand for money over time.

Review Questions and Problems

Review Questions

1 What is the difference between an exogenous variable and an endogenous variable?

2 Explain the difference between general-equilibrium models and partial-equilibrium models. How are the numbers of endogenous and exogenous variables related to whether a model is a partial-equilibrium model or general-equilibrium model?

3 What are the main factors that affect a person's decision about how often to go to an ATM?

4 Describe the main factors at play in the liquidity-preference model. What variables does the model determine?

5 What is the liquidity effect? Why does it occur in the liquidity-preference model?

6 What is the main difference between a static model and a dynamic model?

7 What is meant by the steady state in a dynamic model? Why is a steady state useful to analyze in a dynamic model?

8 What is a shock in a dynamic model? What does a shock do in such a model?

9 In U.S. data, how sensitive is the demand for money to changes in nominal interest rates?

10 Is the demand-for-money function stable over time?

Numerical Exercises

11 Using a spreadsheet program or a calculator, solve Tracy's problem of how often to go to the ATM when the nominal interest rate on her bank account is 10 percent, she spends $30 each day, it costs her $0.50 each time she uses the ATM, and she thinks that there is a 15 percent chance that she will lose her cash or have it stolen. Under these conditions, how often does Tracy go to the ATM, and how much cash does she take out each time?

12 In the model of Tracy's decision about how often to go to the ATM in exercise 11, try to find a combination of parameters that would lead her to

go to the ATM just once every 10 days. You can consider variations in Tracy's spending amount, her cost of using the ATM, the nominal interest rate, and the probability of having her cash lost or stolen. (*Hint:* Use a spreadsheet program or use calculus.)

13 Suppose that the money-demand equation is Equation (4):

$$M^D = P \times [(0.125 \times Y) - (75 \times i)]$$

Suppose initially that $P = 1$, $Y = 7{,}000$, and $i = 5$. If Y falls to 6,500 and the price level does not change, by how much should the Fed change the money supply if it wants to keep the nominal interest rate unchanged? Should the money supply rise or fall, and by how much? Use the liquidity-preference framework.

14 In Equation (6), suppose that the coefficients are estimated as $\alpha = 0$, $\beta = -0.05$, and $\gamma = 1$. If the nominal interest rate were to rise by 1 percentage point and income were to fall by 3 percent, by what percent would the quantity of real money demanded change? If prices were to fall 1 percent, by what percent would the quantity of nominal money demanded change?

Analytical Problems

15 In the liquidity-preference framework, suppose that the Fed changes the money supply to keep the nominal interest rate unchanged whenever the demand for money shifts. Show what happens to the quantity of money and the nominal interest rate if the money-demand curve shifts to the right.

16 Describe how a one-time decline in the money supply in a dynamic model affects the nominal interest rate over time.

17 Suppose that the liquidity effect is small, people monitor changes in the money supply carefully, and prices and inflation expectations adjust rapidly. In this situation, describe the movement of the nominal interest rate when there is a permanent decline in the growth rate of the money supply.

The AGGREGATE-DEMAND/AGGREGATE-SUPPLY MODEL

Over time, the long-term trends in output growth have changed, and the economy has gone through numerous business cycles. We would like to know what causes the changes in those long-term trends and what causes recessions so that we can make better forecasts, interpret historical events, enact policies to increase growth, and reduce the likelihood of recessions.

Understanding what affects long-term output growth and what causes recessions is difficult because the economy is complex; millions of people make independent decisions, each of which has a small effect on the economy. To aid our understanding of how the economy works, we need a model of the economy that is much simpler than the economy itself yet that captures the economy's main features.

In this chapter and in Chapter 13 we will see how economists build models that represent the economy. In this chapter we will look at a particular model, called the *aggregate-demand/aggregate-supply* model, that has been used by macroeconomists for over 40 years. We will discuss other types of models, which have been developed more recently, in Chapter 13.

To begin, we will see how the aggregate-demand/aggregate-supply (*AD–AS*) model is built up from dividing the economy's spending into a number of different categories depending on who buys which goods and services. Because government policy may have a substantial impact on the economy, the second section of this chapter examines how such policy works in the *AD–AS* model. In the 1960s, the *AD–AS* model was the basis for large structural models of the U.S. economy with hundreds of equations and variables that were used for forecasting and analyzing changes in government policy; such models are the subject of the third section. The policy perspective presented at the end of the chapter asks if those large models contributed to the poor performance of the U.S. economy in the 1970s.

12-1 A Model of Aggregate Demand and Aggregate Supply

How can we develop a model of the economy that is simple enough to understand yet rich enough to capture the key factors that influence the economy? After experimenting with a number of alternative methods, economists many years ago discovered a useful way to break down the overall economy into two main components, which they labeled "aggregate demand" and "aggregate supply." The basic idea is that aggregate demand tells us the amount of goods and services being purchased, whereas aggregate supply tells us how much is produced. In equilibrium, the amount purchased equals the amount produced. Together, aggregate demand and aggregate supply determine the amount of output produced and the level of prices in the economy.

In this section we first develop the *AD–AS* model of the economy by investigating the economic variables that influence aggregate demand and those that influence aggregate supply. Then we show how the model reaches equilibrium in the short run and in the long run. Finally, we look at the effects of a shock (an unexpected change in an exogenous variable) and how the economy responds to the shock.

aggregate demand the economy's total demand for goods and services

12-1a Aggregate Demand

Aggregate demand is the total demand for goods and services by everyone in the economy. We divide aggregate demand into various components: consumption (demand by people for consumer goods), investment (demand by business firms for equipment and buildings and demand by people for housing), net exports (demand by foreigners for our goods and services), and government spending (demand by the government for goods and services, as well as government investment spending). We examine each of these components in more detail to see the economic variables that determine each of them.

Consumption. The largest component of aggregate demand is consumption. Consumers buy durable goods (such as automobiles, furniture, and major appliances) that last for a long time, nondurable goods (such as clothing) that do not last as long as durables, and services (such as haircuts) that are consumed immediately. (*Note:* Housing is not considered a durable good but rather an investment good, which we will discuss later.) All together, consumption is about two-thirds of aggregate demand.

What determines the amount of spending by consumers at any given time? The main factors that affect all consumers are their current income, their future income, their wealth, taxes, and the real interest rate. (Another factor is consumers' level of confidence, which is discussed in the Data Bank box "Is Consumer Confidence a Good Indicator of Future Consumer Spending?")

Consumers buy more goods and services when their incomes are higher. A person's current income is not all that matters because people often can borrow against their future income. Thus, future income also affects people's spending; for example, if you are about to inherit $50,000, you may buy a new car today even before you receive the money. In addition, of course, people's wealth affects their spending. Wealth differs from income because income is the amount a person earns in a year, whereas wealth is a person's accumulated assets. For example, one

Consumption spending accounts for two-thirds of aggregate demand and rises and falls over the course of the business cycle. Spending on big-ticket items, especially new houses and automobiles, falls substantially in recessions. Because consumer spending depends in part on consumers' optimism about the future, two organizations, the University of Michigan's Survey Research Center and the Conference Board (a research organization in New York City), survey a sample of consumers on a monthly basis, asking them to report on their current and future spending plans.

Both the Michigan survey of 500 consumers (on the Internet at **www.sca.isr.umich.edu**) and the Conference Board survey of 3,500 consumers (**www.conference-board.org/data/consumerconfidence.cfm**) include five questions about current and future economic conditions. The answers to those questions are then compiled into an index that represents consumer confidence or sentiment. The indexes decline sharply at the start of recessions and rise when the economy is growing well.

Economists have been interested in discovering whether or not the consumer confidence indexes are useful in helping them forecast future consumer spending. There is a strong correlation between consumer confidence and consumer spending. But economists also want to know if the consumer confidence indexes provide information not contained in any other economic variables. To test this hypothesis, my research [in the paper "Do Consumer Confidence Indexes Help Forecast Consumer Spending in Real Time?" *North American Journal of Economics and Finance*, (December 2005), pp. 435–450] modeled consumer spending, investigating how such spending is related to past consumer spending, income, the Treasury bill rate, and the average price of stocks. I used that basic model to forecast future consumer spending. I then investigated whether adding one of the consumer confidence indexes to the model helped to improve the forecasts. I found that the indexes are not helpful at all for forecasting future consumption; in some cases, they actually make the forecasts of consumption significantly worse. This surprising result doesn't mean that consumer confidence indexes are worthless, only that the information they contain for forecasting consumer spending is already included in other variables, such as past consumption spending, income, interest rates, and stock prices.

person might earn an annual salary of $50,000 and have $500,000 in wealth because he saved much of his income over time. Another person might earn an annual salary of $150,000 but have no wealth because she spends everything she earns. Both income and wealth affect a person's spending positively; the wealthier a person is, the more he is likely to spend. Taxes also may affect spending because the more taxes people must pay, the less disposable income they have available for spending. (However, under some circumstances, changes in taxes do not affect spending because higher taxes today may mean lower future taxes.) Finally, the real interest rate may affect consumer spending, as we saw in Chapter 6. The higher the real interest rate, the less likely people are to borrow, and the more likely they are to save; they increase saving by decreasing their spending. The real interest rate, rather than the nominal interest rate, is the most relevant interest rate to consider. A person would be happy to borrow at a 10 percent nominal interest rate when expected inflation is 10 percent because the resulting real interest rate is zero. Even though the nominal interest rate is high, the borrower can repay the loan with dollars that are worth less over time because the inflation rate is so high.

Investment. Investment spending on physical capital constitutes about one-sixth of aggregate demand. Business firms invest in physical capital when they buy equipment, such as computers, or build structures, such as office buildings. People invest in physical capital when they buy houses. Note that because aggregate demand refers only to the purchase of goods and services, financial investment (such as the purchase of stocks and bonds) is not included; we consider only investment in physical capital as part of aggregate demand. **Physical capital** consists of equipment and structures that firms use to produce output and houses that people live in. The total amount of physical capital in all firms and households is called the **capital stock.** When firms or households engage in investment in physical capital, some investment spending replaces old capital that has depreciated—for example, when a business firm purchases a new computer to replace one that is five years old and no longer capable of operating current software. Other investment spending adds to the nation's capital stock, such as the construction of a new office building. Business firms invest in capital to make profits, using the capital combined with labor to produce goods or services that consumers want.

Business investment spending on physical capital thus depends on the size of the existing capital stock compared with businesses' desired capital stock. Businesses want to increase their capital when they anticipate that people will be buying more of their goods and services, so business investment depends on future consumption spending, which, in turn, depends on future income, wealth, taxes, and the real interest rate. The investment a firm puts in place depends not just on future consumption spending but also on the firm's ability to pay for the new capital. Firms often pay for their investment goods out of their profits instead of by

physical capital the equipment and structures that a firm uses to produce its output and houses that people live in

capital stock the total amount of physical capital in all firms and households

John Lund/Marc Romanelli /Blend Images /Getty Images

People invest in physical capital when they buy new houses. Their investment spending is part of aggregate demand and is affected by many of the same factors that influence consumption spending: current and future income, wealth, taxes, and especially, the real interest rate.

borrowing; so if profits are high, they may use some of the profits to buy new capital goods, especially if they find it difficult to obtain loans. The real interest rate represents the opportunity cost of investment because firms could invest profits and earn the real interest rate or borrow and pay the real interest rate. Thus, the lower the real interest rate, the greater investment is. Finally, the more optimistic firms are about their future prospects, the more likely they will invest today.

People's investment in housing depends on the same factors that affect consumption spending: current and future income, wealth, taxes, and the real interest rate. The real interest rate is an even more important variable for investment in housing than for other consumption goods because it affects the amount of a household's mortgage payments. The lower the real interest rate, the more expensive a home a family can buy because it will be better able to afford the monthly payments.

Net exports. In calculating the total demand for goods and services, we account for international trade in the following way. In recent years, about 13 percent of goods and services produced in the United States were sold to foreigners. However, Americans import even more goods and services from foreign countries, an amount equal to about 17 percent of total U.S. output. Because net exports are equal to exports minus imports, our net exports equal about −4 percent of aggregate demand.

Because the influences on imports and exports are complicated, especially the effect of changes in currency exchange rates, we defer a detailed discussion of net exports until Chapter 14. For now, we will just assume that net exports depend on income in the United States and income in foreign countries. When people in the United States have higher incomes, they will spend more on consumer goods, including those from abroad, so net exports will decline. When people in foreign countries have higher incomes, they will buy more from the United States, so net exports will increase.

Government spending. Government spending consists of payments to government workers, purchases of goods and services from businesses, and gross government investment in physical capital, totaling about one-sixth of the economy's aggregate demand. Because government spending is determined through a complicated political process, we will not try to explain what determines its level. Instead, we assume that government spending is chosen exogenously; that is, it is not explained by the *AD–AS* model. We will, however, examine the consequences of changes in the amount of government spending.

The aggregate-demand curve. We have seen that consumption, investment, net exports, and government spending are affected by current income, future income, wealth, taxes, the real interest rate, future consumption, profits, business optimism, and foreign income. We are going to consider all these variables as exogenous except for current income and the real interest rate, which are endogenous. To show how the real interest rate is determined, we rely on results from Chapter 11 on the money market. In the money market, consider all the variables that affect money demand and supply as exogenous except for the price level, current income, and the nominal interest rate. For a given expected inflation rate, Equation (7) from Chapter 6 (*nominal interest rate = real interest rate + expected inflation rate*) ties the two markets (goods and services and money markets) together.

Many imported and exported goods are transported between countries on ships such as the one shown here. Net exports are part of aggregate demand and are affected mainly by income in the United States and in foreign countries.

Aggregate demand is the sum of consumption, investment, net exports, and government spending; that is, all spending in the markets for goods and services. The **aggregate-demand curve** is a curve that shows the combinations of the price level and output that are consistent with equilibrium in the markets for goods and services and money.

Now let us consider the effect of a decline in the price level on aggregate demand. According to our assumptions, none of the components of aggregate demand (consumption, investment, net exports, or government spending) are directly affected by the decline in the price level. However, we learned in Chapter 11 that the demand for money is affected by the price level. A

aggregate-demand (AD) curve shows combinations of the price level and output (which equals income) that are necessary for equilibrium in both the market for goods and services and the money market

FIGURE 12.1 The Money Market After a Decline in the Price Level

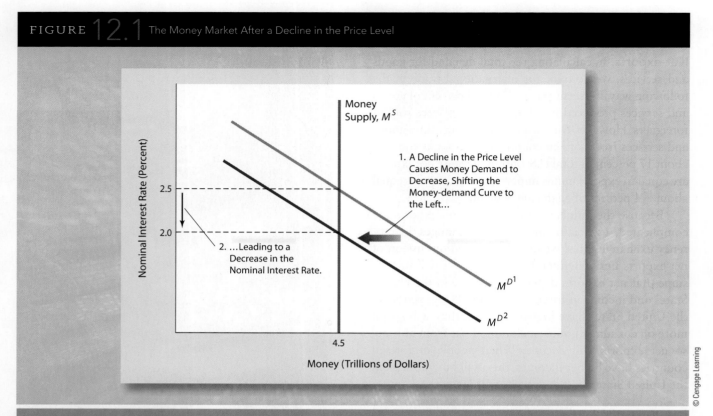

A decline in the price level decreases the demand for money, shifting the money-demand curve to the left. The new equilibrium occurs at a lower nominal interest rate.

decline in the price level reduces the demand for money, causing the money-demand curve to shift to the left, as shown in Figure 12.1. The new equilibrium is one with a lower nominal interest rate. With a lower nominal interest rate but no change in the expected inflation rate, the real interest rate is lower. And now, turning back to the components of aggregate demand, the lower real interest rate is likely to increase consumption and investment spending, thus increasing the total demand for goods and services. Thus, a lower price level is associated with increased aggregate demand. If we plot the aggregate-demand curve, with the price level on the vertical axis and output on the horizontal axis, since output equals aggregate demand in equilibrium, the relationship between the price level and output is shown as a downward-sloping line, as shown in Figure 12.2.

In equilibrium, the quantity of aggregate demand must equal current income because every dollar paid for goods and services is income to someone, either a worker

aggregate supply the economy's total production of goods and services

who earns wages or a firm that earns profits. In addition, output equals current income because every good or service produced leads to income for someone. Thus, we can use current income or output as the horizontal axis label on graphs of aggregate demand; for simplicity, we always use output, but you should remember that in equilibrium, output equals income.

The price level is a key endogenous variable in the *AD–AS* model. Therefore, even though we are treating the price level as exogenous in the money market, it will not be so once we incorporate aggregate supply into the entire model.

Thus, we now have a relationship between the price level and output that tells us about the demand side of the economy. Any of the combinations of the price level and output shown on the *AD* curve is one for which both the goods market and money market are in equilibrium. To find out which combination of the price level and output will occur in equilibrium, we must incorporate information about the supply side of the economy.

12-1b Aggregate Supply

Aggregate supply is the economy's total production of goods and services. To develop aggregate supply in our model, we will derive an aggregate-supply curve, which will show how the price level affects the amount produced.

FIGURE 12.2 The Aggregate-Demand (AD) Curve

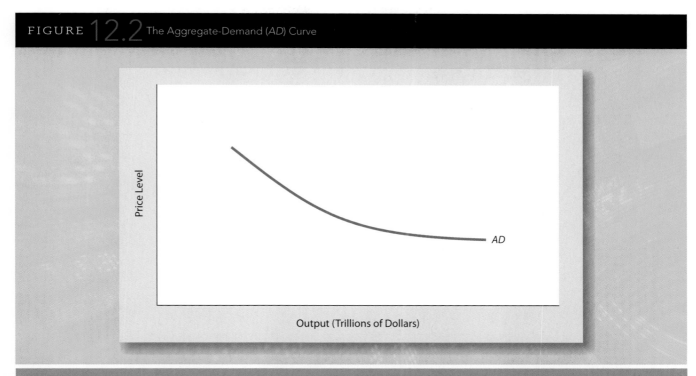

The **aggregate-demand** *(AD)* curve shows combinations of the price level and output (which equals income) that are necessary for equilibrium in both the market for goods and services and the money market.

We first learned about the economy's total production in Chapter 10 when we analyzed how the amount of the economy's output depends on productivity and the amounts of capital and labor used in production. When all the capital and labor is being fully utilized, we say that the economy is at **full employment.** What do economists mean when they discuss labor and capital being fully utilized? They do not mean that the unemployment rate is zero because there is always some unemployment. At any given time, some people are changing jobs voluntarily, and some firms are closing their doors and dismissing their workers. Thus, the term *full employment* takes into account the normal amount of job turnover that always goes on. The unemployment rate reflecting normal job turnover is often called the **natural rate of unemployment.** When the economy is at full employment, the unemployment rate equals the natural rate of unemployment, which is estimated by economists to be currently about 5 or 6 percent. A similar concept applies to physical capital. Physical capital is considered to be fully utilized when most of it is being employed in production; some capital is always being modified, changed, or scrapped, so capital is never used 100 percent. When both labor and capital are fully utilized, the economy is at full employment, and the amount of output produced is called **full-employment output.** In the long run, we assume that the economy will be at full employment, so we show aggregate supply in Figure 12.3 as a vertical line labeled $LRAS$ (long-run aggregate supply) and indicate the amount of full-employment output as $\bar{Y}$. The line is vertical because the amount of full-employment output is not affected by the price level.

In the short run, the capital stock is fixed and cannot be adjusted. In addition, in the short run, we assume that producers of most goods and services are reluctant to change the prices of their products. Then, if the demand for their product is greater than they expected, they will supply goods from inventories they have built up, they will hire additional workers to produce more goods, or perhaps they will ask existing workers to work overtime. They may raise prices a bit, but, because they are not sure if the increase in demand is permanent or temporary, they will be reluctant to raise prices too much.

These assumptions about what firms do in the short run have implications

full employment the situation when all the capital and labor in the economy is being fully utilized

natural rate of unemployment the unemployment rate reflecting normal job turnover

full-employment output the amount of output produced when the economy is at full employment

FIGURE 12.3 Aggregate Supply

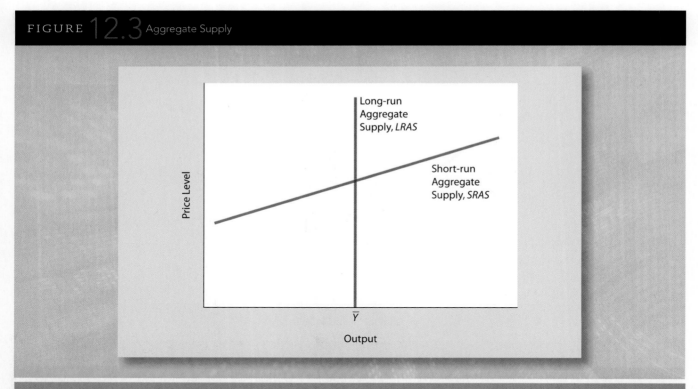

In the long run, the economy will be at full employment, so long-run aggregate supply (LRAS) is shown as a vertical line at the level of full-employment output $\bar{Y}$. In the short run, output increases with the price level. This positive relationship results in an upward-sloping short-run aggregate supply (SRAS) curve.

for the aggregate supply of goods and services. If the average level of prices in the economy rises, the managers of an individual firm might think that the increase in demand they are observing for their product has arisen because the demand curve for their product has shifted to the right. The firm's managers may not recognize that the firm's product has become relatively cheap because its price has not increased in line with other prices. As a result, the firm might raise its price a little, but it also will increase production. In a sense, the firm is fooled into producing too much. If there are many producers in this situation in the short run, each of whom is producing slightly more output and raising prices slightly, the price level (the average price of goods and services) is positively related to the aggregate amount of output produced by firms. This positive relationship results in an upward-sloping aggregate supply curve in the short run, as shown by the curve labeled *SRAS* (which stands for short-run aggregate supply) in Figure 12.3. Thus, the location of the *SRAS* curve depends on firms' expectations about the price level. When the price level is different from what firms expected but they do not recognize it, then the economy will operate at a point

on the *SRAS* curve instead of the *LRAS* curve. Over time, as firms understand what the price level is, their expectations come back into line with the actual price level, and the economy returns to the *LRAS* curve.

In the *AD–AS* model, we will use the short-run aggregate supply (*SRAS*) curve whenever we want to answer questions about the immediate impact of some change in the model's exogenous variables, and we will use the long-run aggregate supply (*LRAS*) curve whenever we want to know about the long-term impact of such a change.

12-1c Putting Aggregate Demand and Aggregate Supply Together

Now that we have derived all these various curves, we can put all the pieces together to form a complete model of the economy. The model can be used to find the two endogenous macroeconomic variables we are interested in: the price level and output. Because output equals income when the goods market is in equilibrium,

FIGURE 12.4 Equilibrium in the AD–AS Model

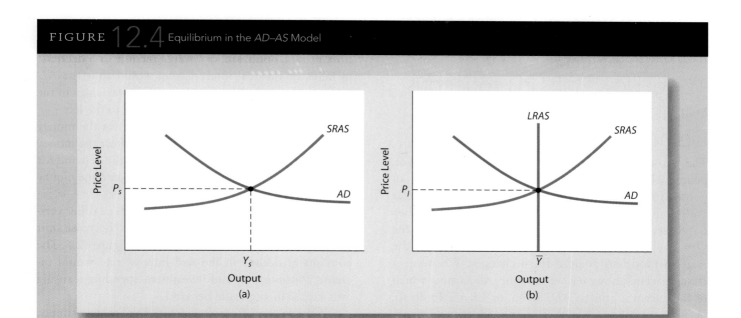

In the short run, equilibrium occurs at the intersection of the *AD* curve and the *SRAS* curve, thus determining the price level and output, as shown in panel (a). The short-run equilibrium level of output Y_s could be less than or greater than the full-employment level of output $\bar{Y}$. In the long run, as shown in panel (b), equilibrium occurs where the *AD* curve intersects the *LRAS* curve, which determines the price level and output. Note that in this case the intersection of the *AD* and *LRAS* curves is also where the *SRAS* curve intersects the other two.

we generally refer to output when drawing graphs of the aggregate-demand and aggregate-supply curves. In the short run, equilibrium occurs at the intersection of the *AD* curve and the *SRAS* curve, thus determining the price level and output, as shown in Figure 12.4a. The short-run equilibrium level of output Y_s could be less than or greater than the full-employment level of output $\bar{Y}$.

In the long run, as shown in Figure 12.4b, equilibrium occurs where the *AD* curve intersects the *LRAS* curve, which determines the price level and output. Note that in this case the intersection of the *AD* and *LRAS* curves is also where the *SRAS* curve intersects the other two, for reasons that will be explained shortly.

12-1d From the Short Run to the Long Run

In setting up the *AD–AS* model, we developed both a long-run and a short-run aggregate-supply curve because economists believe that differences in how supply responds to shocks in the economy are responsible for the fluctuations in economic variables that occur over the business cycle. To understand the business cycle, we would like to know why there is a difference between short- and long-run

aggregate supply and also what forces cause the economy to return to its long-run equilibrium.

What causes the short-run aggregate supply curve to differ from the long-run aggregate supply curve? In our discussion of the short-run aggregate supply curve, we noted that producers might have difficulty distinguishing a change in the prices of their own products from a rise in the overall price level. In addition, both wages and prices may be somewhat slow to adjust to a new long-run equilibrium. For example, wages may need to be negotiated between firms and labor unions. Firms may have distributed catalogs of their products, and they may hesitate to change their prices because of the cost of distributing new catalogs.

Given that misinterpretation of prices and slow adjustment of wages and prices cause the short-run aggregate supply curve to differ from the long-run aggregate supply curve, how does the economy make a transition from the short run to the long run? The answer is that the transition depends on the speed with which producers recognize the difference between changes in their own prices and the general price level and how quickly wages and prices adjust. Before the adjustment takes place, equilibrium is determined by the *AD* and *SRAS* curves, as in Figure 12.4a. After time passes and everyone adjusts, the economy moves to Figure 12.4b because the *SRAS* curve shifts until it moves to the point where the *AD* curve and *LRAS* curves intersect.

12-1e How Shifts in Exogenous Variables Affect Aggregate Demand and Aggregate Supply

The economy is constantly changing. For example, people change their demand for different types of goods, foreign economies go through business cycles and change the amounts of goods and services they purchase, the government changes its spending, and the OPEC oil cartel changes the price it sets. We can use the *AD–AS* model to analyze these changes. Whenever a change occurs, however, we must first determine which of the curves it affects: *AD*, *SRAS*, or *LRAS*. To do so, we now examine each of these curves, identify the exogenous variables that affect it, and show how they shift the curve.

Consider the *AD* curve. We need to know which direction it shifts when variables that affect it change. Because points on the *AD* curve are those for which both the market for goods and services and the money market are in equilibrium, we need to consider each market in turn.

The market for goods and services is affected by changes in future income, wealth, taxes, the real interest rate, future consumption, profits, business optimism, and foreign income. Because output (which equals current income) and the price level are plotted on the axes of the *AD* curve, a change in one of these two variables causes a movement along the curve, not a shift of the curve.

To analyze the impact on the *AD* curve of some event that causes a change in future income, wealth, taxes, the real interest rate, future consumption, profits, business optimism, or foreign income, we ask the question: If the price level or current income did not change, would the demand for goods and services increase or decrease? That is, would consumption, investment, net exports, or government spending increase or decrease? If demand would increase, then the *AD* curve would shift to the right; if demand would decrease, then the *AD* curve would shift to the left.

To illustrate such a shift in the *AD* curve, consider what would happen if corporate profits increased. The higher corporate profits encourage businesses to invest more and lead to increased consumption when those profits are received in the form of dividends by stockholders, so aggregate demand increases, thus shifting the *AD* curve to the right.

Factors that increase aggregate demand, including an increase in future income, wealth, future consumption, profits, optimism, or foreign income or a decrease in taxes or the real interest rate, would shift the *AD* curve to the right. Movements of these variables in the opposite direction would shift the curve to the left.

Next, consider the variables that affect the money market. The exogenous variables that affect the money market include any variables that affect the demand for money, such as the costs of using ATMs, and the money supply.

A decrease in the costs of using ATMs or other variables that cause the demand for money to decrease shift the money-demand curve to the left in Figure 12.5. The consequent decline in the real interest rate would increase consumption and investment spending, causing an increase in aggregate demand.

If the Federal Reserve increased the money supply, the quantity of money demanded would need to increase to restore equilibrium, as shown in Figure 12.6. Returning to equilibrium requires that the nominal interest rate decline, and assuming no change in the expected inflation rate, the real interest rate also would decline. The lower real interest rate would lead to a rise in consumption and investment spending, increasing aggregate demand.

What causes the aggregate supply curve to shift? In the long run, the aggregate supply curve's location is determined by total factor productivity and the size of both the capital stock and the labor supply. Changes in the inputs into the production process, such as the price and quantity of oil, can affect productivity and thus cause the *LRAS* curve to shift. When the *LRAS* curve shifts, the *SRAS* curve also shifts. If productivity increases or the capital stock or labor supply increases, the *LRAS* and *SRAS* curves shift to the right; conversely, if productivity declines or the capital stock or labor supply declines, the *LRAS* and *SRAS* curves shift to the left. In addition, the *SRAS* curve shifts when firms' expectations about the price level change or if the costs of producing output increase. The *SRAS* curve intersects the *LRAS* curve at the point where the expected price level equals the actual price level. As expectations about the price level decline, the *SRAS* curve shifts to the right, so the intersection of the *LRAS* and *SRAS* curves occurs at a lower price level; conversely, if expectations about the price level increase, the *SRAS* curve shifts to the left. Similarly, if the costs of production increase, firms want to produce less output and expect prices to rise, so the *SRAS* curve shifts to the left.

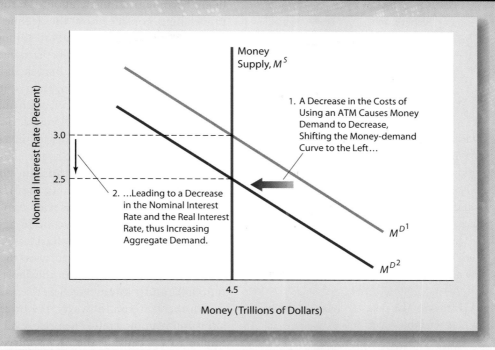

Decrease in the costs of using an ATM causes the demand for money to decrease, so the money-demand curve shifts to the left. The nominal interest rate declines, as shown in the graph, causing the real interest rate to decline, thus increasing aggregate demand.

FIGURE 12.6 The Money Market After an Increase in the Money Supply

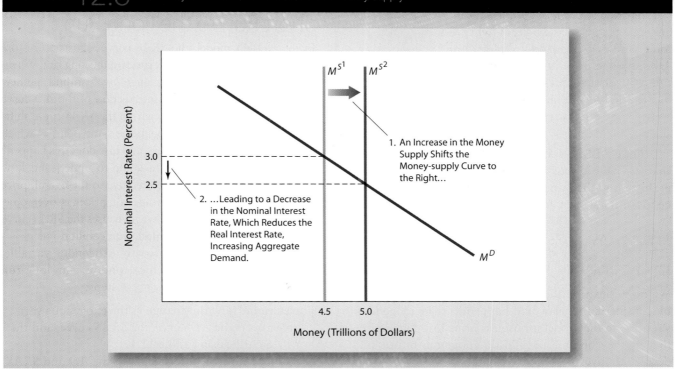

If the Federal Reserve increases the money supply, the quantity of money demanded would need to increase to restore equilibrium. Thus, the nominal interest rate would decline, so the real interest rate would decline, causing an increase in aggregate demand.

| TABLE 12.1 Shifts in the AD, LRAS, and SRAS Curves | | |

An Increase in	Causes This Curve to Shift	In This Direction
Future income	AD	Right
Wealth	AD	Right
Taxes	AD	Left
Real interest rate	AD	Left
Future consumption	AD	Right
Profits	AD	Right
Business optimism	AD	Right
Foreign income	AD	Right
Government spending	AD	Right
ATM costs or other variables that increase money demand	AD	Left
Money supply	AD	Right
Productivity	LRAS SRAS	Right Right
Capital stock	LRAS SRAS	Right Right
Labor force	LRAS SRAS	Right Right
Expected price level	SRAS	Left
Costs of producing output	SRAS	Left

Note: A *decrease* in an exogenous variable in the first column would lead to a shift of each curve in the opposite direction.

© Cengage Learning

Table 12.1 shows each exogenous variable that we have discussed so far, which of these curves is shifted by that variable, and in which direction the curve shifts.

12-1f An Example: A Drop in Business Optimism

We now illustrate the workings of the AD–AS model by considering what would happen to the endogenous variables in the model if business firms lost confidence; that is, they became pessimistic about the future and decided to invest less in new capital.

We begin with the economy in long-run equilibrium. The initial situation is illustrated in Figure 12.7 by the curves AD^1 and $SRAS^1$. Beginning from long-run equilibrium at point 1, imagine that business firms suddenly become pessimistic about the future. To analyze this change, consider how the decline in business optimism would affect the AD, SRAS, and LRAS curves. The decline in optimism is not permanent, so it will not affect the economy's capital stock, labor supply, and productivity in the long run; that is, it will not affect the LRAS curve. In addition, with no change in the expected price level, the SRAS curve does not shift. But the demand by business firms for investment goods is a part of aggregate demand, so the change in optimism will affect the AD curve. Because the change represents a decline in aggregate demand, the AD curve shifts to the left from AD^1 to AD^2, as shown in the graph.

In the short run, the decline in aggregate demand reduces the price level, so businesses produce fewer goods. The shift of the AD curve to the left means that there is a new equilibrium in the short run with lower output Y_2 and a lower price level P_2.

In the long run, however, the price level is able to adjust more completely. The price level declines further, falling to P_3, causing the SRAS curve to shift to the right from $SRAS^1$ to $SRAS^2$. This shift restores equilibrium at full-employment output. In the graph, the price level is now lower at P_3.

12-1g Adjustment from the Short Run to the Long Run

In the AD–AS model, the SRAS curve adjusts to restore equilibrium between the short run and the long run. Whenever an exogenous variable changes, we can find the new short-run equilibrium at the intersection of the AD curve and the SRAS curve. In the long run, the SRAS curve shifts left or right until it goes through the same point at which the AD and LRAS curves intersect. How does this happen? As time passes, business firms come to understand how their own prices have changed relative to the overall price level, and any stickiness of wages or prices is overcome. The adjustment of prices and wages causes the SRAS curve to shift left or right to restore long-run equilibrium.

In analyzing a change to any exogenous variable, we begin by assuming that the economy is in long-run equilibrium. Then we follow these steps:

1. Determine how the change in the exogenous variable affects the AD curve, the SRAS curve, and the LRAS curve, using Table 12.1.
2. Examine how the intersection of the AD and SRAS curves changes, affecting the price level and output in the short run.

FIGURE 12.7 Effects of a Decline in Business Optimism

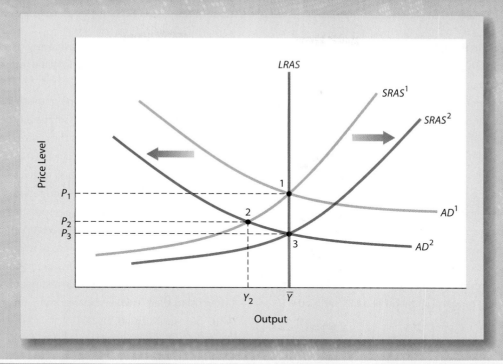

The economy begins in long-run equilibrium, as given by the AD^1 and $SRAS^1$ curves. If business firms suddenly become pessimistic about the future, the AD curve shifts to the left from AD^1 to AD^2. The result is a decline in output to Y_2 and a decline in the price level to P_2. In the long run, the price level declines further, falling to P_3, as the $SRAS$ curve shifts to the right from $SRAS^1$ to $SRAS^2$. This restores equilibrium at full-employment output.

3. Determine how the $SRAS$ curve must shift to restore long-run equilibrium; it must shift left or right to cross the point of intersection of the AD and $LRAS$ curves.

4. Determine the price level and output in the long run.

Following these steps will allow you to analyze a change in any exogenous variable.

The example of a change in business optimism is fairly typical of the response of the economy to shocks to components of aggregate demand. In the short run, output and the price level are affected. In the long run, however, output returns to its original full-employment level. The price level may differ in the long run from its original level, however.

The economy is constantly buffeted by changes in many different exogenous variables. Some such shocks cancel each other out and are not very noticeable. But some shocks are much bigger and have a major impact.

In this model, how does a recession occur? There must be a large change in some exogenous variable or several such shocks simultaneously. (One variable that frequently shifts dramatically in a recession is investment spending. See the Data Bank box "Investment Shocks and the Business Cycle.") For example, suppose that an international crisis caused the demand by other countries for U.S. goods to decline significantly. At the same time, suppose that businesses suddenly became more pessimistic about the possibilities for future profits. The declines in both net exports and investment would shift the AD curve to the left. The analysis would be just like that in Figure 12.7, in which output declines, causing a recession. The decline in output leads to a reduction in businesses' use of both capital and labor. As the economy eventually adjusts through a decline in the price level, output begins to rise again as the $SRAS$ curve shifts to the right until output returns to its equilibrium level. In the recovery phase of the expansion, output usually rises fairly rapidly. Once full employment is restored, the economy's growth follows its long-run trend.

Business cycles occur in the *AD–AS* model when there are shocks (sudden, unexpected changes) to a key variable in the model. In reality, the shocks that drive the business cycle frequently are associated with investment spending, even though investment spending is only about one-sixth of gross domestic product (GDP). Figure 12.A illustrates the notion that large shocks to investment occur over the business cycle by plotting the annual percentage change of investment compared with "Other GDP," which is all the components of GDP except investment (that is, consumption plus net exports plus government spending). The blue-shaded areas represent recessions.

You can see in the graph that other GDP grows at a fairly steady pace. Its growth rate almost never turns negative; it was negative in just four recessions and never fell more than 2 percent. Investment growth, on the other hand, shows dramatic swings over time, decreasing sharply in recessions and

rising sharply in most recoveries. In every recession, investment declines 5 percent or more, and in many recessions it declines 20 percent or more.

Why does investment decline so much in recessions? Investment occurs when business firms buy new machines, computers, and software so that they can increase the amount of goods and services they produce or when they replace obsolete machines, computers, and software. In a recession, though, people buy fewer goods and services, so firms do not need to increase production. As a result, they invest less than in expansions. In addition, part of investment is housing. But people do not build as many homes or renovate their homes in recessions because they may be worried about their incomes falling or losing their jobs. Thus, investment is very volatile, often rising sharply when expansions begin and falling sharply when recessions begin.

FIGURE 12.A Investment Growth and Other GDP Growth

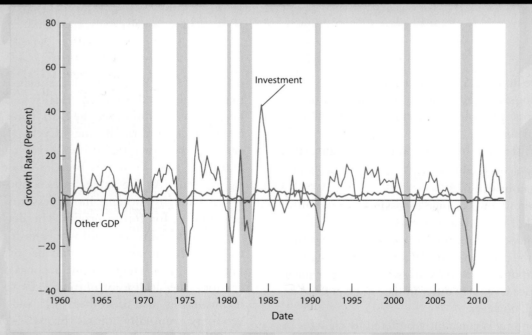

This graph shows time-series plots of the growth rate of investment and other GDP. You can see that investment growth declines sharply in recessions, whereas other GDP (all the components of GDP except investment) does not decline as much. Thus, changes in the growth of investment spending are responsible for much of the change in GDP growth over the business cycle.

1	The *AD–AS* model analyzes the economy by distinguishing aggregate demand (demand for goods and services) from aggregate supply (production of goods and services).
2	Aggregate demand consists of consumption, investment, net exports, and government spending. The aggregate-demand (*AD*) curve shows combinations of the price level and output for which there is equilibrium in both the market for goods and services and the money market
3	Aggregate supply is shown by the vertical *LRAS* curve in the long run and the upward-sloping *SRAS* curve in the short run.
4	Equilibrium in the *AD–AS* model occurs in the long run where the *AD* curve, *LRAS* curve, and *SRAS* curve all intersect. In the short run, equilibrium occurs where the *AD* curve intersects the *SRAS* curve.

12-2 Analyzing Policy Using the *AD–AS* Model

Government policymakers often take actions that attempt to affect output and the price level. In this section we analyze both monetary and fiscal policies using the *AD–AS* model. Monetary and fiscal policies have similar impacts on output and the price level, but they affect the real interest rate in different ways.

12-2a Monetary Policy

Monetary policy consists of Federal Reserve decisions about the amount of the money supply. We have seen that an increase in the money supply causes the *AD* curve to shift to the right and a decline in the money supply shifts the *AD* curve to the left.

Suppose that the economy is in a recession, as shown in Figure 12.8, in which the aggregate-demand curve (AD^1) intersects the short-run aggregate supply curve ($SRAS^1$) at point 1, which is to the left of the *LRAS* curve. Note that AD^1 and $SRAS^1$ intersect at output level Y_1, which is less than full-employment output $\overline{Y}$.

Monetary policy can return the economy to full employment. If the Fed engages in expansionary policy by increasing the money supply, it could restore equilibrium at full employment because the *AD* curve would shift from AD^1 to AD^2. In the graph, the new equilibrium occurs at point 2, at the intersection of the $SRAS^1$, *LRAS*,

and AD^2 curves, with output at its full-employment level $\overline{Y}$ and a higher price level P_2.

Notice the consequences of expansionary monetary policy in this situation. If policy is enacted quickly, then full employment is restored quickly. In addition, the price level is higher than before.

What would have happened if the Fed had not changed monetary policy? In that case, the *SRAS* curve would shift gradually to the right from $SRAS^1$ to $SRAS^2$; there would have been no shift in the aggregate-demand curve, which would have remained at AD^1. Equilibrium occurs at point 3, which is where $SRAS^2$ intersects AD^1 and *LRAS*. Notice that output is at its full-employment level $\overline{Y}$, and the price level P_3 is lower.

Thus, the *AD–AS* model allows us to compare the outcome of expansionary monetary policy with no change in policy. These results are summarized in Table 12.2.

What impact would expansionary monetary policy have if the economy began at full employment rather than in a recession? In that case, output might rise for

TABLE **12.2**	Impact of Expansionary Monetary Policy in a Recession	
Variable	**Expansionary Monetary Policy**	**No Change in Monetary Policy**
Output	Returns to full-employment level quickly	Stays below full-employment level for prolonged period
Price level	Rises quickly	Declines slowly

FIGURE 12.8 Effects of an Increase in the Money Supply in a Recession

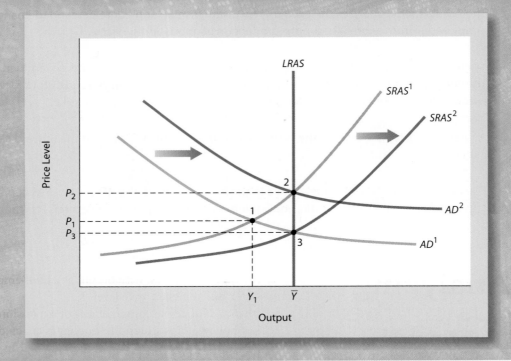

The economy is shown to be in a recession because the aggregate-demand curve (AD^1) intersects the short-run aggregate supply curve ($SRAS^1$) at point 1, which is to the left of the $LRAS$ curve. Note that AD^1 and $SRAS^1$ intersect at output level Y_1, which is less than full-employment output $\bar{Y}$. If the Fed engages in expansionary policy by increasing the money supply, it could shift the AD curve from AD^1 to AD^2. The new equilibrium occurs at point 2, with output at its full-employment level $\bar{Y}$ and a higher price level P_2. If the Fed does not use monetary policy, the economy eventually will return to equilibrium as the price level declines, causing the $SRAS$ curve to shift to the right from $SRAS^1$ to $SRAS^2$. Equilibrium is restored at a lower price level than when expansionary monetary policy is used; output is identical.

a short time beyond its full-employment level $\bar{Y}$. Output can exceed its full-employment level when firms ask workers to put in overtime, and they run their plants all day and all night. However, when output is above the full-employment level, there is a scarcity of resources and a shortage of workers. Consequently, the prices of resources rise, as do wages and salaries for workers. These higher costs to businesses then would cause the short-run aggregate supply curve to shift to the left, reflecting the higher resource costs.

Figure 12.9 illustrates this situation. The economy begins at full employment, with short-run aggregate supply curve $SRAS^1$ and aggregate demand curve AD^1 intersecting at point 1, which is on the $LRAS$ curve. Output is at its full-employment level $\bar{Y}$.

An increase in the money supply shifts the AD curve to the right from AD^1 to AD^2. Output rises from $\bar{Y}$ to Y_2, and the price level rises from P_1 to P_2. Because output is above its full-employment level, over time, the $SRAS$ curve shifts to the left from $SRAS^1$ to $SRAS^2$. As

it does so, output declines from Y_2 to $\bar{Y}$, and the price level rises from P_2 to P_3. Equilibrium occurs at point 3 on the graph, where output is at its full-employment level $\bar{Y}$, but the price level P_3 is higher.

Obviously, if monetary policy did not change and the economy were in the initial situation of full employment, then output and the price level would be unchanged at point 1. The results are summarized in Table 12.3.

TABLE 12.3 Impact of Expansionary Monetary Policy at Full Employment

Variable	Expansionary Monetary Policy	No Change in Monetary Policy
Output	Rises above full-employment level temporarily, then returns	Stays at full-employment level
Price level	Rises relatively quickly as AD curve shifts, then rises more as $SRAS$ shifts	No change

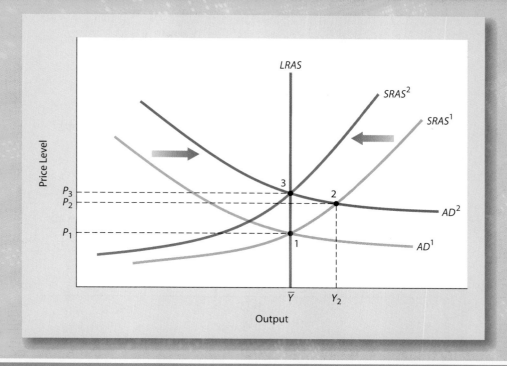

The economy begins at full employment, with short-run aggregate supply curve $SRAS^1$ and aggregate demand curve AD^1 intersecting at point 1, which is on the *LRAS* curve. Output is at its full-employment level $\bar{Y}$. An increase in the money supply shifts the *AD* curve to the right from AD^1 to AD^2. Output rises from $\bar{Y}$ to Y_2, and the price level rises from P_1 to P_2. Because output is above its full-employment level, the *SRAS* curve shifts gradually to the left from $SRAS^1$ to $SRAS^2$. As it does so, output declines from Y_2 to $\bar{Y}$, and the price level rises from P_2 to P_3. Equilibrium occurs at point 3 on the graph.

At first, you might think that using expansionary monetary policy when the economy is at full employment is a good thing; after all, output becomes higher temporarily. But do the costs to the economy because of fluctuations in output and the higher price level exceed the benefits of the higher temporary output? We will look more closely at these costs and benefits in Chapter 17.

If monetary policymakers want to reduce the price level, what should they do? According to this model, they will want to use contractionary monetary policy, reducing the money supply. This will have the opposite effects of those shown in Table 12.3. Output will fall temporarily, and the price level will be permanently lower. Policymakers must make a tradeoff between short-term pain (output below its full-employment level) and long-term gain (lower prices), which we will discuss in greater detail in Chapter 17.

12-2b Effects of Fiscal Policy

The analysis of fiscal policy is similar in impact to that of monetary policy. Of course, fiscal policy works through different channels: through government action to change taxes and government expenditures. Government spending is a component of aggregate demand, and thus changes in government spending affect aggregate demand directly. Changes in taxes also may affect aggregate demand because a decline in taxes might boost spending by consumers or businesses (although in Chapter 13 we will see why a change in taxes might have no effect on spending).

Consider what happens in a recession when the government increases spending. In Figure 12.10, the short-run aggregate supply curve ($SRAS^1$) intersects the aggregate demand curve (AD^1) curve to the left of the *LRAS* curve, so output Y_1 is less than its full-employment level $\bar{Y}$. The price level is P_1.

If the government increases its spending sufficiently, the *AD* curve shifts from AD^1 to AD^2. Equilibrium would occur at point 2 in the graph. This would return output to its full-employment level $\bar{Y}$, and the price level would rise to P_2.

What would happen if there were no change in fiscal policy? As before, the return to full-employment

FIGURE 12.10 Effects of an Increase in Government Spending in a Recession

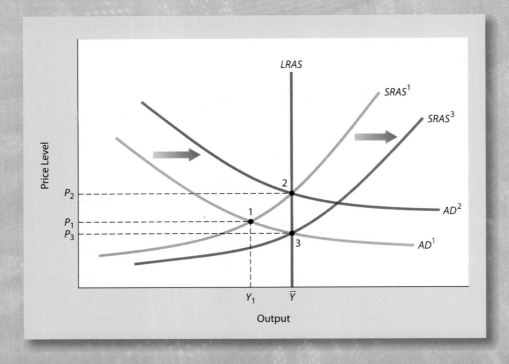

This graph shows the economy in a recession. The short-run aggregate supply curve (SRAS^1) intersects the aggregate demand curve (AD^1) to the left of the LRAS curve, so output Y_1 is less than its full-employment level $\bar{Y}$. If the government increases its spending sufficiently, the AD curve shifts from AD^1 to AD^2. Equilibrium would occur at point 2 in the graph. This would return output to its full-employment level $\bar{Y}$, and the price level would rise to P_2. If the government does not use expansionary policy, the economy eventually will return to equilibrium as the price level declines, causing the SRAS curve to shift to the right from SRAS^1 to SRAS^3. Equilibrium is restored at a lower price level than when expansionary fiscal policy is used; output is identical.

equilibrium would take place more slowly through the adjustment of prices. The price level would decline gradually, causing the SRAS curve to shift to the right from SRAS^1 to SRAS^3. The results are summarized in Table 12.4.

A comparison of the results in Table 12.4 with those in Table 12.2 shows that there is no difference between

the use of fiscal policy and monetary policy to combat recessions in our AD–AS model. However, in more sophisticated models, one difference between fiscal policy and monetary policy is the direction of change of the real interest rate; it rises if the government uses fiscal policy but declines if the government uses monetary policy. This difference suggests that monetary and fiscal policy should be coordinated; using both policies together would allow the government to keep the real interest rate from changing when it uses both fiscal and monetary policy.

Thus, either fiscal or monetary policy can be used to combat recessions, but is it wise to do so? Although the AD–AS model suggests some scope for government action in combating recessions, in practice, policymakers find it very difficult to know how much to do, that is, how much to increase the money supply or how much to increase government spending. To understand these issues, we now turn to how economists have tried to apply the AD–AS model in practice.

TABLE 12.4 Impact of Expansionary Fiscal Policy in a Recession

Variable	Expansionary Monetary Policy	No Change in Monetary Policy
Output	Returns to full-employment level quickly	Stays below full-employment level for prolonged period
Price level	Rises quickly	Declines slowly

1 The *AD–AS* model shows that monetary policy and fiscal policy can be used to combat recessions. Increases in the money supply or increases in government spending can increase output and get the economy out of a recession. If such policies are not used, the economy will return slowly to full employment.

2 If expansionary monetary policy or fiscal policy is used when the economy is at full employment, the price level will increase.

12-3 Large Structural Macroeconomic Models

Economists have spent decades trying to capture the essence of macroeconomic theory, especially the *AD–AS* model, in computer models that can be used for both forecasting and understanding the effects of changes in monetary and fiscal policy. The earliest such efforts came about in the 1950s and 1960s and led to the formation of private-sector forecasting companies that used huge amounts of computing power to forecast with models consisting of hundreds of equations to capture the behavior of many different economic variables. Such work continues today at private forecasting companies, such as Macroeconomic Advisers, and at the Federal Reserve Board of Governors, where economists use more sophisticated versions of the earlier models.

These models are called **large structural macro-economic models** because they consist of hundreds of equations that are thought to model the elements of the entire economy. They stand in contrast to smaller models developed in the past two decades, which use only a few equations and describe only a few of the economy's major variables.

The development of large structural macroeconomic models began in the 1950s and continued in the 1960s and 1970s. Lawrence Klein of the University of Pennsylvania was a key figure in developing such models, for which he was awarded the Nobel Prize in economics in 1980. Klein and his colleagues used the *AD–AS* model as a basic framework, found data to fit the model, developed many more sectors of the model than we described earlier in this chapter, and coded all of this into a large mainframe computer. They then generated forecasts and offered policy advice based on the model.

The development of these models was spearheaded by Keynesian economists, who focused on how shocks to aggregate demand led to business cycles and how the government could use fiscal and monetary policies to reduce the severity of the business cycle.

large structural macroeconomic models models with many equations that describe the economy in great detail; the models are based on the assumption that their equations do not change over time

The large structural macroeconomic models represented the state of the art in econometric modeling for many years, employing the fanciest computational techniques around. Economists used the models to analyze historical events, such as the Great Depression. Policymakers used the models to guide policy. At the Federal Reserve, for example, a large structural macroeconomic model was used to examine how the economy was likely to respond to changes in monetary policy. The Fed policymakers could then tinker with alternative policies and investigate the impact of such changes in the model before trying them out in the real world. Finally, economists used the models to forecast the economy. This turned out to be a most lucrative use. Business firms desired forecasts so that they could plan the amount of output to produce and could form sensible expectations of future prices, and numerous companies started selling them forecasts based on large structural macroeconomic models.

Maintaining these large models was not easy, however. Because the models needed data from many sectors of the economy, hundreds of labor hours were required each month just to keep the data in the models updated. Forecasters discovered that the equations in the models tended to break down; that is, errors made in one period would persist in later periods. To prevent persistent forecast errors, the forecasters started to "add-factor" the models, using their best guesses to change some of the model equations. But then the question arises: Is the forecast being generated by objective data, or is it merely reflecting the subjective opinions of the person running the model?

Economists began to question the structure of the models. Often the models were internally inconsistent; that is, one part of the model contradicted another part. Sometimes in the models variables that were closely related to exogenous variables were treated as endogenous. For example, foreign output often was treated as an exogenous variable that affected the demand for U.S. exports, yet the strength of the U.S. economy was vital for the health of many foreign economies. A second problem with the structure of the models was that individual equations in the model were estimated in isolation from one another when economic theory would suggest that these equations would be interrelated. For example, consumption of durable goods is closely related to consumption of nondurable goods and consumption of services. Yet equations for each of these components of consumption were estimated as if they were independent of each other.

These types of inconsistencies made forecasting with large structural macroeconomic models seem to be more art than science. As a result, economists became skeptical of their value. This skepticism solidified when the models began making erroneous forecasts in much of the 1970s, convincing many economists that a new approach to creating models for forecasting and analysis was needed. Those new models are the subject of Chapter 13. For now, we will look at how the large structural models have been used to analyze changes in policy, and what those models told us about policy in the 1970s.

RECAP

1 Economists used the *AD–AS* model as the basic framework for large structural macroeconomic models that provided analysis and forecasts of many variables.

2 Large structural macroeconomic models were used by policymakers in analyzing the consequences of their actions and by businesses in planning production and forecasting prices.

3 The large structural macroeconomic models developed a number of inconsistencies over time and began making erroneous forecasts in the 1970s.

12-4 Keynesians versus Classicals

The *AD–AS* model in this chapter can be used to illustrate the differences between Keynesian and classical macroeconomists. The two main camps of macroeconomics differ in three major ways, all of which can be seen in the *AD–AS* model. They differ in their views on (1) the speed with which the price level adjusts to restore general equilibrium following a shock to the economy, (2) the knowledge that policymakers possess about the state of the economy, and (3) the implications for the government's ability to engage in stabilization policy.

The primary disagreement between Keynesians and classicals is in the length of time they think it takes for prices and wages to change to restore general equilibrium in the economy. Keynesians generally think it takes a long time for this process to occur, so they think government policymakers have a lot of time to act to help the economy using monetary and fiscal policy. But classical economists think the price-adjustment process works fairly quickly, so that government policy is not needed, as the *SRAS* curve will adjust fairly quickly to restore general equilibrium.

Keynesians and classicals also differ in their beliefs about the ability of policymakers to understand the current state of the economy. In the *AD–AS* model, using monetary policy or fiscal policy effectively requires the policymakers to know where the *LRAS* curve is located. Keynesians believe that policymakers know enough about the location of the *LRAS* curve to be able to use policy effectively. But classical macroeconomists are skeptical because they think it is very difficult to figure out the sources of shocks to the economy. They worry that Keynesians believe that most shocks to the economy are shocks to aggregate demand, but classicals think most shocks are to long-run aggregate supply. If policymakers do not understand where the *LRAS* curve is, perhaps because they cannot tell if the shock to the economy is to aggregate demand or aggregate supply, then they may make severe policy errors. For example, in the 1970s, the Fed used expansionary monetary policy to stimulate the economy, but later we learned that the main shocks to the economy were to aggregate supply, so the Fed's stimulus merely caused inflation and could not increase output.

For these reasons, Keynesians and classicals differ sharply on the ability of policymakers to improve the economy. Keynesians think that monetary policy and fiscal policy can be used to stimulate the economy when it is weak and to slow the economy down when it is strong, keeping output and inflation stable. But classicals believe that the economy will adjust on its own without government policy intervention and that the lack of solid information on the location of the *LRAS*

curve means that policymakers are likely to make mistakes using policy. Therefore, classicals prefer that government policymakers do little to attempt to stabilize the economy.

The debate between Keynesians and classicals intensified following the Great Recession. From 2008 to 2013, Keynesians argued that the main shock was to aggregate demand, not aggregate supply, so the use of monetary and fiscal policy to increase aggregate demand was appropriate. But classicals viewed the shock as mainly affecting aggregate supply, especially because so much time passed, so that surely the price level would have adjusted by 2013 to restore general equilibrium. In support of the classical position, the attempt to use expansionary monetary policy did not seem to be very successful, though perhaps the economy would have done enough worse without it. In support of the Keynesian position, the fact that inflation remained very low in the face of large increases in the money supply suggests that the economy was not on the *LRAS* curve.

RECAP

1 Keynesians think prices and wages adjust slowly, so it takes the economy a long time to return to general equilibrium following a shock. Classicals believe that prices and wages adjust quickly, so the economy is not out of general equilibrium very long.

2 Keynesians believe that policymakers understand enough about the state of the economy and the location of the *LRAS* curve that they can stabilize the economy by using the appropriate level of monetary and fiscal policy. Classicals disagree and cite evidence from the 1970s suggesting that lack of knowledge about the economy can lead policymakers to make poor choices, leading to inflation.

3 Keynesians believe that policymakers can and should act to offset shocks to the economy. Classicals do not think such policy actions are warranted.

Policy→Perspective   Did Large Macro Models Mislead Policymakers in the 1970s

As the 1970s began, macroeconomists were confident that they understood the economy. In the 1960s, they used large structural macroeconomic models and Keynesian theories about manipulating the economy, leading to the longest economic expansion in U.S. history, far longer than any earlier economic expansion.

The expansion began in February 1961 and did not end until December 1969. The 106-month-long expansion was more than two years longer than the most lengthy expansion before, which occurred in the 80 months from June 1938 to February 1945—an expansion led by the military buildup during World War II.

(continued)

In the early 1970s, economists were so confident of their ability to manage the economy successfully that they began talking about how there would be no more need to study macroeconomics at all; the field had been exhausted, and there was nothing else to learn. Professors felt that macroeconomics had become obsolete as a field of study and urged their students to study microeconomics instead, where there was much work to do.

One major assumption of the Keynesian theory embedded in the large structural macroeconomic models was a tradeoff between unemployment and inflation. In most business cycles, inflation and unemployment moved in opposite directions. Unemployment rose in recessions and fell in expansions, whereas inflation rose in expansions and fell in recessions. The tradeoff between inflation and unemployment was a key part of the large structural macroeconomic models and an integral part of Keynesian theory.

In the period from 1973 to 1975, however, something unusual happened. In large part because of higher oil prices dictated by OPEC's monopoly, inflation rose during the recession that lasted from November 1973 to March 1975, peaking at over 12 percent in the middle of the recession. According to both Keynesian theory and the large structural macroeconomic models, the simultaneous increase in the unemployment rate and the inflation rate should not have happened. Forecasters using such models were continually predicting that inflation would decline, and they were continually wrong. As the government used its tools of expansionary monetary and fiscal policy, the large models kept predicting a quick end to the recession, which also did not occur.

The rest of the decade was no better. Although the recession finally ended in early 1975, the economy remained below full-employment output, according to the models. The models were correct in predicting that inflation would decline in the mid-1970s. And with economic performance continuing to be sluggish, the models projected inflation to continue to fall after that, but instead it began rising in 1977 and reached unprecedented heights (exceeding 14 percent) during the recession

rational expectations
the notion that people use all available information in making their economic decisions

that began in January 1980. Again, both Keynesian theory and the large models failed to predict the magnitude or the direction of changes in the inflation rate.

Clearly, economists' confidence in their ability to manage the economy stemmed from their success in the 1960s. But economists are supposed to be a skeptical lot, so it is surprising that they were so self-deceived to believe that they had solved all the major macroeconomic problems by the early 1970s.

Some economists had been skeptical of Keynesian theory and of the large macroeconomic models all along. They inspected the foundations of the theory and the models and found them lacking, especially in how they treated people's expectations for the future. These skeptics were especially critical of the types of policy analyses suggested by such models, and they developed an alternative view of macroeconomics during the late 1970s and early 1980s in what is known as the *rational-expectations revolution.*

Rational expectations means that people use all available information in making their economic decisions. By contrast, the large structural macroeconomic models assumed that people did not have rational expectations. Instead, people were viewed as short-sighted, basing their expectations only on past data, and ignoring other information.

Here is an example. The large macro models take the expected inflation rate in the future as something that can be estimated at a point in time. Thus, for example, the model might have estimated in mid-1973 that the expected inflation rate for the next year would be 6 percent. Economists using the model to analyze monetary policy would take the expected inflation rate as given at 6 percent and then analyze what would happen if the Fed increased the money supply substantially to generate faster economic growth. Thus, the model failed to account for the fact that people's inflation expectations are based on what monetary policy is likely to do. In the 1970s, this proved to be the undoing of the large structural macroeconomic models. The models failed to predict inflation, and they were poor indicators of people's inflation expectations. The models misled the policymakers to conduct a monetary policy that was far too expansionary in the 1970s, resulting in an annual average inflation rate of 8.7 percent from 1973 to 1982. Under rational expectations, people anticipate what the Fed is likely to do.

That is, they observe the Fed's behavior, and if they anticipate that the Fed will increase the growth rate of the money supply, they expect higher inflation. Thus, the model's assumption that expected inflation is independent of monetary policy is incorrect and misleading.

Thus, poor performance by the large structural macroeconomic models may have played a significant role in the high inflation rates of the 1970s. Inflation eventually came down in the early 1980s, but at a substantial cost in terms of economic performance. Monetary policy was very tight from 1979 to 1982 in an effort to wring inflation out of the system. Two recessions occurred in that short time span.

In retrospect, it is not that hard to see what went wrong with the large structural macro models. Nobel Laureate Robert E. Lucas Jr. argued that the large structural macroeconomic models were flawed in a way that could not be fixed. Lucas argued that people and firms make decisions that depend on what they think policymakers will do so that ". . . any change in policy will systematically alter the structure of econometric models."[1] This argument has come to be known as the **Lucas critique.** As we shall see in the next chapter, dealing with the Lucas critique is very difficult. However, as Lucas and his frequent coauthor Thomas Sargent put it, ". . . our intent is to establish that the difficulties are *fatal:* that modern macroeconomic models are of *no* value in guiding policy and that this

condition will not be remedied by modifications along any line which is currently being pursued."[2]

Because the large macro models did not allow for the idea that people learn about the policy process, the models were wrong when it mattered most. If inflation had remained 2 to 3 percent per year, no one would have paid much attention to how monetary policy was set. But because inflation began rising so much, people began to pay attention to it and to examine what policymakers were planning to do.

Lucas critique the argument that a change in policy will systematically alter the structure of econometric models

Thus, to understand the economy, we must model peoples' expectations. The rational-expectations revolution led by Lucas pointed out the vital nature of peoples' expectations clearly and convincingly in the late 1970s, leading economists to pursue an entirely different modeling strategy, as we will see in Chapter 13. Unfortunately, the damage to the economy had already been done. The only hope is that policymakers learned from their mistakes in the 1970s and will never repeat them. However, the economics profession is partly to blame as well—its overconfidence growing out of the 1960s led policymakers down the wrong path. Today, forecasters and policymakers still use variants of the large structural macroeconomic models from the 1970s, but they incorporate rational expectations into the models' structures.

[1] Robert E. Lucas Jr., "Econometric Policy Evaluation: A Critique," *Carnegie-Rochester Conference Series on Public Policy* 1 (1976), p. 41.

[2] Robert E. Lucas Jr. and Thomas J. Sargent, "After Keynesian Macroeconomics." *After the Phillips Curve: Persistence of High Inflation and High Unemployment,* Federal Reserve Bank of Boston, conference series 19, 1978, p. 50.

RECAP

1 The success of the large structural macroeconomic models in the 1960s made macroeconomists overconfident. But reality struck when both unemployment and inflation rose in the 1970s.

2 The downfall of large macro models arose because they did not adequately model people's expectations. Further, the models were subject to the Lucas critique because they did not allow the model's equations to change when policy changed.

Review Questions and Problems

Review Questions

1 What are the two equilibrium conditions needed to determine points on the *AD* curve?

2 Explain the major components of the market for goods and services. What key macroeconomic variables influence spending on those components?

3 What does it mean to say the economy is "at full-employment output"?

4 Why does the *SRAS* curve slope upward?

5 Why is the *LRAS* curve vertical?

6 How does the economy adjust from the short run, in which the *AD* curve intersects the *SRAS* curve at a point that is not on the *LRAS* curve, to the long run, in which all three curves intersect at a common point?

7 What are the consequences of an increase in the money supply on output and the price level? Does your answer depend on where the economy starts (whether it is in long-run equilibrium or not)?

8 Describe the major differences between classical and Keynesian macroeconomists and what they think about the ability of fiscal and monetary policy to control the economy.

9 How did the overconfidence of macroeconomists after the long expansion of the 1960s lead to the inflation of the 1970s?

10 What is the Lucas critique, and how did it expose a fatal flaw in large structural macroeconomic models?

Analytical Problems

11 Describe how a decrease in government defense spending causes the *AD* curve to shift. What is the effect on the price level and output in the short run? In the long run?

12 Show the impact of a reduction in the money supply on the economy. You may assume that the economy begins in long-run equilibrium. Be sure to show the impact on output and the price level in both the short and the long run.

13 Suppose that the government imposed a $1 tax each time someone used an ATM. How would this tax affect output and the price level in the short and the long run?

14 In the late 1990s, a huge increase in the value of the stock market increased the wealth of many consumers. Show how this increase in wealth affected consumption spending, aggregate demand, output, and the price level in the short and the long run.

15 Suppose continued terrorist activity forces business firms and government to devote additional resources to law enforcement and military force, causing a permanent reduction in business productivity. Show the impact in the *AD–AS* model on the long-run level of output and the price level. What is likely to happen to consumption and investment as a result?

16 Suppose that an increase in people's expected inflation rate in the coming year would reduce their demand for money. How would a shock to expected inflation affect output and the price level in the short run and in general equilibrium?

CHAPTER 13

Yadid Levy/Alamy

MODERN MACROECONOMIC MODELS

To understand the long-term growth of the economy and the business cycle, we need to understand the

major factors that influence the economy. In Chapter 12 we learned about the aggregate-demand/ aggregate-supply (*AD–AS*) model, which is an approach to understanding the macroeconomy that was refined in its current form over 30 years ago. In this chapter we examine the two main approaches economists have developed to build macroeconomic models during the past 20 years. The first approach begins with economic theory and attempts to build an economic model that improves on the large structural macroeconomic models of the 1960s and 1970s. Improvement comes from better descriptions of the relationships between variables over time, along with detailed microeconomic foundations, including a model of how people form expectations. The second approach begins by ignoring economic theory altogether and just examining the statistical relationships among economic variables. Further developments of this approach use a few ideas from economic theory to help figure out how policy affects the economy.

Economists have used both approaches to analyze the effects of government policy. Government policymakers would like to pursue policies that increase economic growth and stabilize the business cycle while minimizing the rise in unemployment during recessions and the rise in inflation during expansions. Economists use the models discussed in this chapter to advise policymakers.

13-1 Dynamic Models

The *AD–AS* model of Chapter 12 is a static model that economists criticize for its inconsistent treatment of variables, inadequate treatment of expectations, and susceptibility to the Lucas critique. A **dynamic model** is a model in which actions that occur at one time affect what happens at other times. A model that is not dynamic is called a **static model** because it focuses on what is happening at just one point in time. The main advantages of using dynamic models are that (1) they allow us to model how people form expectations about future economic variables and investigate the role of expectations in influencing the economy, thus not falling prey to the Lucas critique, and (2) they allow us to examine how people are affected by policy actions because the models describe the microeconomic foundations of the macroeconomy. A **model with microeconomic foundations** is based on the decisions of economic agents (rather than starting with equations that describe aggregates, such as aggregate consumption spending, as in the *AD–AS* model). **Economic agents** are households, business firms, governments, and foreigners who make decisions about purchasing or selling goods and services, saving or borrowing, and investing in physical capital. The disadvantage of dynamic models is that they are more complicated than static models.

In this section we develop a dynamic model of consumption spending to illustrate why a dynamic model with microeconomic foundations that incorporates people's expectations is vital for understanding how government policy works. To keep the model simple, we focus just on consumer spending and ignore investment in physical capital, government spending, and net exports.

13-1a A Two-Period Model of Consumption and Saving

We illustrate how dynamic models work using a two-period model of consumption and saving. We make a number of simplifying assumptions to focus on the key elements

dynamic model a model in which actions that occur at one time affect what happens at other times

static model a model that focuses on what is happening at just one point in time

model with microeconomic foundations a model that is based on the decisions of economic agents

economic agents households, business firms, governments, and foreigners who make decisions about purchasing or selling goods and services, saving or borrowing, and investing in physical capital

A dynamic model with microeconomic foundations explains the shopping behavior of economic agents, such as the consumers in this photo.

of people's lifetime spending decisions. We assume that the only economic agents are households and that each household lives for two periods, which we call *period 1* and *period 2*. Each period is fairly long, perhaps 35 years.

Consider a single household and the decisions it makes. Suppose that the household knows what its wwww will be in both periods—$50,000 in period 1 and $75,000 in period 2. Suppose also that either the household can borrow some amount in period 1 and repay that amount plus interest in period 2, or it can save in period 1 and get its savings back plus interest in period 2. The interest rate is 50 percent for either borrowing or lending. (An interest rate of 50 percent might seem high, but remember that a period is about 35 years, so the interest rate averages just over 1 percent per year.) Finally, suppose that there is one consumer good, with a price of $1 per unit in both periods. Because the model assumes the same price in both periods, the inflation rate is zero, so the nominal interest rate equals the real interest rate; both are 50 percent.

Income and the interest rate determine the budget constraint. If this household decides not to borrow or save in period 1, then it would spend $50,000 on the good in period 1 and $75,000 in period 2. Because the price of the consumption good is $1, the household would buy 50,000 goods in period 1 and 75,000 goods in period 2.

If the household decided to save all its income in period 1, not purchasing any goods, its savings would be $50,000. In period 2, the household would receive interest on its savings of

$$\$50,000 \times 0.50 = \$25,000$$

In addition, it would receive repayment of its principal amount of $50,000, and it would receive its period 2 income of $75,000, so its total spending in period 2 would be

$$\$25,000 + \$50,000 + \$75,000 = \$150,000$$

Alternatively, the household might borrow as much as it could and promise to repay the lender with its $75,000 of income in period 2. How much could it borrow? With the interest rate equal to 50 percent, it could borrow as much as

$$\frac{\$75,000}{1.50} = \$50,000$$

By doing so, it would pay interest in period 2 of $50,000 × 0.50 = $25,000 and repay the principal borrowed of $50,000, for a total of $75,000. If the household were to borrow $50,000 in period 1, it would be able to buy consumption goods worth $100,000 in period 1 using its $50,000 of income plus its $50,000 in borrowed funds.

These three possibilities are only a few of the choices available to the household. It also could borrow any amount between $0 and $50,000, or it could save any amount between $0 and $50,000. All these possibilities are shown in Figure 13.1, with dots indicating the three points just described. One point, with consumption in period 1 of 50,000 goods and consumption in period 2 of 75,000 goods, is labeled *Consumption with no borrowing or lending*, which is the first point described. Another point, labeled *Consume all in period 2*, is the second point described, in which the household saves all its income from period 1. A third point, labeled *Consume all in period 1*, is described as the case where the household borrows against its entire income from period 2.

Note in the graph that these three points lie on a straight line. Any other amount of borrowing or lending the household chooses to do is also on that line, which we call the **budget constraint (or budget line)** because it shows all the possible amounts the household can consume, given its budget or income.

A useful way to think about the budget constraint is to use the concept of present value from Chapter 4. The present value of the household's income is

$$\frac{\$50,000}{(1.50)^0} + \frac{\$75,000}{(1.50)^1} = \$50,000 + \$50,000 = \$100,000$$

Note that $100,000 is the amount the household could consume in period 1 if it borrowed everything it could in period 1, spending that amount along with its income from period 1. Each point on the budget line shown in Figure 13.1 has the same present value.

With all these choices, which point is the household likely to choose? That depends on its preferences. Some households will be impatient, desiring more goods today and fewer in the future. They will choose to consume more than 50,000 goods in period 1, which means that they must borrow. As a result, they will consume fewer than 75,000 goods in period 2.

FIGURE 13.1 The Budget Constraint in the Two-Period Model

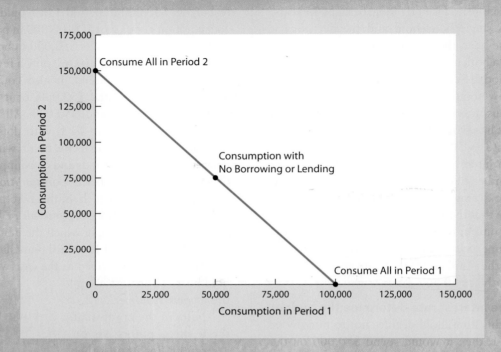

In the two-period model, the household faces a budget constraint based on its income in each period. If the household spends its income each period, it consumes at the point labeled *Consumption with no borrowing or lending*. If the household borrows as much as it can, it reaches the point labeled *Consume all in period 1*. If the household saves as much as it can, it reaches the point labeled *Consume all in period 2*. Intermediate amounts of borrowing or saving allow the household to reach any other point on the budget constraint.

Other households that have the same budget constraint might be more patient. They may choose to be on a point on the budget constraint such that they consume fewer than 50,000 goods in period 1 and more than 75,000 in period 2, which means that they will save in period 1.

Thus, different households facing the same budget line will choose to consume at different points on the budget constraint because they have different preferences—they have differing degrees of patience. In addition, of course, different households may have different amounts of income and thus will choose to consume different amounts.

A change in income affects consumption. What would happen in this model if a household's income in period 1 were higher? Suppose that instead of receiving income of $50,000 in period 1, the household's income were $70,000 in period 1. The household could consume more than before in period 1, in period 2, or in both periods. If the household were to spend the entire

present value of its income in period 1, it would be able to spend

$$\frac{\$70{,}000}{(1.50)^0} + \frac{\$75{,}000}{(1.50)^1} = \$70{,}000 + \$50{,}000 = \$120{,}000$$

Thus, the $20,000 of extra income in period 1 allows the household to purchase an extra 20,000 goods in period 1.

What if the household were to save all its income from period 1? Then its spending in period 2 would be

$$(\$70{,}000 \times 0.50) + \$70{,}000 + \$75{,}000 = \$180{,}000$$

In this case, the household is able to consume an extra 30,000 goods compared with the initial situation in which its income in period 1 was $50,000.

If we plot the initial budget constraint and the new one (Figure 13.2), we see that the increased income in period 1 leads to a parallel shift in the budget constraint.

FIGURE 13.2 Higher Household Income in the Two-Period Model

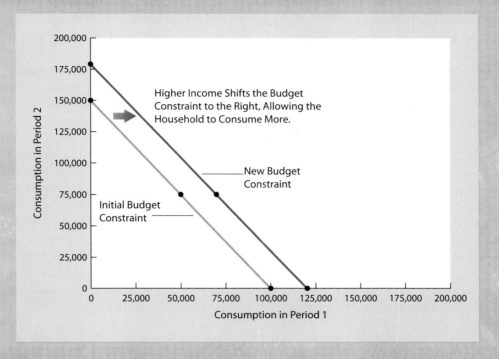

If the household's income is higher, the budget constraint shifts to the right in a parallel fashion. The amount of the shift (in the horizontal direction) equals the present value of the increase in income. The shift of the budget constraint allows the household to consume more goods.

The budget constraint shifts to the right by the amount of the increase in period 1 income divided by $1 (the price of goods), which is 20,000.

The same effect would occur if period 2 income were higher. The amount of the shift to the right in the budget constraint would equal the present value of the increase in income in period 2. For example, if income in period 1 were $50,000 (as in the initial situation), and income in period 2 rose from $75,000 (in the initial situation) to $105,000, the present value of the household's income would be

$$\frac{\$50,000}{(1.50)^0} + \frac{\$105,000}{(1.50)^1} = \$50,000 + \$70,000 = \$120,000$$

Note that this would give the same budget constraint as the one in Figure 13.2 labeled *New budget constraint* because the present value of income is the same in both cases.

Thus, we have seen that an increase in income in either period would lead to a shift to the right in the budget constraint. Following similar reasoning, a decrease in income in either period would lead to a shift to the left in the budget constraint. In either case, the household's consumption in both periods is likely to change.

A change in the interest rate affects consumption. What would happen if the interest rate were to change? The point on the budget constraint at which a household neither borrows nor saves would not be affected because such a household neither pays nor receives interest. However, because all the other points on the budget constraint are those at which the household borrows and thus pays interest or saves and thus receives interest, those points are affected by a change in the interest rate.

Suppose that the interest rate were to decline from 50 percent to zero. With a zero interest rate in the initial situation in which the household's income is $50,000 in period 1 and $75,000 in period 2, if the household borrowed as much as possible and spent the present value of its income in period 1, it would spend

$$\frac{\$50,000}{(1.00)^0} + \frac{\$75,000}{(1.00)^1} = \$50,000 + \$75,000 = \$125,000$$

If the household saved everything in period 1 and spent everything in period 2, it would spend

$$(\$50,000 \times 0.00) + \$50,000 + \$75,000 = \$50,000 + \$75,000 = \$125,000$$

Plotting these points, along with the point at which the household neither borrows nor lends, shows that this decline in the interest rate causes the budget constraint to rotate in a counterclockwise direction (Figure 13.3).

Is a household better off if the interest rate is 50 percent or zero? Consider a household that would have been at point A in Figure 13.3 if the interest rate were 50 percent. Point A is on the initial budget constraint, where the household spends $70,000 in period 1 and $45,000 in period 2. Thus, the household planned to borrow $20,000 to spend in period 1 and repay $30,000 in period 2. Because the household had planned to borrow, a decline in the interest rate from 50 percent to zero means that it will have to repay less in period 2. The new budget constraint is now further to the right, so the household will be able to consume more. The household that initially planned to borrow is clearly better off with the lower interest rate.

What about a household that had planned to save? Consider point B in Figure 13.3. Such a household initially was planning to save when the interest rate was 50 percent. When the interest rate declines, the household realizes that it will receive less interest on its savings. Most likely the lower interest rate makes the household worse off because it gets a lower return on its savings. In some cases, however, the household could switch from being a saver to being a borrower, in which case it actually might be better off.

Therefore, when the interest rate is lower, a household that had planned initially to borrow is definitely better off, and a household that had planned initially to save is most likely worse off.

What happens if the interest rate is higher? Following similar reasoning, a higher interest rate definitely makes households that initially planned to save better off. They were planning to save, so the higher interest rate gives them even more to spend in period 2. Households that initially planned to be borrowers are most likely to be worse off because they must pay a higher interest rate on the amount they borrow. In some cases, however, the effect of the higher interest rate is so large that the household might switch from borrowing to saving, in which case it might become better off.

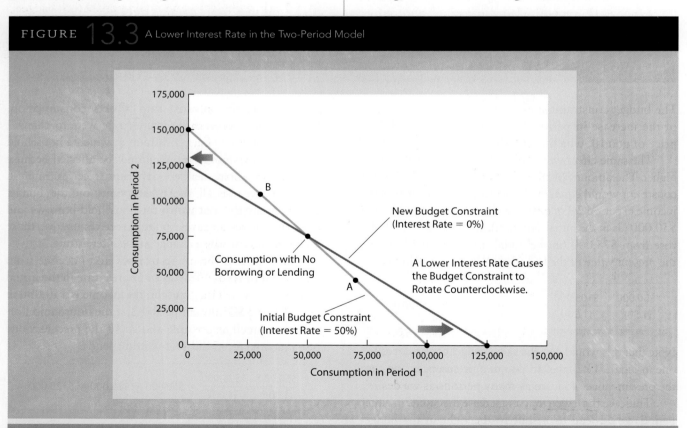

FIGURE 13.3 A Lower Interest Rate in the Two-Period Model

If the interest rate is lower, the budget constraint rotates counterclockwise around the point at which the household neither borrows nor lends. A household that would have been at point A (if the interest rate were 50 percent) is better off with the lower interest rate because it was planning to borrow, and it can now consume more than before. A household that would have been at point B might be worse off with the lower interest rate because it was planning to save, but now it will receive less interest.

To see the effect of a change in the interest rate on the budget constraint, note that the slope of the budget constraint equals $-(1 + i)$, where i is the interest rate (in decimal form). For example, the initial budget constraint had a slope of -1.50 because the interest rate was 50 percent. When the interest rate declined to zero, the slope of the budget constraint became -1.00, which is flatter, as you can see in Figure 13.3. The interest rate represents the relative price of consumption in period 1 relative to period 2 because for every good a consumer buys in period 1, she gives up the opportunity to consume $1 + i$ goods in period 2. Thus, the interest rate represents the opportunity cost of consuming goods in one period instead of another and is represented graphically by the slope of the budget constraint.

Consumption depends on lifetime income. One important lesson from this analysis is that consumption in both periods depends on income in both periods and on the interest rate. Note especially that consumption depends on income in *both* periods. In particular, households anticipate what their income will be in the future and may spend more in period 1 if they know that their incomes will be higher in period 2. An increase in income in either period is likely to lead to higher consumption spending in both periods, assuming that people prefer to spread out their consumption spending over their lifetimes.

Adding realism to the model. This model of consumption may seem unrealistic because there are only two periods. However, using equations to describe the budget constraint and people's preferences, we can extend the model to have as many periods as we desire. Nonetheless, the two-period model gives us the basic insights into consumption behavior.

Another potentially unrealistic assumption of the model is that households face the same interest rate whether they are borrowing or lending. In reality, households often must pay a higher interest rate when they borrow than the interest rate they receive when they lend. It is not difficult to adjust the model to include different interest rates for borrowers and lenders. Because the slope of the budget constraint equals $-(1 + i)$, the budget constraint will be steeper (representing a higher interest rate) when the household borrows and flatter (representing a lower interest rate) when the household saves, as Figure 13.4 shows. Note that now there is a kink in the budget constraint at the point at which the household neither borrows nor lends.

It is also somewhat unrealistic to assume that the household knows what its income in period 2 will be, but we can extend the model to incorporate such uncertainty. Suppose that a household knows that its income in period 1 will be $50,000 but is unsure about its income in period 2. If there is a 50 percent chance that its income will be $75,000 in period 2 and a 50 percent chance that its income will be $105,000 in period 2, then it does not know where its budget constraint will be. In Figure 13.5, the household could be on either of the two budget constraints, and it must decide how much to spend in period 1 before it knows which of the two lines it is on.

When households face uncertainty about their budgets, they often save more than if they were certain about their incomes. The extra amount of savings that they maintain because of uncertainty is called **precautionary savings** because they hold these savings as a precaution against low future income. The more uncertain future income is, the more precautionary savings a household is likely to desire. This idea is confirmed in U.S. data. Farm families traditionally save large fractions of their income, when they are able to do so, because their income is very uncertain. Bad weather can easily change their incomes by a large amount, so they tend to have large precautionary savings. On the other hand, families whose sources of income are secure often have very little savings and may even incur substantial debt. This is especially true if they expect their income to grow over time because they would like to spend some of their future income before they earn it.

> **precautionary savings**
> the extra amount of savings that households maintain because of uncertainty about future income

13-1b General Equilibrium

So far this analysis has considered only the decisions of individual households. We have looked at how households decide what to do and how they react to changes such as an increase in income or the interest rate. Now that we understand the household's decision-making

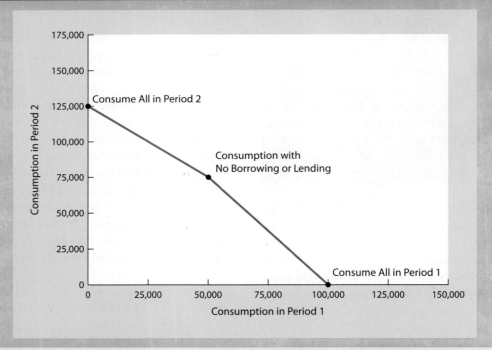

If the interest rate on borrowing is higher than the interest rate on lending, the budget constraint is kinked at the point where the household neither borrows nor lends.

FIGURE 13.5 Uncertainty About Household Income in the Two-Period Model

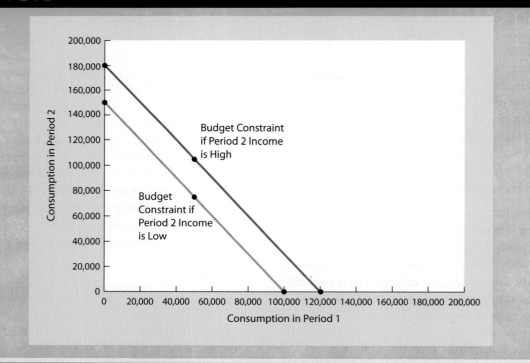

If household income in period 2 is uncertain, the household does not know where its budget constraint will be.

process, we can look at what all households do and find the economy's general equilibrium. **General equilibrium** is a situation in which all markets are in equilibrium and all economic agents have made decisions in their own best interest.

To solve this two-period model and find the general equilibrium, we will make some assumptions about the income of each household and the number of households. Then we will calculate how much each household would borrow or lend for every different value of the interest rate. We then can find the unique equilibrium interest rate that is needed to equate the quantity demanded of borrowed funds with the quantity supplied. Once we have determined the equilibrium interest rate, we can find out how much each household would consume in each period and how much each would save or borrow in period 1.

Suppose that the economy consists of 50 households, each of which has income of $50,000 in period 1. Suppose that 25 of the households have incomes of $75,000 each in period 2 and that the other 25 households have incomes of $105,000 each in period 2. The households all know what their incomes will be, so there is no uncertainty in the model. To keep track of who is who, we use the term *poor* for households that have incomes of $75,000 in period 2 and the term *rich* for those who will earn $105,000 in period 2.

We assume that in period 1 each household decides to consume one-half the present value of its income from both periods. The present value of income of a poor household is

$$PV(poor) = \$50,000 + \frac{\$75,000}{1 + i}$$

where i is the interest rate. It will spend one-half that amount on consumption in period 1, which equals

$$C_1(poor) = \frac{1}{2} \times \left(\$50,000 + \frac{\$75,000}{1 + i} \right) \div \$1 = 25,000 + \frac{37,500}{1 + i} \quad (1)$$

Note that we divided by $1 in this equation because the price of goods is $1 and we need to express consumption in numbers of goods, not dollars. The household's savings equals its income in period 1 ($50,000) minus its spending, so its savings are

$$S(poor) = \$50,000 - \left(\$25,000 + \frac{\$37,500}{1 + i} \right) = \$25,000 - \frac{\$37,500}{1 + i} \quad (2)$$

By similar reasoning, a rich household has savings equal to

$$S(rich) = \$50,000 - \left(\$25,000 + \frac{\$52,500}{1 + i} \right) = \$25,000 - \frac{\$52,500}{1 + i} \quad (3)$$

At this point we do not yet know if savings for any particular household will be positive or negative. That depends on how high the interest rate is in Equations (2) and (3). In our model, households can only borrow from each other, so the interest rate must adjust so that total savings in the economy equals total borrowing; that is, net savings must be zero. Because there are 25 households with each amount of income, this means that

> **general equilibrium** a situation in which all markets are in equilibrium and all economic agents have made decisions in their own best interest

$$\left[25 \times \left(\$25,000 - \frac{\$37,500}{1 + i} \right) \right] + \left[25 \times \left(\$25,000 - \frac{\$52,500}{1 + i} \right) \right] = 0$$

We can divide both sides of this equation by 25 and then bring the terms with the interest rate to the right-hand side of the equation to get

$$\$25,000 + \$25,000 = \frac{\$37,500}{1 + i} + \frac{\$52,500}{1 + i}$$

which can be simplified to

$$\$50,000 = \frac{\$90,000}{1 + i}$$

We can solve for the equilibrium interest rate i by multiplying both sides of the equation by $1 + i$ and then dividing both sides by $50,000 to get

$$1 + i = \frac{\$90,000}{\$50,000} = 1.8$$

so $i = 0.8$, which is 80 percent.

After we have solved the model to find the equilibrium interest rate, we can find the values of other endogenous variables. In equilibrium in this baseline model, the interest rate is 80 percent. The other endogenous variables are the amounts of savings and consumption in each period by each household. Poor households will spend, from Equation (1),

$$C_1(poor) = 25{,}000 + \frac{37{,}500}{1.8} = 45{,}833.33$$

in period 1, and they will save

$$S(poor) = \$50{,}000 - \$45{,}833.33 = \$4{,}166.67$$

Rich households will spend

$$C_1(rich) = 25{,}000 + \frac{52{,}500}{1.8} = 54{,}166.67$$

in period 1, and they will save

$$S(rich) = \$50{,}000 - \$54{,}166.67 = -\$4{,}166.67$$

Because their savings are negative, the rich are borrowers.

Thus, the 25 poor households are savers and the 25 rich households are borrowers. The interest earned by the savers on their savings of $4,166.67 is

$$\$4{,}166.67 \times 0.80 = \$3{,}333.33$$

so the total payment including principal is

$$\$3{,}333.33 + \$4{,}166.67 = \$7{,}500.00$$

In period 2, poor households will consume

$$C_2(poor) = 75{,}000 + 7{,}500 = 82{,}500$$

Rich households will consume

$$C_2(rich) = 105{,}000 - 7{,}500 = 97{,}500$$

To sum up the results, in general equilibrium in our baseline model, (1) the interest rate is 80 percent, (2) poor households will spend $45,833.33 in period 1, will save $4,166.67, and will spend $82,500 in period 2, and (3) rich households will spend $54,166.67 in period 1,

expectations people's beliefs about future economic variables

rational expectations expectations based on using all the information available

will borrow $4,166.67, and will spend $97,500 in period 2. These are all the endogenous variables in the model.

You can follow the same types of steps to see what the equilibrium interest rate would be in other situations. For example, if the high income level is $90,000 instead of $105,000, the interest rate will be 0.65, or 65 percent. If the high income level is $105,000, as before, but the number of people receiving that income is higher, the interest rate rises. For example, if only 10 households earn the low income ($75,000) in period 2 and 40 earn the high income ($105,000), the equilibrium interest rate rises to 0.98, or 98 percent. On the other hand, if the number of households earning the low income in period 2 increases, the interest rate declines. For example, if all 50 households earn the low income ($75,000), the equilibrium interest rate is 0.50, or 50 percent.

Variables that are not endogenous variables are *exogenous* variables, which means that they are determined outside the model. In our model, the exogenous variables are the number of people getting the high income in period 2 and the low income in period 2, the amount of income in period 1, and the two possible amounts of income in period 2.

Understanding which variables are endogenous and which are exogenous is crucial to being able to figure out the sources of changes in the economy. You can only analyze the general-equilibrium impact on endogenous variables of a change in an exogenous variable. For example, we could answer the question: How would consumption spending by poor people in period 1 change if the number of rich people were to rise from 25 to 35? This question can be answered because the number of rich people is an exogenous variable. However, we are unable to answer a question such as: How would consumption spending in period 1 change if the interest rate rises? This question cannot be answered because the interest rate is also an endogenous variable. Answering the question requires that you know the source of the change in the interest rate—that is, you must first answer the question: Which exogenous variable changed to cause the interest rate to rise? And in this case the change in the exogenous variable is the ultimate source of the change in consumption spending, not the change in the interest rate.

13-1c Expectations

Expectations are people's beliefs about future economic variables. If people form their expectations using all the information available to them, they are said to have **rational expectations.** Economic research over the last

20 years suggests that expectations are best modeled as endogenous variables. Doing so means that the decisions by economic agents within the model depend on future variables and that there is some description within the model of how those expectations are formed.

One type of expectations variable affects a single household's budget constraint, such as a worker's expected future income. A worker usually believes that his income will rise over time as he gains on-the-job experience. If the worker has rational expectations, the household realizes this fact and acts on it; it spends more than its income when workers in the household are young, incurring debt and planning to pay off that debt with its higher future income.

A second type of expectations variable affects all the economic agents in the economy, such as the expected inflation rate. If a household chooses to buy a long-term debt security that pays fixed dollar amounts in the future, the real return depends on the inflation rate over the time until the security matures; the inflation rate is the same for all households. How do households form rational expectations about the inflation rate? If inflation has been stable for decades, never changing very much from some level, then households may be safe in assuming that such a trend will continue. If monetary policy has changed from one that stabilizes the inflation rate to one that results in higher inflation rates over time, however, as was the case in the 1970s, then households will adjust their expectations. Thus, a good model of expectations includes a description of how households modify their expectations in response to changes in monetary policy.

If people's expectations about inflation depend on their expectations about future monetary policy, people wish to understand the incentives facing monetary policymakers. If a household can figure out why policymakers make the decisions they do, it is able to form better expectations about future inflation. This is why people carefully monitor the Federal Reserve chairman's every word; they think that it will give them some clue about future monetary policy. We will study this expectations process more carefully in Chapter 18.

13-1d The Impact of Changes in Government Policy

In dynamic models, a key to understanding the impact of government monetary or fiscal policies is to consider how a change in policy affects people's expectations. To illustrate how to model changes in policy in a dynamic model, we return to our two-period model and consider a change in fiscal policy. Suppose that the government of our economy planned to give everyone $1,000 in period 1. (You could think of this as a tax rebate.) The government would get the money to do so by borrowing $50,000 in period 1 and then repaying that money with interest to investors in period 2. Recall that all the households have incomes of $50,000 each in period 1, 25 households have incomes of $75,000 each in period 2, and 25 households have incomes of $105,000 each in period 2. In the benchmark model without the fiscal policy, the equilibrium interest rate was 80 percent.

How do we include the government's fiscal policy actions in the model? Because the government is giving a $1,000 tax rebate to every household in period 1, household income rises to $51,000 in period 1. If people were not rational, they might think that this was a one-time effect and that they were better off by $1,000, so their budget constraint would shift to the right, and they could spend more. However, rational economic agents understand that the government will have to repay its borrowing. This means that households know that they will be taxed in period 2 so that the government can repay its debt. If the interest rate were unaffected by the government's actions and remained at 80 percent, a household could calculate that the government would need to repay

$$(\$50,000 \times 0.80) + \$50,000 = \$90,000$$

in period 2. With 50 households, the government would impose a tax of

$$\frac{\$90,000}{50} = \$1,800$$

on each household.

Thus, the rational household realizes that although it will receive $1,000 from the government in period 1, its income in period 2 will decline by $1,800. The present value of the $1,800 tax in period 2 is exactly equal to the $1,000 received from the government in period 1 because (using the present-value formula)

$$Present\ value = \frac{\$1,800}{1+i}$$
$$= \frac{\$1,800}{1.8}$$
$$= \$1,000$$

Because the present value of its after-tax income has not changed, the household knows that its budget constraint is unaffected by this fiscal policy. (Even if the household considers the possibility that the interest rate might change, it would find that its budget constraint was not affected by the fiscal policy, so its choice of consumption in period 1 would not change. In general equilibrium, the interest rate will not change.) The household therefore will increase its savings by exactly $1,000 in period 1 so that it can pay the taxes in period 2. The fiscal policy therefore has no effect on people's consumption. The view that a change in the timing of taxes does not affect people's consumption is known as the **Ricardian equivalence proposition** after economist David Ricardo, who discussed the idea in the early 1800s. Economists have studied the conditions under which the Ricardian equivalence proposition holds and the conditions under which it does not hold; those conditions depend on people's expectations and whether the present value of a person's lifetime taxes is unchanged when fiscal policy changes.

Ricardian equivalence proposition the result that a change in the timing of taxes does not affect people's consumption

In this example, expectations are the key to understanding why the fiscal policy change has no effect. If people were short-sighted and did not understand that they would need to pay the higher taxes in period 2, they likely would have spent some of the $1,000 they received from the government in period 1. Then the fiscal policy would have an impact. Because people have rational expectations, though, the policy does not change people's spending or affect the interest rate; it just affects their incomes and the amount they save.

Under some circumstances, the fiscal policy might affect some people. If the model were slightly different—for example, if the interest rate on borrowing were higher than the interest rate on lending—the fiscal policy might affect people because the government would need to pay a higher interest rate on its borrowing than people received on their savings. In such a case, people would need to save more than $1,000 in the first period to offset the government's borrowing, so their consumption would be affected. Thus, the fiscal policy could have an effect on consumption and the interest rate. Other complications of the model, such as if people who wanted to borrow were unable to or if people had uncertain future incomes, also could lead to the fiscal policy having some effect. (See the Policy Insider box "Tax Cuts and Consumer Spending" for an analysis of the impact of the tax rebates in 2001.)

This example tells us that to analyze the impact of a tax rebate, we must use a model that includes people's expectations of future taxes. In Chapter 12 we saw that the large, structural macroeconomic models did a poor job of forecasting inflation in the 1970s in part because they did not model expectations properly. If the government changes from a policy that stabilizes inflation to a policy that increases inflation, the model must include people's expectations about future inflation; otherwise, the model will not work well, as was the case with the structural models in the 1970s.

Expectations in a macroeconomic model depend on the decisions made by policymakers. Over time, those decisions may change, and a good macroeconomic model must account for such changes.

RECAP

1 The benefit of using dynamic models is that they allow us to model expectations, avoiding the Lucas critique, and they describe the microeconomic foundations of the economy, which allows us to examine how people are affected by policy actions.

2 The two-period model of consumption and saving illustrates how a dynamic model works, showing the split of variables into those that are exogenous and endogenous, as well as the impact of a policy change on all the endogenous variables.

3 Finding the general equilibrium in a dynamic model requires first finding out how each of the endogenous variables depends on the exogenous variables and then finding out what values of the endogenous variables clear all markets. In the two-period model, the market clears when total saving equals total borrowing; only one value for the interest rate clears the market.

13-2 Dynamic, Stochastic, General-Equilibrium Models

Following the failure of the large, structural macroeconomic models in the 1970s, economists began to build models like the dynamic model we worked with in the preceding section. These new models included decisions by households that make consumption decisions and by firms that act to maximize their profits. The new models included expectations. We describe these models as *dynamic* because they explain how variables change over time. They are *stochastic*, which means they include uncertainty. They are *general equilibrium* because they assume that the price level, wages, and interest rates adjust to bring all markets into equilibrium, with all economic agents making decisions in their own best interest.

Hence these models are called **dynamic stochastic, general-equilibrium (DSGE) models.**

In this section we describe real business-cycle models and newer DSGE models. We discuss the causes of the business cycle and the role of government policy in such models.

> **dynamic stochastic, general-equilibrium (DSGE) models** models incorporating time and uncertainty in which prices, wages, and interest rates adjust to bring all markets to equilibrium and all economic agents make decisions in their own interest

13-2a Real Business-Cycle Models

Early DSGE models focused on the influence of a real economic shock as the key source of business cycles. In particular, researchers found that movements in the economy's total factor productivity were the main causes of business cycles. Because these models suggested that "real" shocks to productivity were the main determinant of the business cycle,

Policy →IN← sider   Tax Cuts and Consumer Spending

In 2001, the U.S. government cut personal tax rates and mailed rebate checks of $300 or $600 to many households. Initially, the plan was to give taxpayers back some of the government's budget surplus, but as the economy weakened, government officials viewed the tax rebate as a policy action to stimulate consumer spending.

Because the stock market declined sharply in 2001, the rebate checks could be seen as an increase in people's wealth to help offset their losses in the stock market. However, to the extent that people accepted the rebates as replacing lost wealth, they might not spend them, which would defeat the government's plan to stimulate spending.

To find out how many taxpayers would spend the rebate checks compared with the number that planned to save the money or to pay off their existing debts, the University of Michigan's Survey Research Center included some additional questions in its monthly survey during several months in 2001 and 2002. The survey questionnaire explained the background of the rebate checks and then asked people: ". . . will the tax

rebate lead you mostly to increase spending, mostly to increase saving, or mostly to pay off debt?"

The results of the survey were analyzed by economists Matthew D. Shapiro and Joel Slemrod ("Did the 2001 Tax Rebate Stimulate Spending? Evidence from Taxpayer Surveys," in *Tax Policy and the Economy*, edited by James Poterba, Cambridge, MA: MIT Press, 2003). They found that slightly less than one-quarter of households said they would mostly spend the rebate. They found very little to explain which households would spend the rebate compared with those who would not, although there was some tendency for both the elderly and the wealthy mostly to spend the rebate. Also, people who thought the economy would be in good shape one year in the future were more likely to spend the rebate.

What impact did the tax rebates have on overall consumer spending? The survey results suggest that the impact on consumption was fairly small. It thus seems unlikely that the tax rebates were very helpful in increasing spending in the economy and offsetting the weakness in output growth that occurred in 2001.

the models were known as **real business-cycle (RBC) models.** In these models, the *level* of total factor productivity is the engine of economic growth, whereas *fluctuations* in total factor productivity are responsible for business cycles. The theory is quite simple because both growth and cycles are explained by movements of a single variable.

RBC theory stands in sharp contrast to other macroeconomic theories. Monetarists argued that the business cycle was attributable to erratic monetary policy. Keynesians viewed the business cycle as emanating from demand shocks from a variety of potential sources. But RBC theory suggests that the business cycle is driven by movements in total factor productivity. When those movements occur, the economy adjusts, and the adjustment process is characterized by business-cycle movements in output: expansions and recessions.

The methods used by RBC researchers differ from those used by other macroeconomists. RBC models are calibrated so that they provide results broadly consistent with the major trends in economic growth and the relationships between variables over the business cycle. To calibrate a model, the researcher picks a few key parameters based on long-run historical averages of the data. For example, in the two-period model of consumption and saving, a researcher might choose the number of poor and rich households in such a way that the interest rate in the model equals the historical average U.S. interest rate. However, RBC researchers do not use the statistical techniques that most other economists use. Because the models are very complicated, with many changes over time and complex decision rules by the economic agents, the models are simulated on a computer—they simply are not solvable using pen and paper. Fortunately, as these models were being developed, technological advances gave researchers dramatically improved computational power on their desktop personal computers (PCs). Without this, research on RBC models could not be done.

RBC models from the late 1980s and early 1990s were able to reproduce some important relationships between variables over the U.S. business cycle. One such relationship is that, over the course of the business cycle, consumption spending and investment spending on physical capital change together,

although the movements of investment spending are much larger in percentage terms. Another relationship is that output growth is closely related to growth in labor hours over the business cycle. RBC models successfully reproduce both relationships. Researchers found that an RBC model could account for as much as 70 percent of the fluctuations in output growth. Thus, RBC theory was considered a success by some economists.

Other economists, however, remain skeptical about the results of RBC models. Some object that RBC models are unable to provide a convincing description of the technology shocks that are the main variable responsible for the business cycle. Others object that RBC models are subject to severe measurement errors and do not do a good job of identifying the reason for the business cycle. Measurement errors arise because the government does not have perfect measures of hours worked that are used in constructing data on total factor productivity. As a result, some fluctuations of productivity may arise because of badly measured changes in hours worked, which makes fluctuations in productivity and output appear to be more closely related than they really are. Another objection is that the data on hours worked and the amount of capital that are used in calculating total factor productivity do not reflect how intensively those factors of production are used. For example, when the economy begins to slow in a recession, production workers may not be laid off immediately but may be asked to perform other tasks that are less productive than usual. Thus, a manufacturing plant that has experienced a decline in the demand for its product may pull workers off the production line (because the company does not need to produce as many goods) and have them paint buildings or repave parking lots. Because the workers continue to work, the number of hours worked does not decline, but the plant's output does, so the statistics show a decline in total factor productivity. The decline in productivity was not the cause of the decline in output, however; both occurred as a result of declining demand. Thus, shocks to total factor productivity may be less important as a source of the business cycle than RBC research suggests.

According to RBC theorists, government policy plays a less important role than suggested by monetarist or Keynesian models. In monetarist models, sharp fluctuations in the money supply are the main cause of the business cycle, so monetarists suggest that the best policy is one with slow, steady growth in the money supply. Keynesians view the business cycle as being caused by shocks to demand in the economy, which government policy can offset by shifting demand in the opposite direction of the shock. But RBC models suggest that government policy plays little, if any, role in the business cycle, except to the extent that it influences total factor productivity. Thus, the government's role should be to not cause business productivity to fluctuate; nothing else the government does matters very much. RBC models suggest that monetary and fiscal policy should be set in predictable ways, for example, by keeping tax rates constant over time and making the money supply grow 3 percent per year. Policy variables should not be adjusted to try to offset the business cycle because they have no effect on the economy unless they cause confusion, thus reducing productivity growth. Therefore, the role of government policy is to stay out of the way!

Over the last decade, these extreme views about RBC models and government's role in the economy have softened considerably. RBC theorists have attempted to add more variables to their models and have discovered subtle ways in which their models do not match U.S. data very well. As they have refined their models, some researchers have included relationships from monetarist and Keynesian models of the economy. In some recent versions of the models, both fiscal and monetary policies play key roles in affecting endogenous variables over the business cycle.

13-2b Modern DSGE Models

Because newer models now show that government policy affects key endogenous variables over the business cycle, they are no longer considered "real" business-cycle models. But the models are dynamic and stochastic and general equilibrium, so the name *dynamic stochastic general-equilibrium (DSGE) models* is now used to describe them. DSGE models are much broader in scope than the original RBC models and are sometimes even used by economists who could be considered monetarists and Keynesians. The DSGE model is now the workhorse model of many macroeconomists.

In recent years, macroeconomists have extended the frontiers of their knowledge about business cycles. Perhaps the most interesting progress has been toward developing models with many different economic agents. The large, structural macroeconomic models and the early RBC models were all based on thinking about an economy in which all households were alike and every business firm was like every other, so such models were known as **homogeneous-agent models.** With the expanding power of computers in recent years, however, economists have begun to construct models with many different households and many different firms, called **heterogeneous-agent models.**

> **homogeneous-agent models** models in which the economic agents are all alike
>
> **heterogeneous-agent models** models that contain many different economic agents

Thus, economic research continues to make progress with more and more realistic models over time. It will be interesting to see if the new DSGE models with heterogeneous agents eventually can provide better forecasts than the large, structural macroeconomic models. Also, it will be interesting to see if policymakers find such models valuable for evaluating alternative policy plans.

Researchers using DSGE models generally proceed in the following way:

1. Pose the question to be answered (for example, can shocks to productivity explain most of the variation in output over the business cycle?).
2. Develop a model containing the major elements needed to answer the question (for example, a model in which households are hired by firms to produce output, and the productivity of workers and capital can change over time). Analyze the decisions that each economic agent must face.
3. Match up the model with economic data, using statistical techniques to calculate the sizes of shocks that occur (for example, the sizes of the shocks to productivity).
4. Simulate the model and compare the statistical properties of the model with those of the data. See if the main variables in the model have the same variability and affect each other in the same way as observed in the data. If the model closely matches the data, the question in part 1 can be answered. If the model does not closely match the data, then the question cannot be answered with the model, and the researcher must modify the model until it more closely matches the data. (For example, an early RBC study found a model that matched the data fairly closely and suggested that 70 percent of the variation in output growth over the business cycle was attributable to shocks to productivity.)

1 Real business-cycle (RBC) models focus on movements over time in total factor productivity as the source of both long-term economic growth and business-cycle fluctuations. RBC models are able to account for as much as 70 percent of the fluctuations in output growth. RBC models suggest that government policy plays little role in output fluctuations, but some economists are skeptical of the value of RBC models.

2 Modern DSGE models allow government policy to play a bigger role than RBC models did and allow for heterogeneous economic agents. Much current economic research uses a DSGE model framework for answering questions about policy and for explaining historical events.

13-3 Statistical Models of the Economy

Some economists who did not like the large, structural macroeconomic models of the 1970s took a different statistical approach. They believed that the problem with those models was not that they lacked theoretical foundations but that they were based too heavily on theory and not enough on data. This group began to model the economy as if it were just a large set of variables that were related to each other in ways that we would never really be able to understand. Because the world is so complex, some argued, economists can do nothing more than identify the way different variables are correlated, without being able to say anything about the economic relationships between variables. The models they built used statistical theory, not economic theory, so we call them *statistical models*.

The simplest statistical model is known as a **univariate time-series model,** which assumes that the value of a variable at any date depends just on its own past values plus an error term. The term *univariate* means that the model uses data from only one variable; the term *time series* refers to the use of past values of the variable.

univariate time-series model a model in which the value of a variable at any date depends just on its own past values plus an error term

For example, in the dynamic model in the preceding section we saw that a household's consumption spending in period 1 was equal to one-half the present value of the household's income, which depended on current and future income, taxes, and the real interest rate. Thus, we could represent the relationship between consumption spending and the other variables in the model with the equation

$$C_1 = \frac{1}{2}\left[(Y_1 - T_1) + \frac{Y_2 - T_2}{1 + r}\right]$$

where C_1 is consumption spending in period 1, Y_1 is income in period 1, Y_2 is income in period 2, T_1 is taxes in period 1, T_2 is taxes in period 2, and r is the real interest rate. Note that consumption depends on the values of specific macroeconomic variables.

By contrast, a univariate time-series model is one in which the only variables affecting consumption are the past values of consumption. For example, a model might have consumption today depend on consumption in the last four quarters, in which case the equation describing consumption would be

$$C_t = a_0 + a_1 C_{t-1} + a_2 C_{t-2} + a_3 C_{t-3} + a_4 C_{t-4} + e_t$$

where the term e_t is an error term that causes consumption spending to move somewhat unpredictably.

Note that the dynamic model provides an economic explanation for the amount of consumption spending; it says that consumption is affected by income, taxes, and the real interest rate in a particular way. The time-series model, on the other hand, suggests only that consumption depends on its own past values and that other variables that affect consumption are unpredictable, entering the model through the error term e_t.

As simple as a univariate time-series model is, forecasts from such models are quite good. For example, in data from the 1950s to the late 1970s, a univariate time-series model produced better forecasts for the U.S. inflation rate than the average from a survey of professional economic forecasters. Thus, many economists, even those who prefer to use structural models, often begin examining the properties of a macroeconomic variable by using a univariate time-series model as a benchmark.

A more complicated statistical model is known as a **vector autoregression (VAR) model,** in which the value of a variable depends on its own past values plus the past values of other variables plus an error term. The equation for consumption spending in a VAR model including income Y and real interest rate r might look something like

$$C_t = a_0 + a_1 C_{t-1} + a_2 C_{t-2} + a_3 C_{t-3} + a_4 C_{t-4} + b_1 Y_{t-1} + b_2 Y_{t-2} + b_3 Y_{t-3}$$
$$+ b_4 Y_{t-4} + c_1 r_{t-1} + c_2 r_{t-2} + c_3 r_{t-3} + c_4 r_{t-4} + e_t$$

The equations for income and the real interest rate would be similar.

The advantages of VAR models are that all the variables in the model are endogenous, and you can see how important one variable is for explaining the movements in other variables. VAR models can be used in place of large, structural macroeconomic models to predict the behavior of major economic variables. In fact, some of the earliest such models were found to be superior to large, structural macroeconomic models in comparisons of forecasts, at least for certain variables. One of the earliest such models used just three variables—output, money, and the price level—yet it was able to produce good forecasts for all three variables that were quite similar to the forecasts from large, structural models with hundreds of equations.

These models posed a strong challenge: Why bother to maintain a large model, keeping track of hundreds of different equations with thousands of hours of work each month, if you can do just as well with a few hours of work using a model that has only three or four variables to keep track of? The only benefit of the large model is that it can provide forecasts of more variables, such as the components of output (consumption, investment, government spending, and net exports). However, if you were interested only in forecasts of the major macroeconomic variables, especially output, prices, interest rates, and money supply, why not use a much simpler VAR model?

Unfortunately, a major problem with VAR models is that although they are clearly usable (and remarkably good) for forecasting, they are much more difficult to use for other purposes. In particular, economists often like to use models to interpret historical events or to analyze how shocks to some variable would affect the economy, but VAR models and univariate time-series models cannot perform either of these tasks in the absence of some additional assumptions.

To use a model to interpret historical events, we must examine the error terms associated with each equation of the model and interpret them. For example, the recession of 1990–1991 occurred when Iraq invaded Kuwait, causing oil prices to rise. If you look at the equations of a large, structural macroeconomic model, you can see that the equation describing consumer spending showed a large negative error term—which means that consumer spending declined more than the variables in the model predicted. Thus, it was consumers' responses to the higher oil prices and the possibility of war in the late summer of 1990 that led to the recession. Analysis such as this is not possible in a simpler model; for example, a simple VAR model (such as one with only output, money, and the price level) does not even have an equation for consumer spending. Thus, for some purposes, a large, structural macroeconomic model may be useful.

Economists often want to use a model to analyze how a shock to some variable would affect endogenous variables such as output, price level, and real interest rate. But VAR models and univariate time-series models cannot perform such a task easily. The models merely describe the correlations between variables over time. Because they provide no useful information about how the variables of the model interact with each other, they cannot answer questions about how changes in one variable might cause changes in other variables. For example, suppose that OPEC announced that oil prices would be raised immediately from $60 per barrel to $100 per barrel and remain there for the next two years. We would like to be able to analyze how this rise in oil prices would affect consumption spending, the price level, and the real interest rate. However, a VAR model with oil prices in it cannot be used to answer the question directly. The same is true for analyzing the effects of changes in monetary and fiscal policy. However, as we will see in "Policy Perspective: Do Modern Macroeconomic Models Have Any Value for Policy?", VAR models can be used to answer such questions if researchers make more assumptions about their structure, thus turning them into a mixture of a statistical model and a structural model.

vector autoregression (VAR) model a model in which the value of a variable depends on its own past values plus the past values of other variables plus an error term

1 Statistical models of the economy are based on statistical theory rather than on economic theory.

2 Univariate time-series models relate a variable's value at one date to its values in the recent past and no additional variables. Forecasts from such simple models are surprisingly good.

3 A vector autoregression (VAR) model is one in which a variable's value at one date depends on the past values of a number of other variables. Forecasts from such models were as good as and sometimes better than those from more complex structural models. But the models are not very good at interpreting historical events or analyzing the effects of changes in policy unless additional assumptions are made.

Policy → Perspective   Do Modern Macroeconomic Models Have Any Value for Policy?

Using a model to analyze the effects of policy means showing how forecasts from the model would change in response to changes in government policy. For example, suppose that the government were to consider two alternative policies for setting the growth rate of the money supply. Policy A would set money-supply growth at 5 percent each year, whereas policy B would set money-supply growth at 3 percent each year. The question is: What happens to output and the price level in the future for each of the two policies?

Large, structural macroeconomic models and some VAR models claim to be able to answer questions such as this. They contain an equation that describes the growth rate of the money supply. One way to analyze this difference in policy is to replace the model's equation describing the growth rate of the money supply with an equation that describes the potential policy. Thus, in our experiment, we would remove the existing equation describing money-supply growth and replace it with an equation that the money supply will grow 5 percent each year (path A) or an equation that the money supply will grow 3 percent each year (path B).

Is this a sensible exercise? It is not sensible, according to many economists, because the Lucas critique (described in Chapter 12) applies. A change in government policy may affect how households and business firms act in a fundamental way that would contradict the model's current structure. The result would be large forecast errors in the model, as was the case with the large, structural macroeconomic models of the 1970s. You cannot simply take one equation out of a model and replace it with another equation without running the risk that the whole enterprise falls apart.

Some economists disagree with this view, notably Chris Sims of Princeton University. Sims and others argue that this method of replacing equations is not necessarily wrong so long as the policies being evaluated are similar to those that have been used in the past. This is a simple, yet powerful argument. If the government at some time made the money supply grow 5 percent each year and at other times made the money supply grow 3 percent a year, then both policies are within the realm of past experience. Past data reflect those policies, and the model is based on that past data.

Although the Lucas critique is correct in principle, Sims and others argue that it does not apply to most policy choices because those choices are similar to choices made by the government in the past. However, a policy that had never been tried before, such as the increased money growth that led to higher inflation in the 1970s, is a novel experience and is likely to change the way people behave. Thus, one should not use statistical models to analyze policies that have never before occurred.

If we accept this argument, we can conclude that economists can use VAR models to evaluate some policy changes, such as the choice between money growth of 5 percent and money growth of 3 percent, but such an analysis would be a poor idea for analyzing a policy that would increase money growth by 30 percent each year, which is an unprecedented event in U.S. history.

In addition to the Lucas critique, VAR models face one more major criticism—that they are unable to isolate the effects of policy variables because those variables are not really exogenous. Recall that, in a large, structural macroeconomic model or in a dynamic, stochastic, general-equilibrium model, we divide variables into those that are endogenous (determined by the model) and those that are exogenous (determined outside the model). Just as one of those models can analyze only the effects of a change in an exogenous variable, the same is true of VAR models. Therefore, to analyze a change in a policy variable, statistical tests must show that such a variable is exogenous. Even if they do, however, there is some chance that the results will be misleading because those statistical tests are not perfect. As a result, the VAR model may provide misleading results on the effects of policy.

The debate over the value of VAR models for analyzing policy led to a modification that adds some economic theory to these statistical models. The idea is to begin with a VAR model but to impose certain additional restrictions on it. Such a system is called a **structural VAR model** because it is a VAR model with some economic structure associated with it. Rather than being based heavily on economic theory, as is the case with large, structural macroeconomic models or DSGE models, structural VAR models are still mostly statistical models, with just a bit of economic theory thrown in to guide them.

The restrictions imposed on structural VAR models are of two main types: short-run restrictions and long-run restrictions. A **short-run restriction** describes the impact of the current-period value of one variable on the current-period value of another variable. For example, suppose that a model includes both output and the money supply. Without a restriction in a VAR model, each variable would affect the other simultaneously. Because economic theory suggests that monetary policy works with a lag, a sensible restriction that many modelers adopt is a restriction that a change in the money supply this month has no immediate effect on output; it can only affect output in the future. (However, a change in output this month may affect the money supply immediately.)

A **long-run restriction** describes the impact of the current-period value of one variable on the value of another variable in the distant future. For example, many economists believe that a change in the money supply has no long-term effect on the economy's output. This belief can be imposed on a structural VAR model through an equation that affects how the model's parameters are estimated.

Both types of restrictions are represented in a model by coefficients in the equations of the VAR model. With such restrictions imposed, the results of the model can be interpreted readily in terms of how an unexpected change in one variable affects other variables. And, in particular, they can be used to show how unexpected changes to policy variables affect other variables. One simply must believe that the short- and long-run restrictions are sensible.

What do such structural VAR models tell us about the effects of changes in policy? Economists have been unable to determine the precise impact of changes in monetary policy on output, prices, and the real interest rate. In recent work, though, research with structural VAR models has now "given us a clearer quantitative picture of the size and dynamics of the effects of monetary policy."[1]

What about the policy implications of DSGE models? One branch of research on them suggests that government policy affects the economy only through changes in total factor productivity. Government policy generally hampers the economy—without improving the well-being of economic agents. As Edward Prescott put it, "The policy implication of this research is that costly efforts at stabilization are likely to be counterproductive."[2]

However, others who do research on DSGE models have become convinced that government policy does matter, and not just through its effects on total factor productivity. They have begun to construct DSGE models in which monetary policy affects output and the real interest rate. In these models, properly timed government policy may help to offset shocks that otherwise would reduce output and employment. (See the box titled "The New Neoclassical Synthesis" for a discussion of these types of models.)

Research on both DSGE and statistical models eventually may provide policymakers with better frameworks for analyzing the effects of policy. Some researchers even have combined both approaches with some success. Eventually, they may be able to build models that will deliver significantly better forecasts than the large, structural macroeconomic models of the 1970s.

structural VAR model a VAR model with some economic structure associated with it

short-run restriction a description of the impact of the current-period value of one variable on the current-period value of another variable

long-run restriction a description of the impact of the current-period value of one variable on the value of another variable in the distant future

[1]Christopher A. Sims, "Macroeconomics and Methodology," *Journal of Economic Perspectives* (Winter 1996), p. 118.
[2]Edward C. Prescott, "Theory Ahead of Business Cycle Measurement," Federal Reserve Bank of Minneapolis *Quarterly Review* (Fall 1986), p. 21.

The New Neoclassical Synthesis

Economists in the classical tradition of macroeconomics (such as economists trained at the University of Chicago) like to work with dynamic models with microeconomic foundations. Until recently, most such models, even many DSGE models, showed that the effects of government policy were very small. Thus, many economists felt that the government's role simply should be to do no harm to the economy and to avoid engaging in policy actions to offset the business cycle.

Recently, however, new research has developed models labeled as the "new neoclassical synthesis." In the 1970s, the neoclassical synthesis was a blend of classical and Keynesian ideas to develop a model of the economy in which government policy could play a prominent role. Most DSGE models developed in the 1990s, however, had no role for government policy. The new neoclassical synthesis uses a basic DSGE framework and then adds frictions to the model that give government policy scope to affect output, interest rates, and other macroeconomic variables.

The new neoclassical synthesis models have a basic RBC model at their core and treat total factor productivity as a key variable in the model determining growth and influencing the business cycle. However, the models then add some Keynesian touches. For example, one such model gets its punch by modeling firms as having some monopoly power, which creates a distortion to the free market. An additional assumption that businesses face costs of adjusting prices leads to some stickiness (or sluggishness) in the adjustment to general equilibrium, which helps to generate a business cycle. [For more details, see the article by Marvin Goodfriend, "Monetary Policy in the New Neoclassical Synthesis: A Primer," *International Finance* (Summer 2002), pp. 165–191.]

In a new neoclassical synthesis model, the government ideally keeps the inflation rate equal to zero because doing so minimizes the costs to firms of changing prices. In addition, the government ideally responds to shocks to the economy. For example, if people become suddenly pessimistic (as measured by changes in consumer confidence), the government should reduce the real interest rate by using expansionary monetary policy; such a policy keeps the pessimism from causing a recession. If the economy suffers a temporary reduction in total factor productivity, however, the government should allow output, income, and consumer spending to decline by raising the real interest rate; such a policy will stabilize both inflation and unemployment.

Thus, the new neoclassical synthesis is a DSGE model with frictions in it that allow a role for government policy. Although such models are just beginning to be explored, they hold the potential for bringing together the classical and Keynesian points of view.

Review Questions and Problems

Review Questions

1 How does a dynamic model differ from a static model? Why is that difference important?

2 In the two-period model of consumption and saving, what element of a graph shows all the possible amounts the household can consume?

3 Under what circumstances will a household have precautionary savings?

4 What are expectations, and why are they important, in macroeconomic models? What would you think about a macroeconomic model that assumed that people's expectations of inflation were constant, even though the inflation rate changed over time?

5 What does it mean to have rational expectations?

6 Describe how macroeconomic models have evolved from the early 1980s through the DSGE models of today.

7 Why are some economists doubtful of the value of RBC models?

8 What is the difference between homogeneous-agent models and heterogeneous-agent models? Which do you think is more realistic? Which do you think is more difficult to work with because it is technically more complicated?

9 How does a univariate time-series model differ from a VAR model?

10 What are the problems a researcher encounters in trying to use a VAR model to investigate the effects of monetary policy? What type of VAR model can be used to solve these problems?

Numerical Exercises

11 Draw a figure showing a household's budget constraint in a two-period model if the household's income is $10,000 in period 1 and $12,000 in period 2, and the interest rate is 20 percent. Assume that the price of the good is $1 in both periods. Show three points on the budget constraint: the point with no borrowing or saving, the point with all consumption in period 2, and the point with all consumption in period 1. Show what happens to the budget constraint if

the interest rate rises to 40 percent. Show the same three points as before.

12 Suppose that a household in a two-period model has income of $30,000 in period 1 and $25,000 in period 2, and the interest rate is 75 percent. Assume that the price of the good is $1 in both periods. Suppose that the household decides to consume 26,000 in period 1 and 32,000 in period 2. Now suppose that the interest rate falls to 50 percent, and the household decides not to borrow or lend at all. Is the household better off or worse off with the higher interest rate?

13 Suppose that an economy consists of 100 households, 50 of which have no income in period 1 and income of $50,000 in period 2 and 50 of which have income of $40,000 in period 1 and no income in period 2. Assume that the price of the good is $1 in both periods. Suppose that each household decides that its consumption in period 1 will equal one-half the present value of its income from both periods. Find the equilibrium value of the interest rate. How much does each household save in period 1 and consume in each period?

14 An economy has 75 households, all of which have incomes of $25,000 each in period 1, 50 of which have incomes of $40,000 each in period 2, and 25 of which have incomes of $20,000 each in period 2. Assume that the price of the good is $1 in both periods. Suppose that each household decides that its consumption in period 1 will equal 50 percent of the present value of its income from both periods.

a Find the equilibrium value of the interest rate.

b Now suppose instead that each household will consume 60 percent of the present value of its income from both periods in period 1. Now what is the equilibrium value of the interest rate?

c Finally, suppose that each household's period 1 consumption equals one-half the present value of its income from both periods, but everyone's income in period 1 is lower: just $20,000. What is the equilibrium value of the interest rate now?

(continued)

Analytical Problems

15 Describe how the budget constraint of a household in a two-period model is affected by each of the following changes. In each case, do you think the household is better off or worse off, or is the answer ambiguous? If ambiguous, what does the answer depend on?

a Period 1 income is lower.

b The interest rate is higher.

c Period 2 income is lower, and the interest rate is lower.

16 How is a household's precautionary savings likely to be affected by the following events?

a The main wage earner in the house switches from a career in management at a large corporation to starting a small consulting business.

b The household is given $5 million from a wealthy relative's estate.

c A couple's last child graduates from college.

17 If inflation has been about 5 percent each year for a long time and you have observed no change in the behavior of monetary policymakers, what is your rational expectation of future inflation? If inflation has been about 5 percent each year for a long time and monetary policymakers have announced that they are planning to increase the growth rate of the money supply by 3 percent, what is your rational expectation of future inflation?

18 In the two-period model described in this chapter, suppose that a household's income in period 1 increases at the same time that the interest rate decreases. Is the household better off or worse off because of this change? What will happen to its savings? You might want to think about a household that was a saver before the change and another that was a borrower.

Currency	We Sell Note	We Buy Note	We Buy T/C
US Dollar	1.448	1.406	1.406
Sterling Pound	2.861	2.751	2.750
Australian Dollar	1.316	1.230	1.230
Canadian Dollar	1.453	1.384	1.384
New Zealand Dollar	1.169	1.092	1.092
EURO	2.144	2.082	2.081
Swiss Franc	1.352	1.300	1.299
Renminbi	20.987	19.799	
Saudi Arabia Riyal	39.063	34.266	
Japanese Yen	1.361	1.309	1.309
Malaysian Ringgit	45.285	43.128	
Hong Kong Dollar	19.277	18.016	18.016
Thai Baht	4.667	4.243	
Philippines Pesos	3.799	3.453	
Taiwan NT	4.800	4.364	
Indonesian Rupiah	0.164	0.149	
India Rupee	40.704	35.705	
Korean Won	1.717	1.506	

外币兑换

ECONOMIC INTERDEPENDENCE

In this chapter we examine questions about how a country is affected by a change in its exchange rate, which is the price of the country's currency in terms of another country's currency. We begin by looking at the relationships between the business cycles of different countries. We then move on to a discussion of exchange rates: what they are, what they mean, how they are determined, and why they are important. We finish the chapter by looking at the Asian financial crisis, the role played by exchange rates in the crisis, and whether anything can be done to prevent similar crises.

14-1 The International Business Cycle

Countries are not independent of each other—a recession in one country often coincides with a recession in other countries. The relationship between the business cycles in different countries is called the *international business cycle*. In this section we seek to answer some questions about the international business cycle:

- What causes the business cycles of different countries to be related to one another?
- Is the whole world at the same phase of the business cycle, or when some countries are doing well, are others doing poorly?
- How are shocks in one country transmitted to other countries?

14-1a Why Is There an International Business Cycle?

Why is the business cycle in one country related to the business cycle in another country? One possibility is that changes in an economic variable directly affect both countries. Another possibility is that the countries are interdependent so that a recession in one country causes a recession in another.

Shocks may affect several countries. Business cycles occur when a shock to the economy (defined in Chapter 11) is large enough that it leads to fluctuations in key macroeconomic variables. If the same shock hits many countries at once, then their business cycles will occur simultaneously. For example, many countries, including the United States, depend on crude oil imported from the Middle East. Suppose that a shock to oil prices (a supply shock) occurs, for example, as happened in 1990 at the start of the Gulf War when uncertainty about the supply of oil drove the price up dramatically. Countries that use oil as a major input into production face higher prices. Of course, not every country will be affected to the same extent because some probably use more oil than others, and some (such as the United States) also produce their own oil to meet some of their needs. If the shock is large, as the 1990 shock was, it can lead to a recession, as it did in the United States.

A shock can be positive as well as negative. For example, new computer technology (a supply shock) in the 1990s was developed mainly in the United States, Europe, and Japan. However, the technological improvements were incorporated into capital equipment (personal computers, cell phones, and personal digital assistants) that was sold throughout the world. The result was a jump in output in many countries simultaneously. Again, each economy may have been affected differently, depending on how quickly the country was able to use the new technology.

Some shocks that cause the economy's output to rise or fall are likely to affect just one country and not have much effect on others, at least not directly. For example, suppose that the government in one country reduces its spending sharply, which leads the economy to slow down because of the resulting reduction in aggregate demand (a demand shock). The direct effect on the citizens of the country is not shared by citizens in other countries.

Some shocks harm one country and benefit another country. For example, suppose that one country specializes in producing chicken and another specializes in producing beef. If an event such as the spread of mad cow disease reduces the demand for beef (a demand shock) and increases the demand for chicken, the chicken-producing country gains at the expense of the beef-producing country.

Shocks may spread because of economic interdependence. A shock that is isolated to one country may be transmitted to other countries indirectly. For example, the country that cut its government spending sharply and thus has lower aggregate demand will purchase fewer goods and services from foreign countries, thus causing the reduction in aggregate demand to spread. The first country's recession influences the growth of output in other countries.

Many countries engage in substantial amounts of foreign trade with a few close trading partners. For example, proximity leads to Canada's main export market being the United States. When the U.S. economy slows, Canada's economy weakens considerably, leading to the adage, "When the U.S. sneezes, Canada catches a cold."

The financial crisis of 2008 originated in the United States and led to a decline of about 9 percent (at an annual rate) in U.S. GDP in the fourth quarter of 2008. But countries that were dependent on exports to the United States, such as Japan and Singapore, saw their GDP decline about 12 percent (at an annual rate) in both of those quarters, twice the decline felt in the United States.

14-1b How Correlated Are the Business Cycles in Different Economies?

The data on the international business cycle from the early 1970s through the mid-1980s showed that business cycles were strongly correlated across countries. The correlation between output growth in the United States and Europe was about 0.7, a value that shows a fairly close relationship between output growth in the two regions. A correlation of 1.0 would mean that output growth in both regions changed at exactly the same time and by a proportionate amount. A correlation of 0.0 would mean that there was no relationship between output in the two regions. A negative correlation would mean that output in the two regions was inversely related: When one rose, the other was likely to fall. The correlation between output in the United States and Canada was about 0.8, and the correlation between output in the United States and Japan was about 0.6. From calculations such as these, economists believed that output in the major industrialized countries tended to move closely together.

In the late 1980s and the 1990s, however, the correlation in output across regions declined sharply. The United States entered a recession in 1990, but the economies of Japan and Europe did not weaken until about two years later. As a result, the correlation between output in the United States and those regions dropped significantly. The correlation between output in the United States and Europe fell to about 0.3, and that between the United States and Japan fell to about 0.0. The business cycles in the United States and Canada remained synchronized because the correlation of output rose slightly from the late 1980s to 2000. In the 2000s, the correlations between output growth in the United States and other countries rose sharply because the financial crisis in 2008 and 2009 hit all countries simultaneously.

In part, the close correlations between the regions in the 1970s and 1980s occurred because the major shocks in that period were the increases in oil prices beginning in 1973 and again in 1980. In the 1990s, events unique to each region had a greater impact on the business cycle in different economies. A weak banking system in the United States, combined with weak growth of construction caused by excess capacity of office space and apartment buildings, led to very slow growth in the early 1990s. Other countries' economies were stronger in that period and did not falter until later in the decade (however, they did slow down slightly). In 1992, European economies faced a crisis in which interest rates rose sharply, causing investment spending on physical capital to be curtailed and sending their economies into recessions. The recession in Europe had some effect on the United States as well, keeping U.S. growth lower than it might have been otherwise.

The financial crisis of 2008 originated in the United States and spread rapidly across the world, leading to a strong correlation of economic activity across countries. Export-oriented economies were damaged more severely than economies that depended less on exports. Overall, however, all the major economies of the world entered severe recessions.

14-1c International Transmission of Shocks

How is a shock that hits one country transmitted to other countries? Shocks are transmitted internationally by means of three mechanisms: (1) trade effects, (2) interest-rate effects, and (3) exchange-rate effects.

The first way in which shocks to one country are transmitted internationally is through the trade of goods and services between countries. We touched on this idea briefly in Chapter 12 when we noted that net exports are a component of aggregate demand. For example, suppose that one country is hit with a shock that reduces its income. Then it will demand fewer imports of goods and services from other countries, thus reducing aggregate demand in those countries.

The second avenue of linkages from one country to another is through interest rates. When people in one country can invest in another, then changes in interest rates in one country affect flows of investment between the countries. Depending on exactly what caused the initial change in the interest rate, output in the two countries could be positively or negatively linked. For example, suppose that the interest rate in the United States rises because of a change in monetary policy that raises the U.S. interest rate and reduces U.S. output. The increase in the interest rate induces investors to reduce their investments in Europe and invest more in the United States. As a result, the interest rate in Europe rises, causing output to decline. Thus, output in both regions is positively correlated. On the other hand, suppose that the interest rate in the United States rose because investors became more optimistic about the prospects for U.S. growth and less optimistic about the prospects for growth in Europe. The increased investment in physical capital in the United States would increase economic activity, and the reduced investment in physical capital in Europe would reduce economic activity. So output is negatively correlated in the two regions.

The third link between countries comes through exchange rates, which are the rates at which the currency of one country trades for currency of another country. Changes in exchange rates affect the demand and supply of both imports and exports of goods and services and also influence how investors decide where to invest their savings, as we shall see in the next section.

RECAP

1 Business cycles are related across countries because shocks may affect several countries, and a shock in one country may spread to other countries because the countries are interdependent.

2 Business cycles were more closely correlated between the United States and Europe and between the United States and Japan from the 1970s to the mid-1980s than from the mid-1980s to the 1990s. More recently, the correlations have increased because the financial crisis that began in 2008 affected most countries all over the world.

3 Shocks are transmitted internationally through trade effects, interest-rate effects, and exchange-rate effects.

14-2 Exchange Rates

The **exchange rate** is the amount of one currency needed to purchase one unit of another currency. Most countries have their own currencies: dollars in the United States, yen in Japan, pounds in the United Kingdom. An exception is that many European nations have joined together to use one currency, the euro. An example of an exchange rate is that 1 euro was worth about 1.32 U.S. dollars at the beginning of 2013. Table 14.1 shows several other exchange rates and how they have changed over time from 1970 to 2013.

Every exchange rate can be written in two ways. Instead of valuing 1 euro at 1.32 dollars, we also could determine the number of euros that would be equivalent to 1 dollar. We find this equivalence by taking the inverse of the number of dollars per 1 euro:

$$\frac{1}{1.32 \text{ dollar/euro}} = 0.76 \text{ euro/dollar}$$

exchange rate the amount of one currency needed to purchase one unit of another currency

Thus, 1 dollar would trade for 0.76 euros. Whenever you want to exchange one currency for another, as you

TABLE **14.1** Exchange Rates Since 1970

	Value on January 1 Each Year				
	1970	**1980**	**1990**	**2000**	**2013**
U.S. dollar/U.K. pound	2.40	2.22	1.61	1.62	1.63
Canadian dollar/U.S. dollar	1.07	1.17	1.16	1.44	1.00
French franc/U.S. dollar	5.55	4.02	5.77	6.51	—
Japanese yen/U.S. dollar	358	240	144	102	87
German mark/U.S. dollar	3.69	1.73	1.69	1.94	—
U.S. dollar/European euro	—	—	—	1.01	1.32

Note: Each exchange rate shows the number of units of the first currency that are needed to obtain one unit of the second currency. For example, the 1970 value for the U.S. dollar/U.K. pound exchange rate of 2.40 means that 2.40 dollars could be traded for 1 pound. The exchange rates are written here as they are quoted most commonly in markets for foreign exchange, that is, in terms of U.S. dollars per 1 U.K. pound in the first row and units of another currency per 1 U.S. dollar in the other rows. The French franc and German mark ceased to exist in 2002, so there is no value for their exchange rates for 2013; the euro came into existence in 1999, so there is no value for it in 1970, 1980, and 1990.

© Cengage Learning

would if you were traveling abroad, you must be careful to note the way the currency conversion is written.

What does it mean when an exchange rate changes? Let's use the euro and the dollar as an example. When the euro was introduced in January 1999, 1 euro traded for 1.18 dollars. By January 2001, 1 euro traded for just 0.94 dollars. This change means that the euro's

value decreased in terms of dollars; alternatively, the dollar's value increased in terms of euros. When the value of a currency decreases in terms of another, it is said to **depreciate** against the other; when the value of a currency increases in terms of another, it is said to **appreciate** against the other. When one currency appreciates, the other depreciates. Thus, the euro depreciated against the dollar from January 1999 to January 2001; stated equivalently, the dollar appreciated against the euro.

To remember when a currency appreciates or depreciates, think about it this way. Consider two currencies; call them Y and Z. The exchange rate Y/Z represents the number of units of currency Y that one unit of currency Z can buy. If we write the exchange rate as Y/Z, then currency Z appreciates if Y/Z rises; currency Z depreciates if Y/Z falls. Remembering this idea will help you to always know whether a currency is appreciating or depreciating. For example, in the euro–dollar example earlier, the number of dollars per 1 euro (dollars/euro) fell from 1.18 to 0.94, so the euro depreciated and thus the dollar appreciated.

14-2a Exchange Rates Matter for the Prices of Goods

Exchange rates determine the prices of goods imported into one country from another. The following example will illustrate how changes in the exchange rate determine prices, based on production costs.

Suppose that companies sell their exported products for a price that equals their cost of production, which includes a normal profit. It costs 1,400 dollars for Apple to produce a laptop computer in the United States, and it costs 2,800,000 yen for Toyota Corporation to produce a Toyota Prius in Japan. The exchange rate is 100 yen per dollar, which also can be written as 0.01 dollar per yen.

> **depreciate** when the value of a currency decreases in terms of another
>
> **appreciate** when the value of a currency increases in terms of another

Apple sells a laptop computer in Japan for its cost of production, translated into yen:

$$1,400 \text{ dollars} \times 100 \frac{\text{yen}}{\text{dollar}} = 140,000 \text{ yen}$$

Similarly, Toyota sells a Prius to U.S. customers for

$$2,800,000 \text{ yen} \times 0.01 \frac{\text{dollar}}{\text{yen}} = 28,000 \text{ dollars}$$

What would happen, however, if the exchange rate were different? Suppose that it were 125 yen per dollar, or 0.008 dollars per yen. Then, following the same steps as above, the price of the Apple laptop sold in Japan is

$$1,400 \text{ dollars} \times 125 \frac{\text{yen}}{\text{dollar}} = 175,000 \text{ yen}$$

The price of the Toyota Prius sold in the United States is

$$2,800,000 \text{ yen} \times 0.008 \frac{\text{dollar}}{\text{yen}} = 22,400 \text{ dollars}$$

The results of this example are summarized in Table 14.2.

As the table shows, the more valuable the dollar is (when 1 dollar is worth 125 yen instead of 100 yen), the higher the price is of the Apple laptop sold in Japan and the lower the price is of the Toyota Prius sold in the United States.

TABLE 14.2 Example of Effect of Exchange Rate on Prices

	Exchange Rate	
	100 Yen per 1 Dollar	125 Yen per 1 Dollar
Price of Apple laptop sold in Japan	140,000 yen	175,000 yen
Price of Toyota Prius sold in U.S.	28,000 dollars	22,400 dollars

Btrenkel/iStockphoto.com

The value of the exchange rate affects the prices of goods and services sold to foreigners. Visitors to Europe from China can travel more cheaply if the euro depreciates relative to the Chinese yuan.

In general, when a country's currency appreciates, its goods become more expensive when sold abroad. When a country's currency depreciates, its goods become cheaper when sold abroad.

Business firms that export their products sell fewer goods when their currency appreciates because their goods become more expensive when sold abroad. The firms sell more units when their currency depreciates because their goods become cheaper abroad. Thus, changes in the exchange rate affect the prices of goods and the amount of imports and exports. For that reason, business firms often say that they would prefer that the currency of their country should depreciate because they could then sell more goods abroad; they also sometimes claim that would make the country better off. But that argument ignores the fact that a depreciation of the currency makes consumers in the country worse off because they face higher prices on the goods they purchase from abroad. Overall, it is not clear whether a country is better off or worse off because of an appreciation of the currency.

In this simple example we used hypothetical exchange rates to illustrate the impact of appreciating and depreciating currency on the demand for goods. We ignored an important question: What determines exchange rates? We now examine the answers to this question.

14-2b How Supply and Demand Determine Exchange Rates

Because an exchange rate is the price of one currency in terms of another, we can use our usual notions of supply and demand in the market for foreign exchange. If the supply of a currency increases, the currency depreciates relative to other currencies, just as the price of any good declines when its supply rises. If the demand for a currency increases, the currency appreciates relative to other currencies, just as the price of any good rises when demand for it increases. Thus, a simple approach to analyzing changes in exchange rates is to identify what changes supply or demand.

When firms or consumers buy foreign goods, they must exchange their domestic currency for foreign currency. When Apple sells its laptops domestically, it earns dollars that it uses to pay suppliers, workers, and stockholders. When it sells its laptops in Japan, it earns yen. Suppliers, workers, and stockholders do not want yen; they want dollars. Therefore, Apple must exchange the yen payments for laptops sold in Japan for dollars.

FIGURE 14.1 Determination of the Exchange Rate

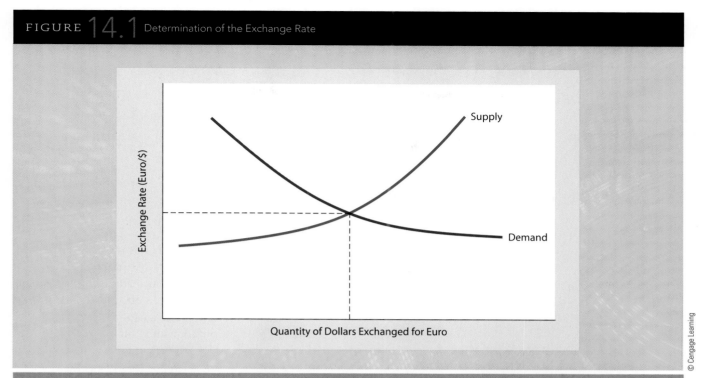

The exchange rate (denoted here in terms of euros per dollar) is determined by the supply of and demand for dollars in exchange for euros. Equilibrium occurs where the supply and demand curves intersect.

After Apple sells laptops to Japan, it will supply the yen it earns to the foreign-exchange market and demand dollars. Similarly, after Toyota sells cars in the United States, it will supply dollars and demand yen in the market. In general, exporters demand their own currency in the market for foreign exchange and supply currency from countries in which they sell their goods.

However, international trade is not the only source of demand and supply for foreign currency. A large part of the market for foreign exchange comes from investors in one country who want to invest in another. If a German citizen wishes to buy British government bonds, for example, he will supply euros in the market and demand British pounds. When he receives interest payments on his bonds, he will be paid interest in pounds and will want to trade them for euros, so he will then supply pounds and demand euros.

Overall, the market for foreign exchange is huge, with trades worth over $3 trillion taking place each day, on average. This amount is roughly 100 times as much as the amount of trade in goods and services, so most of the demand for currency trade arises from transactions between investors, not because of selling goods or services in foreign countries.

Most of the trading in currencies takes place between large commercial banks and investment banks in major financial centers such as London, New York, Tokyo, Frankfurt, Chicago, Los Angeles, Singapore, Hong Kong, Zurich, and Paris. Although we say that these transactions are of one currency for another, they are mostly exchanges of deposits at banks, not actual paper currencies. Trading in foreign exchange takes place 24 hours a day. Most transactions (almost 90 percent) are trades of dollars for another currency. Thus, the dollar is the world's monetary standard.

Figure 14.1 shows how the exchange rate is determined in the market. The diagram depicts the quantity of dollars exchanged for euros on the horizontal axis and the exchange rate (in terms of the number of euros per dollar) on the vertical axis. Suppliers will increase their supply of dollars if they get more euros from them, so the supply curve slopes upward. Demanders will decrease their demand for dollars if it takes more euros to buy a dollar, so the demand curve slopes downward. Equilibrium in the foreign-exchange market occurs when the quantity demanded equals the quantity supplied, at the intersection of the supply and demand curves.

If the demand for the dollar were to increase, perhaps because the United States began producing better goods than European nations, the dollar would appreciate, as shown in Figure 14.2. The increased demand for U.S. goods increases the demand for dollars, which

FIGURE 14.2 Effects of an Increase in the Demand for Dollars

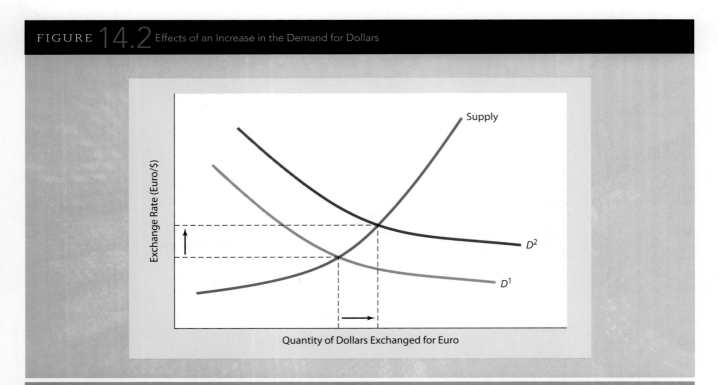

When the demand for dollars rises, the demand curve shifts to the right. The new equilibrium in the foreign-exchange market occurs at a higher exchange rate, which is denoted in euros per dollar. The higher exchange rate thus implies an appreciation of the dollar.

is reflected in the graph as a shift to the right of the demand curve. The new equilibrium occurs at a higher exchange rate. Because the exchange rate is denoted in euros per dollar, the dollar has appreciated.

Similarly, an increased supply of dollars can be analyzed using our supply-and-demand graph. Suppose that people holding dollars abroad increase their supply of dollars, perhaps because they gained more faith in the euro as a store of value. They would increase the supply of dollars in exchange for euros, represented in the graph as a shift to the right of the supply curve, as shown in Figure 14.3. The equilibrium exchange rate would decline, representing a depreciation of the dollar and appreciation of the euro.

14-2c How International Trade Affects the Exchange Rate

Trade between countries has a significant influence on the supply and demand curves in the market for foreign exchange and thus affects the exchange rate. If we focus on the trade of one good between countries, we can see how differences in costs of production limit the movement of exchange rates by influencing the supply and demand for foreign exchange.

Suppose that the only good sold between the United States and Canada is wheat, which both countries produce. The market for wheat determines the price and quantity of wheat in both countries. The cost of producing wheat is 14 U.S. dollars per bushel in the United States and 12 Canadian dollars per bushel in Canada. If the only trades between Canadians and U.S. citizens are for wheat, and if neither country produces enough wheat for both countries, then it seems logical that there should be only one price for wheat; that is, the exchange rate should be such that the Canadian dollar price of wheat equals the U.S. dollar price of wheat times the number of Canadian dollars per U.S. dollar. If that is true, then the exchange rate should be

$$\frac{12}{14} = 0.86 \text{ U.S. Canadian dollar per 1 U.S. dollar}$$

or

$$\frac{14}{12} = 1.17 \text{ U.S. dollars per 1 Canadian dollar}$$

When the exchange rate is 0.86 Canadian dollar per 1 U.S. dollar, then the cost of production of wheat in the United States and Canada is exactly the same when expressed in units of either currency.

FIGURE 14.3 Effects of an Increase in the Supply of Dollars

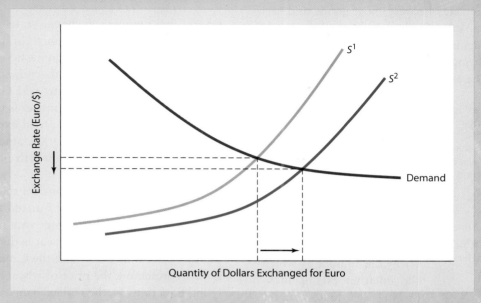

When the supply of dollars rises, the supply curve shifts to the right. The new equilibrium in the foreign-exchange market occurs at a lower exchange rate, which is denoted in euros per dollar. The lower exchange rate thus implies a depreciation of the dollar.

What would happen if the exchange rate were less than 0.86 Canadian dollar per 1 U.S. dollar? If the exchange rate were 0.75 Canadian dollar per 1 U.S. dollar, or 1.33 U.S. dollars per 1 Canadian dollar, then a price of 12 Canadian dollars per bushel is 12 Canadian dollars per bushel × 1.33 U.S. dollars per 1 Canadian dollar = 16 U.S. dollars per bushel. In this case, Canadian wheat imported into the United States would be more expensive ($16) than U.S. wheat ($14), and no one in the United States would want to buy Canadian wheat at that price.

Similarly, the price of 14 U.S. dollars per bushel would translate into Canadian dollars as 14 U.S. dollars per bushel × 0.75 Canadian dollar per 1 U.S. dollar = 10.50 Canadian dollars. Thus, U.S. wheat is cheaper in terms of Canadian dollars (10.50 Canadian dollars per bushel) than Canadian wheat (12.00 Canadian dollars per bushel). In this case, the United States would export wheat to Canada, and Canadians would buy all the U.S. wheat they could. As such transactions occurred, the demand for U.S. dollars would rise, and the demand for Canadian dollars would fall, so the U.S. dollar would appreciate until it reached 0.86 Canadian dollar per 1 U.S. dollar.

It is likely that in equilibrium the exchange rate will equate the prices of goods in different countries. If there is only one good traded between countries, the equilibrium exchange rate is determined such that the **law of one price** holds; that is, the price of the good in the two countries, when expressed in units of the same currency, is the same. If the price of the good is not the same in the two countries, then either exports or imports will occur—the good will be produced in the country where it is cheaper to produce and exported to the country where the price is higher.

In reality, of course, many goods and services are traded between countries, and it is difficult to use the law of one price to figure out what the exchange rate should be. Economists have tried to use the general notion that the exchange rate is determined by the costs of producing goods in different countries. Countries measure the average prices of their goods and services using price indexes. Thus, generalizing the law of one price to many goods and services suggests that the exchange rate depends on the price indexes in different countries. According to the concept of **absolute purchasing-power parity,**

law of one price the idea that the exchange rate is determined such that the price of a good is the same in two countries when expressed in units of the same currency

absolute purchasing-power parity the idea that the exchange rate should equal the ratio of the price indexes of two countries

the exchange rate should equal the ratio of price indexes of different countries. Unfortunately, absolute purchasing-power parity does not appear to be a good guide to exchange rates because most goods and services are not tradable between countries, and the goods usually are not identical between countries. Thus, the notion that equalizing the prices of goods across countries determines the exchange rate seems far-fetched.

An alternative but related view is that exchange rates change as prices change in different countries. This notion is called **relative purchasing-power parity** and means that a currency in one country depreciates relative to the currency in a second country by the amount by which the inflation rate is higher in the first country than in the second country. For example, suppose that the inflation rate is 2.0 percent in the United States and 0.5 percent in Japan; then the inflation rate is 1.5 percent higher in the United States than in Japan. Relative purchasing-power parity implies that the dollar should depreciate 1.5 percent against the yen. There is some evidence that relative purchasing-power parity helps to predict changes in exchange rates, but it takes a long time for the exchange rate to adjust. Other factors seem to matter much more for determining the exchange rate.

Even if the ideas of absolute and relative purchasing-power parity are not very useful in determining the exchange rate, the idea of adjusting the exchange rate for changes in prices in different countries is useful. Economists define the **real exchange rate** as the exchange rate adjusted for changes in prices. (What we have been calling the exchange rate, which is the amount of one currency needed to purchase a unit of another currency, is often called the *nominal exchange rate* because it does not account for changes in prices.) In analyzing the real exchange rate, we must be careful about which currency is being traded for one unit of another. We usually think about this from the point of view of a citizen in one country, which we call the *domestic country,* trading with someone from another country, which we call the *foreign country.* The real exchange rate x equals the nominal exchange rate X times the ratio of the domestic price level P to the foreign price level P^F, that is,

relative purchasing-power parity the idea that a currency in one country should depreciate relative to the currency in a second country by the amount by which the inflation rate is higher in the first country than the second

real exchange rate the exchange rate adjusted for changes in prices in both countries

$$x = X\frac{P}{P^F} \qquad (1)$$

where the nominal exchange rate is expressed in terms of the number of units of the foreign currency per one unit of the domestic currency. Just as a price index can be used to convert nominal gross domestic product (GDP) into real GDP, the ratio of price indexes in different countries is used to convert a nominal exchange rate into a real exchange rate. The real exchange rate is the average amount of goods in the foreign country that are worth one unit of goods in the domestic country.

In the wheat example, consider the United States to be the domestic country and Canada to be the foreign country. The nominal exchange rate is 0.86 Canadian dollar per 1 U.S. dollar. If wheat is the only good, then the U.S. price index is 14 and the Canadian price index is 12 (representing the price of wheat in each country). Using Equation (1), the real exchange rate is

$$x = 0.86\frac{14}{12} = 1$$

Under absolute purchasing-power parity, the real exchange rate always should equal 1, as is the case in this example.

Relative purchasing-power parity, on the other hand, says that the real exchange rate is constant and that changes in prices cause changes in the nominal exchange rate. We can see the influence of prices on the nominal exchange rate if we rewrite Equation (1) in terms of the nominal exchange rate. To do so, begin with Equation (1):

$$x = X\frac{P}{P^F}$$

Then rearrange this expression by switching sides and multiplying both sides by P^F/P:

$$X\frac{P}{P^F}\frac{P^F}{P} = x\frac{P^F}{P}$$

Simplifying this expression gives

$$X = x\frac{P^F}{P}$$

We can use this equation to see how the nominal exchange rate changes when terms on the right-hand side of the equation change. For small changes in the real exchange rate and prices in each country, the percentage change (%Δ) in the nominal exchange rate is related to the percentage changes in the price levels in the two countries:

$$\%\Delta X = \%\Delta x + \%\Delta P^F - \%\Delta P$$

Because the percentage change in the price index is the inflation rate π, this equation can be written as

$$\%\Delta X = \%\Delta x + \pi^F - \pi \qquad (2)$$

If relative purchasing-power parity holds, the real exchange rate remains unaffected by changes in prices, so $\%\Delta x = 0$, and Equation (2) becomes

$$\%\Delta X = \pi^F - \pi$$

That is, the percentage change in the nominal exchange rate in each year equals the difference between the foreign inflation rate and the domestic inflation rate. Thus, in the preceding example in which inflation was 0.5 percent in Japan and 2.0 percent in the United States, the dollar would depreciate by 1.5 percent each year if relative purchasing-power parity holds because

$$\%\Delta X = \pi^F - \pi$$
$$= 0.5\% - 2.0\%$$
$$= -1.5\%$$

14-2d How Financial Investment Affects the Exchange Rate

Because the total amount of foreign-exchange trading far exceeds the amount of goods traded, it makes sense to think that exchange rates are determined by investors buying and selling financial securities in other countries. Consider a U.S. investor deciding where to invest her savings. The investor will look at many possible investments, accounting for differences in risk, liquidity, and the other criteria that we discussed in Chapter 2. She is likely to invest where her expected return is the highest. However, in addition to the risk on the return to the financial securities she buys, if she invests in securities from a foreign country, she faces an additional risk—the risk that the exchange rate will change.

An example will help to illustrate the risk from a change in the exchange rate. Suppose that a U.S. investor with $10,000 to invest can buy a one-year U.S. government bond with a nominal interest rate of 4 percent or a one-year Japanese government bond with a nominal interest rate of 1 percent. Suppose that the current exchange rate is 100 yen per dollar. The U.S. bond pays interest of

$$10,000 \text{ dollars} \times 0.04 = 400 \text{ dollars}$$

To buy the Japanese bond, the investor would exchange her $10,000 for 1,000,000 yen and then buy the bond with those yen. At the end of the year, she will receive 1,010,000 yen (10,000 yen in interest plus the principal of 1,000,000 yen). Next she will have to exchange her yen for dollars. The problem she faces is that at the time she buys the bond, she does not know what the exchange rate will be in one year when she wants to exchange her 1,010,000 yen for dollars.

Suppose, for example, that the exchange rate is 95 yen per dollar at the end of the year, which represents a 5 percent depreciation of the dollar. When the investor exchanges her yen for dollars at the end of the year, she receives

$$\frac{1,010,000 \text{ yen}}{95 \text{ yen/dollar}} = 10,632 \text{ dollars}$$

which represents interest of $632. In this case, she is better off investing in the Japanese bond instead of the U.S. government bond because the U.S. bond would pay only $400 in interest.

However, suppose that the exchange rate is 98 yen per dollar at the end of the year, a 2 percent depreciation of the dollar. Then the investor would receive

$$\frac{1,010,000 \text{ yen}}{98 \text{ yen/dollar}} = 10,306 \text{ dollars}$$

which means that she receives only $306 in interest from the Japanese bond. In this case, she is better off owning the U.S. bond.

Thus, the investor must consider not just the interest rates on the securities in different countries but also whether the exchange rate might change. The investment in the foreign security has an expected return in dollar terms approximately equal to $i^F - \%\Delta X^e$, where i^F is the nominal interest rate in the foreign currency (in percent), X is the nominal exchange rate in terms of units of the foreign currency per unit of the domestic currency, and the superscript e refers to the expected value in one year; thus,

$$\%\Delta X^e = \frac{X^e_{t+1} - X_t}{X_t} \times 100\%$$

The investor knows the current nominal exchange rate X_t when she invests, but she does not know what the exchange rate will be in one year, so she must form some expectation about it, which we denote as X^e_{t+1}. If $\%\Delta X^e$ is positive, the domestic currency is expected to appreciate. If $\%\Delta X^e$ is negative, the domestic currency is expected to depreciate.

In the example, suppose that the investor thought the exchange rate would be 95 yen per dollar in one year. Then the expected depreciation of the dollar would be 5 percent because

$$\%\Delta X^e = \frac{95 - 100}{100} \times 100\% = -5\ percent$$

The expected dollar return to investing in the Japanese bond would be about 1 percent $-$ (-5 percent) $= 6$ percent, which is higher than the 4 percent interest rate on the U.S. bond. If the investor thought that the dollar would appreciate -2 percent, the expected dollar return to investing in the Japanese bond would be about 1 percent $-$ (-2 percent) $= 3$ percent, which is less than the 4 percent interest rate on the U.S. bond.

In general, an investor compares the interest rate on a domestic investment with the interest rate on a foreign investment minus the expected appreciation of the domestic currency. In fact, when the interest rate on a domestic bond just equals the interest rate on a foreign bond minus the expected appreciation of the domestic currency, there is said to be **interest-rate parity**. Interest-rate parity means that

interest-rate parity a situation in which the interest rate on a domestic bond equals the interest rate on a foreign bond minus the expected appreciation of the domestic currency

$$i^D = i^F - \%\Delta X^e \qquad (3)$$

where i^D is the interest rate on the domestic bond (in percent).

Interest-rate parity often does not appear to occur because expected return is not the only factor in the investor's decision. Investing in a foreign country has additional risk because of the need to exchange currencies and the possibility that the exchange rate will change. Thus, investors, who are likely to be risk-averse, may need higher returns to entice them to purchase securities in foreign countries.

14-2e How Has the Dollar's Value Changed over Time?

Movements of the exchange rate between the dollar and every other currency of the world can be tracked over time. Because the United States trades with so many other countries, though, it makes sense to figure out, on average, how the dollar is faring against the other countries taken as a group. The Federal Reserve has devised an index to do so, based on the amount of trade the United States does with each country. One index looks just at the nominal exchange rate. The other index uses the consumer price index in each country to calculate an index in real terms. Both indexes are shown in Figure 14.4.

The figure shows that the dollar appreciated in nominal terms, on average, against other currencies from 1980 to 1985, depreciated slightly from 1985 to 1988, appreciated from 1988 to 2001, depreciated from 2001 to 2008, appreciated sharply during the financial crisis of 2008, depreciated after the crisis ended until 2010, and has been relatively stable since 2010. Much of the overall appreciation of the dollar, however, occurred because U.S. inflation was lower than foreign inflation.

The real index shows that in inflation-adjusted terms the dollar depreciated in the 1970s following the oil-price shocks in that period. The dollar appreciated in the first half of the 1980s because the United States had very high interest rates while it attempted to reduce inflation, thus attracting financial investment from foreign countries. The dollar depreciated in the second half of the 1980s and in the first half of the 1990s because U.S. interest rates were reduced and U.S. citizens sought to diversify their portfolios internationally. The productivity boom of the second half of the 1990s brought a new inflow of capital from foreign countries, and the dollar appreciated again. As the U.S. economy weakened in the early 2000s and U.S. interest rates and stock returns were low, the dollar depreciated in real terms. The dollar continued to depreciate in real terms throughout the 2000s until 2008. During the financial crisis, many investors sought the safety of U.S. investments

FIGURE 14.4 Nominal and Real Indexes of the Foreign-Exchange Value of the U.S. Dollar

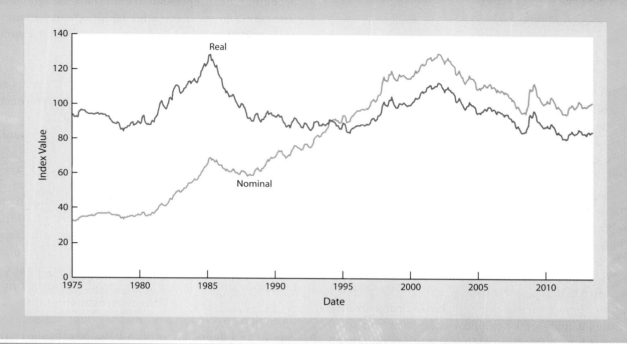

The Federal Reserve's broad index of the foreign-exchange value of the U.S. dollar is shown in both nominal terms and real terms. The figure shows that in nominal terms the dollar appreciated, on average, against other currencies from 1975 to 2013 because U.S. inflation was lower than foreign inflation, on average. The real index shows that in inflation-adjusted terms the dollar has fluctuated around a fairly stable level from 1975 to 2013.

(especially U.S. government bonds) and the dollar appreciated sharply in real terms at the end of 2008 to early 2009. After the crisis ended, the dollar began depreciating again in real terms. Overall, from 1975 to 2013, the dollar has fluctuated around a fairly stable level.

14-2f How Exchange Rates Affect the Economy

Exchange rates affect the economy primarily through their impact on the prices of imports and exports. What effect does a change in the exchange rate have on a country's imports and exports? We noted earlier that if a currency depreciates, a country's exports become cheaper when sold abroad and its imports become more expensive. Because demand depends on price, the amount of exports rises and the amount of imports declines. Thus, net exports rise.

Some accounting will help to clarify the effect of exchange rates on an economy. When we discussed the macroeconomy in Chapter 12, we noted that net

exports were one component of aggregate demand. Aggregate demand in the economy was equal to the sum of consumption C, investment in physical capital I, government spending G, and net exports NX, which must equal the economy's output Y in equilibrium. All the income that people earn must equal the economy's output and must be spent either on consumer goods C or taxes T, or it must be saved S. Thus, we have two equations describing the relationship between these variables:

$$Y = C + I + G + NX$$

and

$$Y = C + S + T$$

Combining the two equations gives

$$C + I + G + NX = C + S + T$$

The C term cancels because it appears on both sides of the equation, and the equation can be rearranged to get

$$S = I + NX + (G - T) \qquad (4)$$

This equation shows that an economy's savings are used for investment in physical capital, net exports, and government deficits $(G - T)$. It might seem odd that savings are used for net exports, but consider what happens when a country exports more than it imports (so that $NX > 0$). The country receives more foreign currency from selling its exports than it spends on imports, so it might buy financial securities in foreign countries. Thus, some of its savings are used for foreign investment.

The idea that savings are used for net exports, investment in physical capital, and government deficits is formalized in the system of international income accounting. This system defines the **balance on current account** as a measure of the flows of goods and services out of a country into other countries or other items that cause payments to flow into the country. The measure equals net exports of goods and services *plus* net income from abroad *plus* net unilateral current transfers (gifts to the country from foreigners minus gifts from the country to foreigners, such as foreign aid). If a country has positive net exports, it exports more goods than it imports, so payments flow into the country, on net. If a country's citizens who work abroad bring income home, or when a country's citizens earn investment income from foreign financial securities, payments flow into the country. When a country gives foreign aid to other countries, payments flow out of the country, so those amounts are subtracted from the balance on current account.

A second concept in the system of international income accounting is the **balance on capital and financial account,** which represents the amount foreign citizens, firms, and governments invest in a country minus the amount that country's citizens, firms, and governments invest abroad.

The balance on the current account plus the balance on the capital and financial account equals zero, by definition, because every international transaction involves offsetting amounts that sum to zero in the current account, the capital and financial account, or both.

For our analysis, we use the international accounting system's capital and financial account. The negative of the balance on the capital and financial account is called **net foreign investment (NFI).** A country's NFI represents investments in other countries, either from purchasing financial securities, called **portfolio investment,** or from installing capital goods and using them to produce output in the other countries, called **direct investment,** minus what foreigners invest in the domestic country. Because the capital and financial account balance plus the current account balance equals zero, and because net foreign investment is the negative of the capital and financial account balance, and assuming that net income from abroad and net unilateral transfers are zero, then NFI equals net exports (NX):

$$NFI = NX$$

Given this, Equation (4) can be rewritten as

$$S = I + NFI + (G - T) \qquad (5)$$

This equation says that savings are used to invest in the domestic country, to invest in foreign countries, or to finance the government's budget deficit (which equals government spending minus taxes). The following box illustrates how savings are used.

Can we predict what happens over the course of a business cycle to the exchange rate? When a country's economy is growing strongly, the expected return on its investments is usually high, so investors tend to invest more in it, causing its currency to appreciate. As an economy weakens in a recession, expected returns generally decline, investors pull out, and the currency depreciates. On the other hand, inflation often increases in expansions, causing

balance on current account net exports of goods and services plus net income from abroad plus net unilateral current transfers

balance on capital and financial account the amount foreign citizens, firms, and governments invest in a country minus the amount that country's citizens, firms, and governments invest abroad

net foreign investment (NFI) investments in other countries in the form of portfolio investment or direct investment minus what foreigners invest in the domestic country

portfolio investment investments in other countries from purchasing financial securities

direct investment investments in other countries from installing capital goods and using them to produce output in the other countries

How Savings Are Used

$$S = I + NFI + (G - T)$$

Savings   Domestic Investment   Net Foreign Investment   Government Budget Deficit

the currency to depreciate; inflation often decreases in recessions, causing the currency to appreciate. Finally, in an economic expansion, people buy more imported goods, selling the domestic currency for foreign currencies, so the domestic currency depreciates; in a recession, people cut back on purchases of imported goods, so the domestic currency appreciates. Thus, the exchange rate is affected by different forces pushing it in different directions—the overall effect is ambiguous. In fact, a look at the broad real exchange-rate index in Figure 14.5 shows very little relationship with the business cycle. In the figure,

recessions are indicated by blue bars. Sometimes the currency appreciates in a recession, but at other times it depreciates.

Why do exchange rates vary so much? Given what we know about the determinants of exchange rates, the changes in exchange rates arise because there are substantial changes in inflation and inflation expectations, government policy concerning international trade, productivity (which affects expected returns), the demand for imports and exports, and monetary policy (which affects expected inflation in the long run and expected returns in the short run). (To see how productivity

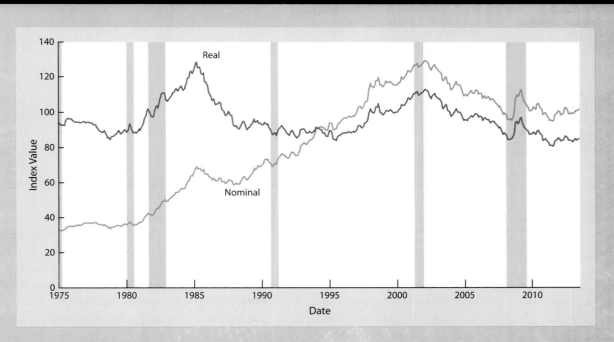

FIGURE 14.5 Recessions and the Foreign-Exchange Value of the U.S. Dollar

The Federal Reserve's broad indexes of the foreign exchange value of the U.S. dollar are shown in both nominal and real terms with recession bars. The figure shows that in recessions, the dollar appreciates sometimes and depreciates sometimes. In expansions, there are periods when the dollar is appreciating and other times when the dollar is depreciating.

Businesspeople who run companies that export goods often complain that as the currency of their home country appreciates, they must raise their prices in foreign countries, and thus they are at a competitive disadvantage. For example, in the late 1990s in the United States, business executives complained about the high value of the dollar to the president and to the Federal Reserve. However, the profits those companies earned abroad rose to record levels at the same time. Why would businesspeople complain when they are making record profits?

What the business executives fail to understand about the appreciation of their currency is that it might be their own success that causes both the appreciation of the currency *and* their record profits. In the late 1990s, for example, productivity in U.S. manufacturing grew dramatically as firms employed new technology effectively. This increase in productivity enabled the firms to reduce their costs of producing goods. The overall increase in productivity in the United States caused profits to rise, leading foreign investors to invest more in the United States, thus raising the value of the dollar and leading those firms to raise their prices abroad. The reduction in production costs also allows the exporting firms to reduce their prices, sell as many goods as before, and make higher profits.

The root cause of both higher overall prices and higher profits is the increase in productivity.

Economists Cedric Tille, Nicolas Stoffels, and Olga Gorbachev ["To What Extent Does Productivity Drive the Dollar?" Federal Reserve Bank of New York, *Current Issues in Economics and Finance* (August 2001)] examined the long-term movements in the real exchange rate over the last 30 years to see if those movements could be explained by movements in productivity. Economic theory suggests that a rise in the productivity of producing goods that are traded across countries should cause the real exchange rate to rise (when the exchange rate is expressed as the number of units of the foreign currency needed to purchase one unit of the domestic currency). But how much of the movement of the real exchange rate is explained by changes in productivity? The researchers found that productivity accounted for two-thirds of the dollar's appreciation relative to the euro in the 1990s and three-fourths of the appreciation of the dollar relative to the yen.

Thus, when U.S. exporters' profits rise and the dollar appreciates, business executives should not complain to the government about it; they should realize that they caused it by their own improvements in productivity.

affects exchange rates, see the Data Bank box "Productivity and Appreciation.")

What are the implications of exchange rates and interdependence of economies for the macroeconomy? We can analyze this in terms of the aggregate-demand/aggregate-supply (*AD–AS*) model of the economy from Chapter 12, noting that current and expected exchange rates affect some of the key variables in the model. In addition, Equation (5) ties together domestic investment in physical capital, foreign investment, and the government budget deficit with the economy's savings. The aggregate-demand and aggregate-supply curves look just as they did in Chapter 12, but now an additional set of equations determine the exchange rate, which feeds back on many of the other variables of the model.

Dynamic models, such as those we discussed in Chapter 13, can easily accommodate an open economy (an economy in which international trade plays a vital

role). The exchange rate, present and future, affects the decisions of economic agents. One more endogenous variable than before, the exchange rate, is determined by the model. Dynamic models get a bit more complicated in an open-economy framework because the decisions of the foreign agents also must be modeled in a consistent way.

How do the results from open-economy models differ from those with a closed economy? They generally show that the outcomes are a bit more complicated because there are more avenues through which variables can be changed. Foreign economies can affect the domestic economy, and there can be feedback between the two. Yet the main direction of changes in major macroeconomic variables remains the same. The following box, "Policy Perspective: How Independent Should a Country Be?" explores the issue of whether a country should allow itself to be influenced by other countries through international investment.

1 Because prices of goods depend on production costs, changes in the exchange rate cause changes in the prices of imported and exported goods. When a country's currency appreciates, its exports become more expensive abroad, and the goods it imports become cheaper; when a country's currency depreciates, its exports decline in price, and its imports become more expensive.

2 Exchange rates are determined by supply and demand for currencies. Supply and demand, in turn, depend on both international trade and financial investment flows between countries.

3 In nominal terms, the dollar has appreciated against the average of other currencies because the U.S. inflation rate has been lower than the inflation rate in other countries. In real terms, the dollar has gone through periods of both appreciation and depreciation.

4 Exchange rates do not move systematically over the business cycle.

Policy➔Perspective   How Independent Should a Country Be?

Economic research shows that an economy can grow faster in the long run if it is open to trade and investment from abroad. Being open, however, allows shocks from abroad to be transmitted to a country. In addition, when a country allows financial capital to flow freely in and out of the country, it must be prepared to face the consequences if foreign investors change their expectations about the profitability of the investments. In the Asian crisis, which began in 1997, investors started to pull out of the entire Asian region, and the results were devastating to those countries, especially Indonesia, Malaysia, South Korea, and Thailand.

What caused investors to conclude that Asia was no longer worth investing in? From the 1970s through the early 1990s, investors flocked to Asia and received a fairly good return. But the accounting systems in place in many Asian countries did not reveal sufficient information to investors and misled investors about the returns on their investments. The banking sectors in those economies were not very strong and were poorly supervised. In addition, government policy came to play a larger and larger role in the region, and investors felt that the governments were determining their returns, not the market; in some cases, corrupt government officials engaged in cronyism by directing investments to their family and friends.

As a result, many investors began to reduce their involvement in the region, selling their investments. With reduced investor confidence, people began to think that the currencies of the Asian economies would depreciate in the future. Because the exchange rate was expected to decline in the future,

investors became even less likely to invest in a country, and the exchange rate began to decline immediately.

Unfortunately, many of the countries had borrowed substantial sums from abroad, denominated in foreign currencies such as dollars. As their currencies depreciated, the countries had to repay the loans with more of their own currency. (To understand why, note that if a firm in South Korea must make an interest payment of $100,000, and the exchange rate has changed from 800 won per dollar to 1,400 won per dollar, then the payment in won has risen from 80,000,000 won to 140,000,000 won, an increase of 75 percent.) The result was an increased risk of default for companies and governments in Asia that borrowed heavily from abroad. When foreign investors pulled out, the interest rate rose, thus discouraging new investment in capital goods by domestic business firms. On the plus side, the decline in the exchange rate reduced the price of a country's exports, so it could sell more goods abroad.

What can a country do when investors withdraw their investments, causing the currency to depreciate, as in the Asian crisis? There are two main possibilities: The countries can try to (1) prop up the currency or (2) limit the movement of capital.

The first possibility, propping up the currency, is very risky. A country that tries this can use its reserves of gold, dollars, and other currencies that it has saved over time, exchanging them all to purchase its own currency in the foreign-exchange market, thus increasing the demand for its currency and causing the currency to appreciate. In doing so, however, the country may find itself

(continued)

quickly running out of reserves, and the effort may fail. Indeed, this happened in a number of the Asian countries and turned out to exacerbate the crisis. An alternative is for a country to reduce the money supply to raise interest rates, trying to attract foreign investors to keep their investments in place because they will be able to earn a higher return. However, this policy often leads to a recession because the high interest rates needed to keep the exchange rate stable choke off investment in capital goods by business firms. The recession increases unemployment and reduces incomes, so the country bears significant costs from such a policy.

The second possibility, restricting the flow of capital, is a desperate measure. In the Asian crisis, the government of Malaysia began to restrict capital flows, blaming the country's troubles on evil foreign investors. A country certainly can kick those investors out completely, but then it cannot attract capital from abroad. The ability to borrow from abroad can help a country grow much more rapidly than it would in the absence of those capital flows. Instead of weathering the crisis, countries such as Malaysia seem to prefer to sacrifice their long-run growth for a short-run solution. In fact, nearly all the Asian countries except Indonesia recovered fairly quickly from the crisis. These nations probably will be hesitant to borrow as much from abroad in the future, especially in terms of loans denominated in units of foreign currency.

To avoid such problems, a country might try to rely less on short-term investments by foreigners. If governments would borrow less from abroad in the form of short-term loans, then in a crisis they would not have so much to repay in a short amount of time. Unfortunately, many foreign investors do not want to commit to long-term loans in a country; the investors *want* short-term loans precisely because they will be able to remove their funds quickly if the country's economy begins to deteriorate.

Can anything else be done, or must a country go it alone? One possibility, similar to the way in which the Federal Reserve can supply funds to a bank that is temporarily in trouble, would be for an international agency to supply funds to a country to help it avoid short-term problems. In fact, the International Monetary Fund (IMF) has the potential to do so. Unfortunately, two major drawbacks prevent the IMF from bailing out countries in crises. First, the IMF does not have enough funds at its disposal to prevent financial crises such as the one in Asia. Usually, the IMF can lend a few billion dollars to help a country weather a crisis, but it often takes more than that for a country to pay off all the short-term loans it has outstanding. Countries sometimes ask the U.S. government for similar loans, but Congress has been reluctant to be the world's lender of last resort, for good reason (in many cases) because the money often would not be returned. Second, the problem with IMF bailouts is one of moral hazard: If countries know that the IMF will bail them out in the event of a crisis, they will not take sufficient steps to prevent the crisis in the first place, and investors will not take as many precautions concerning where to lend, knowing that the IMF effectively will guarantee their loans.

The market for capital can bring a country benefits when capital flows into a country and stays there. In a crisis, the existence of that capital can be disastrous when investors attempt to pull their funds out. Thus, greater economic interaction with the rest of the world can have its drawbacks because it means that a country is more subject to shocks from outside and to swings in the sentiment of investors. However, interdependence also increases an economy's growth.

RECAP

1 The Asian crisis in 1997 revealed that when countries are dependent on capital flows from abroad, they face large risks if foreign investors withdraw their investments.

2 When investors pull their investments out of a country, the country can either try to prop up its currency to prevent depreciation or try to limit the movement of capital. Neither plan is very promising.

3 A country can avoid the problem of foreign investors pulling out by not borrowing much from abroad, but then it may not grow as rapidly.

Review Questions and Problems

Review Questions

1 Why does an oil price shock cause the business cycles of different countries to be synchronized?

2 Why did the business cycles of major industrial countries become unsynchronized in the 1990s?

3 What mechanisms lead to the international transmission of economic shocks? Explain the basic means by which the transmission occurs.

4 What is the difference between the law of one price and purchasing-power parity?

5 Why do investors care about what happens to the exchange rate?

6 What is the difference between the nominal exchange rate and the real exchange rate?

7 How does absolute purchasing-power parity differ from relative purchasing-power parity?

8 What is interest-rate parity?

9 What is the relationship between a country's savings, its government budget deficit, its domestic investment in physical capital, and its foreign investment?

10 What were the main causes of the Asian financial crisis in 1997? What role did exchange rates play in the crisis?

Numerical Exercises

11 Based on the data in Table 14.1, did the dollar depreciate or appreciate against the pound, the Canadian dollar, the franc, the yen, and the mark between 1970 and 1980? Between 1980 and 1990? Between 1990 and 2000? Between 2000 and 2013?

12 Table 14.1 shows the exchange rates of various currencies versus the dollar. Use the information in the table to show how you could have profited by trading currencies if the exchange rate between French francs and German marks was 3 francs per mark on January 1, 1990. Suppose that you began with 10,000 marks. Show what trades you could have made buying or selling francs, marks, and dollars to generate a profit and how much money you could make.

13 Suppose the price level in Japan is 12,000, the price level in the United States is 145, and the price level in Mexico is 500. Suppose the current nominal exchange rates are 115 yen per dollar and 4 pesos per dollar. Calculate the real exchange rates (rounded to two decimal places) between each pair of countries. (That means you should be calculating three real exchange rates.)

14 Suppose that you are an investor who is considering buying a one-year U.S. government bond that has a 5 percent interest rate or a one-year Japanese government bond with a 1 percent interest rate. The exchange rate today is 110 yen per dollar, and you expect the exchange rate to be 105 yen per dollar one year from now.

  a Which bond would you purchase? Why?

  b Suppose that the exchange rate today is 107 yen instead of 110 yen. Would you change your decision about which bond to buy?

  c Suppose that the exchange rate is 110 yen today, and you think that there is a 20 percent chance that the exchange rate will be 100 yen in one year and an 80 percent chance that the exchange rate will be 108 yen in one year. Would you change your decision about which bond to buy?

15 Suppose that the exchange rate adjusts so that interest-rate parity holds. Suppose also that the interest rate on a one-year German bond is 7 percent and the interest rate on a one-year U.S. bond is 4 percent.

  a Suppose that you expect the exchange rate in one year to be 1.2 dollars per euro. What is the exchange rate today?

  b Suppose that relative purchasing-power parity holds and that the inflation rate in Germany is expected to be 2 percent over the next year. What is the expected inflation rate in the United States?

(continued)

Analytical Problems

16 Many countries have taken steps in recent years to increase their trade with other countries, increasing both exports and imports. Given this expansion of trade, should we expect synchronized or unsynchronized business cycles across countries in the future?

17 Some U.S. presidents have pursued a strong dollar policy, taking actions that cause the dollar to appreciate against other currencies. Other presidents have cared less about the value of the dollar, allowing it to depreciate against other currencies. What are the benefits and costs to a nation of appreciation and depreciation?

18 Suppose that you were a politician in a small country that owed millions of dollars (in dollar-denominated loans) to U.S. banks that had lent your country money for investment over the past decade. Most of the investments failed because they went to political cronies rather than to legitimate business firms. Now foreign investors are getting nervous and starting to pull their money out, causing your country's exchange rate to depreciate. What actions should you consider taking to save your country's economy? Will it help to pass a law forbidding foreign investment?

PART 4

MONETARY POLICY

CHAPTER 15

Fstockfoto/shutterstock.com

The FEDERAL RESERVE SYSTEM

The Federal Reserve System (the Fed) is the organization that determines U.S. monetary policy, oversees many

U.S. financial institutions, and ensures the efficient functioning of the payments system. In this chapter we will look at how the Federal Reserve System is organized, where it gets the funds to operate, and how it is related to the U.S. government.

The Federal Reserve System has three main parts: Federal Reserve banks, the Board of Governors, and the Federal Open Market Committee (FOMC), as shown in Figure 15.1. The Board of Governors, located in Washington, D.C., heads up nationwide tasks such as determining banking regulations. The 12 Federal Reserve banks, located around the country, work on local tasks such as examining the banks in their district, counting the money supply, and providing banks with currency and coin.

FIGURE 15.1 The Structure of the Federal Reserve System

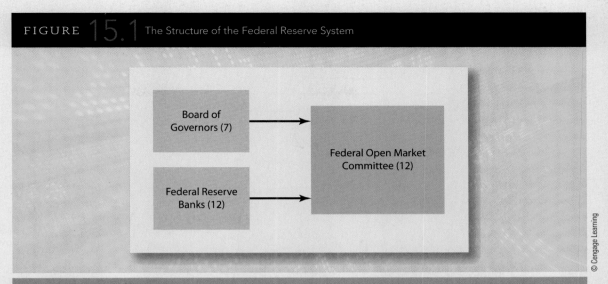

The Federal Reserve System is headed by a seven-member Board of Governors in Washington, D.C. Twelve Federal Reserve banks around the nation serve banks in their districts. The seven governors and five of the Federal Reserve bank presidents are members of the Federal Open Market Committee (FOMC), which determines monetary policy.

The FOMC, which determines monetary policy, is composed of the seven members of the Board of Governors and five of the presidents of Federal Reserve banks. Because the committee receives input from the Federal Reserve banks around the country, it is less likely to be dominated by the viewpoint in New York or Washington. (See the Policy Insider box "Why Power Is Diffuse at the Fed.")

In this chapter we examine how Federal Reserve banks operate on a day-by-day basis and how they influence monetary policy. Then we examine the Board of Governors and its role in overseeing the entire Federal Reserve System, especially the power of the chairman. Next we look at the details of operation of the FOMC, which is the group responsible for setting monetary policy. Finally, we examine the Fed's independence from government and politicians.

15-1 Federal Reserve Banks

The 12 Federal Reserve banks in the United States perform a variety of functions, including supervising and examining state member banks and bank holding companies, tracking the banking statistics on deposits that are part of the monetary aggregates, supplying currency and coin to financial institutions, holding the reserves of financial institutions, serving as the fiscal agent of the U.S. Treasury Department (essentially keeping the government's checkbook), and acting as a lender of last resort. Reserve banks (also called *district banks*) are spread throughout the United States, and each is responsible for some portion of the country, as the map in Figure 15.2 shows. Each Reserve bank's territory is called a *district*, and the districts are numbered sequentially, so the Federal Reserve Bank of Boston is responsible for the first district, the Federal Reserve Bank of New York has the second district, and so on. The Federal Reserve Bank of New York has a special role because it implements monetary policy by buying or selling securities in the open market, as well as buying or selling currencies in the foreign-exchange market.

Why are there 12 Federal Reserve banks located around the country, and why are they located in the cities shown in Figure 15.2? Before the Federal Reserve System was established by law in 1913, the country lacked a system to stabilize interest rates and prevent

FIGURE 15.2 The Federal Reserve System

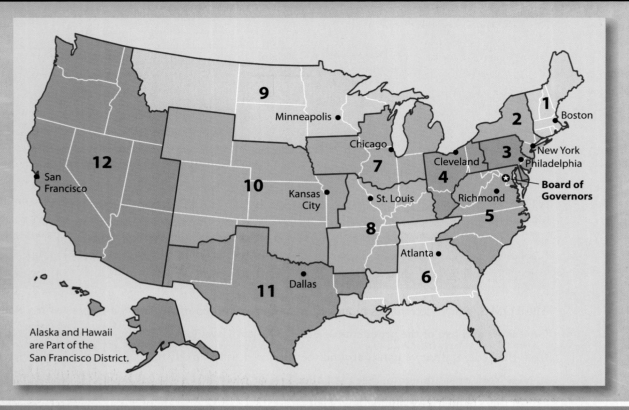

The Federal Reserve System consists of 12 Federal Reserve banks located around the country, each of which is responsible for the payments system in its own district, as shown on the map. The Board of Governors in Washington, D.C., oversees all the activities of the Federal Reserve banks.

banking crises. For this reason, the Fed was given the power both to control the money supply and to regulate banking. In writing the Federal Reserve Act, however, Congress worried that the new organization would place too much power in the hands of just a few policymakers. Thus, Congress gave substantial power to separate Federal Reserve banks around the country, hoping to diffuse power. Once the number of Federal Reserve banks was determined, Congress fought over where they would be, so the locations of the Federal Reserve banks are primarily a reflection of the political power of influential senators and representatives in 1913.

15-1a The Structure of a Federal Reserve Bank

Formally, each of the 12 Federal Reserve banks is a corporation, each with a board of directors and with outstanding equity securities. The banks in each Federal Reserve bank district that are members of the Federal Reserve System own those securities. The member

banks receive periodic dividend payments, just as if they owned shares in any other corporation. However, the banks that own shares in Federal Reserve banks are not allowed to sell their shares or buy additional shares. Their ownership share in the Fed is proportional to their own equity capital, and the dividend is set by law at 6 percent of the capital that banks pay in to purchase their shares. Unlike a private corporation, the Federal Reserve banks are not free to set their budgets without approval by the Board of Governors in Washington, D.C. Thus, a Federal Reserve bank is a corporation that is constrained in what it can do and thus is similar to many government organizations.

The board of directors of each Federal Reserve bank is chosen in a manner that is consistent with the part-private, part-government organization of the Fed. Each Federal Reserve bank has nine board members, as shown in Figure 15.3. Three class A directors are bankers elected by the member banks of the Federal Reserve bank. Three class B directors are prominent business leaders, usually executives of corporations; they are

When the Federal Reserve Act was passed in 1913, the need for a central bank to control the money supply and prevent banking crises was clear. The Panic of 1907 led to the collapse of the banking system and the bankruptcy of many companies. Despite the need for action, however, Congress spent many years debating the Fed's structure, in particular trying to determine a system that would make the central bank effective but not too powerful.

In 1910, a group of prominent bankers and politicians met for 10 days at Jekyll Island, off the coast of Georgia, and debated the pros and cons of various alternative plans for the central bank. They all agreed that a central bank that could act as a lender of last resort was vital. They disagreed, however, about whether the central bank should be a private bank or a government agency, whether there should be one nationwide interest rate on loans from the central bank or different interest rates across the country, and whether there should be one institution or several. One of the key disagreements was whether the central bank should look more like those in Europe, which were completely separate from the government, or whether the American system of political checks and balances should be applied to the central bank, with some degree of independence but some degree of government oversight. Republican Nelson Aldrich, who headed the Senate Finance Committee, was the leader of the group, and from the Jekyll Island meeting he brought forth a plan that he submitted to Congress.

The Aldrich plan called for the creation of a National Reserve Association that would have been run by the banking industry. However, many people and politicians worried that such an entity would be run by the large banks in the East, often referred to as the *Money Trust,* and that the plan did not include a sufficient role for oversight by the U.S. government. A group of businesspeople known as the National Citizens' League for the Promotion of a Sound Banking System became influential and began a national campaign to inform people of the issues involved in setting up a central bank, but they did not endorse the Aldrich plan. Then, when Democrat Woodrow Wilson was elected president in 1912 and Democrats also took control of the House of Representatives, the Aldrich plan was doomed.

After much debate, mainly carried out in the House Banking and Currency Committee under Representative Carter Glass, a new proposal began to take shape. To make the new plan acceptable, key elements of the Aldrich bill were modified to spread power out across the country through the system of Federal Reserve banks, thus taking power away from eastern banks. The new plan also gave the federal government a prominent role in overseeing the new agency, called the *Federal Reserve.* By giving bankers influence on the Fed, bankers were willing to support the new structure. By establishing the Board of Governors in Washington, D.C., it was clear that the federal government would be able to influence the central bank.

Thus, the Federal Reserve was born as a part-private and part-government agency with power and influence decentralized around the country. Bankers had input into the Fed but could not control it. The checks and balances built into the structure thus were similar to those in the setup of the federal government itself. Despite the diffusion of power, many people even today distrust the Federal Reserve, knowing that the original idea for it was hatched by a small group of wealthy men on Jekyll Island.

---

also elected by the member banks. Three class C directors are public-interest directors, often labor leaders or other businesspeople, who are appointed by the Board of Governors in Washington, D.C. The mix of directors is designed to keep bankers from dominating the decision-making process at the Federal Reserve banks and to provide policymakers with alternative points of view about economic issues.

As in any corporation, the board of directors of a Federal Reserve bank is responsible for overseeing the bank's management and approving major initiatives, but day-to-day decisions are made by the bank's management team. In addition, the board of directors is required by law to meet at least every two weeks to set the discount rate, which is the interest rate the Federal Reserve bank charges on loans it makes to financial intermediaries. Each board of directors usually meets in person once each month or two and has phone conference calls between those meetings to set the discount rate. However, the discount rate is coordinated nationally by the Board of Governors in Washington, D.C., so a Federal Reserve bank's board of directors actually cannot change its own discount rate. Instead, it requests that the Board of Governors change the national discount rate. The Board of Governors then may act on such a recommendation or decline to let the discount rate change.

FIGURE 15.3 Board of Directors of a Federal Reserve Bank

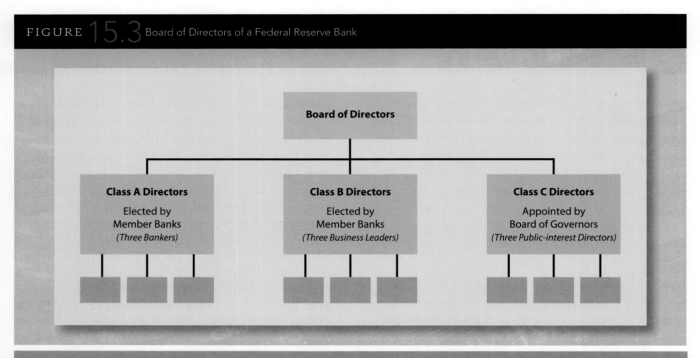

A Federal Reserve bank has nine directors. Three class A directors are bankers who are elected by the member banks in the district. Three class B directors are business leaders elected by the member banks as well. Three class C directors are public-interest directors appointed by the Board of Governors.

The Federal Reserve banks are led by a group of executives known as *officers* who make most of the day-to-day decisions of each bank. They are headed by a president, who is elected by the board of directors (subject to approval by the Board of Governors) to a renewable five-year term. Federal Reserve bank presidents generally remain in office for as long as they wish before taking jobs elsewhere or retiring. The president is usually like a head of state who deals with the overall organization, sets strategy, and acts as the key spokesperson for the bank. Although the president bears ultimate responsibility for the organization, many of the operational tasks required to run the bank are delegated to the first vice president of the bank. Usually, distribution of currency and coin, building maintenance, and computer facilities are managed by the first vice president, whereas bank supervision, statistics, and economic research report directly to the president. In this way, the president focuses on matters related to central banking (monetary policy and bank supervision and regulation), whereas the operations side of the bank is run separately.

Where do the Federal Reserve banks obtain the funds they need to operate? Some parts of the Federal Reserve bank, such as those that provide services for the banking system, charge fees for their services. The same is true of the other departments that run the payments system—including the wire services that allow efficient transfers of funds and securities between many firms and individuals. The central banking parts of the Fed, however, such as the economic research area and the bank supervision and regulation department, cannot charge for their services. The funds to run those parts of the organization come from interest income on the Federal Reserve bank's holdings of financial securities. The annual income from securities far exceeds the annual expenditures of the Federal Reserve bank, as we will discuss later in this chapter.

15-1b Central Bank Functions Performed by Federal Reserve Banks

The Federal Reserve banks perform a number of functions related to both the operation of the payments system and central banking. Operating the payments system requires a Federal Reserve bank to operate wire-transfer systems and to provide currency and coins to other banks. Because we discussed many of the specifics of the operation of the payments system in Chapter 3, in this section we will discuss just the central bank functions that Federal Reserve banks engage in. The main functions related to central banking are economic research, bank supervision and regulation, discount-window lending, monetary statistics, and consumer and community affairs.

Economic research is a key priority for Federal Reserve banks. [Each Federal Reserve bank president attends all meetings of the FOMC, which is the group that determines the nation's monetary policy.] As a result, the president must remain informed about the current state of the national economy, research that pertains to recent economic trends, the condition of financial markets, the well-being of foreign economies, and what forecasts suggest about the future of the economy. The president is usually considered to be an expert on the local economy in the Federal Reserve district. The federal government does not collect much local data, so analysts at Federal Reserve banks often compile such data. In preparing for meetings of the FOMC, regional analysts at each Federal Reserve bank prepare a report on local economic conditions, known as the *Beigebook* for the color of its cover. In the course of their normal duties, the economists at Federal Reserve banks learn about issues that are of interest to the general public. By sharing their expertise, they can teach the public about economic theories and data. For this reason, Federal Reserve banks consider economic education to be a major part of their overall mission—one that they are in a unique position to provide. They educate the public about economics through public speaking and by writing articles that are comprehensible to non-economists.

Economists provide information to policymakers in several different ways. Much of the preparation for discussion of monetary policy is based on understanding the current state of the economy: How fast is output growing? Is the unemployment rate rising or falling? Do people expect inflation to rise or fall? Compiling information on such basic economic variables is known as *up-and-down economics* among Fed staff members. Because the economy is changing constantly, though, more theoretical or speculative economic research is needed to provide insight to policymakers. For example, as the "new" economy appeared in the 1990s, economists at Federal Reserve banks were among the first to recognize that technological change was beginning to cause a large increase in productivity. In such cases, where policy implications are not clear, the Fed's staff economists devote time to novel, often very technical research. The Fed economists' ideas are reviewed by the profession as a whole through publication in academic journals.

Each Federal Reserve bank hires a number of economists—from 15 to 30 at most Federal Reserve banks, more in New York (about 70) and Chicago (about 40) because of the role of those cities as financial centers. Economists' work consists of preparing policy briefings for the bank's president; doing academic-style research, much of which is related to policy issues; writing articles for the general public about the economy; and giving presentations to groups of bankers or citizens about issues of importance to them. Fed economists engage in research covering a wide range of topics. For example, macroeconomists might study the impact of changes in inflation expectations on interest rates, banking economists might examine the impact of technological improvement on the costs and profits of banks, and regional economists might look at how changes in monetary policy affect some regions differently than others. Some of the research develops new economic theories, but much of it examines how data fit existing theories. The economic research group usually is managed by a small group of executives, including a research director, who often reports directly to the Federal Reserve bank president.

The key question when Fed economists brief the president of a Federal Reserve bank is this: What actions, if any, should monetary policymakers take today? To some extent, the discussion about what policymakers should do in the short run is similar in all 12 Federal Reserve banks. However, alternative perspectives also arise because macroeconomists disagree so much among themselves about how the economy works.

Economists at the Federal Reserve Bank of St. Louis, for example, have long promoted monetarism. They have followed the teachings of Nobel Laureate Milton Friedman and based their policy recommendations on that viewpoint. The board of directors at the Federal Reserve Bank of St. Louis has sought to appoint presidents and research directors who are monetarists.

At other Federal Reserve banks, other theories are prominent. For the past two decades, the Federal Reserve Bank of Minneapolis has centered its attention on macroeconomic research. Its group of economists is the smallest (about 15) of any Federal Reserve bank, but its research publication record is the best. The Minneapolis Fed hires many University of Minnesota faculty members as consultants. In the 1970s and 1980s, bank economists and Minnesota faculty at the Minneapolis Fed were leaders in the rational-expectations revolution. Moreover, in the 1980s and 1990s, the Minneapolis Fed was a leader in research on real business-cycle models.

Economists at Federal Reserve banks also help educate the public. Each Federal Reserve bank publishes some type of publication, usually called an *economic review* or something similar, containing articles that are accessible to a broader audience than just professional economists. These articles are often quite useful for college students, which is why so many of them are referenced in this textbook. They are available to the public for free and can be accessed on the Internet. Economists also give speeches to bankers or community groups on issues of importance to them.

The second group within a Federal Reserve bank that performs central banking functions is the supervision and regulation department. The role of this department was described in Chapter 9, which discussed the details of regulating and supervising banks. The Fed has primary responsibility for supervising bank holding companies and state banks that are members of the Federal Reserve System.

There is some interaction between the economic research group and the supervision and regulation group. Economists working on banking research often get information from the supervision and regulation group, whereas the latter often asks for advice from economists in the research group on why banks are engaging in certain activities. Collaboration between the groups has become vital in recent years as banks' balance sheets have become more complicated. For example, many banks now own derivative securities, whose properties may be difficult to understand. In addition, banks have developed new methods to manage risk in recent years, which banking economists can explain to the bank supervisors.

Another central banking task at Federal Reserve banks is providing loans to financial institutions at the discount window. Discount-window lending occurs in a variety of situations. Occasionally, a financial institution will suffer some mechanical breakdown, such as a crash of a key computer system, that will cause it to be short of funds temporarily; it can ask for a discount-window loan to obtain funds. Also, in the process of tightening monetary policy, the Fed sometimes reduces the money supply so quickly that banks must scramble to find enough reserves to meet their reserve requirements. The total amount of reserves in the entire banking system may not be enough, so the Fed can lend to banks temporarily, giving them time to readjust their portfolios to reduce their demand for reserves. In addition, special events sometimes greatly increase the need for reserves, which can be accommodated at the discount window. For example, on September 11, 2001, many large banks housed in or around the World Trade Center were forced to shut down, so routine payments could not flow through the processing system, and many banks were unable to obtain funds in a timely manner. Federal Reserve banks all over the country made a large number of discount loans (as much as $45 billion on September 12) to ensure that the payments system continued to run smoothly.

Another central bank function that Federal Reserve banks perform is collecting data on the money supply. The statistics group collects reports that financial institutions are required to complete periodically on the amounts of various deposit accounts they hold, checks them for accuracy, and then passes the data on to the Board of Governors, where the statistics for the entire nation are calculated. The statistics group is essential in providing information on the nation's money supply and the flow of credit.

Another major group in Federal Reserve banks is concerned with community and consumer affairs and helps to implement laws concerning banking and consumer credit. For example, this group helps banks to meet their responsibilities for community development as required by the Community Reinvestment Act (CRA). In addition, the group investigates consumer complaints about banks.

The Federal Reserve Bank of New York carries out two additional duties beyond those carried out at all the Federal Reserve banks: operating the Open Market Desk and the International Desk. The first desk, the Open Market Desk, is responsible for carrying out the open-market operations of the FOMC, which we discuss shortly. The desk's operations include buying and selling securities in financial markets, so it is located at the Federal Reserve Bank of New York because New York City is the center of the country's financial markets. The second desk, the International Desk, is responsible for carrying out the country's interventions in foreign-exchange markets. As we discussed in Chapter 14, a country sometimes finds it desirable to buy or sell its currency in the foreign-exchange market to influence the exchange rate. In the United States, such operations are decided on by the U.S. Treasury Department and the Federal Reserve Board and are implemented by the International Desk at the New York Fed because New York City is a major location for currency trading.

15-2 The Board of Governors

The Federal Reserve System's Board of Governors (called the Board for short) consists of seven governors and hundreds of support staff. It is much more like a government agency than the Federal Reserve banks. Located in Washington, D.C., the Board has oversight over all the activities of Federal Reserve banks and is subject to much more political scrutiny than the Federal Reserve banks.

The seven governors are appointed by the president of the United States to nonrenewable 14-year terms. The U.S. Senate must confirm their appointments, so appointees must have political skill, as well as economic acumen. The 14-year terms are staggered so that one expires every two years, thus providing stability to the Board. Table 15.1 shows the Board members as of 2013 and when their terms expire.

You might note that even though the terms expire every two years, many of the governors were appointed at about the same time: Tarullo in 2009, Yellen and Raskin in 2010, and Stein and Powell in 2012. Very few governors remain in office for 14 years, so most are serving partial terms. A governor filling a partial term may be reappointed to a full term. For example, former Chairman Alan Greenspan was appointed to a partial term in 1987 that ran through 1992, then was reappointed to a 14-year term that expired in 2006, so he was on the Board of Governors for 18½ years.

The chairman of the Board of Governors is arguably the second most powerful person in the world,

TABLE 15.1 Current Members of the Federal Reserve Board of Governors

	Term Began	Term Expires	Office
Ben S. Bernanke	2006	2020	Chairman since 2006
Janet L. Yellen	2010	2024	Vice chair since 2010
Jerome H. Powell	2012	2014	
Sarah Bloom Raskin	2010	2016	
Jeremy C. Stein	2012	2018	
Daniel K. Tarullo	2009	2022	
vacant		2026	

© Cengage Learning

second only to the president of the United States. The chairman's power comes from the impact that monetary policy has on the U.S. economy and the importance of the U.S. economy in the world. The Federal Reserve System has long had a tradition of speaking with one voice on major issues, and that voice is the chairman's. Behind closed doors, the governors may discuss and disagree, but outside the Board's doors, they support one position so that they can send clear signals about monetary policy. In addition, both Congress and the president of the United States often ask the chairman of the Board of Governors to advise them on economic matters, not just those related to monetary policy. Thus, the chairman wields tremendous power.

The president of the United States appoints one of the seven governors as chairman for a renewable four-year term, which must be confirmed by the Senate. Former Fed Chairman Greenspan was appointed initially by President Reagan in 1987, reappointed by President

Former chairman of the Federal Reserve System Alan Greenspan had great political influence and often gave advice to Congress and the president about economic matters.

Bush in 1991, reappointed again by President Clinton in 1996 and 2000 (the extra year between 1991 and 1996 arose so that Greenspan could start a full 14-year term as a governor with a slot that started in 1992), and reappointed to a final term of chairman by President Bush in 2004 (though he could not stay in office until 2008 because his 14-year term as a governor expired in 2006). Many consider Greenspan to have been the most successful Fed chairman in history because he steered the U.S. economy through a period of great economic growth. He seemed to know more about economic data than any person alive: "His secret for divining the economy's direction lies in understanding the numbers, the thousands and thousands of numbers that describe its complex workings. But, in fact, he relies on a sophisticated

seat-of-the-pants approach to monetary policy, informed by nearly 50 years of pondering the economy."[1]

Not everyone thinks Chairman Greenspan did a great job, however. President George H. Bush blamed his defeat to Bill Clinton in 1992 on the failure of the Fed to cut interest rates fast enough in the recession of 1990–1991. Economist Robert Barro has argued, "The fact is that Greenspan is no more than a competent economist who was fortunate enough to be in office when price stability could be achieved."[2] And Greenspan has been roundly criticized for not doing enough to rein in subprime mortgage lending, which ignited the financial crisis of 2008.

How should we measure the success of a Fed chairman? Ultimately (as we will discuss in the following several chapters), the Federal Reserve can control only the inflation rate. Although the Fed can affect the economy in the short run, the effects of monetary policy on the economy are short-lived, so a chairman's legacy is reflected mainly in the long-run impact on inflation. Fed chairmen since 1951 are listed in Table 15.2, along with the average inflation rate during their terms in office. The inflation rate used in the table is based on the personal consumption expenditures price index (excluding food and energy prices). Food and energy price inflation is excluded because it often distorts the underlying trend in inflation.

Looking at the table, and judging a Fed chairman solely by his performance on inflation, we see support for the notion that Greenspan was a very good

[1]David Wessel, "In Setting Fed's Policy, Chairman Bets Heavily on His Own Judgment," *Wall Street Journal*, January 27, 1997.
[2]Robert J. Barro, "Is Alan Greenspan a Genius—Or Just Plain Lucky?" *Business Week*, August 16, 1999, p. 20.

TABLE 15.2 — Inflation Rate Under Fed Chairmen Since 1959 (PCE Inflation Rate Excluding Food and Energy Prices)

	Average	Start	End	Change	Term in Office
William M. Martin, Jr.	2.3	1.7	4.6	+2.9	Apr. 1951 to Jan. 1970
Arthur F. Burns	5.7	4.6	6.5	+1.9	Feb. 1970 to Jan. 1978
G. William Miller	6.9	6.4	7.1	+0.7	Mar. 1978 to Aug. 1979
Paul A. Volcker	5.6	7.1	3.7	−3.4	Aug. 1979 to Aug. 1987
Alan Greenspan	2.4	3.7	2.0	−1.7	Aug. 1987 to Jan. 2006
Ben S. Bernanke	1.7	2.2	1.1	−1.1	Jan. 2006 to present

Note: Average is the average inflation rate from the start of the chairman's term to the end; *Start* and *End* are the inflation rates over the previous year at the beginning and end of the chairmen's terms; *Change* is the difference between the inflation rate at the beginning and end of the chairmen's terms. Because of data unavailability, results for Martin begin in January 1959, though his term began in April 1951.

FIGURE 15.4 Core Inflation Rate During Fed Chairmanships

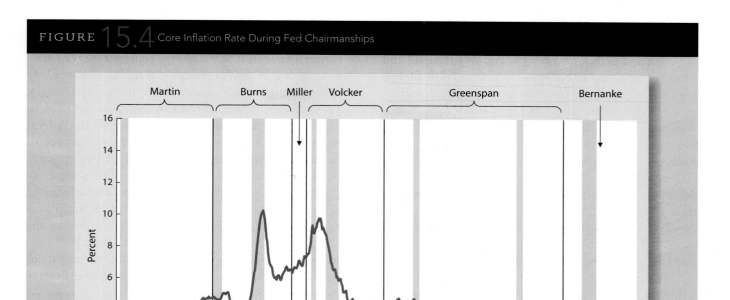

This figure shows the movements of the personal consumption expenditures inflation rate (excluding food and energy prices) over the terms of six Federal Reserve chairmen. The records of Volcker and Greenspan are particularly impressive in reducing inflation, whereas Martin, Burns, and Miller allowed inflation to rise during their terms.

chairman. Inflation averaged just 2.4 percent and fell 1.7 percentage points during his term. A closer look at the change in the inflation rate over time (Figure 15.4) shows how the inflation rate trended steadily downward during much of Greenspan's term, except at the beginning before 1990, around 2000, and from 2004 to 2005. Also impressive was the performance of Paul Volcker, who was appointed to office by President Carter in 1979 to wring inflation out of the economy. He did so by focusing the Fed's actions for a time on the growth rate of the money supply. By reducing the growth rate of the money supply, the Fed was able to reduce inflation to about 4 percent, as the figure shows. Perhaps the worst performance was turned in by Arthur Burns in the 1970s, under whose chairmanship inflation remained at a high level despite several recessions that helped to reduce it. William Miller served a short time and was ineffectual in reducing inflation. William McChesney Martin was chairman in the 1950s and 1960s and was successful for much of his term, but he failed to prevent the run-up of inflation in the late 1960s. Despite that,

Martin is revered in the hallways of the Fed because in the 1950s his actions ensured the Fed's independence from the federal government. (For more on Martin, see the Policy Insider box "William McChesney Martin and the Independence of the Fed.")

Perhaps the average inflation rate or the change in the inflation rate is not the ideal measure with which to measure a Fed chairman's success. For example, the data suggest that both Volcker and Greenspan benefited from calmer world economies than earlier Fed chairmen. Although Arthur Burns's performance is panned widely, he also faced many adverse events, especially the first OPEC oil price shock.

The governors other than the chairman also play important roles in the Federal Reserve System. They work in three major areas: operations, banking regulation, and monetary policy. Part of their role is operational, because they oversee the entire Federal Reserve System. For example, one governor may be assigned to monitor the budgets of Federal Reserve banks, and another governor may investigate the efficiency of the system for distributing currency and coin. The Board of Governors also must approve mergers and acquisitions of banks and determine how the Fed will regulate and supervise banks. But the most important job of Fed governors is to participate in monetary policy decisions, which occur primarily through the FOMC and which will be discussed in more detail in the next section. Also, governors affect monetary policy when they set bank reserve requirements, decide on requests from Federal Reserve banks to change the discount rate, and determine the interest rate the Fed will pay banks on their reserves, which we will discuss in Chapter 16. Finally, the Board of Governors can set margin requirements for the purchase of stock (the percentage of the purchase price of stock that cannot be borrowed), but the Fed has not changed the margin requirement, currently 50 percent, since 1974.

In making its decisions, the Board of Governors obtains input from its constituents through a group of advisory councils. The Federal Advisory Council consists of one banker from each of the 12 Federal Reserve districts, who meet with the Board of Governors four times each year to discuss issues concerning economics and banking. The Consumer Depository Institutions Advisory Council, composed of 12 bankers, meets with the Board to discuss the economy and lending conditions.

Although the chairman is the most powerful of the governors, he can be outvoted. In 1986, several governors joined together and threatened to outvote Chairman Volcker on his proposal to change the discount rate. Although a compromise was reached and Volcker was not formally outvoted, this attempt to outvote the chairman caused a major rift between the chairman and the rest of the governors, and Volcker resigned his position not long after that. Thus, most of the time, the other governors support the chairman, but the consequences are great when they disagree with him.

The balance of power between the Board of Governors and the Federal Reserve banks is sharply divided—the Board is the dominant force. The Board sets standards for Federal Reserve banks to follow and gives them grades for performance on both their operational procedures (for example, the efficiency of their coin and cash distribution process) and their central banking work (for example, the quality of their research output). One advantage of this performance evaluation is that the Board forces the Federal Reserve banks to compete with each other, encouraging them to be efficient in their operations. Because many parts of the Federal Reserve banks do not compete directly against private firms, it would be possible for them to build

empires and become large, bloated bureaucracies. The Board attempts to prevent this by forcing competition between Federal Reserve banks. Federal Reserve banks that get higher grades from the Board are more likely to have their budgets approved without major changes. They also are more likely to be awarded the right to run certain system-wide projects, which the Federal Reserve banks view as prestigious and as a source of power within the Federal Reserve System. For example, one Federal Reserve bank is chosen to host the Fed's Cash Product Office, which coordinates the delivery of currency between the Bureau of Engraving and Printing and all 12 Federal Reserve banks, coordinates the delivery of coins between the U.S. Mint and all 12 Federal Reserve banks, and coordinates the movements of both currency and coin between all 12 Federal Reserve banks and other financial institutions.

The Board has the ultimate authority over Federal Reserve banks because it approves their expenditures and the salaries of their top executives (president and first vice president). In addition, publications by Federal Reserve bank economists are reviewed by the staff economists of the Board before being printed so that the Board can ensure that Federal Reserve banks are not publishing misinformation or discussing sensitive matters in a way that would harm the Federal Reserve System. This oversight has the potential to backfire if it stifles dissent. However, the Federal Reserve Banks of St. Louis and Minneapolis have long held views on monetary policy that differ from the views of the Board without major confrontations. This may be so because the presidents and boards of directors of the Federal Reserve Banks of Minneapolis and St. Louis support their economists and encourage them to explore alternative viewpoints.

The Board has a large staff of over 300 economists who provide information to the governors, just as Federal Reserve bank economists do for their presidents. The economic staff is divided into three main groups: research and statistics, monetary affairs, and international finance. The directors of each group are the chairman's main advisors. As with Federal Reserve banks, the Board wants economists to do cutting-edge research so that they are at the forefront of economic knowledge. However, because the Board oversees the entire system, its economists are called on often to help out whenever there is a crisis somewhere in the world or in the sector of the economy in which they specialize.

As an example of their detailed knowledge, the Fed staff has numerous contacts with major U.S. companies, such as automobile manufacturers. Often the Fed

Although the Federal Reserve was established by law in 1913, it did not act on its own until Chairman William McChesney Martin made it independent in the early 1950s. Prior to Martin's bold push for independence, the Fed generally helped the U.S. government sell its debt in the financial markets. The Federal Reserve Bank of New York dominated the market for U.S. government securities, buying and selling securities whenever necessary to keep interest rates on government securities equal to the Fed's target for such securities. Martin and the Board of Governors wanted to end the role of the Fed in targeting interest rates so tightly so that the government securities market would be subject to free-market pressures rather than being under government control. But power within the Federal Reserve was dominated by the Federal Reserve Bank of New York, which wanted to keep control over the government securities market.

Both the Board of Governors of the Federal Reserve and the U.S. Treasury Department, the government agency that sold bonds to finance U.S. government budget deficits, wanted the government securities market to become free of government control for several reasons. Because the Federal Reserve Bank of New York controlled the market so closely, buyers and sellers in the market merely watched what the Fed did and failed to trade independently. As a result, the market was not very liquid or very deep. Private investment firms did not take on speculative positions in the market, nor did they form their own forecasts of where interest rates might move in the future. In addition, the Board of Governors and the Treasury Department thought that if the government securities market was subject to fluctuations in supply and demand, the Fed would gain insight from the movements of interest rates. For example, if long-term interest rates rose, the Fed might be able to infer that inflation expectations were increasing, which might help to guide monetary policy.

To force the government securities market to become independent of the Federal Reserve Bank of New York, Martin took several steps. First, in 1951, the Treasury and the Fed announced that they had reached an "accord" that would "minimize the monetization of the public debt." *Monetization* referred to the idea that if the Treasury borrowed more, selling new debt securities, the interest rate might increase as the supply of securities increased. The Federal Reserve Bank of New York then would buy debt securities in the market, reducing the interest rate to its original level. The overall effect, however, was that the money supply was higher and the government debt owned by private citizens was unchanged. The accord, though not very specific, was an agreement to stop the monetization of government debt.

The second step in making the government securities market independent came in 1953, when Martin and the Board of Governors declared a "bills only" policy, in which they required the Federal Reserve Bank of New York's Open Market Desk to buy and sell only U.S. Treasury bills, which had times to maturity of less than one year, and to stop buying and selling government securities with longer maturities. Thus, the Fed would influence only short-term interest rates, allowing long-term interest rates to be governed by supply and demand in the private market for securities without Fed intervention.

The final step in the push for independence came in 1955. In that year, Martin and the FOMC forced the Open Market Desk to report to the FOMC instead of to the president and board of directors of the Federal Reserve Bank of New York. The move made it clear that the FOMC would set monetary policy and that the Federal Reserve Bank of New York would implement the FOMC's wishes. Because the FOMC wanted to make monetary policy independently of the government's need to finance its debt, the effect was to make the FOMC independent of the government.

Chairman Martin's actions in the early 1950s allowed the FOMC to begin to use monetary policy to offset the business cycle rather than simply to help the government sell its debt. Martin began a policy of "leaning against the wind," which meant that when the economy was growing unsustainably fast, he slowed it down; when the economy was slowing below trend, he sped it up. He thus transformed the Fed from a sales agent for government bonds to a powerful force affecting the economy independent of the government.

To read more about Martin and the Fed's struggle for independence in the 1950s, see the article "After the Accord: Reminiscences on the Birth of the Modern Fed," by Robert L. Hetzel and Ralph F. Leach, Federal Reserve Bank of Richmond *Economic Quarterly,* Winter 2001, pp. 57–64.

knows more about data such as the breakdown of the number of automobiles sold to businesses and consumers than does the Bureau of Economic Analysis, which reports the gross domestic product (GDP) data.

Some of the governors of the Board have complained that senior staff economists at the Board have more power than they do. If so, that is because the chairman has so much power, and the senior staff members have the chairman's ear. However, the governors are not free to use the staff as they please; only the chairman does. Alan Blinder, who was vice chairman of the Board for several years in the mid-1990s, left the Board after one and one-half years of frustration. He had wanted to sit in on the staff discussions of economic forecasts but was rebuffed. Blinder said, "There's an old admonition that we remember from grade school arithmetic: Show your work."[3] But he was never allowed to see it.

Much of the economic work at the Board is devoted to one major topic—the determination of monetary policy on a short-term basis. Decisions about monetary policy are made by the Federal Open Market Committee (FOMC), which is our next subject.

[3]John M. Berry, "At the Fed, a Power Struggle Over Information," *Washington Post*, July 8, 1996.

RECAP

1 The Board of Governors oversees the Federal Reserve System, with power concentrated in the hands of the chairman. The seven governors are appointed by the president of the United States to nonrenewable 14-year terms.

2 The chair of the Board of Governors is one of the seven governors and is appointed by the president of the United States to a renewable four-year term.

3 If we measure the success of Fed chairmen by the average rate of inflation or the change in inflation over their terms, then Volcker and Greenspan were the most successful chairmen and Burns and Miller were the worst.

15-3 The Federal Open Market Committee

The Federal Open Market Committee (FOMC) influences the money supply through open-market operations. The FOMC consists of the seven governors plus five of the 12 Federal Reserve bank presidents, who serve on a rotating basis. All 12 Federal Reserve bank presidents attend each FOMC meeting and participate in the committee proceedings; only the five official members can vote on decisions, however. The right to vote is rotated among the Federal Reserve banks in the following way: The Federal Reserve Bank of New York always votes because it is the center of the financial industry. Nine of the Federal Reserve banks vote once every three years: Boston, Philadelphia, and Richmond rotate, as do Kansas City, Minneapolis, and San Francisco and Atlanta, Dallas, and St. Louis. Two banks, Chicago and Cleveland, alternate, with each voting every other year.

Despite the apparent importance of being a voting member of the FOMC, the right to vote is not as significant to the bank presidents as the press often suggests. Most often the FOMC reaches its decisions by consensus, so while having the right to vote gets attention in the media, it does not really translate into more power. A Federal Reserve bank president acquires power from persuading other FOMC members about policy issues, not from voting in a particular way. In most cases, the vote at FOMC meetings is not in doubt.

What is it, exactly, that the FOMC decides on when it meets? The FOMC decides how the Fed will conduct its open-market operations during the period until the next FOMC meeting.

15-3a Open-Market Operations

The tool the Fed uses to change the money supply is called **open-market operations,** which are purchases and sales of government securities in the secondary market. These purchases and sales directly affect the amount of reserves in the banking system. If the Fed wants to increase the amount of reserves, it buys government securities in the market in exchange for additional reserves at banks. If the Fed wants to decrease the amount of reserves, it sells government securities in the open market. The money supply changes in the same direction as the change in reserves; for example, if the Fed wants to reduce the money supply, it sells securities in the open market, reducing reserves and thus the money supply. (We'll discuss the effects of changes in reserves on the money supply in more detail in Chapter 16.)

Open-market operations are carried out at the Open Market Desk of the Federal Reserve Bank of New York, which is called *the Desk* for short. The Desk is run by a group of economics and finance professionals who understand financial markets and gather information about them. Every day, the Desk chooses the optimal time and amount of securities to buy or sell in order to accomplish the goals of the FOMC. Prior to their decision, the staff members of the Desk consult with one of the voting members of the FOMC and key staffers of the Board of Governors by conference call early each business day. The day-to-day decisions depend on technical factors, including daily flows of reserve balances throughout the banking system and such esoteric variables as movements of money by the U.S. Treasury Department into and out of banks. The Desk makes the daily purchase or sale of securities early in the morning because, over the course of the day, banks make decisions about what to buy or sell in financial markets. The Desk does not want to find itself unable to carry out its planned operation for the day because banks have already made decisions about their reserves, and the Desk would have no one to trade with. Thus, the Desk operates early in the morning before banks have locked in their decisions.

The interest rate in the market for bank reserves is the **federal funds rate,** which applies to overnight loans of reserves between banks. In making their daily decision, the staff of the Desk knows that in the short run the federal funds rate will rise if the Desk sells securities because the supply of reserves will decrease. The federal funds rate will fall if the Desk buys

securities. Thus, the daily decision of the Desk comes down to this: Given a target for the federal funds rate (which is determined by the FOMC), and given the reserves at banks, is the federal funds rate likely to rise above the target or fall below it if the Desk does not take any action? If the federal funds rate is expected to be above its target, the Desk tries to estimate how many securities it needs to buy to bring the funds rate back to its target. Similarly, if the federal funds rate is expected to be below its target, the Desk estimates how many securities it should sell to bring the funds rate back to its target. (We will discuss this in more detail in Chapter 16.)

The purchases and sales of securities in the open market are arranged between the Desk and a group of **primary government securities dealers,** which are large investment banks and brokers (21 of them in 2013) that meet certain capital requirements and agree to actively transact with the Fed. Being a primary dealer is prestigious in the investment community, so there are benefits to firms to having this status. The Fed expects the primary dealers to buy and sell securities from the Desk regularly to ensure that the reserves market is liquid.

Another factor the Desk must consider in its daily activities is whether it wants its actions to be temporary or permanent. For example, suppose that staff of the Desk estimated that to keep the federal funds rate on target, the Desk should purchase $2 billion in securities today but that the need for an additional $2 billion in reserves is temporary—the Fed will need to sell securities worth $2 billion tomorrow. In such a case, the Fed will not buy $2 billion worth of securities today but instead will enter into repurchase agreements with primary dealers. **Repurchase agreements (repos)** are transactions in which a primary dealer agrees to sell a security to the Fed one day and buy it back the next day or several days later. The Desk uses repos

open-market operations the tool the Fed uses to affect the money supply, consisting of purchases and sales of government securities in the secondary market

federal funds rate the interest rate in the market for bank reserves, which applies to overnight loans of reserves between banks

primary government securities dealers large investment banks and brokers that meet certain capital requirements and agree to actively transact with the Fed when it engages in open-market operations

repurchase agreements (repos) transactions in which a primary dealer agrees to sell a security to the Fed one day and buy it back the next day or several days later

extensively to increase bank reserves temporarily. When the Desk wants to take reserves out of the banking system temporarily, it uses a *reverse repo,* in which the Fed sells securities, thus withdrawing reserves from the banking system, and agrees to buy them back in one or several days, so the reserves are then returned to the banking system.

How does the FOMC affect what the Desk does? Mainly, the FOMC gives the Desk a target for the federal funds rate. The target is the main object of FOMC voting, and it is set forth in the directive, which is the key outcome of an FOMC meeting.

15-3b The FOMC Directive

The FOMC operates by giving a directive to the Desk. The directive is a fairly brief document (usually two sentences) that states the goals of the FOMC and the target for the federal funds rate. The first sentence lists the goals. For example, most of the recent directives begin: "The Federal Open Market Committee seeks monetary and financial conditions that will foster price stability and promote sustainable growth in output." The second sentence of the directive is the operative language, stating how policy should be conducted by the Desk. These days the instructions to the Desk are to maintain a given target for the federal funds rate. Here is an example of the directive language from April 29, 2009: "To further its long-run objectives, the Committee seeks conditions in reserve markets consistent with federal funds trading in a range from 0 to ¼ percent." Prior to August 1997, however, the directive told the Desk to achieve a particular degree of pressure on reserve positions, which is less explicit and is much more open to the Desk's interpretation. The FOMC did this even though the Fed has been targeting the federal funds rate fairly explicitly since 1990. Previously, even when the FOMC publicly announced its directive, it was hard for people to interpret what the language meant. Now the FOMC is explicit and issues a news release about any changes in the target for the federal funds rate immediately on the completion of an FOMC meeting.

What does the FOMC usually vote on? The directive can change the target for the federal funds rate by any amount, but usually the FOMC moves in increments of 25 or 50 basis points. One **basis point** is one-hundredth of a percentage point, so 25 basis points is one-quarter percentage point and 50 basis points is one-half percentage point.

basis point one-hundredth of a percentage point

There are three main options for the FOMC to choose from:

Option A: Reduce the federal funds rate 50 basis points.

Option B: Keep the federal funds rate unchanged.

Option C: Raise the federal funds rate 50 basis points.

However, when the economy is very weak, the FOMC does not even consider option C, and when the economy is very strong, the FOMC does not consider option A. The FOMC often chooses to move only 25 basis points. On rare occasions, the FOMC might consider a move of more than 50 basis points, but it avoids making such a large change in one day because people may interpret it as a sign of panic.

15-3c The FOMC Meeting

The FOMC holds regularly scheduled meetings eight times a year (about every six or seven weeks). Some of the meetings last just one day, but others last two days so that the FOMC can discuss longer-term issues and forecasts. In the aftermath of the financial crisis, most FOMC meetings went two days.

A typical one-day meeting opens with a report on intervention in exchange markets by the manager of the International Desk at the Federal Reserve Bank of New York. The International Desk buys and sells currencies from time to time to maintain orderly markets or at the request of the U.S. Treasury Department or for a foreign central bank. Next, the manager of the Open Market Desk in New York discusses the open-market operations put into place, highlighting any unusual occurrences or difficulties and noting how well the Desk hit its target for the federal funds rate during the intermeeting period (the period between FOMC meetings).

Next, the director of the Research and Statistics Division discusses a document that was circulated in advance, known as the *Tealbook* for the color of its cover. (The Tealbook used to be two separate books, the Greenbook showing forecasts and the Bluebook showing policy options. But recently they were combined into the Tealbook.) The Tealbook discusses data released since the last FOMC meeting and projects how major macroeconomic variables will fare in the next two years, assuming that monetary policy follows a particular path in the future. Often the future path is one in which the federal funds rate remains unchanged over the next few years. Usually, the staff of the Board of Governors bases its projection on that path and does not build in a path of easier or tighter monetary policy because the FOMC may feel that the staff is prejudging its actions. However, when the economy is very weak, the Tealbook will sometimes assume that easier monetary policy will occur in the near future, and when the economy is strong, the Tealbook usually will be based on an assumption of somewhat tighter monetary policy.

When the director of the Research and Statistics Division presents the Tealbook forecasts, he discusses the main assumptions behind the projections, along with an overview of the main issues of concern for policy. The Tealbook often evaluates alternative scenarios so that FOMC members can form some idea of the risks to the forecast, that is, how likely it is that the economy will not perform as projected in the baseline forecast. FOMC members ask questions about the forecast and how to interpret the results.

Once the Tealbook has been discussed, all 19 of the governors and presidents discuss their views of the outlook for the economy. Federal Reserve bank presidents discuss both the local outlook (for their district) and the national outlook, whereas governors usually just discuss the national outlook. In many cases the participants explain how their own personal forecast differs from that in the Tealbook, so the Tealbook is an important central focus of the discussion.

The chairman usually leads the discussion of policy, telling the FOMC what he would like to do. (Sometimes the chairman goes last, in cases where he is undecided on what to do and is willing to be influenced by the others.) The other 18 participants then voice their views on what policy should do or bring up other issues that the FOMC should consider. In this go-around, the participants will say whether they disagree or agree with the chairman. Even if they disagree, they may support the chairman's view; for example, if the chairman wanted to reduce the federal funds rate by 25 basis points, a committee member might say something like, "I would have preferred to cut the rate by 50 basis points, but I'll go along with the recommendation of the chairman."

After every participant has had a chance to speak, the chairman summarizes the views of the voting members. He then asks for a vote. Following the vote, the FOMC decides on language for the statement to accompany the directive. That language is important to the financial markets because it gives them information about what the FOMC thinks about the current situation and how policy may change in the future.

After the statement has been discussed, the FOMC deals with other special topics that may come before it. There might be a briefing about banking legislation or some administrative issues that are not relevant to the decision about monetary policy. The FOMC meeting generally concludes about 2:00 P.M. (Eastern time), and public announcement of the decision is made about 2:15 P.M.

The deliberations of the FOMC are secret. Because policymaking is an ongoing process, the FOMC fears that if too much information about its activities were available too quickly after a meeting, some investors would gain an unfair advantage. In addition, the Fed often uses confidential information that it gets from private companies (for example, car production plans by major automobile makers) and from foreign governments (for example, plans by the Japanese government to purchase dollars in the foreign-exchange market). At the same time, the FOMC wants to communicate its overall views to the public and the financial markets so that investors know what the Fed is thinking about and what its long-term plans are. Consequently, the Fed reveals information in the following way. First, the statement that is released immediately following the FOMC meeting tells everyone, at the same time, what the Fed's short-term policy plans are and what the vote was on the directive, that is, whether anyone dissented. About every other regularly scheduled meeting, the Fed chairman holds a press conference, a practice that began in 2011. Second, the Fed releases the minutes of each FOMC meeting three weeks after the meeting; the time lag ensures that financial investors cannot capitalize on the information. Third, in the intermediate term, the Fed chairman, the governors, and the Federal Reserve bank presidents give public speeches in which they explain the FOMC's opinions about the economy and about policy, as well as their own opinions. Finally, after five years have passed, the Fed makes available verbatim transcripts of the meetings, as well as the Greenbook forecasts. Whether the release of information from the Fed in this way is sufficient to keep the public properly informed about Fed policy is an open question; some economists believe that the Fed should be much more open about its decisions and its interpretation of the economic data.

Until 2000, the Federal Reserve was required by law to report targets for money-supply growth to Congress. However, the legislation expired in 2000, and because the FOMC is no longer convinced that targeting the money supply is useful, the Fed no longer targets money-supply growth.

1 The FOMC, composed of the seven governors and five presidents of Federal Reserve banks, is the main entity in charge of monetary policy because it determines how open-market operations are carried out.

2 The FOMC instructs the Open Market Desk at the Federal Reserve Bank of New York to use open-market operations to hit a particular target for the federal funds rate. The Desk engages in daily transactions with a group of primary government securities dealers. The Desk buys securities to increase the money supply and reduce the federal funds rate; it sells securities to decrease the money supply and increase the federal funds rate.

3 In FOMC meetings, committee members discuss current economic conditions in the districts and the nation, forecasts for key macroeconomic variables, and anecdotal information gathered by Federal Reserve bank presidents. The committee then votes on a policy action.

Policy→Perspective   Should the Federal Reserve Be So Independent?

The Federal Reserve System was established so that it would be independent of the rest of the government. One advantage of this independence is freedom from political pressure in setting monetary policy. Before debating the advantages and disadvantages of the Fed's relationship to government, let's identify the reasons the Fed enjoys this independence.

First, the 14-year terms of governors are so long that no U.S. president can have much impact on the makeup of the Board of Governors. Because a governor cannot be reappointed after a 14-year term, he or she has no incentive to adhere to the political objectives of elected officials and thus is more likely to remain independent. Second, because a governor's term expires just every two years, it takes a U.S. president almost two full terms to have appointed a majority of governors to the Board. Fed appointees generally share the U.S. president's economic objectives, so the ability to appoint like-minded Fed governors is valuable to a president. The inability of a president to appoint too many governors helps to keep the Fed balanced. Third, the Fed's income comes from its holdings of securities, and thus the Fed does not need the government to supply it with operating funds. Therefore, the Fed can assert its independence without fear that its budget will be slashed by an angry Congress. In 2012, for example,

the Fed earned profits of $91.0 billion and had net operating expenses of just $3.7 billion.

Nevertheless, the Fed's power makes it subject to strong political forces. Congress and the U.S. president naturally do not like to share power with the Fed, so they pressure the Fed whenever they think they can. As a result, the Fed needs a very strong chairman to maintain its independence. A strong chairman, such as William M. Martin, Paul Volcker, or Alan Greenspan, does not allow politicians to affect monetary policy and instead influences Congress and the president to choose policies consistent with the Fed's approach.

Why do politicians want to influence monetary policy? The main reason is that monetary policy has a strong short-run influence on the growth rate of output. If output growth is strong and the unemployment rate is low at election time, incumbent politicians, especially the U.S. president, are very likely to be reelected; if the economy is weak, incumbents are often defeated. For example, George H. Bush successfully led the country in quickly defeating Iraq in the Gulf War in 1991, but the economy's slow growth in the early 1990s led to his electoral defeat when he ran for reelection in 1992. Because the strength of the economy has a major influence on elections, incumbent politicians have a strong incentive to be sure that the economy is growing rapidly at election time. Because monetary policy works with a lag, incumbent politicians would like monetary policy to begin easing about a year before the election, with lower interest rates causing increased spending, faster economic growth, and lower unemployment. Nothing is worse for an incumbent than to have monetary policy tighten and the economy slow just as the election nears. The idea that monetary policy eases before elections to favor incumbent politicians is known as the **political business cycle.** Although some economists think that the political business cycle is a reality in the United States, the laws governing the Fed have fairly successfully protected the Fed from political influence, and no political business cycle is readily apparent. In some countries, such as Japan, where the central bank is not independent, the central bank regularly stimulates the economy (increasing money growth and cutting interest rates) just before elections to help ensure the reelection of incumbent politicians. Japan's record is not something the United States would like to emulate.

When researchers compare the inflation performance in different countries with the degree of independence of their central banks, they find that greater independence is associated with lower inflation. The results are very clear in some cases. Historically, Germany, which had a very independent central bank, also had quite low inflation rates, whereas Italy, whose central bank had much less independence, had much higher inflation rates. There are a few exceptions, however. A few central banks in less developed countries with no independence at all in their central banks have very low inflation rates in part because the government itself believes that inflation should be low. In addition, the Bank of Japan is not independent of the government at all yet has managed to achieve extremely low inflation. In general, though, independence is inversely related to inflation. This effect exists only for industrial countries but not for developing countries, most likely because many factors other than the independence of the central bank affect inflation in those countries.

Research also shows that the degree of independence of the central bank mainly affects inflation, not other economic variables. There appears to be no clear relationship between the independence of a country's central bank and its rate of economic growth, for example.

However, the Federal Reserve is not protected by the U.S. Constitution. The law establishing the Fed, the Federal Reserve

Act, could be repealed by Congress and the president at any time. Over the last decade, many legislators have introduced proposals to modify the Fed and reduce its independence. These proposals recommended abolishing the Fed as an independent group, making it part of the U.S. Treasury Department; forcing the Fed to have its budget approved by Congress; removing the presidents of the Federal Reserve banks from the FOMC so that Congress would have more control over FOMC members (because the Senate must approve the appointments of Fed governors); and expanding the FOMC to include additional members who are politicians. The motivation for these changes is to increase Congress's ability to influence the Fed's decisions. These proposals to change the Fed have been rejected, however, perhaps because most members of Congress do not think that it is appropriate to increase the political pressure on the Fed.

political business cycle the idea that monetary policy eases before elections to favor incumbent politicians

While overt attempts to politicize the Fed have been rejected, some people have raised legitimate questions about the Fed's independence. There are two potential problems with the existence of an organization such as the Fed that is separate from the rest of government. First, the organization might build itself into a bloated, inefficient bureaucracy. Second, the organization might perform poorly if it is not somehow accountable for its actions.

Is there any evidence that the Fed has built itself into an inefficient bureaucracy? Some economists think so, noting that the Fed's budget often rises more rapidly than the overall price level, so the Fed is getting bigger in terms of real expenditures. To protect itself from political pressure, the Fed has built a large constituency of bankers and other financial market participants who support the Fed. Consequently, when legislation is introduced into Congress that would change the Fed's role in the economy, bankers are the first group to protest the change and use their political influence to eliminate the threat to the Fed.

The other problem that may be raised by the Fed's independence is its lack of accountability, which some people view as undemocratic. The Fed should be held accountable somehow for its actions. It will always be difficult to know if the Fed could have done a better job in the short run, but in

(continued)

the long run, the Fed is certainly responsible for the overall rate of inflation in the economy. As Figure 15.4 suggests, the Fed failed in its mission in the 1960s and 1970s but succeeded in the 1980s, 1990s, and 2000s. Thus, Congress and the public should have been quite disappointed in the Fed's performance in the former period but should be satisfied with the Fed's actions, at least from a long-term perspective, in the latter period.

If the Fed is really accountable for its actions only in the long run, it is hard to hold it responsible for its short-run policies. There is clearly a tradeoff between accountability and political independence.

What would happen if the Fed were under the control of Congress? No one knows for sure, but in many countries where the central bank is part of the government, there is a clear political business cycle. Such a cycle is bad for a country's economic health because it leads to high costs when inflation is reduced, or else it leads to higher and higher inflation rates, which cause severe economic problems, as we will discuss in Chapter 17. Thus, it seems the best course is to keep the Fed independent and to live with the consequences. In the last 30 years, at least, doing so has been rewarding.

RECAP

1	The Federal Reserve is independent of the government by virtue of the structure of governors' terms and its independent income.
2	Politicians seek to influence monetary policy because the state of the economy affects their chances of being reelected.
3	Although the Fed might have incentive to become an inefficient bureaucracy, the Board of Governors sets up internal competitions to force efficient behavior by Federal Reserve banks.
4	The Fed is accountable for inflation in the long run but cannot be held accountable for its actions in the short run.

Review Questions and Problems

Review Questions

1 In what sense are Federal Reserve banks part of the government? In what ways are they part of the private sector?

2 What are the main activities of Federal Reserve banks?

3 What does an economist in the Federal Reserve System do compared with an economics professor at your college or university?

4 What gives the chairman of the Board of Governors so much power and influence in the world?

5 What do Federal Reserve governors do? Why are they quoted so often in the press?

6 Who serves on the Federal Open Market Committee (FOMC)? How does the vote rotate among the presidents of Federal Reserve banks?

7 What is the FOMC directive, and why is it so important?

8 What is the difference between the Beigebook, and the Tealbook?

9 What factors make the Fed independent from politics? Why is there so much political pressure on the Fed, despite its independence?

10 How does the Fed work to protect itself from political pressure?

Analytical Problems

11 Are there any good reasons to have 12 Federal Reserve banks scattered around the country rather than having everything run by the Board of Governors in Washington, D.C.? What are the costs and benefits?

12 Why have some Federal Reserve governors complained about the economic staff at the Board of Governors? Is their concern about how the staff treats them or about how the chairman treats them?

13 Suppose that you thought that some day you would become a member of the Board of Governors of the Fed. How would you prepare for the job? What would you study in college? What types of jobs would you seek after college?

14 Evaluate the pros and cons of proposed legislation that would make the U.S. Secretary of the Treasury a member of the FOMC.

15 Which Fed chairman has had the lowest average inflation rate? How do you think that chairman will be remembered historically?

MONETARY CONTROL

The Federal Reserve (the Fed) affects interest rates, inflation, and output growth in the economy by controlling the money supply. The Fed does not control the money supply directly but rather indirectly through adjustments in the monetary base. The monetary base is an amount that the Fed determines directly by its open-market operations and the amount of discount loans it makes. The monetary base, in turn, supports a larger money supply through the money-multiplier process, which we will study in this chapter. Thus, to understand how the Fed controls the money supply, we will find it convenient to decompose the money supply according to the equation

$$\text{Money supply} = \text{money multiplier} \times \text{monetary base} \qquad (1)$$

The money supply is a measure of the amount of money held in the economy, such as M1 or M2, which we first discussed in Chapter 3. The money multiplier is a number that is affected by decisions made by people, banks, and the Federal Reserve; this chapter explains how those decisions affect the money multiplier. The monetary base is determined by the Federal Reserve and consists of the currency that people hold plus the reserves that banks hold.

The Federal Reserve can control the money supply by manipulating the money multiplier or the monetary base, but for reasons we will examine later, the Fed controls the money supply mainly by changing the monetary base. The money multiplier depends on decisions that people make concerning how their money is divided into various assets, such as currency, transactions deposits (funds in checking accounts), nontransactions deposits (such as funds in savings accounts), and money-market mutual funds, and on decisions that banks make concerning how much reserves they hold. For a given money multiplier, the Fed can choose the size of the monetary base so that the monetary base times the money multiplier equals the desired money supply. For example, if the Fed wants the money supply to be $1,200 billion and the money multiplier is 2, the Fed will set the monetary base at $600 billion because $2 \times \$600$ billion = $1,200 billion.

In this chapter we begin by showing how money is created or destroyed by the actions of the Federal Reserve interacting with banks. We then look at how a small change in bank reserves supplied by the Fed is multiplied by banks into a much larger change in the economy's total money supply and how people and banks influence the size of that multiplier. Next, we see what tools the Fed has at its disposal for influencing the money supply. Finally, we examine the market for reserves, which is the only market the Fed affects directly with its policy actions, to see how the Fed influences the money supply on a day-to-day basis.

16-1 Money Creation and Destruction by the Fed and by Banks

People carry currency and coins in their pockets and purses and keep funds on deposit in their banks. How does that money get into circulation? In this section we will see how the Federal Reserve and banks create money or destroy money.

The Federal Reserve wants to determine the amount of money in the economy. It cannot do so directly, however, because it has no control over the amount of deposit accounts at banks that are part of the money supply. Instead, the Fed must influence the money supply indirectly using tools that affect the amount of reserves at banks. Banks, in turn, create money as they make loans to businesses and individuals. Thus, to understand the Fed's ability to influence the money supply, we first must see what the Fed controls and then see how banks create money and how the amount of money they create is affected by the Fed's decisions.

Suppose that the Fed took a $20 bill from its vault and used that bill to buy a dozen pens. There now would be $20 more money in circulation in the economy, and the Fed would own pens that it could use to perform its duties. In practice, the Fed changes the money supply not by buying and selling pens but by buying and selling securities in the financial market. Those actions, open-market operations, influence the money supply by affecting banks' assets and liabilities and the Fed's own assets and liabilities.

To understand how open-market operations work, we must begin by examining the balance sheet of the Federal Reserve, which looks like Table 16.1.

The main asset of the Fed is its portfolio of securities—mostly government securities. On the liability

TABLE 16.1 Federal Reserve Balance Sheet, July 24, 2013 (billions of dollars)			
Assets		**Liabilities + Capital**	
Securities	3,297	Monetary base	3,553
Loans	2	Other liabilities	9
Other assets	318	Capital	55
Total assets	3,617	Total liabilities + capital	3,617

© Cengage Learning

side of the balance sheet, the monetary base is the main item. The **monetary base** consists of currency held by the nonbank public and banks' reserves, some of which are currency held in banks' vaults and some of which are held on deposit in banks' accounts at the Fed. Note that the term *banks* here refers to all depositary institutions, including commercial banks, savings banks, savings and loan associations, and credit unions.

If the Fed wants to increase the monetary base, it usually engages in open-market operations (discussed in Chapter 15), purchasing government securities in the open market. (However, in the financial crisis of 2008, the Fed also increased the monetary base by making many more loans to financial institutions, and acquiring assets from institutions such as AIG and Bear Stearns to prevent them from failing.) To pay for the securities, the Fed increases the monetary base by increasing the amount of reserves in banks' deposit accounts at the Fed. For example, suppose that the Fed made an open-market purchase of $4 billion from primary government securities dealers. On the Fed's balance sheet, this transaction would be recorded as an increase of $4 billion on the asset side under government securities and an increase of $4 billion on the liabilities + capital side under monetary base. Where does the $4 billion come from? The Fed merely adds $4 billion to the reserve accounts of the banks where the government securities dealers have their deposit accounts. The bank reserve accounts are nothing more than entries in the Fed's computer system. Thus, money comes into existence simply because the Fed writes a number down on its books. In a similar way, the Fed can sell securities on the open market and reduce bank reserves and the monetary base.

In the example of a $4 billion open-market purchase, the Fed's balance sheet would change in the following way:

Change in Federal Reserve Balance Sheet (billions of dollars)

Change in Assets	Change in Liabilities + Capital
Securities +4.0	Monetary base +4.0

If the Fed changes the monetary base by using open-market operations, how do people get $20 bills in their wallets? The answer is that the Fed supplies currency to banks in whatever amount they ask for, paid for with amounts in their reserve accounts at the Fed. For example, in the holiday shopping season in December, people want more currency, so they withdraw more currency from automatic teller machines (ATMs) and hold less in their bank accounts. The banks must obtain enough currency to meet the needs of their customers, which they buy from the Fed by drawing down their reserve accounts at the Fed. Therefore, when people hold more currency, banks' reserves are reduced.

16-1a How Banks Create or Destroy Money

The Fed can increase or decrease the monetary base as much as it desires. Changes in the monetary base work their way through the banking system, leading banks to create additional money or destroy existing money. Recall that the money supply is not just the amount of currency outstanding but also includes various deposit accounts at banks (transaction accounts in M1 and savings and time deposits in M2). Thus, banks may influence the money supply through their impact on those accounts. The basic idea is that a bank makes a loan that is deposited in other banks, causing increases in the funds on deposit at those banks.

To illustrate how banks create or destroy money, we use a fictional example. Consider a hypothetical bank; call it First Bank. Suppose that it has the following balance sheet:

Balance Sheet for First Bank (amounts in millions of dollars)

Assets		Liabilities + Capital	
Reserves	11.5	Transaction accounts	115.0
Securities	66.0		
Loans	77.5	Nontransaction accounts	30.0
		Capital	10.0
Total assets	155.0	Total liabilities + capital	155.0

To keep our calculations simple, assume that required reserves are 10 percent of all transaction accounts (checkable deposits). In this initial situation, First Bank's required reserves are

$$\$115.0 \text{ million} \times 0.10 = \$11.5 \text{ million}$$

Because this amount is just equal to its reserves, First Bank has no excess reserves.

First Bank's Reserves (millions)	
Total reserves	$11.5
− Required reserves	$11.5
Excess reserves	$ 0.0

Suppose, however, that one of First Bank's customers is a government securities dealer, which sells $4 million in securities to the Federal Reserve when the Fed engages in open-market operations. How is First Bank's balance sheet affected? On the asset side of First Bank's balance sheet, reserves increase by $4 million (from $11.5 million to $15.5 million) as the Fed transfers $4 million to First Bank's reserve account; on the liabilities + capital side of the balance sheet, First Bank adds $4 million in transactions deposits, crediting the account of the securities dealer. Thus, First Bank's balance sheet looks like this:

Balance Sheet for First Bank (amounts in millions of dollars)			
Assets		Liabilities + Capital	
Reserves	15.5	Transaction accounts	119.0
Securities	66.0		
Loans	77.5	Nontransaction accounts	30.0
		Capital	10.0
Total assets	159.0	Total liabilities + capital	159.0

Change in Balance Sheet for First Bank			
Assets		Liabilitie + Capital	
Reserves	+4.0	Transaction accounts	+4.0

Now First Bank's required reserves are

$$\$119.0 \text{ million} \times 0.10 = \$11.9 \text{ million}$$

Because its reserve balance is $15.5 million, First Bank finds itself with excess reserves of $3.6 million because its required reserves have risen $0.4 million and its reserves have increased $4.0 million.

First Bank's Reserves (millions)	
Total reserves	$15.5
− Required reserves	$11.9
Excess reserves	$ 3.6

Suppose that First Bank decides to make a loan to the Stinger Corporation of $3.6 million. It does so by signing a loan agreement with Stinger, thus adding to the total amount of loans on the asset side of its balance sheet. To give the funds to Stinger, First Bank simply adds $3.6 million on its computer system to Stinger's account. This change appears on First Bank's balance sheet as

Balance Sheet for First Bank (amounts in millions of dollars)			
Assets		Liabilities + Capital	
Reserves	15.5	Transaction accounts	122.6
Securities	66.0		
Loans	81.1	Nontransaction accounts	30.0
		Capital	10.0
Total assets	162.6	Total liabilities + capital	162.6

Change in Balance Sheet for First Bank			
Assets		Liabilities + Capital	
Loans	+3.6	Transaction accounts	+3.6

Now, First Bank has required reserves of

$$\$122.6 \text{ million} \times 0.10 = \$12.26 \text{ million}$$

Because its reserve balance is $15.50 million and required reserves are $12.26 million, First Bank has excess reserves of $3.24 million:

First Bank's Reserves (millions)	
Total reserves	$15.50
− Required reserves	$12.26
Excess reserves	$ 3.24

Should First Bank make another loan to another company? Probably not, because Stinger would not borrow $3.6 million and leave the funds in its checking account. Stinger no doubt borrowed the money to spend on an investment project. Suppose that Stinger spends the money by purchasing computer equipment from the Compdell Corporation in Seattle. Stinger writes a check on its account at First Bank to pay for the equipment. Compdell deposits the check in its bank in Seattle, Second Bank, which asks First Bank for the funds. When First Bank delivers the funds, its balance sheet now looks like this:

Balance Sheet for First Bank
(amounts in millions of dollars)

Assets		Liabilities + Capital	
Reserves	11.9	Transaction accounts	119.0
Securities	66.0		
Loans	81.1	Nontransaction accounts	30.0
		Capital	10.0
Total assets	159.0	Total liabilities + capital	159.0

Change in Balance Sheet for First Bank

Assets		Liabilities + Capital	
Reserves	−3.6	Transaction accounts	−3.6

Now First Bank has required reserves of

$$\$119.0 \text{ million} \times 0.10 = \$11.9 \text{ million}$$

Because its reserve balance is $11.9 million, First Bank has no excess reserves:

First Bank's Reserves (millions)

Total reserves	$11.9
− Required reserves	$11.9
Excess reserves	$ 0.0

The final balance sheet for First Bank is very similar to its initial balance sheet, the only changes being that reserves are $0.4 million higher, loans are $3.6 million higher, and transaction accounts are $4.0 million higher:

Balance Sheet for First Bank
(amounts in millions of dollars)
Initial Balance Sheet

Assets		Liabilities + Capital	
Reserves	11.5	Transaction accounts	115.0
Securities	66.0		
Loans	77.5	Nontransaction accounts	30.0
		Capital	10.0
Total assets	155.0	Total liabilities + capital	155.0

Final Balance Sheet

Assets		Liabilities + Capital	
Reserves	11.9	Transaction accounts	119.0
Securities	66.0		
Loans	81.1	Nontransaction accounts	30.0
		Capital	10.0
Total assets	159.0	Total liabilities + capital	159.0

Change in Balance Sheet for First Bank

Assets		Liabilities + Capital	
Reserves	+0.4	Transaction accounts	+4.0
Loans	+3.6		

But the story does not end here. Remember that Compdell Corporation deposited $3.6 million in Second Bank, so we need to see how this transaction affects Second Bank. Suppose that Second Bank has the following balance sheet before the transaction:

Balance Sheet for Second Bank
(amounts in millions of dollars)

Assets		Liabilities + Capital	
Reserves	20.0	Transaction accounts	200.0
Securities	130.0		
Loans	90.0	Nontransaction accounts	25.0
		Capital	15.0
Total assets	240.0	Total liabilities + capital	240.0

Note that Second Bank has no excess reserves because its required reserves are

$$\$200 \text{ million} \times 0.10 = \$20 \text{ million}$$

which is exactly equal to its total reserves.

Second Bank's Reserves (millions)

Total reserves	$20.0
− Required reserves	$20.0
Excess reserves	$ 0.0

After Compdell deposits $3.6 million into the bank and the check has cleared, Second Bank gains $3.6 million in reserves (held in its account at the Federal Reserve Bank of San Francisco) and has $3.6 million more in transaction accounts (in Compdell's account). Its balance sheet now looks like this:

Balance Sheet for Second Bank
(amounts in millions of dollars)

Assets		Liabilities 1 Capital	
Reserves	23.6	Transaction accounts	203.6
Securities	130.0		
Loans	90.0	Nontransaction accounts	25.0
		Capital	15.0
Total assets	243.6	Total liabilities + capital	243.6

Change in Balance Sheet for Second Bank

Assets		Liabilities + Capital	
Reserves	+3.6	Transaction accounts	+3.6

Second Bank's balance sheet now has an extra $3.6 million in transaction accounts, against which it must hold $0.36 million in additional required reserves, leaving it with excess reserves of $3.24 million. That is, required reserves are now

$$\$203.6 \text{ million} \times 0.10 = \$20.36 \text{ million}$$

which is $3.24 million less than its total reserves of $23.6 million:

Second Bank's Reserves (millions)

Total reserves	$23.60
− Required reserves	$20.36
Excess reserves	$ 3.24

Suppose that Second Bank now makes a loan of $3.24 million to another company, which spends the funds, which end up in yet another bank. When the funds are spent, Second Bank's balance sheet will look like this:

Balance Sheet for Second Bank
(amounts in millions of dollars)

Assets		Liabilities + Capital	
Reserves	20.36	Transaction accounts	203.60
Securities	130.00		
Loans	93.24	Nontransaction accounts	25.00
		Capital	15.00
Total assets	243.60	Total liabilities + capital	243.60

Change in Balance Sheet for Second Bank

Assets		Liabilities + Capital
Reserves	−3.24	
Loans	+3.24	

Now Second Bank no longer has any excess reserves because required reserves are

$$\$203.6 \text{ million} \times 0.10 = \$20.36 \text{ million}$$

which is just equal to its total reserves:

Second Bank's Reserves (millions)

Total reserves	$20.36
− Required reserves	$20.36
Excess reserves	$ 0.00

However, now the third bank in line will find itself with excess reserves because it will get a deposit of $3.24 million, against which it must hold $0.324 million in reserves. Suppose that this process continues indefinitely, with each successive bank receiving a smaller deposit than the one before but still having some amount of excess reserves and making a smaller loan than the one before.

TABLE 16.2	Summary of Effects on All Banks from Open-Market Purchase of $4 Million (all amounts in millions of dollars)		
Bank	New Deposits	Additional Reserves	Loans Made
1. First Bank	4.00	0.400	3.60
2. Second Bank	3.60	0.360	3.24
3. Third Bank	3.24	0.324	2.92
4. Fourth Bank	2.92	0.292	2.63
	.	.	.
	.	.	.
	.	.	.
Total	40.00	4.000	36.00

money multiplier the ratio of the money supply to the monetary base

If we add up all the new deposits that come into banks, the additional reserves they hold against those deposits, and the loans they make, we get the outcome shown in Table 16.2. Loans are made by each bank when that bank gains excess reserves. The additional reserves held by each bank are required reserves.

How do we know what the totals of the amounts in each column of Table 16.2 are? To calculate this, we use a mathematical shortcut, which is that the sum of a series of numbers, each of which is a proportion $(1 - q)$ of the number before, equals the first number in the series times $1/q$. (To learn more about this shortcut, see Appendix 16.A.) In this case, q is the reserve requirement of 10 percent, or 0.10, so $1 - q$ is 0.9. Note that each number in each column of the table is 0.9 times the number above it. With $q = 0.10$, then

$$1/q = \frac{1}{0.10}$$
$$= 10$$

Thus, the total amount of new deposits is

$$\$4 \text{ million} \times 10 = \$40 \text{ million}$$

Similarly, the total amount of additional reserves is

$$\$0.4 \text{ million} \times 10 = \$4 \text{ million}$$

And the total amount of loans made is

$$\$3.6 \text{ million} \times 10 = \$36 \text{ million}$$

The overall result from this exercise is that an open-market purchase by the Federal Reserve of $4 million leads to a total increase in transaction accounts of $40 million, with newly created loans in the banking system of $36 million. The original $4 million is held as additional reserves at banks throughout the country.

Because banks bring money into existence when they make new loans, they can destroy money if they make fewer loans than before. If the government securities dealer that is First Bank's customer had purchased securities from the Fed instead of selling them to the Fed, First Bank's required reserves would have exceeded its actual reserves. To make up the reserve shortfall, First Bank would need to take some action, such as not renewing a loan, to reduce the amount of funds it has in transaction accounts. Again, there is a chain reaction throughout the banking system, and the amount of deposits, reserves, and loans throughout the economy would decline. Thus, banks' actions following an open-market sale by the Fed cause the money supply to contract by a multiple of the amount of the open-market sale.

16-1b The Money Multiplier

Because all measures of the money supply include funds in transaction accounts, the example of how banks create money shows that the total increase in the money supply equals a multiple of the original amount of reserves the Fed introduces into the banking system by increasing the monetary base through open-market operations. We call this multiple a **money multiplier.** The money multiplier is defined as the ratio of the money supply to the monetary base:

$$Money\ multiplier = money\ supply \div monetary\ base$$
$$mm = M \div MB \tag{2}$$

where M is a measure of the money supply such as M1 or M2, mm is the money multiplier (a different one for each different measure of the money supply), and MB is the monetary base. Equation (2) comes from dividing Equation (1) through by the monetary base.

Often we want to know how a change in the monetary base affects the money supply, so we use the related formula

$$\text{Change in money supply} = \text{multiplier} \times \text{change in monetary base}$$
$$\Delta M = mm \times \Delta MB \qquad \text{(3)}$$

where the symbol Δ means the change in the variable that follows. Equation (3) is useful for understanding how the money supply changes in the short run because of a change in the monetary base. It is not useful for looking at how the money supply changes over a longer period because the money multiplier may change slowly over time, in which case Equation (3) is not valid because it is based on the assumption that the money multiplier is constant.

In the example in the preceding section showing how banks create money, the money multiplier was equal to the inverse of the reserve requirement q:

$$mm = \frac{1}{q}$$

Because $q = 0.10$,

$$mm = \frac{1}{0.10}$$
$$= 10$$

Thus, the increase in the monetary base of $4 million leads to an increase in the money supply of

high-powered money
another name for the monetary base

$$\Delta M = mm \times \Delta MB$$
$$= 10 \times \$4 \text{ million}$$
$$= \$40 \text{ million}$$

The same formula also works when the Fed reduces the monetary base; the multiplier tells you the multiple by which the money supply contracts relative to the decline in the monetary base. Because a given change in the monetary base gets multiplied to determine the change in the money supply, the monetary base is sometimes referred to as **high-powered money**. It is "high-powered" because any change in it is multiplied to find the total effect on the money supply.

In analyzing how money flows through banks, we must distinguish between the overall effects on the banking system and effects on individual banks. Sometimes one bank gains reserves, and another bank loses reserves. When this happens, the first bank will expand its loan portfolio, and the second bank will contract. On net, there is no change to the total amount of loans made in the banking system. Only when the Fed increases the monetary base can the amount of the money supply increase or decrease, so long as the money multiplier remains constant.

RECAP

1 The Federal Reserve affects the money supply when it changes the monetary base.

2 Banks create money when they make loans; banks destroy money when they reduce the amount of loans outstanding.

3 An increase in the monetary base of a given amount leads to an increase in the money supply equal to the money multiplier times the increase in the monetary base.

16-2 Realistic Money Multipliers

In our example showing how banks create money, we made simplifying assumptions that allowed us to see how the money multiplier arises. The example assumed that the money created by banks remains entirely in those banks and that new deposits stay in the banks in which they were deposited originally. Reality, however, is more complex. People hold new money partly as currency and partly in accounts other than transaction accounts, and banks hold some excess reserves.

To derive money multipliers, allowing for more realistic behavior by people and banks, we must examine

(1) how the monetary base is split up into reserves and currency held by the nonbank public; (2) how the different measures of the money supply are split into their components; (3) how bank reserves are split between required reserves, and excess reserves; and (4) how people split their money holdings into different assets, such as currency, transaction accounts, nontransaction accounts, and money-market mutual funds.

16-2a The Monetary Base

We start our analysis with an expression for the monetary base. The monetary base, you will recall, is equal to the amount of reserves held by banks plus the amount of currency held by the nonbank public:

$$Monetary\ base = reserves + currency$$
$$MB = R + C \qquad (4)$$

16-2b Measures of the Money Supply

Different measures of the money supply will have different multipliers. Thus, for the M1 measure of the money supply, we add currency C and funds in transaction accounts D, counting travelers' checks as part of currency to keep things simple:

$$M1 = transaction\ accounts + currency$$
$$M1 = D + C \qquad (5)$$

The M1 multiplier ($mm1$) is the ratio of M1 to the monetary base:

$$mm1 = M1 \div MB \qquad (6)$$

The M2 measure of the money supply consists of M1 plus deposits in nontransaction accounts N, which consist of savings deposits and small-denomination time deposits, plus retail money-market mutual funds (MMF):

$$M2 = M1 + nontransaction\ accounts + deposits\ in\ money\text{-}market\ mutual\ funds$$
$$= M1 + N + MMF$$

Because M1 = $D + C$ from Equation (5),

$$M2 = M1 + N + MMF$$
$$= D + C + N + MMF \qquad (7)$$

The M2 multiplier ($mm2$) is the ratio of M2 to the monetary base:

$$mm2 = M2 \div MB \qquad (8)$$

16-2c Bank Reserves

Banks hold reserves R because they must hold required reserves RR, and because they may desire to hold some excess reserves ER. Adding these elements together gives the equation for total reserves:

$$Reserves = required\ reserves + excess\ reserves$$
$$R = RR + ER \qquad (9)$$

In the example in the last section of how banks create money, we assumed that required reserves RR at banks equal the reserve requirement q times the amount of funds in transaction accounts at banks. In reality, however, required reserves are more complex because the reserve requirement varies with the amount of transaction accounts a bank holds, as we learned in Chapter 8. Thus, we will assume that the amount of required reserves depends on the amount of transaction accounts, but the ratio of required reserves to transaction accounts RR/D may vary over time even if the reserve requirement does not change.

Because banks are likely to want to hold excess reserves ER as a function of the amount of funds in transaction accounts, we will assume that at any given time (with a given interest rate), banks try to hold the ratio of excess reserves to deposits ER/D at a constant level. However, because interest rates represent the opportunity cost of holding excess reserves, higher interest rates would likely decrease ER/D.

16-2d People's Holdings of Monetary Assets

The M1 and M2 measures of the money supply consist of four different monetary assets: currency C, transaction accounts D, nontransaction accounts N, and money-market mutual funds MMF. How do people choose the ratio of currency to transaction accounts they desire? This choice depends on their spending habits, the costs of getting funds, and the interest rate, as we saw in Chapter 11. Both the choice of nontransaction accounts to transaction accounts and the choice of money-market mutual funds to transaction accounts that people hold depend on their incomes and the relative returns to the different assets.

At any given time, with no change in people's income, the interest rate, spending habits, the costs of getting funds, and the relative returns to different assets, we might expect people to want to hold the assets in a given ratio to the amount of funds they hold in transaction accounts. That is, we assume that people want to maintain a given ratio of currency to transaction accounts C/D, nontransaction accounts to transaction accounts N/D, and deposits in money-market mutual funds to transaction accounts MMF/D.

16-2e Deriving the Multipliers

We now derive the multipliers for M1 and M2. To begin, we break the monetary base down into its components. We start with Equation (4) and then substitute in for R from Equation (9):

$$\begin{aligned} MB &= R + C \\ &= RR + ER + C \end{aligned} \qquad \textbf{(10)}$$

To find the money multiplier for M1, we start with Equation (6), which defines it as

$$mm1 = \frac{M1}{MB}$$

Now use Equation (5) to substitute in for M1 and use Equation (10) to substitute in for MB:

$$\begin{aligned} mm1 &= \frac{M1}{MB} \\ &= \frac{D + C}{RR + ER + C} \end{aligned}$$

If we now divide the top and bottom of this fraction by D, we get

$$mm1 = \frac{1 + C/D}{RR/D + ER/D + C/D} \qquad \textbf{(11)}$$

Notice that if people do not hold currency and banks do not hold excess reserves so that C/D and ER/D are zero, this formula becomes

$$mm1 = \frac{1}{RR/D}$$

Under the simplifying assumption that required reserves RR = reserve requirement $q \times$ transaction accounts D, then $RR/D = q$, so

$$mm1 = \frac{1}{q}$$

which was the simple multiplier in the earlier example.

We can derive the multiplier for M2 in a similar way. From Equation (8),

$$mm2 = \frac{M2}{MB}$$

Now use Equation (7) to substitute in for M2 and use Equation (10) to substitute in for MB:

$$\begin{aligned} mm2 &= \frac{M2}{MB} \\ &= \frac{D + C + N + MMF}{RR + ER + C} \end{aligned}$$

If we now divide the top and bottom of this fraction by D, we get

$$mm2 = \frac{1 + C/D + N/D + MMF/D}{RR/D + ER/D + C/D} \qquad \textbf{(12)}$$

The denominators of both Equations (11) and (12) are the same because the denominator represents where the monetary base ends up: Some is held as required reserves (the RR/D term), some is held as excess reserves (ER/D), and some is held as currency (C/D).

The numerators of Equations (11) and (12) are different because M2 includes more assets than M1 does. The two terms in the M1 multiplier reflect transaction accounts (the 1 term, because everything is measured relative to transaction accounts) and currency (the C/D term). The additional two terms in the numerator of Equation (12) relate to nontransaction accounts (the N/D term) and retail money-market mutual funds (the MMF/D term).

Thus, both multipliers can be thought of in terms of the assets that make up the aggregates represented in the numerator and the uses of the monetary base represented in the denominator. We can use the multiplier formulas to see how the public and banks affect the money supply.

16-2f How People and Banks Affect the Money Supply

Because the money supply (M1 or M2) equals the multiplier times the monetary base, changes in the multiplier affect the money supply. People and banks help to determine the multiplier: (1) People choose the ratio of currency to transaction accounts C/D, the ratio of nontransaction to transaction accounts N/D, and the ratio of retail money-market mutual funds to transaction accounts MMF/D, and (2) banks choose the ratio of excess reserves to transactions accounts ER/D.

Excess reserves ER/D appear only in the denominators of both equations. Thus, an increase in excess reserves reduces the multipliers and therefore reduces the money supply for a given amount of the monetary base. In addition, because the amounts of nontransaction accounts N/D and retail money-market mutual funds MMF/D appear only in the numerator of Equation (12), an increase in either amount increases the M2 multiplier only, thus increasing the M2 measure of the money supply (but not M1) for a given amount of the monetary base.

The outcome of a change by the public in its desire to hold currency (the C/D term) is more difficult to predict because C/D appears in both the numerator and the denominator of the multiplier (for both M1 and M2). An increase in C/D adds the same amount to both the numerator and the denominator, which makes the multiplier closer to 1 than before. If the multiplier is larger than 1, that is, when the money supply (M1 or M2) is larger than the monetary base, when the multiplier gets closer to 1 it becomes smaller.

Before the financial crisis in 2008, both M1 and M2 were always larger than the monetary base, but since the financial crisis, the monetary base has exceeded M1. So, since 2008, an increase in C/D would increase the M1 multiplier.

For example, suppose that $C/D = 0.8$, $RR/D = 0.1$, and $ER/D = 1.4$. Then the M1 multiplier is

$$
\begin{aligned}
mm1 &= \frac{1 + C/D}{RR/D + ER/D + C/D} \\
&= \frac{1 + 0.8}{0.1 + 1.4 + 0.8} \\
&= \frac{1.8}{2.3} \\
&= 0.78
\end{aligned}
$$

Then suppose that people increase their demand for currency relative to transaction accounts, so C/D rises from 0.8 to 1.0. Then the multiplier is

$$
\begin{aligned}
mm1 &= \frac{1 + C/D}{RR/D + ER/D + C/D} \\
&= \frac{1 + 1.0}{0.1 + 1.4 + 1.0} \\
&= \frac{2.0}{2.5} \\
&= 0.80
\end{aligned}
$$

Note that the multiplier has increased from 0.78 to 0.80 and is now closer to 1 than before. Thus, an increase in the ratio of currency to transaction accounts leads to an increase in the multiplier and hence an increase in the money supply for a given size of the monetary base.

Table 16.3 summarizes how the public's and banks' decisions affect the multiplier and the money supply. The results in the table occur in the long run, when the change in demand by people and banks has worked its way through the entire banking system. For example, suppose that people increase their demand for nontransaction accounts. According to the table, people will transfer funds from transaction to nontransaction accounts, so you might think that M1 would decline because of the decline in transaction accounts. However,

TABLE 16.3	How Decisions by People and Banks Affect the Multiplier and the Money Supply		
Who?	**What Do They Change?**	**What Action Do They Take?**	**What Is the Effect on Money Supply?**
People	Increase demand for currency	Withdraw currency from banks and reduce transaction accounts	Reduces multiplier and money supply (both M1 and M2) if multiplier >1; increases multiplier and money supply if multiplier <1
	Increase demand for nontransaction accounts	Transfer funds from transaction accounts to nontransaction accounts	Increases M2 multiplier and M2 (no effect on M1)
	Increase demand for *MMF* holdings	Transfer funds from transaction accounts to *MMF* accounts	Increases M2 multiplier and M2 (no effect on M1)
Banks	Increase demand for excess reserves	Lend a smaller proportion of any excess reserves	Reduces multiplier and money supply (both M1 and M2)

FIGURE 16.1 Money Multipliers

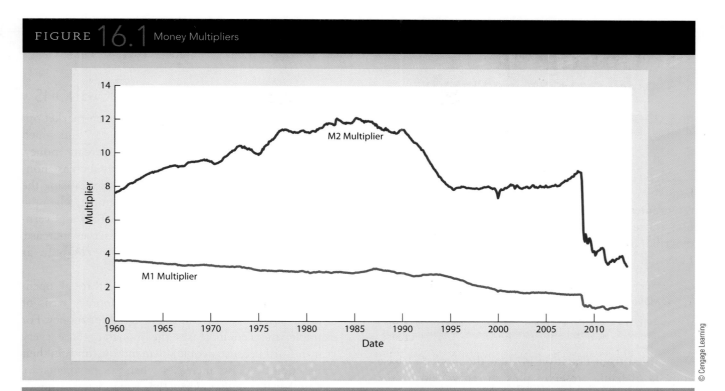

The multipliers for M1 and M2 are shown from January 1960 to June 2013. The M1 multiplier has declined slowly over the entire period, although the rate of decline increased in the late 1990s with the advent of sweep accounts. The M2 multiplier, on the other hand, generally was rising from 1959 to the mid-1980s. From 1990 to 1995, the M2 multiplier fell sharply, but it stabilized from 1995 to 2007. Both multipliers fell sharply during the financial crisis of 2008, as banks began holding a large quantity of excess reserves and have remained low since then.

remember that if the amount of transaction accounts declines, required reserves decline, so banks have more excess reserves than before, so they will make new loans, which will increase the amount of transaction accounts. In the end, the amount of transaction accounts will be the same as it was initially, so M1 will be back to its original level, whereas M2 will increase because of the rise in nontransaction accounts.

Figure 16.1 shows what the multipliers for M1 and M2 have looked like since 1960. Note that the M1 multiplier has declined relatively steadily over time and that the decline has accelerated in recent years; in the financial crisis of 2008, as banks began holding a large number of excess reserves, the M1 multiplier fell sharply. The M2 multiplier was increasing from 1959 to 1985, but fell from 1985 to 1995 and was fairly stable from 1995 to 2007. It rose somewhat in 2007, then fell sharply in the financial crisis of 2008. Both multipliers have remained low since the financial crisis and are likely to remain low if banks continue to hold high levels of excess reserves.

Even though the public and banks affect the money supply by their decisions, the Fed ultimately determines the money supply because it can offset any changes made by banks or the public. Thus, the Fed must decide the extent to which it wants to allow changes in decisions by banks and the public to influence the money supply and the extent to which it wants to offset them. That is the subject of the next section.

RECAP

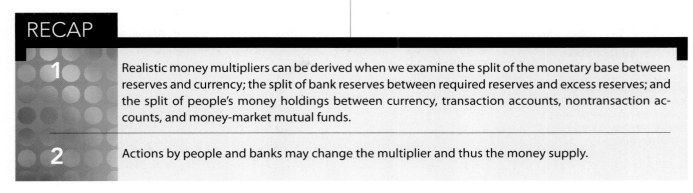

1. Realistic money multipliers can be derived when we examine the split of the monetary base between reserves and currency; the split of bank reserves between required reserves and excess reserves; and the split of people's money holdings between currency, transaction accounts, nontransaction accounts, and money-market mutual funds.

2. Actions by people and banks may change the multiplier and thus the money supply.

16-3 The Fed's Tools for Changing the Money Supply

The Fed has four main tools for affecting the money supply: (1) open-market operations, (2) changes in the discount rate, (3) changes in the interest rate on banks' reserve balances, and (4) changes in reserve requirements. In this section we will learn how the Fed uses those tools to affect the money supply. We can describe how each tool works by breaking down Equation (1) into finer components:

Money supply = money multiplier × monetary base

$$M = mm \times MB$$

We learned from Equation (4) that the monetary base consists of banks' reserves plus currency held by the nonbank public:

Monetary base = reserves + currency

$$MB = R + C$$

Banks' reserves can be broken down into those that are borrowed from the Fed, which equal the amount of discount loans, and nonborrowed reserves:

Reserves = discount loans + nonborrowed reserves

$$R = DL + NBR \tag{13}$$

Beginning with Equation (1), use Equation (4) to substitute for *MB*:

$$\begin{aligned} M &= mm \times MB \\ &= mm \times (R + C) \end{aligned}$$

Now use Equation (13) in this expression to substitute for *R*:

$$\begin{aligned} M &= mm \times (R + C) \\ &= mm \times (DL + NBR + C) \end{aligned} \tag{14}$$

defensive open-market operations open-market activity the Fed undertakes because of seasonal effects or to offset a temporary change in money demand

dynamic open-market operations open-market activity the Fed undertakes when it wants to change monetary policy

We can use Equation (14) to see how the Fed's tools influence the money supply.

16-3a Open-Market Operations

The Fed's most commonly used tool is open-market operations, which we discussed in Chapter 15 and which we used in our example of how banks create money. Purchases of securities by the Fed directly increase non-borrowed reserves and the monetary base, causing the money supply to increase. As in our example, when the Fed purchases securities in the market from a government securities dealer, nonborrowed reserves increase, causing a multiple increase in the money supply, as shown in Equation (3).

Many changes in the monetary base through open-market operations are made on a temporary basis or to offset seasonal swings in the demand for money. For example, the Fed increases the monetary base every year in April because people's demand for funds in their transaction accounts increases when tax payments are due and in December when the demand for currency increases dramatically for the holiday shopping season. When people demand more currency in December, the M1 multiplier typically changes 3 percent from November to December. To prevent this change in the multiplier from affecting M1, the Fed simply changes the monetary base to offset it.

Open-market operations the Fed undertakes because of seasonal effects or because of a temporary change in money demand are called **defensive open-market operations.** The term *defensive* refers to the idea that the Fed is offsetting some factor originating elsewhere—defending against that change causing a movement in the federal funds rate. By contrast, the Fed engages in **dynamic open-market operations** when it wants to actively change monetary policy. For example, when the Fed wanted to ease monetary policy in 2008 to offset the recession, it made numerous open-market purchases, thus increasing the money supply.

16-3b Discount Lending

The Fed's second tool for monetary policy is changing the discount rate, which is the interest rate that banks pay when they borrow from the Fed at the discount window. If the Fed raises the discount rate, banks are likely to borrow less; if the Fed reduces the discount rate, banks are likely to borrow more.

A bank that takes out a discount loan must provide collateral, which consists of assets that the bank promises to give to the Fed if it cannot repay the loan. To protect itself from loss, the Fed takes a **haircut,** which means that it requires collateral valued at more than the amount of the loan. For example, if a bank took out a $3 million loan, it might be required to offer the Fed $3.5 million in collateral; the extra $0.5 million of collateral is the amount of the haircut. By taking a haircut, the Fed will not lose money even if the value of the assets falls slightly and the bank defaults on the loan. If the Fed charges a larger haircut, banks will be discouraged from borrowing.

Banks that are at least adequately capitalized and that have a CAMELS rating (defined in Chapter 9) of 1, 2, or 3 qualify to borrow under the Fed's primary credit program. A bank taking out a **primary credit discount loan** may borrow as much as it would like (up to the amount of collateral it can pledge) on a short-term basis (a day or a few days). The Fed will not question the purpose or nature of such loans. The primary credit program began in 2003; prior to that, even strong banks were reluctant to borrow at the discount window because the Fed might question the purpose of the loan or might audit the bank. Beginning in 2003, the Fed reduced the level of scrutiny for such loans, hoping that banks would be more likely to borrow, especially if the federal funds rate rose higher than the discount rate.

If a bank is not adequately capitalized or has a CAMELS rating of 4 or 5, it may be able to borrow under the Fed's secondary credit program. A **secondary credit discount loan** has a discount rate that is ½ percentage point higher than the discount rate for primary credit. Banks in trouble may borrow under the secondary credit program for an extended period of time, not just for a short term. However, loans under the secondary credit program are subject to careful scrutiny by the Fed, which wants to make sure that borrowing banks are operating in a safe and sound manner.

The Fed also has a program to lend at the discount window to small banks, such as those in farming communities, that have a seasonal demand for credit. The interest rate on a **seasonal credit discount loan** is set by a formula, equal to one-half the average federal funds rate over the previous two-week maintenance period

plus one-half the average rate on negotiable certificates of deposit over the same period.

When the Fed lends at the discount window, how is the money supply affected? To see this, refer to Equation (14):

$$M = mm \times (DL + NBR + C)$$

An increase in the amount of discount loans increases the money supply by the amount of the increase in the discount loans times the money multiplier. For example, suppose that $mm1 = 2$, $DL = 0$, $NBR = 60$, and $C = 400$ (amounts in billions of dollars). Then

$$M1 = 2 \times (0 + 60 + 400) = 2 \times 460 = 920$$

Now if the amount of discount loans increases from 0 to 20, and $mm1$, NBR, and C are unchanged, then

$$M1 = 2 \times (20 + 60 + 400) = 2 \times 480 = 960$$

Thus, M1 increases from $920 billion to $960 billion when the amount of discount loans increases from $0 to $20 billion.

16-3c The Interest Rate on Bank Reserves

The Fed's third tool is the interest rate the Fed pays to banks on their reserve balances held at the Fed. In October 2008, in the middle of the financial crisis, the Fed began paying interest on bank reserves, as we discussed in Chapter 8. The idea was to give banks an incentive to hold reserves for safety's sake and to give the Fed another tool (the interest rate paid on reserve balances) to affect

haircut the extra collateral the Fed requires above the value of a discount loan

primary credit discount loan a loan made by the Fed to a bank that is highly rated, under which the Fed does not question the purpose of the loan

secondary credit discount loan a loan made by the Fed to a bank that is not highly rated, under which the Fed carefully scrutinizes the purpose of the loan and the ability of the bank to repay the loan; the secondary credit discount rate is ½ percentage point higher than the rate for primary credit

seasonal credit discount loan a loan from the Fed to a small agricultural bank

the amount of bank reserves and money. If the Fed increases the interest rate on reserves, banks will hold more excess reserves; if the Fed lowers the interest rate, banks will hold fewer excess reserves. The change in the amount of excess reserves will affect the money multiplier, as you can see in Equations (11) and (12)—an increase in the ratio of excess reserves to deposits will reduce the money multiplier. Further, the interest rate the Fed pays on reserves will put a lower bound on the federal funds rate, as no bank would lend to another in the federal funds market at an interest rate lower than the Fed pays on reserves.

16-3d Reserve Requirements

The Fed's fourth tool is changing the reserve requirement. Historically, an increase in the reserve requirement reduced the money multiplier because banks held more reserves and lent less of any new deposits they received. The decline in the money multiplier reduced the money supply for a given monetary base. Conversely, a decrease in the reserve requirement increased the money multiplier and thus increased the money supply with a given monetary base.

The Fed could have changed the reserve requirement to achieve its policy goals but as a practical matter rarely did so. Small changes in the reserve requirement would have had a strong impact on the amount of required reserves, but usually the Fed did not want to affect the amount of reserves by very much. Changing reserve requirements was simply too blunt an instrument for the Fed to use for minor adjustments to the money supply. The effect of a change in reserve requirements today is less clear than it was historically. Because today banks hold large volumes of excess reserves, an increase in reserve requirements might not cause any change in the amount of reserves that banks hold, or in the money multiplier. In that case, a change in reserve requirements would have no effect on the money multiplier or the money supply. This has been the situation since 2008, when the Fed began paying interest on reserves.

This situation could change if economic conditions normalize and the Fed begins reducing the monetary base by open-market sales of its assets. Then the amount of excess reserves might shrink substantially. In that case, a change in reserve requirements might reduce the money multiplier and the money supply, as was the case before 2008. But for now, at least, a change in reserve requirements would have no effect.

Table 16.4 summarizes how the Fed changes the money supply.

TABLE 16.4 How the Fed Changes the Money Supply		
What Does the Fed Change?	**What Action Does the Fed Take or How Do Banks Respond?**	**What Is the Effect on Money Supply?**
Open-market purchases	Fed buys securities in exchange for reserves	Increases monetary base and money supply
Increase in discount rate	Banks decrease discount borrowing	Decreases monetary base and money supply
Increase in interest rate on bank reserves	Banks hold more excess reserves	Decreases multiplier and money supply
Increase in reserve requirements	Banks increase reserves	Decreases multiplier and money supply before 2008; no effect on multiplier or money supply after 2008

Open-market purchases by the Federal Reserve increase the monetary base and the money supply; open-market sales reduce the monetary base and the money supply.

2 If the Fed reduces the discount rate, the monetary base increases as discount loans rise; the money supply also increases. If the Fed raises the discount rate, the monetary base decreases as discount loans decline, and the money supply also decreases.

3 If the Fed raises the interest rate that it pays on reserves, banks will hold more excess reserves, the money multiplier decreases, and the money supply decreases; a reduction in the interest rate on reserves leads banks to hold fewer excess reserves, increases the money multiplier, and increases the money supply.

4 Before 2008, an increase in the reserve requirement reduced the multiplier and thus decreased the money supply; a decrease in the reserve requirement increased the multiplier and thus increased the money supply. Changes in reserve requirements were not useful for the Fed in making day-to-day adjustments in the money supply. After 2008, because banks hold many excess reserves, any change in reserve requirements would have no effect on the multiplier or the money supply.

16-4 The Market for Bank Reserves

On a day-to-day basis, the Fed engages in open-market operations that affect the size of the monetary base and the amount of bank reserves. To use its tools effectively, the Fed must model the market for reserves. What determines the amount of reserves banks want to hold? The federal funds rate matters because that is the interest rate banks charge each other on overnight loans of reserves. The higher the federal funds rate, the lower the demand for reserves will be. And, of course, banks hold reserves because they are required to hold them against the amount of money deposited in transaction accounts and because they need to clear checks. We learned in Chapter 11 that the amount of transaction accounts is inversely related to the interest rate, so banks' demand for reserves is inversely related to the federal funds rate. However, if the federal funds rate were below the interest rate that the Fed pays on reserves, then banks would borrow in the federal funds market and hold excess reserves, thus making a risk-free profit. Because many banks would try to do this at the same time, they would effectively bid up the federal funds

rate to equal the interest rate on reserves; thus the federal funds rate should never fall below the interest rate on reserves. If we plot the demand for reserves against the federal funds interest rate, as in Figure 16.2, we see that the demand curve slopes downward until it hits the interest rate on reserves (ir), after which it becomes horizontal.

What determines the supply of reserves? Reserves R may be split into nonborrowed reserves NBR plus the amount of discount loans DL:

$$\text{Reserves} = \text{nonborrowed reserves} + \text{discount loans}$$
$$R = NBR + DL \tag{15}$$

What determines the supply of nonborrowed reserves? The Fed determines the monetary base, which consists of reserves plus currency held by the nonbank public, from Equation (4):

$$MB = R + C$$

If we substitute for R from Equation (15), we get

$$MB = R + C$$
$$= NBR + DL + C$$

FIGURE 16.2 The Demand for Reserves

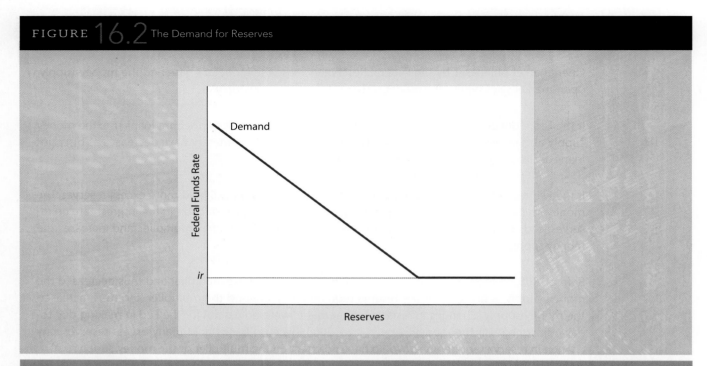

The demand for reserves slopes downward because a lower federal funds rate induces banks to hold more reserves. The federal funds rate cannot fall below the interest rate on reserves (*ir*), so the demand curve becomes horizontal at that interest rate.

Now subtract $DL + C$ from both sides of this equation and reverse the sides of the equation:

$$NBR = MB - (DL + C) \qquad (16)$$

Equation (16) is the basis for the Fed's day-to-day operations in the reserves market. The Fed uses open-market operations to adjust the monetary base, accounting for its estimates of the amount of discount loans and currency held by the nonbank public to determine the amount of nonborrowed reserves.

What determines the amount of discount loans? Some banks take out loans under the Fed's seasonal credit program, in which small farm banks can borrow to meet the seasonal demand for agricultural loans. Also, some banks in financial trouble may take out secondary credit discount loans until they get themselves into better financial condition. Finally, some banks take out primary credit discount loans because of temporary problems, such as the failure of a computer system. We lump all these loans together and call them *discount loans that arise for business needs* (*DL-business*).

However, banks in good standing also may take out primary credit discount loans to make a profit. If the primary credit discount rate is below the federal funds rate, banks could borrow from the Fed at the lower rate (the primary credit discount rate) and lend to other banks at the higher rate (the federal funds rate). Doing so would yield them a profit at very low cost, so banks will be eager to do so. We use the term *discount loans for profit* (*DL-profit*) to refer to the amount of borrowing from the Fed that occurs as banks try to profit. Clearly, if the federal funds rate ever exceeds the discount rate, we should expect banks to take out many discount loans for profit, but if the federal funds rate is below the discount rate, there should be no discount loans for profit (because banks would incur losses).

Therefore, what does the supply curve of reserves look like? The amount of reserves supplied equals

$$
\begin{aligned}
R &= NBR + DL \\
&= NBR + DL\text{-}business + DL\text{-}profit
\end{aligned}
$$

It is reasonable to assume that *NBR* is set by the Fed and that *DL-business* depends on the season of the year (for seasonal credit), the financial conditions of banks (for secondary credit), and random events such as computer failures (for primary credit discount loans for business needs). We will assume that demand for such discount loans is not related to the federal funds rate. Since *NBR* is determined by the Fed through open-market operations, and *DL-business* does not depend on the federal funds rate, then on any given day *NBR* + *DL-business* is an amount

FIGURE 16.3 The Supply of Reserves

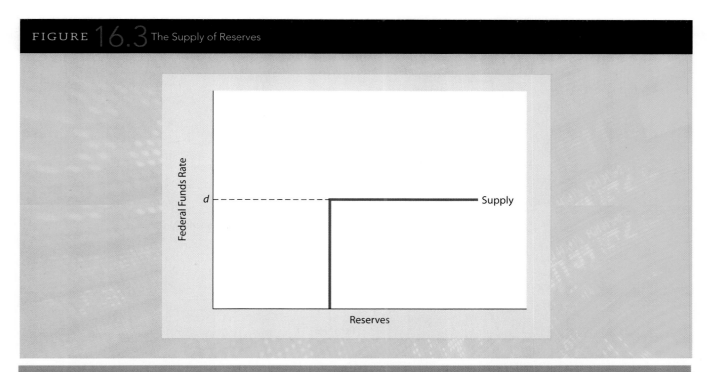

The supply of reserves is vertical when the federal funds rate is less than the primary credit discount rate *d* because banks would not want to take out a primary credit discount loan when a federal funds loan is cheaper. The supply of reserves is horizontal when the federal funds rate equals the primary credit discount rate because banks would be willing to take out primary credit discount loans when the federal funds rate is equal to or above the primary credit discount rate.

that does not depend on the federal funds rate and thus is represented as a vertical line in Figure 16.3. Primary credit discount loans for profit *DL-profit* are shown as the horizontal line segment in the graph; they will be zero whenever the federal funds rate is less than the discount rate, but *DL-profit* will be very large whenever the federal funds rate exceeds the primary credit discount rate.

How do we find equilibrium in the market for bank reserves? Figure 16.4 combines Figures 16.2 and 16.3 to show a normal situation in which there are no discount loans for profit. Equilibrium in the reserves market occurs where the demand curve intersects the supply curve. This point determines the equilibrium amount of reserves R^* and the equilibrium federal funds rate ffr^*. Note that the amount of discount loans equals *DL-business*; there are no primary credit discount loans for profit because the federal funds rate is less than the discount rate. The equilibrium federal funds rate is above the interest rate on reserves *ir*, as well.

Using this diagram, we can understand the daily operation of the Open-Market Desk at the Federal Reserve Bank of New York. Consider Figure 16.5, which shows what the Fed thinks the market for reserves looks like on a particular morning. Suppose that the Fed's target for the federal funds rate (determined by the FOMC) is 4.75 percent and that the Fed thinks

that the demand curve for reserves is given by the line labeled *Demand*. The Fed has estimated the amount of required reserves, excess reserves, and required clearing balances that banks plan to hold that day. The Fed allows for some discount loans for business needs as well. Then the Fed asks: What amount of reserves do we need to add to or take away from the market so that supply and demand intersect at the targeted federal funds rate of 4.75 percent? In the graph, the Fed thinks that the current supply of reserves is given by the curve S_1. However, to hit its target, the Fed must increase the amount of nonborrowed reserves to shift the supply curve to S_2, which requires the addition of reserves in the amount ΔR shown in the graph. The Fed then engages in open-market operations, purchasing ΔR of securities in the open market that morning to hit its target for the federal funds rate. If it does not do this, the federal funds rate will be higher than the target because supply curve S_1 intersects the demand curve at a federal funds rate of 5.50 percent.

The challenge faced by the Desk is correctly estimating the amounts of reserves that are in the market each day. A number of factors influence this amount. A particularly important factor is the change in the balances that the U.S. Treasury holds in banks. As people and business firms pay their taxes, the Treasury keeps those funds

FIGURE 16.4 The Reserves Market

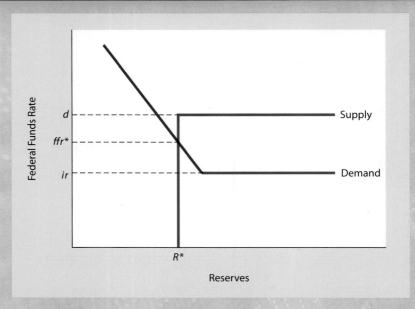

This graph shows equilibrium in the reserves market. Equilibrium occurs where the demand curve for reserves intersects the supply curve. In equilibrium, the federal funds rate is *ffr**, and the amount of reserves is *R**. The primary credit discount rate is d, and there are no primary credit discount loans because *ffr** < *d*.

FIGURE 16.5 Daily Analysis of the Reserves Market

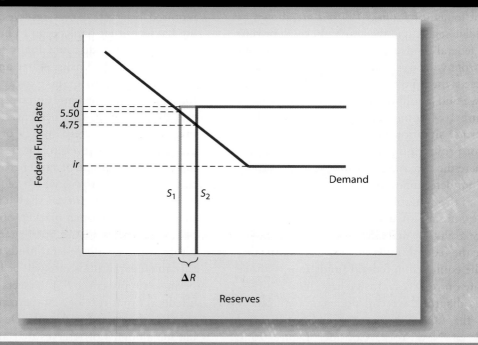

Each day, the staff at the Open-Market Desk at the Federal Reserve Bank of New York estimates what the reserves market will look like. In the graph, the Desk estimates that without any open-market operations, supply curve S_1 will intersect the demand curve at a federal funds rate of 5.50 percent, which exceeds the Fed's target of 4.75 percent. However, if the Fed engages in open-market purchases in the amount ΔR, shifting the supply curve to S_2, the equilibrium federal funds rate will equal the target.

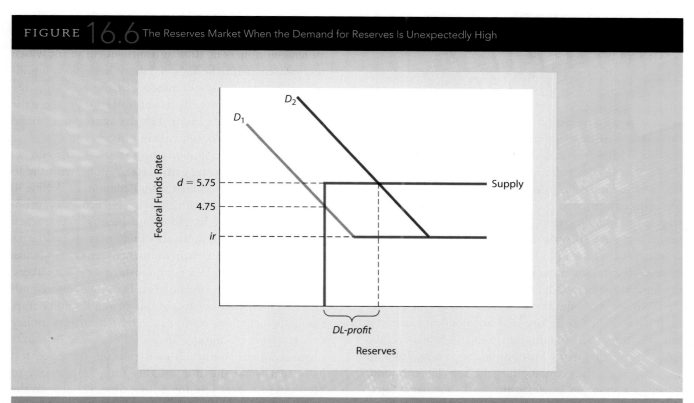

In this graph, the staff at the Fed's Open-Market Desk thinks that the demand for reserves will be D₁, so they supply enough reserves to hit their target for the federal funds rate of 4.75 percent. Suppose, however, that the demand for reserves turns out to be D₂ instead. Then banks take out primary credit discount loans from the Fed in the amount *DL-profit*, and the federal funds rate rises to 5.75 percent, which equals the discount rate.

in accounts at banks until it needs to spend the money. Then the Treasury transfers the funds from banks to the Federal Reserve, where it keeps its checking account. The balances at banks may change significantly from day to day, depending on when the Treasury transfers the funds and when tax payments are made. The Fed consults with the Treasury about its plans each day, so the Fed has a good idea how much those balances are likely to change.

What if the demand for reserves turns out to be substantially higher than the staff at the Open-Market Desk had planned on? Figure 16.6 shows the situation that might occur if the Fed plans for the demand for reserves to be on demand curve D_1, but the actual demand curve for reserves is D_2. The federal funds rate will rise to the primary credit discount rate, 5.75 percent, but no higher as banks take out primary credit discount loans for profit in the amount shown as *DL-profit*. Thus, the procedure established by the Fed for discount lending prevents the federal funds rate from rising above the primary credit discount rate.

RECAP

1 In the market for reserves, demand is determined by the amount of transaction accounts at banks, which varies with the federal funds rate. The supply of reserves is determined by the Federal Reserve's supply of nonborrowed reserves plus the demand for discount loans.

2 The federal funds rate adjusts to equilibrate the market for reserves.

3 In its daily operations, the Fed attempts to manipulate the supply of reserves to hit its target for the federal funds rate.

16-5 Monetary Policy in a Liquidity Trap

The discussion of monetary policy in the earlier part of this chapter showed how the Fed can use its monetary-policy tools to affect the money supply and the federal funds rate. However, since the financial crisis of 2008, the economy reached a situation known as a **liquidity trap**. In a liquidity trap, when the Fed increases the monetary base, people hold the additional base as currency, or banks hold the additional monetary base as reserves, and the money supply does not increase, so the federal funds rate does not decline.

Why does a liquidity trap arise? There have only been a few times in history that an economy entered a liquidity trap, most notably Japan in the 1990s and the United States and many European nations since 2008. In all these cases, the economy hits the **zero lower bound,** which is a situation in which nominal short-term interest rates in the economy become very close to zero. Of course a nominal interest rate on a bond can never fall below zero, because in that situation the nominal return to holding money (which is zero) would exceed the return on the bond, so no one would want to own the bond.

How effective is monetary policy when the economy is at the zero lower bound? Consider the idea that interest rates on short-term bonds are nearly zero, so bonds provide a return that is about the same as cash. If banks are indifferent between holding bonds and holding cash in the form of reserves, then the economy may be in a liquidity trap. If the Fed were to increase the monetary base by buying securities in the open market, banks would sell those securities to the Fed and hold the cash they receive as reserves. Their excess reserves would rise, and the ratio of excess reserves to deposits would rise, but banks would be happy with that because the returns they would earn are the same. If any increase in the monetary base ends up being held as excess reserves by banks, then the money multiplier would decline, just offsetting the increase in the monetary base, and the money supply would not change. That is, in Equation (1), the increase in the monetary base is exactly offset by a decline in the money multiplier, and the Fed cannot change the money supply. Figure 16.1 shows a sharp decline in the money multipliers in 2008 and subsequent years, which is consistent with the U.S. economy being in a liquidity trap. In terms of our models of the economy, the liquidity trap means the Fed is powerless to increase the money supply, so it cannot shift the aggregate demand curve to help the economy get out of recession.

Japan entered a liquidity trap in the 1990s and remained in it during the early 2000s. Along with the liquidity trap, Japan suffered from deflation—a decline in the price level. Deflation causes severe economic problems because most debt is in nominal terms, so that when the price level declines, debtors owe more in real terms and it becomes very difficult for them to repay their loans.

Over the years, U.S. economists and policymakers, including then Fed governor Ben Bernanke, offered advice to Japan on how to get out of the liquidity trap, eliminate deflation, and ensure that monetary policy could help the economy. In a 2004 speech, Bernanke suggested three nontraditional policies for a central bank that is caught in a liquidity trap: (1) promise to keep interest rates low for a long time, (2) change the types of securities the central bank buys, such as buying more long-term securities, and (3) engage in quantitative easing, purchasing many securities in the open market.[1] First, by promising to keep interest rates low for a long time, the central bank hopes to affect long-term interest rates through the term structure, as we discussed in Chapter 5. A promise of low short-term interest rates causes long-term interest rates to be lower than they would be otherwise, and low long-term interest rates should stimulate spending by businesses and households. Second, the central bank could sell short-term securities and buy long-term securities, with the goal of reducing long-term interest rates to stimulate spending. Third, the central bank can use quantitative easing, buying many securities in the market by increasing the monetary base, driving down all interest rates and thus stimulating the economy as the money supply increases.

Though Bernanke and others had discussed what central banks should do in a liquidity trap in the early 2000s, most economists were skeptical that the U.S. economy would ever face such a situation. But in the aftermath of the financial crisis in 2008, the U.S. economy indeed entered a liquidity trap. The Federal Reserve, under Bernanke's leadership, engaged in all three of the activities that he suggested in his 2004 speech.

liquidity trap a situation in which additions to the monetary base do not lead to an increase in the money supply or a decline in the interest rate

zero lower bound a situation in which nominal short-term interest rates are very close to zero

[1]Ben S. Bernanke and Vincent R. Reinhart, "Conducting Monetary Policy at Very Low Short-Term Interest Rates," speech at the American Economic Association annual meeting, San Diego, California, January 3, 2004.

Though the Fed's actions may have helped the economy get out of the liquidity trap, the long-term outcome is not yet clear. Some economists, notably classical economists on the FOMC including Richmond Fed president Jeffrey Lacker and Philadelphia Fed president Charles Plosser, opposed the Fed's nontraditional policies. They believed that the policies would not be effective and posed many risks, especially when the Fed tried to reverse course and tighten policy when the economy rebounded. Other economists, such as Keynesian economists Christina Romer (who had been chair of the Council of Economic Advisers under President Obama) of the University of California and Laurence Ball of Johns Hopkins University, argued that the Fed's policies were not aggressive enough. They argued that the Fed could have quickly gotten out of the liquidity trap by announcing a higher inflation target.[2] Such a policy could affect inflation expectations and raise nominal interest rates, getting them to rise above zero, but has the danger of affecting the central bank's long-run credibility.

[2] See Laurence Ball, "Ben Bernanke and the Zero Bound," National Bureau of Economic Research working paper no. 17836, February 2012.

RECAP

1 When the economy enters a liquidity trap, traditional monetary policy loses its effectiveness.

2 The liquidity trap is caused when interest rates hit the zero lower bound and short-term bonds become perfect substitutes for cash.

3 Getting out of a liquidity trap calls for nontraditional policy measures.

Appendix 16.A

Finding an Infinite Sum

In Table 16.2 we calculated the sum of an infinite series of numbers

$$4.00 + 3.60 + 3.24 + 2.92 + \cdots$$

which we claimed was equal to 40. In general, we calculate this value using a mathematical shortcut, which says that the sum of a series of numbers, each of which is a proportion $(1 - q)$ of the number before, equals the first number in the series times $1/q$. This appendix shows how that shortcut is derived.

In the example, note that each term is 0.9 times the previous term, so $q = 0.1$. The second term is 0.9 times the first term: $3.60 = 0.9 \times 4.00$. The third term is 0.9 times the second term: $3.24 = 0.9 \times 3.60$. And so on. Thus, the infinite sum can be written as

$$4.00 + (0.9 \times 4.00) + [0.9 \times (0.9 \times 4.00)] + \cdots$$

Now each term can be written with powers of 0.9 times 4.00:

$$(0.9^0 \times 4.00) + (0.9^1 \times 4.00) + (0.9^2 \times 4.00) + \cdots$$
$$= 4.00 \times (0.9^0 + 0.9^1 + 0.9^2 + \cdots) \quad (*)$$

Notice what happens if we multiply the second term by $(1 - 0.9)$:

$$(0.9^0 + 0.9^1 + 0.9^2 + \cdots) \times (1 - 0.9)$$
$$= (0.9^0 + 0.9^1 + 0.9^2 + \cdots) \times 1$$
$$\quad - (0.9^0 + 0.9^1 + 0.9^2 + \cdots) \times 0.9$$
$$= 0.9^0 + 0.9^1 + 0.9^2 + \cdots$$
$$\quad - (0.9^1 + 0.9^2 + 0.9^3 + \cdots)$$
$$= 0.9^0$$
$$= 1$$

Because $(0.9^0 + 0.9^1 + 0.9^2 + \cdots) \times (1 - 0.9) = 1$, then

$$(0.9^0 + 0.9^1 + 0.9^2 + \cdots) = \frac{1}{1 - 0.9}$$
$$= \frac{1}{0.1}$$
$$= 10$$

This, is the multiplier of 10 discussed in the text.

Thus, the infinite sum in Equation (*) equals

$$4.00 \times (0.9^0 + 0.9^1 + 0.9^2 + \cdots) = 4.00 \times 10$$
$$= 40$$

In general, if each number in a series is $(1 - q)$ times the number before it, the infinite sum whose first number is N equals

$$N \times [(1 - q)^0 + (1 - q)^1 + (1 - q)^2 + \cdots] = N \times \frac{1}{1 - (1 - q)}$$
$$= N \times \frac{1}{q}$$

Thus, the multiplier is indeed $1/q$, which we set out to prove.

Review Questions and Problems

Review Questions

1 What are the Federal Reserve's major assets and liabilities? What are the relative amounts of each?

2 Explain how the Fed can increase the money supply by engaging in open-market operations. What role do banks play in this process?

3 Define the monetary base, and explain how to use it to analyze changes in the money supply.

4 What decisions do people make that can influence the money multiplier and thus the money supply?

5 What are the Fed's four tools for affecting the money supply? Which tool is used most commonly?

6 Describe the movements in the money multipliers for M1 and M2 over the past 40 years.

7 Describe the shape of the supply curve for reserves, and explain why the curve has that shape.

8 Describe the shape of the demand curve for reserves, and explain why the curve has that shape.

9 What are the maximum and minimum levels that the federal funds rate can reach? What factors determine those levels?

10 What tools are available to a central bank when the economy is in a liquidity trap?

Numerical Exercises

11 Below is the balance sheet of a bank. The reserve requirement is 3 percent on the first $30 million of transaction accounts and 10 percent on transaction accounts in excess of $30 million.

Bank Balance Sheet
(amounts in millions of dollars)

Assets		Liabilities + Capital	
Reserves	15.9	Transaction accounts	180.0
Securities	34.1		
Loans	150.0	Capital	20.0
Total assets	200.0	Total liabilities + capital	200.0

a Calculate the bank's excess reserves.

b Suppose that the bank sells $5 million in securities to get new cash. Draw up the bank's balance sheet after this transaction. What are the bank's excess reserves?

c Suppose that the bank makes a loan to a customer of an amount equal to the amount of its excess reserves from part b. Draw up the bank's balance sheet before the customer spends the proceeds of the loan. What are the bank's excess reserves?

d Now suppose that the customer spends the proceeds of the loan. Draw up the bank's balance sheet, and calculate its excess reserves.

12 Consider the following balance sheet of Princeton Bank:

Balance Sheet for Princeton Bank
(amounts in millions of dollars)

Assets		Liabilities + Capital	
Reserves	30	Transaction accounts	300
Securities	140		
Loans	280	Nontransaction accounts	140
Total assets	450		
		Capital	10
		Total liabilities + capital	450

Statistics for the economy as a whole are
D = $2,000 billion
R = $200 billion
C/D = 0.2 = ratio of currency to transaction accounts
N/D = 2.0 = ratio of nontransaction accounts to transaction accounts
MMF/D = 1.6 = ratio of retail money-market mutual funds to transaction accounts
q = 0.10 = 10 percent = required reserve ratio on transaction accounts = RR/D = ratio of required reserves to transaction accounts

a Calculate the monetary base MB, M1, and M2. Are there any excess reserves in Princeton Bank? Are there any excess reserves in the economy as a whole?

b Calculate the multipliers for M1 and M2.

c Calculate the values of N, D, C, R, and MMF using the fact that C/D = 0.2 and C + D = M1.

d Suppose that the Fed raises the reserve requirement on transactions deposits to 0.20 = 20 percent. What happens to Princeton Bank's balance sheet? Does it have excess reserves, or is it short of reserves? Calculate the new M1 and M2 multipliers. What happens to MB, M1, M2, N, D, C, MMF, and R?

e Suppose that instead of raising the reserve requirements as in part c, the Fed sells $150 billion of securities in the open market, including $30 million to a customer of Princeton Bank. What happens to Princeton Bank's balance sheet? Does it have excess reserves, or is it short of reserves? Calculate the new M1 and M2 multipliers. What happens to MB, M1, M2, N, D, C, MMF, and R?

13 Suppose that the demand for reserves when the federal funds rate exceeds the interest rate on reserves is given by

$$D = 40 - (2 \times i)$$

where i is the federal funds rate in percent and D is expressed in billions of dollars. Suppose that the Fed supplies $28.0 billion in nonborrowed reserves and discount loans for business needs are $1.5 billion. Suppose that the primary credit discount rate is currently set at 6 percent and the interest rate on reserves is 2 percent.

a Calculate the equilibrium federal funds rate, reserves, and the amount of discount loans for profit.

b Suppose that the Fed reduces the supply of nonborrowed reserves to $26.0 billion. Now calculate the equilibrium federal funds rate, reserves, and the amount of discount loans for profit.

14 Suppose that the Fed's Open-Market Desk thinks that the demand for reserves when the federal funds rate exceeds the interest rate on reserves is given by

$$D = 50 - (4 \times i)$$

where i is the federal funds rate in percent and D is expressed in billions of dollars. Suppose that the Fed is currently supplying $29 billion in nonborrowed reserves. Discount loans for business needs are $1 billion. The primary credit discount rate is currently set at 4 percent and the interest rate on reserves is 2 percent. If the Fed's target for the federal funds rate is 3.5 percent, does the Desk need to change the supply of reserves in the market? How much does it need to add or withdraw from the market? After carrying out its daily actions, what will be the equilibrium amount of reserves and discount loans?

Analytical Problems

15 Consider a bank that had excess reserves of $3 million, so it made a loan of that amount to a corporation by adding $3 million to the corporation's checking account in exchange for a loan agreement in which the corporation promised to repay the $3 million plus interest over the next three years. If the reserve requirement is 10 percent, how many excess reserves does the bank now have? Should it make another loan to get rid of these excess reserves? Why or why not?

16 In the financial crisis of 2008, the Fed decided to flood the market with reserves and set the interest rate on reserves equal to its target for the federal funds interest rate. Draw a diagram of the market for reserves showing this situation. In this case, how many federal funds loans are made between banks?

17 In the late 1990s, the Fed worried about the possible disappearance of government securities as the U.S. government ran larger and larger surpluses. Because the Fed uses government securities for its open-market operations, this posed a problem. The Federal Reserve Act does not allow the Fed to buy or sell securities held by private companies with its open-market operations, only U.S. government securities or federal agency securities. What could the Fed do to replace government securities in its portfolio? Would it

(*continued*)

be wise for the Fed to ask Congress to allow it to own securities in private companies? Would there be any drawbacks to such a procedure? If this is not done, what can the Fed do?

18 Describe whether each of the following situations represents defensive open-market operations, dynamic open-market operations, or neither.

a The Fed purchases $40 billion of securities in the open market on September 11, 2001, when a number of major banks face disruptions in their New York operations.

b The Fed reduces the monetary base by $5 billion through open-market sales because inflation has been rising.

c The Fed increases the monetary base by $3 billion because of increased demand by people who want to collect new state quarters.

d The Fed raises the discount rate by half a percentage point.

e The Fed increases the monetary base by $7 billion because a financial crisis in South America increases the demand for U.S. dollar currency that is shipped abroad.

© iStockphoto.com/Sjlocke

Monetary POLICY: GOALS and TRADEOFFS

What should the Federal Reserve (the Fed) do with its monetary policy tools? How should the Fed accomplish its goals? To answer these questions, we need to examine how the Federal Reserve influences the economy, what its goals are in doing so, and how it uses its tools for monetary policy to accomplish those goals. The Fed faces a tradeoff because a change in monetary policy causes the inflation rate and the unemployment rate to change in opposite directions, yet the Fed would like to reduce both of them.

In this chapter we begin by considering the Fed's role in stabilizing the economy over the course of the business cycle. Given the ability of the Fed to stabilize the economy, we look at the Fed's goals in terms of three key macroeconomic variables: output, the unemployment rate, and the inflation rate. We develop the idea that the Fed has an objective function that calculates the loss to the economy when the key variables are different from their ideal levels. The Fed attempts to minimize the objective function by using its policy tools to keep the variables as close as possible to their desired levels.

The Fed faces a tradeoff between the inflation rate and the unemployment rate, which is often depicted in a graph known as the *Phillips curve*. At one time, the Fed tried to reduce the unemployment rate by increasing the inflation rate, but the experiment backfired, and both rates rose. Economists have learned that the tradeoff between the inflation rate and the unemployment rate is quite different in the long run than in the short run, as we see in the Policy Perspective that wraps up this chapter.

17-1 Stabilization Policy

The Fed can use its monetary policy tools, especially dynamic open-market operations, to affect output, the unemployment rate, and the inflation rate over the business cycle. **Expansionary policy** causes the economy to grow faster in the short run; increases in the money supply are expansionary. When the Fed uses expansionary policy, output is higher, the unemployment rate is lower, and the inflation rate is higher over time than it would be if policy were not expansionary. **Contractionary policy** causes the economy to grow more slowly in the short run; decreases in the money supply are contractionary.

When the Fed uses contractionary policy, output is lower, the unemployment rate is higher, and the inflation rate is lower over time than if policy were not contractionary.

Should the Fed use its policy tools to smooth out the business cycle, reducing output during economic expansions and increasing output during recessions? Doing so is known as **stabilization policy.** Consider the graph of the business cycle from Chapter 10, reproduced here in Figure 17.1. In the graph, output is plotted on the vertical axis, and time is shown on the horizontal axis. The graph shows how output would change over the business cycle in the absence of any policy actions explicitly designed to stabilize the economy. When output rises above the trend line, the unemployment rate declines, but the inflation rate rises. When output declines below the trend line, the unemployment rate rises, and the inflation rate declines. As we will see, it is generally best if output is as close as possible to the trend line.

If the Fed were able to use stabilization policy to perfectly smooth out the business cycle, then output would line up with its trend, and the business cycle would be eliminated. Most likely, however, the cycle can be smoothed only imperfectly, as shown in Figure 17.2. In this graph, the line labeled *Neutral policy* shows

---

FIGURE 17.1 The Business Cycle

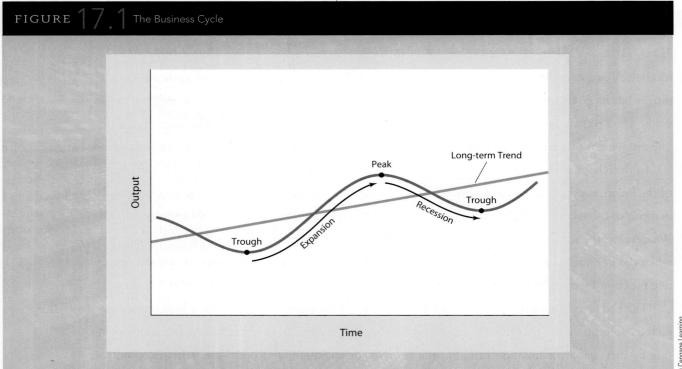

Over the course of the business cycle, output (real gross domestic product [GDP]) fluctuates around a long-term trend. In an economic expansion, output rises at a faster rate than the long-term trend rate of growth. Output reaches a peak at the end of an economic expansion. In a recession, output declines. Output reaches a trough at the end of the recession.

© Cengage Learning

FIGURE 17.2 The Business Cycle with Stabilizing Policy

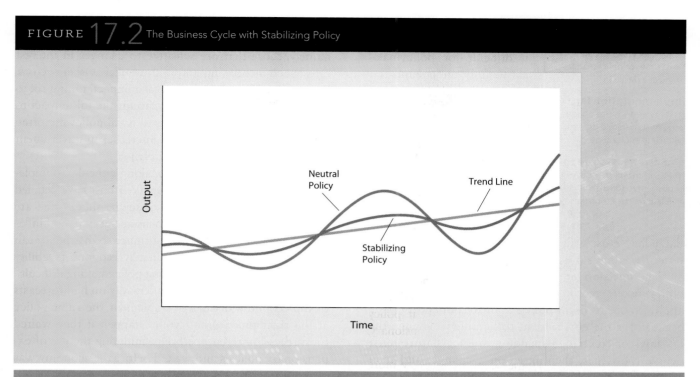

If policy is used successfully to stabilize the economy, then the fluctuations of output over the course of the business cycle are not as severe as they would be if policy were neutral. In economic expansions, output would not rise as much above its long-term trend line under stabilizing policy as it does under neutral policy. In recessions, output would not decline as much below its long-term trend line under stabilizing policy as it does under neutral policy.

what the economy would do in the absence of government attempts to stabilize it; that line is identical to the one in Figure 17.1. The line labeled *Stabilizing policy* shows what might be achieved if monetary policy were able to work effectively. With stabilizing policy, recessions would not be as deep, output would not decline as much, and the unemployment rate would not rise as high as it would with neutral policy. With stabilizing policy, expansions would not be as strong, output would not rise as much, and inflation would not increase as high as it would with neutral policy.

Is there any reason to think that this result is achievable? There might be if the private sector has difficulty adjusting to changes in the growth rate of output. In that case, in the face of some shock to the economy, the Fed may be able to use monetary policy to offset the shock because the private sector is not very adaptable.

17-1a Policy Lags

Are there also reasons to think that the Fed will not be able to achieve such good outcomes? Some economists think so. The problem is that monetary policy requires time to be put into place and to have an effect on the economy. Economists have identified a number of lags that make it difficult to have the right policy in place

at the right time. These are (1) data lag, (2) recognition lag, (3) decision lag, (4) implementation lag, and (5) effectiveness lag. The same lags apply to fiscal policy (changes in government spending and taxes).

The **data lag** means that there is a lag in data availability and quality. For example, the best measure of the economy's overall level of output is real gross domestic product (GDP), data for which are not available until the month after the end of a quarter (e.g., data for the first quarter of the year are released at the end of April). Even monthly data, such as industrial production, are available only with a lag of several weeks to a month, and they tend to be much less reliable than the GDP data. And monthly data do not cover the entire economy, only certain sectors. Thus, policymakers must wait for data before they can take action. Not only is there a delay in the release of the data, but also the initial releases of data are often very preliminary and subject to large revisions. Therefore, the data may not be reliable enough to use for stabilization policy.

The **recognition lag** means that even when data

data lag the lag in data availability and quality

recognition lag the lag that arises because the random nature of the data makes it difficult for policy-makers to fully understand the state of the economy

decision lag the lag in policy that arises because it takes time for policymakers to make a decision

implementation lag the lag between when a change in policy is decided on and when it is implemented

effectiveness lag the time it takes from when a policy is implemented to when it has an effect on the economy

are available, the random nature of the data makes it difficult for policymakers to fully understand the state of the economy. Even the strongest economic expansion often has a weak quarter or two. And even the deepest recession often shows positive signs from time to time. Policymakers cannot react immediately to a change in economic data; they must wait until they recognize a clear pattern of weakness or strength.

The **decision lag** means that it may take time for policymakers to make a decision. The decision lag applies more to fiscal policy than to monetary policy because for the government to be able to change the tax laws or to change spending, the legislature must debate the issues, then agree on a change, and then convince the president of the United States to concur. Each of these steps may take months to accomplish. Monetary policymaking sometimes requires consensus building within the Federal Open Market Committee (FOMC) of the Federal Reserve, which also may take time.

The **implementation lag** refers to the speed with which a change in policy is implemented once a decision is reached. Monetary policy has a short implementation lag because when the Fed decides to change monetary policy, the change can be put in place almost immediately. (In contrast, changes in fiscal policy sometimes have a long implementation lag because even after legislation for additional spending is passed, the funds must be spent by government agencies.)

Finally, there is the **effectiveness lag,** which is the time it takes from when a policy is implemented to when it has an effect on the economy. Monetary policy

takes effect with a long and variable lag. Monetary policy affects a few sectors of the economy fairly quickly—namely, those that are sensitive to changes in interest rates, such as housing and automobiles. Other sectors, however, are fairly slow to feel the impact, taking six to nine months, perhaps even a year, for the full impact to be felt. (By contrast, the effects of fiscal policy are often felt immediately; for example, increases in government spending boost GDP immediately.)

All these lags make policymaking difficult. To implement policy effectively, a policymaker must have detailed knowledge about the economy and the shocks that are hitting it. Forecasts of future economic growth and inflation become of paramount importance so that policy can be set well in advance. Unfortunately, economists' ability to forecast is fairly weak, making policymaking difficult.

What happens if policymakers rely on bad forecasts of the economy or do not implement the right policy at the right time? What would happen if they waited for a recession to end before terminating the use of expansionary policies and waited before the economy was clearly in a recession to stop using contractionary policies? Then, given the lags, they might well be using the wrong policy at the wrong time, making the business cycle worse instead of better. This might lead to the situation shown in Figure 17.3 labeled *Destabilizing policy*.

If policy is destabilizing, the increase in output in expansions is greater than that under neutral policy, and the decline in output in recessions is greater than that under neutral policy. The increased variability in output relative to its trend line leads to greater variability of the unemployment rate and the inflation rate as well. Because of bad forecasts, bad timing of policy, and lags, policy actions make economic performance worse instead of better.

Are fiscal policy and monetary policy stabilizing or destabilizing? Keynesian economists (see Chapter 10) think policy is generally stabilizing, while classical economists think policy is generally destabilizing.

RECAP

1 The Fed engages in expansionary monetary policy by increasing the money supply enough to cause the economy to grow faster. The Fed engages in contractionary monetary policy when changes in the money supply cause the economy to slow.

2 Stabilization policy that works well may help to smooth out the business cycle. But lags in the process may cause policy to be destabilizing, making the business cycle worse than it would be with neutral policy.

FIGURE  17.3 The Business Cycle with Destabilizing Policy

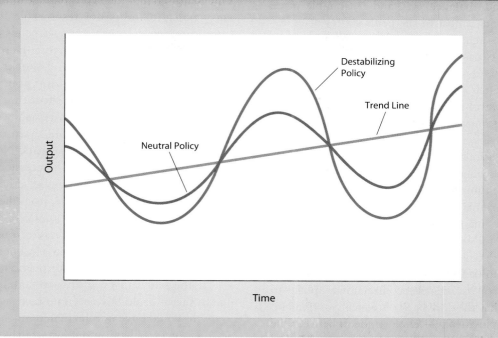

If policy attempts to stabilize the economy but is not successful, then the fluctuations of output over the course of the business cycle are more severe than they would be if policy were neutral. In economic expansions, output would rise more above its long-term trend line under destabilizing policy than it would under neutral policy. In recessions, output would decline further below its long-term trend line under destabilizing policy than it would under neutral policy.

17-2 Goals of Monetary Policy

The Federal Reserve uses its tools for monetary policy to achieve certain goals for the economy's performance. In this section we examine those goals.

The Fed's original goals, as established by the Federal Reserve Act of 1913, were to "provide an elastic currency, to afford means of rediscounting commercial paper, to establish a more effective supervision of banking in the United States, and for other purposes." The need for an elastic currency was clear because the U.S. economy suffered many recessions that resulted from a shortage of money. Time and again, with the money supply determined inelastically by the gold standard, the government's inability to increase the amount of money in circulation led to large increases in interest rates, causing business investment in physical capital to decline and leading to recession. The idea of rediscounting commercial paper was one potential remedy. Banks owned commercial paper (short-term financial securities issued by corporations), and the Fed was authorized to make discount loans to banks, with the commercial paper serving as collateral. In addition, banks sometimes made bad lending decisions, as in the 1920s when they lent funds for people to speculate in the stock market. Thus, the legislation establishing the Fed called for increased supervision of banks to prevent them from making bad loans.

These original goals were directed toward improving the functioning of the payments system and the banking system. The Federal Reserve Act set no goals related to influencing the economy over the business cycle or determining the rate of inflation. However, following the Great Depression and with the advent of Keynesian theory that promoted the use of monetary policy as a tool for stabilizing the economy over the business cycle, lawmakers changed the Fed's goals. According to the Employment Act of 1946, the government (using both fiscal policy and monetary policy) was supposed to use its tools to increase employment and production. This idea was expanded upon in the 1970s, along with the recognition that inflation could be a problem, with the Humphrey–Hawkins Act of 1978. That legislation gave the federal government, including the Fed, a large number of goals, including to "promote full employment and production, increased real income, balanced growth, a balanced Federal budget, adequate productivity growth, proper attention to national priorities, achievement of an improved trade balance, . . . and reasonable price stability." Of course, most of the goals set for the government were not achieved for most of the 20-plus years since the law was passed, especially balancing the government budget and improving the trade balance.

Not all the goals set by the Humphrey–Hawkins Act are under the control of the Fed, so the Fed considers its key goals to be to maximize output and to keep the unemployment rate low in the short run, as well as to maintain a low rate of inflation in the long run. High output and low unemployment go along with strong economic growth, so the Fed considers the Humphrey–Hawkins Act as giving it a "dual mandate" to achieve strong economic growth and low inflation. However, policies to achieve the Fed's goals for output and unemployment usually conflict with the goal for inflation. Expansionary policy that increases output and reduces unemployment has the drawback of increasing inflation; contractionary policy to reduce inflation has the drawback of reducing output and increasing unemployment. Given the tradeoff between the goals, at least in the short run, the best strategy for the Fed to follow is not obvious. Thus, we begin our analysis by examining each goal separately, followed by an analysis of the tradeoff between the goals in the next section.

17-2a Output

One major goal of the Fed is to maximize output. Monetary policy alone is not responsible for the level of output in the economy; output depends on many other factors, including fiscal policy, total factor productivity, the size of the labor force, and shocks such as sharp changes in oil prices. But monetary policy can affect the level of output, at least in the short run.

Figure 17.4 plots quarterly data showing the percentage change in output (real GDP) from one year earlier. Recessions are denoted by blue bars. Note that output growth usually falls below zero in recessions, which means that the level of output is declining, although sometimes not by very much. For example, from the fourth quarter of 1969 to the fourth quarter of 1970, output fell only 0.2 percent, and in the 2001 recession, output declined in the first and third quarters of the year, but the four-quarter growth rate remained positive throughout the recession.

If the Fed had been able to stabilize output perfectly, there would have been no recessions, and output growth would have not fluctuated much over time. The graph suggests that output was fairly stable in most of the 1960s, the 1980s, and the 1990s. In all three of those decades, economic expansions lasted many years, and output growth was fairly steady. In fact, the period

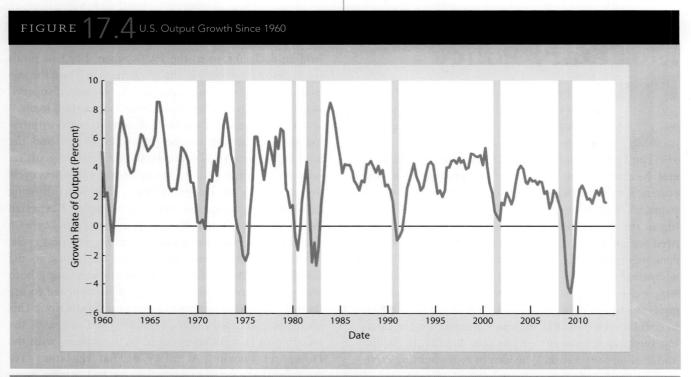

FIGURE 17.4 U.S. Output Growth Since 1960

Output growth (measured by real GDP growth over the past year) has varied substantially over time since 1960. The blue bars denote when recessions occurred. Note that output growth usually falls below zero in recessions.

from 1991 to 2001 was the longest economic expansion in U.S. history. However, the economy was not very stable from 1970 to 1982 because output growth was erratic, and there were four recessions. And the financial crisis of 2008 led to the largest decline in output in the period covered in the graph (since 1960).

The growth of output by itself may not provide all the information we need to analyze the Fed's performance with respect to its goal for output. After all, the long-run growth of output depends on factors the Fed does not control, such as the growth rate of total factor productivity and the growth of the labor force. To account for these factors, economists have developed a concept known as **potential output,** which is the amount of output that would be produced by the economy if resources were being used at a high rate that is sustainable in the long run. Output can exceed potential output in the short run if resources are being used at a very high rate—for example, if production workers work overtime hours. However, such a fast pace of output is not sustainable in the long run.

The growth rate of potential output depends on the growth of the labor force and of productivity; the faster the growth of the labor force or productivity, the more rapid will be the growth rate of potential output. One way to judge how well the economy is doing is to see how close output is to its potential level. If output exceeds potential, workers are spending more time on the job than they would like, and firms are running their equipment more than they would like. Thus, production is not efficient, and the rapid pace of production is not sustainable. If output is below potential, workers are not working as much time as they would like, and equipment is being used less than is ideal. Thus, the economy bears costs if output is either too high or too low. Of course, figuring out exactly what the potential level of output is in the economy is difficult—it requires a judgment about how much workers want to work and the degree to which firms' equipment is used. Economists make educated guesses about the level of potential output by examining economic data on the average workweek and capacity utilization of businesses, as well as data on other variables that are thought to provide information about the economy's potential output, such as the amount of capital.

Figure 17.5 shows one measure of potential output, estimated by the U.S. Congressional Budget Office

> **potential output** the amount of output that would be produced by the economy if resources were being used at a high rate that is sustainable in the long run

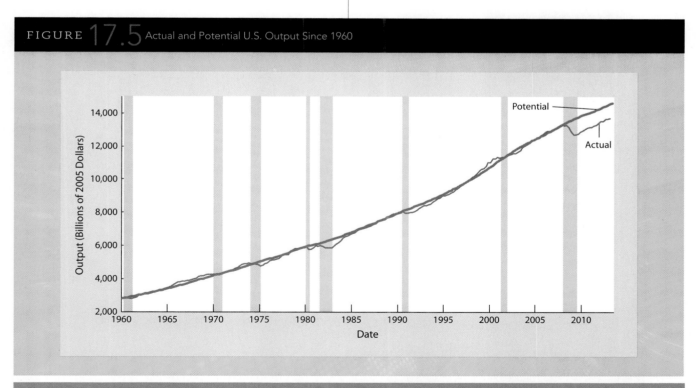

FIGURE 17.5 Actual and Potential U.S. Output Since 1960

This graph plots a measure of potential output, estimated by the U.S. Congressional Budget Office (CBO), and shows how close actual output was to potential output. Output declined below its potential level in every recession and climbed above its potential level in every expansion.

(CBO), and illustrates how close actual output was to potential output. Output declined below its potential level in every recession. There were a few times in economic expansions when output rose substantially above its potential level, most notably in the second half of the 1960s. The graph shows that output rose above potential output for about four years, which means that resources were being used at an unsustainable pace. The consequence was a sharp rise in wages, as firms competed for workers, and an increase in the inflation rate. However, the graph also shows a long period in the late 1990s in which output exceeded potential, but wages and prices did not rise very rapidly in that period.

17-2b Unemployment

A second major goal for the Fed is to keep the unemployment rate low. Generally speaking, the unemployment rate is closely related to output growth; higher output growth is correlated with a decline in the unemployment rate.

Figure 17.6 plots the unemployment rate since 1960. Most significant increases in the unemployment rate occur during recessions. In economic expansions,

the unemployment rate declines gradually. Clearly, the Fed could achieve its goal of keeping the unemployment rate low if it could prevent recessions from occurring.

Looking more closely at short-run movements of the unemployment rate, we can see that after the unemployment rate was driven below 4 percent in the late 1960s, it kept ratcheting up to higher levels in the 1970s, peaking at over 10 percent in the 1981–1982 recession. However, the long boom of the 1980s and 1990s brought unemployment below 4 percent again for the first time in 30 years. Thus, on the unemployment front, most of the 1960s, 1980s, and 1990s brought gains, whereas the 1970s and early 1980s were bad times for workers. The financial crisis of 2008 led to the largest increase in the unemployment rate since the 1980 and 1981–1982 recessions.

In the graph we see that the lowest the unemployment rate has been in the last 40 years is slightly below 4 percent. With new workers, such as college graduates, entering the labor force each year, and workers leaving firms that have suffered reductions in the demand for their products, the unemployment rate never seems to get close to zero. Therefore, even when the economy is producing output at its potential level, the unemployment rate is not insignificant.

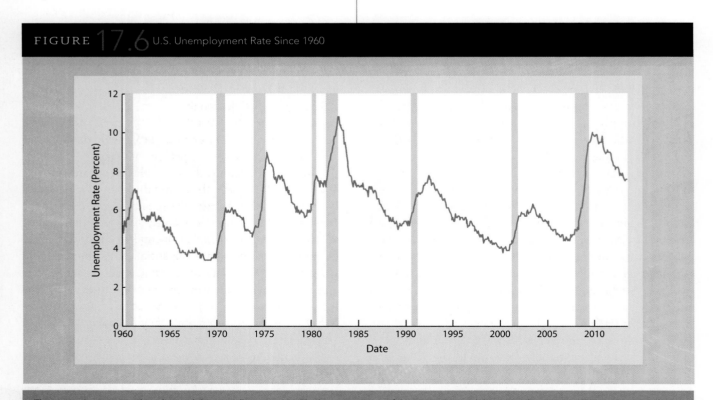

FIGURE 17.6 U.S. Unemployment Rate Since 1960

The unemployment rate has changed dramatically since 1960. The long expansion of the 1960s dropped the unemployment rate below 4 percent, but it ratcheted ever higher after each of the four following recessions. The long boom of the 1980s and 1990s finally brought the unemployment rate back below 4 percent in 2000. The financial crisis of 2008 led to the largest increase in the unemployment rate since the 1980 and 1981–1982 recessions.

FIGURE 17.7 Actual and Natural Rates of U.S. Unemployment Since 1960

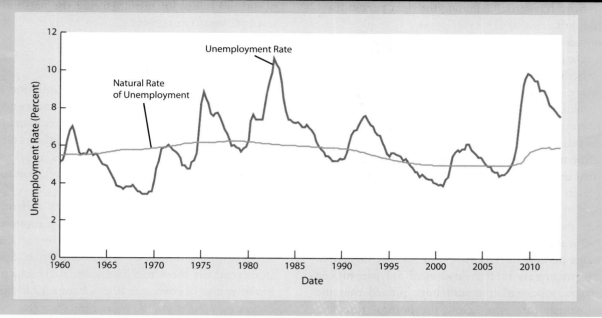

This graph plots annual data on the actual unemployment rate and the natural rate of unemployment, as estimated by the CBO. The natural rate of unemployment rose from 5.5 percent in 1960 to 6.3 percent in 1978, declined gradually to 5.0 percent in 2001, but then rose sharply in the 2008 financial crisis and its aftermath.

The **natural rate of unemployment** refers to the unemployment rate when the economy is producing output equal to its potential. However, economists debate exactly what the value of the natural rate of unemployment is (4 percent? 5 percent?) because no one knows exactly what potential output is. Clearly, the natural rate of unemployment changes over time because of changes in the labor force. For example, in the 1960s and 1970s, as more women entered the labor force, the average amount of work experience declined, and because workers with less experience have higher average unemployment rates, the natural rate of unemployment increased. Similarly, as baby boomers entered the labor force in increasing numbers in the 1960s and 1970s, the natural rate of unemployment increased because young and inexperienced workers are more often unemployed than older and more experienced workers. In the 1980s and 1990s, as women and baby boomers gained experience, the natural rate of unemployment declined.

Economists use demographic information and data on other economic variables to estimate the value of the natural rate of unemployment. One set of estimates, again from the CBO, is shown in Figure 17.7, along with the actual unemployment rate. (The graph is based on quarterly data rather than the monthly data shown in Figure 17.6, so the values for the unemployment rate look slightly different in the two graphs.) In this graph, you can see that the natural rate of unemployment rose from 5.5 percent in 1960 to 6.3 percent in 1978, then declined gradually to 5.0 percent in 2001, and rose during and following the financial crisis in 2008 to about 6.0 percent by 2013.

natural rate of unemployment the unemployment rate when the economy is producing output equal to its potential

In most recessions, the unemployment rate rises far above the natural rate; the higher the unemployment rate is above the natural rate, the greater is the cost to the economy. Unemployment is costly to society because of the direct loss of output that unemployed workers could be producing, along with the social costs raised by idle workers, including increased crime. Fed chairman Ben Bernanke noted that "workers who lose previously stable jobs experience sharp declines in earnings that may last for many years, even after they find new work" and "unemployed people suffer from a higher incidence of stress-related health problems such as depression, stroke, and heart disease, and they may have a lower life expectancy."[1] There also may be costs to the economy from

[1] "Recent Developments in the Labor Market," speech at the National Association for Business Economics meeting, March 26, 2012.

the unemployment rate being far below the natural rate because there is often a mismatch of jobs and workers because firms have trouble finding the right person for a particular job.

Policymakers often examine the unemployment rate in relation to the natural rate of unemployment to judge whether policy should be expansionary or contractionary. To use the natural rate for policy purposes, a policymaker must know what its numerical value is. Unfortunately, the value of the natural rate is difficult to estimate in real time; it is much easier to estimate after time has passed, but that is of little help to policymakers who must make immediate decisions. For example, in 1996 the CBO pegged the natural rate for that year at 5.8 percent; but in 2003, based on more complete data, the CBO thought that the natural rate for 1996 was actually 5.2 percent. The difference of 0.6 percentage point is not insubstantial because the actual unemployment rate in 1996 averaged 5.4 percent. At the time, a policymaker would have judged that the unemployment rate was below the natural rate and might have argued for tighter monetary policy. In retrospect, however, the unemployment rate was still above the natural rate, so tighter policy might have been premature. Policymakers may need to look at economic variables other than the natural rate of unemployment when they set policy; otherwise, they may make policy mistakes because of mismeasuring the natural rate of unemployment in real time.

17-2c Inflation

The third major Fed goal is to keep inflation low. As with output and unemployment, inflation is not determined solely by monetary policy. Shocks to food and energy prices caused by extreme weather conditions, conflict in the Middle East, or changes in prices set by the OPEC oil cartel frequently cause inflation to fluctuate in the short run.

Inflation can be measured in many different ways using measures of prices throughout the economy, such as the GDP price index, or prices faced by particular segments of the economy, such as consumer prices. Such measures generally move together, so we will focus on just a few measures of consumer prices. Figure 17.8 shows two measures of inflation, the overall inflation rate measured by the personal consumption expenditures price index and the inflation rate excluding food and energy prices. The latter measure is more useful for evaluating the long-term trend in inflation because the overall inflation rate

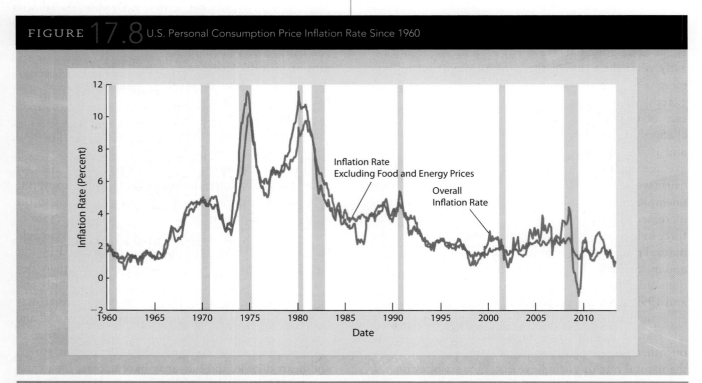

FIGURE 17.8 U.S. Personal Consumption Price Inflation Rate Since 1960

This figure shows the inflation rate of consumer prices, both overall and excluding food and energy prices, since 1960. The trend in the inflation rate increased in the 1960s and 1970s. From the early 1980s to the late 1990s, trend inflation declined. Since the late 1990s, inflation excluding food and energy prices has fluctuated between 1.0 and 2.5 percent.

is often affected by short-term swings in food and energy prices. For example, you can see that in 1986 a sharp, temporary decline in oil prices caused overall inflation to decline to nearly 2 percent. The inflation rate excluding food and energy prices remained just under 4 percent. After oil prices stopped declining, the overall inflation rate rose back to about 4 percent. Thus, the inflation rate excluding food and energy prices is a useful indicator of where inflation may be heading in the long run; it fluctuates less than the overall inflation rate.

Using either inflation measure, the Fed's record from 1965 to 1980 was abysmal. In that period, inflation rose from under 2 percent to about 11 percent. Fed Chairman Paul Volcker took action to reduce inflation in late 1979 and was able to reduce the inflation rate from about 11 percent to about 4 percent when he left office in late 1987. Inflation continued to decline under Fed Chairman Alan Greenspan, bottoming out at 1.2 percent in 1998. Since then, inflation excluding food and energy prices has fluctuated between 1.0 and 2.5 percent, though increases in oil prices have made the overall inflation rate very erratic in the 2000s. Thus, on the inflation front, the Fed seems to be doing well in recent years.

Why does the Fed care so much about inflation? What are the costs to the economy of inflation? Who is harmed by higher inflation rates? We split the costs of inflation into those that arise because inflation is not anticipated and those that arise even when inflation is fully anticipated.

Costs of unanticipated inflation. Inflation hurts people when it is unanticipated because (1) prices are set wrong, (2) wealth is redistributed between borrowers and lenders, and (3) higher inflation leads to greater uncertainty about the future inflation rate. If people do not know what the inflation rate will be in the near future, then businesses face difficulties in setting prices, and workers and firms may have trouble in setting wages. As a result, many prices in the economy may be set at incorrect levels, and someone will lose if inflation is higher than expected, whereas someone else will gain.

Unanticipated inflation also causes a redistribution between borrowers and lenders. When a loan contract is agreed to, nominal interest payments are determined. As we discussed in Chapter 6, borrowers gain at the expense of lenders if the inflation rate turns out to be higher than was expected when the loan was made because borrowers will repay the loan with dollars that are worth less than was expected; that is, the realized real interest rate will be less than the expected real interest rate. Conversely, lenders gain at the expense of borrowers if the inflation rate turns out to be less than

expected; the realized real interest rate will exceed the expected real interest rate.

Unanticipated inflation is a worse problem, the higher the inflation rate. When the inflation rate is high, people do not know if it will head higher or lower, so they face a large degree of uncertainty, which may affect their willingness to make decisions about borrowing and lending. For example, businesses may choose not to invest in physical capital because they will be more uncertain about their profits. If inflation is low, it is usually much less variable, so people are more willing to make decisions and assume that the inflation rate will remain low.

Costs of anticipated inflation. Inflation has costs, even if people anticipate it perfectly, because (1) inflation represents an implicit tax on holding money, (2) firms face menu costs of changing prices, (3) people on fixed nominal incomes are hurt directly, (4) inflation interacts with the tax system to hurt saving and investment in physical capital, and (5) the housing market is distorted by the mortgage-tilt problem.

Inflation causes a reduction in wealth, just like a tax, on anyone holding money or other assets whose nominal rate of return does not change with the inflation rate. Cash pays a zero interest rate, so the higher the inflation rate is, the lower is the real return. People want to avoid losing wealth to inflation, so they will reduce the amount of cash they hold. But reducing cash holdings entails costs. People may hold less cash, as in our automatic teller machine (ATM) model in Chapter 11, so they spend more on transactions costs from going to the ATM more often; economists term such costs "shoe-leather costs" because people wear out their shoes from taking more trips to the ATM. More likely, they spend more on gasoline for their cars for the extra trips to the bank. To avoid having their funds eaten away by inflation, people spend time and energy seeking ways to keep inflation from affecting them. The financial services industry develops assets that protect investors against the ravages of inflation. The employment of people whose job is to protect other people's wealth from inflation represents a cost to society—those people could be better employed doing something productive. People try to avoid being hurt by inflation by buying assets that are hedges against inflation, such as coin and stamp collections, real estate, and artwork, instead of buying assets such as corporate stocks and bonds that may increase the nation's capital stock. Thus, inflation causes a misallocation of resources that could be avoided if inflation were zero or negative.

When inflation occurs, business firms face a cost that is not always trivial: the cost of changing prices. These costs are termed "menu costs" because they resemble the example of a restaurant having to constantly change its prices and print up new menus. However, any firm that offers its goods through a catalog faces similar costs: the cost of printing new catalogs and the confusion customers face because prices are constantly rising. Menu costs could be avoided if inflation were zero.

Some people in society may be living on a given level of nominal income—retirees and pensioners, for example—so inflation hurts them directly because the purchasing power of their incomes falls directly with inflation.

Inflation interacts with the tax system to affect people's decisions about saving, as we learned in Chapter 6. Taxes on interest and dividends are based on nominal income, not real income, so the effective tax rate on real income is much higher than the nominal tax rate. In the 1970s, the effective tax rate on real income was over 100 percent; even in the 1980s and 1990s, the effective tax rate was close to 100 percent at times. Thus, inflation reduces the real return people earn on their savings,

reducing the incentive to save and thus reducing the nation's investment in physical capital and the capital stock.

A major effect that inflation has on the housing market is known as the **mortgage-tilt problem,** which arises because the real value of fixed nominal mortgage payments declines over time.

For example, suppose that a person has a $100,000 mortgage to be paid off over 30 years. If inflation is 5 percent and the mortgage interest rate is 10 percent, the monthly payment is $880, which is calculated using the present-value formula (see Chapter 4). The monthly payment is $880 in the first year, but because inflation occurs at a 5 percent rate, the real value of the mortgage payment in 30 years is just

$$\frac{\$880}{(1.05)^{30}} = \$204$$

Inflation at a steady 5 percent annual rate gradually erodes the real value of the constant-dollar mortgage payment. If we plot the real value of the monthly payment on the vertical axis of a graph, as shown in Figure 17.9,

FIGURE 17.9 The Mortgage-Tilt Problem

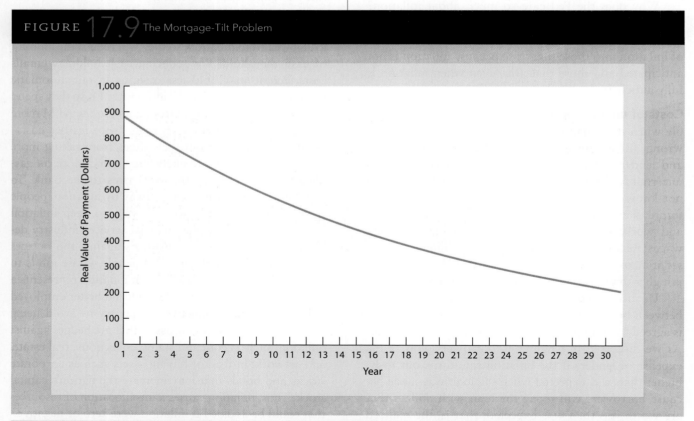

This graph shows the real value of a nominal monthly mortgage payment of $880 when the inflation rate is 5 percent. The real value declines steadily over time from $880 in the first month to $204 in 30 years. Thus, inflation gradually erodes the real value of the constant-dollar mortgage payment. Because the plot tilts down, the problem of declining real payments is known as the *mortgage-tilt problem.*

against time shown on the horizontal axis, the graph tilts down. Consequently, this phenomenon is called the mortgage-tilt problem. This creates a problem because when real payments on a loan are higher early in the life of the loan, borrowers may have problems qualifying for loans and having sufficient cash flow to make their loan payments. As a result, people may buy smaller houses than they desire or take longer to buy homes in the first place. Thus, inflation causes inefficiency in the housing market.

Suppose, however, that the inflation rate is zero. Then, if the mortgage interest rate is 5 percent, the monthly payment is $540, which remains constant over time in both real and nominal terms. The zero inflation rate would remove the mortgage-tilt problem completely, making the housing market work more efficiently.

The ideal inflation rate. The U.S. experience in the 1970s convinced policymakers and economists that high inflation rates lead to low output growth and high unemployment. Ideally, the inflation rate should be so low that it does not cause problems for business planning and investment in physical capital and people's savings decisions. The **ideal inflation rate** π_t^* is an inflation rate that policymakers would like to achieve because it minimizes the costs to society of changing prices. It is usually thought to be about 2 percent and often is assumed to be constant over time. Some economists refer to the ideal inflation rate as the **inflation target** because it represents the Fed's long-term goal for the inflation rate. It is not necessarily 0 because the government's inflation measures are thought to be biased upward, so a measured inflation rate of 1 percent may correspond to a true inflation rate of 0 percent. And, given the recent experience at the zero lower bound (see Chapter 16), many economists think the ideal inflation rate is at least 2 percent. The tradeoff between the costs of inflation and the risks of hitting the zero lower bound led U.S. policymakers at the Fed to formally adopt a 2 percent inflation target in January 2012.

ideal inflation rate an inflation rate that policymakers would like to achieve because it minimizes the costs to society of changing prices; usually thought to be about 2 percent

inflation target another name for the ideal inflation rate

RECAP

1 The Federal Reserve's goals are to maximize output, to keep the unemployment rate low, and to maintain a low inflation rate.

2 Ideally, output equals potential output, and the unemployment rate equals the natural rate of unemployment. Society bears significant costs when output is greater than or less than potential or when the unemployment rate is not equal to the natural rate of unemployment.

3 Inflation imposes significant costs on society. Unanticipated inflation is costly because (a) prices are set wrong, (b) wealth is redistributed between borrowers and lenders, and (c) higher inflation leads to greater uncertainty about the future inflation rate. Anticipated inflation is costly because (a) inflation represents an implicit tax on holding money, (b) firms face menu costs of changing prices, (c) people on fixed nominal incomes are hurt directly, (d) inflation interacts with the tax system to hurt saving and investment in physical capital, and (e) the housing market is distorted by the mortgage-tilt problem.

17-3 The Fed's Objective Function

How can the Fed calculate the best policy to put in place at any time, given the conflict between the short run and the long run? If the Fed focuses only on stabilizing output in the short run, as it did in the 1970s, it may cause inflation to be high in the long run. On the other hand, if the Fed focuses solely on inflation in the long run, it may ignore the possibility of reducing the fluctuations of output and unemployment in the short run. How can the Fed figure out the best way to account for both the short-run impact of policy on output and unemployment and the long-run impact on inflation?

Charting a middle ground is not an easy task, so much of the Fed's strategy, which is the subject of the rest of this chapter, is geared toward making choices about this tradeoff in a sensible way. We do so by developing an equation, called the Fed's *objective function*, that assigns numbers to output, inflation, and unemployment, thus allowing policymakers to assess alternative policies.

17-3a Output Gap

To develop the equation that represents the tradeoff between the Fed's goals, we begin by asking what output would be if the economy worked efficiently and there were never any recessions. We learned in the preceding section that when economic resources are fully used, output equals its potential level. If economic expansions are too strong, output is greater than its potential level because workers are forced to work overtime. When recessions occur, output falls below its potential level because workers become unemployed. Ideally, output always remains at its potential level.

A natural measure of how close output is to the ideal would be to calculate the difference between actual output, denoted y_t, and potential output, denoted y_t^*. We measure that difference in percentage terms, as the **output gap,** denoted $\tilde{y}_t$:

Output gap at time t = percentage deviation of output from potential

= [(actual output − potential output) ÷ potential output] × 100%

$$\tilde{y}_t = \frac{y_t - y_t^*}{y_t^*} \times 100\%$$

(1)

For example, in the fourth quarter of 2012, output was $13,665 billion (in real terms, based on 2005 dollars) and potential output was $14,505 billion, so the output gap was:

$$\tilde{y}_t = \frac{y_t - y_t^*}{y_t^*} \times 100\% = \frac{\$13,665 - \$14,505}{\$14,505} \times 100\% = -5.8\ percent$$

A negative value of the output gap means that output is below potential.

How large are output gaps historically? Figure 17.10 illustrates the size of the output gap since 1960 using the same data on actual output and potential output as shown in Figure 17.5. Output gaps clearly decline and become negative in recessions, as the blue recession bars indicate. The largest negative output gap, −8.1 percent, occurred in the fourth quarter of 1982, when the economy was near the end of a very deep recession. The largest positive output gap, 6.7 percent, occurred in the first quarter of 1966, when the economy was booming at an unsustainably fast pace.

17-3b Unemployment Gap

Following the same idea as the output gap, we may ask how close the unemployment rate is to the natural rate of unemployment. The **unemployment gap** equals the unemployment rate minus the natural rate of unemployment:

Unemployment gap = unemployment rate − natural rate of unemployment

$$\tilde{U} = U - U_N$$

If we plot the values for the output gap over time against the unemployment gap, as shown in Figure 17.11, we find that the data line up reasonably well. The output gap is equal to −2 times the unemployment gap. The negative relationship between the output gap and the unemployment gap is known as **Okun's law** because it was discovered by economist Arthur Okun.

Because the relationship between the unemployment gap and the output gap is relatively tight, we use just the output gap in determining the Fed's objective function. However, we could put the unemployment gap in the Fed's objective function or include both, and the results would not change very much because the output gap and the unemployment gap are so closely correlated.

17-3c Inflation Gap

Following similar reasoning as for the output gap, we can measure the deviation of the inflation rate from the ideal inflation rate, which is the

output gap the percentage deviation of output from potential

unemployment gap the difference between the unemployment rate and the natural rate of unemployment

Okun's law the relationship between the output gap and the unemployment gap, which says that the output gap equals −2 times the unemployment gap

FIGURE 17.10 U.S. Output Gap Since 1960

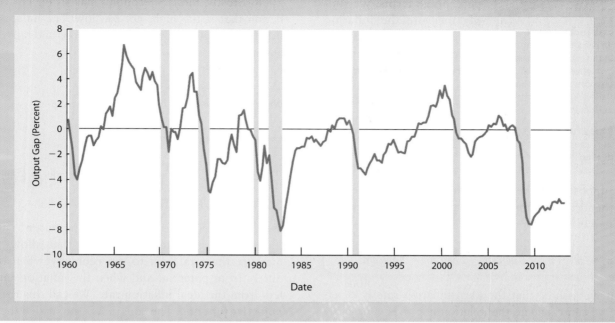

This graph shows the output gap since 1960 using the same data on actual output and potential output as shown in Figure 17.5. Output gaps clearly decline and become negative in recessions, as the blue recession bars indicate, and become positive in expansions.

FIGURE 17.11 Okun's Law in U.S. Data Since 1960

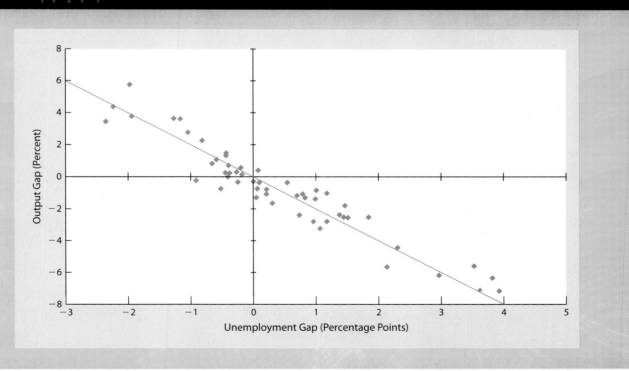

This graph plots the output gap against the unemployment gap. The relationship between the two is fairly tight, with the output gap equal to −2 times the unemployment gap.

inflation gap the actual inflation rate minus the ideal inflation rate

Fed's objective function an equation that summarizes the total cost to the economy when output differs from potential and when the inflation rate differs from the ideal inflation rate

Fed's loss function another name for the Fed's objective function

inflation gap. Because the inflation rate is already in percentage terms, we simply measure the inflation gap ($\tilde{\pi}_t$) as the actual inflation rate (π_t) minus the ideal inflation rate (π_t^*):

Inflation gap at time t = actual inflation rate − ideal inflation rate

$$\tilde{\pi}_t = \pi_t - \pi_t^* \tag{2}$$

has been negative on only a few occasions. However, the inflation gap has been negative most of the time since 2008. Mostly, the U.S. economy has struggled with inflation that is too high, not too low. The inflation gap usually rises late in economic expansions and falls during and after recessions.

Suppose that the actual inflation rate is 5 percent and the ideal inflation rate is 2 percent. Then the inflation gap is

$$\tilde{\pi}_t = \pi_t - \pi_t^* = 5\,percent - 2\,percent = 3\,percent$$

If we assume that the ideal inflation rate is 2 percent, we can calculate the inflation gap over time using the data on the overall inflation rate from Figure 17.8. Figure 17.12 shows the inflation gap since 1960. You can see that it reached a peak in 1974 and 1980 and

17-3d An Equation for the Fed's Objective Function

We can combine the measures of the output gap and the inflation gap into an equation that allows us to measure the total cost to the economy when output differs from potential and when the inflation rate differs from the ideal inflation rate. We call this the **Fed's objective function.** The equation is also called the **Fed's loss function** because the equation measures the economy's loss from having output or inflation differ from the ideal level.

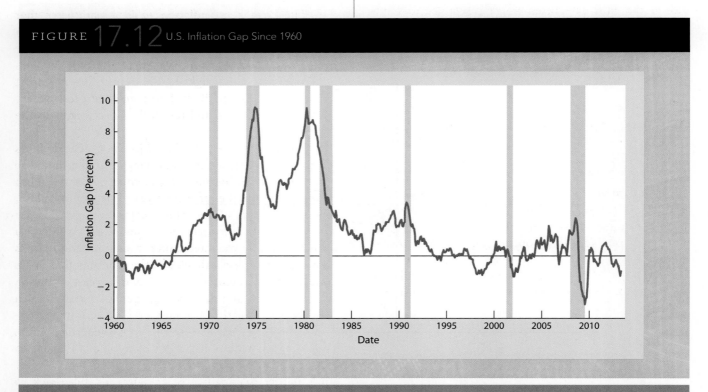

FIGURE 17.12 U.S. Inflation Gap Since 1960

This graph plots the inflation gap over time using the data on the overall inflation rate from Figure 17.8. The inflation gap reached its peak in 1974 and 1980 and has been negative on only a few occasions. However, the inflation gap has been negative most of the time since 2008. The inflation gap usually rises late in economic expansions and falls during and after recessions.

To develop the Fed's objective function, we first need to think about how much to penalize a given difference in output from potential or in the inflation rate from its ideal level. Consider the following example. Suppose that in one year output was 5 percent below potential, so the output gap was −5 percent, and in the next year output equaled potential, so the output gap was 0. Is the economy better off or worse off in this situation than if output were 2.5 percent below potential in both years? Economists generally think that the first situation, in which the output gap is 5 percent in one year and 0 in the next year, is worse than the second situation, in which the output gap is 2.5 percent in both years. The large 5 percent output gap in the first year means that many people are unemployed, and the economy suffers greater problems than two consecutive years of an output gap of 2.5 percent, even though the average output gap in both situations is 2.5 percent. Essentially, the costs to people and businesses from having a nonzero output gap increase exponentially as the output gap increases in size. The same may be true for inflation: The costs of an inflation gap of 7 percent in one year and 0 in the next year are probably far greater than the costs of an inflation gap of 3.5 percent in both years.

Because the costs of output gaps and inflation gaps rise as the gaps get bigger, we represent the loss suffered by the economy by squaring each gap term. For example, an output gap of 5 percent in one year and 0 in the next year has a loss of

$$Loss = 5^2 + 0^2 = 25 + 0 = 25$$

An output gap of 2.5 percent in both years has a loss of

$$Loss = 2.5^2 + 2.5^2 = 6.25 + 6.25 = 12.5$$

In this example, the loss in the first situation is twice the loss in the second situation. Thus, the economy is much better off with smaller, steady output gaps than with one very large output gap and a zero output gap.

Similarly, in the inflation example, if the inflation gap is 7 percent in one year and 0 in the next year, the loss is

$$Loss = 7^2 + 0^2 = 49 + 0 = 49$$

A steady inflation gap of 3.5 percent has a much lower loss:

$$Loss = 3.5^2 + 3.5^2 = 12.25 + 12.25 = 24.5$$

Now that we have determined that each gap will be squared in the Fed's objective function and that we will add up the losses over time, the only remaining decision is how much weight to put on output losses versus inflation losses. The decision about the weight is one over which economists disagree strongly, so we will set up the objective function in a general way and then illustrate what happens as the weight between output losses and inflation losses is changed.

The Fed's objective function is written like this:

$$Total\ loss = sum\ over\ time\ of\ [output\ loss + (w \times inflation\ loss)] = \sum_{time} [\tilde{y}_t^2 + (w \times \tilde{\pi}_t^2)] \qquad (3)$$

where the symbol Σ_{time} means to add up over time the values of the variables that follow, and w stands for the weight on inflation relative to output in the Fed's objective function. The function can be used in a variety of ways: If added up over time in the past, it can be used to evaluate past policies. If added up over future time, it can be used to evaluate alternative future policies. (See the Policy Insider box "A Comparison of the Fed's Loss Function with the Misery Index" for an alternative Fed objective function.)

The weight on inflation w is a parameter that shows the Fed's preferences about missing the inflation target versus missing the output target. If w is large, the Fed gives relatively more weight to the inflation loss and relatively less weight to the output loss in setting policy. If w is small, the Fed gives relatively less weight to the inflation loss and relatively more weight to the output loss.

To demonstrate how this objective function works in practice, consider the following example. Suppose that the level of output and potential output are both 1,000 in year 0, the inflation rate is 2 percent in year 0, the growth rate of potential output is 3 percent per year, w equals 1 so that the output loss and inflation loss are equally weighted, and the ideal inflation rate is 2 percent. Suppose a shock hits the economy that raises output above potential in year 1 and increases inflation in year 2, such as a positive aggregate demand shock in the *AD–AS* model in Chapter 12. The Fed might consider three alternative responses for monetary policy. Policy A tightens policy a bit at a time, sufficient to reduce inflation back to 2 percent in 10 years. Policy B is tighter than policy A, bringing inflation back to 2 percent in 5 years. Policy C is more aggressive, bringing inflation back to 2 percent quickly, but causing output to decline below potential output in year 2.

FIGURE 17.13 Output Under Alternative Policies

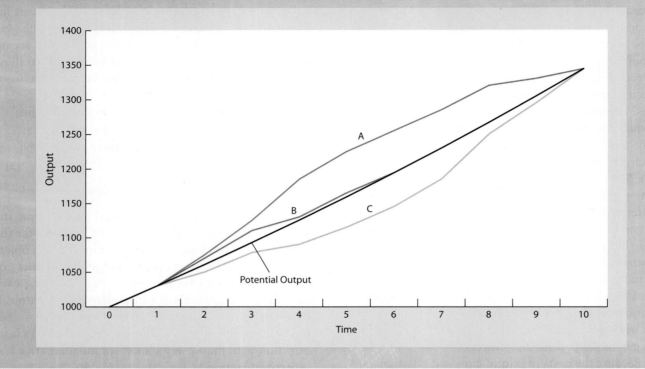

The path of output over time depends on monetary policy. Output is highest under policy A, and lowest under policy C, with output under policy B in the middle. All three policies bring output back to potential by the end of 10 years.

Figure 17.13 shows the response of output under each policy, compared with potential output, over the 10-year period. Output is the highest under policy A, output is lower than that under policy B, and output is the lowest under policy C. All three policies bring output back to potential by the end of 10 years.

Figure 17.14 shows the response of inflation to each policy. Inflation rises in year 2 because of the initial shock. Policy A is not tight enough to prevent inflation from rising further in year 3, but inflation declines in years 4 to 10, reaching the 2 percent target in year 10. Policy B brings inflation back to target by year 6. Policy C is so tight that inflation falls below target by year 5, then rises back to target by year 10.

Which policy is best? To evaluate the policies, we use our loss function in Equation (3). Because all three policies achieve the same result at the end of 10 years, we only need to calculate the loss function for the first 10 years.

With a weight of $w = 1$ on inflation, policy B is best, with a total loss of 6, while policy A has a total loss of 144 and policy C has a loss of 62. Policy A is too slow to bring inflation down, while policy C is a bit too aggressive, overshooting on both output and inflation and causing them both to fall below target.

A different weight on inflation could lead to a change in the ranking of the policies. For example, if the Fed cared mainly about inflation by having a weight of $w = 150$, then policy C would be best with a total loss of 334, followed by policy B with a loss of 355, and policy A would be the worst with a loss of 971.

In general, the weight on inflation in the objective function helps to determine how aggressive monetary policy should be when shocks cause output to deviate from potential or inflation to deviate from its ideal level. If the weight on inflation is low, then the Fed will be more aggressive in acting to return output to its potential level. If the weight on inflation is high, however, the Fed will act more aggressively to return inflation to its ideal level. Thus, the weight on inflation determines how inflation and output change over time after a shock hits the economy.

This example analyzed just three alternative policies. In practice, economists use complete models of

FIGURE 17.14 Inflation Under Alternative Policies

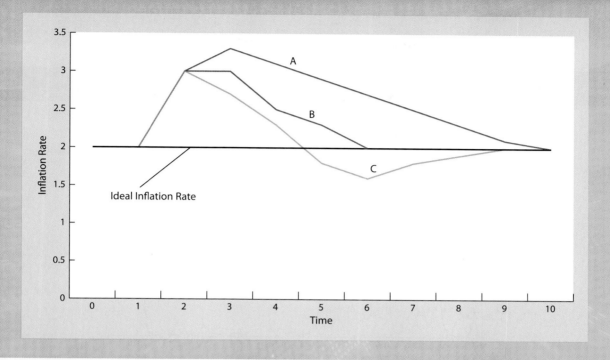

The path of inflation over time depends on monetary policy. Inflation is highest under Policy A, and lowest under Policy C, with Policy B in the middle. All three policies bring inflation back to target by year 10 or earlier.

Policy →IN← sider   A Comparison of the Fed's Loss Function with the Misery Index

In this chapter we have measured the economy's overall performance by the Fed's objective function, which many call the Fed's *loss function* because the higher the value of the function, the worse the economy is doing. In the 1970s, however, economists used a simpler version of the loss function, which they called the *misery index*, equal to the sum of the unemployment rate and the inflation rate. The misery index came into prominence in the election campaign of 1980, when candidate Ronald Reagan used the term to great effect.

If you examine a plot of the Fed's loss function and the misery index, shown in Figure 17.A, you can see why

Reagan focused on the misery index in the campaign. Under President Jimmy Carter, the misery index rose from 13 at the end of 1976 to 18 by the time of the presidential campaign in 1980. The unemployment rate was about 7 percent, and the inflation rate was 11 percent. Reagan had solid ground for complaining about the misery facing the American people.

The graph also shows that the misery index and the Fed's loss function are fairly closely correlated. The biggest spikes, in the mid-1970s and the late 1970s to early 1980s, occur to both the misery index and the loss function. Many

(continued)

FIGURE 17.A   The Fed's Loss Function Versus the Misery Index

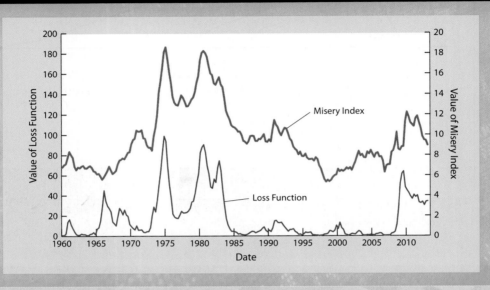

This graph plots the value over time of the Fed's loss function against the misery index, which is the sum of the inflation rate and the unemployment rate. The two measures generally move together and peak at the same time, although there are some differences, as in 1966, 1971, and 1998.

of the general trends in the two measures are the same, although there are some notable differences when one measure spikes up but the other does not, as in 1966 and 1971, or when one measure declines but the other does not, as in 1998. Still, it would not be unreasonable to use either measure as an indicator of overall economic performance. Many economists generally prefer the loss function because it can be adjusted for changes in the growth rate of potential output and the ideal inflation rate, whereas the misery index does not adjust for possible changes in the natural rate of un-employment. The misery index, however, has the advantage of being simpler to calculate. Since it gives the same general result, the simplicity of the misery index may make it prefer-able for general use.

Both measures show fairly similar results in terms of the best years for the U.S. economy. The misery index was less than 7 in 1962–1967 and 1997–2001; the loss function was less than 5 in 1962–1964, 1986, 1994–1997, and 2001–2007. The worst years occurred when the misery index exceeded 15 in 1974–1975 and 1979–1982; the loss function was over 60 in the same years. The financial crisis and the most recent recession led to substantial increases in both the loss function and mis-ery index, but neither was as high in 2009 as they were in the 1974–1975 or 1979–1982 periods.

the economy to analyze many alternative policies. A researcher or economist at a policymaking institu-tion can search over a large number of policies, find-ing the one that works best. Some models, such as the dynamic models with heterogeneous agents discussed in Chapter 13, even can be used to show the impact of alternative policies on different individuals in the economy; for example, the analysis can show differ-ences between the effects of policies on the poor com-pared with the rich.

1 The Fed's objective function adds the squared output gap to the squared inflation gap, with a weight that determines the tradeoff between them.

2 The output gap fluctuates with the business cycle, rising in expansions and falling (and becoming negative) in recessions.

3 The inflation gap is almost always positive; it rises late in economic expansions and declines during and after recessions.

4 The weight on the squared inflation gap in the Fed's objective function determines how aggressive monetary policy will be in response to economic shocks in terms of returning output or inflation to their ideal levels.

Policy → Perspective   The Phillips Curve

Now that we understand the tradeoff between inflation and output (or, equivalently, unemployment) in the Fed's objective function, we turn to an examination of the tradeoff between inflation and unemployment in the data, a tradeoff known as the *Phillips curve*.

In the 1960s, economists discovered that there was a tradeoff in the data between unemployment and inflation, known as the **Phillips curve,** named after British economist A.W. Phillips, who first uncovered the relationship. The existence of such a relationship is logical, according to economic theory, because when output growth increases, the inflation rate often increases, and the unemployment rate declines; when output growth slows, the inflation rate often declines, and the unemployment rate rises. Such a tradeoff occurs in the aggregate-demand/aggregate-supply (*AD–AS*) model of Chapter 12 when the aggregate-demand curve shifts or in a dynamic model such as those described in Chapter 13 if there is an unanticipated change in the money supply.

We can see the relationship between the inflation rate and the unemployment rate in U.S. data from 1948 to 1965 in Figure 17.15. In general, a higher inflation rate is consistent with a lower unemployment rate. Economists looking at this graph in the 1960s naturally thought that the Phillips curve presented a tradeoff they could exploit by picking any point on the trend line.

The Phillips curve was built into many of the large macro-economic models that were in use in the 1960s and 1970s. In equation form, the Phillips curve can be represented as

Phillips curve the tradeoff in the data between unemployment and inflation

$$\pi = \alpha - (\beta \times U) \tag{4}$$

where α and β are coefficients that determine the tradeoff between unemployment and inflation. If we estimate the equation using data on the inflation rate and the unemployment rate from 1948 to 1965, the estimated values of the coefficients are $\alpha = 4.4$ and $\beta = 0.5$, so the equation is

$$\pi = 4.4 - (0.5 \times U)$$

This equation tells you that for every percentage point of higher unemployment, inflation will be 0.5 percentage point lower; equivalently, the unemployment rate will be 2 percentage points lower for every percentage point of additional inflation. For example, if $U = 5$, then

$$\pi = 4.4 - (0.5 \times U) = 4.4 - (0.5 \times 5) = 4.4 - 2.5 = 1.9$$

However, if $U = 3$, then

$$\pi = 4.4 - (0.5 \times U) = 4.4 - (0.5 \times 3) = 4.4 - 1.5 = 2.9$$

(*continued*)

FIGURE 17.15 Phillips Curve from 1948 to 1965

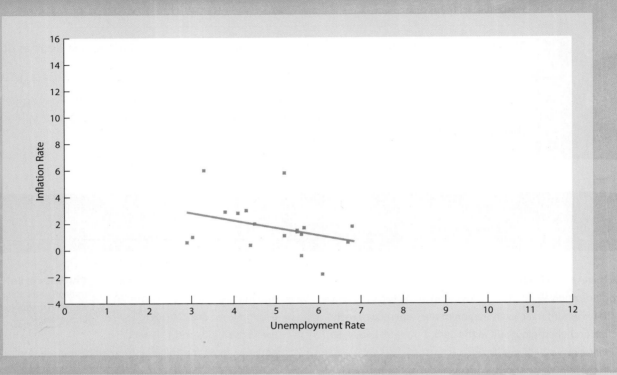

In the 1960s and 1970s, many economists thought that the Phillips curve presented a tradeoff they could exploit by picking any point on the curve. The graph plots points showing the annual average inflation rate against the annual average unemployment rate for 1948 to 1965. There appears to be a tradeoff between inflation and unemployment, shown by the solid trend line.

Thus, the Phillips curve implies that policymakers can choose between having an unemployment rate of 5 percent with an inflation rate of 1.9 percent or having an unemployment rate of 3 percent with an inflation rate of 2.9 percent.

Unfortunately, the Phillips curve tradeoff appears to have disappeared since the 1960s, as Figure 17.16 shows using data from 1948 on. Not only is there no longer a tradeoff between higher inflation and lower unemployment, but also a trend line drawn through the points also now appears to be upward sloping, suggesting that high inflation is associated with high unemployment—the tradeoff has been reversed.

Although Figure 17.16 suggests that the Phillips curve tradeoff that existed from 1948 to 1965 disappeared after

that period, economists have been reluctant to give up the notion of the Phillips curve because economic theory suggests that the tradeoff between inflation and unemployment should still exist. After all, if monetary policy eases, most of our economic models tell us that output will increase for a while, so unemployment will decrease, and that, over time, inflation will increase. Rather than give up their economic models, economists developed a better explanation, adding one more variable to the Phillips curve equation: the expected inflation rate. The idea is this: In the short run, when people expect a particular inflation rate, for example, 3 percent, there is a tradeoff between inflation and unemployment. But the short-run Phillips curve shifts when the expected inflation rate changes.

FIGURE 17.16 Phillips Curve Since 1948

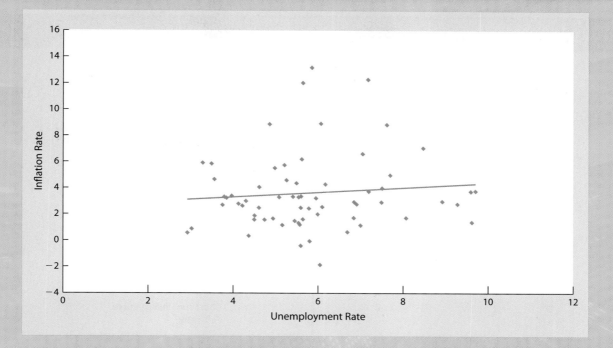

The Phillips curve is no longer apparent in the data. Not only is there not a tradeoff between inflation and unemployment, but also a trend line drawn through the points also now appears to be upward-sloping, suggesting that high inflation is associated with high unemployment.

The Phillips curve, modified with the addition of expected inflation into the analysis, is known as the **expectations-augmented Phillips curve,** which is graphed in Figure 17.17. Just like the original Phillips curve, the tradeoff between inflation and unemployment is shown by a down-ward-sloping line. Now, however, the location of that line de-pends on the inflation rate that people expect. The vertical line denotes the natural rate of unemployment. That line is vertical because the natural rate of unemployment does not change as a result of a change in the inflation rate. The key idea is this: In the short run, inflation and unemployment can be on any spot on the downward-sloping short-run Phillips curve. However, long-run equilibrium occurs on the vertical line denoting the natural rate of unemployment; that vertical line is thus the long-run Phillips curve. At the long-run equilibrium point, the actual inflation rate (shown on the vertical axis of the graph) must equal the inflation rate that people expect (denoted π^e), which is at point A where the short- and long-run Phillips curves intersect.

How does a change in monetary policy affect the economy? Suppose that the economy is in equilibrium at the intersection of the short-run Phillips curve and the long-run Phillips curve, depicted as point A in Figure 17.18. At that point, the unemployment rate equals the natural rate of unemployment of 5 percent, and the inflation rate equals the expected inflation rate of 3 percent. Now suppose that the Fed suddenly and unexpectedly increases the money supply. In the AD–AS model of Chapter 12, this increase in the money supply shifts the AD curve to the right, thus increasing output, reducing unemployment, and increasing prices and the infla-tion rate. In a dynamic model, such as those in Chapter 13, the unanticipated increase in the money supply would reduce

(*continued*)

expectations-augmented Phillips curve a Phillips curve tradeoff between inflation and unemployment in the short run but not in the long run; the short-run Phillips curve is associated with a particular level of expected inflation, and the long-run Phillips curve is a vertical line at the natural rate of unemployment

FIGURE 17.17   The Expectations-Augmented Phillips Curve

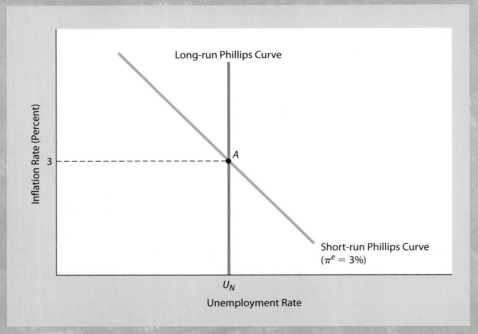

There is a Phillips curve tradeoff between inflation and unemployment in the short run but not in the long-run, so the short-run Phillips curve is repre-sented as a downward-sloping line, whereas the long-run Phillips curve is vertical at the natural rate of unemployment U_N. The short-run Phillips curve is associated with a particular expected inflation rate π^e, which is 3 percent in this case. At point A, where the short-run Phillips curve intersects the long-run Phillips curve, the expected inflation rate equals the actual inflation rate of 3 percent.

the interest rate, causing output to rise temporarily and thus reducing unemployment and increasing inflation. Therefore, in both models the outcome is the same and is shown in Figure 17.18 as a movement up the short-run Phillips curve to point B, where the inflation rate is 5 percent and the unemploy-ment rate is 4 percent. However, the higher inflation rate and lower unemployment rates are temporary. In due course, the economy adjusts to return to long-run equilibrium. Because the increase in the money supply was a one-time event, the inflation rate begins to decline, and the unemployment rate begins to rise. Before too long, in both the dynamic model and the AD–AS model, equilibrium is restored at point A.

What if, instead of a temporary increase in the money supply, the Fed permanently increased the growth rate of the money supply, thus changing the inflation rate in the long run? As you might imagine, this policy change has substantial

effects because it changes the expected inflation rate. The situation is depicted in Figure 17.19. Initially, the inflation rate is 3 percent, and people expect it to be 3 percent, so the initial equilibrium is at point A on short-run Phillips curve PC_1. The location of the short-run Phillips curve depends on the expected inflation rate, denoted π^e, which is 3 percent on curve PC_1. At point A, the unemployment rate equals the natural rate of unemployment, which is 5 percent. Now suppose that expansionary monetary policy moves the economy up the short-run Phillips curve, causing higher inflation (rising to 6 percent) and lower unemployment (falling to 3 percent), as shown at point B. If the expansionary policy is persistent so that the growth rate of the money supply remains higher than it was before, then the inflation rate will be higher in the long run, and people will come to expect the higher inflation rate. As people adjust their expected inflation rate to a higher level, the

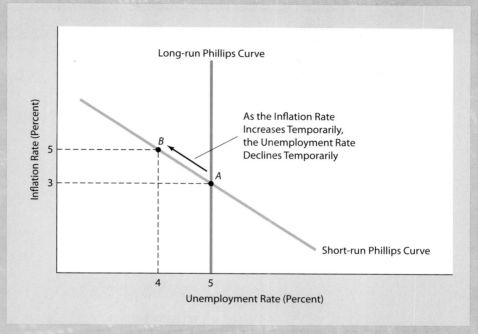

As the Inflation Rate
Increases Temporarily,
the Unemployment Rate
Declines Temporarily

In this graph, the economy is initially in equilibrium at the intersection of the short-run Phillips curve and the long-run Phillips curve, depicted as point A, where the unemployment rate equals the natural rate of unemployment of 5 percent and the inflation rate equals the expected inflation rate of 3 percent. When the Fed suddenly and unexpectedly increases the money supply, it causes a temporary movement up the short-run Phillips curve to point B, where the inflation rate is 5 percent and the unemployment rate is 4 percent. As the economy adjusts to return to long-run equilibrium, the inflation rate begins to decline, and the unemployment rate rises, with equilibrium restored at point A.

short-run Phillips curve shifts from PC_1 to PC_2, at which people expect the inflation rate to be 6 percent. In the long run, the unemployment rate must return to its natural rate of 5 percent, and now inflation is higher at 6 percent, as shown at point C.

Do the data show evidence of short-run Phillips curves that have shifted periodically? If we look at the data on inflation and unemployment since 1948, we are able to show several different short-run Phillips curves in Figure 17.20. The graph suggests that from 1948 to 1965, the economy was on a low Phillips curve; the data from 1948 to 1965 are shown as small circles; the trend line through those circles is the lowest trend line in the graph, labeled "PC (1948–1965, 1997–2008)." From 1966 to 1973, the economy was in transition between Phillips curves, so the data from that period are not shown. The economy was on a much higher Phillips curve from 1974 to 1983, where the data points are shown as triangles and the trend line through those points is labeled "PC (1974–1983)."

After the Fed engaged in tight monetary policy for several years, the short-run Phillips curve shifted down to a new curve from 1984 to 1996, with data points from those years shown as squares and the trend line labeled "PC (1984–1996)." From 1997 to 2008, the data are again consistent with the first short-run Phillips curve from 1948 to 1965, where data points from 1997 to 2008 are shown as diamonds; that trend line is labeled "PC (1948–1965, 1997–2008)." Data from 2009 to 2012 are shown as large circles; it appears that the Phillips curve shifted in 2009, perhaps to the same level as it was from 1984 to 1996, but it is too early to tell for sure.

Economists have discovered an even better way to represent the expectations-augmented Phillips curve. Economic theory suggests that, at equilibrium, the unemployment rate will equal the natural rate of unemployment, and the inflation rate will equal the expected inflation rate. When the economy moves up along the short-run Phillips curve, as it does in

(continued)

FIGURE 17.19 The Effects on the Phillips Curve of a Permanent Increase in the Growth Rate of the Money Supply

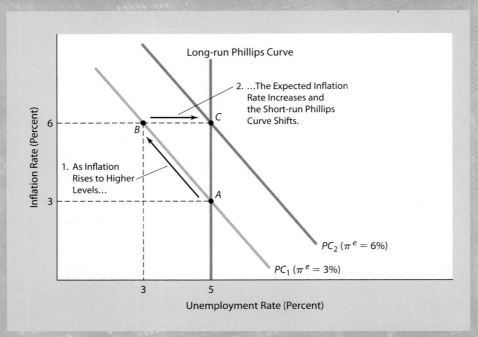

In the short run, with inflation expectations fixed at some level, such as along curve PC_1, in which people expect inflation of 3 percent ($\pi^e = 3$ percent), expansionary monetary policy moves the economy up the curve from point A to point B, causing higher inflation and lower unemployment. However, if such policy persists, the expected inflation rate adjusts to a higher level, and the short-run Phillips curve shifts from PC_1 to PC_2, in which people expect inflation of 6 percent ($\pi^e = 6$ percent), and the economy moves from point B to point C. In the long run, the unemployment rate must return to its natural rate of 5 percent.

Figure 17.19, the inflation rate rises above the expected inflation rate, and the unemployment rate falls below the natural rate of unemployment. If the economy moves down along the short-run Phillips curve, the inflation rate declines below the expected inflation rate, and the unemployment rate rises above the natural rate of unemployment. Thus, we can represent the expectations-augmented Phillips curve in the following way:

> Inflation rate = expected inflation rate
> $- (\beta \times$ unemployment gap) **(5)**
> $\pi = \pi^e - [\beta \times (U - U_N)]$

In this equation, when the unemployment rate U equals the natural rate of unemployment U_N, the unemployment gap

is zero, and the inflation rate π equals the expected inflation rate π^e. If the unemployment gap is negative ($U < U_N$), then in the short run the inflation rate is higher than the expected inflation rate ($\pi > \pi^e$). Because people have rational expectations, however, this situation cannot persist. If the inflation rate remains above the expected inflation rate for long, people adjust their expectations, increasing the expected inflation rate, and the short-run Phillips curve shifts up to a higher level.

This equation appears to fit the data well. If we subtract the expected inflation rate π^e from both sides of Equation (5), we get

> $\pi - \pi^e = -\beta \times (U - U_N)$ or
> **(6)**
> Inflation surprise $= -\beta \times$ unemployment gap

FIGURE 17.20 The Shifting Short-Run U.S. Phillips Curve Since 1948

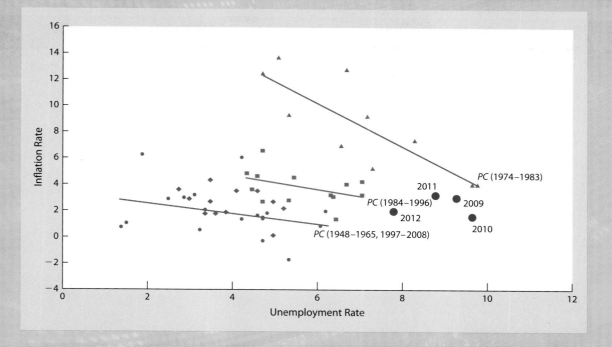

Data on inflation and unemployment since 1948 show several different short-run Phillips curves. From 1948 to 1965, the data shown as small circles indicate that the economy was on the low Phillips curve with the trend line PC (1948–1965, 1997–2008). Data from 1966 to 1973 are not shown because the economy was in transition between Phillips curves. From 1974 to 1983, the data points shown as triangles indicate that the economy was on the short-run Phillips curve with trend line PC (1974–1983). From 1984 to 1996, the data points shown as squares indicate that the economy was on the short-run Phillips curve with trend line PC (1984–1996). From 1997 to 2008, the data shown as diamonds indicate that the economy was back on the short-run Phillips curve with the trend line PC (1948–1965, 1997–2008). It appears that the data from 2009 to 2012 are on a higher Phillips curve, but it is too early to be sure.

The difference between the actual inflation rate and the expected inflation rate is called the **inflation surprise.** Thus, Equation (6) tells us the relationship between surprises in inflation and the unemployment gap.

How well does Equation (6) fit the data? Figure 17.21 shows the data from 1960 on using a survey of economists to measure the expected inflation rate and using the measure of the natural rate of unemployment that we used in Figure 17.7. The graph plots the unemployment gap on the horizontal axis and the inflation surprise on the vertical axis. The points in the graph are reasonably close to the trend line, except for the data from 1973, 1974, and 1979, when the inflation surprise was very large. The data from 2009 to 2012 are shown but they seem reasonably close to the line showing the expectations-augmented Phillips curve. Therefore, we conclude that the expectations-augmented Phillips curve provides a fairly good interpretation of the data.

In setting policy, the Fed must consider two tradeoffs: (1) the tradeoff between output and inflation in its objective function and (2) the tradeoff between unemployment and inflation on the expectations-augmented Phillips curve. These tradeoffs are central to understanding how monetary policy is conducted.

inflation surprise the difference between the actual inflation rate and the expected inflation rate

(continued)

FIGURE 17.21 Expectations-Augmented Phillips Curve Since 1960

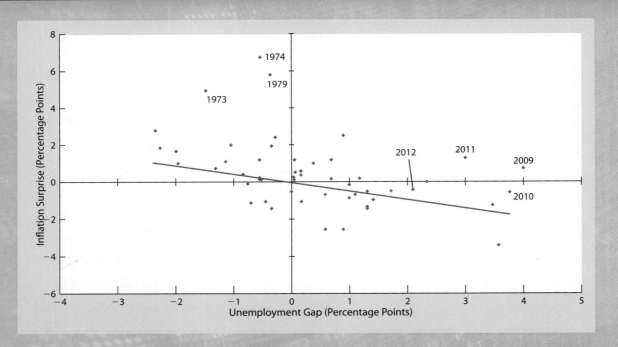

This graph plots the unemployment gap against the inflation surprise since 1960 using a survey of economists to measure the expected inflation rate and using the measure of the natural rate of unemployment that we employed in Figure 17.7. The points in the graph are reasonably close to the trend line, except for the data from 1973, 1974, and 1979, when the inflation surprise was very large.

RECAP

1 There was an apparent Phillips curve tradeoff between inflation and unemployment from 1948 to 1965.

2 The attempt by policymakers to exploit the tradeoff in the 1960s and 1970s caused the expected inflation rate to rise, leading to a higher unemployment rate and a higher inflation rate as the short-run Phillips curve shifted up.

3 There is a short-run tradeoff between unemployment and inflation, but there is no long-run tradeoff; the long-run Phillips curve is vertical.

Review Questions and Problems

Review Questions

1. What is the main goal of stabilization policy? If successful, what does stabilization policy do?

2. Why might stabilization policy lead to an outcome that is worse than if the Fed used neutral monetary policy?

3. Describe the major goals of the Fed and how well they have been achieved in the past 20 years.

4. What is the output gap? Is it measured precisely?

5. What is the unemployment gap? How is it related to the output gap?

6. What is the inflation gap? What is the ideal inflation rate? Is there widespread agreement about the value of the ideal inflation rate?

7. Describe the Fed's objective function and how it can be used with an economic model to evaluate alternative monetary policies.

8. Why didn't policy based on the Phillips curve work to help the Fed reduce the unemployment rate to a lower level than before? What happened in the 1970s as the Fed tried to take advantage of the tradeoff between inflation and unemployment?

9. What caused the increase in inflation in the 1960s and 1970s?

10. Where is the Phillips curve now compared with its location in the 1970s and 1980s?

Numerical Exercises

11. Consider three alternative policies, each with a different set of outcomes in terms of output and inflation, as shown in the following table:

Potential output is 500 in period 1 and rises 3 percent per year. The Fed's objective function is

$$\sum_{time} [\bar{y}_t^2 + (w \times \tilde{\pi}_t^2)]$$

where $w = 1$, and the inflation target is 2.0 percent.

a. Calculate the value of the objective function over the five-year period for each of the three policies.

b. Which policy is best? Why? Which policy is worst?

c. Would your answer to part b change if $w = 5$? Explain.

12. The relationship between inflation and unemployment is given by

$$\pi = \pi^e - 3(U - 6)$$

a. Graph the long-run Phillips curve and three different short-run Phillips curves.

b. What is the value of the natural rate of unemployment?

c. If actual inflation is 2 percent and expected inflation is 5 percent, what is the unemployment rate?

d. If actual inflation is 8 percent and expected inflation is 5 percent, what is the unemployment rate?

13. Policymaking is much easier when the state of the economy is easily observable than when there is uncertainty about how the economy is doing, as this problem illustrates. Suppose that the economy is either in an expansion or a recession. Suppose that in an expansion, monetary policy

	Output Policy A	Output Policy B	Output Policy C	Inflation Policy A	Inflation Policy B	Inflation Policy C
1	500.0	500.0	500.0	2.0	2.0	2.0
2	515.0	500.0	520.0	2.0	1.9	3.0
3	530.5	520.0	535.0	2.0	1.8	4.0
4	546.4	540.0	550.0	2.0	1.9	3.0
5	562.8	562.8	562.8	2.0	2.0	2.0

(*continued*)

ideally sets the interest rate on federal funds (loans between banks) at 6 percent, whereas if the economy is in a recession, the federal funds rate is ideally set at 2 percent. If monetary policymakers know the state of the economy when they set policy, then policymaking is easy—set the fed funds rate at 6 percent when in expansion and at 2 percent when in recession. Suppose, however, that policymakers cannot easily observe the current state of the economy. They know only what the state of the economy was three months ago. Suppose that if the economy was in an expansion three months ago, there is a 90 percent chance the economy is still in an expansion (and thus a 10 percent chance that it is now in a recession). And suppose that if the economy was in a recession three months ago, there is a 75 percent chance that it is still in a recession (and a 25 percent chance that it is now in an expansion). Given these probabilities, what would you guess is the right setting for the federal funds rate if the economy was in a recession three months ago? What is the right setting for the federal funds rate if the economy was in an expansion three months ago? (*Note:* To answer these questions, you must make an assumption about the ideal federal funds rate when you do not know what the state of the economy is—you may make any reasonable assumption you want, but you must justify it.)

Analytical Problems

14 Why doesn't the Fed simply keep increasing the growth rate of the money supply at faster and faster rates to drive the unemployment rate lower and lower? Wouldn't the gains in terms of faster output growth far exceed the losses from inflation?

15 A new Fed governor argues during FOMC meetings that the Fed has not sufficiently achieved the goal of helping the economy reach its potential level of output. She asks the committee to be more aggressive, using expansionary monetary policy to increase the growth rate of output. What are the likely consequences of such a policy? Illustrate your answer using the expectations-augmented Phillips curve.

16 Suppose that the members of the FOMC agree about the state of the economy at any time but have widely different views about the weight that should be placed on inflation in the Fed's objective function. How is monetary policy likely to be determined?

Michael Norcia/Sygma/Corbis

Rules for MONETARY POLICY

Monetary policy is determined by a country's central bank, but economists have long debated what
procedures central banks should follow. If monetary policy decisions seem random, then decisions by people and businesses about saving and investing in physical capital may be different from what they would be if they had a better idea about what monetary policy would do. For this reason, many economists have suggested that central banks establish rules for setting monetary policy that everyone would know and understand. Then monetary policy would be predictable, and people and businesses could make informed decisions.

In this chapter we first examine the economic theory concerning the benefits of having monetary policy determined by rules rather than by the discretion of policymakers. We examine rules based on setting money growth at a particular rate. Then we move on to look at a more sophisticated rule that allows monetary policy to respond to the business cycle. Under such a rule, the central bank would set monetary policy differently depending on how fast the economy is growing and how high the inflation rate is. Then we look at the procedure known as *inflation targeting*, which is not a rule but which helps to reduce policymakers' discretion. Finally, we examine the policy issue: Why don't policymakers follow rules? In this chapter we consider central banks in other countries as well as the Federal Reserve (the Fed) in the United States because many other central banks have more experience with different rules for monetary policy than the Fed has followed.

18-1 Rules versus Discretion

Some economists think that central banks should set policy based on a rule instead of having policy set by policymakers using their discretion at each policy meeting. A **rule for monetary policy** is the systematic setting of policy according to a formula. For example, the rule might set the growth rate of the money supply at 3 percent each year. Here is another example: The Fed might set the federal funds rate at 2 percent when the economy is in a recession and at 5 percent when the economy is in an expansion. Any systematic relationship that a central bank chooses for a variable under its control, such as the growth rate of the money supply or the federal funds rate in the preceding examples, can serve as a rule for monetary policy. If monetary policy is not set by a rule, it is said to be set by **discretion.** Under discretionary monetary policy, the central bank does not choose policy in a systematic manner but instead makes a decision about policy at each policy meeting. In the United States, the Fed's choice at each meeting is usually to **ease policy** by increasing money growth and reducing the federal funds rate, to **tighten policy** by decreasing money growth and raising the federal funds rate, or to keep policy unchanged. (Sometimes, whether policy is easy or tight is difficult to judge, as discussed in the Policy Insider box "What Is the Stance of Monetary Policy?") Other central banks face similar choices, although the tools they use sometimes vary. In most cases there is an interest rate that the central bank influences, similar to the federal funds rate in the United States.

In this section we evaluate the costs and benefits if policymakers were to set monetary policy by a rule compared with discretion. Central banks seem to have wide-ranging discretion to do whatever they want. Discretion, however, may lead to problems that could be avoided if the central bank used a rule.

18-1a Expectations Trap

One problem with choosing monetary policy based on discretion is that a central bank can find itself trapped by people's expectations. For example, suppose that people thought that the Fed planned to reduce the federal funds rate at the next few Federal Open Market Committee (FOMC) meetings. People might conclude that the inflation rate would rise as a result, thus increasing the inflation rate they expect for the future. The increase in the expected inflation rate raises long-term interest rates, causing the economy to slow. To keep the economy from slowing down, the Fed must ease policy, reducing the federal funds rate and increasing inflation. Thus, people's expectations about the Fed's future policy actions force the Fed to do something it might not have done. This situation is known as an **expectations trap,** which occurs when policymakers must increase inflation in response to an increase in the expected inflation rate.

An expectations trap is an example of a fairly common phenomenon in economics in which expectations are self-fulfilling. The central bank must accommodate people's expectations of higher inflation by easing policy, or else a recession may result. If the central bank wants to avoid finding itself in an expectations trap, it must prevent the rise in inflation expectations in the first place.

Why do people think that the central bank will ease monetary policy? There are several possibilities. People might think that the central bank will ease policy just before elections to help incumbent politicians retain their positions if those politicians appointed the policymakers who control monetary policy. Or people might expect the central bank to ease monetary policy because potential output growth has slowed but policymakers do not realize it, so they erroneously think that the output gap is negative, as happened in the 1970s in the United States.

18-1b Time Inconsistency

A more subtle reason that people might expect the central bank to ease policy is time inconsistency. **Time inconsistency** exists when the central bank chooses a policy at one date that leads people to make decisions based on that policy, which then causes the central

rule for monetary policy the systematic setting of policy according to a formula

discretion the situation where monetary policy is not set by a rule

ease policy what a central bank does when it increases money growth and reduces the interest rate

tighten policy what a central bank does when it decreases money growth and increases the interest rate

expectations trap a situation in which policymakers must increase the inflation rate in response to an increase in the expected inflation rate

time inconsistency the difficulty that arises when policymakers have discretion over policy and choose a policy at one date that leads people to make decisions based on that policy, which then causes the policymakers to choose a different policy at a later date

One of the difficult issues policymakers face is figuring out whether policy is easy or tight. They know that if they increase the federal funds rate and decrease money growth, policy is tighter than before, and if they reduce the federal funds rate and increase money growth, policy is easier than before. But how tight or how easy is policy at any point in time? The degree of tightness or ease is known as the *stance of monetary policy.*

To determine the stance of monetary policy, economists have developed a number of measures. Because monetary policy determines the growth rate of the money supply, one of the earliest ways to measure the stance of policy was to plot money growth over time, as shown in Figure 18.A. In this graph you can see that money growth (using the M2 measure of the money supply) has changed over time. The money growth rate was over 10 percent in much of the 1970s, averaged about 7 percent in the early 1980s, declined from the mid-1980s to the early 1990s, increased in the second half of the 1990s, averaging 6 percent from 1995 to 2007, and grew substantially in the financial crisis of 2008 and its aftermath, as people sought to keep their wealth in the safety of government-insured bank accounts.

To see how money growth has influenced inflation, the graph also shows the average inflation rate for the following three years. The graph shows how money growth at one date is related to future inflation. You can see that in the 1970s, when money grew over 10 percent in many years, future inflation increased. In the early 1980s, when money growth was reduced, future inflation declined. In the late 1980s and early 1990s, as money growth fell, so did future inflation. Later in the 1990s, however, even though money growth rose, future inflation

FIGURE 18.A M2 Growth and the Future Inflation Rate

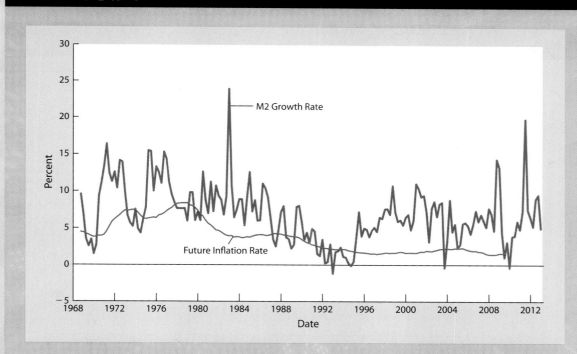

This graph shows money growth over time. Money growth (using the M2 measure of the money supply) has changed over time. The money growth rate was over 10 percent in much of the 1970s, averaged about 7 percent in the early 1980s, declined from the mid-1980s to the early 1990s, increased in the second half of the 1990s, averaging 6 percent from 1995 to 2007, and grew substantially in the financial crisis of 2008 and its aftermath, as people sought to keep their wealth in the safety of government-insured bank accounts. Fast money growth is associated with an increase in the future inflation rate; slower money growth was associated with a decline in the future inflation rate before the mid-1990s, but that relationship has since disappeared.

(continued)

continued to decline. Money growth averaged 6 percent from 1995 to 2007, but inflation remained fairly low and steady, fluctuating between 1.5 percent and 2 percent. And rapid money growth in the financial crisis is correlated with a decline in inflation.

In the 1990s, the Fed stopped targeting money growth because of the erratic behavior of the demand for money, which was caused by financial innovation. Thus, the disconnect between money growth and the inflation rate in the 1990s is not too surprising. Instead, the Fed began focusing more on the real federal funds rate as a guide to the stance of monetary policy.

Figure 18.B shows the stance of monetary policy, as measured by the real federal funds rate. When the real federal funds rate is low, monetary policy is easy; when the real federal funds rate is high, monetary policy is tight.

In several periods in the early 1970s, the graph shows that the real federal funds rate was quite low, and future inflation rose. In the early 1980s, as the real federal funds rate increased, future inflation declined steadily. Monetary policy remained fairly tight in the late 1980s, bringing future inflation down further. But future inflation declined in the early 1990s despite fairly easy monetary policy. Monetary policy in the second half of the 1990s kept the real federal funds rate over 3 percent, which seemed to be effective at keeping the future inflation rate from rising. However, the negative level of the real federal funds rate in the early 2000s allowed the inflation rate to creep up from about 1.5 percent to over 2 percent. So far, however, the negative real federal funds rate from 2008 to 2013 has not led to higher inflation.

Both the growth rate of the money supply and the real federal funds rate are useful indicators of the stance of monetary policy. But they are far from perfect, and sometimes inflation moves in the opposite direction from what the indicators suggest.

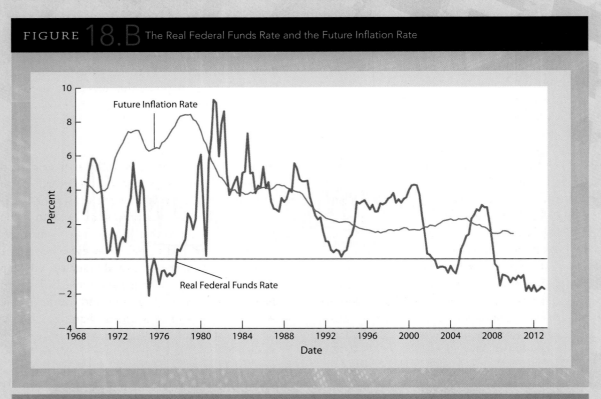

FIGURE 18.B   The Real Federal Funds Rate and the Future Inflation Rate

This graph shows the stance of monetary policy, as measured by the real federal funds rate. When the real federal funds rate is low, monetary policy is easy, and future inflation often increases; when the real federal funds rate is high, monetary policy is tight, and future inflation often declines.

bank to choose a different policy at a later date. Here is an example.

Suppose that the central bank were to announce that its policies would lead to the price level being constant over time instead of rising. Now, as a result, suppose that business firms and workers negotiate labor contracts, agreeing to wages at a particular level, say, $15 per hour. Once that agreement has been made, however, the central bank knows that it could make the economy grow more rapidly by reneging on its promise to keep the price level steady. Suppose that the central bank realizes that it could increase the economy's output if it were to cause prices to rise 10 percent. Then the real (inflation-adjusted) wage would be 10 percent lower than workers and firms expected. With a lower real wage rate, firms hire more workers, and the economy's output increases. By fooling people, the central bank has increased the economy's output.

This type of policy is time-inconsistent because what is optimal for the central bank to do initially (namely, to keep the price level constant) is not the same as what it is optimal for it to do at a later time. In this example, once firms and workers have negotiated a set nominal wage of $15 per hour, the optimal policy by the central bank changes to something different—in this case, to increase the price level by 10 percent.

However, this is not the end of the story. People anticipate what the central bank will do; if they think that the central bank has the incentive to engage in time-inconsistent policymaking, they will ignore the central bank's initial announcement that it will keep prices constant. Instead, they will realize that whatever they agree to, the central bank will then modify by easing policy. They will figure out that the nominal wage level should rise over time at 10 percent per year, so the central bank's optimal response is to cause the inflation rate to be 10 percent per year. If workers and firms have calculated correctly, the resulting real wage is exactly the one they anticipated: the same real wage that would exist if prices were constant and the nominal wage were $15 per hour. Thus, rational expectations by people and firms prevent the central bank from using discretionary policy to fool them. The only drawback is that because of time inconsistency, the inflation rate is 10 percent higher than if the central bank kept the price level fixed. Note that once nominal wages are set to grow 10 percent per year, the central bank finds itself in an expectations trap. If the central bank did not cause the price level to rise 10 percent per year, the real wage would be too high, firms would hire fewer workers, and the economy would slow. Thus, the central

bank likely will ratify people's and firms' expectations for monetary policy, resulting in inflation.

18-1c How to Defeat Time Inconsistency

Is there any way to defeat time inconsistency? What if the salaries of policymakers were tied directly to the inflation rate? The lower the inflation rate is, the higher would be the policymakers' salaries. However, this salary adjustment may not work well because, in the short run, the inflation rate may be buffeted by events such as oil price shocks that are out of the policymakers' control, possibly penalizing good leaders. Also, having the central bank focus on inflation in the short run may be bad for the economy's health. Any monetary policymaker can reduce inflation simply by tightening monetary policy substantially and causing a severe recession. This type of policy is probably undesirable.

Another way to defeat time inconsistency is for the central bank to convince people that it cares only about inflation in the long run. For example, it could tell people that it puts a large weight on inflation in its objective function [Equation (3) in Chapter 17]. An announcement alone would not do the trick, however. The central bank's announcement would have to be credible—that is, people have to believe the central bank will do what it says—or the central bank would have to somehow prove that it is committed to keeping inflation low.

18-1d Credibility

A central bank needs credibility if it wants people to believe it when it says that its actions will not be time-inconsistent. One way that the central bank could become credible is if its only goal were to achieve low inflation. In the United States, this would require a change in the Fed's goals, however, because the Fed would have to ignore the dual mandate, which requires the Fed not just to keep inflation low, but also gives the Fed the goals of high output and low unemployment. Another way to give a central bank credibility would be to make it more independent so that there would be even less pressure on the central bank to increase output to make politicians happy. There is some evidence in favor of this method in that countries with the most independent central banks tend to have the lowest inflation rates. Another method for giving the central bank credibility is simply to choose very conservative people as monetary policymakers—those who have made it clear that they would put a high weight on inflation in the central bank's objective function.

A central bank also could gain credibility by establishing a good reputation over time. In the 1990s and early 2000s, Federal Reserve Chairman Alan Greenspan had tremendous credibility. He gained credibility by tightening policy whenever it appeared that inflation would rise. During such times, policymakers may feel that they are in an expectations trap and have no choice but to ratify people's expectations. If they respond to higher expected inflation by tightening monetary policy, the economy indeed may slow down for a short time. However, the policymaker will gain credibility for combating inflation, which will prove valuable in getting out of expectations traps. If a policymaker does this a few times, people will be convinced that the policymaker is serious about keeping inflation low. Then people will realize that the policymaker will not try to surprise them, and there will be no time inconsistency in policy. If a central bank cannot gain credibility, the alternative mechanism for defeating time inconsistency is commitment.

18-1e Commitment

An alternative to establishing credibility is for the central bank to commit to following a particular rule or to behaving a certain way. Ideally, the central bank would somehow "tie its hands" and always follow a particular rule. However, if the central bank has discretion to choose a rule, it is difficult to see how it could tie its hands sufficiently to prevent time inconsistency.

Some countries have established commitment by eliminating any role for discretion in monetary policy. The central banks in those countries are forced to follow a very rigid rule. For example, in Argentina from 1991 to 2001, the central bank had its power to issue money curtailed by a rule, known as a *currency board*, that required the central bank to own one U.S. dollar for every Argentine peso it issued. The exchange rate between U.S. dollars and Argentine pesos was fixed at one dollar per peso. The problem with such a setup is that monetary policy cannot be used either for stabilization or for affecting inflation. Instead, the inflation rate will equal whatever inflation rate is imported from abroad. Such a policy may go too far in eliminating discretion—it eliminates monetary policy altogether. In fact, the Argentine currency board was abandoned in 2002 because of a deep recession and a large government budget deficit.

Discretion by a central bank is the ultimate source of time inconsistency. If, somehow, a central bank credibly followed a rule for monetary policy or somehow committed to following such a rule, its policy would not be time inconsistent, and the problem would be solved.

RECAP

1 Some economists believe that central banks should follow a rule for monetary policy instead of using discretion.

2 With discretionary policy, a central bank can find itself in an expectations trap, forced to ratify people's expectations.

3 People might expect the central bank to ease policy if policy is time-inconsistent, that is, if the central bank uses discretionary policy to take advantage of people's decisions.

4 The central bank could avoid the time inconsistency of discretionary policy if it could credibly convince people that it put a high weight on inflation in its objective function or if it could commit to a rule that ensured low inflation.

18-2 Money-Growth Rules

Economists who are convinced that a central bank's discretionary policymaking does not serve the public good have suggested that central banks be forced to follow an explicit, verifiable rule for setting monetary policy. Such a rule would eliminate the time-inconsistency problem because the rule allows no scope for the central bank to take advantage of people's decisions.

The first type of rule that economists proposed focused only on the growth rate of money in the economy—a **money-growth rule.** Under such a rule, the central bank simply would set money growth in the long run, ignoring short-run fluctuations in the economy. Not surprisingly, the group of economists in favor of such a policy is the monetarists, whose views on the economy we discussed in Chapter 10.

Why do monetarists think central banks should target money growth? Monetarists point to evidence that money growth is closely related to inflation in the long run. In addition, they believe that the demand for money is fairly stable or at least predictable much of the time.

18-2a The Equation of Exchange

The monetarists' claims about the benefits of a rule based on money growth have their roots in an equation called the **equation of exchange.** The equation of exchange is based on the notion that the amount of money in circulation must be used in transactions a certain number of times to support a given amount of spending. For example, if a person's total spending in one year is $10,000 and the person's average money holdings are $100, then each dollar is used in transactions, on average, 100 times because $100 \times \$100 = \$10,000$. The number of times money is used in transactions is called the **velocity of money,** which is 100 in this example.

We can relate the money supply and the velocity of money to total spending using the equation of exchange:

$$Money \times velocity = average\ price \times quantity\ of\ goods$$
$$= total\ spending$$

or

$$M \times V = P \times Y \qquad \textbf{(1)}$$

where M is a measure of the money supply, V is the velocity of money, P is the average price of goods and services, and Y is the level of real output of goods and services. The right-hand side of the equation, $P \times Y$, equals the dollar value of total spending. For each different measure of money (M1 or M2), there is a different value for velocity. Velocity can be calculated as

$$V = \frac{P \times Y}{M}$$

In the first quarter of 2013, nominal gross domestic product (GDP) in the economy, which is $P \times Y$, was $15,984 billion. Since M1 in that quarter was $2,469 billion, the velocity of M1 was

$$V = \frac{P \times Y}{M}$$
$$= \frac{\$15,984}{\$2,469}$$
$$= 6.47$$

Similarly, with M2 = $10,444 billion, the velocity of M2 is

$$V = \frac{P \times Y}{M}$$
$$= \frac{\$15,984}{\$10,444}$$
$$= 1.53$$

18-2b A Policy of Setting Constant Money Growth

The equation of exchange can be expressed in terms of the growth rates of each variable to arrive at an equation that is useful for examining monetary policy. We use the symbol %Δ to stand for the percentage change in a variable and then modify Equation (1) by calculating the growth rate of each term to obtain

money-growth rule a rule that focuses only on the growth rate of money in the economy; under such a rule, the central bank simply would set money growth in the long run, ignoring short-run fluctuations in the economy

equation of exchange an equation that relates total spending to the amount of money available to be spent; the equation says that money times velocity equals the price level times output

velocity of money the average number of times a dollar of money is used in transactions over the course of a year

$$\text{Money growth} + \text{velocity growth} = \text{inflation rate} + \text{output growth}$$
$$\%\Delta M + \%\Delta V = \%\Delta P + \%\Delta Y \qquad \textbf{(2)}$$
$$= \pi + \%\Delta Y$$

where π is the inflation rate, which equals the percentage change in prices.

Given this equation, how should a central bank set the growth rate of the money supply? Suppose that policymakers want to set the money growth rate permanently to achieve a particular inflation rate in the long run π^T, for example, 2 percent; the target may or may not be equal to the ideal inflation rate (see Chapter 17), as we will discuss later. The policymakers know that in the long run, output Y will grow at the same rate as potential output Y^*, so they can substitute potential output into the equation. If we make those substitutions and subtract velocity growth from both sides of the equation, the new equation is

$$\%\Delta M = \pi^T + \%\Delta Y^* - \%\Delta V \qquad \textbf{(3)}$$

Monetarists originally argued that Equation (3) could be used to set monetary policy because velocity was fairly stable, so $\%\Delta V = 0$. If potential output $\%\Delta Y^*$ grows at about 3 percent per year, and the target inflation rate π^T is 2 percent, then the central bank should set money growth at

$$\%\Delta M = \pi^T + \%\Delta Y^* - \%\Delta V$$
$$= 2 \, percent + 3 \, percent - 0 \, percent$$
$$= 5 \, percent$$

Monetarists even argued that the rule of setting the growth rate of the money supply at a constant rate would work well even if the growth rate of velocity changed over time so long as such changes were reasonably predictable. Then the central bank could substitute the expected growth rate of velocity into Equation (3). For example, if the target inflation rate is 2 percent and potential output growth is 3 percent per year, and if the central bank expected velocity to grow 2 percent each year, then the optimal growth rate for the money supply would be

$$\%\Delta M = \pi^T + \%\Delta Y^* - \%\Delta V^e$$
$$= 2 \, percent + 3 \, percent - 2 \, percent$$
$$= 3 \, percent$$

Thus, even when velocity changes over time, as long as it is predictable, Equation (3) can be used to control the money supply and hit the target for inflation.

18-2c Instability of the Money-Growth Rule

Unfortunately for the monetarists, there have been several instances when financial innovations changed the relationship between money and other variables, and velocity became much less predictable. For example, in late 1986 and early 1987, monetarists noted the very rapid growth of the M1 measure of the money supply, which exceeded 15 percent per year, as you can see in Figure 18.1. They argued that the Fed was repeating the mistakes of the 1970s and predicted that inflation would soon hit double-digit levels again. However, the Fed argued that innovations in the financial system, in particular the introduction of interest-bearing checking accounts, had increased the growth rate of M1 temporarily but reduced velocity growth and thus would not lead to higher inflation. As you can see by the lack of increase in inflation shown in the graph, the Fed was right, and the monetarists were wrong. The innovations in the financial system led to a tremendous decline in the velocity of M1, as you also can see in the graph.

In the 1980s, economists in favor of money-growth rules paid more attention to M2 growth as an indicator

"Here's a leading economic indicator, Dad. It's only Tuesday and my weekly allowance is shot."

George B. Abbott

FIGURE  18.1 M1 Growth, M1 Velocity Growth, and the Inflation Rate

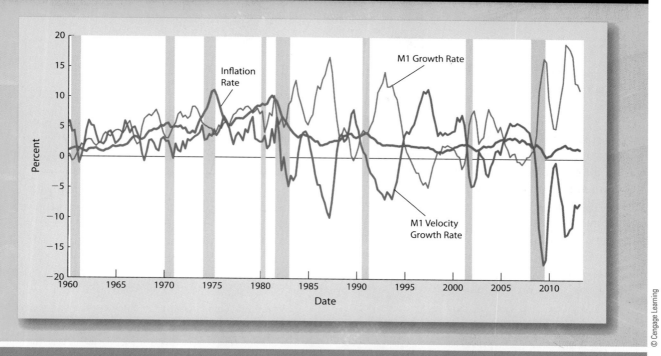

This graph plots the growth rate of the M1 measure of the money supply, the growth rate of the velocity of M1, and the inflation rate since 1960. M1 growth and velocity growth became much more volatile after 1980, whereas the inflation rate became more stable. The large rise in M1 growth in 1986 and 1987 did not lead to increased inflation.

than to M1. The Fed even developed a sophisticated model of the opportunity cost of the various types of financial assets in the M2 measure of the money supply. That model became worthless in the early 1990s, however, because velocity growth changed in ways not predicted by the Fed's model. Figure 18.2 illustrates the movement of velocity growth in the 1990s. Even though M2 growth rose dramatically from 1995 to 2001, inflation hardly budged.

18-2d Activist versus Nonactivist Rules

We have seen that unpredictable shifts in velocity caused the money-growth rule to fail. However, U.S. policymakers never embraced such a rule in the first place, in part because the rule did not change the growth rate of the money supply in response to economic conditions. When the economy is in a recession, policymakers would like to use expansionary monetary policy by increasing money growth to increase output. A rule that allows for this is an **activist rule** because it changes monetary policy as the economy

weakens or strengthens. However, the money-growth rule tells policymakers to keep the growth rate for money constant and to ignore the business cycle. Such a rule is a **nonactivist rule** because under such a rule the central bank maintains the same monetary policy whether the economy is in a recession or an expansion.

Monetarists argue that monetary policy should be nonactivist; that is, monetary policymakers should not engage in stabilization policy. Monetarists believe that the long and variable lags in monetary policy prevent the central bank from accomplishing anything productive with stabilization policy; attempts to counteract the business cycle are destabilizing.

Policymakers wanted a rule that was simple yet could allow some scope for activist policymaking. A rule with those attributes was developed in the 1990s and is the subject of the next section.

activist rule a rule for monetary policy under which monetary policy is allowed to change over the course of the business cycle

nonactivist rule a rule for monetary policy under which the same monetary policy is pursued whether the economy is in a recession or an expansion

FIGURE 18.2 M2 Growth, M2 Velocity Growth, and the Inflation Rate

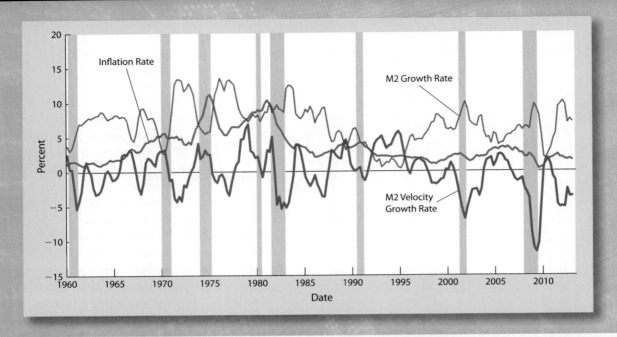

This graph plots the growth rate of the M2 measure of the money supply, the growth rate of the velocity of M2, and the inflation rate since 1960. The growth rate of velocity appeared to be on a downward trend from 1994 to 2001, whereas the M2 growth rate trended up, yet the inflation rate declined. In the 2000s, money growth declined until the financial crisis of 2008, while inflation held fairly steady.

RECAP

1 Money-growth rules originate from the equation of exchange.

2 If velocity is constant, then the central bank can hit its inflation target by setting money growth equal to the sum of the inflation target and the growth rate of potential output.

3 If velocity changes over time but is predictable, the central bank can hit its inflation target by setting money growth equal to the inflation target plus the growth rate of potential output minus the expected growth rate of velocity.

4 The unpredictability of velocity growth in the 1980s and 1990s led researchers and policymakers to abandon money-growth rules.

18-3 The Taylor Rule

John Taylor of Stanford University developed a rule for monetary policy in 1993. Taylor's original intent was to use the rule to describe how the Fed had behaved over the preceding six years from 1987 to 1992, not to suggest that the Fed's policy would be improved by following the rule. Under the **Taylor rule,** monetary policy sets the federal funds rate in response to deviations of real output and inflation from their targets.

The basic idea of the Taylor rule is simple: Set the federal funds rate equal to a baseline rate, and then adjust it up or down depending on the size of the output gap or inflation gap. The baseline rate equals the equilibrium real federal funds rate plus the average inflation rate over the last year. The nominal federal funds rate is increased if there is a positive output gap or inflation gap or decreased if the output gap or inflation gap is negative.

The equation that represents the Taylor rule is

Federal funds rate = equilibrium real federal funds rate + average inflation rate
$$+ (w_1 \times \text{output gap}) + (w_2 \times \text{inflation gap}) \qquad (4)$$
$$i = r^* + \pi + (w_1 \times \tilde{Y}) + (w_2 \times \tilde{\pi})$$

where all variables are measured in percentage points, i is the nominal federal funds rate, r^* is the equilibrium value of the real federal funds rate, π is the inflation rate over the last four quarters, w_1 is the weight on the output gap, $\tilde{Y}$ is the output gap, w_2 is the weight on the inflation gap, and $\tilde{\pi}$ is the inflation gap. The output gap is

$$\tilde{Y} = \frac{Y - Y^*}{Y^*} \times 100\%$$

which is the percentage deviation by which output Y exceeds potential output Y^*. The inflation gap is

$$\tilde{\pi} = \pi - \pi^T$$

which is the amount that the inflation rate π exceeds the Fed's inflation target π^T, which may or may not be equal to the ideal inflation rate.

The first term on the right-hand side of the equation for the Taylor rule, r^*, is the equilibrium value of the real federal funds rate, which represents the level of the real federal funds rate associated with neutral monetary policy. Tight monetary policy means that the real federal funds rate is higher than the equilibrium real fed funds rate; easy policy means that the real fed funds rate is less than the equilibrium real federal funds rate. Many policymakers and researchers using the Taylor rule estimate that the equilibrium real federal funds rate equals its historical average, which Taylor calculated as 2 percent.

The second term in the equation for the Taylor rule, the inflation rate over the last four quarters π, allows the nominal federal funds rate to rise with inflation. By taking the average over four quarters, short-term fluctuations in the inflation rate do not affect the rule's recommendation for the federal funds rate, but persistent movements in the inflation rate do.

The third term in the Taylor rule is the weighted output gap, with a weight w_1, multiplied by the output gap $\tilde{Y}$. In Taylor's original version of the rule, he set w_1 to 0.5. When the output gap is negative, the economy is producing less than its potential, and more than the usual number of people are unemployed. In this case the Taylor rule implies that the Fed should ease monetary policy by reducing the federal funds rate. Easier monetary policy would increase future output, helping to close the output gap. When the output gap is positive, the economy is producing more than its potential, which is possible in the short run as people work overtime, but not in the long run, and leads to higher future inflation. In this case the third term in the Taylor rule is positive, so the Fed would increase the federal funds rate, making monetary policy tighter. Tighter monetary policy would reduce future output, helping to close the output gap.

The fourth term in the equation for the Taylor rule is the weighted inflation gap, with a weight w_2, multiplied by the inflation gap $\tilde{\pi}$. In Taylor's original version of the rule, he set w_2 to 0.5. When the actual inflation rate is below the target, the term $\pi - \pi^T$ is negative. Since w_2 is positive, the Fed will reduce the federal funds rate when the inflation gap is negative, easing monetary policy. Easier policy will increase the inflation rate, bringing it back up to its target. Conversely, when the inflation rate exceeds its target, the inflation gap is positive, so the Fed raises the federal funds rate, tightening monetary policy. Tighter monetary policy will reduce the inflation rate, bringing it down to its target.

To see how the Taylor rule recommends different values for the federal funds rate in different situations, Table 18.1 shows eight different scenarios. The benchmark case is shown in row A; then we examine differences in the value of the equilibrium real federal funds rate in row B, the inflation rate and inflation gap in rows C and E, the weight on the inflation gap in row D, the output gap in rows F and H, and the weight on the output gap in row G to see how those differences affect the rule's prescription for policy.

Taylor rule an activist rule for monetary policy that changes the federal funds rate in response to output gaps and inflation gaps

TABLE 18.1 Examples of the Taylor Rule

	r^*	π	w_1	Y	Y^*	$\tilde{Y}$	w_2	π^T	$\tilde{\pi}$	i
A	2	2	0.5	10.0	10.0	0	0.5	2	0	**4.0**
B	**3**	2	0.5	10.0	10.0	0	0.5	2	0	**5.0**
C	2	**3**	0.5	10.0	10.0	0	0.5	2	**1**	**5.5**
D	2	**3**	0.5	10.0	10.0	0	**1.0**	2	**1**	**6.0**
E	2	**1**	0.5	10.0	10.0	0	0.5	2	**−1**	**2.5**
F	2	2	0.5	**10.2**	10.0	**2**	0.5	2	0	**5.0**
G	2	2	**1.0**	**10.2**	10.0	**2**	0.5	2	0	**6.0**
H	2	2	0.5	**9.8**	10.0	**−2**	0.5	2	0	**3.0**

Notes: Row A is the benchmark; numbers in subsequent rows that differ from the benchmark are shown in bold. The column headings are r^* = Equilibrium real federal funds rate (in percent); π = Inflation rate, averaged over last four quarters (in percent); w_1 = Weight on deviations of output from its target; Y = Actual level of output (real GDP) (in trillions of chain-weighted dollars); Y^* = Level of potential output (in trillions of chain-weighted dollars); $\tilde{Y}$ = Output gap (in percent); w_2 = Weight on deviations of inflation from its target; π^T = Target inflation rate (in percent); $\tilde{\pi}$ = Inflation gap (in percent); and i = Federal funds rate recommended by the Taylor rule (in percent).

In the benchmark case, row A, the equilibrium real federal funds rate is 2 percent; the four-quarter average inflation rate π is 2 percent; the weight on the output gap w_1 is 0.5; output Y is $10.0 trillion (in chain-weighted dollars), which equals potential output Y^*, so the output gap $\tilde{Y}$ is zero; the weight on the inflation gap w_2 is 0.5, and the inflation target π^T is 2 percent, so the inflation gap $\tilde{\pi}$ is 0. In this situation, the Taylor rule suggests that the Fed should set the federal funds rate at

$$i = r^* + \pi + (w_1 \times \tilde{Y}) + (w_2 \times \tilde{\pi})$$
$$= (2\ percent + 2\ percent) + (0.5 \times 0\ percent) + (0.5 \times 0\ percent)$$
$$= 4\ percent$$

which is shown in the last column of row A. In the benchmark case, the Fed should set the federal funds rate at 4 percent, according to the Taylor rule.

What if the equilibrium real federal funds rate were higher? In row B, we keep everything the same, except that the equilibrium real federal funds rate is 3 percent instead of 2 percent. Then the Fed should set the federal funds rate at 5 percent instead of 4 percent, as shown in the last column. For every percentage point higher the equilibrium real federal funds rate goes, the rule says that the nominal federal funds rate should be 1 percentage point higher. Similarly, for every point lower the equilibrium real federal funds rate goes, the nominal federal funds rate should be 1 percentage point lower.

If the inflation rate over the last four quarters has been 3 percent instead of 2 percent as in the benchmark case, then the inflation gap is positive, as row C shows. The higher inflation rate leads the rule to recommend tighter policy, increasing the federal funds rate to 5.5 percent. However, if the weight on the inflation gap were 1 instead of 0.5, as shown in row D, the federal funds rate would increase to 6 percent. On the other hand, if the inflation rate over the last four quarters has been 1 percent, then the negative inflation gap causes the rule to recommend easier policy, reducing the federal funds rate to 2.5 percent, as shown in row E.

If output is above potential, as shown in row F, then the rule leads the Fed to tighten policy; the 2 percent output gap causes the Fed to increase the federal funds rate to 5 percent. However, if the weight on the output gap were 1 instead of 0.5, as shown in row G, the federal funds rate would increase to 6 percent. If output is below potential, as shown in row H, the Fed should reduce the federal funds rate, in this case to 3 percent.

The Taylor rule is an activist rule for policy, which was proposed initially as a description of how the Fed actually behaves. It has been studied extensively by economists around the world for a decade. In many models of the economy, economists assume that the central bank follows a Taylor rule because such a rule provides a reasonable overall description of how the central bank acts. Recent research has promoted the use of the Taylor rule not only as a description of how central banks have set monetary policy historically but also as a recommendation for how the central bank should behave. The Taylor rule has wide appeal because (1) the rule is fairly simple, (2) many economists who do not usually believe in government intervention in the economy favor rules for monetary policy instead of discretion, and (3) economists who believe in government intervention in the economy like it because it is an activist rule. As a result, in the past decade, policymakers and researchers in numerous countries have embraced the Taylor rule both as a description of how central banks have set policy in the past and as a guideline for how they should set policy in the future.

18-3a The Taylor Rule in Practice

How might a policymaker use the Taylor rule in practice? He must first decide what to pick as the inflation target. That target will not necessarily be the ideal inflation rate (discussed in Chapter 17) because the Taylor rule will take swift action to return the inflation rate to its target. If the inflation rate were 10 percent and the inflation target were 2 percent, the federal funds rate would be raised more rapidly than policymakers are likely to accept, especially because doing so probably would cause a recession. Instead, the policymaker might pick an inflation target in the following way: If the inflation rate over the past year was 3 percent or less, the target inflation rate would be 2 percent; if the inflation rate over the past year was more than 3 percent, the target inflation rate would be chosen to be 1 percentage point less than the inflation rate over the past year. The reasoning behind this method of choosing an inflation target is that it would reduce the inflation rate gradually, 1 percentage point at a time, rather than trying to target a 2 percent inflation rate immediately.

Suppose that the policymaker argued at each FOMC meeting that the Fed should set its policy using the Taylor rule instead of the policy actually chosen by the FOMC. What target for the federal funds rate would such a policymaker have argued for, and how would that recommendation compare with what the Fed actually did? The answer is shown in Figure 18.3a for 1955 to the present. The results are based on the Taylor rule using the method of picking an inflation target described in the preceding paragraph and employing the potential output series created by the U.S. Congressional Budget Office (CBO), assuming that the equilibrium real federal funds rate is 2 percent and using weights of one-half each on the output gap and inflation gap. Note that this is not a simulation of what

would happen if the Fed used the Taylor rule but rather a description of what a policymaker using the Taylor rule would have recommended at the FOMC meetings in terms of setting the target for the federal funds rate.

Figure 18.3a shows that such a policymaker would have recommended that monetary policy be tighter in the 1950s, late 1960s, 1970s, and 2000s and easier in the 1980s and 1990s. The actual inflation rate is shown in Figure 18.3b so that we can see how inflation changed over time.

In general, periods in which the Taylor rule suggested tighter monetary policy than the Fed actually put in place are periods of rising inflation—the mid-1950s, the second half of the 1960s, most of the 1970s, and the early 2000s. The exception is the mid- to late 2000s, when monetary policy was easier than the Taylor rule suggested, but inflation declined. Periods in which the Taylor rule suggested that monetary policy should be easier than the Fed actually put in place are periods of declining inflation—the early 1980s and the second half of the 1990s. Therefore, the Taylor rule likely would have kept the inflation rate more stable than the Fed's actual policy.

In the period from 1955 to 1958, a policymaker using the Taylor rule would have recommended much tighter policy than the Fed actually followed, which you can see because the line labeled *Taylor rule* is higher than the line labeled *Actual* in this period. The difference between the two policies is sometimes quite large—as much as 5 percentage points. Note that this period is one in which the inflation rate rose from 1 to 4 percent—perhaps not surprising, given that monetary policy was much too easy in that period. A policymaker using the Taylor rule would have been reasonably satisfied with the Fed's actions from 1959 to 1964; in that period, the Taylor rule line and the actual line are very close, and the inflation rate was fairly stable at about 1 percent. From 1965 to 1969, however, the policymaker would have wanted significantly tighter policy than the Fed actually engaged in, desiring a federal funds rate that was 3 percentage points higher in much of the period. Note that inflation rose sharply in this period. Similarly, the Taylor rule would have suggested a higher federal funds rate in the early and late 1970s, again both periods in which the inflation rate rose sharply.

The situation was quite different in the 1980s and 1990s, however. A policymaker using the Taylor rule would have recommended easier policy in much of those two decades, especially the period from 1980 to 1989. The difference between the actual federal funds rate and what the Taylor rule suggests is as much as

FIGURE 18.3 Actual Federal Funds Rate and the Taylor Rule Recommendation

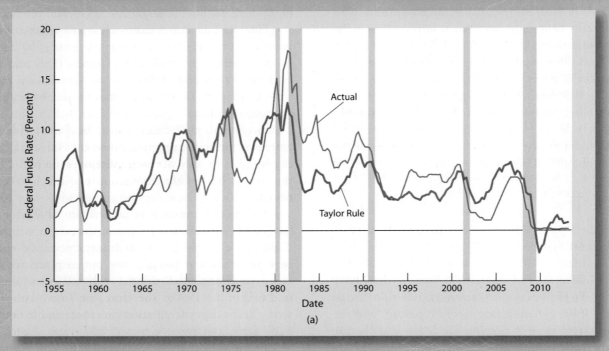

(a)

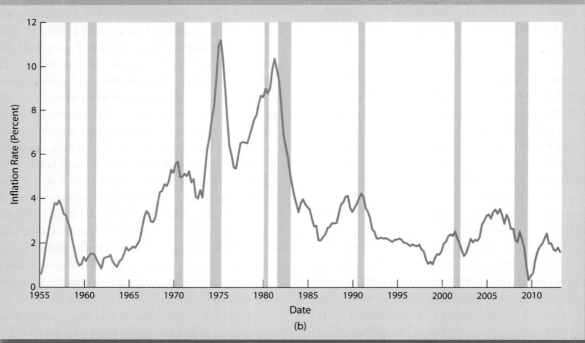

(b)

(a) The Taylor rule sets the nominal federal funds rate as the sum of a long-run equilibrium real rate, inflation over the past year, a response to the output gap, and a response to the inflation gap. A policymaker following the Taylor rule generally would have wanted tighter policy in the 1950s, late 1960s, 1970s, and 2000s and easier policy in the 1980s and 1990s. (b) The inflation rate often rose in periods when the actual federal funds rate was below that suggested by the Taylor rule. Inflation declined in the period when the actual federal funds rate was above that called for by the Taylor rule.

6 percentage points. However, in this period there were two recessions and a major decline in inflation. The Taylor rule would have cushioned the economy somewhat, so the recessions may not have been as deep, but inflation would not have declined as much. From 1990 to 1994, the Taylor rule matched the Fed's actual policy more closely than at other times. In the second half of the 1990s, however, the Taylor rule would have suggested easier policy than the Fed actually conducted; note that in this period inflation trended down significantly. In the 2001 recession, the Fed reduced the federal funds rate more than the Taylor rule suggested and kept it lower throughout the 2000s. This led to a small rise in inflation in the first half of the 2000s, but then inflation declined in the second half of the decade.

Overall, the Taylor rule implies that monetary policy should have been tighter in the 1950s, late 1960s, 1970s, and early 2000s and looser in the 1980s and 1990s. Tighter policy in the earlier period would have prevented inflation from rising as much as it did; looser policy in the later period would have kept inflation from falling as much as it did.

The Taylor rule's response to recessions varies over time. Sometimes the rule suggests that the federal funds rate should be reduced sharply (that is, the slope of the line for the Taylor rule is very steep in Figure 18.3a), as in the recessions of 1957–1958, 1981–1982, and 2007–2009. Other times the rule suggests that the federal funds rate should be reduced, but at a relatively slow pace, as in 1960–1961, 1970, 1990–1991, and 2001. In one case, the recession of 1974–1975, the Taylor rule even suggests that the federal funds rate should be increased because inflation was so high. In the recession of 1957–1958, a policymaker using the Taylor rule might have argued for tightening policy during the recession because that line started out so high above the line that shows the actual federal funds rate. Most of the time during recessions, however, the direction of change in the federal funds rate suggested by the Taylor rule is the same as the actual federal funds rate, although the rate of change (the slopes of the two lines) may be different. For example, the Fed eased monetary policy substantially more in the 1974–1975 and 2001 recessions than the Taylor rule would have suggested. In the 2007–2009 recession, the Taylor rule recommended reducing the federal funds rate to a negative value, which is impossible, as we discussed in Chapter 16. As a result, the Fed engaged in nontraditional policies in an attempt to stimulate the economy.

18-3b Issues in Using the Taylor Rule

Policymakers and researchers who use the Taylor rule face a number of challenges: They must estimate potential output, they need to account for changes in the equilibrium real federal funds rate, and they must understand the impact of data revisions. In addition, researchers trying to estimate what the Taylor rule suggested in the past face other difficulties: They need to explain differences in the rule when different variables are used, they must account for changes in the weights in the rule over time, and they must figure out if there were changes in the inflation target over time.

To use the Taylor rule in practice, the Fed must have a good estimate of the level of potential output. If the Fed does not know the level of potential output very precisely, it may make severe policy mistakes. In fact, research on the Taylor rule shows that the increase in the inflation rate in the 1970s may be attributable to the Fed making large errors in estimating the output gap—that is, in judging how actual output compared with potential output. In particular, the Fed (and most economists) thought that actual output growth was lower than potential output growth in the middle to late 1970s when, in fact, the growth rate of potential output had slowed, but that change was not recognized at the time. Thus, the Fed may have responded to deviations in output from potential and to deviations in inflation from its target according to the Taylor rule, but it kept the federal funds rate too low because it thought the output gap was much more negative than it really was. In practice, economists have used many different techniques to estimate the level of potential output. However, every method has flaws, so the estimate of potential output may be quite different from true potential output. See the Policy Insider box "Was the Fed Misled by Basing Policy on Bad Estimates of Potential Output?" for an illustration of the consequences if the Fed does not have a good estimate of potential output.

The Taylor rule assumes that the equilibrium real federal funds rate is constant over time. However, economists have found compelling evidence that the equilibrium real federal funds rate changes over time. During times of technological improvement, as in the second half of the 1990s, the equilibrium real federal funds rate increases; in times of severe supply shocks, as in the 1970s, the equilibrium real federal funds rate declines. Also, Taylor picked 2 percent for the equilibrium real federal funds rate

Was the Fed Misled by Basing Policy on Bad Estimates of Potential Output?

In the 1970s, the Federal Reserve erred in setting monetary policy. Inflation rose to double-digit levels on several occasions, and the trend in the inflation rate seemed to be heading higher nearly every year. One explanation for the increasing rate of inflation is that the Fed desired to make output grow faster than potential output. In particular, Arthur Burns, who was the Fed chairman for much of the decade, wanted to gain political favor with President Nixon and kept monetary policy too easy. Another explanation is that the Fed was misguided because it wanted to increase inflation to reduce unemployment, believing in a fixed Phillips curve. Still another explanation blames the inflation on the oil price shocks generated by OPEC. And, of course, time inconsistency could be the main cause.

One new hypothesis about the underlying reason for the Fed's error in the 1970s is that the Fed had poor measures of the output gap. In recent years, both economic theorists and empirical researchers have examined this view. Some of the theoretical research has shown that if potential output growth occasionally shifts to a persistently higher or lower rate, then it will take policymakers and researchers some time to catch on to the change. Productivity growth is quite volatile in the short run, so a persistent increase or decrease in the long-run growth rate may be masked by the short-run noise in the data. Simulation studies have shown that if the Fed bases its policy decisions on a rule (such as the Taylor rule) that depends on knowing potential output, then swings in productivity (such as those experienced with the oil price shocks of the 1970s) can lead to substantial policy errors.

Economists also have examined some of the measures of the output gap that the Federal Reserve and other government agencies were looking at in the 1970s when they made their decisions. It appears that those measures were misleading. Because the trend in productivity growth was high in the 1950s and 1960s, economists projected those rates into the future and expected potential output growth to be substantial in the 1970s. However, in fact, as we know now, the trend in productivity growth dropped sharply in about 1973 and remained low for nearly 25 years.

Does the finding that potential output was mismeasured in the 1970s absolve policymakers from blame for the high inflation rates in that era? There are two reasons to think policymakers still deserve blame: (1) because they should not have believed the numbers, based on observations of how the economy was faring, and (2) because they should not have based their policy on a concept that was subject to such large mismeasurement.

Policymakers should not have believed the potential output numbers being bandied about because they should have realized that such numbers were based on unrealistic projections. Some measures of potential output were based purely on extrapolating the trend in productivity from the 1960s. When the oil price shocks hit, however, any economist should have realized that the higher price and shortage of this key resource effectively would slow productivity growth. Further, as the decade went on, policy-makers should have known that data on employment and other variables were inconsistent with the measures of potential output being used. In fact, numerous economists warned of the dangers of basing policy on measures that were as imprecise as potential output and the natural rate of unemployment.

Policymakers also may be faulted for basing policy on a concept that was subject to so much mismeasurement. The reality is that a good measure of potential output is available only years after the fact. That is, in 2013, our estimate about potential output in 2013 is very uncertain. We only know what potential output is for 2013 with precision about three or even five years later, once we have seen how productivity growth has changed and observed the long-run trends in the data.

Thus, even though economists have developed theory and evidence that mismeasurement of potential output is partly to blame for the rise in trend inflation in the 1970s, the blame rests mainly with the monetary policymakers at the Fed.

because that was the long-run historical average of the actual real federal funds rate, but over that historical period, the inflation rate, on average, was much higher than is desirable. Thus, using the long-run historical average is likely to provide weak performance on inflation. Instead, it would be better to look at periods in which inflation was fairly stable or declining and use the average real federal funds rate in that period. Doing so would suggest an equilibrium real federal funds rate of about 3 percent, 1 percentage point higher than in the original Taylor rule.

The Taylor rule may be a poor guide to policy because data are measured with error. For example, the output gap for last quarter based on the latest GDP report may be misleading if the GDP data are later revised. Data revisions can be quite large—as much as several percentage points. As a result, if the Taylor rule is based on the latest data that are poorly measured, monetary policy may move in the wrong direction.

Researchers investigating whether the Fed might have based policy as if it were following the Taylor rule in the past have found that small variations in the exact variables used in the equation for the Taylor rule can lead to large differences in the federal funds rate. The choice of a different measure of inflation, use of inflation expectations instead of past inflation, and use of a different measure of potential output all lead to differences in what the rule implies about the federal funds rate. Reasonable alternatives lead to differences in the nominal federal funds rate of as much as 2 percentage points.

Another problem researchers face is that they do not know if the Fed has changed the weights on the output gap and inflation gap. Research by John Judd and Glenn Rudebusch has shown that the weights seem to be different for each chairman of the Federal Reserve.[1] They show that if the Fed had used the original Taylor rule with weights of 0.5 on the output gap and inflation gap in Equation (4), the federal funds rate would have been higher than it actually was during the chairmanship of Arthur Burns and lower than it actually

[1] "Taylor's Rule and the Fed: 1970–1997," Federal Reserve Bank of San Francisco *Economic Review* (1998, Number 3), pp. 3–16.

was during the chairmanship of Paul Volcker. The rule works well mainly as a description of the Fed's behavior during the chairmanship of Alan Greenspan.

Economists estimating how the Fed would have acted if it had used the Taylor rule usually assume that the Fed's target for inflation did not change over time. In Taylor's original version of the rule, the inflation target was assumed to be 2 percent. This was a reasonable description of the Fed's goals in the late 1980s or early 1990s, which was the period that Taylor was evaluating. However, the target the Fed used probably was quite a bit higher in the 1970s. Even in the early 1980s, many economists thought the inflation rate might never again be as low as 2 percent.

Several of these problems may occur simultaneously. For example, in Figure 18.3a, the Taylor rule suggests that monetary policy should have been easier in the late 1980s (from 1987 to 1989) than actually was the case. However, when Taylor first proposed the rule, his calculations showed that monetary policy was almost perfectly on target in this period. The calculations in Figure 18.3a, though, are based on a different view of potential output than Taylor used and on revised data on real GDP and prices. These differences have caused a change of 1 to 2 percentage points in the rule's implication for the federal funds rate in that period.

Despite all the potential problems with the Taylor rule, it is used widely as a benchmark for monetary policy by researchers and policymakers in central banks throughout the world. Even if policymakers disagree about what the federal funds rate should be, if the Taylor rule suggests a significant change in the federal funds rate, it provides a useful signal to policymakers. Economic conditions may have changed enough that policy should respond.

RECAP

1 The Taylor rule describes how the Fed responds to output gaps and inflation gaps by changing the federal funds rate.

2 A policymaker basing policy recommendations on the Taylor rule would have wanted tighter policy in the 1950s, late 1960s, 1970s, and 2000s but would have pushed for easier policy in the 1980s and the second half of the 1990s.

3 Implementing the Taylor rule requires that a policymaker have a good estimate of potential output and the equilibrium real federal funds rate and be able to handle the uncertainty that arises because data are revised. Economists estimating if the Fed has acted as if it used the Taylor rule must deal with these issues and also must determine the appropriate variables to use in the rule, how the weights in the rule may have changed over time, and how the inflation target may have changed over time.

18-4 Inflation Targeting

In several countries in the 1990s, central banks, which are the agencies responsible for setting monetary policy, introduced a procedure known as inflation targeting. Under **inflation targeting,** the central bank tries to achieve an explicit target for the inflation rate within some period. In some cases, the country's government requires the central bank to target a particular inflation rate; in other cases, the central bank selects its own target.

Usually the target is specified in terms of a **target band,** which is a range that represents the goal for the inflation rate. For example, a target band of 0 to 2 percent means that the central bank has achieved its goal as long as the inflation rate is between 0 and 2 percent. The band allows for shocks, such as an unexpected increase in oil prices, to change the inflation rate temporarily. For example, if the target band is 0 to 2 percent and the inflation rate is currently 1 percent, in the middle of the band, a shock to oil prices might raise the inflation rate, perhaps to 1.8 percent, which is still within the target band. Target bands should not be too narrow, or the inflation rate constantly will be moving outside the band, and the central bank will lose credibility. On the other hand, bands that are too wide have no effect. Most central banks choose bands that are about 2 or 3 percentage points wide.

The first country to engage in inflation targeting was New Zealand, which started doing so in 1990. The inflation target band that first year was 3 to 5 percent. The central bank in New Zealand gradually brought the target down over time so that it now has a target band of 1 to 3 percent. The central bank is required to publish information on inflation and forecasts of inflation and to publicly explain its actions to hit the inflation target. If the target is missed, the governor who runs the central bank can be fired immediately by the government.

For most of the 1990s, New Zealand's central bank was able to hit its inflation target. In early 1990, when the target band was 3 to 5 percent, inflation was about 7 percent, but by the end of that year it was just under 5 percent. In 1991, with a target band of 2.5 to 4.5 percent, and 1992, with a target band of 1.5 to 3.5 percent, inflation fell even more than planned, to about 1 percent, dropping below the lower band of the target range. Inflation fell to near zero in 1994 but rose just above the upper limit of the target band (2 percent at the time) in 1996. The central bank explained that this was a temporary outcome and that it was taking immediate action to tighten monetary policy to reduce inflation. As a result, inflation fell below 2 percent, and the governor of the central bank was allowed to remain in office, although he could have been fired. The government and central bank agreed to widen the target band to allow for sudden changes in the inflation rate as in 1996, so for 1997 and after, the target band was widened by ½ percentage point on each side—in 1996 the band was 0 to 2 percent, but it has been 1 to 3 percent since 2002. The results have continued to be quite good. New Zealand, which had been a poor performer on inflation in the 1970s and 1980s (far worse than the United States, Germany, or Japan), has transformed into a country with a low and stable inflation rate.

Why did inflation targeting work so well in New Zealand? Probably the most important reason was the change in the law to require the central bank to reduce inflation. Because inflation had been so high for so long in New Zealand, if the central bank had simply said, "Now we are going to reduce inflation," it would have lacked credibility. The change in the law, however, made the government's resolve to reduce inflation clear to the public by setting guidelines for the central bank's performance and establishing an explicit mechanism for accountability: the provision to fire the governor if the central bank missed its target. Thus, the legal change gave the central bank instant credibility, therefore avoiding a time-inconsistency problem.

One of the major advantages of inflation targeting in New Zealand was that it made the goal of the central bank explicit. After the law was passed, everybody in the country knew what the central bank was planning to do. The detailed information that the central bank provides about inflation and forecasts of inflation also gave the public an understanding of how the central bank planned to achieve its objectives. When a central bank is explicit about its goals and plans, it is said to be **transparent.** This transparency about the central bank's operations also improves its credibility, thus allowing it to avoid expectations traps.

Because of the success of inflation targeting in New Zealand, more than 20 other countries have begun to use inflation targeting. They all target a measure of inflation in consumer prices. Because shocks to food and energy

inflation targeting a system in which the central bank tries to achieve an explicit target for the inflation rate within some period

target band a range that represents the goal for the inflation rate

transparent a description of a central bank that is explicit about its goals and plans

prices often cause short-term swings in the overall inflation rate, some countries base their target on a "core" inflation measure that excludes those prices. The width of the target band varies across countries, with some countries not using bands but trying to achieve a particular inflation rate, others having bands only 1 percentage point wide, and still others, especially where inflation is high and variable, having bands as wide as 5 percentage points (for example, in Chile and Peru in their first years of targeting inflation). Most of the targets are for a low but positive inflation rate, which allows for some mismeasurement of inflation and prevents the costs that an economy may incur when deflation occurs. Many inflation-targeting arrangements provide escape clauses for unusual events, such as a large oil price shock, although some do not. Escape clauses keep monetary policy from doing the wrong thing at the wrong time and also raise concerns about the central bank's credibility. In most cases, the target must be hit annually, although sometimes (as in Australia) the target is the average inflation rate over the business cycle. The inflation target itself usually is set by negotiation between the government and central bank, although in some countries the government sets the target on its own, whereas in others the central bank chooses its target. Finally, in almost all the inflation-targeting countries, the central bank provides a detailed inflation report in which it discusses monetary policy, data on inflation, and forecasts of inflation.

The inflation report that each central bank writes is probably the most important part of inflation targeting. In some countries, the central bank's policies and procedures are cloaked in mystery; no one really understands what the central bank does or why it does it. In countries that use inflation targeting, though, the inflation report is a great communications device, helping the central bank clarify its goals and its plans. Instead of being detrimental to the central bank because it revealed too much, as many central bankers initially feared, the inflation report has turned out to make monetary policy easier to implement and helps the public understand what the central bank is doing.

Should the Federal Reserve change its policies to follow an inflation-targeting system? Some economists think that it should, and they would like to see the Fed formalize its procedures along the lines of inflation-targeting central banks. The Fed debated the pros and cons of inflation targeting, but in October 2007 announced that it was not going to pursue such a procedure because of perceptions that the Fed would then focus too much on inflation and not enough on stabilizing the economy, and thus would not be fulfilling its dual mandate. However, the Fed has acted much like other inflation-targeting countries by providing more information to the public about how it determines policy and providing more detailed forecasts to the public. In 2012, the Fed announced for the first time that its long-run inflation target was a 2 percent inflation rate in the PCE price index. But the Fed also made it clear that it would strive to fulfill its dual mandate and was not focusing solely on inflation.

In inflation targeting, forecasts of inflation play an important role. Because monetary policy affects inflation with a lag, policymakers must make decisions today to affect inflation one or two years in the future, so policy is based not on the inflation rate today but on the forecast for future inflation. Unfortunately, inflation forecasts are simply not all that accurate. In most of the 1990s, for example, forecasters thought inflation would rise in the coming year. Yet inflation trended down over the entire decade. Thus, if the Fed had used inflation targeting based on inflation forecasts, monetary policy might well have been tighter in the 1990s than it actually was. This might have led to lower inflation and also to slower economic growth.

One disadvantage of inflation targeting is that it reduces the flexibility of the central bank. The central bank cares about goals other than reducing inflation, such as stabilizing output. Think about a country that has experienced an oil price shock that has driven the economy into a recession and raised inflation above its target band. The law may require the central bank to tighten monetary policy, thus making the recession worse. Some countries have solved this problem by giving the central bank the option to ignore the inflation target temporarily in a recession, but in many countries, no such option is available.

One difficult question for central banks that use inflation targeting is how quickly they should try to reduce inflation in the face of a shock that has raised inflation above the target. Some economists believe that inflation should be reduced immediately with tight monetary policy regardless of the cost in terms of lost output. Such diehard devotion to an inflation target, however, is not generally acceptable by people or governments—almost no one thinks that the central bank should be concerned only with inflation and nothing else. Using monetary policy for stabilization purposes is acceptable within the context of inflation targeting, as long as inflation remains on target on average in the long run. Thus, if a shock raises inflation above target, the central bank should reduce it, but it also should consider the state of the economy while doing so. The speed of the central bank's actions should depend on the exact costs in terms of lost output, which are likely to be specific to the situation. If inflation has risen because of an oil price shock, the central bank may be slower to tighten policy than if inflation rose because of increased demand for goods by foreign countries. That is, shocks to the economy's aggregate supply of goods (as measured by costs of production) will be treated differently from shocks to the economy's aggregate demand for goods. Therefore, it is not clear that a country is better off with *only* an inflation target and without having a goal for full employment or output as well. It is true that in the long run a central bank can only affect the inflation rate. The problem is that if the central bank adheres too closely to an inflation target in the short run, it can damage the economy with overly tight monetary policy in a recession.

The use of inflation targeting has helped to reduce inflation around the world. Inflation targeting provides a goal for central banks to follow and increases the accountability of the central bank, making it clearly responsible for the inflation rate in the long run. Inflation targeting also makes the policies of the central bank more transparent to everyone. It is risky, however, in the sense that it may reduce the central bank's flexibility in responding to shocks, especially if the central bank is not also given a goal (or at least a secondary objective) of maintaining economic growth.

The 1990s, when many countries began inflation targeting, were characterized by increased economic growth throughout most of the world, very few military conflicts between countries, few oil price shocks, and falling inflation in almost every country—not just those using inflation targeting. In the financial crisis of 2008, inflation-targeting countries were a bit slower to ease monetary policy than countries that were not inflation targeters. However, their performance in the aftermath of the financial crisis did not appear to be any worse than in other countries that were not inflation targeters. So inflation targeting appears to allow enough flexibility that it did not force inflation targeters to maintain overly tight policy.

RECAP

1 Under a system of inflation targeting, a central bank tries to keep the inflation rate within a target band. A number of countries have used inflation targeting successfully to bring their inflation rates down over time.

2 The success of inflation targeting in countries such as New Zealand is attributable to the gain in credibility for the central bank. Under inflation targeting, the central bank's actions are transparent because the central bank issues a lot of information about its goals and plans. Particularly important is the inflation report issued by the central bank, which communicates the central bank's views to the public.

3 Disadvantages of inflation targeting include the use of inflation forecasts, which may not be accurate, and the loss of flexibility by policymakers.

Policy → Perspective   Why Don't Policymakers Follow Rules?

Given all the good reasons for a central bank to follow a rule for monetary policy, why are so many policymakers, especially in the United States, reluctant to embrace the idea? Their main fear is that once they have locked themselves into a particular rule, then structural change in the economy will cause the rule to generate bad policy. U.S. policymakers cite the breakdown of the once-stable relationship between the velocity of money and its opportunity cost as a case in point. If velocity is unpredictable and volatile, no rule based on the equation of exchange can work. Other rules, such as the Taylor rule, also may break down if some fundamental change occurs in the economy. For example, during the "new economy" of the late 1990s, the increase in productivity growth increased potential output growth. A policymaker following the Taylor rule who did not realize that potential output was higher might have argued for tighter monetary policy because he would have thought there was a positive output gap.

Fed Chairman Alan Greenspan expressed the situation well in a speech in 1997 when he noted: "But we have found that very often historical regularities have been disrupted by unanticipated change, especially in technologies. . . . In an ever-changing world, some element of discretion appears to be an unavoidable aspect of policymaking.[2]" He cited the increased unpredictability of the demand for money as a case in point. Greenspan also discussed the Taylor rule but suggested that "these types of formulations are at best 'guideposts' to help central banks, not inflexible rules that eliminate discretion."

There is no doubt that policymakers use rules as general guides, as Greenspan suggests. For example, the recommendations for policy of the Taylor rule and other rules are posted on the Web site of the Federal Reserve Bank of St. Louis and graphed in the publication *Monetary Trends*.

Thus, policymakers buy into the idea of using rules for monetary policy as general guides to policy but are quite reluctant to follow them blindly. They think they can make policy better than the rules do, as Fed Governor Janet Yellen noted in 1996: "The Taylor rule is no more than a rule of thumb which works tolerably well in promoting dual objectives under conditions of uncertainty. In contrast, the Fed is constantly striving to improve its understanding of the economy's structure, to uncover the source of shocks and to devise policies to accomplish more precisely our objectives.[3]" The hundreds of economists who work for the Fed are engaged in cutting-edge research to do what Governor Yellen suggests, so it is logical to think that they must contribute to making policy better than a simple rule.

Policymakers make a compelling case that changes to the economy's structure will prevent any rule from working well for long and that spending many resources to improve discretionary policy is necessary. On the other hand, some economists worry about the human element in policymaking. They worry that policymakers not following a rule will be tempted, from time to time, to pursue time-inconsistent policies. They are concerned that even though monetary policy seemed to succeed at reducing inflation under Greenspan, the reduction in inflation may have been more good luck than good policy. These same economists think that policymakers tend to make policy more volatile than it should be because of the lags in policy and because policymakers are humans who may not take a scientific approach but rather want to appear to be "doing something" if the economy is not running perfectly. For example, it always will be difficult for a policymaker to want tighter monetary policy, even if inflation is rising, if the economy is in a recession. Yet, if the recession is mild and inflation is rising rapidly, a rule might call for tighter policy.

Thus, U.S. policymakers are unlikely to ever adhere strictly to rules. Therefore, policy always will be discretionary, which does not bode well for keeping inflation low.

[2] Alan Greenspan, "Rules vs. Discretionary Monetary Policy," September 5, 1997. Available at www.federalreserve.gov/boarddocs/speeches/1997/19970905.htm.

[3] Janet L. Yellen, "Monetary Policy: Goals and Strategy," Remarks at the National Association of Business Economists, Washington, D.C., March 13, 1996.

RECAP

1 Policymakers do not want to be tied to a rule for monetary policy because they fear that structural change will make the rule work poorly.

2 But policymakers seem quite willing to look at the recommendations of rules to see what advice they give. Then they may adjust policy relative to the rule's suggestion to reflect special circumstances or structural change.

3 Some economists worry that the human element in policymaking will lead to an inflation rate that is higher than ideal because policymakers want to be perceived as doing something to help the economy grow.

Review Questions and Problems

Review Questions

1 What is an expectations trap? If people thought that the central bank was likely to raise the inflation rate to 3 percent from 2 percent, how might that lead to an expectations trap?

2 Describe the idea of time inconsistency in general terms. How can the problem be prevented?

3 How can the central bank establish credibility for keeping inflation low?

4 Why have rules for monetary policy based on money growth been unsuccessful in recent years?

5 Describe how activist rules differ from nonactivist rules. Give an example of each.

6 On average, would inflation over the last 45 years have been higher or lower if the Fed had followed the Taylor rule? In what periods would monetary policy have been tighter? When would it have been easier?

7 Does an inflation-targeting country follow a particular rule for monetary policy, such as the Taylor rule?

8 Describe New Zealand's approach to inflation targeting. What are the advantages and disadvantages of that system?

9 Why is the inflation report such an important part of an inflation-targeting system?

10 Why don't policymakers want to adopt rules for monetary policy?

Numerical Exercises

11 Suppose that the Fed's inflation target is 2 percent, potential output growth is 3.5 percent, and velocity is a function of how much the interest rate differs from 5 percent:

$$\%\Delta V = 0.5 \times (i - 5)$$

Suppose that a model of the economy suggests that the real interest rate is determined by the equation

$$r = 8.5 - \%\Delta Y$$

where Y is the level of output, so $\%\Delta Y$ is the growth rate of output. Suppose that people expect the Fed to hit its inflation target.

a Calculate the optimal money growth rate needed for the Fed to hit its inflation target in the long run.

b In the short run, if output growth is just 2 percent for two years and the equation determining the real interest rate changes to $r = 4.5 - \%\Delta Y$, what money growth rate should the Fed aim for to hit its inflation target in that period?

c If the Fed instead maintained the money growth rate from part a, what is likely to happen to inflation?

d Which policy do you think is better in the short run? Which is better in the long run?

12 Suppose that the economy is thought to be 3 percent below potential when potential output grows 3.5 percent per year. Suppose that the Fed is following the Taylor rule (with the equilibrium real federal funds rate assumed to be 2 percent and the weights on the inflation gap and output gap both equal to ½). The inflation rate was 3 percent over the past year. The federal funds rate is currently 4 percent.

a What is the Fed's target for the inflation rate?

b Suppose that a year has gone by, output is now just 1 percent below potential, and the inflation rate was 2.5 percent over the year. What federal funds rate should the Fed now set (assuming that the inflation target does not change)?

13 Suppose that the economy is thought to be 2 percent above potential (that is, the output gap is 2 percent) when potential output grows 4 percent per year. Suppose also that the Fed is following the Taylor rule, with an inflation rate of 2 percent over the past year. The federal funds rate is currently 3 percent. The equilibrium real federal funds rate is 3 percent, and the weights on the output gap and inflation gap are 0.5 each. The inflation target is 1 percent.

a Is the federal funds rate currently too high or too low? By how much? Show your work.

b Suppose that a year has gone by, output is now just 1 percent above potential, and the inflation rate was 1.5 percent over the year. What federal funds rate should the Fed now set (assuming that the inflation target does not change)?

14 a Write down the equation for the Taylor rule for monetary policy. Explain what each term in the equation means, in one sentence.

b Suppose the Fed is following the Taylor rule. Suppose the growth rate of potential output is 3 percent, the output gap is −6 percent, the weights on the output gap and inflation gap are each ½, the Fed's inflation target is 2 percent, the Fed believes the equilibrium real federal funds rate is 3 percent, and the inflation rate has been 2 percent over the past year. At what level does the Fed set the federal funds rate?

c Suppose the Fed thinks that the equilibrium federal funds rate is 3 percent, as in part b above, but in fact the equilibrium real fed funds rate is 4 percent. What do you think will happen to the inflation rate in the long run?

Analytical Problems

15 What would have happened to the money supply in the United States in the 1990s if the Federal Reserve had adhered to a policy of targeting monetary base growth of 3 percent each year regardless of the demand for currency? Note that currency growth averaged 5 percent each year in that period largely owing to the demand from abroad.

16 Looking at the historical record for the Taylor rule, were there any periods when the rule gave bad advice? That is, are there periods when the rule would have tightened policy in the face of weak economic growth or periods when the rule would have eased policy even though inflation was rising?

17 In some macroeconomic models, the equilibrium real federal funds rate changes percentage point for percentage point with the growth rate of output. If the Fed believed such models and was following the Taylor rule, how would the Fed need to adjust its rule in the "new economy" of the second half of the 1990s as productivity growth increased?

18 Would it make sense for a central bank to try inflation targeting by using the Taylor rule? What problems might the central bank encounter in trying to do so?

absolute purchasing-power parity   the idea that the exchange rate should equal the ratio of the price indexes of two countries

activist rule   a rule for monetary policy under which monetary policy is allowed to change over the course of the business cycle

adverse selection   the problem that people or firms that are worse than average risks are more likely to seek out loans than borrowers that are better than average risks

after-tax expected return   the expected return after taxes are paid

aggregate demand   the demand for all goods and services in the economy at a given time

aggregate-demand (AD) curve   shows combinations of the price level and output (which equals income) that are necessary for equilibrium in both the market for goods and services and the money market

aggregate supply   the economy's total production of goods and services

amortization   a process in which the principal amount of a security is repaid gradually over time

anomalies   incidents of predictable patterns to stock prices that investors could exploit, even accounting for risk aversion

appreciate   when the value of a currency increases in terms of another

arbitrage-pricing theory (APT)   a model of stock prices that allows for more sources of risk than just the stock market's excess return

asymmetric information   a situation in which one party in a transaction knows more than another

balance on capital and financial account   the amount foreign citizens, firms, and governments invest in a country minus the amount that country's citizens, firms, and governments invest abroad

balance on current account   net exports of goods and services plus net income from abroad plus net unilateral current transfers

bank   a financial intermediary that accepts deposits from savers and makes loans to borrowers; includes commercial banks, savings banks, savings-and-loan associations, and credit unions

bank run   a situation in which many depositors go to a bank at the same time to withdraw their money

basis point   one-hundredth of a percentage point

budget constraint (or budget line)   a line showing all the possible amounts the household can consume, given its budget (that is, the amount of income it has)

business cycle   the short-term movement of output and other key economic variables around their long-term trends

CAMELS rating system   a system used by banking supervisors in which banks are rated on their (1) capital adequacy, (2) asset quality, (3) management, (4) earnings, (5) liquidity, and (6) sensitivity to risk

capital asset pricing model (CAPM)   a model of stock prices that explains the returns to a stock as depending on how risky the stock is compared with the market average

capital gain   the increase in the dollar value of a financial investment in some period

capital-gains yield   the capital gain divided by the value of the security at the beginning of the period

capital stock   the total amount of physical capital in all firms and households

collateral   an asset that a borrower promises to give to the bank if that borrower is unable to repay the bank's loan

classical economists   economists who believe the economy will return to equilibrium quickly without the need for government intervention

commodity money   money whose value is determined by its value as a material, such as the value of gold used in jewelry; also called **full-bodied money**

Community Reinvestment Act (CRA)   a law requiring banks to serve their local communities; the purpose of the law is to prevent discrimination, especially on the basis of race, in granting credit

compensation   wages and salaries plus benefits earned by workers

compounding   earning interest on interest that was earned in prior years

contagion   the spread of a bank run from one bank to another

contractionary policy   policy that causes the economy to grow more slowly in the short run; a decrease in the money supply is contractionary

coupon bond   a security that pays a regular interest payment until the maturity date, at which time the face value is repaid

covenant   a part of a loan contract that requires the borrower to act in a certain way or to use the borrowed funds for a particular purpose

credit crunch   a situation in which banks do not lend money as they ordinarily would but rather have much higher requirements for borrowers to qualify for loans than normal

current yield   the income the investor receives in some period divided by the value of the security at the beginning of that period

data lag   the lag in data availability and quality

debt security   a contract that promises to pay a given amount of money to the owner of the security at specific dates in the future

decision lag   the lag in policy that arises because it takes time for policymakers to make a decision

default   the situation when the issuer fails to make a payment promised by a debt security

default risk   the possibility that a bank's loan customers might not repay their loans as specified in the loan agreement or that the issuer of securities (other than loans) the bank owns will not pay interest or principal when due; also called **credit risk**

defensive open-market operations   open-market activity the Fed undertakes because of seasonal effects or to offset a temporary change in money demand

depreciate   when the value of a currency decreases in terms of another

depression   a particularly bad recession, in which output declines much more than usual for a recession

direct finance   when savers buy securities directly from borrowers

direct investment   investments in other countries from installing capital goods and using them to produce output in the other countries

discount bond   a debt security with just one payment

discount factor   the amount by which a future value is divided to obtain its present value, which equals $(1 + i)^N$ for an amount to be received or paid in N years, where i is the rate of discount

discount rate   the interest rate a bank pays on a loan from the Fed's discount window

discount window   the place where banks can request loans from the Federal Reserve

discounting   the process of dividing a future value by the discount factor to obtain the present value

discretion   the situation where monetary policy is not set by a rule

diversification   ownership of a variety of securities by an investor

dividend   the periodic payment made on an equity security

dual banking system   a system in which a bank may choose whether to be chartered by federal government authorities or by a state government

dynamic model   a model that allows variables to change over time; a model in which actions that occur at one time affect what happens at other times

dynamic open-market operations   open-market activity the Fed undertakes when it wants to change monetary policy

dynamic, stochastic, general-equilibrium (DSGE) models   models incorporating time and uncertainty in which prices, wages, and interest rates adjust to bring all markets to equilibrium and all economic agents make decisions in their own interest

ease policy   what a central bank does when it increases money growth and reduces the interest rate

econometrics   the use of statistical techniques on economic data to investigate how economic variables are related

economic agents   households, business firms, governments, and foreigners who make decisions about purchasing or selling goods and services, saving or borrowing, and investing in physical capital

effectiveness lag   the time it takes from when a policy is implemented to when it has an effect on the economy

efficient markets hypothesis   the idea that stock prices fully reflect all available information

endogenous variable   a variable that is determined within the model

equation of exchange   an equation that relates total spending to the amount of money available to be spent; the equation says that money times velocity equals the price level times output

equity premium   the average amount (in terms of percentage return) by which the return on stocks exceeds the return on debt securities

equity-premium puzzle   the surprising result that people will not pay much to avoid risk in everyday situations, but when it comes to the stock market, people are willing to give up large potential returns to stocks in order to buy safer Treasury securities

equity security   a contract that makes the owner of a security a part owner of the company that issued the security

excess reserves a bank's total reserves minus its required reserves

exchange rate the amount of one currency needed to purchase one unit of another currency

exogenous variable a variable that is determined outside the model or taken to be given by the model

expansion the state of the economy in which output is rising, along with other key variables such as income and employment

expansionary policy policy that causes the economy to grow faster in the short run; an increase in the money supply is expansionary

expectations people's beliefs about future economic variables

expectations-augmented Phillips curve a Phillips curve tradeoff between inflation and unemployment in the short run but not in the long run; the short-run Phillips curve is associated with a particular level of expected inflation, and the long-run Phillips curve is a vertical line at the natural rate of unemployment

expectations theory of the term structure of interest rates the theory that a long-term interest rate is equal to the average of current and expected future short-term interest rates on securities maturing on the same date as the long-term security

expectations trap a situation in which policymakers must increase the inflation rate in response to an increase in the expected inflation rate

expected real interest rate the nominal interest rate adjusted for expected inflation; also called the **ex-ante real interest rate**

expected return the gain that an investor anticipates making, on average, from a financial security

face value the principal amount repaid by a coupon bond at maturity

federal funds market the market in which banks with excess reserves lend them to banks that desire additional reserves

federal funds rate the interest rate in the market for bank reserves (the federal funds market), which applies to overnight loans of reserves between banks

Fed's loss function another name for the Fed's objective function

Fed's objective function an equation that summarizes the total cost to the economy when output differs from potential and when the inflation rate differs from the ideal inflation rate

fiat money money that has value mainly because the government decrees that it has value for payment of taxes

financial holding company (FHC) a new financial structure, created by the Gramm–Leach–Bliley Act, in which a company can own a bank, a securities firm, and an insurance company

financial intermediary a company that transfers funds from savers to borrowers by receiving funds from savers and investing in securities issued by borrowers

financial market a place or a mechanism by which borrowers, savers, and financial intermediaries trade securities

financial security a contract in which a borrower, who seeks to obtain money from someone, promises to compensate the lender in the future

financial system the securities, intermediaries, and markets that exist to match savers and borrowers

Fisher hypothesis the argument that an increase in the inflation rate, in equilibrium, will cause an increase in the nominal interest rate but will not change the expected real interest rate

fixed-payment security a security in which the dollar payment on the security is the same every year so that the principal is amortized

full employment the situation when all the capital and labor in the economy is being fully utilized

full-employment output the amount of output produced when the economy is at full employment

fundamental value the present value of expected earnings of a company or of all companies in the stock market as a whole

future inflation discount factor for every dollar's worth of goods and services bought today, how much money it will take in N years to buy the same amount of goods and services when the average future inflation rate is π^e

general equilibrium a situation in which all markets are in equilibrium and all economic agents have made decisions in their own best interest

general-equilibrium model a model in which all the key macroeconomic variables, such as the nominal interest rate, are endogenous; a model in which all prices are endogenous in markets where individuals or firms make a choice that affects the supply or demand in those markets

Glass–Steagall Act the law, passed in 1933, that kept banks out of the securities industry

Gramm–Leach–Bliley Act the law, passed in 1999, that allowed banks back into the securities (and insurance) industries

haircut the extra collateral the Fed requires above the value of a discount loan

Herfindahl–Hirschman index (HHI) a statistic used to measure the amount of competition in a banking market

heterogeneous-agent models models that contain many different economic agents.

high-powered money another name for the monetary base

homogeneous-agent models models in which the economic agents are all alike

hyperinflation a very high rate of inflation, often taken to be 50 percent per month (13,000 percent per year) or higher

ideal inflation rate an inflation rate that policymakers would like to achieve because it minimizes the costs to society of changing prices; usually thought to be about 2 percent

idiosyncratic (unsystematic) risk risk that can be eliminated by diversification

implementation lag the lag between when a change in policy is decided on and when it is implemented

implicit capital gains capital gains that have been accrued but not yet realized

income effect the situation when a higher nominal interest rate results from an increase in income that increases the demand for money

index fund a mutual fund that tries to mimic a stock index, such as the S&P 500

indirect finance when savers invest through financial intermediaries, which buy securities from borrowers

inflation gap the actual inflation rate minus the ideal inflation rate

inflation surprise the difference between the actual inflation rate and the expected inflation rate

inflation target another name for the ideal inflation rate

inflation targeting a system in which the central bank tries to achieve an explicit target for the inflation rate within some period

inside money money that is created in the private sector

interest a payment (or series of payments) made by the borrower to the investor in a debt security in addition to repayment of the principal

interest-rate parity a situation in which the interest rate on a domestic bond equals the interest rate on a foreign bond minus the expected appreciation of the domestic currency

interest-rate risk the risk that a change in market interest rates will affect the value of financial assets

inverted yield curve a downward-sloping yield curve

investor the owner of a financial security

irrational expectations a theory that investors do not have rational expectations, so the stock market goes through periods in which stock prices rise higher than their fundamental value and other periods in which stock prices fall below their fundamental value

Keynesians economists who follow the ideas of British economist John Maynard Keynes; they believe that the key element in business cycles is the economy's inability to return to equilibrium immediately following a shift in aggregate demand because wages and prices are sticky and do not adjust right away

labor force the supply of workers, which consists of people who are either employed (they have jobs) or unemployed (they desire to have jobs)

labor-force participation rate the ratio of the labor force to the working-age population

labor productivity a measure of productivity per worker, calculated as output divided by the number of hours worked

large, structural macroeconomic models models with many equations that describe the economy in great detail; the models are based on the assumption that their equations do not change over time

law of one price the idea that the exchange rate is determined such that the price of a good is the same in two countries when expressed in units of the same currency

legal tender the condition that a lender must accept money in the repayment of debts, by law

lender of last resort the service provided by the government that lends funds to a bank when needed

liquidity how easy it is to buy or sell a security in the secondary market when you want to without incurring significant costs; how quickly and easily a type of money can be used to purchase goods and services

liquidity effect the inverse relationship between the money supply and the nominal interest rate

liquidity-preference model a model in which money demand and supply determine the nominal interest rate

lock-in effect the idea that investors who own stock that has appreciated significantly feel locked into holding that stock forever to avoid paying capital-gains taxes

long-run restriction a description of the impact of the current-period value of one variable on the value of another variable in the distant future

Lucas critique the argument that a change in policy will systematically alter the structure of econometric models

M1 the Federal Reserve's measure of money consisting of coins, paper currency, amounts in checking accounts, and traveler's checks

M2 the Federal Reserve's measure of money consisting of M1 plus amounts in savings accounts, money-market mutual funds (held by individuals), and small time deposits (under $100,000)

market (systematic) risk risk that cannot be removed by diversification

marketable security a security that can be sold to another investor

maturity the time until borrowed funds are repaid

medium of exchange the function that money serves when people exchange money for goods and services

model with microeconomic foundations a model that is based on the decisions of economic agents

monetarists economists who believe that erratic growth of the money supply is the main cause of business cycles

monetary aggregate a measure of the total supply of money in the economy

monetary base the sum of currency held by the nonbank public and banks' reserves

money-growth rule a rule that focuses only on the growth rate of money in the economy; under such a rule, the central bank simply would set money growth in the long run, ignoring short-run fluctuations in the economy

money multiplier the ratio of the money supply to the monetary base

moral hazard   the situation in which the existence of a contract changes the behavior of a party to the contract; for example, if a firm receiving a bank loan behaves differently because it has the loan than if it didn't have the loan, in a way that harms the bank

mortgage-tilt problem   the problem that arises when the real value of fixed nominal mortgage payments declines over time because of inflation

mutual fund   an investment company that pools the funds of many investors and buys a large number of different stocks (or other securities)

natural rate of unemployment   the unemployment rate reflecting normal job turnover; equivalently, the unemployment rate when the economy is producing output equal to its potential

net foreign investment (NFI)   investments in other countries in the form of portfolio investment or direct investment minus what foreigners invest in the domestic country

nominal interest rate   the amount of interest paid on a debt security in nominal (dollar) terms as a percentage of the principal (in dollar terms)

nonactivist rule   a rule for monetary policy under which the same monetary policy is pursued whether the economy is in a recession or an expansion

nonmarketable security   a security that cannot be sold to another investor

off-the-run security   a U.S. Treasury security that is not the most recently issued

Okun's law   the relationship between the output gap and the unemployment gap, which says that the output gap equals −2 times the unemployment gap

on-the-run security   the U.S. Treasury security (for a given time to maturity) that was issued most recently in the primary market

open-market operations   the tool the Fed uses to affect the money supply, consisting of purchases and sales of government securities in the secondary market

output gap   the percentage deviation of output from potential

outside money   money created by the government or by nature, not by groups or institutions in the private sector

overvalued   a situation in which stock prices exceed their fundamental value

partial-equilibrium model   a model in which some key macroeconomic variables, such as the nominal interest rate, are exogenous; a model in which individuals or firms make a choice that affects the supply or demand in a market whose price is exogenous

past inflation discount factor   for every dollar's worth of goods and services bought at an earlier date, how much money it would take now to buy the same amount of goods and services after N years of inflation at rate π

past return   the average annual return that a security or a portfolio has produced in the past

payments system   the mechanisms by which cash, checks, and electronic payments flow from buyers to sellers; equivalently, the set of mechanisms used for making transactions

peak   the end of an expansion, when output, income, and employment begin to decline

perpetuity   a debt security that pays interest forever and never repays principal

Phillips curve   the tradeoff in the data between unemployment and inflation

physical capital   the equipment and structures that a firm uses to produce its output and houses that people live in

political business cycle   the idea that monetary policy eases before elections to favor incumbent politicians

portfolio   the collection of securities an investor owns

portfolio investment   investments in other countries from purchasing financial securities

potential output   the amount of output that would be produced by the economy if resources were being used at a high rate that is sustainable in the long run

precautionary savings   the extra amount of savings that households maintain because of uncertainty about future income

present value   the amount of money you need to invest today to yield a given future amount

present-value formula   an equation that can be used to calculate the present value of almost any financial security

price-level effect   the situation when a higher nominal interest rate results from an increase in the price level that increases the demand for money

primary credit discount loan   a loan made by the Fed to a bank that is highly rated, under which the Fed does not question the purpose of the loan

primary government securities dealers   large investment banks and brokers that meet certain capital requirements and agree to actively transact with the Fed when it engages in open-market operations

primary market   the market in which a security is initially sold to an investor by a borrower

principal   the amount of money invested in a financial security or deposited in a financial intermediary

random walk   the idea that movements of stock prices from day to day, year to year, or decade to decade are not predictable

rate of discount   the term i in the discount factor

rational expectations   a theory that investors use all the information available to them about companies' future prospects in determining their buying and selling decisions, in which case stock prices always equal their fundamental value; the notion that people use all available information in making their economic decisions

real business cycle (RBC) models   models suggesting that "real" shocks to productivity, not shocks to monetary policy, cause the business cycle

real business cycle (RBC) theory   a theory that business cycles are caused by shocks to productivity

real exchange rate   the exchange rate adjusted for changes in prices in both countries

real interest rate   the nominal interest rate adjusted for expected or actual inflation

real money-demand function   the function $m(Y, i)$, which is a useful summary of the relationship between the real demand for money, real income, and the nominal interest rate

realized capital gains   profits that an investor receives by actually selling stock

realized real interest rate   the nominal interest rate adjusted for actual inflation; also called the **ex-post real interest rate**

recession   a period when output, income, and employment are declining

recognition lag   the lag that arises because the random nature of the data makes it difficult for policymakers to fully understand the state of the economy

regression analysis   the key method in econometrics in which the coefficients of an equation are calculated by finding values for them that make the sum of the squared error terms as small as possible

relative purchasing-power parity   the idea that a currency in one country should depreciate relative to the currency in a second country by the amount by which the inflation rate is higher in the first country than the second

repurchase agreements (repos)   transactions in which a primary dealer agrees to sell a security to the Fed one day and buy it back the next day or several days later

required clearing balances   amounts held by banks at the Federal Reserve that help to ensure that the check-clearing process runs smoothly; amounts are negotiated between the Fed and banks, and banks receive credits from the Fed that they can use to pay for Fed services

reserves   a bank's vault cash plus its deposits at its Federal Reserve bank

return   the income from a security plus the change in the value of the security as a percentage of the security's initial value

Ricardian equivalence proposition   the result that a change in the timing of taxes does not affect people's consumption

risk   the amount of uncertainty about the return on a security

rule for monetary policy   the systematic setting of policy according to a formula

seasonal credit discount loan   a loan from the Fed to a small agricultural bank

secondary credit discount loan   a loan made by the Fed to a bank that is not highly rated, under which the Fed carefully scrutinizes the purpose of the loan and the ability of the bank to repay the loan; the secondary credit discount rate is ½ percentage point higher than the rate for primary credit

secondary market   the market in which a security is sold from one investor to another

securitization   the process by which financial intermediaries that own assets (such as mortgage loans) sell them off to another company, which in turn sells bonds to investors; the interest payments on those bonds are paid from the interest payments on the original assets (such as mortgage payments)

shareholders   investors who own stock in a corporation; also called **stockholders**

shock   a change to a variable in a model that causes other variables to deviate from their long-run equilibrium values in the short run (or to differ over time from the path they would take in a steady state) or in the long run

short-run restriction   a description of the impact of the current-period value of one variable on the current-period value of another variable

spread   the difference between the average interest rate on a bank's assets and the average interest rate on its liabilities

stabilization policy   policy that attempts to smooth out the business cycle

standard deviation   a measure of the risk to a security

standard of deferred payment   the function that money serves when people buy something one day and pay for it later, and the repayment is denoted in terms of money

static model   a model that does not allow variables to change over time; a model that focuses on what is happening at just one point in time

steady state   the long-run equilibrium of a model, which describes what the endogenous variables in the model will do if they are not disturbed by any other variable in the model; the key variables in the model are constant or else they are growing at a constant rate

stock   another name for an equity security

stock exchange   a place where people buy or sell stocks; also called a **stock market**

stock index   the average price of a collection of stocks

store of value   the function that money serves when people keep money for some period instead of spending it or investing it

structural VAR model   a VAR model with some economic structure associated with it

systematic risk   the risk to a stock's return that is attributable to the fluctuations in the market; also called **market risk**

target band   a range that represents the goal for the inflation rate

Taylor rule   an activist rule for monetary policy that changes the federal funds rate in response to output gaps and inflation gaps

term premium   the difference between the interest rate on a longer-term bond and the average interest rate on shorter-term bonds, which arises from interest-rate risk

term spread the interest rate on a long-term debt security minus the interest rate on a short-term debt security

term structure of interest rates the relationship between interest rates with differing times to maturity

tighten policy what a central bank does when it decreases money growth and increases the interest rate

time inconsistency the difficulty that arises when policy-makers have discretion over policy and choose a policy at one date that leads people to make decisions based on that policy, which then causes the policymakers to choose a different policy at a later date

too-big-to-fail policy a policy under which bank regulators will not close a bank that is deemed to be so large that its closure would affect the financial system and cause other banks to fail; instead, the government will make loans to the bank to keep it afloat

total factor productivity (TFP) a measure of productivity that explains changes in output other than those attributable to the amount of labor and capital, which is calculated by estimating the contributions of the quantity of capital and the quantity of labor to total output and then figuring out what is left over

transactions costs costs of trading, such as time spent shopping and negotiating

transparent a description of a central bank that is explicit about its goals and plans

trough the end of a recession, when output, income, and employment begin to rise

undervalued a situation in which stock prices are below their fundamental value

unemployment gap the difference between the unemployment rate and the natural rate of unemployment

unemployment rate the number of unemployed workers as a fraction of the labor force

unit of account the function that money serves when prices are denoted in terms of money

univariate time-series model a model in which the value of a variable at any date depends just on its own past values plus an error term

unsystematic risk the risk to a stock's return that is not explained by movements in the market; also called **idiosyncratic risk**

vector autoregression (VAR) model a model in which the value of a variable depends on its own past values plus the past values of other variables plus an error term

velocity of money the average number of times a dollar of money is used in transactions over the course of a year

yield curve a plot of interest rates for a given date for debt securities with different times to maturity in which the yield to maturity is shown on the vertical axis and the time to maturity is shown on the horizontal axis

yield to maturity the average annual return to a security if you purchase the security in the market today and hold it until it matures

Andrey Prokhorov/iStockphoto.com

C

CAMELS rating system
    defined, 190
    discount lending, 345
Capital, 248
Capital, economic growth, 209–210
Capital adequacy, 190
Capital asset pricing model (CAPM),
    146–147
Capital gain, 26, 27
Capital-gains yield, 26, 27
Capital stock, 248
CAPM, 146–147
Car
    buying/leasing, 63–64
    negotiating payments, 71–72
Carter, Jimmy, 375
Cash Product Office, 322
CD. *See* Certificate of deposit (CD)
Central bank. *See* Federal Reserve System
CEO, 135
Certificate of deposit (CD)
    measuring money supply, 45
    personal saving via indirect finance, 77
CFO, 135
Chartered bank, 188
Checking account, 43
    as inside money, 43
    liquidity of funds in, 45
    measuring money supply, 44
Checks, 43
Chief executive officer (CEO), 135
Chief financial officer (CFO), 135
Cigarettes, as medium of exchange, 38
Classical economists, 215
Clinton, Bill, 320
Cochrane, John H., 150, 151n, 153, 153n
Coins
    Coinstar machines, 49
    gold, 39, 42
    seignorage revenue, 49
    shortage of (1999-2000), 49
    silver, 39, 42
    state quarters, 49
Coinstar, 49

Collateral, 160, 161
Commercial banks, 188
Commercial firms, 181
Commercial paper, 79
Commodity money, 42
Community Reinvestment Act (CRA), 182, 191
Compensation, 217
Compound interest, 4–5
Compounding, 54–55
Consumer confidence, 247
Consumer credit, 14
Consumer spending, 281
Consumption
    aggregate demand, 246–248
    consumer confidence, 246–248
    lifetime income, 275
    two-period model of consumption and saving,
        270–275
Contagion, 179
Continental Illinois, 185
Contractionary policy, 358
Control. *See* Monetary control
Counterfeit currency, 42
Coupon bond, 59–60, 69–70
Covenant, 161
CRA, 182, 191
Creation of money, 8
Credibility, Fed, 391–392
Credit card, 44
    inside money, 43
    interest rates, 171
Credit crunch, 164
Credit risk, 172–173
Credit union, 188, 189
Crises. *See* Financial crises
Currency
    counterfeit, 42
    creation/destruction, 333–339
    exchange rate fluctuations, 307, 308
    gold coins, 39, 42
    M1, and, 46
    paper, 42
    silver coins, 39, 42
    supply control, 181
Currency boards, 392
Current yield, 26, 27
Curry, Timothy, 163n

CHAPTER SUMMARY

1. The two major types of financial securities are debt and equity. Households, business firms, foreigners, and governments issue debt or equity as a means to obtain funds; those groups are also investors in those securities.

2. Debt and equity securities differ in terms of two major details: how long it will be before the borrowed funds are repaid (debt specifies a maturity date; equity does not) and what type of periodic payment will be made (debt pays interest; equity pays dividends).

3. Direct finance occurs when a saver buys a financial security issued by a borrower; indirect finance occurs when a saver transfers funds to an intermediary, which then buys a security issued by a borrower.

4. Financial intermediaries transfer funds from savers to borrowers and offer such services as providing diversification, pooling the funds of many people, taking short-term deposits and making long-term loans, gathering information, and reducing transactions costs.

5. Borrowers issue new securities to investors in the primary market. Investors sell securities to each other in the secondary market.

6. As in other markets, the price of a security depends on supply and demand.

7. An efficient financial system promotes economic growth.

8. A financial system that works poorly causes problems, such as a lower standard of living.

9. Investors care about expected return, risk, liquidity, taxes, and maturity.

10. Because people have different attitudes toward risk, there is not an optimal portfolio that everyone should own. People who do not like risk will have safer portfolios; those who do not mind risk as much will have riskier portfolios.

KEY EQUATIONS

The general formula for the expected return to a security is

$$E = p_1 X_1 + p_2 X_2 + \cdots + p_N X_N \qquad (1)$$

where there are N possible outcomes and a given outcome X_i ($i = 1, 2, \ldots, N$) occurs with probability p_i. The sum of the probabilities $p_1 + p_2 + \cdots + p_N$ must equal 1.

The standard deviation of the return to a security is given by the formula.

$$S = [p_1(X_1 - E)^2 + p_2(X_2 - E)^2 + \cdots + p_N(X_N - E)^2]^{1/2} \qquad (2)$$

where E is the expected return from Equation (1) and S stands for standard deviation.

KEY TERMS

after-tax expected return   the expected return after taxes are paid (p. 33)

capital gain   the increase in the dollar value of a financial investment in some period (p. 26)

capital-gains yield   the capital gain divided by the value of the security at the beginning of the period (p. 26)

current yield   the income the investor receives in some period divided by the value of the security at the beginning of that period (p. 26)

debt security   a contract that promises to pay a given amount of money to the owner of the security at specific dates in the future (p. 14)

default   the situation when the issuer fails to make a payment promised by a debt security (p. 27)

direct finance   when savers buy securities directly from borrowers (p. 17)

diversification   ownership of a variety of securities by an investor (p. 19)

dividend   the periodic payment made on an equity security (p. 16)

equity security   a contract that makes the owner of a security a part owner of the company that issued the security (p. 14)

expected return   the gain that an investor anticipates making, on average, from a financial security (p. 26)

financial intermediary   a company that transfers funds from savers to borrowers by receiving funds from savers and investing in securities issued by borrowers (p. 17)

financial market   a place or a mechanism by which borrowers, savers, and financial intermediaries trade securities (p. 20)

financial security   a contract in which a borrower, who seeks to obtain money from someone, promises to compensate the lender in the future (p. 14)

financial system   the securities, intermediaries, and markets that exist to match savers and borrowers (p. 13)

idiosyncratic (unsystematic) risk   risk that can be eliminated by diversification (p. 34)

indirect finance when savers invest through financial intermediaries, which buy securities from borrowers *(p. 17)*

interest a payment (or series of payments) made by the borrower to the investor in a debt security in addition to repayment of the principal *(p. 16)*

investor the owner of a financial security *(p. 14)*

liquidity how easy it is to buy or sell a security in the secondary market when you want to without incurring significant costs; how quickly and easily a type of money can be used to purchase goods and services *(p. 33)*

market (systematic) risk risk that cannot be removed by diversification *(p. 34)*

marketable security a security that can be sold to another investor *(p. 33)*

maturity the time until borrowed funds are repaid *(p. 16)*

nonmarketable security a security that cannot be sold to another investor *(p. 33)*

portfolio the collection of securities an investor owns *(p. 34)*

primary market the market in which a security is initially sold to an investor by a borrower *(p. 20)*

principal the amount of money invested in a financial security or deposited in a financial intermediary *(p. 16)*

return the income from a security plus the change in the value of the security as a percentage of the security's initial value *(p. 26)*

risk the amount of uncertainty about the return on a security *(p. 27)*

secondary market the market in which a security is sold from one investor to another *(p. 20)*

standard deviation a measure of the risk to a security *(p. 28)*

stock another name for an equity security *(p. 14)*

CHAPTER SUMMARY

1. Money is a medium of exchange when it is traded for goods and services. Money's role as a medium of exchange is important because money reduces transactions costs.

2. Money serves as a unit of account—the measure by which prices are denoted.

3. Money is used as a store of value by people who save money now to buy something in the future.

4. Money is a standard of deferred payment when a borrower agrees to repay a loan in terms of money at some time in the future.

5. Outside money, which is money created by nature or by the government, has evolved over time from commodity money, such as gold coins, to fiat money, such as paper dollars that cannot be redeemed for gold.

6. Inside money is created by banks and includes balances in checking accounts.

7. Electronic payments are growing in popularity but may never be as popular as checks because of concerns over fraud and security.

8. The Federal Reserve monitors the money supply by adding up various types of accounts that serve as money according to their liquidity and size. Though M1 seems to be the most money-like aggregate, its behavior in recent years has made it less useful as a measure of the money supply than M2.

9. The amount of U.S. currency in circulation per citizen is very high because many dollars are used overseas.

10. Coin shortages arise when people hoard coins and do not spend them or find ways to return them to circulation.

KEY TERMS

commodity money   money whose value is determined by its value as a material, such as the value of gold used in jewelry; also called full-bodied money *(p. 42)*

fiat money   money that has value mainly because the government decrees that it has value for payment of taxes *(p. 42)*

hyperinflation   a very high rate of inflation, often taken to be 50 percent per month (13,000 percent per year) or higher *(p. 40)*

inside money   money that is created in the private sector *(p. 43)*

legal tender   the condition that a lender must accept money in the repayment of debts, by law *(p. 41)*

liquidity   how easy it is to buy or sell a security in the secondary market when you want to without incurring significant costs; how quickly and easily a type of money can be used to purchase goods and services *(p. 45)*

M1   the Federal Reserve's measure of money consisting of coins, paper currency, amounts in checking accounts, and traveler's checks *(p. 45)*

M2   the Federal Reserve's measure of money consisting of M1 plus amounts in savings accounts, money-market mutual funds (held by individuals), and small time deposits (under $100,000) *(p. 46)*

medium of exchange   the function that money serves when people exchange money for goods and services *(p. 38)*

monetary aggregate   a measure of the total supply of money in the economy *(p. 45)*

outside money   money created by the government or by nature, not by groups or institutions in the private sector *(p. 41)*

payments system   the mechanisms by which cash, checks, and electronic payments flow from buyers to sellers; equivalently, the set of mechanisms used for making transactions *(p. 41)*

standard of deferred payment   the function that money serves when people buy something one day and pay for it later, and the repayment is denoted in terms of money *(p. 41)*

store of value   the function that money serves when people keep money for some period instead of spending it or investing it *(p. 40)*

transactions costs   costs of trading, such as time spent shopping and negotiating *(p. 38)*

unit of account   the function that money serves when prices are denoted in terms of money *(p. 39)*

CHAPTER SUMMARY

1. The present value of an amount to be received in the future is simply the amount of money you would need to start with today, invested at the current market interest rate, to yield the given future amount.

2. Compounding is earning interest on interest from previous periods.

3. Discounting is accomplished by dividing a future amount by the discount factor to determine the present value.

4. The present value of any future amount of money is inversely related to the rate of discount.

5. Timelines are graphic devices used to illustrate the payments made by a financial security.

6. Variations of the present-value formula are used to evaluate a perpetuity (a security that never matures), a fixed-payment security (a security with a constant payment over time that amortizes the principal), and a coupon bond (a debt security that makes periodic interest payments and repays the principal at maturity).

7. Slight adjustments to the present-value formula allow us to handle the case when compounding occurs more than once a year.

8. When market interest rates change, so do prices of securities in the secondary market.

9. For a given principal amount and interest rate, the present-value formula can be used to determine future payments. The present-value formula can be used to calculate past return, expected return, and yield to maturity.

10. An automobile lease is similar to an automobile loan. Evaluating both of them requires the use of the present-value formula.

KEY EQUATIONS

The value of an investment after N years (where N can be any positive number) is

$$\text{Value after N years} = (1 + i)^N \times P \tag{1}$$

where i is the annual interest rate, and P is the principal amount of the investment.

The present value of some amount F that you will receive one year from now is

$$P = \frac{F}{1 + i} \tag{2}$$

where i is the rate of discount.

The present value of the future amount F to be received in N years is

$$P = \frac{F}{(1 + i)^N} \tag{3}$$

where i is the rate of discount.

If multiple payments are being made over many years, then the present value is

$$P = \frac{F_1}{(1 + i)^1} + \frac{F_2}{(1 + i)^2} + \cdots + \frac{F_N}{(1 + i)^N} \tag{4}$$

where each F_t term is the amount to be received t years in the future for $t = 1, 2, \ldots, N$, and i is the rate of discount.

The present value of a perpetuity that pays amount F each year forever is

$$P = \frac{F}{i} \tag{5}$$

where i is the rate of discount.

The present value of a fixed-payment security that pays the amount F at the end of each of the next N years, when the rate of discount is i, is

$$P = \frac{F}{(1 + i)^1} + \frac{F}{(1 + i)^2} + \cdots + \frac{F}{(1 + i)^N}$$
$$= F \times \frac{1 - [1/(1 + i)]^N}{i} \tag{6}$$

The present value of a coupon bond that pays the amount F each year for N years and that repays the face value V at the end of N years, when the rate of discount is i, is

$$P = \left\{ F \times \frac{1 - [1/(1 + i)]^N}{i} \right\} + \frac{V}{(1 + i)^N} \tag{7}$$

The payment amount for a fixed-payment security when the amount P is borrowed for N years and when the rate of discount is i is

$$F = P \times \frac{i}{1 - [1/(1 + i)]^N} \tag{8}$$

The past return, expected return, or yield to maturity for a security making one payment in one year can be calculated with the equation

$$i = \frac{F}{P} - 1 \tag{9}$$

The past return, expected return, or yield to maturity for a security making one payment in N years can be calculated with the equation

$$i = \left(\frac{F}{P}\right)^{1/N} - 1 \qquad \textbf{(10)}$$

In the case of a perpetuity, the past return, yield to maturity, or expected return are found using the equation

$$i = \frac{F}{P} \qquad \textbf{(11)}$$

For a fixed-payment security, the past return, yield to maturity, or expected return can be found using the equation

$$\frac{P}{F} = \frac{1 - [1/(1+i)]^N}{i} \qquad \textbf{(12)}$$

The equation cannot be solved directly.

KEY TERMS

amortization a process in which the principal amount of a security is repaid gradually over time *(p. 59)*

compounding earning interest on interest that was earned in prior years *(p. 54)*

coupon bond a security that pays a regular interest payment until the maturity date, at which time the face value is repaid *(p. 59)*

discount bond a debt security with just one payment *(p. 56)*

discount factor the amount by which a future value is divided to obtain its present value, which equals $(1 + i)^N$ for an amount to be received or paid in N years, where i is the rate of discount *(p. 55)*

discounting the process of dividing a future value by the discount factor to obtain the present value *(p. 55)*

face value the principal amount repaid by a coupon bond at maturity *(p. 59)*

fixed-payment security a security in which the dollar payment on the security is the same every year so that the principal is amortized *(p. 59)*

interest-rate risk the risk of a change in the price of a security in the secondary market because of a change in the market interest rate *(p. 64)*

past return the average annual return that a security or a portfolio has produced in the past *(p. 67)*

perpetuity a debt security that pays interest forever and never repays principal *(p. 58)*

present value the amount of money you need to invest today to yield a given future amount *(p. 53)*

present-value formula an equation that can be used to calculate the present value of almost any financial security *(p. 57)*

principal the amount of money invested in a financial security or deposited in a financial intermediary *(p. 53)*

rate of discount the term i in the discount factor *(p. 56)*

yield to maturity the average annual return to a security if you purchase the security in the market today and hold it until it matures *(p. 68)*

CHAPTER SUMMARY

1. There are many different debt securities, each with a different interest rate.

2. The interest rates on debt securities change with supply and demand in both the primary and secondary markets.

3. An investor compares the average interest rate on current and future short-term bonds with the interest rate on a long-term bond, choosing whichever has the higher return (in the absence of transactions costs, uncertainty about future interest rates, or concern about risk).

4. The choice of buying short- or long-term bonds depends on transactions costs and uncertainty about future interest rates.

5. According to the expectations theory of the term structure of interest rates, if investors are not concerned about risk, the equilibrium interest rate on a long-term bond equals the average of interest rates on current and future short-term bonds.

6. A yield curve is a plot of interest rates on bonds with different times to maturity, with the yield to maturity shown on the vertical axis and the time to maturity shown on the horizontal axis.

7. According to the expectations theory of the term structure of interest rates, the yield curve should be flat when short-term interest rates are not expected to change, the yield curve should slope upward when short-term interest rates are expected to rise, and the yield curve should slope downward when short-term interest rates are expected to decline.

8. The longer the term to maturity of a debt security, the greater is the interest-rate risk.

9. Because investors are concerned about interest-rate risk, long-term interest rates equal average expected short-term interest rates plus a term premium.

10. The longer the maturity of the bond is, the larger the term premium will be. The term premium varies over time.

11. Yield curves are flat or downward sloping at the start of recessions, sharply upward sloping at the start of economic expansions, and somewhat upward sloping in the middle of economic expansions.

12. The term spread between interest rates on long- and short-term bonds is helpful in predicting recessions. The smaller the spread, the greater is the probability of a recession.

KEY TERMS

basis point   one-hundredth of a percentage point *(p. 80)*

expectations theory of the term structure of interest rates   the theory that a long-term interest rate is equal to the average of current and expected future short-term interest rates on securities maturing on the same date as the long-term security *(p. 89)*

inverted yield curve   a downward-sloping yield curve *(p. 102)*

off-the-run security   a U.S. Treasury security (for a given time to maturity) that is not the most recently issued *(p. 80)*

on-the-run security   the U.S. Treasury security (for a given time to maturity) that was issued most recently in the primary market *(p. 80)*

securitization   the process by which financial intermediaries that own assets (such as mortgage loans) sell them off to another company, which in turn sells bonds to investors; the interest payments on those bonds are paid from the interest payments on the original assets (such as mortgage payments) *(p. 79)*

term premium   the difference between the interest rate on a longer-term bond and the average interest rate on shorter-term bonds, which arises from interest-rate risk *(p. 96)*

term spread   the interest rate on a long-term debt security minus the interest rate on a short-term debt security *(p. 104)*

term structure of interest rates   the relationship between interest rates with differing times to maturity *(p. 84)*

yield curve   a plot of interest rates for a given date for debt securities with different times to maturity in which the yield to maturity is shown on the vertical axis and the time to maturity is shown on the horizontal axis *(p. 84)*

CHAPTER SUMMARY

1. Real interest rates are interest rates adjusted for inflation. The expected (ex-ante) real interest rate is based on the expected inflation rate, and the realized (ex-post) real interest rate is based on the actual inflation rate.

2. When the inflation rate is higher than expected, the realized real interest rate is lower than the expected real interest rate; so borrowers are better off and lenders are worse off. When the inflation rate is lower than expected, the realized real interest rate is higher than the expected real interest rate; so borrowers are worse off and lenders are better off.

3. Investors dislike unexpected inflation and uncertainty about the inflation rate.

4. The real present-value formula uses the same form as the nominal present-value formula but with all terms adjusted for expected or actual inflation.

5. Measures of expected real interest rates based on survey data on the expected inflation rate show that expected real interest rates were low in the 1970s, high in the early 1980s, and moderate from the mid-1980s to the late 1990s. Since 2000, they have been volatile and often negative.

6. The Fisher hypothesis suggests that the nominal interest rate rises one-for-one with the expected inflation rate, keeping the expected real interest rate unchanged, assuming no other changes in the economy. The data show that expected real interest rates change over time, but that is not necessarily evidence against the Fisher hypothesis because of changes in the economy other than changes in the expected inflation rate.

7. Expected real interest rates, both short and long term, change over time. They fall when the economy is in a recession.

8. Inflation interacts with the tax system and damages the economy by effectively raising the government's tax rate on investors' real returns, thus discouraging saving and investment.

9. Under some conditions, the after-tax expected real interest rate could be independent of the expected inflation rate. In that case, the expected real interest rate rises as the expected inflation rate rises; so the nominal interest rate rises even more.

10. The interaction of inflation and taxation can be eliminated either by modifying the tax system so that taxes are imposed only on real returns or by reducing the inflation rate to zero.

KEY EQUATIONS

The expected real interest rate is

$$r = \frac{1+i}{1+\pi^e} - 1 \tag{1}$$

where i is the nominal interest rate, r is the expected real interest rate, and π^e is the expected rate of inflation. A useful approximation is

$$r = i - \pi^e \tag{2}$$

The realized real interest rate is

$$rr = \frac{1+i}{1+\pi} - 1 \tag{5}$$

or the approximation

$$rr = i - \pi \tag{6}$$

where rr is the realized real interest rate and π is the actual inflation rate.

The relationship between the expected real interest rate and the realized real interest rate is

$$r - rr = \pi - \pi^e \tag{9}$$

The real present-value formula is given by

$$P = \frac{f_1}{(1+r)^1} + \frac{f_2}{(1+r)^2} + \cdots + \frac{f_N}{(1+r)^N} \tag{10}$$

where the future payment amounts are in real terms:

$$f_1 = F_1/(1+\pi^e)^1, f_2 = F_2/(1+\pi^e)^2, \ldots$$
$$f_N = F_N/(1+\pi^e)^N$$

where f_1 is the expected real payment in one year, f_2 is the expected real payment in two years, and so on.

The after-tax expected real interest rate is

$$r_a = [(1-t) \times i] - \pi^e \tag{12}$$

where t is the investor's tax rate. Similarly, the after-tax realized real interest rate is

$$rr_a = [(1-t) \times i] - \pi \tag{13}$$

KEY TERMS

expected real interest rate   the nominal interest rate adjusted for expected inflation; also called the ex-ante real interest rate *(p. 110)*

Fisher hypothesis   the argument that an increase in the inflation rate, in equilibrium, will cause an increase in the nominal interest rate but will not change the expected real interest rate *(p. 122)*

future inflation discount factor   for every dollar's worth of goods and services bought today, how much money it will take in N years to buy the same amount of goods and services when the average future inflation rate is π^e *(p. 118)*

nominal interest rate   the amount of interest paid on a debt security in nominal (dollar) terms as a percentage of the principal (in dollar terms) *(p. 110)*

past inflation discount factor   for every dollar's worth of goods and services bought at an earlier date, how much money it would take now to buy the same amount of goods and services after N years of inflation at rate π *(p. 118)*

real interest rate   the nominal interest rate adjusted for expected or actual inflation *(p. 110)*

realized real interest rate   the nominal interest rate adjusted for actual inflation; also called the ex-post real interest rate *(p. 111)*

CHAPTER SUMMARY

1. Stock exchanges allow people to trade stocks with one another; they are efficient means of bringing together buyers and sellers of stocks.

2. Stock indexes are useful summaries of the overall movements of stock prices.

3. Mutual funds help investors to diversify at low cost.

4. Tax rules sometimes cause investors to be locked into stock holdings, thus reducing the efficiency of the stock market.

5. Inflation affects stock returns, which are best measured in real (inflation-adjusted) terms.

6. If stock markets are efficient, and if investors do not care about risk, stock prices should follow a random walk.

7. Predictability of stock prices means that investors are risk averse or that the stock market is not perfectly efficient.

8. Anomalies are situations in which stock prices are predictable, even accounting for risk.

9. Accounting for the risk aversion of investors requires a model of how stock returns vary with risk factors. Two popular models are the CAPM and APT.

10. The fundamental value of the stock market can be estimated using the present-value formula. Stock prices should equal the present value of expected future corporate earnings.

11. The equity premium is very large, which means that the returns to stocks are dramatically higher than the returns to bonds.

KEY EQUATIONS

The total return on stock equals the dividend yield (D_t/P_{t-1}) plus the capital-gains yield $[(P_t - P_{t-1})/P_{t-1}]$:

$$Total\ return = \frac{D_t}{P_{t-1}} + \frac{P_t - P_{t-1}}{P_{t-1}} \qquad (1)$$

The capital asset pricing model (CAPM) relates the realized return to holding stock i at date t (R_t^i) to the interest rate on a risk-free bond (r_t), the market's excess return ($R_t - r_t$), the average return to all stocks in the market (R_t), and the part of the return that is unexplained by the market's return, called unsystematic risk (ε_t^i):

$$R_t^i = r_t + \beta^i(R_t - r_t) + \varepsilon_t^i \qquad (2)$$

The arbitrage-pricing theory (APT) describes the return to a particular stock as a function of k different factors that affect the return to the stock:

$$R_t^i = r_t + \beta^{1i}f_t^1 + \beta^{2i}f_t^2 + \cdots + \beta^{ki}f_t^k + \varepsilon_t^i \qquad (3)$$

When earnings grow at a constant rate (g), then the fundamental value of the stock market can be found as a function of g, the rate of discount (R), and last year's earnings (e_0):

$$V = \frac{1 + g}{R - g} \times e_0 \qquad (4)$$

KEY TERMS

anomalies incidents of predictable patterns to stock prices that investors could exploit, even accounting for risk aversion *(p. 145)*

arbitrage-pricing theory (APT) a model of stock prices that allows for more sources of risk than just the stock market's excess return *(p. 147)*

capital asset pricing model (CAPM) a model of stock prices that explains the returns to a stock as depending on how risky the stock is compared with the market average *(p. 146)*

efficient markets hypothesis the idea that stock prices fully reflect all available information *(p. 144)*

equity premium the average amount (in terms of percentage return) by which the return on stocks exceeds the return on debt securities *(p. 152)*

equity-premium puzzle the surprising result that people will not pay much to avoid risk in everyday situations, but when it comes to the stock market, people are willing to give up large potential returns to stocks in order to buy safer Treasury securities *(p. 152)*

fundamental value the present value of expected earnings of a company or of all companies in the stock market as a whole *(p. 148)*

implicit capital gains capital gains that have been accrued but not yet realized *(p. 138)*

index fund a mutual fund that tries to mimic a stock index, such as the S&P 500 *(p. 136)*

irrational expectations a theory that investors do not have rational expectations; so the stock market goes through periods in which stock prices rise higher than their fundamental value and other periods in which stock prices fall below their fundamental value *(p. 149)*

lock-in effect the idea that investors who own stock that has appreciated significantly feel locked into holding that stock forever to avoid paying capital-gains taxes *(p. 138)*

mutual fund an investment company that pools the funds of many investors and buys a large number of different stocks (or other securities) *(p. 136)*

overvalued a situation in which stock prices exceed their fundamental value *(p. 149)*

random walk the idea that movements of stock prices from day to day, year to year, or decade to decade are not predictable *(p. 145)*

rational expectations a theory that investors use all the information available to them about companies' future prospects in determining their buying and selling decisions, in which case stock prices always equal their fundamental value; the notion that

people use all available information in making their economic decisions *(p. 149)*

realized capital gains profits that an investor receives by actually selling stock *(p. 138)*

shareholders investors who own stock in a corporation; also called **stockholders** *(p. 135)*

stock exchange a place where people buy or sell stocks; also called a **stock market** *(p. 135)*

stock index the average price of a collection of stocks *(p. 135)*

systematic risk the risk to a stock's return that is attributable to the fluctuations in the market; also called **market risk** *(p. 146)*

undervalued a situation in which stock prices are below their fundamental value *(p. 149)*

unsystematic risk the risk to a stock's return that is not explained by movements in the market; also called **idiosyncratic risk** *(p. 146)*

CHAPTER SUMMARY

1. Banks are institutions that accept deposits and make loans; they include commercial banks, thrift institutions (savings banks and savings-and-loan associations), and credit unions.

2. Banks pool funds, and they specialize in gathering information, both of which make the financial system run more efficiently.

3. Banks face asymmetric-information problems because borrowers know more about their prospects than the bank does.

4. Adverse selection arises because bad borrowers are more likely to ask for a loan than good borrowers.

5. Moral hazard arises when borrowers change their plans after receiving a loan, to the detriment of the bank that made the loan.

6. Banks reduce asymmetric-information problems by asking for collateral, imposing net-worth requirements, and imposing covenants on loan contracts.

7. The banking system breaks down at times, failing to deliver funds efficiently from lenders to borrowers. This breakdown occurs during credit crunches and in crises, such as the savings-and-loan crisis and in the financial crisis of 2008.

8. On banks' balance sheets, assets (mainly reserves, securities, and loans) equal liabilities (mainly transactions deposits, nontransactions deposits, and borrowings) plus equity capital.

9. Banks are required to hold reserves, which consist of their vault cash and deposits at their Federal Reserve bank.

10. Banks that have excess reserves will hold them, lend them to another bank in the federal funds market, buy securities with them, or make new loans with them. Banks that have a reserve deficiency will borrow from another bank in the federal funds market, borrow from the Federal Reserve, sell securities, reduce their outstanding loans, or issue new CDs to attract funds.

11. The profits a bank earns depend on the spread, which is the difference between the average interest rate received on the bank's assets and the average interest rate paid on its liabilities.

12. The Fed began to pay interest to banks on their reserves in October 2008. As a result, banks began holding large amounts of excess reserves, mainly for safety reasons during the financial crisis. The Fed can now affect the amount of reserves banks hold by varying the federal funds rate and the interest rate it pays on reserves.

KEY EQUATIONS

Accounting rules are set up so that a bank's balance sheet must satisfy the equation

$$Assets = liabilities + equity\ capital \qquad (1)$$

Reserves consist of vault cash and deposits at the Fed:

$$Reserves = vault\ cash + deposits\ at\ the\ Federal\ Reserve \quad (2)$$

KEY TERMS

adverse selection   the problem that people or firms that are worse than average risks are more likely to seek out loans than borrowers that are better than average risks *(p. 159)*

asymmetric information   a situation in which one party in a transaction knows more than another *(p. 159)*

bank   a financial intermediary that accepts deposits from savers and makes loans to borrowers; includes commercial banks, savings banks, savings-and-loan associations, and credit unions *(p. 1579*

collateral   an asset that a borrower promises to give to the bank if that borrower is unable to repay the bank's loan *(p. 160)*

covenant   a part of a loan contract that requires the borrower to act in a certain way or to use the borrowed funds for a particular purpose *(p. 161)*

credit crunch   a situation in which banks do not lend money as they ordinarily would but rather have much higher requirements for borrowers to qualify for loans than normal *(p. 164)*

default risk   the possibility that a bank's loan customers might not repay their loans as specified in the loan agreement or that the issuer of securities (other than loans) the bank owns will not pay interest or principal when due; also called **credit risk** *(p. 172)*

discount rate   the interest rate a bank pays on a loan from the Fed's discount window *(p. 169)*

discount window   the place where banks can request loans from the Federal Reserve *(p. 169)*

excess reserves   a bank's total reserves minus its required reserves *(p. 169)*

federal funds market   the market in which banks with excess reserves lend them to banks that desire additional reserves *(p. 169)*

federal funds rate   the interest rate in the market for bank reserves (the federal funds market), which applies to overnight loans of reserves between banks *(p. 169)*

interest-rate risk   the risk of a change in the price of a security in the secondary market because of a change in the market interest rate *(p. 172)*

moral hazard   the situation in which the existence of a contract changes the behavior of a party to the contract; for example, if a firm receiving a bank loan behaves differently because it has the loan than if it

didn't have the loan, in a way that harms the bank *(p. 160)*

reserves   a bank's vault cash plus its deposits at its Federal Reserve bank *(p. 167)*

securitization   the process by which financial intermediaries that own assets (such as mortgage loans) sell them off to another company, which in turn sells bonds to investors; the interest payments on those bonds are paid from the interest payments on the original assets (such as mortgage payments) *(p. 173)*

spread   the difference between the average interest rate on a bank's assets and the average interest rate on its liabilities *(p. 170)*

CHAPTER SUMMARY

1. Banks are regulated because the government wants to reduce the externalities caused by bank failures, to keep banks small, to prevent bank runs, to ensure the efficiency of the payments system, and to control the money supply.

2. To achieve its goals, the government supervises banks closely, restricts mergers and bank activities, provides a safety net for banks, offers payment services to banks, and requires banks to hold a certain level of reserves.

3. Banks are subject to scrutiny from a variety of different supervisors depending on what type they are (commercial bank, thrift, or credit union), how they are chartered (federal or state), who insures them (FDIC or NCUSIF), and whether they are members of the Federal Reserve System.

4. Banks pay deposit insurance premiums depending on the riskiness of their assets, as determined by their government supervisors.

5. Banks are rated according to the CAMELS system, which examines their capital adequacy, asset quality, management, earnings, liquidity, and sensitivity to risk.

6. Banks are evaluated on the adequacy of their capital according to international standards, which require a certain amount of capital relative to the riskiness of the assets.

7. Banks must comply with the Community Reinvestment Act, which requires them to make loans in areas where they take deposits.

8. The government evaluates bank mergers on the basis of the effects on competition, the adequacy of the financial and managerial resources of the new bank, the ability of the bank to meet the convenience and needs of the community, and whether the bank provided complete information about the merger or acquisition to the banking authorities.

9. A merger can be challenged if the HHI after the merger would exceed 1,800 and if the change in the HHI would exceed 200 or if the new bank would have a market share exceeding 35 percent. The merger can also be challenged if the new bank would have more than 10 percent of the nation's deposits or more than 30 percent of a state's deposits. However, mitigating factors also may be considered.

10. Banks' profits increase after mergers both because costs are reduced and because competition is reduced.

KEY EQUATIONS

The HHI is defined as:

$$HHI = s_1^2 + s_2^2 + \cdots + s_N^2 \qquad (1)$$

where the terms on the right-hand side of the equation are the squared values of the market shares of each bank (in percentage terms).

KEY TERMS

bank run a situation in which many depositors go to a bank at the same time to withdraw their money *(p. 179)*

CAMELS rating system a system used by banking supervisors in which banks are rated on their (1) *c*apital adequacy, (2) *a*sset quality, (3) *m*anagement, (4) *e*arnings, (5) *l*iquidity, and (6) *s*ensitivity to risk *(p. 190)*

Community Reinvestment Act a law requiring banks to serve their local communities; the purpose of the law is to prevent discrimination, especially on the basis of race, in granting credit *(p. 191)*

contagion the spread of a bank run from one bank to another *(p. 179)*

dual banking system a system in which a bank may choose whether to be chartered by federal government authorities or by a state government *(p. 188)*

financial holding company a new financial structure, created by the Gramm–Leach–Bliley Act, in which a company can own a bank, a securities firm, and an insurance company *(p. 184)*

Glass–Steagall Act the law, passed in 1933, that kept banks out of the securities industry *(p. 183)*

Gramm–Leach–Bliley Act the law, passed in 1999, that allowed banks back into the securities (and insurance) industries *(p. 184)*

Herfindahl–Hirschman index (HHI) a statistic used to measure the amount of competition in a banking market *(p. 192)*

lender of last resort the service provided by the government that lends funds to a bank when needed *(p. 184)*

payments system   the mechanisms by which cash, checks, and electronic payments flow from buyers to sellers; equivalently, the set of mechanisms used for making transactions *(p. 180)*

too-big-to-fail policy   a policy under which bank regulators will not close a bank that is deemed to be so large that its closure would affect the financial system and cause other banks to fail; instead, the government will make loans to the bank to keep it afloat *(p. 185)*

CHAPTER SUMMARY

1. The trend growth rate of output has changed over time mostly because of changes in the trend growth rate of labor productivity, according to the view of economic growth based on labor data.

2. Trend growth in total factor productivity, which accounts for increases in both capital and labor, mirrors the trend in labor productivity.

3. Business cycles are the fluctuations of output and other key economic variables about their long-term trends.

4. Output rises in an expansion and falls in a recession.

5. The National Bureau of Economic Research determines when recessions begin and end.

6. Over the course of a business cycle, many variables move together and tend to be above or below trend for some time.

7. Business cycles may be caused by erratic growth of the money supply, swings in business capital investment spending, changes in productivity growth, and changes in the prices of factors of production such as oil. No one explanation is sufficient to explain all business cycles.

8. Workers' compensation per hour mirrored gains in labor productivity in the Economic Liftoff period, fell slightly behind productivity gains in the Reorganization period, and lagged far behind in the Long Boom.

KEY EQUATIONS

Output is related to labor productivity and the amount of hours worked:

$$Output = labor\ productivity \times hours\ worked \qquad (1)$$

The growth-rate form of Equation (1) is

$$Output\ growth = labor\ productivity\ growth + growth\ of\ hours\ worked$$

$$\%\Delta\ Output = \%\Delta\ labor\ productivity + \%\Delta\ hours\ worked \qquad (2)$$

A specific equation relating output to capital and labor that fits the data well is

$$Y = A \times K^a \times L^{1-a} \qquad (4)$$

where Y is output, K is capital, L is labor, a is a coefficient, and A is total factor productivity (TFP).

Economists calculate TFP growth from the available data, using the equation

$$\%\Delta\ A = \%\Delta\ Y - (a \times \%\Delta\ K) - [(1 - a) \times \%\Delta\ L] \qquad (6)$$

KEY TERMS

aggregate demand   the demand for all goods and services in the economy at a given time *(p. 215)*

business cycle   the short-term movement of output and other key economic variables around their long-term trends *(p. 211)*

classical economists   economists who believe the economy will return to equilibrium quickly without the need for government intervention *(p. 215)*

compensation   wages and salaries plus benefits earned by workers *(p. 217)*

depression   a particularly bad recession, in which output declines much more than usual for a recession *(p. 211)*

expansion   the state of the economy in which output is rising, along with other key variables such as income and employment *(p. 211)*

Keynesians   economists who follow the ideas of British economist John Maynard Keynes; they believe that the key element in business cycles is the economy's inability to return to equilibrium immediately following a shift in aggregate demand because wages and prices are sticky and do not adjust right away *(p. 215)*

labor force   the supply of workers, which consists of people who are either employed (they have jobs) or unemployed (they desire to have jobs) *(p. 201)*

labor-force participation rate   the ratio of the labor force to the working-age population *(p. 201)*

labor productivity   a measure of productivity per worker, calculated as output divided by the number of hours worked *(p. 203)*

monetarists   economists who believe that erratic growth of the money supply is the main cause of business cycles *(p. 215)*

peak   the end of an expansion, when output, income, and employment begin to decline *(p. 211)*

real business cycle (RBC) theory models suggesting that "real" shocks to productivity, not shocks to monetary policy, cause the business cycle *(p. 215)*

recession a period when output, income, and employment are declining *(p. 211)*

total factor productivity (TFP) a measure of productivity that explains changes in output other than those attributable to the amount of labor and capital, which is calculated by estimating the contributions of the quantity of capital and the quantity of labor to total output and then figuring out what is left over *(p. 209)*

trough the end of a recession, when output, income, and employment begin to rise *(p. 211)*

unemployment rate the number of unemployed workers as a fraction of the labor force *(p. 201)*

CHAPTER SUMMARY

1. The ATM model shows that a person's decision about how often to withdraw cash from an ATM depends on the person's spending habits, the opportunity cost of holding money (which depends on the nominal interest rate on the person's checking account), the costs of going to the ATM, and the chance of loss or theft.

2. Exogenous variables are those determined outside a model; endogenous variables are those determined within a model.

3. In a partial-equilibrium model, key variables are exogenous; in a general-equilibrium model, all key variables are endogenous.

4. The liquidity-preference model is a model in which the supply of and demand for money determine the nominal interest rate.

5. The liquidity effect occurs when an increase in the money supply causes a decline in the nominal interest rate or when a decrease in the money supply causes an increase in the nominal interest rate.

6. A dynamic model of money is one in which the movements over time of money, nominal interest rates, and other macroeconomic variables are examined. The steady state of the model is the long-run equilibrium in which the key variables are constant or growing at a constant rate.

7. In a dynamic model of money, shocks affect the movement of variables. A one-time increase in the money supply leads to a higher price level in the long run but no changes in other variables such as the nominal interest rate or real incomes. The nominal interest rate declines at first (the liquidity effect) and then rises, finally settling back to its original level.

8. An increase in the growth rate of the money supply leads to a higher inflation rate and a higher nominal interest rate. The movement of the nominal interest rate over time depends on how fast prices adjust and on people's expectations about inflation.

9. Empirical estimates of the money-demand function have changed significantly over time perhaps because of insufficient data. Recent estimates suggest that the money-demand function may be fairly stable, with coefficients that are lower than researchers thought before.

KEY EQUATIONS

The demand for money is modeled as

$$M^D = P \times m(Y, i) \tag{3}$$

where M^D is the total quantity of money demanded, P is the price level, and m is a function relating the nominal interest rate i and people's total real income Y to the demand for money.

In real terms, the demand for money is written as

$$\frac{M^D}{P} = m(Y, i) \tag{5}$$

where the real demand for money depends on total income and the nominal interest rate.

A model of money that is commonly estimated by researchers is

$$\log(M^D/P) = \alpha + \beta i + \gamma \log(Y) + \varepsilon \tag{6}$$

where the logarithm of the real demand for money depends on a constant term α, the level of the nominal interest rate i times its coefficient β, the logarithm of the level of real income Y times its coefficient γ, and an error term ε.

KEY TERMS

dynamic model   a model that allows variables to change over time; a model in which actions that occur at one time affect what happens at other times *(p. 234)*

econometrics   the use of statistical techniques on economic data to investigate how economic variables are related *(p. 240)*

endogenous variable   a variable that is determined within the model *(p. 228)*

exogenous variable   a variable that is determined outside the model or taken to be given by the model *(p. 228)*

general-equilibrium model   a model in which all the key macroeconomic variables, such as the nominal interest rate, are endogenous; a model in which all prices are endogenous in markets where individuals or firms make a choice that affects the supply or demand in those markets *(p. 228)*

income effect the situation when a higher nominal interest rate results from an increase in income that increases the demand for money *(p. 237)*

liquidity effect the inverse relationship between the money supply and the nominal interest rate *(p. 232)*

liquidity-preference model a model in which money demand and supply determine the nominal interest rate *(p. 229)*

partial-equilibrium model a model in which some key macroeconomic variables, such as the nominal interest rate, are exogenous; a model in which individuals or firms make a choice that affects the supply or demand in a market whose price is exogenous *(p. 228)*

price-level effect the situation when a higher nominal interest rate results from an increase in the price level that increases the demand for money *(p. 237)*

real money-demand function the function $m(Y, i)$, which is a useful summary of the relationship between the real demand for money, real income, and the nominal interest rate *(p. 233)*

regression analysis the key method in econometrics in which the coefficients of an equation are calculated by finding values for them that make the sum of the squared error terms as small as possible *(p. 240)*

shock an unexpected change in an exogenous variable; a change to a variable in a model that causes other variables to deviate from their long-run equilibrium values in the short run (or to differ over time from the path they would take in a steady state) or in the long run *(p. 235)*

static model a model that does not allow variables to change over time; a model that focuses on what is happening at just one point in time *(p. 234)*

steady state the long-run equilibrium of a model, which describes what the endogenous variables in the model will do if they are not disturbed by any other variable in the model; the key variables in the model are constant or else they are growing at a constant rate *(p. 234)*

CHAPTER SUMMARY

1. The aggregate-demand/aggregate-supply *(AD–AS)* model is built around the concepts of aggregate demand, which is the amount of goods and services that people want to buy, and aggregate supply, which is the amount of goods and services that firms produce.

2. Aggregate demand depends on the demand for consumption goods, investment goods, net exports, and government spending. The aggregate-demand curve shows the price level and output consistent with equilibrium in both the market for goods and services and the money market.

3. In the long run (when prices have fully adjusted), aggregate supply is the same no matter what the price level is; so the long-run aggregate supply curve is vertical. In the short run, the aggregate quantity of goods and services supplied depends on the price level; output is higher when the price level is higher; so the short-run aggregate supply curve is upward sloping.

4. Prices adjust so that the economy returns to full employment in the long run. In long-run equilibrium, the *AD* curve intersects the *SRAS* curve and the *LRAS* curve at the same point.

5. Business cycles occur when there are sudden changes to exogenous variables. Those shocks cause movement in the *AD*, *SRAS*, and/or *LRAS* curves, leading to adjustments in the short run until the economy returns to long-run equilibrium.

6. The effects of policy actions on the economy can be traced by looking at how policy affects the *AD* curve in the short run and how the *SRAS* curve shifts to restore equilibrium in the long run.

7. Large structural macroeconomic models were developed using the *AD–AS* model as a framework, but they were expanded to include many additional variables.

8. Keynesian and classical macroeconomists differ in the speed at which they think prices adjust to restore general equilibrium, the knowledge of policymakers about the state of the economy, and the ability of policymakers to stabilize the economy.

9. Large macro models provided poor forecasts in the 1970s, misleading policymakers and contributing to the high rates of inflation experienced from 1973 to 1982. Their fundamental flaw was in not modeling people's expectations as rational, thus falling prey to the Lucas critique.

KEY TERMS

aggregate demand the demand for all goods and services in the economy at a given time *(p. 246)*

aggregate-demand (*AD*) curve shows combinations of the price level and output (which equals income) that are necessary for equilibrium in both the market for goods and services and the money market *(p. 249)*

aggregate supply the economy's total production of goods and services *(p. 250)*

capital stock the total amount of physical capital in all firms and households *(p. 248)*

full employment the situation when all the capital and labor in the economy is being fully utilized *(p. 251)*

full-employment output the amount of output produced when the economy is at full employment *(p. 251)*

large structural macroeconomic models models with many equations that describe the economy in great detail; the models are based on the assumption that their equations do not change over time *(p. 263)*

Lucas critique the argument that a change in policy will systematically alter the structure of econometric models *(p. 267)*

natural rate of unemployment the unemployment rate reflecting normal job turnover; equivalently, the unemployment rate when the economy is producing output equal to its potential *(p. 251)*

physical capital the equipment and structures that a firm uses to produce its output and houses that people live in *(p. 248)*

rational expectations a theory that investors use all the information available to them about companies' future prospects in determining their buying and selling decisions, in which case stock prices always equal their fundamental value; the notion that people use all available information in making their economic decisions *(p. 266)*

CHAPTER SUMMARY

1. Dynamic models have a number of advantages over static models. They show that many variables are relevant in determining the economy's general equilibrium, they allow expectations to be modeled, and they model the economy's microeconomic foundations, allowing us to analyze the effects of shocks to economic variables.

2. Dynamic models show how economic agents are affected by changes in exogenous variables and how those agents' decisions determine the economy's general equilibrium.

3. In a two-period model of the economy, the budget constraint shows how much a household can spend in each period. The budget constraint shifts when income changes and rotates when the interest rate changes.

4. The economy is in general equilibrium when prices, wages, and interest rates have adjusted to bring markets for goods, services, labor, money, and securities into equilibrium, with all economic agents making decisions in their own best interests.

5. In dynamic models, people have rational expectations if they use all the information available to them in forming their expectations.

6. The effects of policy in a dynamic model can be examined by seeing how a change in policy affects the endogenous variables of the model. Some policy changes may have no effect, as in the case of the Ricardian equivalence proposition, which shows that a household's budget constraint may not be affected by a tax cut.

7. RBC models suggest that movements in the economy's total factor productivity are the main source of business-cycle fluctuations. The models use numerical methods because the models are too complicated to solve analytically.

8. A promising new avenue of research on DSGE models is heterogeneous-agent models.

9. Statistical models of the economy do not use economic theory but instead use statistical theory. They include univariate time-series models and VAR models. However, statistical models cannot be used easily to interpret historical events or to analyze policy effects without additional assumptions.

10. Statistical models are hard to use for analyzing policy because of the Lucas critique and because policy variables may not be exogenous. However, short- and long-run restrictions imposed in a structural VAR model may allow policy to be analyzed.

KEY TERMS

budget constraint (or **budget line**)   a line showing all the possible amounts the household can consume, given its budget (that is, the amount of income it has) *(p. 271)*

dynamic model   a model that allows variables to change over time; a model in which actions that occur at one time affect what happens at other times *(p. 270)*

dynamic stochastic, general-equilibrium (DSGE) models   models incorporating time and uncertainty in which prices, wages, and interest rates adjust to bring all markets to equilibrium and all economic agents make decisions in their own interest *(p. 281)*

economic agents   households, business firms, governments, and foreigners who make decisions about purchasing or selling goods and services, saving or borrowing, and investing in physical capital *(p. 270)*

expectations   people's beliefs about future economic variables *(p. 278)*

general equilibrium   a situation in which all markets are in equilibrium and all economic agents have made decisions in their own best interest *(p. 277)*

heterogeneous-agent models   models that contain many different economic agents *(p. 283)*

homogeneous-agent models   models in which the economic agents are all alike *(p. 283)*

long-run restriction   a description of the impact of the current-period value of one variable on the value of another variable in the distant future *(p. 287)*

model with microeconomic foundations   a model that is based on the decisions of economic agents *(p. 270)*

precautionary savings   the extra amount of savings that households maintain because of uncertainty about future income *(p. 275)*

rational expectations   a theory that investors use all the information available to them about companies' future prospects in determining their buying and selling decisions, in which case stock prices always equal their fundamental value; the notion that people use all available information in making their economic decisions *(p. 278)*

real business cycle (RBC) models   models suggesting that "real" shocks to productivity, not shocks to monetary policy, cause the business cycle *((p. 282)*

Ricardian equivalence proposition   the result that a change in the timing of taxes does not affect people's consumption *(p. 280)*

short-run restriction   a description of the impact of the current-period value of one variable on the current-period value of another variable *(p. 287)*

static model   a model that does not allow variables to change over time; a model that focuses on what is happening at just one point in time *(p. 270)*

structural VAR model   a VAR model with some economic structure associated with it *(p. 287)*

univariate time-series model   a model in which the value of a variable at any date depends just on its own past values plus an error term *(p. 284)*

vector autoregression (VAR) model   a model in which the value of a variable depends on its own past values plus the past values of other variables plus an error term *(p. 285)*

CHAPTER SUMMARY

1. Business cycles in different countries are related because shocks hit several countries at once (as in the case of an increase in oil prices) and because countries are interdependent.

2. The correlation of business cycles across countries was higher in the 1970s and 1980s than in the 1990s. Because of the worldwide financial crisis in 2008, the correlation increased substantially.

3. Shocks are transmitted internationally through trade effects, interest-rate effects, and exchange-rate effects.

4. An exchange rate is the amount of one currency needed to purchase a unit of another currency.

5. Changes in exchange rates affect the prices of goods that are imported or exported.

6. Supply and demand determine the exchange rate. Explanations for the supply and demand of currencies, and hence the exchange rate, include trade-related theories (purchasing-power parity) and investment-related theories (interest-rate parity).

7. In real terms, the U.S. dollar depreciated in the 1970s, appreciated in the first half of the 1980s, depreciated in the second half of the 1980s and first half of the 1990s, appreciated in the second half of the 1990s, and depreciated in the 2000s until the financial crisis of 2008. Overall, the real value of the dollar fluctuated around a fairly stable level.

8. A country's savings are used to invest in physical capital domestically, to invest in foreign countries, or to finance the government's budget deficit.

9. Open-economy models of the economy yield results similar to closed-economy models, but there is more feedback from one country to another the more interdependent the economies are.

10. In the Asian crisis, investors pulled out of many Asian countries when they realized that their returns would be lower than expected. Those countries suffered recessions as a result because their short-term debt to other countries became more expensive when their currencies depreciated.

KEY EQUATIONS

The real exchange rate x is related to the nominal exchange rate X, the domestic price level P, and the foreign price level P^F via the equation

$$x = X\frac{P}{P^F} \tag{1}$$

The nominal exchange rate is in terms of the number of units of the foreign currency per unit of the domestic currency. The real exchange rate is the average amount of foreign goods per unit of domestic goods.

The percentage change in the nominal exchange rate is related to the percentage change in the real exchange rate and the inflation rates (in percent) in both countries according to the formula

$$\%\Delta X = \%\Delta x + \pi^F - \pi \tag{2}$$

Interest-rate parity means that

$$i^D = i^F - \%\Delta X^e \tag{3}$$

where i^D is the interest rate (in percent) on the domestic bond and i^F is the interest rate (in percent) on the foreign bond.

A country's savings S are used to invest in physical capital in the domestic country (I), to invest in foreign countries (NFI), or to finance the government's budget deficit ($G - T$), so

$$S = I + NFI + (G - T) \tag{5}$$

KEY TERMS

absolute purchasing-power parity   the idea that the exchange rate should equal the ratio of the price indexes of two countries *(p. 299)*

appreciate   when the value of a currency increases in terms of another *(p. 295)*

balance on capital and financial account   the amount foreign citizens, firms, and governments invest in a country minus the amount that country's citizens, firms, and governments invest abroad *(p. 304)*

balance on current account   net exports of goods and services plus net income from abroad plus net unilateral current transfers *(p. 304)*

depreciate   when the value of a currency decreases in terms of another *(p. 295)*

direct investment   investments in other countries from installing capital goods and using them to produce output in the other countries *(p. 304)*

exchange rate   the amount of one currency needed to purchase one unit of another currency *(p. 294)*

interest-rate parity   a situation in which the interest rate on a domestic bond equals the interest rate on a foreign bond minus the expected appreciation of the domestic currency *(p. 302)*

law of one price   the idea that the exchange rate is determined such that the price of a good is the same in two countries when expressed in units of the same currency *(p. 299)*

net foreign investment (NFI)   investments in other countries in the form of portfolio investment or direct investment minus what foreigners invest in the domestic country *(p. 304)*

portfolio investment   investments in other countries from purchasing financial securities *(p. 304)*

real exchange rate   the exchange rate adjusted for changes in prices in both countries *(p. 300)*

relative purchasing-power parity   the idea that a currency in one country should depreciate relative to the currency in a second country by the amount by which the inflation rate is higher in the first country than the second *(p. 300)*

CHAPTER SUMMARY

1. Federal Reserve banks are corporations owned by the member banks in the district.

2. The board of directors of a Federal Reserve bank is partly elected by member banks and partly selected by the Board of Governors of the Federal Reserve. Only three members of each nine-member board are bankers.

3. Federal Reserve banks are responsible for central banking functions that include economic research, bank supervision and regulation, discount-window lending, monetary statistics, and consumer and community affairs.

4. The Board of Governors oversees the entire Federal Reserve System from its headquarters in Washington, D.C.

5. The chairman of the Board of Governors is one of the most powerful people in the world because monetary policy has a strong impact on the U.S. and world economies.

6. Judged by the impact on inflation over their terms, Paul Volcker and Alan Greenspan have been the best Fed chairmen in the last half century.

7. The Federal Open Market Committee (FOMC) is the group primarily responsible for monetary policy in the United States. It consists of the seven members of the Board of Governors and five Federal Reserve bank presidents.

8. Monetary policy is implemented through the use of open-market operations, which are purchases or sales of securities made by the Fed's Open Market Desk in New York.

9. The Federal Reserve is relatively independent from politics because of the structure of the members' terms and the source of its income. Nonetheless, politicians are constantly pressuring the Fed to do their bidding.

10. A potential problem with the Fed's independence is a lack of accountability, at least in the short run. In the long run, however, the Fed can be judged on its inflation record.

KEY TERMS

basis point   one-hundredth of a percentage point *(p. 326)*

federal funds rate   the interest rate in the market for bank reserves (the federal funds market), which applies to overnight loans of reserves between banks *(p. 325)*

open-market operations   the tool the Fed uses to affect the money supply, consisting of purchases and sales of government securities in the secondary market *(p. 325)*

political business cycle   the idea that monetary policy eases before elections to favor incumbent politicians *(p. 329)*

primary government securities dealers   large investment banks and brokers that meet certain capital requirements and agree to actively transact with the Fed when it engages in open-market operations *(p. 325)*

repurchase agreements (repos)   transactions in which a primary dealer agrees to sell a security to the Fed one day and buy it back the next day or several days later *(p. 325)*

CHAPTER SUMMARY

1. The Federal Reserve controls the money supply by determining the monetary base and influencing the multiplier.

2. Banks create money when the Fed increases the monetary base because they gain excess reserves; so they make additional loans. The total amount of new loans and transaction accounts in the banking system are multiples of the increase in the monetary base.

3. The money multiplier equals the money supply divided by the monetary base.

4. Money multipliers depend on people's choices of how much currency, nontransaction accounts, and money-market mutual fund deposits to hold relative to their transaction accounts, banks' choices of how much to hold in excess reserves, and the Fed's choice of the reserve requirement.

5. In addition to open-market operations, the Fed can increase the monetary base by reducing the discount rate.

6. The Fed can increase the money multiplier by reducing reserve requirements or by reducing the interest rate it pays on reserves.

7. Most of the Fed's day-to-day open-market operations are defensive—offsetting temporary swings in the demand for reserves. The Fed occasionally engages in dynamic open-market operations when it wants to actively change monetary policy.

8. Equilibrium in the reserves market is determined by the demand for reserves by banks and the supply of reserves by the Federal Reserve; the federal funds rate equilibrates supply and demand in the reserves market.

9. The setup of discount lending is designed to ensure that the federal funds rate will not rise above the primary credit discount rate. The interest rate on reserves puts a lower bound on the federal funds rate.

10. When the economy enters a liquidity trap, traditional monetary policy loses its effectiveness. The liquidity trap is caused when interest rates hit the zero lower bound and short-term bonds become perfect substitutes for cash. Getting out of a liquidity trap calls for nontraditional policy measures.

KEY EQUATIONS

The money supply is a multiple of the monetary base:

$$\text{Money supply} = \text{money multiplier} \times \text{monetary base} \quad \text{(1)}$$

The monetary base, or high-powered money, equals the amount of reserves that banks hold (either as vault cash or as deposits at Federal Reserve banks) plus the amount of currency held by the nonbank public:

$$\text{Monetary base} = \text{reserves} + \text{currency}$$
$$MB = R + C \quad \text{(4)}$$

The multiplier for M1 is

$$mm1 = \frac{1 + C/D}{RR/D + ER/D + C/D} \quad \text{(11)}$$

C/D is the ratio of currency to transactions deposits, RR/D is the ratio of required reserves to transactions deposits, and ER/D is the ratio of banks' holdings of excess reserves to transactions deposits.

The multiplier for M2 is

$$mm2 = \frac{1 + C/D + N/D + MMF/D}{RR/D + ER/D + C/D} \quad \text{(12)}$$

where most of the components are the same as those for the M1 multiplier, with the addition of N/D, which is the ratio of nontransactions deposits to transactions deposits, and MMF/D, which is the ratio of retail money-market mutual fund holdings to transactions deposits.

KEY TERMS

defensive open-market operations   open-market activity the Fed undertakes because of seasonal effects or to offset a temporary change in money demand *(p. 344)*

dynamic open-market operations   open-market activity the Fed undertakes when it wants to change monetary policy *(p. 344)*

haircut   the extra collateral the Fed requires above the value of a discount loan *(p. 345)*

high-powered money   another name for the monetary base *(p. 339)*

liquidity trap   a situation in which additions to the monetary base do not lead to an increase in the money supply or a decline in the interest rate *(p. 352)*

monetary base   the sum of currency held by the nonbank public and banks' reserves *(p. 334)*

money multiplier   the ratio of the money supply to the monetary base *(p. 338)*

primary credit discount loan a loan made by the Fed to a bank that is highly rated, under which the Fed does not question the purpose of the loan *(p. 345)*

seasonal credit discount loan a loan from the Fed to a small agricultural bank *(p. 345)*

secondary credit discount loan a loan made by the Fed to a bank that is not highly rated, under which the

Fed carefully scrutinizes the purpose of the loan and the ability of the bank to repay the loan; the secondary credit discount rate is ½ percentage point higher than the rate for primary credit *(p. 345)*

zero lower bound a situation in which nominal short-term interest rates are very close to zero *(p. 352)*

CHAPTER SUMMARY

1. Monetary policymakers may try to stabilize the economy by smoothing out the business cycle.

2. Lags in policymaking, such as the data lag, recognition lag, decision lag, implementation lag, and effectiveness lag, make stabilization policy difficult to implement; such lags may even lead to destabilizing policy.

3. The Fed's main goals are to maximize output, to keep the unemployment rate low, and to maintain a low inflation rate.

4. The Fed's objective function summarizes its goals in a simple way that can be used in economic modeling.

5. The economy bears costs when output differs from potential output and when the unemployment rate differs from the natural rate of unemployment. When output exceeds potential output and when the unemployment rate is below the natural rate of unemployment, people are working more than they want to, and equipment is being used at an unsustainable pace. When output is below potential and the unemployment rate is below the natural rate, the economy's resources are not fully used, causing production to be inefficient and leading to social problems, such as crime.

6. Unanticipated inflation is costly because (a) prices are set wrong, (b) wealth is redistributed between borrowers and lenders, and (c) higher inflation leads to greater uncertainty about the future inflation rate.

7. Anticipated inflation is costly because (a) inflation represents an implicit tax on holding money, (b) firms face menu costs of changing prices, (c) people on fixed nominal incomes are hurt directly, (d) inflation interacts with the tax system to hurt saving and investment in physical capital, and (e) the housing market is distorted by the mortgage-tilt problem.

8. The weight that inflation has in the Fed's objective function determines how aggressive policy is in returning output to potential and returning the inflation rate to the ideal inflation rate.

9. The attempt by policymakers to exploit the Phillips curve tradeoff in the 1960s and 1970s caused higher and higher rates of inflation, which were matched by higher expected inflation.

10. The expectations-augmented Phillips curve shows the short-run tradeoff between inflation and unemployment. But the long-run Phillips curve is vertical at the natural rate of unemployment because there is no long-run tradeoff.

KEY EQUATIONS

The output gap measures how far actual output is from potential output:

Output gap at time t = percentage deviation of output from potential

= [(actual output − potential output) ÷ potential output] × 100%

$$\tilde{y}_t = \frac{y_t - y_t^*}{y_t^*} \times 100\% \qquad (1)$$

where actual output is denoted y_t, potential output is denoted y_t^* and the output gap is denoted $\tilde{y}_t$.

The deviation of the inflation rate from the ideal inflation rate is the inflation gap:

Inflation gap at time t = actual inflation rate − ideal inflation rate

$$\tilde{\pi}_t = \pi_t - \pi_t^* \qquad (2)$$

where the ideal inflation rate π_t^* is an inflation rate that policymakers would like to achieve because it minimizes the costs to society of changing prices.

The Fed's objective function summarizes the Fed's goals for output and inflation:

Total loss = sum over time of [output loss + (w × inflation loss)]

$$= \sum_{time} [\tilde{y}_t^2 + (w \times \tilde{\pi}_t^2)] \qquad (3)$$

where the symbol $\sum_{time}$ means to add up over time the values of the variables that follow, and w stands for the weight on inflation, which is a parameter that shows the Fed's preferences about the inflation loss versus the output loss.

The Phillips curve, as it was used in the 1960s and 1970s, is

$$\pi = \alpha - (\beta \times U) \qquad (4)$$

where U is the unemployment rate, π is the inflation rate, and α and β are coefficients that determine the tradeoff between unemployment and inflation.

The expectations-augmented Phillips curve is

$$\pi = \pi^e - [\beta \times (U - U_N)] \qquad (5)$$

When the unemployment rate U equals the natural rate of unemployment U_N, the inflation rate π equals the expected inflation rate π^e.

KEY TERMS

contractionary policy policy that causes the economy to grow more slowly in the short run; a decrease in the money supply is contractionary *(p. 358)*

data lag the lag in data availability *(p. 359)*

decision lag the lag in policy that arises because it takes time for policymakers to make a decision *(p. 360)*

effectiveness lag the time it takes from when a policy is implemented to when it has an effect on the economy *(p. 360)*

expansionary policy policy that causes the economy to grow faster in the short run; an increase in the money supply is expansionary *(p. 358)*

expectations-augmented Phillips curve a Phillips curve tradeoff between inflation and unemployment in the short run but not in the long run; the short-run Phillips curve is associated with a particular level of expected inflation, and the long-run Phillips curve is a vertical line at the natural rate of unemployment *(p. 379)*

Fed's loss function another name for the Fed's objective function *(p. 372)*

Fed's objective function an equation that summarizes the total cost to the economy when output differs from potential and when the inflation rate differs from the ideal inflation rate *(p. 372)*

ideal inflation rate an inflation rate that policymakers would like to achieve because it minimizes the costs to society of changing prices; usually thought to be between 0 and 2 percent *(p. 369)*

implementation lag the lag between when a change in policy is decided on and when it is implemented *(p. 360)*

inflation gap the actual inflation rate minus the ideal inflation rate *(p. 372)*

inflation surprise the difference between the actual inflation rate and the expected inflation rate *(p. 383)*

inflation target another name for the ideal inflation rate *(p. 369)*

mortgage-tilt problem the problem that arises when the real value of fixed nominal mortgage payments declines over time because of inflation *(p. 368)*

natural rate of unemployment the unemployment rate reflecting normal job turnover; equivalently, the unemployment rate when the economy is producing output equal to its potential *(p. 365)*

Okun's law the relationship between the output gap and the unemployment gap, which says that the output gap equals -1.7 times the unemployment gap *(p. 370)*

output gap the percentage deviation of output from potential *(p. 370)*

Phillips curve the tradeoff in the data between unemployment and inflation *(p. 377)*

potential output the amount of output that would be produced by the economy if resources were being used at a high rate that is sustainable in the long run *(p. 363)*

recognition lag the lag that arises because the random nature of the data makes it difficult for policymakers to fully understand the state of the economy *(p. 359)*

stabilization policy policy that attempts to smooth out the business cycle *(p. 358)*

unemployment gap the difference between the unemployment rate and the natural rate of unemployment *(p. 370)*

CHAPTER SUMMARY

1. If a central bank uses discretion, rather than following a rule, it may be caught in an expectations trap that arises when people's expectations about inflation rise. Then the central bank must ease monetary policy, causing inflation, or allow the economy to slow.

2. An expectations trap may arise because discretionary policy is time-inconsistent; the central bank may renege on a promise of low inflation once people's expectations are set. The central bank can defeat time inconsistency by tying the salaries of its leaders inversely to the inflation rate or by credibly announcing a policy of low inflation.

3. A central bank can establish credibility in many ways, even if it does not follow rules. In the United States, the Fed gained credibility by establishing a reputation for reducing inflation, even when doing so entailed costs.

4. Monetarists proposed a rule to target the growth rate of the money supply. But unpredictable shifts in money demand have made such a rule seem undesirable.

5. Policymakers and researchers debate whether activist policy, which responds to the business cycle, is better than nonactivist policy, which does not respond to the business cycle.

6. A number of countries have switched to inflation targeting in recent years, beginning with New Zealand in 1990. They focus monetary policy on hitting a particular target for inflation without following specific rules for monetary policy, such as the Taylor rule.

7. An important part of an inflation-targeting system is the central bank's inflation report, in which the factors causing the inflation rate to change are explained, forecasts for inflation are discussed, and the central bank's strategy for reducing inflation is revealed. The inflation report provides useful information to investors and other people, helping them to understand what the central bank is doing and making monetary policy transparent.

8. The Taylor rule sets the federal funds rate in response to the output gap and inflation gap. Had monetary policy followed the Taylor rule, it would have been tighter in the 1950s, late 1960s, 1970s, and 2000s and easier in the 1980s and 1990s.

9. Policymakers and researchers using the Taylor rule face many difficulties: They must estimate potential output, they need to account for changes in the equilibrium real federal funds rate, and they must understand the impact of data revisions. In addition, researchers trying to estimate whether the Fed acted as if it followed the Taylor rule face other difficulties: They need to explain differences in the rule when different variables are used, they must account for changes in the weights in the rule over time, and they must figure out if there were changes in the inflation target over time.

10. In practice, policymakers are unlikely to ever adopt explicit rules but prefer to use rules as guidelines.

KEY EQUATIONS

The equation of exchange relates the money supply and the velocity of money to total spending:

$$M \times V = P \times Y \qquad \text{(1)}$$

where M is a measure of the money supply, V is the velocity of money, P is the price level, and Y is the level of output of goods and services.

Using the equation of exchange, a money-growth rule is one that sets the growth rate of the money supply according to

$$\%\Delta M = \pi^T + \%\Delta Y^* - \%\Delta V \qquad \text{(3)}$$

where Y^* is potential output, and π^T is the inflation target.

The Taylor rule is given by the equation

$$i = r^* + \pi + (w_1 \times \tilde{Y}) + (w_2 \times \tilde{\pi}) \qquad \text{(4)}$$

where all variables are measured in percentage points, i is the nominal federal funds rate, r^* is the equilibrium value of the real federal funds rate, π is the inflation rate over the last four quarters, w_1 is the weight on the output gap, $\tilde{Y}$ is the output gap, w_2 is the weight on the inflation gap, and $\tilde{\pi}$ is the inflation gap.

KEY TERMS

activist rule a rule for monetary policy under which monetary policy is allowed to change over the course of the business cycle *(p. 395)*

discretion the situation where monetary policy is not set by a rule *(p. 388)*

ease policy what a central bank does when it increases money growth and reduces the interest rate *(p. 388)*

equation of exchange an equation that relates total spending to the amount of money available to be spent; the equation says that money times velocity equals the price level times output *(p. 393)*

expectations trap a situation in which policymakers must increase the inflation rate in response to an increase in the expected inflation rate *(p. 388)*

inflation targeting a system in which the central bank tries to achieve an explicit target for the inflation rate within some period *(p. 404)*

money-growth rule a rule that focuses only on the growth rate of money in the economy; under such a rule, the central bank simply would set money growth in the long run, ignoring short-run fluctuations in the economy *(p. 393)*

nonactivist rule a rule for monetary policy under which the same monetary policy is pursued whether the economy is in a recession or an expansion *(p. 395)*

rule for monetary policy the systematic setting of policy according to a formula *(p. 388)*

target band a range that represents the goal for the inflation rate *(p. 404)*

Taylor rule an activist rule for monetary policy that changes the federal funds rate in response to output gaps and inflation gaps *(p. 397)*

tighten policy what a central bank does when it decreases money growth and increases the interest rate *(p. 388)*

time inconsistency the difficulty that arises when policymakers have discretion over policy and choose a policy at one date that leads people to make decisions based on that policy, which then causes the policymakers to choose a different policy at a later date *(p. 388)*

transparent a description of a central bank that is explicit about its goals and plans *(p. 404)*

velocity of money the average number of times a dollar of money is used in transactions over the course of a year *(p. 393)*